Strategies for Teaching
English Learners

THIRD EDITION

Strategies for Teaching English Learners

Lynne T. Díaz-Rico

California State University, San Bernardino

PEARSON

Boston ■ Columbus ■ Indianapolis ■ New York ■ San Francisco ■ Upper Saddle River
Amsterdam ■ Cape Town ■ Dubai ■ London ■ Madrid ■ Milan ■ Munich ■ Paris ■ Montreal ■ Toronto
Delhi ■ Mexico City ■ São Paulo ■ Sydney ■ Hong Kong ■ Seoul ■ Singapore ■ Taipei ■ Tokyo

Vice President, Editor-in-Chief: Aurora Martínez Ramos
Editor: Erin Grelak
Editorial Assistant: Michelle Hochberg
Marketing Manager: Krista Clark
Production Editor: Mary Beth Finch
Editorial Production Service: Electronic Publishing Services Inc.
Manufacturing Buyer: Megan Cochran
Electronic Composition: Jouve
Interior Design: Electronic Publishing Services Inc.
Photo Researcher: Bill Smith Group
Cover Designer: Jennifer Hart

A previous edition was published under the title *Teaching English Learners: Strategies and Methods*, copyright © 2004.

Library of Congress Cataloging-in-Publication Data

Díaz-Rico, Lynne T.
  Strategies for teaching English learners / Lynne T. Díaz-Rico. — 3rd ed.
      p.   cm.
  Includes bibliographical references and index.
  ISBN-13: 978-0-13-268518-4 (pbk.)
  ISBN-10: 0-13-268518-3 (pbk.)
  1. English language—Study and teaching—Foreign speakers.   I. Title.
  PE1128.A2D453 2013
  428.0071—dc23

                                        2011046824

10 9 8 7 6 5 4 3 2 1

ISBN-10: 0-13-268518-3
ISBN-13: 978-0-13-268518-4

To Phillip, Voltaire, Daniel, and Eva:
Thank you for your love and care.

To my mother and father,
Sarah Pack Thomas and Horace J. Thomas III

To my students, who work so hard as learners and as teachers:
Thank you for your devotion to the success of English learners.

To my colleagues:
Thank you for making TESOL a worthy profession.

To all my teachers, past, present, and future:
Thank you for your help and guidance.

About the Author

Lynne Díaz-Rico is professor of education at California State University, San Bernardino. She has worked with public and private teacher education institutions and agencies around the world to prepare teachers for classrooms with diverse students and English language pedagogy. Her books *Crosscultural, Language, and Academic Development Handbook* and *A Course for Teaching English Learners* are widely used to educate English-language development teachers. Her research interests are in pedagogies for multilingual classrooms; creative, innovative English teaching strategies; critical discourse analysis; and visual literacy.

Brief Contents

Contents

1 Who Are English Learners and Their Teachers?   1

2 Critical Roles for Teachers   23

4 Performance-Based Learning 67

5 Learner Strategies and Learner-Focused Teaching   99

6 Oracy Instruction That Builds on the First Language 137

7 Literacy Instruction for English-Language Development 161

8 Learning Processes and the Imaginary   199

9 Grammar through Integrated Language Skills and Wonderful English   237

10 Culturally Based Language Teaching   263

11   Discourse in the Classrooms of English Learners   291

12   Dual-Language Proficiency   307

13 Teaching English in Context   327

14 Building a Community of Learners   345

15 Project-Based Learning and Service Learning   375

Preface

Strategies for Teaching English Learners offers an overview of basic principles, practices, and methods for educating English learners, including such topics as the influence of culture on schooling, the cultural practices of schooling, and the sociopolitical context of education. This book is designed to increase teachers' effectiveness in expanding English learners' access to the core curriculum, instructing all students with a rich and demanding curriculum, and making crosscultural connections by means of teaching practices and curricular content.

ESL (English as a second language) and EFL (English as a foreign language) teachers with multicultural sensitivity and knowledge of intercultural communication can be expected to actively build a base of personal knowledge about the ways in which language, culture, and schooling are connected. This book is designed to work at many levels simultaneously so that participants can organize and verbalize what they know, make professional presentations, and grow toward a teaching career graced with knowledge, empathy, and dedication. The best teaching model is one that is stimulating and furthers understanding, encouraging the learner actively to reach out to apply what is learned.

Teacher education is open-ended and never ending. This book does not use a behaviorist model of teacher training (in which one is told exactly how to behave as a teacher), but rather a cognitive/humanist/constructivist model of teacher education, in which one receives fundamental principles in order to fashion one's own version of what constitutes good teaching.

Simultaneously, a dedication to social equity and justice broadens the focus of education to include attention to issues of social context, cultural values, and individual rights and responsibilities within a democratic framework. This adherence to democratic ideals is a given, despite the wide variety of cultures and societies that now use English for their own purposes. Although English grew from a small language of five to seven million speakers to a global language through a combination of imperialism, global militarism, and ambitious economic agendas, it is still the language of the Declaration of Independence and the Bill of Rights. One must never lose sight while teaching English of the possibilities of human freedom, equality of opportunity, and justice—ideals exquisitely expressed in the English language.

In this book, I use the term *strategy* to mean "a conscious plan for achieving learning." This book features a range of strategies that the prospective teacher can acquire and deploy as a learner of teacher education. Some strategies, in turn, are appropriate for the second-language learner to use to increase autonomous learning

I use the term *megastrategy set* to denote "large ideas that guide practice and that hosts a set of matching strategies consonant with its theme." There are fifteen sets of megastrategies, one corresponding to each of the fifteen chapters of the book.

Sixty-six matching strategies align with these megastrategies. Each strategy is accompanied by a set of recommended practices.

This book is built on a fundamental rejection of any dichotomy of theory and practice. I visualize the tool kit of theory and the practice as components in a cycle of stance (see Figure P.1). Gramsci (Adamson, 1980) has conceptualized theory and practice as a linked set, in which theory and practice are linked by the identification of how individuals come to constitute—and therefore also can reconstitute—their worlds. In this instance, I conceive of *theory* as a tool kit of megastrategies and strategies. By *practice* I mean the deployment of actions with a repertoire of these megastrategies and strategies within a specific context. (Critical theorists might call this *praxis* rather than practice.) *Insight* into a specific occurrence, plus the *creation of stance and voice*, then the *ongoing affirmation of the stance* in view of real consequences, becomes the chief technology (set of techniques) of deploying the self (Foucault, 1988) within an individual's profession.

FIGURE P.1 *Components in a cycle of stance*

X = Experiences in world
Y = Technologies of the self

The concept of *stance* is an individual instantiation of what Gramsci called the "war of position" (Simon, 1982). The power exercised by the status quo is often unquestioned; to create social change, members of society who wish to transform relationships within the civil society must deliberately take positions to interrupt this status quo. For this reason, I consider stance an individual analog of the war of position, in which individuals engage in transformative practices using a cycle of stance.

What kinds of transformative practices are required? Experienced teachers assert themselves on a daily basis to sustain support for effective teaching. Educators who teach English learners in the United States sometimes face multiple obstacles to school success: poverty, stress, discrimination, and increasing academic demands are often blamed as educators struggle to explain the frustration faced by English learners. Educators who teach English as a foreign language abroad face a different set of frustrations—the risks of marginalization or intercultural miscommunication. Appendix A includes a discussion of how U.S.-based educators can exert power to maintain their profession on the cutting edge of educational progress. Similar techniques can be adapted for teaching abroad, taking into consideration the particular context.

In the process of using the cycle of stance, an individual chooses a particular challenge to face. This might include trying a new teaching practice or asserting influence within an institution. Employing that practice creates a critical incident. By applying reflective insight, the practitioner evaluates the incident and creates a stance. The stance is a position taken by a practitioner with a voice. The voice speaks up for change; if the practice failed for a specific reason, the voice advocates for change in the social context to allow the next trial of the practice to be a success. The cycle continues as the consequences of this re-experience with voice are examined. If the stance is affirmed, the practice, with its attendant social change, was successful. If so, the cycle spirals to a new level of implementation. If not, the failure becomes a new critical incident. Thus, the individual creates experiences in the world using technologies of the self.

The cycle of stance provides a clear process for utilizing and evaluating various practices. It does not, however, place blame on the practice or the practitioner if success is not attained. Neither does it encourage the practitioner to quit trying. Rather, it acknowledges that the practitioner needs to examine the incident, choose points of leverage in the stance to apply the self within the social context, and then re-experience and evaluate the consequences. Only in this way can the practitioner learn to understand the social context and act meaningfully within that context.

Use of a carefully structured tool kit of megastrategies and strategies permits the educator to act clearly and consistently as a professional. In addition, the educator can attain a lucid and concise picture of a complex and demanding profession. In reality, the complex texture of native and target cultures, native languages, social and political situations, socioeconomic status, and individual differences in learners that one faces when teaching English learners means that one must continually innovate and experiment with teaching and learning strategies.

This book emphasizes a commitment to social justice and a moral commitment to democracy. I offer my thanks and tribute to colleagues in the profession of teaching

English learners whose like-minded dedication has sustained and inspired me throughout my professional life. If the reader finds argument with this subject position and does not support these social goals, I invite dialogue, autonomy, and resistance, using a cycle of reflection, stance, and voice.

Changes in the Third Edition

This edition includes several new or expanded features. Chapter 1 describes the unique contributions nonnative-English-speaking teachers make to the teaching of English, plus up-to-date information on the demographics of English learners and the demand for English teachers worldwide. Chapter 2 provides examples of innovative social justice curricula. New ways to connect brain research with reading instruction are presented in Chapter 3, and Chapter 4 updates the reader with developments in standards for English teaching, along with standardized assessments. Chapter 5 offers suggestions about the use of learning centers in English-as-a-foreign-language elementary classrooms, along with an expanded discussion of computer-assisted language learning; Chapters 6 and 7 present multimedia tools, social media, and other Internet-based technologies for instruction in literacy and oracy (listening and speaking). Strategies for oracy and literacy are augmented, with an increased attention to vocabulary acquisition.

Chapter 10 features an expanded definition of culture to include a contemporary emphasis on identity and expanded coverage of issues in the education of gay, lesbian, bisexual, and transgendered students. The foundations of bilingual education are summarized in a handy reference section in Chapter 12. Chapter 14 includes new ways to incorporate volunteers into classroom instruction and ways to encourage "virtual volunteering." Project-based learning and service learning are creatively combined in Chapter 15 as ways to link English learners with the larger community. Appendix B presents an expanded treatment of special education for English learners. Each chapter concludes with a discussion exercise called "Exploratory Break" to augment and reinforce the concepts presented in each chapter.

New! CourseSmart eBook and Other eBook Options Available

CourseSmart is an exciting new choice for purchasing this book. As an alternative to purchasing the printed book, you may purchase an electronic version of the same content via CourseSmart for reading on PC, Mac, as well as Android devices, iPad, iPhone, and iPod Touch with CourseSmart Apps. With a CourseSmart eBook, readers can search the text, make notes online, and bookmark important passages for later review. For more information or to purchase access to the CourseSmart eBook, visit http://www.coursesmart.com. Also look for availability of this book on a number of other eBook devices and platforms.

Acknowledgments

This edition was made possible through the help of many people. I credit my editor, Aurora Martínez Ramos, with the persuasive power that moved me to undertake the project. I thank my colleague Dr. María V. Balderrama for her help. I acknowledge the support of my students, who gave me feedback on early drafts. Thanks to Dr. Jay Fiene, dean of the College of Education at CSUSB, and my colleagues for their patience.

I would like to thank the reviewers of this edition for their insight and feedback: Rui Cheng, Nazareth College; Lynn Henrichsen, Brigham Young University; and Julieta Martinez (Beam), Kaplan University.

Strategies for Teaching English Learners: A Summary

<u>*Megastrategy* **SET 1**</u> **Professionalize the teaching of English learners.**

Megastrategy **1.1** Become familiar with the profession of teaching English learners.

Megastrategy **1.2** Know who your learners are and why they need English.

Megastrategy **1.3** Join with other professionals to facilitate teaching.

<u>*Megastrategy* **SET 2**</u> **Advance the interests of the learner.**

Megastrategy **2.1** Set professional goals with the learner's best interests in mind, as the learner defines them.

Megastrategy **2.2** Critique the social conditions of the learner.

Megastrategy **2.3** Use power and policy issues to support English learners.

<u>*Megastrategy* **SET 3**</u> **Teach the whole person—beliefs, body, brain, emotions, and culture—within a positive social environment.**

Megastrategy **3.1** Take into consideration your philosophy and beliefs, as well as the philosophies and beliefs of the learner.

Megastrategy **3.2** Use behavioral training for accurate pronunciation and rote memory of information such as object and motor vocabulary.

Megastrategy **3.3** Align learning with the brain and its natural ways of knowledge acquisition.

Megastrategy **3.4** Reduce tension and support a positive emotional state in the learner.

Megastrategy **3.5** Be aware of the effect of the sociocultural context on cognitive and language development.

Megastrategy **3.6** Place learning in the context of contemporary social change.

Megastrategy **SET 8**   **Use English to explore the imaginary as a language-learning tool.**

Megastrategy **8.1**   Explore the concept of the imaginary as a language-learning tool.

Megastrategy **8.2**   Empower the emotional imagination with drama.

Megastrategy **8.3**   Stimulate the linguistic imagination with poetry.

Megastrategy **8.4**   Celebrate a sense of joy with music and other oral activities.

Megastrategy **SET 9**   **Teach language in a way that arouses a genuine interest in the history and beauty of English.**

Megastrategy **9.1**   Treat language as whole and integrate skills.

Megastrategy **9.2**   Arouse interest in the history of English.

Megastrategy **9.3**   Arouse interest in English as a language.

Megastrategy **9.4**   Teach the structure of English explicitly but contextually.

Megastrategy **9.5**   Teach respect for correct usage in English.

Megastrategy **SET 10**   **Use culture to teach language.**

Megastrategy **10.1**   Learn about how culture affects learning.

Megastrategy **10.2**   Align the culture of schooling and the learner's culture.

Megastrategy **10.3**   Motivate the learner to achieve cultural fluency.

Megastrategy **10.4**   Teach English using the learner's culture as well as the target culture.

Megastrategy **10.5**   Teach English by comparing cultures.

Megastrategy **10.6**   Use intercultural communication to teach English.

Megastrategy **SET 11**   **Understand cultural patterns of instruction.**

Megastrategy **11.1**   Understand the role of language and culture in instruction.

Megastrategy **11.2**   Understand typical U.S. classroom instructional patterns.

Megastrategy **11.3**   Promote the learner's use of cognitive academic language.

Megastrategy **11.4**   Help the learner to construct meaning.

Megastrategy **SET 12**   **Develop cognitive academic language proficiency in two languages.**

Megastrategy **12.1**   Support enriched education in dual-language programs.

Megastrategy **12.2**   Teach literacy and oracy in two languages.

Megastrategy **12.3**   Teach for transfer between the primary language and English.

Megastrategy **12.4**   Provide cultural support for dual-language learning.

Megastrategy **SET 13**   **Teach respect for contextual usage of English.**

Megastrategy **13.1**   Honor the dialect of the learner.

Megastrategy **13.2**   Teach a variety of registers and styles.

Megastrategy **13.3**   Teach academic registers and standard usage.

Megastrategy **SET 14**   **Make the classroom a community, and bring the community into the classroom—parents, families, neighborhoods, and culture.**

Megastrategy **14.1**   Make the classroom a learning community.

Megastrategy **14.2**   Involve families as partners in learning.

Megastrategy **14.3**   Affirm and build on what the community values as knowledge.

Megastrategy **14.4**   Form partnerships with the community to involve students in community activities and social action.

Megastrategy **SET 15**   **Involve the learner in projects that offer long-term, meaningful learning; serve and learn in the community.**

Megastrategy **15.1**   Negotiate the project topic with the learners.

Megastrategy **15.2**   Delimit and focus project activities.

Megastrategy **15.3**   Document and assess the progress and outcome of the project.

Megastrategy **15.4**   Form partnerships with the community to involve students in community activities and social action.

Megastrategy **15.5**   Design a service-learning project.

Megastrategy **15.6**   Perform and evaluate service.

Strategies for Teaching
English Learners

Chapter *1*

Who Are English Learners and Their Teachers?

The Profession of Teaching English Learners

Language is a powerful means of communicating the deepest and highest desires, dreams, and ideals of humanity. Language helps us to fulfill our potential, to share our inner selves with others, or to act on the world powerfully. We use language to participate in private and public life with our families, community, or nation. As teachers, we use language to help others reach higher states of knowledge, emotion, or spirit. These are among the strongest drives of humankind, and language has proved to be a superior tool for those ends. But how frustrating that no common language exists among peoples of the world! The world today stands on the brink of an opportunity never before available: the use of a world language, English, that can sustain intercultural contact between individuals who would otherwise have no mutual means of communication. However, the role of English entails a host of social, economic, and political issues.

English Language Development

Before looking at English teaching around the world, some fundamental questions need to be posed. Asking these questions helps frame the context for English instruction (Kaplan, 2001).

> Why will English be taught, and what variety?
> Who are the learners?
> Who are the teachers, and how are they trained?

English learners consti-
tute a growing proportion
of schoolchildren in the
United States.
© Darrin Henry/Shutterstock.com

When will instruction begin, how long will it last, and who will pay the expenses?

Who prepares the syllabus and teaching materials?

Who determines what methods are appropriate, how the success of students is assessed, and whether the teaching program is effective?

What role do the learners, or parents of learners, play in decision making?

From these questions, it is clear that language teaching is intricately interwoven with language planning and policy decisions (see chapter 2).

Teaching English learners is one of the fastest-growing professions in today's world. But who are "English learners"? In countries such as the United States, Canada, the United Kingdom, and Australia, native speakers of English study their own language as they progress through school. Such instruction is not considered "teaching English learners"; even though English is being taught on a daily basis, the fact that the learners are native speakers of English means they are not "English learners." The term *English learners* means those who are learning English as non-native speakers.

However, in many English-speaking countries, traditional academic English classes increasingly serve students who, although schooled entirely in English, speak other languages at home. These have been called "Generation 1.5 students" (Rumbaut & Portes, 2001; Roberge, 2009)—caught between generations, having acquired some proficiency in two or more languages but not truly native speakers of English. Even though they take classes with native speakers, they may not actually have attained academic competence in English. To teach these students, English teachers in classes designed for native speakers may also benefit from a focus on "English learners."

Therefore, the answer to the question "Who is an English learner?" may not simply be, "One who is taught by an ESL/EFL teacher." English learners are also taught by teachers whose primary responsibility is to teach a primary language in a so-called bilingual classroom, as well as by English and other elementary school teachers who treat their students as native English speakers even if they are not. This situation creates a complex set of professional loyalties on the part of teachers.

Megastrategy **1.1**

Become familiar with the profession of teaching English learners

The term *teachers of English to speakers of other languages* (TESOL) includes those who teach English learners in general, although classroom teachers may think of themselves as "elementary teachers," "bilingual teachers," or "English teachers." Teaching English learners is a broad and flexible profession: TESOL educators can be found in kindergartens in Seattle, college classrooms in Korea, adult education classes in Texas, "cram" schools in Thailand, precollege preparation courses in Michigan, middle school social studies classes in California, five-year vocational colleges in Taiwan, private schools in the United Arab Emirates, or summer intensive programs in Uzbekistan. They operate at a myriad of levels in a host of countries around the world, working with learners at levels ranging from preschool to postgraduate. TESOL educators are represented professionally by the organization TESOL International Association (www.tesol.org).

The field of teaching English learners is equally open to those whose native language is English and those who are nonnative speakers. Positions are available worldwide with employers who recognize that those who have learned English as an additional language and have achieved some measure of bilingual competence are uniquely qualified to understand the needs of English learners (see Brutt-Griffler & Samimy, 1999). TESOL's Nonnative English Speakers in TESOL (NNEST) Interest Section (http://nnest.asu.edu) can provide more information about this topic.

It is widely acknowledged that the majority of English teachers worldwide are NNESTs (Liu, 1999). It is also a fact that in EFL settings such as China, Japan, Vietnam, South Korea, and Thailand, studying English with instructors whose mother tongue is the same as that of the students is not only realistic, but it is also very successful because such teachers have unique characteristics. In July 2011, a group of South Korean teachers studying at CSU, San Bernadino, suggested that NNESTS can be as effective as native-English-speaking teachers, in these ways:

- Teach language-learning strategies in L1
- Be more empathic to the needs and problems of learners
- Anticipate transfer problems between L1 and English
- Explain complex grammar points in L1
- Maintain classroom discipline and study routines according to native cultural contexts
- Enlist parental support and intervention more effectively

Nonnative-English-speaking teachers teach English in classrooms around the world.
© GG Pro Photo/Shutterstock.com

The Internet can help to provide a broad picture of the possibilities available to those who specialize in teaching English learners. Bilingual and ESL educators in the United States may enjoy the professional information available from the National Clearinghouse for English Language Acquisition and Language Instruction Programs (NCELA) (www.ncela.gwu.edu/), including the online library (hundreds of full-text articles and other documents for educators); useful links to national, regional, and state educational resources and databases; a conference calendar; lesson plans; and other practical classroom information. Dave's ESL Cafe (online at www.eslcafe.com) is a popular site for English learning, featuring chatrooms; a "bookstore"; job listings; and sections on slang, idioms, and other language-teaching tips. The *Internet TESOL Journal* (http://iteslj.org) connects to 3,500 additional links of interest to ESL/EFL students and teachers. Boot up, click, and enjoy the international flavor of the profession of teaching English learners.

PRACTICES FOR TEACHERS
Finding Out More about Teaching English Learners

■ Investigate the career possibilities of teaching English learners using the Internet.

■ Job shadow an educator to observe the challenges and opportunities.

Once the door to English is opened, learners who acquire basic tools of language acquisition can proceed at their own pace. In some countries, English skills can be a key to social and economic success. However, in the United States, as in other target cultures, entrenched social class privileges, politics, and economic realities present obstacles that must be overcome. Assisting English learners to adapt to or adopt the ways of a particular target culture as they learn English is an increasingly important facet of teaching. In the process, educators of many backgrounds, not solely native speakers of English, may learn much about themselves. Such cultural broadening as an outcome of teaching offers the possibility of valuable personal growth.

Aside from the intellectual and pedagogical challenges of teaching in a language-acquisition classroom, those who teach in such classrooms reap what they sow. Those who offer cultural understanding receive it; those who offer language exchange expand their foreign-language skills; those who offer empathy grow as human beings. No other area of teaching extends as rich an opportunity for intercultural communication, literacy development, creative instructional delivery, or reflective social praxis. And few other teaching areas involve such hard work!

Language learning is a complex, dynamic process that forms the foundation for academic skills. Beginning with basic communication skills, English learners face an uphill battle to acquire the sophisticated verbal skills needed for college entry or career success. Part of the challenge of educating learners of a second language is discovering what works and doing more of it, and then supporting other educators who are making similar discoveries and achieving similar successes.

In the past, students without English skills may have sat silent, excluded from instruction, because the classroom teacher was unable to teach them. In contrast, teachers today are challenged to prepare all students to succeed in life, including those learners who enter schools speaking a language other than English. Part of the repertoire of the contemporary teacher is a set of English-teaching strategies to reach those students whose English proficiency is emergent.

Educational Terminology

As in other professions, teaching English learners requires mastering a unique jargon. Table 1.1 offers a look at the terminology in this field.

As in other fields, when teaching English learners, one occasionally meets controversy over terminology. This book uses the term *English learner* rather than the term *language minority student*, although Skutnabb-Kangas insists that the term *minority* is correct, and its use in reference to populations whose language is a minority actually preserves legal protections for students' language rights under international agreements (see Wink, 2000).

The term *bilingual* has a wide variety of meanings and connotations. It can be used to designate the linguistic skills of individuals competent in two or more languages. The term *bilingual education* is also used to characterize types of educational programs (see Díaz-Rico & Weed, 2010). Many other terms will arise in the glossary of words useful in teaching English learners. These will be defined as they arise.

Teachers of English learners draw on such disciplines as linguistics, English literature and language study, foreign-language teaching pedagogy, sociology, anthropology, psychology, philosophy, and computer-assisted learning, as well as specific fields of study (medicine, engineering, aviation) that have their own distinctive

TABLE 1.1 *Educational Terminology for Teachers of English Learners*

Term	Meaning
English learners, EL students	Anyone learning to speak English whose native language is not English
Teachers of English to Speakers of Other Languages (TESOL)	The discipline of instructing English learners
Teachers of English to Speakers of Other Languages International Association	International professional association that represents TESOL educators
English as a second language (ESL)	Learners whose primary language is not English, yet who live in places where English has some sort of special status or public availability
Teaching English as a second language (TESL)	Teacher education programs whose candidates will teach ESL
English as a foreign language (EFL)	Learners of English who live in places where English is, by and large, an academic subject, functioning narrowly in that culture as a tool for communicating with outsiders
Teaching English as a foreign language (TEFL)	Teacher education programs whose candidates will teach EFL
English-language development (ELD)	Term used in the United States to refer to ESL services
English-language teaching or English-language training (ELT)	Term used internationally to refer to EFL services
Language acquisition (includes language learning)	Learning language in a natural context or formally through rules of grammar and usage
First language (L1)	The language learned at home from the primary caregivers (mother tongue, primary language, or native language)
First-language acquisition (FLA)	Acquiring mother tongue, primary language, or native language
Second language (L2)	Any language (whether third or twentieth) that is learned after the first language
Second-language acquisition (SLA)	Learning any language (whether third or twentieth) in school or in some other way after the first language
Target language (TL)	The language that is being learned in SLA
Minority-language student	Student whose native language is not the main language spoken in that country (a misleading term, perhaps, because a language other than English is the *majority* language in many classrooms of English learners)
ELL	English-language learner (English learner)

glossaries in English (creating the field known as English for special purposes, or ESP). Terminology from these associated disciplines will be introduced throughout this book as needed.

Critical Perspectives

This book adopts a critical perspective in regard to the education of English learners. A critical perspective is one that looks at broad social issues of dual-language proficiency and language policy from a point of view that promotes social transformation. It asks teachers to develop a deeper understanding of the effects of culture and language on the success—or disenfranchisement—of minority students by school culture, curriculum, and instructional methods in order to promote social change toward increased social equity and social justice.

As Wink (2000) has stated, "Critical does not mean to criticize. Rather, it means seeing beyond. It means looking within and without and seeing more deeply into the complexities of teaching and learning" (p. 29). It is my hope that those who use this book will become inspired to look within, around, and beyond social and educational issues; to ask probing questions concerning the role of educators in the struggle to attain fairness, justice, equity, and equal opportunity in the world; and also to work toward social equity and justice as part of their role as language educators.

Equity issues connected to the teaching of English do not disappear when English is taught as a foreign language. The same social, political, and economic forces that have mandated English learning in countries around the world have created layers of access and disenfranchisement that facilitate enrollment in English courses for social elites while barring the door to the poor. English as an international language (EIL) is an area of sociological and linguistic study that traces the impact of English on societies around the world. Those who equate English with traditions of social justice and democracy may be in for a rude awakening, for English is deployed within a wide variety of nations without democratic goals and ideals as well as in countries that share liberal Western cultural values.

Who are English Learners and What are Their Needs?

"What's that?" Jenny Wright asks fourth grader Michael Lopez, pointing to a drawing of a foot.

The boy shrugs.

This fall afternoon, as the rest of Wright's remedial reading class at Park Hill Elementary School in San Jacinto, California, completes language exercises on worksheets or computers, Wright is coaching her newest student, Michael, one on one.

He knows what a foot is, of course, but to him, it's *el pie*. The nine-year-old arrived last year from Culiacan, Mexico, and speaks barely a word of English.

Scenes like this unfold in nearly every classroom on Park Hill's tidy campus, where teachers struggle daily to balance the intense needs of immigrant students with the overall demands of educating everyone (Rosenblatt, 2007).

The following overview of the education of English learners in the United States and in selected countries around the world is presented with this question in mind: Who are English learners and what are their needs?

U.S. Demographics

> *Megastrategy* **1.2**
> Know who your learners are and why they need English

Higher birthrates among nonwhites than among whites, together with steady immigration rates, have impacted U.S. demographics and created a need for ESL services. California still leads the United States in demographic changes, as "minorities" became the majority in California in the year 2000.

In 2008–2009, there were 49,487,174 students enrolled in K–12 schools in the United States. Of these students, 5,346,673 are English learners (NCELA, 2009). This represents a 51 percent gain since 1997–1998. In nine states (California, Oregon, Nevada, Colorado, Arizona, New Mexico, Texas, Illinois, and Florida) over 10 percent of students are English learners. The greatest growth in percent of population, however, has taken place in ten states, mostly clustered in the South: Alabama, Georgia, Arkansas, North Carolina, South Carolina, Virginia, Tennessee, and Kentucky, as well as Indiana and Colorado (NCELA, 2009). Five states—California, Texas, New York, Florida, and Illinois—are home to almost 70 percent of all English learners in elementary schools (Cosentino de Cohen & Clewell, 2007).

In 2000, 32.8 million Latinos resided in the United States, accounting for 12 percent of the total U.S. population (the terms *Hispanic* and *Latino* are used interchangeably in the 2000 census reports). From 2000 to 2004, Latino populations grew more than 40 percent in six metropolitan areas: Atlanta; Cape Coral, Florida; Charlotte, North Carolina; Indianapolis; Nashville; and Raleigh, North Carolina (Associated Press International, 2006). Latinos of Mexican origin live mostly in the West (56.8 percent) and South (32.6 percent); Cubans predominate in the South (80.1 percent); Puerto Ricans in the Northeast (63.9 percent); and Central and South Americans in the Northeast (32.3 percent), the South (34.6 percent), and the West (28.2 percent) (U.S. Census Bureau, 2001b).

In 2010, the Asian and Pacific Islander population in the United States numbered 18.5 million, constituting 6 percent of the population. (*Asian* refers to those belonging to any of the original peoples of the Far East, Southeast Asia, or the Indian subcontinent, including Cambodia, China, India, Japan, Korea, Malaysia, Pakistan, the Philippine Islands, Thailand, and Vietnam. *Pacific Islander* refers to those belonging to any of the original peoples of Hawai'i, Guam, Samoa, or other Pacific islands.) Approximately 2 percent of these Asians are Chinese speakers, and of these more than 80 percent prefer to speak Chinese at home (Wallraff, 2000). Nationally, the growth of the Asian and Pacific Islander population at 46 percent between 2001 and 2010 is the largest of any racial or ethnic group, suggesting a proportional increase in the English-language teaching needs of these students (http://2010.census.gov/news/releases/operations/cb11-cn123.html).

Nationwide, in 1990 about one in seven people spoke a language other than English at home. By 2010, that number had risen to 20 percent of the population (U.S. Census Bureau, 2001c). States vary in this percentage, with California leading at 40 percent, followed by New Mexico at 36 percent and Texas at 32 percent. Swerdlow's (2001) detailed population maps show when and where immigration has occurred within the continental United States. In 2010, California, with a school enrollment of approximately 1.6 million English learners, led the states in the need for ESL services at the K–12 level (California Department of Education, 2010).

ELD Services for English Learners

By and large, then, in the United States, those who educate English learners are most likely to find employment in California, New Mexico, New York, or Texas, and in schools in city centers serving Hispanics or Asians and Pacific Islanders. Aside from this employment likelihood, demographics indicate that services for English learners are needed in every state and large city. For example, a major employer in the Cedar Falls/Waterloo metropolitan area is the meatpacking industry. Although Iowa in general is not a magnet for immigrants, many immigrants are attracted every year because of the high turnover of employees in the dangerous and low-paying meatpacking industry. Many such immigrants—mostly from Mexico, but also from Bosnia and Vietnam—bring with them schoolchildren; the ESL population in the local schools has gone from 50 in 1996 to more than 800 in 2001 (Milambiling, 2002).

From these demographics, it should be clear that ESL education in the United States is deeply bound up with the problems of inner-city education. As of 2007, about 46 percent of schools with high levels of English learner enrollment were in urban settings, versus about 24 percent of the low- and no-English-learner schools. Schools with no English learners tended to be in rural parts of the country, and those with low numbers were in suburban areas. Racial differences in schools correlated with large numbers of English learners. Rural areas served a 76 percent White student population, whereas at schools with high numbers of English learners, minority students accounted for 77 percent of the student body. These differences were largely driven by Hispanic students, who made up 53 percent of the students enrolled in schools with high numbers of English learners (Cosentino de Cohen & Clewell, 2007).

There are many English learners among the 50 percent yearly dropout population of the Boston public school system, or the 70 percent dropout population in the New York public schools. Macedo and Freire (1998, p. ix) claimed that the United States is experiencing the "Third-Worldization" of North America, with high levels of poverty, violence, homelessness, and human misery in the inner cities that approach proportions seen in the shantytowns of the disadvantaged nations of the world. The percentage of poor children, represented by the share qualifying for free and/or reduced-price school lunches, was significantly higher (72 percent) in schools with high numbers of English learners compared to schools with few English learners (about 40 percent). In fact, poverty was cited as a "serious problem" by more than 40 percent of principals and teachers at schools impacted by English learners, versus 20 percent or less of staff at other schools. Student health problems, likely also related to poverty, were identified as "serious" and "moderate" more frequently in high- than in low-English-learners-impacted schools (Cosentino de Cohen & Clewell, 2007, p. 3).

To educate these students, resources are badly needed, resources that are often not available to inner-city schools. The richest school districts spend 56 percent more per student than do the poorest; schools with large numbers of poor children tend to have fewer books and supplies and teachers with less training and experience. Thus, the urgent need for excellence in education for English learners is further complicated by the fact that many of the very students enrolled in these programs in the United States are poor and attend poorly equipped schools.

Did You Know?

Hispanic College Degrees

Leaders of society continually emphasize the importance of a college degree in the U.S.'s knowledge-driven economy, yet in 2007, only 13 percent of Hispanics age 25 and over had earned a bachelor's degree or higher; in 2003–2004, only 3 percent of all doctoral degree and 5 percent of master's degree recipients in the United States were Latino/a. Given the projected Latino demographic growth in the future, it is time to say to our Latino/a youth: "Latinos are critical to our nation's future and we will not let you fail" (S. E. Brown, 2009, p. 160).

International Demographics of English

Shakespeare's English at the end of the sixteenth century was the native speech of between 5 and 7 million Britons. Today, English is used by at least 750 million people, although only about 427 million speak it as a mother tongue. In fact, despite the establishment of 23 languages with equal rights in the European Union, English is nudging out French as the language of diplomacy in Europe (Phillipson, 2003).

No one is sure, moreover, what level of mastery of English determines whether a user of the language is proficient. Richard Parker, in his book *Mixed Signals: Prospects for Global Television News* (1995), reported that a study in the early 1990s tested 4,500 Europeans for "perceived" versus "actual" English skills and found that in countries such as France, Spain, and Italy, fewer than 3 percent had an excellent command of English. Only in Scandinavia, the Netherlands, and Belgium did the number rise above 10 percent. These sobering statistics indicate that English may not, after all, be the perfect international communication tool. In fact, several factors may be putting at serious risk the idea that English will continue to dominate world-wide discourse (Wallraff, 2000): the backlash against American values and culture in the Middle East and other places; the rise of regional trading zones in Asia, Latin America, and the Middle East; and the demographic surge of young non–English speakers in Asia, Africa, and the Middle East.

Many have touted the Internet as a medium that will circulate English around the world. However, as the technology becomes more widely available, people will naturally prefer to use the Web in their home language. No matter how much material is available on the Web, one cannot simply assume that people will use the medium as a tool to practice English. As the Internet is more widely available for recreation and entertainment, it may become more and more similar to television: People may consume and use it in their native language in preference to English. After all, more than six billion people in the world are *not* native speakers of English.

Given these conditions, one cannot simply assume that the demand for English will develop apace with world population growth. But the presence of a variety of trends argues as much *for* the increasing role of global English as *against*. Whatever the long-range opportunities, for the present, teaching English learners is among the world's fastest-growing occupations.

Contexts for Teaching English Worldwide

Despite concerns that call into question the value and utility of English to the world's cultures and peoples, there is no doubt that many countries are eager to employ English teachers. Following is a brief sampling of the conditions in which English is taught in various countries and areas of the world. In Japan it is widely believed that people who can speak English well have an advantage in obtaining and advancing their careers; however, few Japanese people need English skills in their everyday lives. Teachers who are native speakers of English are employed by the Japanese Exchange Teacher (JET) program at the high school level, but there is also work in the private *eikaiwa* (conversation) schools (G. Morrison, 1997).

In South Korea, English plays a crucial role in academic performance as a requirement for admission to competitive universities, as well as in entering prestigious occupations and, later, obtaining advancement at work. An impetus to learning English for many Koreans is the desire to live in the United States, which is home to over 1.4 million expatriate Koreans, many of whom live in the Los Angeles area (van der Woude, 1998).

In Taiwan, most students study English beginning in junior high school or earlier. About 80 percent of the economy of Taiwan relies on importing and exporting, with English being the most commonly used language in the global economic system as well as in trade between other Asian countries. English is largely a tool for passing senior high school or university entrance examinations. English teaching jobs are available in the private after-school or after-work "cram" schools, in which creative alternatives to rote classroom instruction are possible.

In the People's Republic of China, English is widely taught, although the preferred target language is still British English. The demand for teachers who are native speakers of English is high, although the pay is low by Western standards. Those who have an MA in TESOL may find themselves teaching English teachers or preparing advanced students for the required nationwide English examinations. Conversational classes are also popular (Ness, 1998).

In 2001, France announced a package of government reforms aimed at lowering the age at which French children start studying a foreign language to six in 2004 and five in 2005. These changes will require the employment of 1,850 language assistants in the schools each year. Not all French citizens are happy with these policies, however. Many teachers fear that the new policy will result in the dominance of English (Pugliese, 2001).

In Tunisia, most students learn English as a fourth language, after Tunisian Arabic, classical Arabic, and French. Despite the dominance of French as a Western language, English is gradually gaining ground in some sectors of society (Battenberg, 1997).

In Israel, all university students need a high level of reading comprehension in English, for the vast majority of courses feature reading assignments in English. However, as written and oral assignments and class lectures take place in Hebrew, students tend to prioritize learning the meaning of technical vocabulary words in English (Kirschner, 1993).

In Eastern Europe, the breakup of the Soviet Union and the declining influence of Russian culture and language has brought new life into English studies in former Soviet-bloc countries such as Hungary, the Czech Republic, and Poland. In former republics of the Soviet Union, however, the surge of nationalist sentiments and the scramble for economic survival has served to emphasize communication in the native language and in the language of nearby trading partners over a large-scale push for English proficiency. However, outside Moscow or St. Petersburg, there are few opportunities to use English outside the classroom. Teaching positions for foreigners are limited at the primary and secondary levels, but institutions of higher education and foreign-language institutes employ native speakers, and exchange programs are available (Menconi, 1996).

Indonesia, as the world's fourth most populous country, developed a national English-teaching syllabus as early as 1950, when English was chosen as the country's official "first foreign language." Students receive most of their English in high school, where it is a required subject. Currently, there are thousands of native-English-speaking teachers working in schools, universities, and private institutes all over Indonesia, supported by government-to-government agreements and university exchange programs (Musthafa, 2002).

In Mexico, English is in high demand. Anglo-American culture is popular, represented by subtitled Hollywood movies, dubbed American television shows, American baseball and football news, and various forms of pop and rock music in English on radio and television. Positions for English teachers are found mainly in private schools, in private English institutes, or in businesses, particularly in larger cities.

In Colombia, the extreme economic and security situation, as well as the number of multinational companies doing business in Colombia, have created a surge of interest in engineering and technical English (Deer, 2001). Ecuador has much to offer EFL teachers with MA degrees, who may receive a reasonable teaching load at a provincial university, free health insurance, and paid vacations (Owens, 1998). In Uruguay,

English is taught as a required subject at the secondary level and, since 1993, in the primary schools. Even small towns have English institutes, in which students work to complete international certificates. Teacher training is also available through distance learning (Pérez de Lima, 1996).

From these examples, it is evident that English learners are found throughout the world, making the teaching of English an international profession.

Career Preparation for Teaching English Learners

To prepare for teaching English learners, one can pursue various stages of career preparation, from BA programs with a special emphasis on language teaching through twelve-hour certificate or endorsement programs to MA programs to doctoral study in academic departments of education, linguistics, applied linguistics, or English. Despite the widely varying career ladders available to educators, the demand for professional English-language teachers has grown steadily around the world. In all parts of the world, at all times of the day, someone is teaching or studying English.

Teaching ELD in the United States

In states that support bilingual education, teachers with bilingual fluency who can deliver K–6 primary-language education in the languages of demand often receive hiring preference over educators who do not have bilingual certification. In the course of their primary-language instruction in literacy and in content areas, these teachers are expected also to deliver English-language development (ELD) instruction. In states where structured immersion (content delivery in English, usually without support for primary-language literacy) is the norm for K–12 English learners, teachers may be asked to use specially designed academic instruction in English (SDAIE) strategies (see Chapter 5) in addition to ELD. Elementary and secondary school teachers in most states must have a degree in education. Most elementary or secondary education teaching positions in school districts heavily impacted by English learners also require ESL/TESL/ESOL/TESOL certification or an add-on endorsement in ESL.

> Ramon Espinal teaches first grade. His class consists of twenty students, all of whom speak Spanish as their primary language. Fifteen of the students attended the school during the previous year and speak a limited amount of English. He has two students who are in their first year of formal schooling and are new to the United States. The other three students have come from other schools within the district and speak no English. Espinal partners with two other first-grade teachers. These three teachers teach specialized courses in the afternoons and rotate and integrate their students for language experience. (Frey & Fisher, 2007)

For teacher education positions as well as community college and precollege preparation of international students (intensive English programs, or IEPs), an MA degree is the basic requirement. The website www.tesol.org offers an online directory of teacher education programs in North America.

Teaching adult immigrants to function successfully in an ESL environment can be richly rewarding, for seldom does one find a more grateful or devoted group of students. Aside from the level of survival skills (gaining employment, finding housing, and providing vocational English), higher levels of professional ESP can include work-site training for engineering and computer professionals and other career-enhancing efforts.

Certification for teaching in adult English programs in the United States is less standardized than are requirements in K–12 schools. Some states have statewide certification, but in others the professional requirements vary from one service provider to the next. Each employer can make the local requirements and training options available to prospective employees.

The availability of teaching employment in the United States, then, depends on the population, the role of ELD teaching in relation to bilingual education, and the local need for qualified ESOL experts. One fact, however, remains a constant: The current shortage of teachers in U.S. classrooms will worsen in the decade 2010–2020, with urban school districts facing the most extreme shortfalls. The United States is expected to need ESL-trained teachers in affected rural areas (Chan, 2004). Districts are setting aside funds for teacher bonuses, training, and recruitment; raising starting salaries for teachers; and recruiting abroad for teachers in such specialty areas as bilingual education. The employability outlook remains constant for teachers who specialize in teaching English learners.

PRACTICES FOR TEACHERS

Increasing U.S. Employability

- Be aware of the connection between local language populations and career opportunities in teaching.
- Engage in career preparation that certifies instruction at more than a single level.
- Find out what specific kind of ESOL instruction is offered at various levels of education.

Teaching English Around the World

English teaching is an attractive international career, one that, although imperfect, offers interesting professional and personal growth opportunities. Teaching English in a foreign country has its own rewards: viewing your native language from another perspective, living and working in a foreign country, experiencing intercultural communication on a daily basis, and learning about the learners' culture at close range.

TESOL professionals seeking to work globally may find that the era is over in which native English speakers could be hired to teach English solely on the basis of their native speech. There is increasing evidence that being a native English speaker will be less of a hiring advantage in the coming years. In fact, as the twenty-first century advances, English will be shaped less by the cultures of English-speaking countries and will show more evidence that English has been localized and influenced by the native language.

One is best advised to prepare carefully for a job overseas; www.tesol.org offers articles in the Placement E-Bulletin (PEB) that often suggest additional articles and tips for working outside the United States (sample tip: Candidates should take plenty of official transcripts and copies if planning to teach abroad—they may need to change jobs while overseas). Whether you are looking for a teaching position or are just curious about ESL/EFL employment trends, PEB is a useful resource. To subscribe to PEB, you must be a member of the TESOL International Association.

PRACTICES FOR TEACHERS
Teaching Successfully Abroad

- Be prepared for local adaptation and adjust your teaching to local needs.
- Even though you may have native-like or native-speaker proficiency in English, face the fact that you may not understand the English of the natives!
- Negotiate job details carefully before accepting an overseas position.

Challenges for Teachers of English Learners

The first challenge is to teach English effectively, to motivate English learners to achieve the highest possible level of proficiency under the circumstances, and to gain a sensitive and complex understanding of the target culture. In this process, teachers of English who represent the highest ideals of the American target culture will work to create a classroom environment characterized by equal opportunity and democratic process.

The second challenge for the teacher of English learners is to respect the native language and the rights of its speakers. English teachers must be aware that for young children, learning English may put their knowledge and use of the heritage language at risk. Teachers must make every effort to support and enhance student's heritage language skills.

English teachers who make sincere attempts to learn the languages of their students and build English on students' prior language expertise will model expert learning. Teachers of English learners are intercultural educators whose understanding of crosscultural similarities and differences will further the abilities of the learners to acquire an appreciation for the target culture.

English as an International Language (EIL)

No one will question the claim that English has achieved some sort of global status. Three linked events created the opportunity for English to spread worldwide and fulfill social and economic functions in the lives of people from many nations: (1) the global military, political, and economic imperialism of Great Britain and the United States; (2) the defeat of Japan and Germany in World War II, with the subsequent reconstruction of their cultures and economies more aligned with English-speaking cultures; and (3) the global deployment of the Internet, resulting from a communication matrix connecting the technical and scientific universities in the United States (Wark, 2001). As such, English has become an international language, used by many the world over as a common linguistic currency.

Is English Natural, Neutral, and Beneficial?

Many regard the spread of English around the world as the beneficial result of a natural process in which English is benignly chosen as a trade lingo of choice because, as a language, it is somehow neutral in its social, political, and economic entailment. In reality, nothing could be further from the truth. Researchers who have looked closely at the role of English as an international language have challenged the spread of English in its global and local contexts. What are the implications of using English globally? Pennycook (1994) frames the issue with the following questions: To what uses is English put? What different meanings does it come to carry? Is the spread of English indeed *natural, neutral,* and *beneficial*?

Is English Natural?   To see the domination of English as *natural* is to believe that EIL is the result of inevitable global forces; that some language would eventually come to dominate others; and that, as it happened, English filled this slot. However, the spread of English is in fact due to politics and economics. To choose one example, the use of English on the part of the people of Puerto Rico, a commonwealth associated with the United States, is the result of a series of coercive government policies that have mandated English instruction at one level or another in Puerto Rican schools from 1905 to the present (Pousada, 1999). Another example is the way in which U.S. foreign policy created connections with populations abroad that pulled certain groups to the United States. For example, the conquest of the Philippines at the beginning of the twentieth century eventually resulted in significant Philippine immigration to the United States. Later, during the Vietnam War and its aftermath, Cambodians who cooperated with the U.S. military immigrated to the United States (Gillett, 1989). Basically, English has spread around the world because of war, colonization, and global trade.

Is English Neutral?   Is English a *neutral,* transparent medium of communication, detached from its original cultural contexts and not ideologically encumbered? First, we may hope that English will remain "ideologically encumbered" with the highest ideals: equality of opportunity, social justice, and human rights. However, it is naive to believe that people around the world are choosing to study English in a neutral way. To do so would be tantamount to denying that English proficiency worldwide is associated with middle- or upper-class status, access to higher education, and cultural encumbrances including the embrace of modernity.

EIL is heavily implicated in many social systems abroad that reproduce inequities in wealth, power, and privilege. Because English is the means to achieve education, employment, and social position, its use creates and maintains social divisions dominated by elites. Like access to technology, English is a player in a system that is widening the gap between global haves and have-nots, with the ownership of knowledge becoming ever more one-sided. In many countries, not speaking or reading English is an assurance that one will remain in an unskilled job.

Is English Beneficial?   One final question that Pennycook (1994) posed is this: Is the spread of English *beneficial*? Such a belief assumes that this spread occurs on cooperative and equitable footing, denying the role that English plays in many countries as a gatekeeper to social and economic progress. Like the spread of capitalism, international development aid, American media-disseminated popular culture, and international academic relations, the drive to attain English proficiency has its good and bad points. Just as consumers can become dependent on store-bought goods that were not considered necessary in traditional cultures, students can become dependent not only on knowing English for academic purposes but also on English-language media to spur desires that are, in the final analysis, irrelevant for their own best needs and purposes. This is the danger inherent in a world language when the world is not an equal playing field.

The changing nature of English—its evolution en route to becoming "the world's language," and the pros and cons of this process—are a part of the curriculum in educating teachers of English to speakers of other languages. Teachers are becoming increasingly aware that like many other aspects of teaching, teaching English involves power and politics.

PRACTICES FOR TEACHERS
Concerning English as an International Language

■ Don't be naive about the social and economic forces that coexist with the demand for English worldwide.

Languages at Risk

Unfortunately, the rich linguistic heritage of the peoples on earth today is at risk. Of course, the dominant languages of the world are not threatened—the 1,113 million Chinese speakers, for example, outnumber the native 352 million English speakers

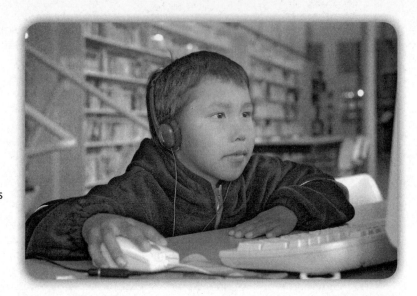

Native American students are using a rich set of computer programs to learn their heritage languages.
© Design Pics Inc./Alamy

by a ratio of three to one. By the year 2050, 556 million speakers of Urdu and Hindi, 486 million speakers of Spanish, and 482 million speakers of Arabic will more than hold their own numerically against 508 million speakers of English (Wallraff, 2000).

Minor languages, however, are in jeopardy. According to Woodbury (2001), there are roughly 5,000 to 6,000 languages spoken in today's world. A century from now, the number will almost certainly fall to the low thousands or even the hundreds. Even now, fewer than 300 of these languages have more than one million speakers; half of the world's languages have fewer than 10,000 users (Skutnabb-Kangas, 2001). Nearly half of the world's languages are already moribund, that is, they are no longer being learned by children. The linguistic diversity most at risk includes the tribes of Papua New Guinea, who alone speak as many as 900 languages; the native peoples of the Americas, who in ever-smaller numbers still retain 900 or so of their indigenous languages; national and tribal minorities of Africa, Asia, and Oceania, speaking several thousand more languages; and marginalized European peoples such as the Irish, the Frisians, the Provençaux, and the Basques.

The single greatest threat to languages with tiny numbers of speakers is often the language of the colonizer, of the most profitable trading partner, or of a more numerous and aggressive nearby population. In California, for example, the number of speakers of the 100 Native American languages spoken 150 years ago at the time of the arrival of English-speaking settlers has dwindled decade by decade. At present, there are about 1,000 speakers of these languages, representing 27 languages or language families (Hinton & Montijo, 1994). English is the native language of the children of these native groups, with the exception of the Spanish-speaking Indian people (Kumeyaay, Ipai, Tipai, and Quechan) residing on the border of Mexico and the United States.

What happens when a language dies? Woodbury (2001, p. 1) described this damage in eloquent terms: "Language loss entails the loss of much of the cultural, spiritual, and intellectual life of a people as experienced through language, ranging from prayers, myths, ceremonies, poetry, oratory, and technical vocabulary, to everyday greetings, leave-takings, conversational styles, humor, ways of speaking to children, and unique terms for habits, behavior, and emotions." When a language is lost, there is no guarantee that all this can be refashioned in the new language; when it does take place, such refashioning involves abrupt loss of tradition.

Aside from the toll on specific human cultures, social groups, and individuals' personal identities, the impending loss of linguistic diversity will limit scientific knowledge about the human mind. Language diversity tells us about the types of languages people can and cannot learn, how these differ, what such limitations may reveal about human cognition, and what this can tell us about the ways in which infants and young children acquire the range of diverse language structures now known to us.

Educators can address the problem of language endangerment in two positive ways. One is to volunteer to work with communities around the world who wish to preserve their languages, offering technical and other assistance in programs of language teaching, language maintenance, and even language revival. The other approach is to help English learners grow toward full bilinguality while documenting the primary language using videotape, audiotape, and written records of both formal and informal language use.

Box 1.1 **Preserving the Hopi Way of Life**

About 10,000 Hopi Indians have lived on their 1.8-million-acre reservation in Arizona for over 1,000 years. Their language is used for ritual purposes and is still spoken by all generations in the course of daily life, although now interjected with many English terms. Hopi educators are currently developing thematic educational units on such cultural content as Hopi legends, stories, and narratives; children's games; and history, including clan and village histories. Even though Hopis live in the modern world, they are raising their consciousness of the danger of language loss and reaffirming their identities as Hopi through schooling and literacy practices.

Each Hopi ceremonial dance begins with these words:

Pay yeesiwni.

Sopkyawat sinom wuyomiqhaqami qatsit naavokyawintiwni.

Paypu okiwa.

This invocation can only be roughly translated into English:

> We journey together in the Hopi Way immersed in the good things in life, our deepest values rooted in the cornfields; we Hopi aspire to experience the highest in life, and pursue this with humbleness and industry, so that each can reach self-fulfillment on behalf of the whole.
> (Sekaquaptewa, quoted in Nicolas, 2005)

English-language development teachers can show support for indigenous languages by integrating local indigenous culture into English language learning—not only to educate learners about indigenous people in their own countries and throughout the world, but also so that students from indigenous cultures can recognize their own culture(s) in the curriculum. Barfield and Uzarski (2009) give examples of using the history and design of Maori tattoos for English learners in New Zealand, using stories from the Bantu culture in EFL classes in Mozambique, incorporating the colors of Tibetan prayer flags into English teaching using environmental awareness as a theme, and basing ESL lessons in North American classrooms on ideas and designs drawn from Native American start quilts. Thus, despite the loss or future loss of an indigenous language, elements of culture can be preserved during English lessons. Only in the context of full support for the bilingual, bicultural learner does the teaching of English respect the learner's linguistic and cultural heritage. Chapter 2 and Appendix A explore in more depth the role of educators in language planning and policy issues, and Chapter 14 examines ways in which educators can involve the broader heritage–language community in English learning.

PRACTICES FOR TEACHERS

To Support Endangered Languages

- Further the teaching of English while respecting native-language rights.
- Encourage speakers of endangered languages to speak, read, or write in that language (if a writing system exists for that language).

Professional Organizations for Teachers of English Learners

TESOL International Association as an Organization

Megastrategy 1.3

Join with other professionals to facilitate teaching

The TESOL International Association promotes excellence in education for English learners and a high-quality professional environment for their teachers. TESOL's mission is to develop the expertise of its members and others involved in teaching English to speakers of other languages to help them foster effective communication in diverse settings while respecting individuals' language rights. To this end, TESOL articulates and advances standards for professional preparation and employment, continuing education, and student programs; enhances communication among language specialists; produces high-quality programs, services, and products; and promotes sound, research-based education policy and practices that increase awareness of the strengths and needs of English learners and further appreciation of diverse linguistic and cultural backgrounds.

TESOL is organized around twenty-two interest sections, offering the opportunity for members to focus on particular areas of expertise such as teacher education, adult education, intercultural communications, and computer-assisted language learning, to name a few. Associated regional organizations comprise more than one hundred affiliates, with such titles as Thailand TESOL (ThaiTESOL), IATEFL Hungary, Moroccan Association of Teachers of English (MATE), and California/ Nevada TESOL (CATESOL). Most affiliates hold yearly conferences or institutes for professional development so that teachers, administrators, and researchers with a distinct focus on areas such as elementary, secondary, adult, and university education can meet and share expertise.

Other Professional Organizations

However, many teachers of English learners do not identify themselves as TESOL educators. They may choose other professional affiliations, such as the National Association for Bilingual Education (NABE, www.nabe.org); National Council of Teachers of English (NCTE, www.ncte.org); International Reading Association (IRA, www.ira.org); International Association of Teachers of English as a Foreign Language (IATEFL, www.iatefl.org); or state, regional, or local affiliates of these organizations. Although these organizations increasingly focus on the education of English learners in their publications and conference sessions, the TESOL International Association is the only U.S.-based professional organization whose central mission is the teaching of English to speakers of other languages.

PRACTICES FOR TEACHERS

Meeting, Networking, and Enhancing Employment Options

- Investigate the local and regional TESOL affiliates.
- Explore the TESOL interest sections available with membership.
- Use sample job search Internet programs.

The best educators of English learners are those whose passion for teaching and learning nurtures within their students the capacity for critical literacy and joyful lifelong learning along with a sense of respect and pride regarding human diversity and the desire to promote intercultural understanding. This accomplishment is made possible through professional collaboration between colleagues who together undertake the task of achieving full literacy and social justice accompanied by equal access to, and opportunity for, quality education for all students. Critical educators become advocates for a more inclusive society, in which language, literacy, and culture play a central, integrated role in the understanding, communication, and respect needed to improve and transform education in local and global communities.

Those who teach English learners work within a full range of social, cultural, and linguistic contexts. They engage in reflective practice, promote reciprocal teaching and learning relationships, develop pedagogical knowledge that is socioculturally based, and honor in themselves and others the diversity in culture, language, socioeconomic status, and talent that makes us all uniquely human.

Exploratory Break

- Describe the demographic profile of the English learner population at your school site or in your local area. What specific linguistic or cultural needs should be incorporated into your curriculum or lesson plans?
- If you are a new teacher, what support do you think you will need during your first year of teaching to succeed as an ELD educator?

Chapter *2*

Critical Roles for Teachers

Teachers influence the daily lives of students in their classrooms. They can create a climate of warmth, acceptance, and high achievement for English learners, supporting the home language while fostering the growth of English. Conversely, they can allow policies of the school to benefit English-dominant students at the expense of English learners. As relative newcomers to English, English learners may need their instructor's support to negotiate their way in a new culture. Teachers of English learners cannot ignore the effects of power and policy issues. A critical stance is necessary to understand these issues.

> *Megastrategy* **SET 2**
>
> **Advance the interests of the learner**

Educators as Critical Pedagogists

Teachers of English learners have a special role in the classroom: as language emissaries and mediators, as agents of introduction to the target culture, and as sources of professional knowledge for their colleagues. Teachers who are aware of students' needs at various stages of their adjustment to the academic demands of schools and the stresses of life will help students to be more successful learners and intellectual partners.

What Is Critical Pedagogy?

The term *critical pedagogy* originated in the work of Paulo Freire. In the 1950s and early 1960s, Freire ran an adult native-language literacy project in northeast Brazil. Rather than using a standard text, Freire and his teachers taught using "generative" words based on the learners' social conditions and environment, such as *slum, land, salary, government, wealth*, and so on. Freire chose these words because they had special affective importance to the learners and reflected their social, cultural, and political contexts (Spener, 1992).

> *Megastrategy* **2.1**
>
> **Set professional goals with the learner's best interests in mind, as the learner defines them**

Using this method, Freire aimed to develop literacy built on the themes and actions identified in everyday life. By learning to read and write, students would also learn to criticize and act on their conditions (C. Brown, 1987). They could seize ownership of the written code to change their lives and social circumstances and gain the confidence to begin to free themselves from oppression and exploitation. Freire (1973) believed that one of the main tasks of adult education was to increase people's belief in themselves.

Glass (2001) offered a eulogy to Freire that is both eloquent and comprehensive:

> Nearly four years after his death, a world still mourns Paulo Freire. Freire's theory about the relationship between liberation and education has inspired and informed countless efforts to make life more human for those oppressed by economic and ideological structures that denied them their dignity, rights, and self-determination. The ideas in *Pedagogy of the Oppressed* (1970) have been applied in every continent, in projects ranging from grassroots basic literacy programs to national educational policies. Many people engaged in progressive struggles for justice—teachers, students, community organizers, workers, movement activists, and citizens from every walk of life—who studied his work discovered practices worth translating into their own contexts. Freire's legacy is unprecedented for an educator: None other has influenced practice in such a wide array of contexts and cultures, or helped to enable so many of the world's disempowered turn education toward their own dreams. (p. 15)

Educators around the world who understand his pedagogy of hope (Freire, 1987, 1994, 1998) have adopted Freire's learner-centered literacy approach in native- and second-language literacy projects in both rural and urban settings. In the United States, many community-based organizations have used the approach to developing basic literacy in English, in native languages other than English, and in English as a second language. In the process, these methods, originally designed for native-language literacy, are adapted to the education of English learners (see Auerbach, 1995). As Hones (1999) put it, "Critical pedagogy is a way of teaching and learning that poses problems about the world, with the goal of helping all participants become more fully human and transform the reality around them" (p. 27).

Critical Pedagogy as a Method

Critical pedagogy begins with *problem posing*. Teachers help learners draw on their experiences, culture, and personal strengths to try to resolve problems in their everyday lives. Teachers learn about problems in the community by walking through students' neighborhoods with students or alone, talking to people on the street, and observing living conditions, habits, and material objects. Conversations with students reveal as much as they are willing to relate about their home countries, how their lives compare in their previous and new countries, and what values they want to retain.

To verify what topics are vital for the students, teachers select and present familiar situations to students. Photographs, drawings, collages, stories, written dialogues, movies, or songs are used as stimulus situations called *codes*. Each situation involves personal or social conflicts that are emotionally charged. The teacher asks a series of open-ended questions about these materials so that students can elaborate on what they see, in this way defining the real-life problem being represented, discussing its causes, and proposing actions that can be taken to solve it.

Inductive questions move students from the concrete to a more analytical level: "What do you see?" (students describe and name the problem); "How does this apply to you?" (students define and personalize the problem); "How does the problem apply to your own situations?" (students describe connections); "Why does this problem exist?" (students fit their individual experiences into a larger historical, social, or cultural context); "What are some solutions?" (students discuss alternatives). This last step leads students into plans for action.

Contrasting Critical Pedagogy with Banking Models of Instruction

The technique described above clearly contrasts with ELD lessons that stem from what Freire calls the "banking model" of education, in which the teacher treats students as though their minds are empty accounts in which to deposit information. The banking model is predicated on two deeply entrenched misconceptions. The first is the belief that learners are empty, devoid of useful culture and knowledge. To the contrary, learners are not empty—they lead complex lives full of thoughts, dreams, emotions, families, loyalties, problems, friendships, and enmities that can enrich their language life in L2 as in L1.

The second misconception of the banking model is that "standard" knowledge is useful for everyone. In fact, this material is drawn from a "central bank of knowledge" selected and authorized by those with the power to set standards. When students generate their own dialogues, they have a greater chance to address those issues that they find meaningful.

The U.S. system of justice furnishes rich discussion. Hones (1999) used ESL instruction based on social studies to study the incarceration of Philadelphia death-row inmate Mumia Abu-Jamal. During reading assignments, class discussions, debates, and field trips to local courts, police stations, and protest sites, students posed problems relating to the criminal justice system in the United States, especially for prisoners whose race, socioeconomic status, and/or politics differ significantly from the mainstream. Hones specifically related race relations to Foucault's analysis of discipline and punishment (Foucault, 1979). Because Hones's students were drawn from a variety of nations, their contrasting views and experiences with social justice enabled a rich dialogue among students.

Using these methods to generate student language using codes drawn from both students' daily lives and current social issues, teachers bring English into the classroom that is useful and powerful in ways that students need it to be powerful. Chapter 15, which discusses project-based service learning, lays out a rapidly growing alternative to lockstep, sequenced, banking-model lesson planning. Both approaches hold fruitful potential for teaching English learners.

PRACTICES FOR TEACHERS

Seeing the Possibilities of English Learners as Problem Solvers

■ Listen and observe as learners tell you who they are and what their passions are.

■ Build codes based on students' lives to stimulate discussion.

■ Invest in long-term issues in order to develop language that is meaningful to students.

A Critical Sociological Look at Language and Power

Megastrategy 2.2

Critique the social conditions of the learner

Teaching methods are not carried out in a vacuum. Sociologists and social philosophers who study language and society have urged a wider perspective on the social tensions that underlie educational language usage. Critical language theorists offer tools of analysis that unveil language–power relations. Teachers who take a critical stance understand that the everyday realities of schooling—including the oral language of the classroom, the texts, and the written and unwritten practices and policies at the school site, district, and government levels—work in powerful ways to benefit or disadvantage English learners. Critical analysis can uncover ways to oppose discriminatory institutional and social inequities.

A critical perspective, one that looks at broad social issues of dual-language proficiency and language policy, has developed from the work of five theorists in particular: Tollefson, Foucault, Bourdieu, Cummins, and Fairclough. These five theorists represent critical sociological points of view and offer insights about language policies in education.

Tollefson: Power and Inequality in Language Education

James Tollefson (1995) has compared language policy issues across a variety of countries, researching the inequity created by social policies and practices that undermine the academic achievement of nonnative language speakers. He has laid the foundation for a worldwide vision of language equity issues.

Tollefson contrasted *descriptive* and *evaluative* ways to understand language behavior (1991). The descriptive approach examines such linguistic phenomena as low-status versus high-status language, code-switching by bilingual speakers in various social contexts, and the way language is used to establish and maintain social position. An evaluative approach, on the other hand, looks at efforts to standardize or purify language, to preserve or revive endangered languages, to establish national languages, or to legislate language usage. Both approaches help us to understand issues relating to language and power.

One might view language diversity as a problem, a right, or a resource (Ruiz, 1984). The view that bilingualism is a *problem* is at best socially and economically shortsighted. A country with bilingual citizens benefits economically and socially in commerce with other countries. Those who view language diversity as a *right* understand language rights in two ways: "(1) the right of freedom from discrimination on the basis of language; and (2) the right to use your language(s) in the activities of communal life" (Macías, 1979, p. 41). As a *resource,* dual-language proficiency, the attainment of advanced skills in more than one language, will be the source of employment advancement for job seekers in the global economy. Tollefson and his colleagues have documented that the struggle to achieve language equity has profound worldwide ramifications.

Foucault: The Power of Discursive Practices

Michel Foucault, a twentieth-century social historian, documented the means by which language practices sustain the spread of power relations in the modern world. Foucault emphasized that the struggle for power is "a struggle for the control of discourses" (Corson, 1999, p. 15). In several important treatises (1973, 1979, 1980, 1984, 1988), Foucault outlined the ways in which authorities have used language to repress and disempower social groups in favor of those in power, and how certain social groups have appropriated language practices for their own ends.

Foucault's contribution to the study of language policy, although indirect, is profound. He has shown that language is not neutral; language is inseparable from the workings of power. Power, however, is neutral; it can be either a creative force for those who use discourse masterfully or a destructive force that excludes those without effective language practices. As Ewald (1992) put it, "We have a responsibility with regard to the way we exercise power: we must not lose the idea that we could exercise it differently" (p. 334).

Bourdieu: Language as Social Capital

According to the French sociologist Pierre Bourdieu, language functions as *social capital,* a major form of cultural capital—that is, as a part of the social "goods" that people accumulate and use to assert power and social class advantage. Language is an asset, just as physical resources are. In a capitalist society, those who are native speakers of a high-status language receive their language skills as a part of their social capital, but those born into a language with lower social status have a lack of language capital to overcome. Those without capital largely remain in that condition.

Bourdieu (1977, 1991) recognized the key role of education in the determination of social success, emphasizing that schools reproduce the existing distribution of capital, permitting the haves to succeed at the expense of the have nots. In the classroom, those children who already appear to be successful can attract a teacher's attention, admiration, and reinforcement at the expense of those who appear to lack social capital. The teacher's attention is an important facet of a teacher's social capital. Bourdieu placed schooling, with its behaviors and practices, squarely in the context of the surrounding economic reality.

Cummins: Language Policies as Emancipatory

Jim Cummins (1989, 1996) contrasted educational practices that serve as *collaborative* relations of power with those that are *coercive*. He cautioned that children who enter schools in which diversity is not affirmed soon perceive that their "difference" is not honored. Often English learners are not encouraged to think critically, to reflect, and to solve problems. This attitude on the part of teachers communicates a sense of reduced worth, resulting in poor motivation to achieve.

Pressuring students to conform to schooling practices that are unfair or discriminatory results in a loss of their identity as human beings. Cummins called this "identity eradication." To counteract this devaluation of students, teachers who are dedicated to social change must help students to develop the confidence and motivation to succeed academically: They must also be aware of the ways in which spoken and unspoken language can circulate positive attitudes, building strong personal and social identities. Cummins's work highlights the need for schools to support the academic success of English learners.

Fairclough: Critical Language Analysis

Norman Fairclough (1989, 1992) offered critical language analysis (CLA) as a structured means to analyze how power messages are conveyed. Fairclough conceived of discourse as a nested set of boxes: In the inside box is the text itself, the language of the message. In the middle box is the institutional influence on the message. The outer box denotes the social and cultural meanings embedded in the message. Any text, whether spoken or written, has features at these three levels.

In the innermost box, a set of tools is available to describe the features of the text. One might ask, What is the origin of the text? What is the style of writing, level of vocabulary, complexity of syntax, and tone of the message? What is said? What is unsaid but implied? Does the text assume prior knowledge on the part of the reader? Who is responsible for the actions, opinions, or stance taken in the text?

At the middle layer of analysis, one can interpret the institutional influence on the text, asking such questions as, What institution originated the message? What social group (school, club, etc.) supplied the paper, the computer or word processor, or the microphone? Who stands to benefit from the message? What invisible rules or constraints shape or delimit the message?

The outermost layer of analysis is sociocultural. One might ask, How did society's attitudes and treatment of age, gender, and culture influence the text? Is the text biased? How might the text have been different had its origin been a person of different culture, gender, or age? What hidden messages can be understood about this message knowing its social origin?

Fairclough's CLA can be used to examine any item of discourse. For example, one might use CLA to scrutinize an editorial written by an English learner in a high school newspaper. The editorial criticizes local police officers who target minority youth whom they suspect are members of street gangs by stopping individuals on the street and detaining them for informal questioning. The editorial denounces this practice and calls for an immediate end to it. At the level of *text*, the editorial appears to be two columns wide, five paragraphs long, and prominently placed on the editorial page. The text is well edited, and the sentences are simple and uncomplicated. The choice of words—"Unjustified police action," "illegal," "unwarranted"—is unequivocal. The editorial is unsigned.

At the level of *institution*, the editorial is a part of the "school homecoming edition" of the paper, thus ensuring that many townspeople and alumni will read the accusations against the police. One must use prior knowledge about newspapers to identify the paper's editor as the author. The editorial reflects on the school because the newspaper is the official student "voice" of the school.

At the *sociocultural* level, the text assumes that the newspaper staff feel free to criticize the actions of the local police. Publication of the editorial is predicated on the support of the teacher who acts as the faculty sponsor of the student staff. The author of the editorial obviously sides with the minority youth who are being targeted by the police action.

One can see from this example that no published text is devoid of social and political consequences. CLA is a structured means of creating awareness of hidden levels of language. This awareness can then be used to tap previously unacknowledged information about the relationship between power and language and to confront assumptions and practices that lie beneath schooling practices. As an analytical tool, it is simple yet easy enough to teach to English learners as they become aware of what is said—and unsaid—in discourse.

Before continuing, two important terms come to mind when critical views are presented: *pedagogy* and *empowerment*. McLaren (1989) suggested that pedagogy is "the process through which students learn to critically appropriate knowledge existing outside their immediate experience in order to broaden their understanding of themselves, the world, and the possibilities for transforming the taken-for-granted assumptions about the way we live" (p. 186). J. Banks (1991) set empowerment in the context of personal and social change: "A curriculum designed to empower students must be transformative in nature and help students to develop the knowledge, skills, and values needed to become social critics who can make reflective decisions and implement their decisions in effective personal, social, political, and economic action" (p. 131). Wink (2000) cautioned that the verb *empower* should not be used with a direct object because it is patronizing to believe that one can empower someone else.

To summarize the contributions of the critical social theorists, societies around the world hide power relations within language issues. Language is a chief vehicle for deploying power, whether constructively or destructively. Language is a kind of social asset, and schools are agencies in which language is often used to benefit the privileged and disenfranchise the powerless. Schooling practices can empower or disempower, depending on the language and cultural policies of the school. The tools of the social language critic work to clarify and reveal covert language power relations.

Teaching for Social Justice

Teachers can collaborate as teams to incorporate social justice ideals into their practice. Cummins, Brown, and Sayers (2007) described a social justice–oriented curriculum in Los Angeles:

> In 2002, fourth-grade teacher Salina Gray and colleagues at the 99th St. Elementary School began participating in a local university program to explore social-justice pedagogy in urban schooling contexts. Their school, located at the border of Compton and Watts in South-Central Los Angeles, was sixty percent Latino and forty percent African American, and featured a regimented curriculum with a basic-skills approach to classroom instruction that was disconnected from students' lives.
>
> They found that by layering a media-analysis approach to literacy over the state-mandated scripted language-arts curriculum they could engage students in deeper critical inquiry. Films and Internet articles brought the world into the classroom; technical and scientific vocabulary from the media engaged students with higher-level language than usual; and hot-button topics like access to health care were introduced using such sources as *John Q*, a movie starring Denzel Washington as a father whose son was denied access to a crucial heart operation. As a result of this curriculum, test scores soared and many students won awards for high achievement. Gray writes,
>
> > Far too often, scripted reading programs take the power away from the teacher to be creative and decide what is best for students. I resent the fact that often teachers are not treated as professionals. Districts and administrators tell teachers that they need to have high expectations if they want their students to succeed. Well, I say the same thing to them—that they need to have high expectations of teachers and allow us to do what we need to do. (p. 246)

One way to add a critical perspective to the curriculum is to integrate social studies and history with English-language development. Bigelow (2010/2011) describes an assignment in which he asked students to write an "autobiography" of themselves as members of "The American Anti-Slavery Society" as a way to help students make personal connections to the role abolitionists played in the struggle to end slavery in the United States. Mariya Koroteyev, a Russian immigrant, responded with a first-person narrative of herself as the pre–Civil War slave, "Maggie":

> I leaned against the tree with closed eyes. "You!" I heard the watcher yell. "Get moving. Don't waste precious time!" So once more I took my heavy basket and began to pick. Row by row, basket by basket, under the burning sun . . .

Mariya's narrative continues, following Maggie's escape to Canada and subsequent life as a host for the Underground Railroad, helping other slaves to gain their freedom. This role-play exercise helps students to understand the critical importance of personal involvement in the struggle to obtain and maintain personal freedoms that most Americans take for granted.

A social justice pedagogy encourages teachers to act as intellectual leaders in education rather than as dutiful technicians. Students who are expected to think deeply about their world will rise to the occasion, and teachers who engage students in critical inquiry are the mentors of the citizens and teachers of tomorrow. The goal is to guard the students' best interests as the heart of schooling.

Profession, Policy, and Power in the Education of English Learners

Language policies such as class size, allocation of classrooms, availability of primary-language instruction, availability of support services for English learners, and funds for curricular materials are determined by policies at the school, district, local, state, and federal levels. Even the day-to-day influence of teachers amounts to a de facto language policy. Educators can promote the interests of English learners by taking an active role in language policy issues.

Examining the power issues that underlie the social uses of language helps to provide a broader perspective on language policy issues in education. Educators with a critical perspective may choose to influence policy matters at various levels to foster educational opportunities for English learners.

Language policies are written descriptions or unwritten actions that are taken to support certain languages.

Policies can be formal and official, or they can be informal, such as efforts made to manipulate attitudes toward languages and dialects (Corson, 1990). Language policies are not only enacted in government offices and

Megastrategy **2.3**

Use power and policy issues to support English learners

legislative bodies but are also debated in public forums such as newspapers, school board meetings, and radio talk shows. Attitudes toward second-language teaching and usage in schools overlap with other kinds of attitudes, such as support for immigration or racial prejudice against speakers of other languages; these attitudes in turn affect language policies. Both formal and informal policies have an impact on teachers, who often work under conditions that are highly political. Appendix A presents ways in which educators can influence policies to benefit English learners.

In the United States the language skills and rights of minorities are a fragile resource. These same issues resonate in other countries. Teachers need to use the leadership of large professional organizations wisely to effect constructive change in the education of English learners. Teachers must be willing to step outside the confines of the classroom to help students be successful and learn how to influence policy on a larger scale. As Kubota (1998) noted,

> Teachers who engage in critical pedagogy thus challenge and question the knowledge that is taken for granted, and explore the creation of new knowledge. In this view, the teacher's role shifts from that of apolitical technician merely transmitting information to a "transforming intellectual" (Giroux, 1991), critically aware of power and discourse, who addresses social and political issues. Thus, teaching is never neutral or apolitical; it legitimizes or challenges a particular discourse that controls social practices. (p. 303)

A teacher who believes in English learners' potential for success is in a strong position to fight for the recognition of their rights and the allocation of resources that make educational success possible. An excellent resource for student projects in the community, including those that deal with social justice issues, is B. Lewis's *The Kid's Guide to Social Action: How to Solve the Social Problems You Choose—And Turn Creative Thinking into Positive Action*. This book explains how to organize students to carry out projects such as having a proclamation issued, circulating a petition, and calling public officials—important ways that students can become involved in social issues and influence public policy in a democracy.

Marshall and Oliva (2006) sum up the role of socially conscious educators:

> School leaders sometimes do equity work when they implement equity-related policies. . . . Some go further, demanding better than the letter of the law, for example, by joining in political coalitions or in legal actions for school finance equity, for the preservation of bilingual programs, and the like. However, the activist, interventionist stance of social justice leadership goes even further, inspired not just by an intellectual ideal, but also by moral outrage at the unmet needs of students and a desire for a caring community where relationships matter. . . . Social justice leadership reconnects with emotional and idealistic stances. It supports leaders' . . . efforts to conceptualize and articulate models of leadership that incorporate democratic community engagement, spirituality and emotion, and caring and compassion. (pp. 7–8)

Exploratory Break

- Some educators argue that the emphasis on reading and mathematics proficiency under the federal mandates of No Child Left Behind (NCLB) is reducing students' exposure to history and social studies, thus limiting their understanding of how to become better citizens using the existing political systems. Do you think the emphasis on reading proficiency under NCLB is limiting students' ability to become good citizens?

- What social justice issues might prospective teachers of English learners face when looking for employment?

Chapter *3*

Views of Teaching and Learning

Philosophy, Psychology, Anthropology, Sociology, and Postmodern Pedagogy

Education is the key not only to survival but also to prosperity. This has been the message to young people throughout the history of human beings. When knowledge was whole—not divided into disciplines and specializations—wisdom was integrated into holistic views about nature and human nature, craft and sorcery, men's and women's knowledge, earth and the universe. Later, the study of ideas, human nature, culture, and language separated into disciplines such as philosophy, psychology, anthropology, and linguistics.

In the late twentieth century, these disciplines came together again in the complex endeavor of teaching English to speakers of other languages. Few undertakings combine so many disparate areas of knowledge. It is rare in this age of specialization to encounter a teaching discipline that demands the range of cross-disciplinary expertise required of those who educate English learners.

Second-language acquisition (SLA) is difficult, for it requires attaining linguistic and cultural proficiency, precise control of meaning, careful attunement to intonation, and mastery of behavioral subtlety. Unlike other areas of learning, however, prior knowledge of one's own language and culture assists this learning only to a degree and may actually be counterproductive: What is right at home may be exactly wrong abroad.

To make matters worse, whereas second-language mistakes are often forgiven in a rank novice ("charming accent," "how good of you to try our language"), an advanced speaker of a foreign language faces increasingly negative sanctions for error. Often, "almost there" is more threatening to native speakers than the failings of a beginner, and the better one becomes as a learner, the less one's errors are tolerated. Added to this difficulty is the seductive ease of lapsing into one's native language. Thus, there are multiple cognitive and emotional obstacles to second-language proficiency.

The particular nature of English as a target language compounds this difficulty. The huge vocabulary is a burden. Cultural invention of all kinds promotes continuous linguistic and cultural innovation, making learning English like swimming after a moving ship. Spelling is a learner's headache (compare *come* and *home*). Idiomatic verb–particle combinations provide challenges (compare "put up with" versus "put down" versus "put on"). Finally, different varieties of English worldwide may already be mutually incomprehensible—to pick just two examples, the English spoken in Jamaica versus that spoken in Taiwan.

Educators need every possible tool to create successful learning in the face of these challenges. Pedagogy for English learners draws on philosophy, psychology, anthropology, and sociology. Today, TESOL is a worldwide pedagogy. In this, it must be experimental. Language teachers must be unafraid to be risk takers and innovators in their teaching and must actively apply teaching and learning strategies using a broad, interdisciplinary approach.

Teaching the Whole Person

> *Megastrategy* **SET 3**
>
> Teach the whole person—beliefs, body, brain, emotions, and culture—within a positive social environment

Learning a second language involves the whole person. When a word or phrase comes out exactly right, accurate and appropriate for the situation, the whole person benefits. Educators who devote their attention to the whole learner reap the reward of rich person-to-person interaction. Such education draws on philosophy, psychology, sociology, and anthropology.

Philosophical Foundations of Education

> *Megastrategy* **3.1**
>
> Take into consideration your philosophy and beliefs as well as the philosophies and beliefs of the learner

Teaching strategies in many parts of the world are based on philosophy. In societies around the world, dominant systems of thought and governing ideologies are closely aligned with the policies and curricula in schools. Instruction is designed not to conflict with prevailing values and norms. English instruction in these countries is no exception.

In the United States, however, laws prevent public schools from promoting specific religious, political, or social philosophies. English teachers who go abroad may find no such prohibition.

Progressivism

In the twentieth century, education in the United States was influenced by John Dewey's *progressivism,* which sought to embody in educational practices the American ideals of individual rights, freedom, and creativity. According to Dewey (1916/1963), the learner must participate in forming purposes that direct learning so that education can develop thinking citizens in a democracy. This philosophy has justified pedagogy based on active learning and liberal social beliefs.

Traditionalism

However strong an influence Dewey has had on education, traditional schooling persists. Traditional schooling features an emphasis on the authority of the teacher and school administration; learning is based on the discipline of bodies and acquisition of a predetermined body of authorized knowledge.

English is taught in many countries in highly traditional contexts, and may be framed by philosophical beliefs such as Confucianist, Buddhist, or Islamic values that underlie educational principles. Educators in countries with a Western European cultural heritage believe in individual liberty and devotion to the worth of the individual stemming from the Renaissance and Enlightenment eras, beliefs that are often labeled "humanistic."

Belief Systems and Teaching

An educator's personal philosophy inevitably shapes and underlies classroom instruction. Challenges to one's personal philosophy may be superficial or profound, depending on the degree of difference between the cultures of the teacher and students. Intercultural educators are wise to pursue a deeper understanding of philosophical differences in discussions with peers, rather than students, and outside class time. In response, practitioners may adopt educational strategies that are psychological, rather than philosophical, in origin.

Teachers may face ethical dilemmas if they feel at odds with a given student's cultural background. Note the differences between Chad's values and that of the student's family in Box 3.1 (the incident is based on a real occurrence). What should be the recommended course of action in this situation?

PRACTICES FOR TEACHERS
Contrasting Teacher–Student Philosophical Belief Systems

- Learn more about the philosophical beliefs of students by finding a neutral context for discussion that does not jeopardize teaching and learning activities.

- Develop intercultural communication skills to frame discussions of comparative philosophical systems and the effect these may have on TESOL instruction.

- Be aware that in some cultures, authorities negatively sanction discussion of personal beliefs.

Box 3.1   To Mentor or Not to Mentor?

Chad is a journalism teacher in a large urban high school and the adviser to the school newspaper. Khalia is a young woman who enrolled in an introductory journalism class as a junior. Although English was not her first language, she showed unusual ability and creativity in writing the stories to which she was assigned. Chad routinely advises students on their vocational choices, writes letters of recommendation for them when they apply to college, and encourages those who want to further their education. Khalia has told Chad of her difficulty in winning support from her parents to attend college. Her father has already warned her that if her older sister does not receive a proposal of marriage within the year, he will approach a matchmaker to find Khalia a husband. Khalia does not want to enter an arranged marriage and has asked Chad for help in applying to college. Should Chad help Khalia?

Educational Psychology: Behavioral Methods

Megastrategy 3.2

Use behavioral training for accurate pronunciation and rote memory of information such as object and motor vocabulary

Psychology provides a second main foundation for instructional practices. The teaching of English has benefited as a discipline from psychological research on teaching and learning. The most successful paradigm in the early days of educational psychology was behaviorism.

Grammar Translation

The earliest type of language teaching was predicated on authorities having strict control over the learners' behavior. Grammar-translation pedagogy can be seen as a traditional form of behaviorism. As teachers explain the meaning of vocabulary words and the structure of sentences, students learn only what is required, in a system in which the rewards are explicitly connected to precisely defined actions.

The strengths of this methodology are twofold. First, when rewards are explicit, students have a clear choice of how much effort is needed to attain socially sanctioned goals; school success clearly predicts social success. Second, the curriculum can be carefully structured and controlled, with students' access to L2 limited to that which the teacher or other authorities determine to be valuable.

There are drawbacks to traditional behaviorism. First, students have little choice in what they might find motivating. Rewards are limited to those aligned with success in the native culture, even if a separate set of rewards may be a vailable in the target culture. Second, grammar translation as a methodology goes against the intrinsic nature of cognition: stimulation of curiosity, playfulness, and exploration. Third, there is often little independent language acquisition. Limited access to the target language and culture means little social interaction with actual speakers of the target language.

The Rise of Experimental Behaviorism

B. F. Skinner's success in formulating principles of behavior management established behaviorism as the dominant paradigm used to explain language-learning behavior. Behaviorism emphasizes the importance of external rewards and incentives. Providing grades, stars, and so on to reward learning—or imposing demerits for misbehavior—is an attempt to motivate students by extrinsic means.

Practices in descriptive and structural linguistics during this era resulted in a kind of behaviorist language-teaching methodology. Linguists believed that second-language teaching should be based on training the learners to perform accurate sound and sentence structure behavior. Their findings led to the development of the audiolingual method.

The Audiolingual Method

Based on behavioral principles, audiolingual instruction was designed to create correct pronunciation in a second language through oral practice. Students developed correct language habits by repetitious training, often using technology such as tape recordings in language laboratories. The role of the teacher was to direct and control students' behavior, provide a model, and reinforce correct responses (Doggett, 1986). Errors were corrected immediately to discourage "bad" habit formation. Reading and writing were often delayed until the student had an adequate oral base. However, audiolingual instruction alone did not seem to be very successful for second-language instruction beyond a basic level.

Total Physical Response

Total physical response (TPR) was invented by Asher (1982) based on the association between language and body movement. Even though Asher aligned his teaching with Krashen and Terrell's Natural Approach, much of TPR teaching follows behavioral methods of teaching, such as shaping of response and fading of reward. In TPR, students respond to oral commands that are simultaneously modeled; for example, the teacher says "Stand" while standing up and "Sit" while sitting down, and students follow along. The instructor repeats the commands followed by the appropriate action until students perform them without hesitation.

Eventually, the number of commands is increased, and novel commands are given that combine previously learned commands in a new way. For example, if the students learn "run" and "touch the chair," they may be given "run to the chair." Students continue to respond in a nonverbal manner until they feel comfortable issuing their own commands. TPR is associated with early stages of second-language learning, although efforts have been made to use advanced techniques at higher levels (see the section on TPR storytelling in Chapter 8).

Total physical response
involves active learning.
© Michael Newman/PhotoEdit

Direct Teaching and Mastery Learning

In direct teaching, the instructor maximizes learning time by careful classroom management, makes clear and organized presentations, and moves at a steady pace to cover key topics. This type of behavioral learning emphasizes explicit instructional objectives for students and promotes the learning of facts, sequenced steps, or rules. A clear and consistent match of instructional objectives with assessment helps students know the goals of study and guides the teacher's content delivery.

Another type of behaviorist instruction is mastery learning. A course of study is divided into small units with specific objectives. Students progress at their own rate and demonstrate mastery of each unit before proceeding to the next, thus developing basic skills before moving on to more complex skills. Students are gradually taught how to self-monitor, regulate, and reward their own actions; to monitor their progress, for example, through journals or study schedules.

Advantages of Behavioral Methods

Methods that focus on training the body (oral language behavior as well as kinesthetics) continue to be used in TESOL education. The strength of the audiolingual method is its focus on correct pronunciation. The strength of TPR is the reinforcement to memory provided by physical action. The strength of direct teaching and mastery learning is the ability to build discrete skills.

Disadvantages of Behavioral Methods

A weakness of grammar-translation pedagogy is that it limits exposure to target culture and self-motivated language acquisition. The weakest feature of audiolingual

instruction is that learners pressured to perform accurately under classroom or laboratory conditions often find it difficult to communicate spontaneously with native
speakers. The drawback of TPR is the tendency to focus on sensorimotor actions. The
weakest part of direct teaching is students' lack of ownership of the goals of learning,
even though mastery learning may permit students to control their own instructional
pacing. Balancing the strengths and weaknesses of behavior-based pedagogy, one
might conclude that these teaching techniques have a distinct, yet limited, role in
instruction.

PRACTICES FOR TEACHERS

Using Behavioral Approaches to Second-Language Acquisition

- Direct teaching is useful for teaching such topics as precise mastery of grammar, vocabulary, or pronunciation.

- Careful alignment of instructional objectives, direct teaching, and assessment is useful for mastering a highly structured curriculum.

- Mastery learning supplements direct instruction by encouraging students to achieve incremental, precisely defined objectives.

Educational Psychology: Cognitive Methods

Megastrategy **3.3**

Align learning with the brain and its natural ways of knowledge acquisition

The 1960s saw the birth of cognitive psychology, brought
forth through a combination of Piaget's developmental
work with children, Chomsky's focus on innate language
processing, and the application of information-processing
models to human thinking. Cognitive psychologists studied human thinking directly, rather than basing principles
of behavior on animal studies. This research gave rise to
studies in generative grammar, information-processing theories of the mind, brain-
compatible learning, and neurolinguistics.

Generative Grammar

Chomsky's devastating critique of Skinner's book *Verbal Behavior* (Chomsky, 1959)
claimed that language is not learned solely through a process of behavioral reinforcement, but that the mind contains an active language processor, the language
acquisition device (LAD), which generates rules through the unconscious acquisition
of grammar.

The fact that preschool children, for example, master complex aspects of their native language's syntax and semantics suggests that certain aspects of language need not be taught to children. Linguists postulate the existence of a human biological blueprint for language development to explain why the first language is mastered so rapidly.

Researchers studying generative grammar examine the language of native speakers, looking for rules used to master syntax. The syntax used by those acquiring a second language often shows characteristic errors, which also demonstrates their use of rules, even if the rules are not correct. Selinker (1972, 1991) used the term *interlanguage* to describe the language created by second-language learners. Interlanguage researchers look for ways in which the rules of both the first and the target language influence language learning, as well as asking what rules, and what kinds of rules, are universal to the human mind.

Krashen's Monitor Model

An idea similar to that of Chomsky's LAD was incorporated by Krashen's (1981, 1982) theory of SLA. Krashen's theory included five hypotheses. The *acquisition-learning hypothesis* distinguished acquisition (an unconscious process that occurs when language is used for real communication) from learning (which involves "knowing about" language and its rules). Krashen deemphasized direct instruction of syntax rules.

Krashen's *natural order hypothesis* asserted that language rules are acquired in a predictable order. Children acquire correct usage of grammatical structures in their first language (L1) gradually, as do children acquiring a second language (L2).

The *monitor hypothesis* postulated that the mind employs an editor, the monitor, which scans utterances for accuracy. When an individual initiates an utterance, that individual's monitor confirms or repairs the utterance either before or after attempted communication.

The *input hypothesis* claimed that language is acquired in an "amazingly simple way—when we understand messages" (Krashen, 1985, p. vii). Simply immersing a learner in a second language is not sufficient. Second-language learners are challenged by language that is slightly more complex than they can themselves easily understand. Peer conversation that mixes more and less skilled speakers is the chief means of accelerating a student's SLA.

Teachers may vary their speech to make comprehensible input for students, using shorter sentences, simple sentence structures, and restricted vocabulary and range of topics; focusing on the message and its relevance for the language learner within the environment; and using a variety of modalities, including visual and kinesthetic, to ensure that speech is comprehensible.

Krashen's *affective filter hypothesis* described the mental and emotional blocks that can prevent language acquirers from fully comprehending input. People acquire a second language only if their affective filters are low enough to allow them to receive adequate input.

Krashen's monitor model provided the theoretical base for the Natural Approach, which has had a great impact on second-language instruction in the United States.

> ### PRACTICES FOR TEACHERS
> ## Using the Natural Approach
> - Emphasize language acquisition as a by-product of interesting learning activities.
> - If the class as a whole has attained a certain level of fluency but one or two students have not, use specific techniques to include the lower-level students during instruction.

Stages of Development

There appear to be some generally accepted stages of development through which second-language learners progress in spite of human differences. The stages described by the Natural Approach are *preproduction, early production, speech emergence,* and *intermediate fluency*. In natural situations, second-language learners progress through these stages in a predictable order and at their own pace.

In preproduction (also called the *silent period*) the learner absorbs the sounds and rhythms of the new language, learns to identify specific words, relies on contextual clues for understanding key words, and generally communicates nonverbally. Once a learner feels more confident (the early production stage), words and phrases are attempted, and responses can consist of single words ("yes," "OK," "come"), two- or three-word combinations ("gimme the ball," "don't go"), utterances learned in one piece ("Can-I-go-to-the-bathroom?"), and simple poems and songs. In the third stage (speech emergence), utterances become longer and more complex. In the fourth stage (intermediate fluency), students begin to sustain conversations and can recognize and correct their own errors.

Recommendations for managing multilevel classes (those that contain students at different levels of proficiency) are the following: Plan a curriculum in which daily lesson plans feature a variety of activities geared toward different skill levels. Use assessment frequently and flexibly so that students receive instruction matched to their skill levels. Group students cooperatively and heterogeneously so that skill levels can be combined for effective peer language input or, alternatively, homogeneously so that students at the same skill level can be taught using the same materials and expectations. Vary the size of groups, from pairs to whole-class activities. Provide individual self-access material so that students can work alone. Ask tutors and volunteers to work with students in need of additional mediation.

Information-Processing Theories of Mental Functioning

For information-processing theorists, the computer serves as a metaphor for human mental activity: The mind processes information by gathering and recognizing it, storing it, retrieving it when needed, and generating responses. The perception

TABLE 3.1 *Ways to Enhance Students' Perception*

Explanation	Practices for Teachers
Variation in properties of written or spoken words: intensity, pitch, size, color, or novelty	Use various colored markers on the board; use volume change-up (soft, soft, loud, soft).
Manipulating posture, gestures, and movements	Use accompanying gestures to teach action words.
Use of emotion: vivid mental images, metaphors	Use reading material that quickens the pulse.

(input/recognition), short-term memory (information encoding), and long-term memory (storage) work together during learning.

Stating the *purpose* of a lesson helps students to focus on how the material will be useful or important to them. Giving lessons that require students to touch, smell, or taste shifts sensory channels. Using movements, gestures, and voice inflection (speaking softly and then more emphatically) stimulates perception (see Table 3.1).

The next phase, short-term memory (STM), receives patterns of images or sounds. Such information lasts only about twenty to thirty seconds at the most; it must be kept activated (by rehearsing or repetition) to be retained. STM is sometimes known as *working memory.*

To enhance STM, teachers can play short-term memory games such as Fruit Clap-Clap-Click-Click. (Students stand in a circle, and all clap their hands twice and snap their fingers twice; when it is a person's turn, he or she repeats the name of a fruit said by the previous person on the first click and adds a new fruit on the second click. The turn moves around the circle.) To stretch STM for actions, teachers can use a series of three or four commands in TPR situations.

Long-term memory (LTM) is the permanent store of knowledge. To move information into LTM requires time and effort, but once it is securely stored, it can remain there permanently. A *schema* is a structure for organizing information or concepts. A *script* stores a common behavioral sequence.

Teachers can help students store data in and retrieve information from LTM (see Table 3.2). Whatever devices are used, students get better as they practice, developing their own organizational and elaboration strategies as they mature.

Alternative Theories of Mental Functioning

Some linguists believe that parallel-processing computing models the operation of the brain. Parallel or distributed processing involves a simultaneous adjustment of a net of neural connections in the brain. As information is received, the brain creates a pattern across the net, adjusted over time by repeated exposure (see Clark, 1993). This model is closer to the LAD in operation. It is not, however, as good a model for conscious or strategic learning.

TABLE 3.2 *Ways to Enhance Storage and Retrieval of Information from LTM*

Prioritizing	Separating essential from nonessential details and focusing on meaning
Elaboration	Adding meaning to new information by connecting new with existing knowledge to increase retrieval cues
Organization	Placing new information in a structure that serves as a guide for retrieval
Context	Learning physical or emotional cues connected with information to enhance retrieval cues
Repetition, review	Repeated acts of storage and retrieval

Edelman (1992) saw the development of the brain as a process of evolution, with synapses evolving and competing with one another. In his view, it is more useful to think of the brain as a messy terrain in which competing capacities vie for dominance. The environment selects from among the built-in options available so that one set of propensities wins out over others (Sylwester, 1995; see also Clark, 1997).

Ratey (2001) used a metaphor of the brain as ecosystem. Four theaters (perception, function, consciousness, and identity) alternately take precedence, depending on task and predilection. His view, that function and consciousness are partially separate theaters, is an interesting way to look at the use of language, a human skill that often involves simultaneous conscious and unconscious performance. Even in this model, language is a central player, whatever theater is prominent at the moment.

To summarize these alternative views of how the brain functions during learning, learning stimulates the brain to search for the best response to the immediate challenge. The brain contains a basic set of neurons that interconnect to respond to the environment. On top of this innate capacity, culture has added technological components (computers, books) that continually interact with the internal biological brain but in themselves create new stresses and challenges to the brain's innate ability to solve problems (Sylwester & Cho, 1992/1993).

We must be flexible in the discourse we construct about the mind as we evolve the capacity to model a set of ever-more-complex systems based on qualitatively distinct, situationally responsive modular subsystems that afford humans the capacity to process information and to communicate.

Brain-Compatible Learning

Recent research on how the brain learns has led to new ideas about optimizing learning environments. The greatest challenge of brain research for educators lies in comprehending the vastness, complexity, and potential of the human brain. Brain-compatible learning helps to reconceptualize teaching by taking into consideration how the brain learns (D'Arcangelo, 1998; Jensen, 1998).

Brain-compatible teaching emphasizes the way the brain learns naturally; it is a comprehensive approach to teaching that uses contemporary research from neuroscience to create effective strategies. Given what is known about learner differences, brain-compatible teaching offers multisensory, multimodal pathways to learning that are brain-friendly and biologically driven (Haley, 2010; Armstrong, 1994).

The brain is a parallel processor that performs many functions simultaneously. Learning engages the entire physiology and is as natural to humans as breathing. Brain-compatible teaching must fully incorporate stress management, nutrition, exercise, drug education, and other facets of health into the learning process in order to respect and support the brain's complicated functioning.

The brain attempts to discern and understand patterns as they occur and to express unique and creative patterns of its own (Caine & Caine, 1997). The search for meaning cannot be stopped, only channeled and focused. Brain-compatible education addresses the brain's need for complex and meaningful challenges.

Students remember not what they are told but what they experience. Teachers should use a great deal of real-life activity, including classroom demonstrations, projects, field trips, visual imagery, stories, metaphor, drama, interaction of different subjects, and so on that immerse the learner in complex and interactive experiences (Jensen, 1998).

Emotions and cognition cannot be separated. Optimal cognitive functioning depends on a classroom emotional climate that is supportive and respectful, and creates a state of relaxed alertness in students. Under stress, the brain "downshifts" (Hart, 1983) as we literally lose access to portions of the brain. Students need projects that include a public demonstration so that they can experience anticipation, concern, excitement, and suspense (D'Arcangelo, 1998).

Mental processes are integrated differently in each person's brain. Teaching should be multifaceted to allow students to express visual, tactile, emotional, or auditory preferences and individual interests. This is the key to optimal brain functioning (Caine & Caine, 1994, 1997).

Are we stuck with same brains that our hunter-gather ancestors used? A group of cognitive scientists and neuroscientists says no—although the brain is highly structured, it is more plastic and influenced by experience than we might think. Each new generation of brains grows up in the environment that its parents have created, and can be "wired" in a different way. But at least one research finds that this is an exciting shift.

> ...the dance through time between old brains and new ones, parents and children, tradition and innovation, is itself a deep part of human nature, perhaps the deepest part...But surely, in the end, the story of the reading, learning, hyperlinking, endlessly rewiring brain is more hopeful than sad. (Gopnik, 2010, p. 15)

What are implications for teachers from the brain-based learning literature? Slavkin (2004) has the following comment:

> It is very likely that brain-based learning will continue to grow in popularity as our knowledge of the brain increases...Teachers already might be using brain-based

Box 3.2 **Can Brain Research Improve Reading Skills?**

At least one brain-based reading researcher takes pains to emphasize that the brain itself has placed limits on the reading process. No matter what the writing system, the brain has evolved to match sounds to symbols, relying on a limited inventory of shapes to convey sounds that correspond to meaning (Dehaene, 2009). The neuronal constrictions of the functional processing of the brain while reading define the scope of human cultural invention. So it is not the case that brain-based reading will allow teachers to discover entirely new ways for students to read—but rather ways to make the decoding and meaning-making process easier for all students, regardless of their brain processing strengths and limitations.

methods in their classrooms just by assessing students' learning styles and varying their instructional methods to accommodate the needs of students. Instead of teaching the lessons directly out of the teaching manual, children can be called upon to participate actively in learning by having a stake and a say in what occurs within the learning environment…when brain-based learning is successfully implemented in a classroom, no child is left behind. (p. 53)

Multiple Intelligences   A popular form of brain-compatible teaching is Howard Gardner's theory of multiple intelligences. Gardner (1983) defined intelligence as the ability to solve problems or make things that are culturally valued. According to Gardner, children possess different abilities that naturally direct them to learn in different ways and have at least eight separate kinds of "intelligences": linguistic (verbal), musical, spatial, logical-mathematical, bodily-kinesthetic, interpersonal (understanding of others), intrapersonal (understanding of self), and natural (using cues from nature). Gardner (1993) further stated that teachers who respect multiple intelligences offer a variety of materials and help to ease children into activities they may find threatening.

Emotional Intelligence   Emotional intelligence (EI) is a construct proposed by Salovey and Mayer (1990) and popularized by Goleman (1998). According to Goleman, emotional intelligence is "the capacity for recognizing our own feelings and those of others, for motivating ourselves, and for managing emotions well in ourselves and in our relationships" (p. 317). EI consists of self-awareness, self-regulation, motivation, social skills, and empathy. The term *EI* is a useful shorthand for discussing competencies that need to be encouraged in educating English learners.

Emotional scaffolding is a term that Fredericks-Malone and Gadbois (2005/2006) use to mean the following: "when a teacher designs a lesson plan, activity or approach to a subject that incorporates the students' personal lives, including ethnicity, socioeconomic group, history, and culture" (p. 21). They adapted the term from Rosiek (2003), with the idea that emotional engagement, in addition to intellectual engagement, is key to higher academic performance. Teachers' powers of observation and experience are invaluable tools to discovering what aspects of the students' lives—what topics they gravitate to in their personal lives—will spur self-motivation.

Educators are increasingly aware that schools should promote not only academic competence, but also teach students to interact in socially skilled and respectful ways, with positive, safe, and healthy lifestyles and behaviors; and that schools should foster the goal of contributing to society with ethical attitudes and actions, solid work habits, and values that include responsibility and engaged citizenship. Jennings and Greenberg (2009) presented research that ties the social and emotional competence (SEC) of teachers to their ability to create healthy teacher–student relationships and bring about a classroom environment that supports social and emotional learning (SEL).

Teachers with adequate SEC can regulate their own emotions to prevent professional burnout, especially if their classroom management skills prevent emotional stress from accumulating. Teachers who are unable to regulate their own stress response cannot promote positive relations with students, leading directly to poor student learning outcomes. The teacher's emotional intelligence is thus a key factor in student learning—promoting empathy, a sense of shared responsibility for co-creation of a healthy learning environment, and a mutual understanding and respect for the importance of emotions.

PRACTICES FOR TEACHERS
Involving the Whole Brain in Learning

- Vary methods and media for presentation of new information and problem solving.
- Provide opportunities for students to develop skills in areas of strength and weakness, especially using both heterogeneous and homogeneous groupings of students based on strengths.
- Invite role models to visit the classroom to offer students contact with someone in their area of strength.

Source: Moorman & Haller, 2011.

Neurolinguistic Research Based on Study of Brain Function

How does the brain store words once learned? Do bilinguals store their separate languages in two different parts of the brain? Is the left side of the brain really the language side? Do people who read languages written from left to right (like English) think differently from people who read languages written from right to left (like Hebrew and Arabic)? What about languages written using some other kind of symbols, such as Chinese or Japanese?

Box 3.3 Reducing Verbal Emotional Violence

John Ash teaches eighth-grade social studies. His students are similar to other students. They talk about clothes, video games, and the opposite sex. They also put each other down.

Tired of battling the verbal violence, John taught his students about put-downs. He shared and solicited examples of put-downs. He led a discussion on what it felt like to both send and receive put-downs.

Without exception, John responded to put-downs identically: "We don't use put-downs in eighth grade. What we do here is tell the other person how we are feeling and what we want to have happen."

In less than a month, John had drastically reduced the incidents of verbal violence in his classroom. "Some people think 'safe' refers only to physical safety," he said. "But it also means emotional safety. If I don't provide an environment where students are safe emotionally, how much learning do you think will occur?"

Source: Moorman & Haller, 2011.

Neurolinguists use techniques like event-related potential (ERP), which can show finer and finer details of the brain's constantly changing activity, and functional magnetic resonance imaging (FMRI), which can be used to picture the brain's tissues and functions. However, simple answers about language and the brain are not forthcoming.

Human brains are not all organized in the same way. Everybody's brain is different in terms of size, structure, and function, independent of the effects of experience and aging (Hotz, 2001). Language is one of the most complex of all human cognitive abilities. For one thing, the use of language is universal; all normally developing children learn to speak at least one language, and many learn more than one. By contrast, not everyone becomes proficient at complex mathematical reasoning, few people learn to paint well, and many people cannot carry a tune.

Cognitive Teaching Means a Focus on Learning

In summary, cognitive psychology studies how people transform, elaborate, store, and recover information. According to this view, active learners are people who initiate experiences, seek out information, and reorganize what they already know to achieve new insights, pursue goals, solve personally relevant problems, and attempt to make sense of the world. Various automatic mental control processes, schemata, and other mental mechanisms help the brain to deal with both familiar and unfamiliar situations.

Teachers motivate students best by providing course activities and projects that tap students' natural abilities and interests and develop their confidence in their ability to think. Teachers who ask thought-provoking questions and use concrete examples, activities, and demonstrations stimulate students' imaginations and critical thinking skills. This process includes *metacognition* in the form of cognitive self-knowledge, goal setting, planning, self-monitoring, and self-evaluating.

TABLE 3.3 *Comparing Behaviorist and Cognitivist Views of Learning*

Component of Learning	Behaviorist	Cognitivist
Belief about the mind	The mind is a blank slate.	The mind is an active organizer.
	All minds are basically alike.	Brains vary, with multiple intelligences and learning styles.
Goal setting	Teacher plans and sets goals.	Students participate in planning and goal setting.
Motivation	Reward is a motivator.	Learning is a motivator.
Teaching styles	Teacher teaches his/her way; one "best" way.	Teacher teaches with variety; no one "best" way.
Content of curriculum	Students are taught "what."	Students are taught "what" and "how."
Assessment: who does it	Teacher assesses.	Students are actively involved in peer and self-assessment.
Role of culture	Culture is irrelevant.	Culture is the basis for social interaction patterns; learning results from social interaction.

Cognitive training includes the use of learning strategies, study skills, memory enhancement, text-processing skills, note taking, research skills, test-taking skills, problem solving, making use of transfer, use of graphic organizers, information-processing tips, as well as learning the characteristics of the brain. A cognitivist view of learning means teaching students how to learn. A cognitive lesson needs two kinds of objectives: *content objectives* and *learning-strategy objectives*. Teaching content involves knowledge of subject matter. Teaching learning strategies builds cognition.

Comparing the Cognitive View with Behaviorism

Since the era in which behaviorism was dominant, much has been learned about making fuller use of higher-order cognitive functions during learning. Table 3.3 contrasts basic behaviorist assumptions about the nature of learning with later cognitivist views.

Learning Styles and Strategies

A large part of the shift toward a cognitive view of learning has involved research on learning styles and strategies. Chapter 5 explores these areas.

Constructivist Learning

Constructivism is an offshoot of the cognitivist tradition, in which complex, challenging learning environments help students to take responsibility for constructing their own knowledge. As students deal with complex situations, the teacher provides support. Thus, students and teachers share responsibility for the knowledge construction process. Constructivist methods make minimal use of rote memorization and instead focus on problem solving. Students discuss, ask questions, give explanations to one another, and present ideas and solve problems together.

Key elements of constructivist learning are particularly relevant to learning in multicultural classrooms: the encouragement of student autonomy and initiative, expectation that student responses will drive lesson content and instructional strategies, focus on students' concept understanding, and emphasis on critical thinking and student dialogue. A constructivist learning environment is of vital importance in enabling students to balance global issues and understanding—they will, after all, live in a different world than currently exists—with the need to achieve their own orientation to the world's challenges (Brown & Kysilka, 2002).

Constructivist learning in the elementary years helps students to maintain their curiosity and zest for learning. English develops as students talk, listen, read, write, and are involved with authentic tasks. At the middle and high school levels, students use research resources featuring various types of information representation. Project-based learning (PBL), for example, is a constructivist technique in which teams of students pool resources and expertise in the service of large undertakings (see Chapter 15).

PRACTICES FOR TEACHERS

Promoting Students' Construction of Knowledge

- Ensure that instructional objectives involving authentic learning are both compelling and comprehensible.
- Realize that complex problems require teachers as well as students to become learners. Constructivism is not for teachers who already know everything!
- In schools where students are exposed to a variety of representational formats for knowledge (text, visual, oral, figurative, etc.), students can choose to which modes they are most receptive and in which modes they are most productive.
- Facilitate working in teams and develop students' conflict resolution skills.

Humanistic Education: Affective and Emotional Factors

Megastrategy 3.4
Reduce tension and support a positive emotional state in the learner

Integrating Cognitive and Affective Learning

Educators have long recognized the advantages of developing both cognitive and affective (emotional) aspects of learning: the head *and* the heart. Students who explore content that interests them, work cooperatively with others, and accept the emotions that accompany learning (joy, curiosity, and excitement as well as frustration and anxiety) will mature as people with unique gifts and talents. Positive emotional factors help language acquisition to take place.

Self-Esteem

Self-esteem can be defined as having a positive self-concept or evaluation of oneself. High self-esteem may *cause* language success or *result from* language success. Students who feel proud of their successes and abilities and who have enhanced images of self, family, and culture are better second-language learners.

Of course, the most powerful sense of self-esteem is the result not solely of one's beliefs about oneself but also of successful learning experiences. Practices of schooling that damage self-esteem, such as tracking and competitive grading, undermine authentic cooperation and a sense of accomplishment on the part of English learners.

Classroom texts are available that offer literature and anecdotal readings aimed at the enhancement of identity and self-esteem. *Identity* (Raimes, 1996) includes authentic texts grouped into chapters titled "Name," "Appearance, Age, and Abilities," "Ethnic Affiliation and Class," "Family Ties," and so forth, best used in high school ESL classes of intermediate fluency and above. Another entry in this genre is *Who Am I* from Perfection Learning (2000), a collection of essays and stories that help students (middle school and above) to examine their identities and values.

Materials in the self-esteem genre can be divided into four parts using Siccone's (1995) typology: Type I activities promote an internal sense of individual esteem; Type II enhance students' sense of interdependence, or group esteem; Type III advance a personal sense of responsibility; and Type IV help students to feel a sense of social responsibility. Suggested activities for self-esteem building, along with recommended grade levels for each activity, are presented in Table 3.4.

Sapon-Shevin (1999) provides resources for various ages in many self-esteem genres, including books about self-affirmation, family diversity, peers helping one another, social inclusiveness, and social justice, as well as lists of organizations devoted to social change, songs, and cooperative games.

Ways of organizing the classroom can boost students' self-esteem:

> [The students'] first assignment was to introduce themselves to [the teacher] and to their classmates. "Spread yourself along a wall" was the way [the teacher] put it.
>
> What he had done before they arrived was to attach 30 numbered slips of paper on various surfaces of different sizes and shapes—surface areas of windows, walls, chalkboards, file cabinets, doors, an area under a table, inside a drawer, and so forth. He asked students to elect a numbered area that intrigued them and then sign their ownership of it on a numbered form on his desk.
>
> He then brought out boxes of construction paper, magazines with lots of pictures, wallpaper samples, colored yarn, scissors, marking pens, and masking tape—everything a student might want to develop a display that would be interesting self-advertisement.
>
> The students obviously loved the assignment, and the room was glorious.
> (Sylwester, 2003, p. 92)

TABLE 3.4 *A Sampling of Self-Esteem-Building Activities by Grade Level*

Activity	Description	Grade	Source
The Name Game	Students introduce themselves by first name, adding a word that describes how they are feeling today—using a word that begins with the same letter as their first name. (The teacher may provide English learners with an alphabetized list of adjectives so they can prepare in advance.) Each subsequent person repeats what the others have said in sequence.	3–12	Siccone(1995)
Name Interviews	Students work in pairs using a teacher-provided questionnaire: "What do you like about your name? Who named you? Were you named for someone? Are there members of your family who have the same name?"	1–12 (adapt to grade)	Siccone(1995)
Class Name/ Theme	Class decides on a name and theme. Students must not choose a name that is a put-down ("The Losers") or reflects a competitive orientation ("The Best Third Grade").	1–12	Sapon-Shevin(1999)
Maybe Yes, Maybe No	Students use a Chinese folktale to learn that events in one's life can be interpreted positively or negatively.	4–12	Siccone(1995)
Lend a Hand	Using a poster displaying prints of everyone's hands, students plan/celebrate giving or receiving help.	1–12	Siccone(1995)
A Kid's Guide to Resources for Social Action	Provides a comprehensive list of organizations available for resources on projects of social change.	4–12	Lewis et al. (1998)

Related to self-esteem is the concept of *inhibition.* Students are inhibited when they defend themselves against new experiences and feelings. Emphasizing fluency over accuracy in the first stages of language learning may help students feel less inhibited.

The ability to *take risks,* to "gamble," may facilitate SLA. Learners who are willing to guess at unclear meanings and to risk making errors will progress in language skills more rapidly than their more inhibited colleagues. As D. Brown (2000) pointed out, however, students who make random guesses and blurt out meaningless phrases have not been as successful. It appears that moderate risk takers stand the best chance of language development.

Extroversion can be seen as the need to receive ego enhancement or information from other people. Although the extrovert may be perceived as a person who takes more risks with language, an introverted or more reserved person may show more intuitive understanding or empathy with others.

Empathy aids language acquisition if the learner is aware of another's feelings, understands the intentions and emotions of a speaker, and attempts to comprehend the message.

Motivation

Motivation has been defined as the impulse, emotion, or desire that causes one to act in a certain way. Humans strive to actively acquire knowledge, explore, enhance the ego, achieve an identity within a group, and learn about their world. Various individual, sociocultural, and instructional factors impact motivation. Gardner and Lambert (1972) postulated two types of motivation in learning a second language: *instrumental* motivation, the need to acquire a language for a specific purpose such as getting a job, and *integrative* motivation, the desire to affiliate with members of the second-language group. Most students experience a mixture of both types of motivation.

B. N. Pierce (1995) has reconceptualized motivation in terms of investment, identity, and language choice. As Brutt-Griffler and Samimy (1999) pointed out, the basic social construction of the identity of native versus nonnative speaker influences motivation. A nonnative speaker must accept the status of a permanent learner (and unfortunately, even at the present time, someone who must learn is socially positioned as unfinished and intellectually marginal). This can result in reduced motivation.

Motivation can be seen as being a trait that is relatively consistent and persistent or as a state, a more temporary condition that can be influenced by the use of interesting materials or activities, reward, or punishment. Much depends on a teacher's definition of motivation. The belief that motivation is a *trait* may lead teachers to blame the student, parents, or culture for low student interest or achievement. Conversely, teachers who believe that motivation is a *state* may be motivated to alter their teaching if students appear unmotivated, to make lessons more interesting and involving.

Anxiety

Anxiety about language learning resembles communication anxiety, that is, feelings of self-consciousness, desire to speak perfectly, and fear of making mistakes. SLA anxiety is like other feelings of tension that students may experience in the classroom. Using a foreign language can threaten a person's sense of self because speakers know they cannot represent themselves fully in a new language or understand others readily.

Because students learn better in a supportive, nonthreatening environment, several language educators have developed methodologies that reduce tension. Student-to-student communication increases with peer work, small-group work, games, simulations, and an atmosphere of warmth and friendliness.

Several types of activities allow all students to participate with little apprehension. Beginning students tend to feel comfortable in activities that require sensorimotor involvement, such as TPR and playing games that require a combination of language and physical activity.

Anxiety-reducing tasks at the level of early production might involve hands-on tasks such as working with maps or creating simple puppet shows in which the puppeteer is behind a curtain or below a table. Speech emergence activities might include singing in a group or creating activity books such as "Autumn Leaf Poems." At the level of intermediate fluency, pair interviews help students get to know a classmate.

PRACTICES FOR TEACHERS

Reducing Student Anxiety

- Monitor activities to reduce undue pressure.
- Give students in competitive tasks a reasonable chance to succeed.
- Avoid making anxious students perform in front of large groups.
- Give examples or models of how the task is done when starting a new type of task.
- Teach skills explicitly and provide study guides.
- Vary assignments over different modes of language learning.
- Energize students by giving them a chance to be physically active.

(Adapted from Woolfolk, 2007)

Attitudes of the Learner

Attitudes toward self, language, peers, the teacher, and the classroom environment play a critical role in learning English. One's *attitude toward the self* involves self-esteem and related emotions, what one believes about one's ability in general as well as the ability to learn language. These cognitions and feelings are often hidden and may be slow to change.

Attitudes toward English, or the primary language, and those who speak it are largely influenced by peers and parents, as well as by prior experience. Negative reactions are often the result of negative stereotypes, discrimination, or racism. If English learners are made to feel inferior because of accent or language status, they may have a defensive reaction or ambivalent feelings about their L1. Conversely, students who acquire English while neglecting their primary language may be considered traitors by their peers or families. Either of these situations can cause problems within the family and create a backlash against English or against maintenance of the primary language.

Attitudes toward the teacher and the classroom environment play an important role. Families' positive attitudes toward school can influence their children's success. However, Ogbu and Matute-Bianchi (1986) stated that parents who have had negative experiences at school may subconsciously pass along these attitudes to their children. Students may cling to language behavior that characterizes their group, as opposed to the language group represented by the school, and engage in resistance in the form of misbehavior, vandalism, and poor relationships with teachers (Nieto, 2008). Self-esteem-building techniques can counteract resistance and foster positive attitudes.

Motivating Students Humanistically

Humanistic approaches promote positive feelings toward learning and respect for the value of every student. Students feel cared for, encouraged, and supported as they learn from their successes and failures, make choices, seek new experiences, work independently, and self-reflect. Students feel able to use their inner resources, competence, and autonomy in the pursuit of knowledge. However, high-quality education is not free of stress. Students need an optimum level of stress for school to be effective.

Humanistic education places emphasis on the worth of the individual, trusting and accepting the strengths and weaknesses of learners and empathizing with their thoughts and feelings. Good teachers target a level of performance that is within the learners' skills and abilities. They give positive feedback as often as possible as students pursue personal inquiry and collaboration, and offer the chance for input into course design so that students can explore issues that interest them.

Evidence shows, however, that promoting self-esteem and a warm relationship between teacher and student is not in itself enough to achieve effective education. A caring classroom cannot entirely overcome the negative quality of dehumanizing "get tough" administrative policies of inner-city schools, or the negative messages that students may receive about their home cultures.

PRACTICES FOR TEACHERS
Seeking to Motivate Students Humanistically

- Tell students you care for them and that your high standards for them are the highest form of caring.
- Demonstrate that you value creativity and individual uniqueness.
- Help students distinguish between "eustress" (good stress) and unwarranted pressure.
- Listen to students' opinions about classroom occurrences they deem unfair, teaching practices that bore them, or ideas that would benefit the whole group.

The Teacher as Counselor

English learners may need assistance during their adjustment to language and schooling in a new culture. Teachers may be called on to do more than facilitate cognitive or language development. They may need to address students' emotional needs by responding to emotional problems or crises, resolving interpersonal conflicts, or otherwise assessing and guiding students' emotional and social growth.

Teachers can help students adjust to school and to life's ups and downs in three ways. First, educators can teach in a way that fosters tolerance, cooperation, and self-respect. Second, teachers can help students to deal with stresses in daily life, either by one-on-one conversation, by group discussion, or by using a story in class that touches on a theme relevant to common problems. Last, when events occur such as a student's suicide or a community crisis, teachers can offer help in focusing students on their schoolwork or dealing with their emotional unrest.

Bullying—defined as a single or series of intentionally cruel incidents in which the intent is to put the victim in distress—may be a problem for non-English-speaking students as it is for many others. Students who are the victims of bullying can become suicidal or suffer lifelong emotional scars. The incidence of bullying is greater than most people believe: One-third of students reported bullying or having been bullied. Victims are more likely to dislike and perform poorly in school (Mestel, 2001; Mestel & Groves, 2001). Schools may benefit from clear antidiscrimination policies, supported with examples of what may be considered prohibited behaviors. Encouraging structured programs of intercultural communication can reduce stress for students in K–12.

PRACTICES FOR TEACHERS

Teachers May Play a Counseling Role

- Be willing to take time outside class to hear about a student's personal life, if this is appropriate in the context of the school.

- Understand that trust and mutual respect take time to develop, yet all cultures expect a certain level of automatic respect from students toward teachers.

- Nonjudgmental listening holds back both quick praise and facile advice; students are helped to discover their own solutions to their problems.

Cultural Anthropology and Education

In recent years, cultural anthropologists have contributed rich insights into the practices of schools, investigating the relative successes and failures of members of various subcultures of, or immigrants to, the United States who have attended public schools. This cultural perspective has also been applied to the study of English

> ### *Megastrategy* 3.5
> Be aware of the effect of the sociocultural context on cognitive and language development

teaching in a variety of settings. From this perspective has emerged a vision of TESOL as one of the first truly intercultural teaching professions.

Communicative Competence

Hymes (1972, 1974) introduced the term *communicative competence,* meaning the ability that enables language users to "convey and interpret messages and to negotiate meanings interpersonally within specific contexts" (D. Brown, 1994, p. 227). Rather than merely knowing grammatical forms, the competent speaker is recognized as one who knows when, where, and how to use language appropriately.

Canale (1983) expanded the components of communicative competence beyond grammatical competence to include sociolinguistic competence, strategic competence, and discourse competence. *Grammatical competence* focuses on accurate knowledge of sentence formation, vocabulary, and so forth. *Sociolinguistic competence* involves producing and understanding language in different social contexts. Strategic competence involves using language to meet communicative goals, compensate for breakdowns in communication, or enhance the effectiveness of communication. *Discourse competence* involves the ability to combine utterances (spoken) and sentences (written) into a meaningful spoken conversation or written text.

Teachers can help students to increase their skills in sociolinguistic, strategic, and discourse competence by building experiences into the curriculum that involve solving problems, exploring students' areas of interest, and designing projects. Students carry over knowledge of how to communicate from experiences in their first language. This knowledge can be tapped as they develop specific forms and usage in English.

> In a high school ESL class, Mr. Thurmond demonstrated grammatical, sociolinguistic, strategic, and discourse competence to students by having them role-play a job interview. As students conducted and analyzed the interview situation, they identified such aspects as the need for forms of politeness and the inappropriate use of slang. The final winner was the applicant who, having at first been turned down, used strategic competence—she asked to be put on a waiting list and then got the job when the first-choice candidate accepted "a better offer"!

Communicative Language Teaching   Communicative competence theory has given rise to communicative language teaching involving social functions of language; for example, talking about oneself, requesting, agreeing, refusing, telling a story, expressing disappointment, and so forth. Students may use conversational gambits such as those for the expression of opinions ("In my opinion...," "I personally believe...," "You might disagree, but I think...") or expressions used to change a subject ("Speaking of...," "That reminds me...," "By the way...," "Oh, before I forget..."). Even at the beginning level, one learns how to have one's needs met through communication in L2.

Students might listen and repeat conversations or role plays in which someone makes a complaint ("Look, I'm sorry to bother you, but . . .") or an apology ("I can't tell you how sorry I am . . ."). Communicative dialogues help students to identify what functional language is needed in a situation (persuading, stating preferences, etc.), and then provide a variety of ways to express the function ("It might be a good idea to . . . ," "Have you ever thought of . . . ?" "Why don't you . . . ?"). At the intermediate level, students also work to expand their repertoire of common phrases, such as, "How's it going?" "I hope so," "I doubt it," and a hundred other useful expressions (see *Common American Phrases in Everyday Contexts,* Spears, 1992).

At the advanced level of instruction, communicative competence helps the learner to achieve personal goals and desires. For example, Goodale's *The Language of Meetings* (1987, p. 9) gives this example of a communicative interchange:

> **SPEAKER A:** (wants to say) I want to meet on the 24th.
> **SPEAKER A:** (actually says) I was wondering if we could meet again on the 24th.
> **SPEAKER B:** (wants to say) That's not suitable. I want the 31st.
> **SPEAKER B:** (actually says) As a matter of fact, I'm afraid that might be a bit difficult, as I have to contact one or two colleagues who are out of town at the moment. Perhaps we could give ourselves an extra week. Wouldn't the following Thursday, the 31st, be better?

Goodale includes an analysis of the strategic features of this interchange: the use of modals (*could, might*) to make a statement more tentative; using questions rather than statements; adding "I'm afraid" to make it clear that the speaker recognizes the unhelpfulness of the message; using qualifying words ("a bit," "a slight problem") and the continuous form ("I was wondering . . .") to make the position more flexible; and using a comparative ("more convenient") to soften the message. Language is thus taught in a strategic/pragmatic/contextual form, and the learning is immediately useful outside the classroom setting.

Communicative language teaching has also led to greater use of games and communicative activities, which lighten the spirit of learning, reduce the affective filter, add excitement to the lesson, and make review and practice more fun. Box 3.4 offers a variety of resources for communicative games.

Box 3.4 **Resources for Communicative Games**

Lewis, G., & Bedson, G. (1999). *Games for children.* Oxford: Oxford University Press.

Lewis, M. (1997). *New ways in teaching adults.* Alexandria, VA: Teachers of English to Speakers of Other Languages.

Nation, P. (1994). *New ways in teaching vocabulary.* Alexandria, VA: Teachers of English to Speakers of Other Languages.

Communicative language teaching must do more than entertain students. As B. P. Taylor (1987) noted,

> Real communication is a shared activity which requires the active involvement of its participants.... We have a responsibility to create an atmosphere in which communication is possible, one in which students can feel free to take communicating initiative and are motivated to do so....
>
> But creating a supportive, student-centered environment...is not enough. True communication to which students are committed will only take place if we also have engaging content that will involve the participants and in which those participants have a stake...basing our instruction on task-oriented activities in the target language which focus on issues that are relevant and meaningful to students. (p. 49)

Social Contexts for Language Learning

The Russian psychologist Lev Vygotsky emphasized the role of social interaction in the development of language and thought: Language joins with thought to create meaning (Wink, 2000). Interaction occurs in a cultural, historical, and institutional context, which shapes the availability and quality of the tools and signs that mediate higher mental functions.

According to Vygotsky, teaching must take into consideration the student's "zone of proximal development," defined as "the distance between the actual developmental level as determined by independent problem solving and the level of potential development...under adult guidance or in collaboration with more capable peers" (1981, p. 86). Social interaction between adults and students operates within this zone.

Children's knowledge develops through their "taking for themselves" the ways of thinking and talking provided by their culture (Kozulin & Presseisen, 1995). This *mediation* of learning—assisting students' performance—requires teachers to adapt to the level of the student, to provide help when needed, and to help students work with one another and the teacher to co-construct meaning. Students benefit from communication with one another, members of the school community, and members of the community at large.

Vygotsky recognized that all teaching and learning takes place within the context of the memories, experiences, and cultural habits that are found within families. The wise teacher draws on families' stories and social histories to enrich the classroom. Self-esteem and identity are strengthened as themes and values are expressed through the words of students and their families.

Communities of Practice

Learning is not a separate and independent activity of individuals, but an integral part of participation in a community (Lave & Wenger, 1991). Children return to dynamic and interactive communities after a day of school. Teachers must come to know and respect what the community offers students and encourage knowledge to travel a two-way path as it circulates from school to home and back to school. Thus, learning is both an individual and a communal activity (McCaleb, 1994). The "funds of knowledge" approach (see Chapter 14) uses the cultural practices of households and communities as the resources within the students' world that can be connected in a meaningful way to the school curriculum.

Culture and Schooling

Schools, as institutions of learning and socialization, represent the larger culture. Culture, though largely invisible, influences instruction, policy, and learning in schools. A knowledge of the deeper elements of culture—beyond superficial aspects such as food, clothing, holidays, and celebrations—can give teachers a crosscultural perspective that enables them to educate students to the greatest extent possible. Chapter 10 treats this topic in depth.

The Study of Classroom Discourse

Schools, as institutions of learning and socialization, are representatives of a particular society, a *macroculture*. Moreoever, each classroom has a unique *microculture*. Understanding the discourse practices used in the classroom is an important step forward for students who are new to English. Classroom discourse practices are analyzed in Chapter 11.

Culturally Responsive Teaching

Intercultural educators have a repertoire of teaching and learning strategies available for use in a given context. Should students outside the mainstream change their cultural patterns to match those of the society at large, and should they seek success in mainstream terms? This is an *assimilationist* view. Other teachers believe in *accommodating* instruction to facilitate learning for such students. Culturally responsive teaching strategies help teachers to use the students' own cultures to support their learning. These are further explored in Chapter 10.

Looking Forward: Postmodernism

Modernism versus Postmodernism

Schools are among those institutions that discipline and shape daily life. Education has gained in importance as daily life has become ever more knowledge-driven. Formal schooling may eventually be replaced by more powerful modes of interactive learning. However, at this moment schooling still retains its role as the chief means by which society produces leaders and reproduces followers.

Megastrategy **3.6**

Place learning in the context of contemporary social change

Applying ideas adapted from postmodern theory may enable us to learn enough about schools to change them, just in time to preserve them. Apart from public schooling, there is no other shared institution in which all become citizens together. As society pulls people deeper into enclaves separated from common ideals, public schooling is at risk.

The modern world encompassed the eighteenth to the twentieth centuries. The Enlightenment led European cultures to a new freedom to pursue scientific questions using rational methods without fear of reprisal from religious authorities. Individuals took on surnames that permitted them to be known outside their village and were thus able to carry this identity forth to trade goods and knowledge, and to build empires capitalized by wealth resulting from new worlds of exploitable raw materials, cheap labor, and mechanization, served by an increasingly large managerial class.

Based on these trends, mass marketing spread the belief that mass consumption results in a secure, middle-class existence and access to a mass culture for everyone, underpinned by a number of specific certainties: that there exists a unified, centered self; that hierarchies based on social class are natural and inevitable; that the possession of "original" and expensive objects and experiences defines "value," whereas analysis and access to these objects and experiences constitutes "culture"; and that books contain knowledge.

However, one by one these beliefs have been challenged by developments that have taken place in the twenty-first century: an awareness of the limitations of rationality, a shift in what constitutes identity, a loss of belief in progress. It has become difficult to sustain a consistent view of change and growth.

Postmodernism is a movement in arts and culture that contradicts, subverts, or resists the prevailing assumptions of modernism. The term *postmodern* recognizes that globalization of cultures, races, images, and products has eroded national, linguistic, ethnic, and cultural identities, resulting in a global mixing of cultures on a scale unknown to societies before the information era. The individual is often adrift as multiple, conflicting identities, housed in alternative family units, combine with bionic mixes of organic and inorganic, human and electronic, to create a consciousness beyond reality saturated by images that may never have been "real." People may no longer identify solely with one native culture or language.

Implications of Postmodernism for Educators

Teaching English in a postmodern world is a career predicated on uncertainty. Like colonized people, those who learn English as a second or foreign language may simultaneously love and hate the colonizer, English. The mother tongue that has nurtured them is no longer sufficient in and of itself, and it cannot be protected from the cultural change that has brought the learner to the point of needing a second means of communication. Modernity has caused tensions and contradictions, yet postmodern pedagogies offer possibilities. The four most important implications of postmodernism for teachers of English learners are in areas of teachers' and learners' identities, technologies of knowledge, understandings about power, and changes in the English language.

Identity   In the modern world, one's *identity* was imprinted by one's primary socialization and encoded in one's native language. In the postmodern shift, identity is investment (see B. N. Pierce, 1995). Identity is seen as an internal resource. What time, energy, and personal characteristics is the learner willing to invest in L2, and how is this done?

Postmodern identity is flexible, multiple, and extended (Weedon, 1987). Postmodern learners are polycultural, as identity boundaries dissolve and people resonate in brotherhoods and sisterhoods that are self-created.

Identity is a powerful engine for SLA because cultural resistance is acknowledged in the postmodern shift. Many learners nurture a secret fear that conflicting loyalties between L1/culture 1 versus English-language target cultures will disrupt family life or cause irreversible change. Teachers can openly discuss fears of cultural detriment and/or change or loss of identity. English is not the enemy of tradition, but rather a vehicle for cultural change. Something is lost and something is gained when cultures change. Dealing with resistance directly makes new identity investments possible, for both the learner and the teacher. Intercultural educators benefit greatly from becoming bicultural, achieving what J. M. Bennett (1999) called "dynamic in-betweenness."

By acknowledging inner resistance, the learner is free to adopt a more flexible orientation toward identity. This can foster additive rather than subtractive identity. Teachers of L2 embrace identity 2 and nourish multicultural hybrid identities that activate and energize SLA and create new connections between motivation and methods.

Technologies of Knowledge   *Technologies of knowledge* will dramatically change in the postmodern world. The four major components of postmodern techniques of knowledge are constructivism, intercultural positioning, metarational thinking, and cybertutorial technologies (Díaz-Rico, 1999b). *Constructivism* endorses interactive creation of meaning. In the postmodern world, teachers leave behind one-size-fits-all methods and negotiate activities and objectives based on the needs of the learner, using knowledge of learning styles and multiple intelligences, and encouraging metacognition and self-reflection.

English teachers will find increasingly powerful ways to incorporate the primary language and the primary culture of the learner. This new emphasis—*intercultural positioning*—radically repositions the teacher and learner in the postmodern classroom. Educators who become learners about the language and culture of the students will serve as a model for learners.

Metarational thinking acknowledges that postmodern technologies do not engage solely the rational mind. Good teachers dip into the imaginary to teach, to use that primordial realm of "prepossibility" where dreams originate. This protects the learner from the belief that rationality is the only desirable mode of thinking, permits the yoking of emotion to logic, and sanctions solutions that are neither wholly right nor wholly wrong (see Chapter 8).

Cybertutorial technologies will characterize the computer–learner connection. They offer learner-managed information access, with project-based learning at the core. Students who surf the Web to complete projects for class can process English purposefully and independently, becoming, in effect, their own tutors.

New Conceptions of Power   Postmodernism will circulate altered understandings about power. In classrooms of the monolingual era, students spoke one language or remained silent. The institution controlled the goals and purposes of students' L2. In the postmodern world, however, power circulates, as dual-language acquisition

Box 3.5   How Is the Identity of a Young Child Affected by Learning a New Language?

Researchers who study English learners within a critical and sociocultural perspective view identity as socially situated. Their position is that the learner is a social agent, located with a network of social relations, using language as a social practice. Within this matrix, language helps to forge a complex identity that changes over time and space. Table 3.5 offers a synopsis of five identity-related research findings.

TABLE 3.5   *Research on Identity Issues for English Learners*

Publication	Findings
E. M. Day (2002)	The research studied the social relationships of a Punjabi-speaking English learner in a Canadian elementary school, showing the critical role his relationships played in the identities he could negotiate and the access, participation, and opportunities for language learning he could therefore gain.
Gutierrez (1994)	Contexts for learning were constructed differently, in three different classrooms, leading to differential access to learning on the part of Latino elementary children, who took up a broad range of tasks and roles in the more collaborative setting.
Hunter (1997)	The author analyzed the multiple and often contradictory positioning of Roberto, a Portuguese/English bilingual child, whose identity in relation to school expectations often conflicted with his identity among peers, and the effect this had on his second-language acquisition.
Litowitz (1997)	It is important to reexamine not only "what we are asking the learner to *do* but whom we are asking the learner to *be*" (p. 479).
McKay & Wong (1996)	In a two-year study of four Mandarin/English bilingual students in a California school, the author traced how students' activity negotiated their identities, positioning and repositioning themselves, resisting positioning, and setting up "counter discourses" that shaped their investment toward learning English.
Toohey (2000)	The identities of six children in a Canadian elementary classroom were differently constructed along various dimensions of competence (physical, behavioral, social, and linguistic); for some, their identities were constructed as deficient, and for others, more favorably.
Willet (1995)	Three female English learners who were allowed to sit together in an elementary classroom gained identities as good students by cooperating and supporting one another; whereas a male student placed between two English-speaking girls who did not help him became more reliant on the teacher and gained a less savory reputation as a needy, dependent child.

rotates power between peoples and among cultures. Students now have the power to speak and to use a public voice toward their self-determined ends.

English as a Language Will Become Postmodern   English will become not "world English" but "the world's English." English as an international language has multiple vernaculars, and speakers have their own dialects and purposes. This notion may be liberating, expanding the rights of others to access English. The best teachers are not necessarily native speakers, but rather those who love English.

Just the fact that English as an international language has multiple purposes, however, does not mean that all of these purposes are noble. Some, indeed, may not be democratic, may not be benevolent, and may not promote human rights. One would hope that the English that is learned favors humanity, equality, and environmental sustainability.

New Roles for English Educators

English-language teachers are poised at the edge of new opportunities; they are teachers with a truly global mission. Dedication to local learning means taking on flexible identities, affirming primary socialization while adopting a polycultural repertoire. Exploring the mind deeply, evoking its potential for self-regulatory and accelerated learning, and honoring the English of international speakers frees teachers of English learners to embrace postmodernism. Tomorrow calls!

PRACTICES FOR TEACHERS

Postmodern Education

- Help learners accept that having a second language means developing a more complex identity, and nurture that complexity.
- Encourage the learner to find meaning using new techniques of imagination, intercultural communication, and computer technologies.
- Examine the social relations of the classroom to see if learners have equal access to power and are treated fairly by the institution.
- Embrace polyvarietal English as equal in status to native speakers' or standard English.

Exploratory Break

- Review the suggestions on brain-based teaching in this chapter. Discuss which you will use in your teaching to enhance instruction.

Chapter *4*

Performance-Based Learning

Why Performance-Based Learning?

Megastrategy SET 4

Maximize learning by basing performance on measurable outcomes

Teaching is both a humanistic endeavor and a science. It is a humanistic endeavor because many psychological and sociocultural factors must be balanced in order to evoke the highest-quality learning from each student. It is a science because the current emphasis on outcome-based learning is based on careful research on teaching and learning over the past one hundred years. Assumptions that underlie this approach are straightforward. To achieve learning, one must do the following:

1. Describe what students are expected to accomplish or perform.
2. Detail what kind of evidence will substantiate this performance.
3. Design learning activities that will accumulate the desired evidence.

Given the complicated social context of schools with English learners, and the students' pressures to acquire English as rapidly as possible, one can begin to appreciate the complex terrain in which teachers of English learners are employed. Stakes are high. In a sense, the entire community is invested in the learning that takes place in a classroom, and the entire community suffers if the learning impetus of the young is misdirected, quashed, or squandered. Teachers must help learners use psychological tools that are designed for contemporary minds.

What Is Performance-Based Learning?

English is taught for purposes of communication and/or academic achievement. Therefore, a classroom lesson contains content. Moreover, the current emphasis on students learning *how to learn* entails some learning-strategy objective in each lesson. Additionally, because students are English learners, a third type of objective develops language. Thus, the objectives for an optimal lesson for English learners fall into three categories:

- Content (knowledge or skill in a subject area)
- Learning to learn (knowledge, skill, or learning strategy that teaches the student how to acquire or process information)
- Language (knowledge or skill in some facet of English)

How are these objectives chosen? Schools, school districts, or state agencies publish standards documents that spell out what students should know and be able to do. Curricular programs follow the goals put forth in the documents. A classroom teacher plans instruction using curriculum guides at the specific grade level. Units may be organized based on a theme or, if the course is text-driven, on chapters in the text (instructional planning is presented in greater detail later in this chapter). Units or chapters are further divided into specific lessons. Each lesson contains the essential content area objectives. The classroom teacher is responsible for presenting the material in an understandable way, arranging for students to participate in learning activities, and then measuring the extent of the student's mastery of the material. Thus, instruction and assessment are linked.

Objectives may include more than one content area. The teacher considers the various tasks that language users must be able to perform in the unit (listening, speaking, reading, writing) and makes provision for learning the vocabulary and concepts needed in the discourse of the content areas involved.

The objectives chosen must be matched to a specific level of performance that students will demonstrate. This process is central to the contemporary focus on accountability because the specific performance expected of the student as a learning outcome can be directly linked to some standard for the performance. Together, these constitute *standards-based learning*.

Standards-Based Learning

At the 1989 Education Summit in Charlottesville, Virginia, President George H. W. Bush and the nation's governors proposed a long-term national education strategy (often referred to as Goals 2000). The call went out for national professional organizations to articulate clear, high standards for what students should know (content standards) and how well they should know it (performance standards). Then the states were supposed to establish delivery standards declaring what all schools must provide in order for students to achieve these standards. All students were henceforth to be measured at intervals (say, fourth, eighth, and tenth or twelfth grade). This emphasis on standards led to the No Child Left Behind Act of 2002.

Megastrategy **4.1**

Align instruction with local, state, and national standards

TESOL Standards

The TESOL International Organization responded to the call for professional standards by adopting the Pre-K–12 English Language Proficiency Standards (see www.tesol .org). The document serves as a complement to other standards documents and specifies the proficiency that English learners need in order to become fully fluent in English. The standards do not prescribe instructional practices that match the proficiency goals. These aspects are covered in five useful volumes: *Integrating the ESL Standards into Classroom Practice: Grades Pre-K–2* (Smallwood, 2001); *Integrating the ESL Standards into Classroom Practice: Grades 3–5* (Samway, 2001); *Integrating the ESL Standards into Classroom Practice: Grades 6–8* (Irujo, 2001); *Integrating the ESL Standards into Classroom Practice: Grades 9–12* (Agor, 2001); and *Scenarios for ESL Standards-Based Assessment* (TESOL, 2001). Together, these volumes contain curricular units that demonstrate how classroom teachers organize standards-based instruction.

State English-Language-Development Standards

Texas adopted English Language Proficiency Standards (ELPS) in 2007 to replace the English as a Second Language Texas Essential Knowledge and Skills (ESL TEKS) beginning in the 2008–2009 school year. The standards are online at *http://www.tea .state.tx.us/curriculum/biling/elps.html*. Florida adopted the *Reading/Language Arts Standards with English Language Proficiency Standards* in 2007 as part of the Sunshine State Standards. In New York, the *Teaching of Language Arts to Limited English Proficient/English Language Learners: Learning Standards for English as a Second Language* document (*http://www.emsc.nysed.gov/biling/resource/ESL/standards.html*) was adopted to serve as the foundation for ESL curriculum, instruction, and assessment in grades pre-K through 12, and to serve as the framework for the New York State ESL Achievement Test (NYSESLAT), which is administered annually to all English learners in New York.

Common Core Standards

The National Governors Association Center for Best Practices and the Council of Chief State School Officers have collaborated with a variety of content experts, state education and school-level administrators, teachers, and parents to develop education standards called the Common Core State Standards. The goal of this effort is to provide English-language arts and mathematics standards for grades K–12 that are aligned and consistent across various states, so that students regardless of where they live are held to the same norms.

One drawback of these standards is that it is unclear how English learners will be assessed. At present, there are no recommendations for adapted testing either for English learners or for students with disabilities. The Common Core Standards website (http://corestandards.org/) indicates that information is available for these populations, but there is no standard adaptation per se.

Instruction Aligned with TESOL Standards

"The Most Beautiful Place in the World" is an instructional unit based on the book by the same title (Cameron, 1988) about a young boy in Guatemala who longs to attend school and learn to read (L. N. Levine, 2000). Levine found that the Spanish words, foods, and other cultural aspects incorporated in the novel were particularly appropriate for her class, who were all from Spanish-speaking families. The unit also integrated social studies curricular goals as students studied map locations, compass directions, and cultural comparisons. To fulfill language arts goals, they read for comprehension and enjoyment, read for specific information, predicted and inferred from text, answered questions using oral and written sentences, and acquired academic vocabulary. To meet affective goals, they learned to listen to and show respect for peers, help one another learn, and feel secure and successful. To achieve study skills goals, they learned specific techniques to learn vocabulary.

At the middle school level, Sillivan (2000) used the unit "Mastering the Art of Persuasion: Marketing and the Media" to culminate a yearlong ESL/language arts course. Students worked their way through a standards chart that stipulated the language functions and critical thinking skills used in persuasive media-based writing (creating print, radio, and television advertising). Students analyzed and created print ads, critiqued radio ads, and wrote and evaluated their own ad copy. Rubrics were used throughout the unit so that students could evaluate their own work as well as that of their peers.

In a high school intermediate/advanced ESL/social studies class using specially designed academic instruction in English (SDAIE, see Chapter 5), standards-based instruction was incorporated into the unit "Exploring World Religions" (Riles & Lenarcic, 2000). Students developed a word web journal to define religion, used reading passages and journals to discuss religion, and conducted library and Internet research to identify important religious figures. Final portfolios were used to archive students' essays and other writings. Throughout the unit, note-taking skills, outlines, time lines, maps, games, and other knowledge technologies were incorporated into group research, oral presentations, paragraph writing, and grammar work.

English-Language Development Standards

The TESOL standards do not define what students should know or be able to do in each level of proficiency. Nor does this document provide educators with directions and strategies to assist English learners. In contrast, California has prepared *English Language Development (ELD) Standards* (California Department of Education, 1999a) to ensure that English learners develop proficiency in both the English language and the concepts and skills contained in the English-Language Arts (ELA) Content Standards (California Department of Education, 1999b) (see Box 4.1 for first-grade ELA standards). Like the

Box 4.1 **Grade 1: English-Language Arts Content Standards**

Reading

1.0 Word Analysis, Fluency, and Systematic Vocabulary Development
Students understand the basic features of reading. They select letter patterns and know how to translate them into spoken language by using phonics, syllabication, and word parts. They apply this knowledge to achieve fluent oral and silent reading.

Concepts about Print
1.1 Match oral words to printed words.
1.2 Identify the title and author of a reading selection.
1.3 Identify letters, words, and sentences.

Phonemic Awareness
1.4 Distinguish initial, medial, and final sounds in single-syllable words.
1.5 Distinguish long- and short-vowel sounds in orally stated single-syllable words (e.g., *bit/bite*).
1.6 Create and state a series of rhyming words, including consonant blends.
1.7 Add, delete, or change target sounds to change words (e.g., change *cow* to *how*; *pan* to *an*).
1.8 Blend one to four phonemes into recognizable words (e.g., /c/ /a/ /t/ = cat; /f/ /l/ /a/ /t/ = flat).
1.9 Segment single syllable words into their components (e.g., /c/ /a/ /t/ = cat; /s/ /p/ /l/ /a/ /t/ = splat; /r/ /i/ /c/ /h/ = rich).

Decoding and Word Recognition
1.10 Generate the sounds from all the letters and letter patterns, including consonant blends and long- and short-vowel patterns (i.e., phonograms), and blend those sounds into recognizable words.
1.11 Read common, irregular sight words (e.g., *the, have, said, come, give, of*).
1.12 Use knowledge of vowel digraphs and *r*-controlled letter-sound associations to read words.

1.13 Read compound words and contractions.
1.14 Read inflectional forms (e.g., *-s, -ed, -ing*) and root words (e.g., *look, looked, looking*).
1.15 Read common word families (e.g., *-ite, -ate*).
1.16 Read aloud with fluency in a manner that sounds like natural speech.

Vocabulary and Concept Development
1.17 Classify grade-appropriate categories of words (e.g., concrete collections of animals, foods, toys).

2.0 Reading Comprehension
Students read and understand grade-level-appropriate material. They draw upon a variety of comprehension strategies as needed (e.g., generating and responding to essential questions, making predictions, comparing information from several sources). The selections in *Recommended Readings in Literature, Kindergarten through Grade Eight* illustrate the quality and complexity of the materials to be read by students. In addition to their regular school reading, by grade 4, students read one-half million words annually, including a good representation of grade-level-appropriate narrative and expository text (e.g., classic and contemporary literature, magazines, newspapers, online information). In grade 1, students begin to make progress toward this goal.

Structural Features of Informational Materials
2.1 Identify text that uses sequence or other logical order.

Comprehension and Analysis of Grade-Level-Appropriate Text
2.2 Respond to *who, what, when, where,* and *how* questions.
2.3 Follow one-step written instructions.

(continued)

Box 4.1 *(Continued)*

2.4 Use context to resolve ambiguities about word and sentence meanings.

2.5 Confirm predictions about what will happen next in a text by identifying key words (i.e., signpost words).

2.6 Relate prior knowledge to textual information.

2.7 Retell the central ideas of simple expository or narrative passages.

3.0 Literary Response and Analysis

Students read and respond to a wide variety of significant works of children's literature. They distinguish between the structural features of the text and the literary terms or elements (e.g., theme, plot, setting, characters). The selections in *Recommended Readings in Literature, Kindergarten through Grade Eight* illustrate the quality and complexity of the materials to be read by students.

Narrative Analysis of Grade-Level-Appropriate Text

3.1 Identify and describe the elements of plot, setting, and character(s) in a story, as well as the story's beginning, middle, and ending.

3.2 Describe the roles of authors and illustrators and their contributions to print materials.

3.3 Recollect, talk, and write about books read during the school year.

Writing

1.0 Writing Strategies

Students write clear and coherent sentences and paragraphs that develop a central idea. Their writing shows they consider the audience and purpose. Students progress through the stages of the writing process (e.g., prewriting, drafting, revising, editing successive versions).

Organization and Focus

1.1 Select a focus when writing.

1.2 Use descriptive words when writing.

Penmanship

1.3 Print legibly and space letters, words, and sentences appropriately.

2.0 Writing Applications (Genres and Their Characteristics)

Students write compositions that describe and explain familar objects, events, and experiences. Student writing demonstrates a command of standard American English and the drafting, research, and organizational strategies outlined in Writing Standard 1.0.

Using the writing strategies of grade 1 outlined in Writing Standard 1.0, students:

2.1 Write brief narratives (e.g., fictional, autobiographical) describing an experience.

2.2 Write brief expository descriptions of a real object, person, place, or event, using sensory details.

Written and Oral English Language Conventions

The standards for written and oral English language conventions have been placed between those for writing and for listening and speaking because these conventions are essential to both sets of skills.

1.0 Written and Oral English Language Conventions

Students write and speak with a command of standard English conventions appropriate to this grade level.

Sentence Structure

1.1 Write and speak in complete, coherent sentences.

Grammar

1.2 Identify and correctly use singular and plural nouns.

1.3 Identify and correctly use contractions (e.g., *isn't, aren't, can't, won't*) and singular possessive pronouns (e.g., *my/mine, his/her, hers, your/s*) in writing and speaking.

Punctuation

1.4 Distinguish between declarative, exclamatory, and interrogative sentences.

(continued)

Box 4.1 *(Continued)*

1.5 Use a period, exclamation point, or question mark at the end of sentences.
1.6 Use knowledge of the basic rules of punctuation and capitalization when writing.

Capitalization
1.7 Capitalize the first word of a sentence, names of people, and the pronoun *I.*
Spelling
1.8 Spell three- and four-letter short-vowel words and grade-level-appropriate sight words correctly.

Listening and Speaking

1.0   Listening and Speaking Strategies
Students listen critically and respond appropriately to oral communication. They speak in a manner that guides the listener to understand important ideas by using proper phrasing, pitch, and modulation.

Comprehension
1.1 Listen attentively.
1.2 Ask questions for clarification and understanding.
1.3 Give, restate, and follow simple two-step directions.

Organization and Delivery of Oral Communication
1.4 Stay on topic when speaking.
1.5 Use descriptive words when speaking about people, places, things, and events.

2.0   Speaking Applications (Genres and Their Characteristics)
Students deliver brief recitations and oral presentations about familiar experiences or interests that are organized around a coherent thesis statement. Student speaking demonstrates a command of standard American English and the organizational and delivery strategies outlined in Listening and Speaking Standard 1.0.

Using the speaking strategies of grade 1 outlined in Listening and Speaking Standard 1.0, students:
2.1 Recite poems, rhymes, songs, and stories.
2.2 Retell stories using basic story grammar and relating the sequence of story events by answering *who, what, when, where, why,* and *how* questions.
2.3 Relate an important life event or personal experience in a simple sequence.
2.4 Provide descriptions with careful attention to sensory detail.

Source: © 1999 by the California Department of Education.

ELA standards, the California *ELD Standards* are organized into areas of reading, writing, and listening/speaking. The California English Language Development Test (CELDT) is aligned with the standards as a placement and achievement test. Using the ELD and ELA standards, teachers can work with students through a developmental framework that stipulates the requirements of each proficiency level.

Incorporating Standards into Lesson Plans

A standard becomes useful to teachers only when they can identify when the standard has been met or progress is being made toward meeting it. Moreover, when schools communicate performance standards to students, the students know what is considered important for them to be able to do and can more easily judge where they stand within the full range of performance expectations. Assessment should provide information on what students already do well and pinpoint what they still need to learn. In this way, assessment can provide information about what aspects of instruction need to be redesigned so that both student and teacher performance improves.

What Is the Best Use of Assessment?

Assessment means more than scoring high marks on a test, getting good grades, or satisfying the accountability demands of an external authority. Assessment plays a vital role in supporting and enhancing learning. Assessment is a process for determining the current level of a learner's performance or knowledge. Assessment for the purpose of placement informs educators about the strengths and needs of the language learner so that students can be appropriately instructed. Classroom instruction that is directly linked to placement tests for English learners permits teachers to begin using effective instructional practices as soon as students enter the classroom. Ongoing assessment informs parents and school authorities of the student's progress and ensures continuous progress. In the current climate of standards-driven instruction, the results of assessment may also be used to assess the effectiveness of the teacher's instruction.

Megastrategy 4.2

Understand the purposes and functions of assessment

Various evaluation methods have been used with English learners. Some are required by government programs and legal mandates; others, more informal, are devised by classroom teachers. Assessment should be used not merely for labeling and placing students but also for designing instruction that advances students' understanding and abilities, helping students to seek meaning and use a second language to fulfill academic and personal goals.

The Changing Nature of Assessment

Three major factors have converged to intensify the focus on new forms of assessment. First, advances in cognitive psychology have led educators to recognize the complex nature of learning. Assessment must be diverse to capture this complexity accurately and fairly. Second, many educators have acknowledged that multiple-choice, standardized achievement tests do not measure the complexity of learning processes despite the fact that educators are increasingly pressured to use such measures to document school improvement. Third, tests are increasingly being used to measure the success of school reform and to document accountability. Tests used as criteria should be dependable and credible measures of student learning (Linn, 2000).

Traditional views of testing were based on the behaviorists' belief that knowledge can be analyzed into small skill units that could be taught, measured, and reinforced separately. Objective tests, administered uniformly to all students, were believed to represent scientific measurement of learning.

Classroom assessment based on constructivist, cognitive, and sociocultural theory, in contrast, offered a radically different focus. Rather than seeing the capacity to acquire knowledge as an inborn skill, Vygotsky and his colleagues argued that knowledge is based on a set of cognitive structures that are created through a dynamic, socially based process of meaning making. As a result of this view, thinking and problem-solving skills have come to the fore. Assessment is still used to report to others on students' ability, but it also provides direct feedback to learners so that they can take responsibility for self-correction and improvement.

Standardized testing will probably persist because of the economic and political investment in the type of assessment that compares students with one another. Too often, however, social and economic pressures from testing overshadow the curriculum and the affective goals of schooling. The judgments resulting from this testing may affect students' present adjustment to school and their future academic and social successes, effectively undermining their ability to plan their own learning strategies, activities, and use of time and resources (O'Malley & Pierce, 1996).

Overall, assessment used wisely can become a source of insight, helping to achieve high standards for schooling. Involving students and teachers in collaborative, informative assessment makes the process more authentic and equitable, and "makes it possible to hold students to higher standards because the criteria are clear and reasonable" (Wiggins, 1992, p. 30).

Assessment and No Child Left Behind

The No Child Left Behind Act (2001) requires that all students be "proficient" in reading and mathematics by the school year 2013–14. Beginning in 2005–06, all public school students in grades 3 through 8 had to be tested annually, using state achievement tests. This group includes English learners, who must be assessed in a valid and reasonable manner that includes reasonable accommodations and, to the extent practicable, testing in the primary language. Those students who have completed thirty months of schooling must, however, be tested in English reading (special exemptions can be applied for on a case-by-case basis, and students living in Puerto Rico are automatically exempted). States must establish baseline proficiency goals to which yearly progress is compared.

In the current climate of standards-driven instruction, the results of assessment are often used to assess the effectiveness of the teacher's instruction. Often, funds are augmented for schools that show increased test scores or, conversely, withheld from schools in which test scores have not risen over a given period. Under NCLB, schools that fail to make acceptable yearly progress (AYP) for two years in a row are subject to corrective action. This is "high-stakes" assessment—the reputation and resources of schools and teachers rest on students' test performance.

The increased emphasis on accountability testing results in increased pressure on teachers of English learners to prepare students to succeed on standardized tests. The pressure for students to perform well on these tests may detract from time spent on language development activities. Educators have argued that these nationally standardized tests penalize English learners, causing schools with large percentages of English learners to rank comparatively poorly on school achievement indices (Groves, 2000).

Haycock (2001) has documented that students at risk of failure are more likely to have insufficient resources; less experienced teachers, who are not prepared for the subjects they teach; and a watered-down curriculum, combined with low expectations for student achievement. This calls into question whether state standards and assessments can achieve educational equity.

One effect of high-stakes testing is the attempt to exclude English learners from testing when scores would penalize schools:

> School officials in Port Chester, N.Y. would rather neither Dayana nor Israel [third graders from Latino immigrant families] takes the New York State English-language-arts test when it is given statewide. They say they do not want such children to be embarrassed by their scores. But they also do not want those scores [to count when] 90 percent of fourth graders score well enough to be regarded as proficient readers.
>
> But that statistic is not a true reflection of the district because so many students from immigrant families [had] been exempted from taking the test. . . . [L]ast June, the U.S. Department of Education required all students in school for more than a year to take regular tests.
>
> That was bad news for Port Chester. Officials here now predict that the proportion of proficient students will drop into the 70s . . . and their schools will be branded in need of improvement and suffer penalties. (Berg, 2006)

Although the No Child Left Behind (NCLB) Act mandated that states desiring federal funds require adequate yearly progress reporting for students with limited English proficiency (LEP), deep-seated structural flaws undermine the validity and reliability of the data that has been collected to date (Abedi, Hofstetter, & Lord, 2004). Problems include the following: the category of "English learner" is not defined in similar ways across states, and in many states, the sparse population of English learners makes comparisons with mainstream populations statistically unreliable. The largest problem, however, is inherent in the logic of the category itself. When an English learner is redesignated, he or she is no longer a member of the subgroup, so the subgroup does not measure its most successful members.

The difficulties for English learners inherent in NCLB legislation have galvanized professional organizations. The TESOL International Association has issued a Statement of Principles and Preliminary Recommendations for the Reauthorization of the Elementary and Secondary Education Act (2006b), including a request that clear guidance be provided for testing accommodations for English learners as well as provision that local educational agencies be permitted to determine when English learners must be tested in reading, math, and science. The National Council of Teachers of English (NCTE) has issued a statement reflecting the changes requested in the No Child Left Behind Act when it is reauthorized. It should:

> support policies that reward rather than punish teachers who choose to work in the nations' most challenging schools; abandon impoverished assessment systems and support the development of multiple tools that measure the complexity of student literacy and learning; and shift the focus from packaged reading programs to initiatives that support teachers' expertise in educating all children to read and write. (P. Harris, 2006, p. 1)

What Is Performance-Based Assessment?

Performance-based testing procedures can be based on tasks that students are asked to do, including essays, demonstrations, computer simulations, performance events, and open-ended problem solving. Collectively, these measures are referred to as *authentic assessments,* because they are related to a student's ability to think knowledgeably about real-life problems.

In an example of performance-based assessment, a beginning English learner might be given clues to a treasure hunt to practice the vocabulary associated with schoolroom objects (eraser, chalk, globe). The teacher might observe the student's ability to collect all the relevant items in an informal assessment. The performance assessment is authentic because the student actually needs to learn the names of common classroom objects and where to find them.

An ideal performance test for reading would be one that contained materials similar to that found in real books, rather than one that reproduced paragraphs written with a controlled vocabulary. The test would be observational and interactional, but scores would also be valid and reliable, and available for comparison and reporting purposes. The test would be diagnostic in order to offer a picture of the student's reading strengths and weaknesses. Ideally, it would be motivating and fun so that students, by taking it, would be encouraged to read more (Bembridge, 1992).

The benefits of performance-based assessments are the match of assessment with instruction and the satisfying feedback provided to the teacher and learner alike about areas of satisfactory attainment and areas of needed improvement. Assessment is an integral part of the instructional process, rather than an "add-on" at the end. At the same time, it provides evidence that a standard of quality has been accomplished. Performance-based assessment is directly related to classroom performance and permits teachers to design and offer the extra mediation that students may need as determined by the assessment.

Performance rubrics are often used to assign grades to performance-based assessment. Students have these available as they begin the task. Students, together with the teacher, make judgments about the progress being made in language. Multiple measures may be used for assessment, incorporating nontraditional domains such as the arts and thus providing a wide range of evidence on which to evaluate a student's competence. Some of these methods are discussed below.

Methods of Assessment

Before taking a closer look at performance-based assessment as a method, let us survey a broad range of assessment types and take a closer look at some terms that are used to compare types of assessment. This examination may assist in identifying what separates performance assessment from other approaches.

Assessment Terms

The assessment literature has developed a rich vocabulary of concepts. Allen, Noel, and Rienzi (2001) offer a glossary of terms (see Table 4.1).

TABLE 4.1 *Assessment Glossary*

Type of Assessment	Definition
Traditional measurement	The teachers assesses the extent to which students have achieved an objective by using traditional tests, such as multiple-choice, essay, or short-answer test questions.
Performance measure	Students provide evidence of how well they have achieved an objective by doing it, such as making a speech.
Authentic assessment	The assessment process is embedded in relevant real-world activities, or resembles real-world events, such as everyday conversations or dialogues.
Quantitative assessment	Assessment results are represented by a numerical score.
Qualitative assessment	Assessment results are described verbally and may involve scoring rubrics, rating scales, or other summary indices.
Embedded assessment	Students receive grades on classwork.
Formative assessment	Formative assessment is designed to give feedback to improve what is being assessed, often by means of checklists or the teacher's verbal coaching.
Summative assessment	Summative assessment provides an end-of-lesson or end-of-unit evaluation, usually accompanied by a score or letter grade.

Standardized and Less Standardized Assessment

Methods for assessing a performance can be *standardized* (students are scored according to a predetermined outcome) and *less standardized* (scoring is flexibly tailored to the product). A combination of assessment (standardized and less standardized) provides a cross-check of student capabilities. For example, a teacher uses a structured observation checklist to circulate among students while they are working and monitors specific skills, such as emergent literacy, word identification, and oral reading. The advantage of a standardized assessment is its speed of scoring through the use of predetermined questions and answer keys.

Less standardized, open-ended assessment, on the other hand, may be more labor-intensive and subjective. Generally speaking, open-ended assessments may feature longer problem-solving exercises, assignments that involve performances or exhibitions, and/or portfolios that contain student work gathered over a longer period of time, such as a semester. Despite the potential drawbacks of open-ended assessment, it can furnish valuable information about students' abilities.

Standardized Proficiency Tests

Several large-scale standardized proficiency tests are available for English learners. For example, the Test of English as a Foreign Language (TOEFL), developed by the

Educational Testing Service in Princeton, New Jersey, is a test used for nonnative speakers of English who wish to study at universities and colleges in the United States. The benefits of standardized tests include speed in administration and convenience in scoring.

Norm-referenced standardized tests compare student scores against a population of students with which the test has been standardized. Examples of norm-referenced tests are the Language Assessment Scales (LAS), a test designed to measure oral language skills in English and Spanish, and the Woodcock-Muñoz Language Assessment. Results from these assessments are used for multiple purposes, including student placement, school accountability, and program improvement. *Criterion-referenced* standardized tests are used principally to find out how much of a clearly defined domain of language skills or materials students have learned. The focus is on how the students achieve in relation to the material, rather than to one another or to a national sample. In an ELD program with many levels, students may be required to pass criterion-referenced tests to progress from one level to the next.

Teacher- and Student-Created Rubrics

Instructionally sound assessment requires more than implementing meaningful tasks and standards. Teachers must develop the capacity to analyze student work, as well as train students to do this analysis. Together, teachers and students need to practice self-assessment on a daily, ongoing basis so that students can regularly make judgments about their own progress as learners, with the teacher's help.

A rubric is a scoring guide that provides criteria to describe various requirements or levels of student performance. The use of rubrics helps to score student work more accurately, quickly, fairly, and reliably and can lead to shared standards among faculty about what constitutes quality in a response. If the students are given the rubric in advance or if they help to create it, they can self-assess their work before completion and offer feedback to their peers.

Developing a rubric first requires decoding what criteria define "quality performance." Next, samples of work must be assembled that demonstrate a range of quality, according to a three-, four-, or five-point scale. Following this step, samples of student work need to be separated into the quality levels represented by the rubric. Finally, reliable samples of good, average, and poor work can be shown to students to help them understand the quality levels.

Some teachers work with students to analyze the standards required for the task and design rubrics together with the students, thus underscoring the importance of the specific criteria. With the evaluative criteria as well as the standards in mind, students are more likely to complete work they can honor (Perrone, 1994).

A scoring rubric that provides clear criteria for scoring student work increases the consistency of assessment. It clarifies the expectations for the assignment so that students can focus on what is important; if they ask for a family member's help on an assignment, others can see clearly what is expected. Using the rubric, students can monitor and critique their own work, adding to a sense of ownership of the knowledge they gain (Airasian, 2005).

English learners with special needs may need testing adaptations.
© Mitch Diamond/Alamy

Teacher-Constructed Tests

Teacher-constructed tests can assess skills in reading comprehension, oral fluency, grammatical accuracy, writing proficiency, and listening. Although they may not be as reliable and valid as tests that have been standardized, the ease of their construction and administration and their relevance to classroom learning have made them a popular basis for awarding grades. Different types of tests have different advantages and disadvantages (see Table 4.2).

Portfolio Assessment

The purpose of portfolio assessment is to maintain a long-term record of students' progress, to provide a clear and understandable measure of student productivity, to improve student self-esteem through demonstrating progress and accomplishment, to recognize different learning styles, and to provide an active role for students in self-assessment (Gottlieb, 1995). Portfolios may include writing samples (compositions, letters, reports, drawings, dictation); student self-assessments; audio recordings (retellings, oral think-alouds); photographs and video recordings; semantic webs and concept maps; and/or teacher notes about students (Glaser & Brown, 1993).

No matter what kind of a portfolio system is developed, some common questions arise: What goes into the portfolio? Who decides? Who "keeps" the portfolio, and where? How are the contents of the portfolio used for grading? A *best-works* portfolio might feature the works of which the student is most proud, with reflective writing or audiotaping from the student explaining why the particular works were chosen. A *selection* portfolio contains work samples, for example, what a student considers the most difficult task. A *process* portfolio

TABLE 4.2 *Advantages and Disadvantages of Various Types of Tests*

Test Type	Advantages	Disadvantages
Multiple choice	Easy and reliable to score using answer key.	Evaluates only recognition knowledge.
True/False	Quick selection from two alternatives; easy to score.	Questions may be easy to misunderstand.
Matching items	Appropriate for content such as vocabulary/definitions.	One error can lead to others.
Short-answer and fill-in-the-blank	Students must generate the answer.	Scoring may be difficult to standardize, leading to unreliability.
Essay	Requires students to organize and synthesize their knowledge.	Students may find writing difficult, and answers are more difficult to score, leading to unreliability.
Oral	Students must speak.	Oral responses are difficult to judge as accurate without strict criteria.
Self-assessment	Students take ownership of the process and may become more motivated to improve.	Students may over- or underestimate their products or performances.

Source: Based on Farrell (2006, pp. 126–131).

might contain evidence of developmental work. L. V. Pierce (1998) and Wolfe-Quintero (1998) offer practical guidelines on planning and implementing portfolio assessment for ESL students.

In many classrooms, students use technology to archive digital portfolios that can store both words and images. O'Bannon and Puckett (2007) outline the format and contents of such a portfolio. Barrett (2000) emphasizes that neither the media nor the contents of a portfolio create learning; it is the student's reflection and thought during and after the process—without this, a multimedia presentation is merely a digital scrapbook.

Teacher Observation and Evaluation

Teachers are in the best position to diagnose needs and document student progress. As students interact and communicate using language, an observant teacher can record how a collaborative group works together or how students use oral language. These observations may extend across all areas of the curriculum and in all types of interactional situations. Observations may be formal (e.g., miscue analysis) or informal. They may be based on highly structured content or on divergent and creative activities. Multiple observations show student progress (Crawford, 1993).

Grading

A variety of approaches have been used to assign grades to English learners. Some teachers of English learners assign a traditional A–F grade scale in accordance with grade-level expectations. Performance standards are not lowered for ELD students, although assignments are adjusted to meet the students' language levels. Alternatively, a pass/fail grade scale is used to avoid comparing English learners with English-proficient classmates. A modified A–F grade scale may used for ESL classes, with A–F grades given based on achievement, effort, and behavior and report card grades modified by a qualifier signifying work performed above, at, or below grade level.

Student Self-Assessment and Peer Assessment

Many teachers have used self-assessment and peer assessment (including student portfolios) to help students take responsibility for their own learning. As part of the reflection on their learning, students can include in the portfolio a letter to the teacher that describes the areas in which they achieved the most growth over a stipulated period, what are now their strongest and weakest areas and why, what their plan is for improving their weakest area, and what grade they would give themselves and why. This task is supplemented by a learning log in which students evaluate their practice and make plans for future effort (McNamara, 1998a). McNamara recommends that teachers offer three types of feedback to this log: *cheerleading*

Box 4.1 Questions to Ask when Determining a Student's Final Grade

Reflective teachers realize that students need to be motivated to "engage, aspire, take risks during learning endeavors" (Herrera, Murry, & Cabral, 2007, p. 260). How do report card grades support this? Only when students take part in authentic learning experiences and activities, have opportunities for supervised practice, and receive timely feedback can this take place. Under standards-based assessment, grades should reflect mastery of the given curricular standards; yet teachers still control what is taught, and to whom.

The following questions can guide decisions about a student's final grade:

- What score information is the basis of the grade?
- Is this reflective of linguistic, academic, cognitive, and sociocultural aspects of performance?
- Are some aspects of learning weighted more than others?
- What role does cooperation, attitude, and motivation play in the final grade?

feedback, in which the teacher celebrates, suggests, or offers encouragement; *instructional feedback,* in which the teacher suggests strategies or materials; and *reality-check feedback,* in which the teacher helps students to set more realistic goals or soften their self-criticism.

Student self-assessment can take several forms. Students can discuss their progress with one another, write reflection logs, use checklists and inventories, and participate in reading and writing conferences to determine their progress and needs for growth. They can ask themselves the following questions: What did I learn? What did I do well? What am I still confused about? What do I need help with? What do I want to learn more about? What am I going to work on next?

J. D. Brown (1998) offers a rich source for peer and self-assessments in ESL/EFL, including assessment of group work, oral presentation, natural communication, interviews, and so forth. O'Malley and Pierce (1996) provided a useful compendium of assessments for educators, including peer and self-assessments.

Other Types of Tests

Not all testing is performance based. Several types of tests are reviewed below, along with some cautions about the use of assessment. Proficiency tests determine a student's level of performance; diagnostic and placement tests provide information to place students in the appropriate level of academic or linguistic courses; achievement tests assess the student's previous learning; and competency tests assess whether a student can be promoted or advanced. Teachers and school administrators sometimes have a choice about which tests are used and for what purposes, but often tests are mandated by state authorities. It is usually up to teachers to develop effective grading procedures and communicate assessment results to students, parents, and other educators (Ward & Murray-Ward, 1999).

Proficiency Tests   Proficiency tests measure overall ability in English. By definition, proficiency tests are not authentic measures of language skill; they are designed to be independent of the curriculum and do not measure the extent to which a student has worked to acquire meaning. Educators should be cautious about using proficiency tests to predict academic or vocational success because language is only one element among many that contribute to success.

Diagnosis and Placement Tests   Diagnosis and placement tests are proficiency tests that are used to determine the academic level or the grade level into which students need to be placed. In addition to identifying students who are English learners and determining the level of proficiency, placement tests can be used to monitor the progress of English learners in acquiring English and to assist in transferring students to mainstream classrooms.

Achievement Tests   Achievement tests measure a student's success in learning specific instructional content. A curriculum-based achievement test is given after instruction has taken place and contains only material that was actually taught. However, many contemporary standardized achievement tests are not aligned with specific curricular content. Teachers who understand the needs of English learners can adjust their instruction to balance lesson planning with the need to prepare students to perform well on standardized achievement tests.

Competency Tests   Competency tests are achievement tests that are used to identify students who can be promoted or graduate. Some states have provisions that modify or exempt testing for English learners until they are ready for standardized testing. Other states offer modifications in the testing such as extended time, a separate site, small-group testing, or testing supervised by a familiar person.

Identification, Assessment, and Placement of English Learners in the Schools

Many states have specific laws and provide procedural guidelines regarding identification procedures for English learners; others do not have state laws but do provide guidelines for assessment. Many states also have procedures for redesignating students and for placing them in mainstream classes. Generally speaking, when students enroll in school, if they are identified as needing ELD services, they are given placement tests that correspond directly to an instructional plan that can be implemented by a classroom teacher. Once in a program, students are then periodically reevaluated for purposes of reclassification.

Identification Procedures for English Learners

A variety of methods are used to identify English learners needing services. The *home-language survey* is a short form administered by school districts to determine the language spoken at home, but students can be identified by other measures. Among these are registration and enrollment information; staff observation; and interviews or referrals made by teachers, counselors, parents, administrators, or community members.

Cheng (1987) recommended other ways to gain information about students' language abilities that can be helpful in making placement decisions: Observe students in multiple settings (classroom, home, and playground); obtain history (medical, family, previous education, immigration experience, home languages); interview current or previous classroom teachers for information about learning styles and classroom behavior; seek information from other school personnel (counselor, nurse); and ask the student's parents to characterize a student's language and performance skills in the home and the community. Educators who draw from a variety of information sources can see the students' needs in a broader context and thus design a language program to meet these needs.

Assessment for Placement

Ideally, once students are identified, bilingual staff conduct an assessment to determine placement. In addition, parents and students should be given an orientation about the assessment and placement process and informed about the services of the school system.

Some districts place students using the LAS to measure oral language skills in English and Spanish. Another frequently used proficiency test is the Bilingual Syntax Measure (BSM), which measures oral proficiency in English and/or Spanish grammatical structures and language dominance. The Basic Inventory of Natural Language (BINL) determines oral proficiency in English by means of pictures that are used to elicit natural speech; spoken sentences are analyzed for fluency, average length of utterance, and level of syntactic complexity.

Even after administering placement tests and gathering information, appropriate academic placement may be difficult. Placement tests measure only language proficiency; they are not informative about a student's academic background, which may vary from strong to weak depending on the subject area. Placement by age can also be a problem. Students may need much more time in the system to learn English, but placement in an earlier grade may lead to social adjustment problems. Teacher-devised checklists and observational data from the classroom can be used to confirm or adjust student placement.

Redesignation and Exit Procedures

School districts use specific criteria to determine when English learners have attained the language skills necessary to succeed in an English-only classroom. This reclassification (redesignation or exiting) process may use multiple criteria, such as measures of speaking, comprehension, reading, and writing as well as evidence that students can participate meaningfully in the general program. Some districts organize bilingual education advisory committees to ensure ethnic parent representation and participation in implementing redesignation criteria that are reliable, valid, and useful.

In summary, the decisions about identifying and placing English learners are as follows: When a student enrolls in a school district, administer the home-language survey. If the student has a primary language other than English, administer an English-language proficiency test. If the student is an English learner, administer achievement and placement tests in English and in the primary language. If the student is eligible for support services, notify parents of options and proceed with placement (Gottlieb, 2006).

Limitations of Assessment

Tests play a large role in placing and reclassifying English learners. Often pressure is applied for programs to redesignate students as fluent English speakers in a short period of time, perhaps before they are ready. Continuing support—such as tutoring, follow-up assessment, and primary-language help—is often not available after reclassification.

Standardized tests, though designed to be fair, are not necessarily well suited as measures of language ability or achievement for English learners. In fact, both the testing situation and the test content may be rife with difficulties and bias for EL students.

Difficulties in the Testing Situation

The context in which a test is administered needs to be examined to understand how students may be affected. Factors within the context of testing such as anxiety, lack of experience with testing materials, time limitations, and lack of rapport with the test administrator may cause difficulties for culturally and linguistically diverse students.

All students experience test anxiety, but this anxiety can be compounded if the test is alien to the students' cultural backgrounds and experiences. Allowing students to take practice exams may familiarize them with the test formats and reduce test anxiety. Moreover, students may take longer to answer individual questions because they need more time for mental translation and to formulate a response. Some students may need a time extension or should be given untimed tests.

When testers and students do not share the same language or dialect, the success of the testing may be reduced. Students may not verbalize freely if they are shy or wary about test taking, feel defensive about teachers' negative stereotypes, or resent the testing situation itself. Those from cultures that discourage individuals from displaying knowledge may not be quick to answer questions and may be reluctant to guess unless they are certain they are right (Cloud, Genesee, & Hamayan, 2000).

Tests, particularly achievement tests, may have bias that affects the performance of English learners. *Language-specific bias* is created when a test developed for use with one language is simply translated into another language; the translation may fail to furnish equivalent vocabulary items. *Geographic bias* happens when test items feature terms used only in particular geographic regions. *Dialect bias* occurs when certain expressions are used that are relevant only to certain dialect speakers. *Cultural bias* may be present when English learners understand test items derived from mainstream culture differently or not at all. Many students are completely unfamiliar with common European American food items, sports, musical instruments, nursery rhymes, or children's stories. Test content may represent *class bias;* for example, *vacuum cleaner* may be a term familiar only among the middle class.

Cautions about Testing

Researchers have the following recommendations for effective practice in the assessment of English learners (August & Pease-Alvarez, 1996; Navarrete & Gustke, 1996):

- Test both content knowledge and language proficiency in the native language and in English.
- Use a variety of techniques to measure content knowledge and skills (e.g., portfolios, observations, anecdotal records, interviews, checklists, exhibits, students' self-appraisals, writing samples, dramatic renditions, and criterion-referenced tests).

- Take students' backgrounds into account, including their educational experiences and parents' literacy.

- Add context to assessment tasks by incorporating familiar classroom material (brief quotations, charts, graphics, cartoons, works of art) as a stimulus and including questions for small-group discussion and individual writing.

- Mirror learning processes with which students are familiar, such as the writing process and reading conferences.

- Give students extra time to complete or respond to assessment tasks, making accommodations such as simplifying directions in English and/or paraphrasing in the student's native language, as well as permitting students to use dictionaries or word lists.

A final comment about standardized testing raises questions about the long-term effects of testing on culturally and linguistically diverse students:

> What effect does the unrelenting emphasis on standardized literacy testing have on students' perception of the purposes and possibilities of literacy? By extension, what effect does testing have on their perception of the possibilities for themselves as readers and writers? Many concerns about identity and standardized testing have been framed in terms of race and social class. . . . Students whose race or social class is not a part of the dominant culture often face more complex challenges in meeting the standards of that dominant culture. (B. T. Williams, 2007, pp. 70–71)

Academic Expectations

How can English learners achieve the highest possible performance? Without question, there is a connection between teacher expectations for English learners and their subsequent school success, or lack of it. The next section examines teacher expectations for student performance. Overall, the effect of teacher expectations amounts to a de facto ongoing assessment of students' worth and capabilities. Addressing these expectations and how they operate is therefore an integral part of examining the role of performance outcomes in the achievement of English learners.

Megastrategy **4.3**

Expect the highest performance possible in the time available

How Teacher Expectations Are Formed and Communicated to Students and How Students Respond

How can teachers communicate positive expectations in order to increase the academic achievement of these students? How do teachers form expectations about student achievement and communicate these during instruction? How do students react?

Students may perform at levels consistent with the teacher's expectations. Although the expectation may have no basis in fact, the student's behavior comes to match the expectation. This effect can be positive (a teacher overestimates a student's abilities, and the student is stimulated to perform well), or it can be negative (a teacher expects very little from a student and communicates this expectation so clearly that student performance is affected adversely).

Jussim (1986) offered a general framework for the operation of expectancy effects: Teachers develop expectations, teachers treat students differently depending on their expectations, and students react to this differential treatment in ways that confirm the expectations. According to Jussim, expectation operates through a set of mediating factors, described as follows.

Teachers Form Expectations.   Teachers first form expectations about students based on prejudgments (a student's reputation, inferences from information in cumulative files, experience with older siblings, or anecdotes from other teachers); racial and cultural stereotypes; scores from placement or standardized tests; observations of a student's classroom performance compared against memories of previous successful and unsuccessful students; and naive predictions and fallacies, such as exaggerating the salience of a few examples of behavior. Together, these factors create an image in a teacher's mind about the likely success or failure of a student.

Differential Treatment of Students.   Expectations and treatment of students are linked. *Attributions* may explain why students of whom teachers have high expectations receive positive attention. Teachers tend to prefer students who are attentive, cooperative, and conscientious, and who time their questions, interruptions, requests, and misbehavior appropriately. They perceive that high-performing students hold similar academic values to their own, and they tend to spend more time with those students to whom they attribute the most potential payoff for their instructional investment. This may explain why teachers spend more time coaching "highs" with more cues and prompts; offer them more feedback, prompts, and response opportunities; are less accepting of poor-quality answers from such students; and design more challenging assignments for them. This closer communication is a factor in students' academic success.

The social context of the learning environment permeates teachers' expectations. A teacher's behavior must be consonant with the motivational climate of school. If the discipline climate in the school is punitive, a less punitive discipline style on the part of the teacher may be perceived as weak. Conversely, if school discipline is lax, the teaching staff may fail in efforts to create high expectations for homework completion. Students participating in a resistance culture may see teachers' motivational efforts as evidence of weakness or react in a hostile manner to teacher demands (see Díaz-Rico, 1993).

Students' Reactions.   Differential treatment received by students alters the potential for achievement. Being called on less and having attempts to speak cut short reduces the chance to think spontaneously and to articulate ideas. If teachers attribute poor performance to students' lack of ability, this assessment is communicated to students, who are likely to lower their level of aspiration.

Minority-group students may sometimes be victims of well-meaning pity from teachers who "ease up" on requirements so that students will "experience success" and "feel good about themselves." This attitude, however well-meaning, may also communicate the message, "You don't have the ability to do this, so I will overlook your failure." Rather than pitying or excusing students who need additional academic support, teachers can teach them how to learn and hold them accountable.

Attention, participation, and cooperation on the part of students may *cause* positive or negative teacher evaluation or *result* from it. Decreased motivation may follow lowered expectations, and lower motivation may in turn lead to lowered performance, which serves to confirm teacher expectations. Cooperation and participation may be enhanced by an understanding of students' differing ability to understand the participation expectations and perform in ways that are consonant with the culture of the classroom.

Planning Instruction

Effective teaching makes a strong connection between goals and outcomes. A teacher who sets precise, well-delineated objectives, plans instruction to teach the targeted skills clearly, and then carefully assesses the results can usually count on most of the students achieving the desired objectives. Despite the seductive clarity of this approach, it is based on the underlying assumption that good teaching causes learning. The reality of the teaching–learning connection is much more complex. Students who are not involved in the process of setting goals miss out on the opportunity to desire to learn.

The desire to learn, like other kinds of desires, has a specific object. A person who desires, desires *something*—usually something tangible, like a new car, a better house, a video game. People can be socialized to desire intangibles, such as victory in a soccer game, more power at work, or high grades at school. But the desire to learn is a tricky intangible, because learning is destabilizing. In Piaget's terms, learning causes disequilibration. Many people dislike learning; they wish to be satisfied by a life in which every question has an answer and every problem has a simple solution. But the central question that drives high-quality teaching is one that in itself is complex, ill defined, and unsettling: What makes someone want to learn? How can a teacher plan lessons based on the learners' desires to learn?

> *Megastrategy* **4.4**
>
> **Plan cooperatively and flexibly for maximum student involvement and achievement**

Constructivist Planning

Constructivist teaching asks, "What is interesting here? What about this subject provokes us? What makes us wonder? Why do we care?" Structures such as K-W-L (see Chapter 5) help teachers bring students' knowledge and interests into the planning cycle. In the long run, the learner is fully engaged only when there is a sense of co-ownership of the learning process so that the learner has a sense of involvement and shared control. This situation is not easy to achieve.

When curriculum and content standards are set by external governing agencies, neither students nor teachers have complete freedom to study what they will. Yet co-planning, co-monitoring, and co-evaluation are the hallmark of co-ownership of the instructional process. How can they fit within a standards-driven curriculum?

In its most inclusive sense, a lesson is a plan that affords or allows learning. The teacher's role is to help the learner to design and perform learning, set learning in motion, identify important problems and make them comprehensible, and set up times and places to showcase discovery and report results. This is the best use of instructional planning.

Modifying the Direct Teaching Model

The seven-step lesson plan is a popular one, stemming from the days of direct teaching. In this model, the teacher determines the objectives of the lesson; teaching then begins with an anticipatory set, in which the teaching materials are displayed and students are told the key topics to be covered. Next, direct instruction takes place, in which the teacher presents information and models the activity that constitutes the learning. Guided instruction follows, as the teacher continues to model and guide students before they engage in independent practice. At this point, there may be supplementary activities before the evaluation/summary/closure (Molina, Hanson, & Siegel, 1997).

Critics of the direct instruction model see a lack of student "ownership" of the design and implementation of this kind of lesson. However, the seven-step model does not have to be teacher-driven. For example, the teacher might involve students in thematic planning before the start of the unit of instruction. The anticipatory set can be used as a means of bringing forth prior knowledge. Direct teaching can be done by students or the teacher, or it can be a very brief stage setting forth instructions for a prolonged practice phase. Students might choose among several different activities to achieve the objective. Finally, students can self-assess or peer-assess in addition to undergoing teacher assessment.

In the long run, however, two major paradigm shifts (learning-centered instruction and standards-based instruction) have made the direct teaching model useful only for small, turnaround lessons that demonstrate a specific skill. Project-based learning—with its extended time frame, complex set of skills to be acquired, and highly visible set of outcomes—is a more robust and authentic model of learning that makes the direct instruction model seem inauthentic.

Matching Performance and Assessment

Megastrategy **4.5**

Set criteria for effective performance and assess attainment of those criteria

Learning goals, lesson plans, classroom activities, and evaluations of student learning must be consistent. Most teachers know that they need to plan stimulating, intellectually challenging tasks for students. Performance-based assessments cannot by themselves bring about significant changes in learning unless classroom instruction improves.

Setting Objectives

The cycle of planning begins with a rich question that "stirs up" swirls of interest. Together the teacher and learner plan how questions that arise can be addressed. The teacher helps to refine goals, discover means, set time lines, and define performances that will help students showcase their learning. In this process, content, learning, and language objectives go hand in hand as language is used to acquire information and perform written or spoken outcomes.

After teachers and students have determined objectives, they can plan to use many means, such as dramatizing, creating songs, or rewriting stories to demonstrate their performance. The learning tasks then become ways to meet the standards that have been set. A variety of ways can be used to employ students' language skills: dramatic, visual, or oral presentations; readers theater; or slide, video, or computer-based audiovisual shows. Re-presentation of knowledge is an important means by which teachers assess student learning and pinpoint areas for reteaching, expansion, and/or modification. In this manner, assessment becomes a part of the learning cycle.

Authentic tasks provide a rich means of assessing English learners. In one community college English class that had been in session one block away from the World Trade Center when it crumbled, students gathered when class resumed to speak of their shock and horror. The class debated what type of writing project they could initiate that would serve as a collection of their thoughts and reactions and convey their response to the tragedy (Abdoh, 2001). This situation is typical of the power of student-determined goals.

Lessons are performance based when the objective is stated in measurable terms: What is the student expected to be able to do, or perform, when the objective is mastered? Therefore, the wording of the objective is active, as in the following samples:

- Students will survey a variety of weather charts.
- Students will ask for and give opinions and advice.
- Students will describe a sequence of events.

Tasks as Objectives

In *task-based learning* (Nunan, 1989), the goal or objective is linked to the learning activities through *tasks*. A task is "a piece of classroom work which involves learners in comprehending, manipulating, producing, or interacting in the target language while their attention is principally focused on meaning rather than on form" (p. 10). Communication and learning tasks are the central building blocks of a lesson plan.

A classroom lesson involves a clear connection between the objectives, activities, and assessment. After the objectives have been determined, activities are designed that will accomplish these objectives. Tasks are linked to the objectives of the lesson by means of task chains.

Task Chains

A task chain is a linked series of actions that accomplishes a specific objective, performed by the learner under the supervision of the teacher. Tasks are linked thematically to the objective. They may involve a variety of language modes, such as listening and speaking, reading, writing, and critical thinking.

In the curriculum *Atlas* (Level 2, Unit 3, "Old Friends"), the first unit goal is to "Talk about Friends" (see Nunan, 1995, pp. 25–27). Task Chain 1 ("Close Friends") is designed to accomplish this goal. Several of the tasks in Task Chain 1 are summarized as follows (some tasks have been omitted):

Task 1. (Pair work). Circle which of the words below (eleven adjectives are given) that describe your best friend.

(Pair work). Think of three friends and make statements about them using words from the list.

Task 2. Listen to the tape-recorded conversation in which Tony is talking about his best friends. Using the given chart, circle the names he mentions and write the correct occupation beside each name.

Task 4. (Group discussion). What does Tony do? Is this an unusual occupation for a man? What about in your country? Do men do this type of job? What jobs do men rarely do? Women?

Task 6. Think of three friends and then complete the chart. (The chart has five columns: "Name," "Things You Do Together," "Things You Talk About," "Occupation, " and "Where You Met.")

(Pair work). Use the chart to talk about your friends with a partner.

Assessing the Task Chain

The success of a task chain is evaluated in several ways, through assessment activities at the end of the chain or through a final assessment at the end of the lesson. Using assessment, the teacher is able to measure directly the extent to which students have mastered the objective. Based on this information, the teacher can choose to reteach the task to all or some of the students, or the class can move forward to the next objective.

Figure 4.1 offers a set of criteria for assessing an instructional plan based on task chains. Each objective of the plan is assessed during the task chain or at the end. The tasks themselves are supported by four kinds of materials. *Posters* offer large, whole-class presentation of information; *focus sheets* offer information that can be used as a component of instruction but are not written on by students during the lesson and can be collected for reuse; *worksheets* are completed during the lesson; and *assessment sheets* are used as the test and scored by the teacher or by peers. This can include peer- or self-assessment sheets.

Figures 4.2 through 4.4 show how a TPR-based lesson features some of these components.

FIGURE 4.1 *MA in Education, TESOL Option Program Outcome Assessment Criteria for Instructional Plan, Standards-Based*

Candidate _____   Assignment: A B C D E

Component of Plan   Point Value/Critique

Introductory Information   ___/10
- Unit/lesson has relevant and appropriate title.
- Level, characteristics of students are specified.
- Materials are listed.
- Provision is made for involving students.

Performance Indicators   ___/10
- Specific
- Feasible in time allotted
- Indicate adequate content
- Matched to TESOL, ELD, district standards

Task Chains   ___/10
- Content is supported using focus sheets or other source materials; matched to performance indicator.
- Activities are relevant; adequate to attain indicator; matched to performance indicator.
- Activity is supported using worksheets or other practice materials.
- Focus sheets and worksheets are referenced and source(s) cited.

Assessment   ___/10
- Formative assessment is relevant and adequate to measure attainment of indicator; performance criteria are specified.
- Summative assessment is supported using assessment sheets or other materials.
- Assessment sheets are referenced and source(s) cited.

Format   ___/10
- Consistent format is used throughout.
- Appearance is professional, word-processed.
- Titles of supporting materials match presentation in lesson plan.

TOTAL   _____/50

FIGURE 4.2 *Demonstration Instructional Plan: Making Flowers from Tissue Paper*

Level: Adult—Speech Emergence

Performance Indicators:

Learning Strategy Objective	1. To sequence written directions using context cues
Language Objective	2. To acquire vocabulary for simple sensorimotor actions
Content Objective	3. To make flowers from tissue paper

Warm-Up: Pass out tissue paper flowers and ask who knows how to make one. If someone knows, recruit him/her as assistant in Task Chain 3.

TESOL Standard: Standard 1. English language learners communicate for social, intercultural, and instructional purposes within the school setting.

Task Chain 1. *Sequencing written directions using context cues*

1. Instructor explains task: Sequence written directions using context cues.
2. Pair students. Each pair receives an envelope with directions on how to make a tissue paper flower (Focus Sheet 1, cut up). Each pair sequences the strips to re-create the proper sequence of instructions.
3. When sequencing task is completed, instructor shows solution on overhead (transparency of Focus Sheet 1).
4. Pairs self-assess their versions for accuracy, recordering if necessary. (Pairs keep directions spread out before them.)

Task Chain 2. *Acquiring vocabulary for simple sensorimotor actions*

1. Each pair chooses ten new words from the directions.
2. First pair writes their ten new words on board. Second pair writes their ten words; if one of their words is already on the board, they put a check beside it, writing only words that have not appeared already.
3. When enough pairs have written their words, instructor takes ten words with the highest number of checks as vocabulary. These are circled on transparency and pronounced together. Students act out sensorimotor actions.
4. Students put strips back in envelopes and return them to instructor.

Task Chain 3. *Making flowers from tissue paper*

1. Instructor demonstrates how to make a flower following directions on transparency (see Focus Sheet 1), accentuating (acting out) verbs that are circled as vocabulary items.
2. Students choose tissue paper colors and follow instructions from overhead.
3. Students process-check against models of partially made flowers.

Final Assessment: *Making flowers from tissue paper*

1. Using the Assessment Sheet, students check their awareness of sequence, knowledge of vocabulary, and context for sensorimotor actions, Scoring: 18–20, Flower, 15–17, Bud; 12–15, Leaf; 8–11, Stem; below 7, Root.

Formative Assessment

As students are engaged in the activity system, the teacher can help them maintain momentum and solve ongoing problems through formative assessment. This process involves progress checks that help students evaluate their efforts in light of their goals and stay on track with benchmark performance measures. The teacher may require formal weekly progress reports, ask for partial products at predetermined times, or set deadlines for circulation of rough drafts. Rich documentation of the progress of an ongoing project helps to create a final product that is not overly dependent on one final spurt of activity that can cause tension and frustration. These requirements help students avoid procrastination and keep their projects moving forward.

Summative Assessment, Culminating Performance, and Metalearning

A final performance on a certain day—a play with other students as audience, an exhibit for parents, or a publication with a printer's deadline—helps students to understand the real world of promise and fulfillment. The excitement that these events generate helps to provide community pressure and support for achievement. Despite the satisfaction these culminating events offer, the substance of assessment remains with the content standards that have been achieved. Peer evaluation, self-evaluation, and teacher evaluation together identify the final wisdom: What did the project achieve? What was learned about the content? What was learned about the process? And, most exciting, what is still not known? What remains to be discovered? This summative assessment is the basis for metalearning, learning about improving learning.

FIGURE 4.3 *Focus Sheet I: Sequencing Written Directions Using Context Cues*

1. Select six sheets of tissue paper, each 10 inches by 15 inches.
2. Stack neatly. For variety, the four on top should be color A, the other two color B.
3. Stack all six layers together and fold into accordion pleats. The pleat should be 10 inches long. Each pleat should measure about 1.5 inches wide.
4. Fold the pleated strip in half at the 5-inch point.
5. Pinch and wrap tightly in wire. The result should look like a bow tie.
6. Shape ends of petals by making either curved or pointed cuts at both ends of tissue paper "bow." For curved petals, cut a semicircle at each end of the bow tie. For pointed petals, cut a triangle at the ends.
7. With fingertips, stretch folds outward to shape tissue paper into a bowl.
8. Delicately fluff out the petals, using a gentle touch to separate the layers of tissue.
9. Holding the floral tape in one hand, wind the tape around the wire stem in a spiral, working from the center of the bow to the end of the wire.

FIGURE 4.4 *Assessment Sheet: Making Flowers from Tissue Paper*

I. *Awareness of Sequence.* Number these steps in the correct order.

_____ Pinch and wrap in wire.

_____ Wind the tape around the wire stem.

_____ Fold the pleated strip in half.

_____ Stretch folds outward.

_____ Fluff out the petals.

_____ Fold in accordion pleats.

_____ Select paper.

_____ Stack neatly.

_____ Cut ends of petals.

II. *Vocabulary for Simple Sensorimotor Actions.* Draw a circle around the words that describe an *action* that takes place in the directions above.

wire	pinch	outward
wrap	pleated	cut
stem	strip	around
wind	tape	stretch
petal	half	out
pleats	fold	ends
select	accordion	paper
fluff	neatly	stack

III. *Context for Sensorimotor Actions.* Write "Yes" if the bold word is used correctly in the sentence. Write "No" if it is not.

1. _____ We **wrap** gifts in gift wrap paper.

2. _____ **Wind** the turkey in the oven.

3. _____ **Stack** the clean clothes.

4. _____ **Stretch** your legs before running.

5. _____ **Fluff** the dirt under the bed.

6. _____ We can use an **accordion** to play music.

Monitoring and Adjusting Instruction

Formative evaluation can permit much valuable ongoing readjustment of the learning process. The responsibility for this monitoring is shared between teacher and learners, but much of the responsibility for adjustment falls on the learner.

> *Megastrategy* **4.6**
> **Adjust instruction to attain performance criteria**

Teachers exercise patience in helping students to monitor and adjust their learning to meet the desired performance standards; vanquish the students' habits of sloth or procrastination, if that is a problem; conquer the students' lack of faith in themselves by providing encouragement, structure, and guidelines; overcome students' impatient desire to improve instantly, as they perhaps try and fail several times before succeeding; help students to accept the disappointment of failure if there is some aspect of a complex problem that eludes solution; or make themselves available during the basic struggle to use English as a means of expression.

Not all learning is successful. Sometimes problems that are worth addressing are beyond comprehension, and sometimes problems that are comprehensible are simply not interesting. Most teachers do everything possible to facilitate successful learning. In the last analysis, however, it is not the teacher's job to rescue students from disappointment or failure; these are a part of authentic learning. Sometimes the metalearning—the wisdom about learning—that takes place comes after the learning has taken place, in a process of reflection and hindsight.

The teacher can take into consideration the struggles and triumphs of one year's students in order to modify instruction the next time. What is exciting about teaching is the opportunity for metalearning—that is, learning better and better how to learn. This goal is not easily achieved, for one must look clearly at the failure that took place as well as the success. Without failure there is no learning; there is only the "already known." For in the last analysis, errors—when assessment shows these clearly and precisely—are the best teachers, providing the opportunity for failure to be converted to wisdom.

Exploratory Break

- Discuss the following: as you make lesson plans, how well do you take into account the various cultural and linguistic backgrounds, interests, and abilities of your students in your class?

- List some advantages and disadvantages of self versus peer assessment and compare your opinion to what you read in the text.

Chapter *5*

Learner Strategies and Learner-Focused Teaching

Learner Control and Academic Competence

This chapter explores the concepts of learner control: how the learner takes responsibility for second-language acquisition (SLA) and what strategies can be used to foster the ability of the learner to be in charge. To accomplish this, two topics follow: first, a look at learner autonomy as an overall topic and second, a focus on learner strategies.

Learner autonomy can be defined as the learners' feeling that studying is taking place due to their own volition. This autonomy is the basis for self-managed, self-motivated instruction. Such autonomy is more than a preference or strategy by the learner; it must be supported in a systematic way by the teacher and curriculum for the learner to benefit.

> *Megastrategy* **SET 5**
>
> **Increase the learner's control, self-management, and self-motivation**

Given the limited time available for in-class instruction in relation to the vast amount of language there is to learn, educators acknowledge that it is impossible to teach learners everything they need to know while they are in class. Therefore, a major aim of classroom instruction should be to equip learners with learning skills that they can employ on their own. These include the following:

- Learning strategies that promote self-managed learning
- Identification of their preferred learning styles and strategies
- Encouragement to monitor and evaluate their own learning
- Support for realistic time management
- Skills in self-assessment

Unfortunately, too often educators assume that students at the beginning level of proficiency in English cannot learn advanced skills. In response to this misconception, the intellectual level of the curriculum is adjusted downward to teach isolated skills that do not foster the cognitive processes necessary for self-directed learning. Strategic teaching addresses the need for educators to promote high-level instruction that will allow English learners to extend their academic potential.

This chapter details a variety of strategies that individuals can use to achieve academic competence. This book is devoted to strategies used by teachers in schools—hence the emphasis on academic competence—but strategies are also used by second-language learners outside the school setting (see Figure 5.1). The emphasis on self-directed and self-motivated learning acknowledges that successful SLA takes place outside as well as inside the classroom.

In Figure 5.1 (from Yeh, 2001), academic competence is divided into learner strategies (indirect and direct) and academic/survival skills. Within the category of learner strategies, some are general; that is, they are not specifically for SLA but can be applied to other content. This chapter focuses not on general strategies but on learner strategies applied to the SLA context.

Cohen (1996) divides learner strategies applied to the SLA context into two parts: second-language use strategies (employed, for the most part, when the learner must extemporaneously speak) and second-language learning strategies (those that assist

FIGURE 5.1 *A Model of Strategies to Achieve Academic Competence*

Academic competence	Learner strategies (indirect and direct)	General strategies applied to non-SLA context		
		Learner strategies applied to SLA context	Indirect: Learning styles	
			Indirect: Second-language use strategies	Rehearsal
				Retrieval
				Communication
				Cover
			Direct: Second-language learning strategies	Literacy, oracy strategies
				Cognitive, meta-cognitive, and social-affective strategies
	Academic survival strategies	Cultural skills	NL cultural skills	
			TL cultural skills	
			Academic (TL) cultural skills	
		Study skills	Time management	
			Text processing	

Source: Based on Yeh (2001).

learners to improve their knowledge in a target language). Language-use strategies primarily employ language that learners already have in their interlanguage; in contrast, language-learning strategies assist learners in learning a new target language.

A third kind of learner strategy, learning styles, like other indirect strategies tends to originate at a level of unconscious or automated performance. Like other indirect strategies, these can be made explicit and used or altered in a conscious manner.

Academic/survival skills, the other aspect of academic competence, comprise cultural skills (native language, target language, and the culture of academia in the target language) and study skills (time management and text processing, among others). Although there may be other important strategies for the learner to acquire and use, this set will serve for now.

Learner Autonomy: Self-Motivation and Self-Management

Autonomy enables students to feel pride in their own achievements. If learning is too externally controlled, a student can feel other emotions (gratitude for the teacher's help, or relief not to have failed) but may not feel a personal sense of success. Intense pressure to acquire English, whether as a newcomer to U.S. schools or as a student at a school in which English learning is mandated by examination competition, causes external obligations to succeed. Moreover, a second language is usually "owned" by native speakers, making a sense of autonomy elusive for nonnative speakers. In the final analysis, however, second-language proficiency is an individual achievement. One can *teach* the learner a second language—but only the learner can *learn* it.

Self-Managed Instruction

What energizes and directs behavior? The explanation could be drives, needs, fear, goals, social pressure, interests, expectations, curiosity, and so forth. *Intrinsic motivation* is a term used to explain internal, personal traits. Raffini (1996) defined intrinsic motivation as "what motivates us to do something when we don't *have* to do it" (p. 3). The opposite is *extrinsic motivation,* when the activity is done for a reward or to avoid a punishment. Usually, students do not perform activities solely for either intrinsic or extrinsic reasons, but rather because of a combination of the two.

Learner autonomy as a concept goes beyond internalized self-motivation to include the additional factor of self-managed instruction. Three areas of learner autonomy are particularly important for students: control over topics (goals), freedom of choice in activity (means), and belief in themselves as agents of their own success (self-efficacy). Students' control over topics was covered briefly in Chapter 3 (constructivist teaching). Students' freedom of choice in activity (means) will be covered in sections that follow dealing with indirect and direct strategies.

Lo (2006) described a multi-age EFL program in Taiwan that incorporated five student self-learning centers. The computer center contained theme-based multimedia, CD-ROMs, activity books, and teacher's guides for students to color, calculate, practice oral and listening skills, and categorize objects. The listening center, equipped with cassette players and headphones, encouraged students to sit or lie on pillows and listen along with reading storybooks. The reading center used Big Books, trade books, and flash cards to stimulate students' independent reading. The writing center furnished clay for shaping letters, crayons, paper, scissors, and glue for hands-on activity. The video center was equipped with two video players so students could watch videotapes three times (once with Chinese captions, once with English captions, and once without captions) before completing a worksheet. These centers offered the choice of multiple language-learning tasks.

Self-Efficacy

Students' belief in themselves as agents of their own success (self-efficacy) can be fostered systematically in language used by the teacher. At the beginning of the course, teachers who introduce the idea of autonomy set a tone of "working together" toward mutual goals. Consistent rhetoric that speaks of goals, together with strategies to achieve these goals, maintains the tone of self-control. Those who are successful as well as those who underachieve can learn to take responsibility for themselves. Doing so means also being able to undertake self-assessment to evaluate goal attainment (McNamara, 1998b).

Autonomy can be fostered by encouraging students to access learning for themselves by drawing on resources outside the classroom. Santás (1996) offered a checklist with which students can check their own self-access language-learning behavior. It includes suggestions such as "Watch films in English with subtitles in your own language"; "Read books, either in the original version or in simplified readers"; "Remember that some readers come with an audiotape"; and "Whenever you can afford it, go to a bookshop and look at the English-language section. Some of the many interesting materials are famous stories with audiotapes, videotapes with sing-along songs, simplified readers, comics, magazines, and computer games. Share what you find with your classmates" (p. 19).

Student Responsibility for Learning

B. Marshall (1999a, 1999b) offered classroom management strategies that foster a sense of responsibility for learning. These include assigning regular duties to all learners within the classroom; expecting all students to answer when a question is asked and using question-and-answer techniques to make this possible; and teaching critical thinking skills explicitly so that these can be used on a daily basis during instruction.

What Are Learner Strategies?

One must distinguish such terms as *strategy, megastrategy, technique, principle, practice,* and *method*. The term *strategy* denotes both general approaches and specific actions taken to learn a second language (see Cohen, 1996). Larsen-Freeman and Long (1991) used the terms *macrostrategies, microstrategies,* and *tactics;* D. Brown (2000) talked about *principles.* I use the term *megastrategy* to denote "a large idea that guides practice and that hosts a set of matching strategies consonant with its theme."

In this book, I use the term *strategy* to mean "an idea that a learner can employ to increase learning." Each strategy in this book is a direct strategy that the prospective teacher can acquire and use *as a learner of teacher education.* Some learner strategies in turn are appropriate for the second-language learner. Tudor (1996) supplied a definition for a second-language learner strategy: "any purposeful activity that learners engage in to promote their learning and knowledge of the target language" (p. 38). So the term *strategy* is used in this book at two levels; it refers both to a strategy used by teachers and to learner strategies employed by English learners.

Indirect and Direct Strategies

Learner strategies are defined as "systematic plans, designs, procedures, or maneuvers used during learning." These can be divided into *indirect* and *direct.* Indirect strategies tend to originate at a level of unconscious or automated performance and may or may not enter consciousness during operation. If the behavior is one that potentially can come under conscious control, however, it should be called a strategy.

As an example of an indirect strategy, suppose a given person has a preference for learning by listening rather than reading. The person probably did not consciously acquire this preference. Once the person becomes aware that listening is a preferred means of input, though, that person has a choice whether to maintain that preference or try to modify it by, for example, consciously trying to read more.

Direct strategies, in contrast, are used by the learner in a directed way, that is, they tend to originate at a level of conscious performance and may or may not become unconscious, or automated, during operation. A person may be taught a strategy, try it, reflect on its success, and eventually either decide to add it to the ongoing repertoire of behaviors or not, depending on its perceived utility. Like other acquired cognitive functions, once in the repertoire, the strategy may be used often or seldom.

Strategy-Based Instruction

What can an educator hope to accomplish by the use of strategy-based instruction? The instructor can provide this instruction for the following purposes:

> (1) Promote self-managed goal-setting; (2) help learners to develop an expanded repertoire of strategies; (3) explicitly teach learning strategies as a part of lesson objectives; and (4) raise learners' awareness of effective and ineffective strategies depending on the nature of the task.

How does the instructor train learners to use these strategies? *Awareness training* helps the learner to become aware of strategies already in use by such means as structured self-observation (taking open-ended notes or using checklists); interviews and think-aloud procedures; keeping notes, diaries, or journals; or taking self-report surveys (Oxford, 1990).

One-time strategy training is another way to teach learning strategies. In this approach, the learner acquires and practices one or two strategies that are matched to specific tasks. Although it does not provide long-term intervention, it is useful for the learner with a particular, focused need.

Long-term strategy training is the most valuable overall, being more prolonged and covering a broader terrain of strategies. This type of training may be tied to the objectives of the overall language program (Oxford, 1990).

Indirect Strategies: Second-Language Acquisition and Use

Megastrategy **5.1**

Honor learners' second-language use strategies

What Are Second-Language Use Strategies?

A second-language use strategy is employed for transmitting an idea when the learner cannot produce precise linguistic forms. Cohen (1996) defined four second-language use strategies: *rehearsal, retrieval, communication,* and *cover.*

- Rehearsal is used to store a correct language form in long-term memory (LTM).
- Retrieval is used to call to mind the correct form from LTM.
- Communication indicates an attempt to convey meaning even when no attempt is made to memorize a form.
- Cover strategies are used to create the impression that the learner is in control when in fact there are gaps in proficiency; for example, a speaker may fail to remember a word and must use gestures or a synonym to compensate.

Second-language use strategies are valuable not only as tools that facilitate the learner's language reception and production but also as a means to interpret the learner's interlanguage. Examining the learner's attempts to express or decode meaning in a given situation provides interesting material not only for the teacher but also for the interlanguage researcher, because it emphasizes the learner's creativity in the face of difficulty.

Examples of Second-Language Use Strategies.   Chesterfield and Chesterfield (1985) found that Mexican-American children used a set of language-use strategies when learning English that incorporated sociolinguistic, discourse, and strategic factors. These include repeating words they heard, using verbal attention-getters to initiate interaction ("Hey!"), appealing for assistance, asking the speaker to clarify or repeat, and using formulaic expressions that function as a unit ("Hi-how-are-you").

D. Brown (2000) examined five broad categories of what he calls "communication strategies" based on Tarone's work (1981). These strategies (see Table 5.1) make

TABLE 5.1 *Categories of Communication Strategies*

Language-Use Strategy	Definition
Prefabricated patterns	Memorizing stock phrases to rely on when all else fails
Appeals for help	Asking a conversant for help or pausing to consult a dictionary
Cognitive and personality styles	Employing one's personality to compensate for unknown language structures
Avoidance	Evading the use of sounds, structures, or topics that are beyond current proficiency
Language switch	Falling back on the primary language for help in communication

Source: Based on D. Brown (2000).

conscious use of both verbal and nonverbal devices. The first category, prefabricated patterns, is the same as "formulaic expressions" (see above). The second, "appeals for help," is also covered above. The third category, "cognitive and personality styles," is covered at greater length in the next section.

Code-Switching.   The last strategy, often called *code-switching,* alternates between two languages on the word, phrase, clause, or sentence level. In addition to its use as a second-language use strategy, code-switching is also used to clarify or emphasize a point, to cross social or ethnic boundaries, to express group identity and status and/ or to be accepted by a group, to quote someone, to interject in a conversation, to exclude someone, and to ease tension in a conversation (Baker, 1993). In classrooms, students should learn in whatever manner they feel most comfortable, including code-switching, if it reduces anxiety or increases group solidarity.

Box 5.1   **When Can a Bilingual Speaker Code-Switch?**

In the increasingly complex linguistic terrain of the United States, one can insult by speaking, for example, Spanish to someone before knowing if they are Spanish-speaking (even if someone has an accent, addressing him or her too quickly in Spanish may convey, "I think you can't speak English"). On the other hand, if one doesn't speak Spanish when addressed in that language, "you also risk coming across as aloof or superior, more Americanized, or not one of them" (Silverstein,

2007, p. A17). The solution? Silverstein's recommendations are as follows:

- *Follow the leader.* If someone opens the conversation in one language, answer in kind.
- *Ask permission.* If you want to switch languages, see if it's OK.
- *Drop hints.* Some bilingual speakers drop some Spanish into an English conversation to subtly signal that it's OK to switch languages.

PRACTICES FOR TEACHERS

To Facilitate Second-Language Use

■ Familiarize language learners with second-language use strategies so that they can recognize them when they occur.

■ Practice with students a set of formulaic expressions to cover most interactions so that they feel comfortable in routine language use.

■ Recognize that in a bilingual context, code-switching is common and relieves anxiety; too much code-switching, however, may interfere with second-language use.

Indirect Strategies: Learning Style Preferences

Equity and excellence may seem like competing values (adjusting to learner variance versus attaining learning standards); they must be carefully balanced. Is it reasonable to expect a class of learners to do the same activities, with the same goals, in the same period of time?

The nature of teaching in U.S. classrooms is that students are increasingly heterogeneous in an array of ways beyond language: religion; mainstreamed students with disabilities (see Kaye, H. S., 1997); race/ethnicity (one-third of the U.S. school population is nonwhite; see Marlowe & Page [1999]); and mobility (43 million people in the United States move every year; see Hodgkinson [1998]). The challenge is clear: How can curriculum, instruction, and assessment be responsive to this learner diversity?

Megastrategy **5.2**

Adapt instruction to learners' varying styles

A key element of diversity is learning style, defined by D. Brown (1987) as "a consistent and rather enduring tendency or preference within an individual" (p. 79). "Learning styles are the preferences students have for thinking, relating to others, and for particular types of classroom environments and experiences" (Grasha, 1990, p. 23). Knowing these preferences can help instructors to anticipate the different needs and perspectives of students, help students to understand themselves as learners, and use the information to plan and modify certain aspects of courses and assignments. There are many typologies of learning styles.

Typologies of Learning Styles

Hruska-Reichmann and Grasha.   Hruska-Riechmann and Grasha (1982) offered three contrasting pairs of learning styles: competitive versus cooperative, dependent versus independent, and participant versus avoidant (see also Grasha, 1996). Students may show characteristics of more than one of these styles.

Keefe. Keefe (1987) divided learning style variables into four categories: physiological, affective, incentive, and cognitive. Physiological variables influence personal nutrition, health, time-of-day preferences, sleeping and waking habits, need for mobility, and need for and response to varying levels of light, sound, and temperature. Affective variables include the amount of structure or supervision students need, what anxiety and curiosity they display, and what degree of persistence they use to pursue a task. Incentive variables cover students' levels of achievement motivation; enjoyment of competition versus cooperation; risk taking versus caution; reaction to rewards and punishment; social motivation arising from family, school, and ethnic background; and locus of control (internal—seeing oneself as responsible for own behavior—or external—attributing circumstances to luck, chance, or other people).

Cognitive learning style variables for Keefe (1987) include field independent versus field dependent; conceptual/analytical versus perceptual/concrete; broad versus focused attention; easily distracted versus capable of controlled concentration; leveling (tendency to lump new experiences with previous ones) versus sharpening (the ability to distinguish small differences); and high cognitive complexity (accepting of diverse, perhaps conflicting input) versus low cognitive complexity (tendency to reduce conflicting information to a minimum).

Sonbuchner. Sonbuchner (1991) referred to learning styles as a combination of information-processing styles (preferences for reading, writing, listening, speaking, visualizing, or manipulating) and work environment preferences (differences in motivation, concentration, length of study sessions, involvement with others, level of organization, prime times for study, amount of noise, amount of light, amount of heat, and need for food/drink).

Tharp. Tharp (1989) suggested two sets of contrasting learning styles: visual/verbal, and holistic/analytic. Schools tend to reward students who are both verbal and analytic. In contrast, students who have a more visual orientation and learn by observing may find schools mystifying until they adjust to a different cognitive style. A student with more holistic thought processes may understand pieces of a process only when the whole pattern is visible.

Cognitive style differences are evident in this excerpt from a dialogue I had with Martha Chacon, the matriarch of the local San Manuel Band of Mission Indians, when I wrote a book on their cultural beliefs. One can see here that the interviewer is struggling for analysis, whereas the interviewee has a holistic cognitive style.

> **L D-R.** So, the *hukat* is the giant deer that appears when someone dies. When was the last time it came?
>
> **M. C.** When my Aunt Luisa died. It was down on the road. When the ambulance came up the road, they said they saw it in their headlights.
>
> **L D-R.** I'm not quite clear here. Are you saying that the deer came for Aunt Luisa?

> **M. C.**   It was because she died.
>
> **L D-R.**   Uh, did the deer come to, a . . . carry away her spirit? Or did Aunt Luisa . . . turn into the deer? Or do you mean that the deer . . . well, stood for her . . . like a symbol?
>
> **M. C.**   Yes.

Kolb.   The adult learner has been the focus of Kolb's theory of experiential learning. Kolb (1976) described this as a four-stage process: a learner's concrete experience forms the basis for observation and reflection, which in turn enables the learner to make decisions and solve problems, thus creating a basis for new experiences. Kolb's four learning types are cast into two dimensions: (1) active experimentation versus reflective observation and (2) abstract conceptualization versus concrete experience. Various types of learners fall along these two dimensions.

McCarthy.   Four learning styles similar to Kolb's are the result of McCarthy's 4-MAT system (McCarthy, 1983): innovative, analytic, commonsense, and dynamic. The innovative learner needs to be personally involved through social interaction. The analytic learner thinks through ideas and concepts. The commonsense learner needs hands-on experience and enjoys solving practical problems. The dynamic learner uses intuition and trial and error, taking risks and jumping to conclusions.

Gregorc.   Gregorc (1982) explored the mismatch between teaching styles and student learning styles as a means of using style diagnostics to improve student learning. According to Gregorc, learners can be categorized into four types: (1) abstract random, (2) abstract sequential, (3) concrete random, and (4) concrete sequential. The abstract/concrete dimension resembles Kolb's abstract/concrete dimension, and the random/sequential distinction is reminiscent of Tharp's holistic/analytic dichotomy.

Myers/Briggs.   Carl Jung's theory of personality is the basis for the Myers/Briggs Type Indicator. Four opposing pairs of personality dimensions (introversion/extroversion, sensing/perception, thinking/feeling, and judging/perceiving) make up the sixteen personality types. The Myers/Briggs Type Indicator has been extensively popularized in easy-to-understand versions such as J. M. Murphy's *The Eight Disciplines* (1998) and Keirsey's *Please Understand Me II* (1998).

Learning Styles Applied to the ESL/EFL Classroom

The use of learning styles is based on a few basic hypotheses: (1) that every learner—and teacher—has learning style preferences; (2) that all styles are equally valid, although the educational context may value some over others; (3) that being aware of one's preferences, and acquiring styles other than one's preference, may assist students in learning; and (4) that learning strategies are linked to learning styles (J. M. Reid, 1995). Teachers can manage the complexity of the learning style typologies by surveying various systems, analyzing themselves, and settling on one or two systems that both explain individual differences and offer accessible ways to accommodate instruction to learner differences.

Cultural Differences in Learning Styles

Some researchers claim that many aspects of cognitive style have demonstrated cultural differences. For example, Nelson (1995) characterized middle-class U.S. public school techniques as appealing to the field-independent, analytical, visual learner, whereas Native Hawaiian and Native American learning environments by contrast favored the field-sensitive, global, and kinesthetic learner. However, norms may not be available that help see a learner's response in the context of his or her native culture.

Measuring Learning Styles

Individuals' learning styles can be measured in four ways.

1. Self-report instruments or questionnaires, usually by means of a forced-choice task (Kolb's self-test is a forced choice among four adjectives: Are you receptive, relevant, analytical, or impartial? Are you accepting, a risk taker, evaluative, or aware?)
2. An open-ended interview
3. Observations of individuals as they work, tracked through anecdotal notes or by means of a checklist
4. Review of what students produce, as seen in the results of their projects or in the types of errors they make

Helping Students Develop a Personal Set of Learning Strategies

Teachers can help students to get to know their own learning strategies and help them to acquire a more flexible repertoire. Students can . . .

- describe how they came up with an answer, solution, or process;
- listen to one another's explanations and acquire alternative ways to solve problems;
- persevere with resilience when they try a new strategy that does not work easily;
- seek out diverse strategies. (Gregory & Kuzmich, 2005)

Adapting Instruction to Learning Styles

In the typical classroom, some modification can be made that takes learning styles into account. If students as a group are both competitive and dependent, for example, assignments that enhance other characteristics (such as collaborative and independent learning) might be developed. Teachers can use a variety of learning activities to accommodate distinct learning styles.

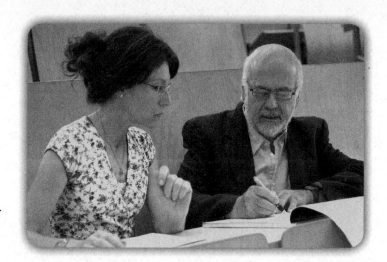

Teachers can coach one another
to diversify their teaching.
©GoGo Images Corporation/Alamy

Cognitive coaching is a peer-coaching process for teachers developed by Garmston and Costa (cf. Garmston, 1987) that helps teachers explore the thinking behind their classroom practices. As teachers talk aloud with a peer about their instruction, they become clearer about the underlying bases for their decisions and increase their awareness of how they might expand their teaching repertoire. This reflective process has been particularly effective in helping teachers become more aware of learner diversity and of the ways in which learners' styles differ from that of the teacher.

One teacher, Jan Whitaker, prided herself on detailed and organized lessons. Her questioning style while teaching tended to call for specific, quantitative answers. By means of cognitive coaching, she altered her style to elicit creativity and higher-order thinking from students. She was able to relax and let students search for their own answers, building self-esteem and self-managed learning along the way (Garmston, Linder, & Whitaker, 1993).

PRACTICES FOR TEACHERS

Incorporating Learning Styles into the Classroom

- Diagnose your own learning style preferences so that you understand yourself as a teacher.

- Settle on one system, or one set of preferences, that you find useful to know about your students.

- Find or create a questionnaire or observation survey that measures these preferences.

- Find a way to add variety to instructional plans that makes a difference on this set of preferences.

Direct Strategies: Cognitive

> *Megastrategy* **5.3**
>
> **Teach cognitive strategies**

Cognitive strategies are the strategies a person thinks and acts on in order to complete a task. They can be divided into three areas: (1) brain-compatible teaching; (2) study skills; (3) and enhancement of cognitive functions by the use of specific psychological tools, including schema building, scaffolding, use of alternative information representations such as graphic organizers, and critical and creative thinking. Brain-compatible teaching was addressed in Chapter 3, and study skills will be introduced later in this chapter.

Schema Building

A *schema* (plural *schemata*) is a unit of understanding that can be used to store knowledge in LTM. Students use existing schemata when they recognize a connection between what they know and the learning experience. In addition to evoking prior knowledge, teachers build schemata, providing new experiences that arouse interest and attention to a topic. These may include field trips, guest speakers, films, experiments, classroom discovery centers, computer simulations, and so on. By recalling their own experiences and engaging in new experiences with their classmates, students can associate what they already know with these new experiences. If there is little prior knowledge of the topic at hand, students will need more instructional support.

Scaffolding

In the world of construction, a scaffold is a temporary support for workers as they build a new edifice. In constructivist teaching, scaffolding is used to help the learner construct knowledge (see Berk & Winsler, 1995). During scaffolding, the teacher helps to focus the learner's attention on relevant parts of the task by asking key questions that help the learner to think and talk about the task, by dividing the task into smaller, manageable subcomponents, and by sensitively withdrawing assistance when it is no longer required. By using scaffolding techniques, teachers can help students build schemata.

The Cognitive Academic Language Learning Approach (CALLA) (Chamot & O'Malley, 1987, 1994) was designed for English learners at the advanced-beginning and intermediate levels. The CALLA model includes the development of academic language skills and explicit instruction in learning strategies for both content and language acquisition. Content topics are introduced by using extensive contextual supports or by reducing language demands. Academic language skills include all four language modes in daily content lessons, as well as language functions important for specific curricular areas, such as analyzing, evaluating, justifying, and persuading. Learning strategies are those used in scientific inquiry; gathering, analyzing, and interpreting data; explaining, inferring, and predicting; and communicating results.

Alternative Information Representation and Graphic Organizers

A graphic organizer is a visual frame used to represent and organize information, "a diagram showing how concepts are related" (McKenna & Robinson, 1997, p. 117). Graphic organizers present ideas visually. Many kinds of graphic organizers can also be used to help students focus their thoughts and reactions, for example, as they read a literature selection. Because graphic organizers balance visual with verbal representation, they can help to make visible the conceptual structures that underlie content. This technique helps students to make models for understanding ideas and outcomes.

Graphic organizers are particularly useful in classrooms in which English learners face challenging academic content. By using mind maps or other information organizers, students can interact with the concepts presented in various content areas in a way that supplements verbal text. Thus, English learners can access core content even when their reading skills are weak. As a result, students become more engaged in their learning.

Graphic organizers have at least three major applications. First, *generative*: They are used to promote language related to content. Students can talk or write about the information presented on a chart. Second, *representative/explanatory*: They are used to increase content understanding, either to build background knowledge before reading a text, to read interactively with the help of an organizer, or to synthesize new information that is gained from a text. Third, *evaluative*: They are used to assess understanding of content.

Sequential organizers show events in order. Sequential organizers include the use of the alphabet, parts of a book, parts of a letter, parts of a paragraph, parts of an essay, a chain of events in a story plot, and a set of steps in written directions (Kagan, 1998). Figure 5.2 shows a sample sequential organizer used to list the beginning, middle, and end of a story. Figure 5.3 shows the problem–solution chain in a Native American "coyote" story. A picture of a chain of boxes horizontally or vertically can represent a sequence, as can a picture of the steps of a ladder. If the events repeat, a cycle graph might be used. A sequence of pictures makes a cartoon or picture strip,

---

FIGURE 5.2   *Sample Sequential Organizer: Story Sequence Chart*

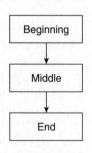

FIGURE 5.3 *Sample Sequential Organizer:*
Problems and Solutions in a Story

Problem 1
Solution 1
Problem 2
Solution 2

and a set of dates can be sequenced on a time line. A step chart with lower to higher steps set up from left to right can represent a set of steps in written directions.

Compare–contrast organizers can be used in language arts to compare characters in the same story or in different stories, types of correspondence (business versus friendly letters), or genres of reading (fiction versus nonfiction). Visually, these comparison charts can be of three types: a Venn diagram (see Figure 5.4), a T-chart (see Figure 5.5), or a comparison chart (see Figure 5.6).

FIGURE 5.4 *Sample Venn Diagram Used*
for the Questions, "How are
two things alike? How are they
different?"

What A is like | How A and B are the same | What B is like

FIGURE 5.5 *Sample T-chart: Comparison*
of Same and Different

Same   Different

FIGURE 5.6 *Sample Comparison Chart: Comparison by Attributes*

Comparison of Civilizations		
	Egypt	United States
Duration	More than 4,000 years	About 400 years
Political structure	Towns united by centralized government	Hierarchy: towns, counties, states, federal government
Religion . (etc.)	Pharaotic, later Islam	Predominantly Protestant Christian, then Catholic Christian, then Jewish, Islam, other

Relational organizers other than compare-and-contrast models show concepts that are embedded (see Figure 5.7), whole–part (see Figure 5.8), or cause–effect (see Figure 5.9).

Classification organizers are used to create hierarchies, matrixes, or other concept relations that show specific structures. Figure 5.10 shows a hierarchy format, Figure 5.11 shows a matrix, Figure 5.12 shows a two-dimensional plot, and Figure 5.13 shows an alternative way to display a hierarchy.

FIGURE 5.7 *Sample Relational Organizer: Embedded Concepts (a Teacher's Phenomenal Field of Person Relations in the Role of Teacher)*

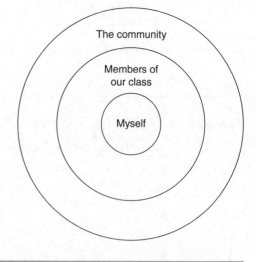

The community

Members of our class

Myself

FIGURE 5.8   *Sample Relational Organizer: Whole–Part (Parts of the Atom)*

Atom	Nucleus	Protons
		Neutrons
	Electrons	

FIGURE 5.9   *Sample Relational Organizer: Cause–Effect (Possible Causes of Lightbulb Nonfunctioning)*

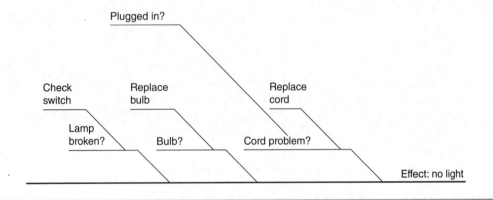

FIGURE 5.10   *Sample Classification Chart: Main Ideas*

FIGURE 5.11   *Sample Classification Chart: Matrix*

	Boys	Girls	Total
Blue-eyed	4	7	11
Brown-eyed	13	10	23
Total	17	17	34

FIGURE 5.12   *Sample Classification Chart: Dimensions (Learning Styles)*

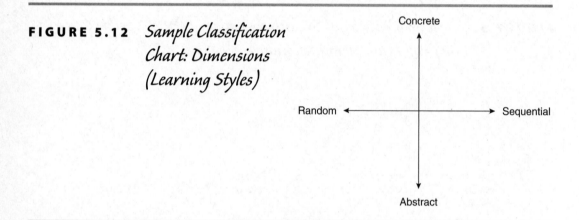

FIGURE 5.13   *Sample Classification Chart: Hierarchy*

FIGURE 5.14 *Sample Concept Development Chart: K–W–L*

What we know	What we want to know	What we have learned

FIGURE 5.15 *Sample Concept Development Chart: Mind Map or Idea Web*

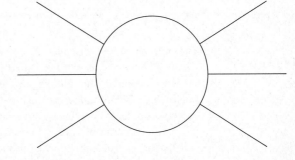

Concept development organizers are used to brainstorm. The K-W-L chart is used to introduce a theme, a lesson, or a reading. It can help generate student interest in a topic and assist students in using their prior knowledge as they read. Students can enter K (what we Know), W (what we Want to know), and L (what we Learned), completing the chart at the end of the unit or lesson (see Figure 5.14). The mind map is basically a circle with the concept or topic in the center, surrounded by lines, bubbles, arrows, or other connectors that group students' ideas to the concept or topic (see Figures 5.15 and 5.16). Concept charts are concept development organizers, primarily lists in no particular order encased in boxes (see Figure 5.17).

Evaluation organizers show degree of positivity (Kagan, 1998). These can be grade scales (A–F); Likert scales (1 = strongly disagree and, at the other extreme, 1 = strongly agree); rubric scales (needs work → satisfactory → good → excellent); two boxes ("I like/agree with" versus "I dislike/disagree with"); or three boxes, indicating plus/minus interest.

Semantic mapping proved to be a successful approach for the three English learners, two boys ages 5 and 9 and their sister, age 10, whom Judy was tutoring. She searched for an interesting topic that would increase their vocabulary in English.

FIGURE 5.16 *Sample Concept Development Chart: Character Trait Web*

The children chose "Halloween." Starting with words they knew in English (skeleton, witch), Judy wrote the words on chart paper and the children copied the words in their notebooks. The children gave other words in Spanish, and Judy found the English equivalents and wrote them, too. Using a fresh piece of chart paper, Judy asked the students how the list of words could be grouped into categories. The activity continued until the words had been grouped into categories, Animals, Monsters, and Trick-or-Treat. Judy followed this activity by reading a book on Halloween, *Rotten Ralph's Trick or Treat*. When they came to a word on the chart, Judy pointed this out for reinforcement. (Brisk & Harrington, 2000, pp. 71–72)

FIGURE 5.17 *Sample Concept Chart: Story Elements Chart*

Once students and teachers become familiar with graphic organizers, they can help English learners grasp basic concepts without depending on language as the sole source of understanding.

Critical Thinking

An important aspect of schooling in a democracy is the ability to think for oneself, analyze ideas, separate fact from opinion, support opinions from reading, draw inferences, and solve problems. Critical thinking can create self-understanding, as a person might approach significant issues in life differently following the acquisition of analytic skills. Paul, Binker, Jensen, and Kreklau (1990) offered a strategy list of the dimensions of critical thought as an organized introduction to this complex field. The four-volume set *Critical Thinking Handbook* (grades K–3, 4–6, 7–9, and high school) presents lesson plans that have been remodeled to include critical thinking strategies (available from the Center for Critical Thinking at Sonoma State University).

Creative Thinking

A whole range of activities, from creative movement and manipulatory activities to brainstorming and story creation, can promote creative thinking. Turner (1990) featured "101 Things to Be: And Then Some"—ideas for creative movement, including being a ball in a pinball machine, a letter of the alphabet, an angry animal, a kite, an umbrella opening and closing, and so on. In Name Puzzle, students print their names in large block letters on brown paper and paint the names and the surrounding space. The students then cut the paper into a puzzle, each keeping a puzzle piece as a souvenir. In Magic Auction, students make a list of things they would wish for (a formula for instant water, a flying carpet) and then hold an auction in groups for these items using play money.

The genre of brain puzzles is also mentally stimulating. The *MENSA Mind Maze Challenge* (Bremmer, 1999) is one huge puzzle from the front to the back of the book, with more than 150 interlinked brainteasers. *Brain Quest* (Feder, 1992) is a series of grade-appropriate card sets with questions and answers that draw on a student's general cultural knowledge. Students can play these in pairs or teams of four. Here are some sample questions from Deck 2: "Order from east to west: India, Japan, Vietnam, Iran"; "What star is closest to earth?"; "Where is a person's diaphragm?"

Both critical and creative thinking are integral parts of the human mind that enrich any part of the curriculum. Thinking is the key to the creation of meaning, in which children learn to react not just in response to the real world immediately before them but also in accord with their internal world, the world of ideas. Channeling the power of thought is an important part of language education in the context of cognitive development.

Direct Strategies: Metacognitive

Metacognitive development involves direct teaching of strategies that help students plan what and how they want to learn; monitor, manage, and motivate while they are learning; and evaluate what they have learned and how they did so. Metacognition is "the ability to think about your thinking—to make your thinking visible. Metacognition results in critical but healthy reflection and evaluation of your thinking, both of which may result in specific changes in how you teach or learn" (N. J. Anderson, 2002, p. 1).

Megastrategy **5.4**

Teach metacognitive strategies

The term *metacognition* means "a person's cognition about cognition." Jacobson (1998) used the term *metacognition* to describe the self-monitoring and conscious use of learning strategies.

Flavell's research on metamemory (see Flavell, 1979, 1985) showed that children's awareness of memory develops gradually over the school years, until they are able to choose selectively which memory strategies are most effective with what kinds of memory tasks. Control over one's own cognition involves the ability to think about thought, to be aware of the relative difficulty of mental tasks and to adjust mental performance in accord with these differences, and to assess and monitor the state of one's own mind.

Chamot and O'Malley (1994) divided metacognitive strategies into three areas: planning, monitoring, and evaluating. *Planning strategies* help students learn how to organize themselves for a learning task. *Monitoring strategies* help students check their comprehension in listening and reading and their production while speaking and writing. *Performance evaluation strategies* teach students how to assess their own performance on a task, using learning logs or other reflective tools to keep track of their progress.

Planning strategies play a role in instruction. For example, if students know that an essay is due in one week, they can plan to gather information for the first three days, draft their composition over the next two days, and finally proofread their writing. Monitoring strategies can be student-used comprehension checks that help students pause and quiz themselves periodically to see if they comprehend the main ideas when reading, or to see if they are writing what they intend to say in a rough draft. Students can self-evaluate outcomes to judge how much they have learned, and this self-evaluation can be compared to the teacher's assessment.

Additional kinds of metacognition in the area of self-knowledge are knowledge of one's own learning styles and preferences, knowledge of one's own strategy repertoire, and knowledge of one's own schemata.

Although to some extent metacognition is innate, it is not self-evident to everyone. Instead, like other strategy training, it must be modeled and integrated into learning through regular guided practice. Metacognitive strategy use takes its place as one more piece within the overall framework of cognitively stimulating teaching.

PRACTICES FOR TEACHERS

Developing Students' Metacognitive Strategies

- Model metacognitive processes such as self-checks and self-awareness.
- Make time during instruction to plan, monitor, and reflect as a group.
- Match self-reflection to replanning and setting new goals.

Direct Strategies: Social-Affective

Social-affective strategies teach how to elicit needed clarification, how to work cooperatively with peers in problem solving, and how to use mental techniques or self-talk to reduce anxiety and increase a sense of personal competency.

Megastrategy 5.5

Teach social-affective strategies

Social strategies represent the actions that learners choose to take in order to interact or communicate with other learners, with the teacher, or with native speakers. This supports or advances learning and helps the learner to "take control of the social environment in learning tasks and/or situations of use" (Tudor, 1996, p. 207).

Affective strategies are defined by Oxford (1990) as "emotions, attitudes, motivations, and values" (p. 140). These strategies help language learners to lower their anxiety, encourage themselves through positive self-talk and a positive attitude, and reward themselves when they have accomplished their learning goals.

However, beyond the control and fostering of positive emotional states, teachers may promote positive character traits, including thinking independently, exercising fair-mindedness, and developing intellectual humility, courage, integrity, and perseverance.

Student Opportunities to Cooperate

In planning for the development of a positive emotional climate in the classroom, many teachers include opportunities for students to talk about key concepts, perhaps using their primary language to clarify the concepts. Teachers ensure that students have numerous conversational partners and opportunities to interact within the context of lessons.

Material presented in a mainstream class may be difficult for English learners if the topics are cognitively complex and highly language dependent. Using cooperative learning, English learners have increased opportunities to verify their comprehension by receiving explanations from their peers and sharing prior knowledge. This technique helps them to clarify and familiarize themselves with the lesson content. Cooperative learning strategies are offered in Chapter 14 in the context of engagement with the community.

Support in the affective domain for English learners outside the classroom may include special home visits by released time teachers, counselors, or outreach workers and informal counseling by teachers. Monitoring of academic progress by counselors helps to encourage students with language needs.

Maintaining the First Language as an Affective Strategy

Students achieve more when they use and develop their native language (Ramírez, 1992). Teachers can use several strategies to support students' L1 in the classroom. Students can also keep reading logs or journals in their native language. Aides and tutors can assist in explaining difficult passages and help students summarize their understanding. Books, magazines, films, and other materials in the native language relating to the topic or theme of the lesson can support and augment students' learning.

PRACTICES FOR TEACHERS

Developing Students' Social-Affective Strategies

- Help students identify their own characteristic negative affective thoughts and formulate positive verbal affirmations.
- Watch for signs of discouragement and pause for encouragement at that point.
- Discuss positive character traits with students and praise students when they exercise them.
- Use L1 support strategies.

Direct Strategies: Academic Survival and Study Skills

Megastrategy 5.6
Teach academic survival and study skills

Academic survival skills are an aspect of academic competence. For English learners, academic experiences in the first language provide a foundation for L2 educational success. These students then acquire target-language skills to supplement this prior experience.

Academic Survival Skills

For many students, college is a necessity, not an option. To bridge the gap between ESL and college content courses, students must grapple with academic material that is challenging and relatively complex (J. N. Gardner, 1997). Students who aim to attend college in English face extensive learning and study demands. Many aspects of higher education follow unwritten cultural rules and practices that may take time to acquire. Discourse practices in U.S. K–12 classrooms are discussed in Chapter 11.

Native-Language Cultural Skills and Experiences

Students with prior success in schooling may know how to use reference materials, how to act like serious students, and how and when to ask for help from peers and authority figures. ELD students have access to a cultural body of knowledge that can be used as topics for essays, term papers, or autobiographic writing. Leki (1995) described an international student in a writing class at a U.S. university who consistently used the native culture as a theme. Even when the instructor asked her to find other themes, she persisted, gradually wearing down the instructor's protests, and received an A in the course. One might call this native-culture guerrilla warfare!

Target-Language Cultural Skills

Students can use target-language cultural skills to achieve academically. Knowing how to solicit cooperation from English-speaking peers is vital. Moreover, in many ways appearances are important in American culture. Presenting oneself as a cultural "player" with access to pop culture, slang expressions, and other accoutrements of "cool" helps gain the respect of peers. Learning one's way around a campus and its activities is a key to success. Those who participate in after-class activities are more likely to be successful in school than those who do not (McWhorter, 1995).

Knowledge about the Culture of Academia in the Target Language

For both immigrants and international students, speaking and listening in class is a hurdle. Instructors in U.S. classrooms tend to expect students to be active participants in class discussion under highly structured conditions. However, this is difficult for many English learners. The students may have learned English by means of curricula based on grammar, reading, and vocabulary without the opportunity to speak English or interact with native English speakers. Often, U.S. teachers spend much time talking or lecturing, or they interact verbally in question-and-answer sessions with students; again, this behavior follows traditional cultural patterns (see Chapter 11).

Use of *clarifying strategies* is the preeminent speaking/listening skill (Leki, 1995). Students use these to make sure they understand the assignment and the tasks they are expected to do. If a student has a particular question or does not understand, it is incumbent on that student to ask for clarification.

Behavioral expectations in an academic setting govern both students and instructors. Students are expected to be on time to class, and good attendance may be a critical factor in the grades received. Students remain sitting during class unless instructed otherwise and are expected to listen while the instructor is speaking. Students are responsible for their own work, and it must be submitted when due. Students are also responsible for their own learning.

Proper forms of address may vary from context to context, but K–12 teachers are generally addressed as "Mr.," "Miss," or "Mrs." Many teachers are annoyed when a student addresses them as "Teacher." Parts of the United States may be more formal than others; for example, instructors in the southeastern United States may require more formal address, with answers accompanied by "Sir" or "Ma'am."

The environment of a classroom is expected to be sociable, but nonacademic activities such as buying or selling items or promoting social clubs are frowned on. Making friends in class is optional. The instructor has discretion in assigning seats or mixing people within working groups. Most K–12 schools have a dress code for students as well as instructors.

Handbooks or other school publications contain regulations that govern the lives of students, and once these are made publicly available, students and/or their families are responsible for abiding by them. Cultural practices are not so publicly stated. For the most part, mainstream Americans do not help induct foreigners into their culture. The newcomer is expected to bear the burden of assimilation or accommodation—to "sink or swim" culturally.

Study Skills

One might think that knowing how to study is a universal skill, but study skills vary across cultures. Some students are trained to memorize, and the instructor is expected to define and delimit exactly what must be learned by rote. These students may not function well when the expectation shifts from dutiful pupil to active scholar. Students may need explicit training from an instructor on specific required skills, such as taking notes, making an outline, and using a library. For example, to help students prepare for writing a term paper, step-by-step preparation may be needed that includes partial credit for an early reference list or draft, as well as provision for in-class peer editing and review.

Keeping track of assignments and notes is an important academic skill. Some students need reminders to copy assignments and to marshal the necessary materials, such as taking the relevant textbook home from school. Time management, textbook reading, academic scheduling, and stress management are integral to academic success. Gardner and Jewell's (1997) handbook includes many such strategies for academic success.

The ability to take tests is another aspect of study skills. However, some strategies that are commonly assumed to be helpful are actually not. The adage "Work as quickly as you can" contradicts research showing that it is not the total time spent on a task that is important, but rather how one allocates and budgets one's time. One should prepare a range of strategies and be able to select strategies intelligently.

Assistance from organizations and volunteers outside the classroom is often available to English learners. This assistance can come from academic summer programs, additional instructional services such as after-school programs and peer tutoring, and dial-a-teacher for homework help in both English and the primary language.

Text Processing and Time Management

Academic reading presents the biggest challenge for English learners. During the period of an average academic semester, students may be faced with hundreds of pages of reading with the expectation that the material must be thoroughly mastered. The term *text processing* is distinct from reading comprehension in that it connotes strategic planning: the ability to manage large reading assignments wisely and to prepare to respond to large amounts of information. Strategic reading is a natural part of this process (see Chapter 7).

Requirements vary depending on the type of assessment. The type of text processing needed depends on the type of thinking that will be required; a good student presses the instructor for indications about the assessment keyed to the reading.

Effective time management divides text processing into phases: early, middle, and late. In the early phase of any assignment, the scholar identifies requirements and assembles materials, setting aside additional time for research-related reading. In the middle phase of the assignment, the scholar processes the text, allowing extra time for difficult reading and distributing the reading evenly over the time allotted. In the late phase, cramming for examinations or pounding out a term paper for a deadline, the scholar takes advantage of prior preparation and does not stay up all night at the expense of other responsibilities.

PRACTICES FOR TEACHERS

Developing Students' Academic/Survival Strategies

- Native culture: Remind students to draw on prior experience to know how to do well in class.

- Target culture: Provide cooperative tasks during class time that pair native and nonnative speakers of English, and encourage assignments in groups so students can make friends with their classmates.

- Academic culture: Provide specific orientation to classroom operations and school rules, including an introduction to library procedures, support personnel, and research skills.

- Study skills: Include in-class test review and term paper draft editing; give students course credit for assembling class notes; provide outlines of class lectures for the purpose of note taking.

- Time management: Employ frequent reminders for longer assignments; require partial products such as notes from reading; call in students who do not perform well at midterm for extra supervision.

ELD in the Content Areas

With the increase of English learners in K–12 schools, school personnel recognize that these students need to keep up academically with their native-English-speaking peers while learning English. Two approaches, *content-based ELD* and *sheltered instruction* (or SDAIE), are used to connect ELD teaching with academic work in K–12 content areas such as mathematics, social studies, and science.

Content-Based Instruction and ELD

Megastrategy **5.7**

Combine English and content teaching

Content literacy is one of four main types of literacy, according to McKenna and Robinson (1997); the others are emergent literacy, functional literacy, and workplace literacy. Content literacy is "the ability to use reading and writing for the acquisition of new content in a given discipline" (McKenna & Robinson, 1997, p. 8). In content-based instruction (CBI) ELD classrooms, ELD educators, collaborating with content teachers, organize learning objectives around academic subjects in order to prepare students to master grade-level curricula as a supplement to the students' English class.

Content literacy is content specific; an individual who can read and write about science may not be able to do so in mathematics. However, being able to think clearly, understand key concepts, and express oneself are cognitive skills that do generalize across disciplines, so that efforts to promote content literacy in one subject can positively affect learning in other subjects.

CBI can be of great benefit if learners, content instructors, and language teachers can work together to provide systematic, planned instruction of vocabulary, concepts, and structures that are required for mastery of the content. Providing English instruction coupled with CBI increases the likelihood of academic success.

Is the collaboration between ELD and content instructors reciprocal? If ELD teachers teach content, the content teachers should include language-development objectives along with content objectives. This is an important feature of SDAIE instruction. The content instructor who promotes content literacy is a more responsible and active partner for collaborative CBI-ELDs.

In CBI-ELD, the content to be taught, general instructional goals, and time available for instruction are negotiated with the content teacher. One important factor in the success of CBI-ELD is the ELD teacher's past experiences in teaching similar content or ability to transfer knowledge gained from teaching similar concepts in other disciplines.

When curriculum is coordinated, two or more teachers in different disciplines connect, reinforce, and extend the knowledge they impart by dealing with complementary subject matter. This may be done through an interdisciplinary approach using an integrated curriculum that focuses on themes, problems, or issues rather than on discipline-specific content.

PRACTICES FOR TEACHERS

Developing Students' Content-Based Strategies

- Develop a collaboration with content instructors that is two-way.
- Include a wide range of learning strategies.
- Both ELD and content instructors are responsible for assessment.

Specially Designed Academic Instruction in English (SDAIE)

Many schools and teachers today use SDAIE to address the academic learning needs of English learners whose English is in an early developmental stage. SDAIE provides additional support to these students rather than leaving them to "sink or swim" in a content class designed for native English speakers. SDAIE combines SLA principles with teaching modifications to make a lesson understandable to students (Echevarria, Vogt, & Short, 2007).

SDAIE features content instruction taught by content area teachers (science, history, mathematics) with English-language support. In contrast, CBI-ELD is taught by ELD teachers using content area materials as texts. SDAIE helps English learners to learn grade-appropriate content featuring "academic" English.

SDAIE teachers support students' academic English by the use of visuals, hands-on props and manipulatives, and cooperative learning. However, the use of such materials may inadvertently be misused to water down content, a practice that decreases the information available to students rather than increasing their ability to comprehend complex content. SDAIE instructional techniques help students to master demanding content areas without overly simplifying the curriculum. SDAIE teachers also modify their oral teaching to make themselves more understandable to English learners.

SDAIE: Determining Content, Language, and Learning-Strategy Objectives. An SDAIE teacher incorporates tasks in the content area and language that take into account the specific language of the discipline. In reviewing the language objectives, the teacher can keep the following questions in mind: (1) What are the key concepts to demonstrate and illustrate? (2) What structures and discourse of the discipline are included in the language objectives? (3) Are all four language modes—listening, speaking, reading, writing—included in planning? Of course, SDAIE lessons should also include learning-strategy objectives, as shown in Figure 5.18.

SDAIE: Modifying Instructional Materials and Activities. The teacher selects, modifies, and organizes text material to accommodate the needs of English learners. In modifying text, the goal is to improve comprehensibility through such means as providing study guides or defining new content vocabulary by showing vocabulary

FIGURE 5.18   *Rain Forest Unit: Content, Language, and Learning-Strategy Objectives*

Science

To name four layers of the rain forest and distinguish the different species that live in the different layers

To compare life cycles of these species for similarities and differences

To study the effect of the surrounding environment on various animals' life cycles

Language

To predict what will happen in the story "The Great Kapok Tree" by looking at the pictures

To explain why the Great Kapok tree was so special

To read aloud parts of the story using appropriate voices to represent characters

To read information from a nonfiction source and compare it with information gained from the story

To recognize vocabulary from the story and pronounce it correctly when reading to a peer

Learning Strategy

To work cooperatively with a learning group

To keep a personal vocabulary "new word" book

To create a comparison chart for information gained from the story and nonfiction sources

---

pictorially. Focus questions or concept maps serve as advance organizers. Selected passages may be tape-recorded for students to listen to as they read along in the text. As students' language proficiency increases, so should the complexity of their reading material. The goal is for students to progress toward the ability to work with unmodified texts.

Student learning activities should develop students' interactive language but not disadvantage an English learner. Collaborative, problem-solving teams include member roles that provide a variety of input and output modalities to balance the English skills and nonverbal talents of students. English learners can benefit from the use of media, realia, science equipment, diagrams, models, experiments, manipulatives, and other modalities that make language more comprehensible.

SDAIE: Increasing Teacher Understandability.   Teachers must ensure that students understand what is said in the classroom. Teachers in SDAIE classrooms devote particular attention to four communication strategies: (1) language contextualization, (2) teacher's speech modification, (3) use of paraphrase and repetition, and (4) use of clarification checks.

Language contextualization means focusing teaching on the context of the immediate task, augmenting vocabulary with gestures, pictures, realia, and so on to convey instructions or key words and concepts. This approach provides a rich visual and/or kinesthetic environment (e.g., through drama and skits).

Teacher's speech modification means adjusting speech from the customary native speech patterns. This takes place at many linguistic levels: phonological (precise articulation); syntactic (shorter sentences, with subject-verb-object word order); semantic (more concrete, basic vocabulary, with fewer idioms); pragmatic (frequent and longer pauses, slower delivery, and exaggerated intonation, especially placing more stress on important new concepts); and discourse (self-repetition; main idea easily recognized and supporting information following immediately). Teachers in SDAIE classrooms also talk less in the classroom, encouraging students to talk.

Use of repetition and paraphrase involves verbal repetition (for example, using the same type of directions throughout various lessons) and organizational repetition (lessons that occur at specific times, lessons with clearly marked verbal and nonverbal boundaries, such as "Now it's time to . . . ,"). Concepts are presented numerous times through various means.

Clarification checks are strategies to monitor listening and reading comprehension at intervals to give the teacher a sense of the students' ability to understand. Teachers may need to rephrase questions and information. The teacher might pause to ask a question requiring a simple response, such as "Show me how you are going to begin your work," or ask individual students to restate the instruction using their own words.

Skilled questioning using a linguistic hierarchy of question types helps teachers to ascertain students' understanding. For students in the "silent period," questions elicit a nonverbal response—a head movement, pointing, or manipulation of materials. Once students begin to speak, they can choose the correct word or phrase to demonstrate understanding of either/or questions: "Is the water evaporating or condensing?" "Did explorers come to the Americas from Europe or Asia?" Once students are more comfortable in producing language, *wh-* questions are used: "What is happening to the water?" "Which countries sent explorers to the Americas?" "What was the purpose of their exploration?" (Díaz-Rico & Weed, 2010).

Although SDAIE teaching involves presentation of subject matter in English, opportunities are available throughout the lesson for students to clarify their understanding using their primary language, supplemented whenever possible by primary-language resources (print, electronic, personnel) that can help students with key concepts.

The scope of this book does not permit an exhaustive discussion of SDAIE. For an excellent, in-depth treatment, refer to *Making Content Comprehensible for English Language Learners: The SIOP Model* (Echevarria, Vogt, & Short, 2007).

PRACTICES FOR TEACHERS

Using SDAIE Strategies

- Teach content and language with two modalities if possible; for example, supplement listening with pictures.
- Cover content with as much richness and depth as possible, without watering down the curriculum or slowing the pace.
- Strive to give students comprehensible input.

Computer-Assisted Language Learning/ Computer-Mediated Communication

Computer-assisted instruction (CAI) has been available for classroom use since the earliest days of word processing (late 1970s). Tutoring programs soon followed. The early 1980s saw the advent of commercially available instructional software, in which multiple-choice answer formats enabled the individual user to attempt repeated answers and receive error feedback without public embarrassment. Computer-assisted language learning (CALL) applied to English learning soon moved beyond skill drills into more innovative applications. *Computer-mediated communication (CMC)* is a term that describes the role of computers in allowing people to communicate virtually (see Herring, 1996).

Megastrategy **5.8**

Use computers to assist language learning

Language classrooms have been transformed through multimedia computing and the Internet. The digital revolution is changing the way people spend their free time— playing video and computer games, chatting on the Internet, conducting business transactions, and much more—and also changing the way people learn. From home, people can access educational experiences that formerly required attending classes. CALL has the potential to extend learning far beyond the four walls of the classroom. Websites offer lesson plans, quizzes, chat rooms, and bulletin boards that allow the learner to sample English idioms, prepare for standardized tests, or connect with English learners in other parts of the world. Many language teachers benefit from an Internet hookup in the classroom or language laboratory.

Computer configurations are changing with dizzying rapidity, and TESOL educators must continually adapt their instruction accordingly:

> Around the world, companies are rolling out a new kind of service that brings broadband power to mobile personal devices. Commonly known as 3rd Generation, or 3G, this upgrade in cellular networks means that any media will be able to stream easily to our devices in full motion, including all manner of television programs, movies, videoconferencing, music, and multimedia. Next will come 4G, in which data rates are expected to be 100 times faster that those in this first 3G wave. As the delivery platform of broadband content and functionality shifts from computer to personal devices, we will be surrounded by a multimedia aura that accompanies us wherever we go. In this way, the New WWW is unlike anything humans have yet experienced. (March, 2007, p. 213)

CALL and Second-Language Acquisition

SLA theory interfaces with CALL around issues such as classroom interaction; physical design of the classroom to facilitate student interaction; the nature of computer-based language-learning tasks; the variety of software and hardware configurations, their uses, strengths, and weaknesses; and computer-based language assessment. It is important that CALL include discussion of pedagogical issues, because the earliest uses of the computer did not foster constructivist pedagogy (cf. D. N. Perkins, 1992).

One problem inherent in the use of technology is the "digital divide." If access to digital information or the ability to use technology separates students across geographic, ethnic, language, financial, disability, gender, or political barriers, then technology becomes exploitative. For example, research has shown that boys embrace technology more readily than girls, creating a gender gap. Moreover, schools with predominantly minority enrollments are more likely to use technology for drill, practice, and test taking. Thus, gender and race act as dividers in the acquisition of computer skills (Cavanaugh, 2006). In contrast, computers can be used in more exciting ways, to model weather systems, to visualize molecular science, and to map complex ideas and concepts (Jonassen, 2006).

Laboratory Skills. Students in schools across the United States are using multimedia computer tools for video and film production, using QuickTime and other digital video production techniques to add sound effects, animation, and other presentation enhancements to create unique works. Bitter and Legacy (2005) have included a host of classroom-friendly multimedia production tools, both software and hardware. English learners should have access to these tools on a par with other learners.

For teachers, hands-on laboratory skills are necessary in addition to a general introduction to CALL to demonstrate the instructional and communicative use of the Internet, CD-ROM–based software, and other CMC tools. Some such courses introduce computer-managed instruction (CMI) techniques such as the use of programs that manage students' grades and perform database management.

Strategic CALL. CALL supports strategic language learning. For example, word processing supports the formal writing process by allowing students to organize, draft, revise, edit, and even publish their work electronically. They can write informal e-mails with "keypals" in different areas of the world or use writing-based chatrooms online in real time. Students can develop oral skills by using presentation or authoring software to create professional-looking oral presentations, and they can use both aural and oral skills in Web-enabled telephone conversations.

Both software programs and online resources are used in classrooms involved in CALL to help students achieve their language-learning goals. Software programs include traditional drill-and-practice programs that focus on vocabulary or discrete grammar points; tutorials; games; simulations that present students with real-life situations in the language and culture they are learning; productivity tools, such as word processing, databases, spreadsheets, graphics, and desktop publishing (DTP); and presentation or authoring programs. Material from encyclopedias and even *National Geographic* are available on CD-ROM.

Instant communication afforded through the Internet connects students with other parts of the world, with speakers of English, and with rich sources of

Computers can be used in a dual-language immersion setting for second-language acquisition.
©Monkey Business Images/ Shutterstock.com

information. The World Wide Web delivers authentic materials including texts, images, sound recording, video clips, virtual reality worlds, and dynamic interactive presentations. Streaming audio and video connect students with native speakers and authentic audiovisual materials by virtually transporting the target-language environment to the second-language classroom. Students can listen to live radio stations from around the world or hear prerecorded broadcasts of music, news, sports, and weather. Search engines (e.g., Yahoo, Google) help the student find authentic materials on classroom, group, or individual research topics.

WebQuests are a popular form of Internet-based instruction because teachers can use the www.webquest.org template to adapt material to their own lessons. Ideally, WebQuests involve students in using the Internet to carry out inquiry-based tasks in which students pose interesting, open-ended questions. Such questions spark true learning: They require students to think for themselves and to analyze, synthesize, and evaluate the information they find on the Web (Cunningham & Billingsley, 2006).

Bitter and Pierson (2006) cautioned that use of the Internet must be evaluated by guidelines that ensure validity of information as well as usability of the search tools provided. On a website, the author of the information should be clearly stated, including credentials and contact information; the date of the site's most recent update is also helpful. The content should be current, accurate, and free of bias. The text and graphics of a high-quality website are easy to read and developmentally appropriate for the intended reader. The site should be easy to navigate, with links that work and that are connected to relevant other sites. Media elements (audio, video, animation, etc.) should enhance the content. The site should be accessible to individuals with disabilities.

CALL Supports Learner Autonomy.   The computer is a powerful learning tool that requires the teacher to organize, plan, teach, and monitor. Computer technology can provide students with the means to control their own learning, to construct meaning, and to evaluate and monitor their own performance.

> Abdel uses the Internet in the language-learning lab to research current events and cultural topics for a conversation class at the International Extension Program (IEP). He also converses with native speakers who are paired with class members via e-mail. To practice pronunciation, he uses software that enables him to click on a word or sentence to hear it repeatedly, look up a meaning, see a related picture or video clip and/or read a related text, listen to a sentence, compare his voice to a computer model of the correct response, and have the computer judge the accuracy of his attempts.

Computer-Mediated Communication

Computer-mediated communication (CMC) is a field in which publications are burgeoning. Articles have appeared on hypertext poetics, visual rhetoric, cyberspace aesthetics, hyperrhetoric, electronic literacy, metamedia literacy, iconology, teletheory, hybrid literacies, and design discourse (see Handa [2001] for a selected bibliography of digital literacy and rhetoric). English is fast becoming fused to an iconic or visually enhanced version of itself, as the sociology of knowledge undergoes a concomitant rapid transformation. It is not clear at this time in what direction the volatile mix of English as an international language and CMC will lead.

Internet technologies have been developed that support a community of learning in the classroom. Holding e-mail discussions by means of a listserv or group e-mail list automates the process of broadcasting one posting to an entire group. Listservs can also distribute electronic journals, e-magazines, or e-newsletters. A teacher can "prime" the list by asking thoughtful questions, recommending useful resources, or requiring students to post a minimum number of messages or responses. Bulletin board discussions resemble e-lists, but the discussions can be structured to maintain the order and topics of discussion and make the entire "conversation" visible. In addition to these asynchronous methods (students do not have to be present simultaneously), synchronous chatrooms make it possible for participants to chat simultaneously (Mills, 2006).

CALL teachers help students to carefully plan and organize learning experiences, rehearse useful language, and understand the physical operation of the Internet.

Digital Online Activity

Digital games and online activities are stimulating students' language activities in ways that were unavailable in the past and threaten to outshine the input students receive in school. Gee (2007) identified a wide range of technical vocabulary, multisyllabic words, and complex syntax in the popular *Yu-Gi-Oh* children's card game that far surpassed the language that many young children encounter in their schoolbooks.

Box 5.2   Upcoming Technologies

How can the technologies that are now becoming part of students' lives motivate them to engage in learning English? Table 5.2 describes these technologies and suggests possible uses in the classroom.

Research on the online activities of a community of Korean-American teenagers in the Midwestern United States who had grown up partly in the United States and partly in Korea and partly found that their instant messaging and web postings to each other within the local peer group contained copious mixing of English and Korean and frequent references to school culture, music, and other forms of popular culture in both Korea and the United States (Yi, 2009).

Technological Literacy

Technological literacy involves both technology and CALL. Charp (1996) stated, "literacy goes beyond the basic skills of reading, writing, and arithmetic and includes

TABLE 5.2   *Some ELD Uses for New Technologies*

Technological Innovation	Possible Classroom Use
Social Networking	Sites devoted to educational communities, such as www.ning.com, allow teachers to use social networking whose content can be managed and made available only to invitees and yet allows students to chat, post blog entries, and interact.
Microblogging and Twitter	Students can follow tweets from famous people; teachers can receive updates on areas of teaching technology. Teachers can ask students to store and analyze the language sent on tweets.
Gaming	Students can write about the problem solving, characters, and other literacy practices needed to master various games.
Mobile Tools	Teen novels have been written in "texting talk," resembling a set of text messages between high school friends. Such writing can be used to carry a narrative.
wiki	Group input sites that allow entries, edits, and publication from multiple authors can be used to host class books and other writings, as well as group digital stories, photos, and links.

Source: Based on Wilber, 2010.

Box 5.3   Point/Counterpoint: Do Mobile Devices Help Language Learning?

Cell phones, iPods, iPads, netbooks—do they have a place in schools, or should they be confiscated at the metal detector before a student can set foot on school grounds? (New York City Schools tried this in 2008 and found that several models of Samsung cell phones are totally plastic and can slip through!)

Point: Mobile technology is here to stay; schools need to take full advantage of immediate-access, immediate-feedback forms of second-language learning. Learning can take place using a highly motivating platform that features high-definition graphics, sounds, and fast-paced interactivity.

Counterpoint: Stationary technology—classroom desktop computers—are easier to monitor for student attention. Today's students are highly distractible, often unable to separate schoolwork, entertainment, and their private lives. "Given human nature and the power of new computer/Internet connections, it is little wonder that some students go down the path of usage that is anti-social and dysfunctional" (Adams & Angeles, 2008, p. 37).

computer and other technology-related skills in the context of the workplace" (p. 6). Hansen (2000) defined technological literacy as "a personal ability to adopt, adapt, or invent proper technological tools in an information society to positively affect his or her life, community, and environment" (p. 31). More than five million jobs added to the workforce since 1993 require professional, management, or technical skills (Charp, 1996). As people recognize its importance, technological literacy will become a growing field, standing as it does at the intersection of ESP, CALL/CMC, and vocational ESL (VESL)/workplace ESL.

WebQuests are a popular form of Internet-based instruction.

©Monkey Business Images/
Shutterstock.com

PRACTICES FOR TEACHERS

Using CALL To Enhance Students' English Acquisition

- Use CALL not as an end in itself but as a means to enhance other learning strategies.

- Expose students to a variety of CALL modes of interaction for reading, listening, speaking, writing, and critical thinking.

- Encourage students to work collaboratively with others to see CALL as a group activity that encourages face-to-face language use.

Equipped with strategies for language learning and use as well as academic and survival skills, students can take more responsibility for improving both their language abilities and their learning processes. Teachers who directly teach strategies will see students gain in language proficiency and self-confidence. Teachers can also encourage students to share their favorite strategies for accomplishing certain tasks during class. As students learn how to succeed with second-language learning, they gain the tools they need to become lifelong learners.

Exploratory Break

- Recall the strategies you may have used when you learned a second/foreign language. Were they taught in class, or did you discover them on your own?

- Choose two second-language acquisition strategies from Chapter 5 and reflect on your own language learning experience: Were these strategies useful for you?

- What CALL strategies are you familiar with? Consider your school site—are these available for your students?

Chapter *6*

Oracy Instruction That Builds on the First Language

According to Plato, the only knowledge humans acquire is that which they already learned in the pure world of Forms. If this were true, teachers would be in the business of teaching people what they already know! In a sense, this is exactly what happens in classrooms. Students learn best when they already know something about the subject matter and can draw from this prior knowledge. The most profound prior knowledge that English learners possess is knowledge *of* their first language and knowledge *in* their first language. This is, as Bourdieu (1977) puts it, their "cultural capital." This is the capital that teachers build on in dual-language acquisition. This chapter discusses the oracy processes—how people learn to listen and speak in a second language—that make academic success possible.

Megastrategy **SET 6**

Teach oracy systematically, building on primary-language skills

Vygotsky believed that children learn to engage in higher-level thinking by learning first how to communicate (including speaking, listening, writing, and reading). The more that students can use language in the classroom environment, the more they will learn how to think. This means that the natural sociability of children in their first language is the foundation for their intellectual development. This chapter presents ways in which oracy develops within a social context and is enhanced by strategic teaching, based on a foundation of how the mind functions. Imaginative ways of using literacy and oracy are addressed in Chapter 8.

Oracy skills are essential if English learners are to participate fully in a democratic society. Speaking involves a number of complex skills and strategies—not only the stringing together of words in proper grammatical sequence but also the organizing of those words into coherent, powerful messages that help the speaker attain personal goals. Listening and speaking are integral to communicative competence—knowing what to say, to whom, and how to shape that discourse in the most effective way. This ability begins with oracy training in English-language development.

Listening Processes

Part of the knowledge needed to comprehend oral discourse is the ability to separate meaningful units from the stream of speech. Although listening may be seen as a "receptive" skill, it is by no means a passive act. According to the sociocognitive approach to learning, listening is an act of constructing meaning. Listeners draw on their store of background knowledge and their expectation of the message to be conveyed as they actively work at understanding a conversation or oral presentation. The role of the teacher is to set up situations in which students can develop their own purposes and goals for listening, acquire the English that is most useful in their daily lives, feel a sense of purpose, and engage in real communication.

A Social Constructionist View of Listening

Looking at learners through a social constructionist lens means seeing human beings as participants in, and creators of meaning—meaning that is achieved as learners interact, speaking and listening to one another, working toward mutual understanding. Even though a cognitive view uses computer metaphors such as "input" and "processing," this "inevitably underestimates the active participation of the successful listener in interaction" (Lynch, 2009, p. 13).

> *Megastrategy* **6.1**
>
> Teach listening in a way that builds interest, information acquisition, and lifelong literacy

Although the current emphasis is on communicating for authentic purposes, a number of guided listening techniques have come from more traditional language-teaching methodologies. For purposes of simplification, listening activities are discussed here under the categories of listening to repeat, listening to understand, and listening for communication.

Listening to Repeat: Updating the Audiolingual Approach

In audiolingual teaching, students repeat exactly what they hear, with an emphasis on correct pronunciation. Minimal pair pattern practice is a common strategy; students are asked to repeat simple phrases that differ by only one phoneme, for example: "It is a ship/It is a sheep"; "He is skipping/He is slipping." Current methods encourage students to listen to minimal pairs within meaningful contexts. Teachers use poems, nursery rhymes, and songs to introduce "rhyming words," asking students to fill in the blanks at the end of lines to demonstrate their knowledge of phonemic difference and context-appropriate words. In addition, teachers can read aloud books featuring wordplay, alliteration, and tongue twisters, encouraging students to talk about how the author manipulates words. Graham (1988) has created jazz chants from fairy tales, giving younger and less proficient students the opportunity to work with longer texts. Such activities help students to hear the language and to develop phonemic awareness.

Box 6.1   **Point/Counterpoint: Should Listening Input Be Slowed Down for Beginners?**

Point: This makes the content more understandable

Counterpoint: The speed is not authentic

Resolution: When the task is to listen for just certain things, the stimulus does not have to be slowed because one does not expect listeners to get every word—just to complete the task (picking out just certain words, etc.). If the stimulus is slowed down, the listener should be told that it is slow; and then, depending on the time available, it can be given again at a normal pace. (Some input cannot be slowed, such as a musical recording.)

A listening area can be set up in which the English learners can listen to books on tape, with picture books or models nearby to support understanding of what is heard. Two such stations might be set up side by side so that students can share this listening experience with a friend. It may be comforting to a child if the voice on the tape speaks English that is accented the same way that people from his or her primary-language community sound. A bilingual English speaker who lives in the neighborhood or a parent can help.

Listening to Understand: The Task Approach

In addition to repeating, students are being asked to demonstrate comprehension as well, not through exact repetition but through performing tasks such as writing the correct response or selecting the correct answer. To be successful, students must listen carefully. Typical classroom tasks are listening to an audiotape and completing true/false exercises based on the content, listening to a prerecorded speech and circling vocabulary items on a list, and listening to a lecture and completing an outline of the notes. Students may be asked to listen for the main idea, for specific information, for synonyms, or for vocabulary in context (Leshinsky, 1995). Other listening activities might include listening for focal stress or listening for syllables.

Autonomy in language learning is encouraged by assigning students to create listening journal entries. Three times a week students summarize what they have listened to—for example, a television program, a video, a movie, or a lecture—with a minimum requirement of thirty minutes of listening at a time.

Contemporary language-teaching methods emphasize the interactional aspects of language and recognize the importance of the listener's construction of meaning. The first stage of language acquisition is now seen as listening rather than repeating. During the initial "silent period," learners actively listen, segmenting the sound stream, absorbing intonation patterns, and becoming comfortable in the second-language environment. They demonstrate comprehension through nonverbal means. With this methodology, academic subjects can be included, even in the early stages of language acquisition (see TPR and Natural Approach, Chapter 3).

Listening to understand features listening activities based primarily on three types of sources. The first type of source is prerecorded selections by various speakers, usually (though not always) native speakers. At this level excerpts are usually based on simulations of actual conversations or other input. For example, Randall's Listening Lab (www.esl-lab.com) uses a limited range of speakers, and topics vary.

A second source of listening material is audiotaped selections culled from a variety of sources. To create listening input materials for *The Heart of the Matter* (Vai, 1998), the author used a tape recorder to interview a wide array of musicians, artists, entrepreneurs, and other professionals on a host of topics. Each lesson was organized around a brief, formal lecture that introduced a topic, a listening activity that presented material of a more informal and subjective nature, and a third listening exercise that asked several speakers "from the street" for their reaction to the second exercise. The usual workbook activities rounded out these listening opportunities with comprehension, vocabulary development, and critical thinking exercises.

A third type of source consists of listening to the "real world." *Talk It Over!* (Kozyrev, 1998) assigns students the task of watching a television game show and answering workbook questions about the nature of the contestants, the content and format of the show, and the kinds of possible prizes. In another section of the same series, students watch television commercials and decide if they are effective tools of persuasion. Thus, students are expected to seek out their own input and do a task based on the assigned listening.

For a more interactive adaptation of these listening procedures, the teacher and students can discuss the topic of an upcoming talk by a guest speaker and brainstorm questions and comments the students might like to make. During the talk, students listen for answers to their questions. The talk can be tape-recorded and the tape subsequently put into a listening center. Students can then listen again, making note of ideas they want to share in the class follow-up activities.

In an adult ESL class at a local church, instructor Jeff Adams used taped monologues at listening centers for students to listen to and repeat. In one such center, students recorded themselves giving oral descriptions, telling short stories, and giving speeches. In addition, students could check out tape recorders to work on oral journal assignments and reports. In spite of these efforts, progress was slow. Jeff wondered if he should rethink the listening centers. (Egbert & Petrie, 2005, pp. 92–93)

Listening for Communication

The emphasis at this level is on developing students' abilities to communicate fluently and accurately by integrating listening, speaking, and pronunciation practice and developing skills in anticipating questions, understanding suggestions, and note taking. In the communicative approach, once listeners are beyond the initial stage, interviews are often used to augment listening skills. Listening can also be used in problem-solving situations by means of riddles, logic puzzles, and brainteasers as well as more traditional mathematical problems. Listening, far from being a merely receptive skill, can be successfully combined with other language modes as part of an integrated approach to English-language acquisition.

Table 6.1 provides listening comprehension activities within each of the three levels discussed above.

Before Listening

Explicit instruction in listening can be organized in "into," "through," and "beyond" stages in a similar fashion to reading instruction. Prelistening tasks can include a preview of vocabulary, a cue to the type of rhetoric expected (such as chronological order), or attention to a map that cues a spatial setting for the listening task. Chapter 1, "The American Civil War," in Unit 5 of Dunkel and Lim's *Intermediate Listening Comprehension* (1994) offers a prelistening preparation task defining "civil war," introducing key vocabulary and previewing the rhetorical structure of causal explanation. At a more advanced level, Dunkel, Pialorsi, and Kozyrev's *Advanced Listening Comprehension* (1996) presents a preview of the content of

TABLE 6.1 *Activities for Listening Comprehension*

Repeating	Understanding	Communicating

To hear sound patterns:
  Rhyming poems
  Songs
  Couplets
  Tongue twisters
  Jingles
  Alliterative poems and books
	Listening to answer factual questions orally or in writing:
	  Dialogues
	  Talks
	  Lectures
	  Arguments
		Playing games:
		  Twenty Questions
		  Pictionary
		  Password
		  Simon Says
		  Mother, May I?

To listen to sentences:
  Jazz chants
  Dialogues
  Skits
	Listening to make notes:
	  Support an argument
	  Persuade
		Open-ended sentences
		Conversation starters
		Cooperative problem-solving activities:
		  Riddles
		  Logic puzzles
		  Brainteasers

Source: Díaz-Rico & Weed (2010).

Box 6.2 A Learner-Strategy Approach to Listening

In this exercise, students are asked, as a pre-listening activity, to think of situations in which they might have to listen for specific information. In this way, they are made aware that trying to listen for details is sometimes a useful strategy.

Task: In this situations, listen carefully to the (prerecorded) information. See if you can collect accurate details.

You are inviting some friends for a barbeque meal tonight, but you are not sure if the weather will be good enough to eat outside. Listen to the weather forecast and decide if you can go ahead with your plans. (Flowerdew & Miller, 2005, p. 17)

the listening tasks as well as a lengthy outline to help the listener understand the rhetorical organization of the excerpt. In contrast, in Chapter 8 of *Talk It Over!* (Kozyrev, 1998), students first interview classmates or people outside class to find out why they watch television and then listen to an interview with David Bianculi, television critic for the *New York Daily News*. This prepares students to listen in a different way.

While Listening

Students can follow an outline as they listen, take notes cued by a set of questions, or take notes in a variety of ways, using idea maps, outlines, paragraphs, or lists. They can listen several times with a slightly different purpose each time: main idea, supporting details, or attitude of the speaker. They can listen to the lecture or conversation recorded several times, using speakers from contrasting dialects.

If the teacher feels the need to lecture, a helpful strategy for English learners is to videotape a lesson while students simply listen to the lecture, concentrating on understanding and writing down only questions or parts of the lecture they do not fully understand. Later, the videotape is played, and the teacher and several students take notes on the board. The teacher can model the type of outline that indicates the main ideas and supporting details. After a few minutes, the videotape is stopped and the discussion then highlights various note-taking and other strategies. This activity can be used on a periodic basis to enhance students' ability to comprehend lectures and take effective notes.

Teachers in content classes in which English learners are mainstreamed need to attend to the listening skills of these students. Frequent comprehension checks are helpful. When a difficult concept is presented, the teacher can ask the entire class to indicate with a (chest-high) thumbs up/thumbs-down sign if they understand a new concept well enough for the class to continue. This public, yet private, gesture can offer feedback to the instructor about the general level of comprehension without stigmatizing the English learners.

After Listening

Many kinds of activities can follow up a listening task. Students can write, discuss, read, draw, or act out their interpretation of the content. They can attend to the linguistic aspects of what they have heard by completing worksheets on word meaning, idiomatic usage, formal versus informal English, words that compare and contrast, or words that introduce causal statements. The focus can be on cultural aspects of the reading, content applications across the disciplines, or critical thinking including problem solving. In Leshinsky (1995), students listen to a recording about two people who have just signed a lease; following this activity, they work on paraphrasing, discussing the relaxed pronunciation of the speakers (use of filler words like *y'know* and contractions), writing a summary of what was learned about the rights and responsibilities of landlords and tenants, or role-playing renegotiating a lease.

Authentic Tasks in and out of the Real World

An effective listening curriculum exposes students to a variety of speakers for a variety of tasks on a variety of topics for a variety of purposes. Language should resemble speech used in real life, whether short and direct, rambling and indirect, formal or informal, or curt and incoherent. How is one to assess the response to such varied stimuli? The most useful approach is one that increases in complexity as students become more capable and exposes them to the real world when they can handle authentic interactions.

Of course, aside from classroom exercises, the real listening skill is going out into the real world. Comprehending carefully selected three- to seven-minute chunks of language is much simpler than listening to actual spoken discourse. Listeners must bring a relatively sophisticated set of understandings to bear on a number of factors: what to expect from the speaker, the setting in time and place, the topic, the genre of the text and the co-text, or accompanying clues to meaning. A great deal of unconscious work goes into the task of real-world listening to create both cultural and linguistic understanding.

But despite the complexity of listening tasks and the emphasis on communicative approaches, listening is only half the work; one must also learn to speak.

Listening Tasks to Measure Listening Comprehension

There are numerous ways to assess listening comprehension, ranging from those useful at the beginning level to those more appropriate for advanced learners (see Table 6.2).

TABLE 6.2 *Listening Assessment Tailored to SLA Level*

Type of Assessment	Recommended SLA Level	The learner can...
Doing	Beginning	. . . respond physically such as in Total Physical Response (TPR)
Choosing	Beginning	. . . select from alternatives such as pictures, objects, texts, or actions
Duplicating	Early Intermediate	. . . simply repeat or translate the message
Transferring	Early Intermediate	. . . transform the message such as drawing a route on map, or filling in a chart
Answering	Intermediate	. . . answer questions about the text
Conversing	Intermediate	. . . actively participate in face-to-face conversation
Condensing	Early Advanced	. . . take notes or make an outline
Extending	Early Advanced	. . . go beyond the text by continuing the story or solving a problem
Summarizing	Advanced	. . . make a summary by reviewing, inferring, or comparing details and evaluating main ideas
Modeling	Advanced	. . . perform a similar task, e.g., give instructions to a coworker after listening to a model

---

PRACTICES FOR TEACHERS

Improving Listening Comprehension

Listening is a complex activity. S. Brown (2006) offers the following tips for improving listening comprehension:

- Activate prior knowledge before listening by drawing upon—or building up—students' schemata so that what they hear will make sense.

- Make sure students have a clear purpose for listening: Will the emphasis be on the main idea, details, or making inferences?

- Place a listening task in a real-world context so students are learning cultural information that makes language useful

- Listening is more likely to lead to comprehension when followed by speaking tasks that require students to draw upon personalized knowledge, using topics that are interesting for them to discuss.

Speaking Processes

Oral work in English has generally been considered to rest on the concept that oracy lacks a social or political dimension. However, acknowledging that discourses are influenced by uneven distributions of power leads to teaching skills that are grounded in the realities of knowledge and power practices. Oracy is inextricably joined with cultural identity and social differences, and opportunities to listen and speak are differentiated according to the individual's relationship to institutions and sociocultural contexts. Direct connections to the community and to the circulation of power (Foucault, 1980, 1984) strengthen the chance that individuals' investments in learning to speak and listen will actually enhance their cultural capital.

Speaking involves a number of complex skills and strategies. Spoken discourse can be informal, as in conversations between friends, or formal, as in academic lectures. Informal conversations are interactive; speaker and listener share common knowledge and support each other with nonverbal cues. On the other hand, a lecturer assumes that the listener can supply a complex background or context; the listener is less able to interact with the speaker to negotiate meaning.

Part of the role of the teacher is to help students assimilate and produce discourse not only for the purpose of basic interpersonal communication (informal) but also for the comprehension and production of cognitive academic language (formal). In addition, the teacher provides opportunities for students to express themselves in a wide range of language functions.

Focus on Fluency

Fluency is the most important speaking skill. L. Jones (2007) defines fluency in this way:

> Fluency doesn't mean speaking really fast without hesitating. It's being able to express yourself despite gaps in your knowledge, despite the mistakes you're making, despite not knowing all the vocabulary you might need. . . . The opposite of fluency is being tongue-tied and embarrassed when speaking English—or not speaking at all. Fluency means speaking slowly and clearly, not speaking fast and unclearly. Fluency depends on knowing more vocabulary and on confidence—and on not worrying about losing face by making mistakes. Another component of fluency is being able to articulate easily and comprehensively. (p. 18)

Megastrategy 6.2

Teach speaking in a way that sustains self-esteem and lifelong self-expression

Difficulties with Spoken Discourse

Today's universities enroll many undergraduates whose first language is not English, including an increasing number of foreign students. It is not uncommon for these students to attend class for an entire semester without speaking once in class. Similar situations exist in K–12 classrooms in U.S. schools, in which large numbers of English learners are main-streamed into contexts that render them silent as a result. It is therefore vital that teachers help students overcome their oral language quietude and help them to develop their speaking abilities. Accepting English learners' use of both languages during instruction may help reduce their anxiety about speaking English (Pappamihiel, 2002).

Basic Interpersonal Communication Skills

A newcomer to the English language needs to learn basic interpersonal communication skills (BICS) that permit adjustment to the routines of schooling and the comforts of peer interaction. This accomplishment enables the student to perform classroom chores, chat with peers, or consume instructional media. The importance of BICS is that students can begin to understand and communicate with their teacher, develop and fine-tune their interpersonal skills, and begin to overcome culture shock.

The focus in BICS is on getting across a message, with little regard for sentence structure and word choice. Cummins (1984) calls BICS *context embedded,* because factors apart from the linguistic code can furnish meaning. For example, one student asks another for an eraser: "Mine's gone. You got one?" The student points to the pencil eraser and beckons for a loan. The item itself provides the context rather than the language. Other cues that add meaning to BICS in this situation are the tone of voice (supplicating) and the gesture ("Give me").

Studies have shown that conversational skills can approach native-like levels within two years of exposure to English (Collier, 1987; Cummins, 1981a). Fluency in BICS often leads parents or other adults to assume that the child has mastered English. However, this apparent fluency can be misleading. Students who may appear to be fluent enough in English to survive in an all-English classroom may in fact have significant gaps in the development of academic aspects of English.

Teachers can encourage newcomers' acquisition of basic social language in several ways. First, pairing a new student with a bilingual buddy who speaks the same primary language as well as English eases the pain of culture shock. Seating newcomers so that they can be involved with other pupils and can participate with other students can help to keep the new students alert and interactive.

A "Newcomer Handbook" is helpful during the earliest stages of BICS acquisition. Students can help to create this orientation guide. Sections of this guide might feature simple school rules and procedures; English phrases to use for various social functions (asking for help, volunteering for class jobs, etc.); and guides for homework help. It might include a simple map of the school with bilingual labels. Teachers may wish to furnish a bilingual picture dictionary.

Cooperative tasks of all kinds provide opportunities for students to speak with one another. Cooperative groups with mixed abilities permit students some measure of participation even though all roles may not require a high level of verbal ability in English.

Developing Oral Language

An encouraging classroom climate helps students to feel confident, to speak freely and make mistakes, and to believe that their way of speaking is respected and their opinions are taken seriously. A noncompetitive atmosphere encourages the sharing of ideas through interaction, especially at a dedicated sharing time every day. A "productively talkative" work environment is not so noisy that a timid child feels overwhelmed. Even in a "normally noisy" class, a shy student may need a "home corner" where he or she can listen to tapes in the primary language or engage in nonverbal play in which English is not necessary. This space provides a respite from the stress of foreign-language immersion.

Separate or Integrated Oral Language Development?

English oral language development is essential to the education of English learners. Virtually all educators agree that such learners need daily oral English practice until some minimum level of competence is reached. However, there is some disagreement on whether this practice should take place in a "pull-out" program or, conversely, integrated into reading/language arts instruction. In English immersion programs, one might question whether a separate block of time is needed for oral English development, because English learners are immersed in English throughout the day. Conversely, in primary-language maintenance programs, educators may lose focus on oral English development.

Using a multisite analysis of kindergarten students in four different kinds of program models, Saunders, Foorman, and Carlson (2006) concluded that students in programs having a separate ELBD block showed modest achievement gains over those students in other models. An interesting by-product of this analysis, however, showed that regardless of program type, students spent most of their oral language time on listening and discussing and very little time on academic topics, target-language vocabulary, or language structure. The challenge? A more structured oral English curriculum, even in kindergarten, lays a more solid foundation for future academic success.

Situations for Spoken Discourse

Students need opportunities to talk in natural interactional contexts and for a variety of purposes: to establish and maintain social relationships; to express reactions; to give and seek information; to solve problems, discuss ideas, or teach and learn a skill; to entertain or play with language; or to display achievement. In addition, students need to learn to interact with a variety of conversational partners: other students, the teacher, other adults at school, cross-age peers, guests, and so on.

English learners need environments that help them to meet the social, emotional, cognitive, and linguistic demands of their lives in and out of school. Students need an *emotional setting,* a climate of trust and respect, in which they need not fear ridicule from their peers or correction from the teacher. Teachers can encourage students to respect the language of their peers, can model respectful listening when students speak, and can work with students to establish classroom rules of respect and support. Students need a *physical setting for talk* that features flexibility for working and interacting: round or rectangular tables, clusters of desks, workstations, and centers. In addition, classrooms need to contain *things to talk about*: fish tanks and nature displays; flags, maps, and artifacts; and a variety of print material. Finally, students need *frequent opportunities to talk;* flexible grouping allows work with a variety of classmates, cross-age tutors, aides, parent volunteers, and volunteer "grandparents" (Dudley-Marling & Searle, 1991).

Speaking can be integrated with other literacy and oracy activities. Students can retell the stories they hear in storytelling or sharing time and finish them in new ways. They can listen to the sharing time of others and use these as starting points for their own "adventures." As they become aware of the patterns within stories and the needs of the audience, they can embellish their storytelling. Inviting storytellers and community elders to tell stories in class provides rich stimuli; and when the visitors are gone, the students can finish these stories to continue the entertainment.

Oral presentations—those in which participants address an audience—provide rich opportunities for English learners to use reading and writing skills to gather information from libraries or online, or to use speaking and listening skills to interview sources. During presentations, peers can use a presentation rubric to offer feedback. Iberri-Shea (2009, p. 36) includes a scoring rubric in which aspects of language (vocabulary, usage, intonation, diction, and pace) and content (organization, introduction, body, and conclusion) are each worth 1–5 points.

If structured public speaking is important in the content of the class, students are given a tight outline and timetable for each presentation. The teacher might invite students to meet outside class to rehearse before the presentation. Other students can help by participating in a peer-scoring rubric in which content is emphasized over understandability. It is wise not to surprise students with requests for extemporaneous speaking.

Resources for Spoken Discourse

Opportunities for oral discourse range from those that are carefully constructed to those that are completely student generated. Several kinds of speaking activities can be included in daily lessons, including problem solving in small groups, practicing persuasive or entertaining speeches, role plays, interviews, chain stories, talks, problems, and discussions (see Zelman, 1996). *Discussion Starters* (Folse, 1996) offers speaking activities that build oral fluency using exercises specifically designed for group participation. The discussion prompts are based on role plays, "finish-the-story" situations, problems that can be solved only if members of a group work together, and real court cases for groups to play "judge."

Preparing for a Public Speech: Resources

Finding resources to help students prepare for a public speech is easier than one might think. One secret is to find people to interview who can add relevant information derived from their own experiences. Another tip is to use the Internet to locate resources. Jabr (2010) lists these Internet search engines to use as resource locators.

Alta Vista: www.altavista.com

Excite: www.excite.com

MSN: www.msn.com

Google: www.google.com

Yahoo: www.yahoo.com

Lycos: www.lycos.com

Virtual Library: vlib.org/overview.html

ERIC (Educational Resource Information Center): http://www.eric.ed.gov/

Sociofil: http://www.library.pitt.edu/articles/database_info/sociofile.html

Table 6.3 organizes representative oral activities into three categories, ranging from tightly structured on the left to freely constructed on the right.

Improving Pronunciation

English learners need a comprehensible control of the English sound system. Pronunciation involves the correct *articulation* of the individual sounds of English as well as the proper *stress* and *pitch* within syllables, words, and phrases. Longer stretches of speech require correct *intonation* patterns. However, the goal of teaching English pronunciation is not necessarily to make second-language speakers sound like native speakers of English. Some English learners do not wish to have a native-like pronunciation but prefer instead to retain an accent that indicates their first-language roots and allows them to be identified with their

TABLE 6.3 *Formats for Oral Practice in the ELD Classroom*

Guided Practice	Communicative Practice	Free Conversation
Formulaic exchanges:	Simulations	Discussion groups
Greetings	Guessing games	Debates
Congratulations	Group puzzles	Panel discussions
Apologies	Rank-order problems	Group picture story
Leave taking	Values continuum	Socializing
Dialogues	Categories of preference:	Storytelling/retelling
Mini-conversations	Opinion polls	Discussions of:
Role plays	Survey taking	Films
Skits	Interviews	Shared experiences
Oral descriptions	Brainstorming	Literature
Strip stories	News reports	
Oral games	Research reports	
	Storytelling	

Source: Díaz-Rico & Weed 2010.

ethnic community. Still others may wish to integrate actively into the mainstream culture and thus are motivated to try to attain a native accent in English. Teachers need to recognize these individual goals and enable learners to achieve pronunciation that does not detract from their ability to communicate.

Students' attempts to reproduce correct word stress, sentence rhythm, and intonation may improve by exposure to native-speaker models. The teacher's role in this case is to create a nonthreatening environment that stimulates and interests students enough for them to participate actively in producing speech. Clarification checks may be interjected politely when communication is impaired. Correction or completion by the teacher may be given after the teacher has allowed ample "wait time."

Communicative games are useful for practicing various aspects of intonation, syllabification, stress, and so on. Syl/la/bles and Linking is an activity proposed by Benson (1999): Students in pairs practice separating words into syllables by clapping along with the instructor as words are said in syllables. Then students mark the syllables in a written paragraph as the instructor reads. Decide which syllables students will learn to link (example: hear_us, told_us). Students in pairs play a game; the instructor reads a list of word phrases, some of which have linked words and some of which do not. Students link arms if the words are linked. Students are out of the game if they link arms incorrectly.

Mahoney (1999b) proposed a game for practicing stress and sentence intonation: Stress Clapping. A student comes to the front of the room, pulls a

---

Box 6.3   The INTeRn3T i5 THr3@+EN1n9 t0 Ch@n93 thE W4Y wE $p34k

Is the Internet threatening to change the way we speak? Rhoads (2007) reported that words used online are finding their way into popular speech. Some people say "my BFF" (best friend forever) instead of "best friend," and "OMG" (Oh my God) as an exclamation. At the same time, aural elements are evident in the way that the textuality of writing is used to perform the textual qualities of speech. Many young people prefer texting to speaking in person. Is the thumb replacing the tongue? Should we rename TESOL to TETOL: "Teaching English to Thumbers of Other Languages"?

---

sentence written on a folded overhead transparency strip out of a box, and displays the sentence on the overhead projector (sentences are taken from song lyrics, poems, or limericks). The student must read the sentence aloud and clap each time there is a stressed word. The student's team receives a point for each stressed word correctly identified.

Using a computer program for practice is a self-tutoring way in which students can improve their pronunciation. Such programs are fun and easy to use.

Before Speaking

Prespeaking activities warm the students to the topic and activate or provide some prior knowledge. In Huizenga and Thomas-Ruzic's (1992) *All Talk*, Unit 13 ("Pick Your Perfect Vacation"), students warm up to the task of interviewing a partner by circling new words in vacation ads. These activities help students to practice vocabulary and survey the content terrain before speaking.

Students can prepare for an impromptu speech on the subject of a news story by watching the evening news on television, listening to a news radio station, reading the editorial page of a local newspaper, reading a newsmagazine such as *Time* or *Newsweek*, and/or talking to people outside the class about selected issues. Students who must prepare for a formal public presentation need a more structured approach, with an advance outline that includes an attention-getting opener, a preview of what will be said, enough substance to complete the main body of the speech, a summary of the main points, and a memorable conclusion. Rehearsal in advance of the delivery—whether out loud to oneself, via an audio- or videotape, or before a critical audience—helps the presenter pace the delivery, create a natural tone, and practice difficult pronunciation (M. S. Wong, 1998).

While Speaking

Teachers working in mixed-ability classrooms can plan group activities that help students in different ways. Students can work in homogeneous groups when the goal of the activity is accuracy and in heterogeneous groups when the goal is fluency.

For example, to develop accuracy, first-grade students can listen to a reading of the story "The Three Little Pigs." A group of beginning students can retell the story using pictures and then talk about the pictures. Intermediate students can retell the story to the teacher or a cross-age tutor who can write their story for them; students can then reread, illustrate, and rearrange the story from sentence strips. A group of more proficient students can create a new group story.

Informal class discussions are a low-key way to practice speaking. While speaking, students make eye contact with listeners, and the volume is appropriate to the distance between the speakers. A speaker usually does not use notes when chatting with a classmate, but sometimes such notes are available from a previous brainstorming session. Turns are usually shared in small groups, and one person does not monopolize discussion.

Correction while a person is speaking is seldom appropriate. A teacher who does correct may seem overly dominant and cause the speaker to become tense and unable to be fluent or creative. Reformulation is the best alternative; if the

TABLE 6.4   *How Learners at the Intermediate Level Fail to Advance and Recommended Solutions*

Difficulties	Proposed Solutions
A gap between *receptive* (listening and reading) and *productive* (writing and speaking) competence	Encourage learners to notice their errors, and increase feedback for the learners' output.
Fluency (including use of lower-level grammar and limited vocabulary) may be ahead of *complexity* (grammar that is closer to native-speaker usage)	■ Employ an intensive language focus before, during, and after lesson activities, giving time to pre-teach and then review necessary forms ■ Reduce task difficulty to increase language complexity
Language production *does not resemble natural speech*	■ Expect learners to master a wide variety of formulaic, conversational utterances that native speakers use ("as I was saying . . . .")
Errors are persistent and little change is evident	■ Focus lessons on grammar ■ Ask learners to record and monitor their own output ■ Use activities that "stretch" syntactic knowledge toward more complex structures ■ Reduce complexity of error correction to focus on a few aspects at a time

Source: Based on Richards (2008).

teacher hears an incorrect utterance, a similar sentence can be repeated to the student naturally and in the context of the conversation without embarrassing the student (Bartram & Walton, 1994). Finders and Hynds (2007) pointed out that a strong focus on correctness may stifle students' enthusiasm and creativity—the emphasis should be on "progress, not perfection" (p. 97). Richards (2008) offers suggestions for improving fluency at the intermediate stage of second-language acquisition (see Table 6.4).

Oral presentations can be assessed using *holistic scoring* (see Figure 6.1) or *analytic scoring* (see Figure 6.2).

FIGURE 6.1 *A Holistic Scoring Criteria for Seventh- or Eighth-Grade Oral Presentations*

A good presentation:
1. Falls within the assigned time limit (or is reasonably close)
2. Has a clearly identifiable speech purpose and a thesis statement
3. Has an introduction, body, and conclusion
4. Shows a basic understanding of effective verbal and nonverbal delivery
5. Shows respect for the audience

An excellent presentation, in addition to meeting the above criteria:
1. Deals with an interesting and challenging topic (if student was allowed to choose topic)
2. Includes both a strong introduction and a conclusion that achieve all their major functions
3. Is well organized
4. Develops points with appropriate supporting materials (relevant, credible)
5. Is skillfully delivered (verbal and nonverbal delivery)

A superior presentation meets all of the above criteria, and:
1. Uses clear, appropriate, and vivid oral language
2. Is delivered fluently and in a polished manner
3. Is interesting and well adapted to the audience
4. Supports points with provocative and compelling supporting material
5. Constitutes a general contribution to the knowledge and/or beliefs of the audience

A fair presentation meets some, but not all, of the grading criteria for a good presentation.

A poor presentation meets almost none of the requirements for a good presentation.

Source: Chaney & Burk (1998, p. 119).

FIGURE 6.2 *An Analytic Scoring Evaluation for an Oral Presentation*

Speaker's Name: _____ Topic: _____

CONTENT	Superior	Excellent	Good	Fair	Poor
Introduction					
Caught attention, stated topic and purpose of speech, previewed main points	5	4	3	2	1
Body					
Main points were clear, distinct, and supported the purpose of the speech	5	4	3	2	1
Organization was clear and consistent throughout	5	4	3	2	1
Logic and analysis (if a persuasive speech) were strong	5	4	3	2	1
Supporting materials were credible, useful, appropriately cited, and adequate for each main point	5	4	3	2	1
Language choice was interesting, appropriate for the occasion and audience, with appropriate grammar	5	4	3	2	1
Conclusion					
Concluded with psychological impact, summarized main points, brought closure to the speech	5	4	3	2	1
DELIVERY					
Audience Adaptation					
Adapted to the physical characteristics of the speaking situation	5	4	3	2	1
Adapted to the background and perspective of the audience	5	4	3	2	1
Chose words and language that were meaningful to, and demonstrated respect for, the audience	5	4	3	2	1
Vocal Delivery					
Appropriate volume, rate, pitch, and variety of expression	5	4	3	2	1
Avoided too many nonfluencies (e.g., "uh," "um," "like," "okay," "y'know")	5	4	3	2	1
Used pauses and silences effectively (if a speech that lends itself to drama)	5	4	3	2	1

(continued)

Physical Delivery

Good posture; absence of nervous shifting of body weight, twisting at the waist, leaning on podium, etc.	5	4	3	2	1
Gestures and facial expressions were well-timed, natural, expressive	5	4	3	2	1
Eye contact was direct, sustained, inclusive	5	4	3	2	1

Additional comments:

Total Score: _____ (out of a possible 80 points)

Source: Chaney & Burk (1998, p. 122).

After Speaking

Sometimes the class as a whole supplies feedback to the speaker in the form of structured peer review. Many kinds of activities can follow up a speaking task. As in the listening task, students can write, discuss, read, draw, or act out their interpretation of the content, attending to the linguistic or cultural aspects of what they have heard. For the most part, oral discussion is a vital part of any other task and should be developed as a top priority. When students have been outside the classroom on a service-learning project, debriefing is needed in order for students to reflect on and share with one another what they have learned.

Speaking Games and Tasks

Shameem and Tickoo (1999) have compiled a variety of listening and speaking games that can be used in a variety of contexts. Table 6.5 lists these and their contributors.

One-on-one read-alouds offer individualized speaking opportunities.

©David R. Frazier Photolibrary, Inc./Alamy

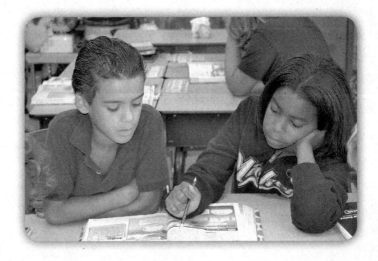

TABLE 6.5 *Activities for Listening and Speaking*

Name of Activity	Directions for the Teacher
Shadow tableaux	Pass around a bag and have each student put in a small personal object. Spread the objects out on an overhead projector so that only their shadows can be seen. Have students work in pairs to name all the objects. (1)
Headline news	Cut out interesting headlines and their corresponding photographs from newspapers. Cut the headlines in half (do not split word phrases). Paste the beginnings and endings of the headlines onto index cards. Students in group A receive photographs, group B receives headline beginnings, and group C receives headline endings. Students move around the room, asking one another (not showing) the content of their card. The first group to identify its members wins the game. (2)
Animal psychology	Pair off students and have them jot on index cards three main characteristics or activities of their favorite animal. Then have partners swap index cards and read each other's phrases, guessing the animal by writing it on the front of the card. After this activity, use the phrases and cards on the overhead projector to generate and practice vocabulary. (3)
Give me a word that . . .	Prepare index cards (one for each student) with fifteen to twenty vocabulary questions starting with the phrase, "Give me a word that . . ." For example, A word that dances . . . (ballerina, Madonna) A word that runs . . . (runner, river) A blue word (sky) A cold word (ice, winter) Student A reads the word; first student in group B and C has thirty seconds to give an answer. Whoever is first wins that round. (4)
So did I	Students report something they did over the weekend ("I visited my grandmother"). Other learners respond "So did I" or "I didn't." The learner must come up with a new idea if someone answers "So did I." (After three reports, move on to the next student.) (5)
Spontaneous oral development of group stories	Seat students in groups of three to six and give them a number corresponding to the order of their sentence in the story. The first student gives the opening sentence of the story; the second gives the second. Before the third, the first two repeat their sentences in order. When the story is completed, one of the students transcribes it, and when all groups are ready, they tell their stories to the class, each repeating one sentence. (6)

Sources: (1) Mahoney, 1999a; (2) Hetherton, 1999; (3) Becker, 1999; (4) Mansour, 1999; (5) Sick, 1999; (6) Larking, 1999.

Oral Discourse and Critical Communicative Competence

Since the time of Socrates, educators have advocated a type of teaching that does more than transmit knowledge and skills. Contemporary educators have sought discussion formats that engage students in critical thinking and intellectually productive social interaction. The instructional conversation (IC) is a small-group, semistructured discourse format in which the instructor functions as "thinker-leader" while encouraging voluntary oral participation (see Chapter 11). CommuniConfidence is an oral language development program specifically tailored for university students that took place for several years at California State University, San Bernardino (Díaz-Rico & Young, 1998). CommuniConfidence sessions were designed to bring together native and nonnative speakers of English in a weekly one-hour chat session.

Discussions were based on a discussion prompt consisting of a one-paragraph vignette that described some small, complex situation involving a protagonist aged twenty-one to thirty (for a sample prompt, see Box 6.4). The prompts were intentionally written to encourage some opinionated interchanges based on participants' personal experiences. The prompts also called forth some deeper understandings of human motivation and values; however, in each situation there were no right or wrong answers. For each conversation (the ideal size for each small group is six to eight members), a thinker-leader guided the flow of the discourse.

Graduate students in the MA program's Teaching Speakers of Other Languages option in the College of Education acted as thinker-leaders for the discussions. These included both English learners who had originally learned English without attaining oral fluency and native speakers of English. The opportunity to assume the leader function in discussions permitted these students to practice thinking fast on their feet as well as to achieve oral and aural proficiency. The thinker-leaders were given two one-hour preliminary training sessions so that they understood how to begin, sustain, and close a discussion.

Box 6.4 **Sample Prompt for CommuniConfidence**

Prompt: "Marriage at Her Age?"

All of Brenda's aunts and uncles, as well as her parents, are upset because Frances, Brenda's grandmother, has a new boyfriend. Frances is eighty years old and has been visiting the Senior Citizens' Center to play mah-jongg twice a week. She met Harvey, who is seventy-eight years old, at the center. Harvey is a widower, and Frances is a widow. Brenda's grandfather died at the age of seventy-five just three years ago. Frances and Harvey have been talking about getting married so that they can live together. Brenda's family is afraid that if Frances remarries, she will alter her will to leave her money to Harvey when she dies. Harvey has three daughters who are always asking him for money. Besides, Brenda's family thinks Frances is too old to remarry.

CommuniConfidence was held in the informal environment of a staff lounge. This provided a relaxing environment that helped to create a sense of community among participants. At the beginning of each hour, participants were welcomed to the session as they signed in and donned name tags so that participants could address one another by first name in conversation if they so wished. This system also ensured that participants became acquainted with one another. Each participant was then given a copy of a prompt.

First-time participants were welcomed with an explanation of the discourse procedure and offered suggestions about turn taking (see Box 6.5). A few students were silent for the first few sessions and then gradually spoke more. Other students were fairly fluent as soon as they acquired the specific turn-taking skills. No feedback was given to participants after each discussion, except for general praise offered by the thinker-leader. New participants who remained silent throughout the conversation were approached individually after each discussion to see if they needed help understanding how to obtain a turn.

Naturally, some prompts were better than others in triggering rich thematic material from participants. One successful prompt was the story of a young man whose mother always bragged about and overstated his academic achievements at family gatherings, ignoring his achievements in art, his desired vocation. Several students from Asian family backgrounds found much in common with this protagonist, and the conversation was long and lively.

Box 6.5   **Get Your Turn (Handout for Participants)**

Get Your Turn

Even when you have something to say, it is sometimes hard to get a turn in the conversation.

Two ways to get a turn

Nonverbal

- Make eye contact with the current speaker.
- Lean forward as if you will be next.
- Interrupt in a small way and then stop.
- Be ready to start your turn at the slightest pause.

Verbal

When your idea is *connected* to the current speaker:

- I'd like to add to that . . .
- Oh, yes, and besides . . .
- Yes, and . . .
- Well, I see it like this . . .

When your idea has *no connection* to the current one:

- Here's a different idea . . .
- I see things a little differently . . .
- Going back to what ___ said, . . .
- Changing the topic somewhat, I'd like to mention . . .

The IC Model.   The IC model developed by Goldenberg and Gallimore (1991) has both instructional and conversational elements. The most important instructional element is the establishment of a thematic focus. The text that participants all read before beginning the conversation provides the basis for the theme. Because the goal of the IC is to develop a more complex understanding of the prompt, a good theme is one that is flexible enough to grow out of the ideas of the participants without being superimposed on the group by the leader. This flexibility encourages the participants to share responsibility for the discussion. At the same time, however, the leader's responsibility is to see that the theme has a genuine connection to the prompt.

The conversation elements include those aspects that defuse anxiety and promote verbal interaction. Another conversational element is the establishment of a challenging, nonthreatening atmosphere for the participants. Disagreement and differences of opinion are protected, although part of the challenging atmosphere is for students to find a way to evaluate one another's viewpoints.

Using IC in the Classroom.   Many instructors are eager to find ways to promote oral participation in the classroom as an alternative to lectures. However, educators may perceive that IC is hard to use in a class with fixed seating and a tradition of lectures. Despite these drawbacks, IC as a discussion format has broad utility in education. In classes of between twenty and thirty-five students, students can break up into small groups using peers as thinker-leaders. Other instructors may offer after-hours sessions with interested students on a voluntary basis on selected course-related topics of interest to students. Students who are assigned group projects as a course requirement may be able to use class time for planning while the instructor pulls aside a discussion group on a rotating basis.

The conversational elements of IC are perhaps the most difficult to incorporate in a traditional classroom because students are not often given the opportunity to converse. However, the instructor may function as a thinker-leader by asking open-ended questions, responding positively to student ideas, and weaving ideas that are volunteered by class members into the instructional content.

Summary: The Conversant Student

The instructional conversation helps students learn to speak English more fluently, to have faith that their opinions will be recognized and honored, and to believe that their ideas are important and valued. Overall, the oracy processes discussed in this chapter—retaining information, listening, and speaking in a second language—share the characteristic that if they are performed naturally in the context of a rich, interesting experience, the learner acquires the skill almost unnoticed. If the pressure is on, however—a test, a public performance—the skill must be learned with focus and determination, with full faculties devoted to the process involved. Both kinds of learning have their place.

Ideally, most English learners will continue to advance oracy skills in their primary language as they learn English. Classroom teachers must therefore model respect for bilingual oracy. The goal is to balance fluency and accuracy in English with respect for the communicative needs of the learners, so they can listen and speak with power, expressing their point of view and listening respectfully to others, contributing positively to their bilingual worlds.

Exploratory Break

- Do you think it is more important for English learners to speak with correct grammar or correct fluency? Illustrate your answer with anecdotes from your teaching or personal experience.
- Discuss the functional and interactional purposes for which an English learner needs listening skills in English in the classroom. How can a teacher assess an English learner's skills for these functions?

Chapter 7

Literacy Instruction for English-Language Development

Learning to read is a process of connecting the sight of written words with the sounds and meanings of words stored in the mind. Learning to read in one's own language requires not only systematic instruction in sound–symbol connection but also acquisition of the love of reading, an intangible gift that is passed from one avid reader to another. The great challenge is when a child—or an adult—must acquire the sounds and meanings of a second language along with initial reading instruction. This is literacy instruction in English-language development. Building on a student's primary-language skills is essential. And in the special case of an older child or adult who is nonliterate in the primary language, dual-language reading instruction is key.

Literacy instruction within a sociocultural framework features a highly interactive classroom, in which students talk as they read, collaborate as they write, listen to one another's ideas, and give presentations about projects. Language skills are integrated and the primary language is developed along-side English. This chapter features English-language development based on a sociocultural, dual-language model. Ideally, this is the English side of literacy instruction in a two-way immersion model.

> *Megastrategy* **SET 7**
> Teach literacy skills systematically, building on primary-language skills

Literacy and Power

Before launching into literacy instruction, one must ask, "Whose purposes does literacy serve?" One cannot "simply" teach English learners to read, write, speak, listen, or think. Learners must select and acquire those aspects of the target language and culture that offer the most reward for their investment of time and energy and provide them with the basis for transforming their lives, rather than simply finding a place in the existing social order (Giroux & McLaren, 1986).

Unfortunately, too often English learners' best interests are sacrificed in the call for mastery of a common national language, accompanied by the need for statistics to show that this task is being successfully accomplished. Gramsci (1971) identified this as a movement toward *hegemony* (defined as the attempt by the dominant class to persuade the subordinated classes to act in the interests of the dominant class). When English learners are led to believe that only literacy in English is socially useful and acceptable—and are then given literacy education that emphasizes narrow decoding skills at the expense of their reading and writing about the world as they see it—the literacy that they acquire, often imperfectly, serves the interests of others.

Macedo cautioned that educators of English learners must pay greater attention to sociocultural context for literacy to be transformational:

> I want to propose that the attempt to institute proper and more effective methods of educating non-English-speaking students cannot be reduced to issues of language but rests on a full understanding of the ideological elements that generate and sustain linguistic, racial, and sex discrimination. (1994, p. 126)

Critical Literacy

Cummins (1996) is also a vocal advocate of "critical literacy" as an essential component of educational reform to promote achievement for Latino/Latina students. According to Cummins, students who achieve only "functional literacy" often fail to develop a sense of empowerment through acquisition of cultural and critical literacy, and cannot successfully challenge the "status quo" in which their culture and language is relegated to a second-class status.

Literacy and Identity.　Schools, communities, and personal literacies co-contribute to the development of identities. As Unrau (2008) put it,

> . . . students use multiple literacies, including those of school, community, and self, to construct visions of who they are, the worlds they inhabit, what they will be like in the future, and how they could be that person. Stories students tell themselves and others about who they are, their realities, their futures, and the paths to be taken to those futures are often composed in our school's classrooms, corridors, and playing fields. (p. 13)

During the entire process of teaching reading, educators who also function as sensitive ethnographers and "child watchers" take note of what reading "lights a fire" in the learners and take care to balance students' receptive and productive skills within a learning environment that respects culture, human interests, and imagination.

Reading Processes

Reading has become an essential skill. Adults who cannot read are hampered when shopping for groceries, filling out applications for work, or obtaining a driver's license. Children who do not learn to read in elementary school enter secondary education as severe underachievers and are at risk for dropping out. Research has shown that English learners often learn to read by becoming efficient "word callers" (Goldenberg, 1992) but may fail to attain comprehension or higher-order thinking skills. How can teachers encourage English learners to acquire skills that will result in academic achievement and an enjoyment of reading?

Reading has become an arena of conflict between advocates of literature-based, whole-language approaches and supporters of bottom-up phonics (Wolfe & Poynor [2001] for a discussion of the politics of reading instruction). Politics aside, this chapter examines various approaches to reading, along with the integration of reading with writing. More complete instruction in reading pedagogy can be found in Peregoy's *Reading, Writing, and Learning in ESL* (2008).

Purposes for Reading

> *Megastrategy* **7.1**
> Teach reading in a way that builds interest, information acquisition, and lifelong literacy

During the advent of the era of television, critics asked, "Is reading dead?" Again, during the information age of the Internet, people are asking the same question, as they see young people inundated with images and sounds that flout classic print conventions. At the same time, however, more individuals are expected to be literate than ever before, as employment in modern technology requires advanced reading and writing skills.

However, in the midst of calls for skills-based literacy, McLaren (1995) has called for a more comprehensive approach to literacy, one that teaches a critical stance, especially toward the media. He called for media studies to be a central focus of school curricula lest learners divest themselves of their specific culture in the attempt to gain access to the social and economic resources they see displayed before them in mass media marketing, or the "mall culture" (S. L. Shepard, 2001, p. 603). This puts into perspective the impulse to impose on learners a functional literacy that serves the purpose of the school but perhaps not the purpose of the individual (see Barton, Hamilton, & Ivanič, 2000).

The search for reading strategies that fit the generic learner quickly runs afoul not only of current calls for situated literacy but also of the impossibility of finding a "best" method (see Bartolomé, 1994). Certainly, contextual and instructional variation complicate matters. Older learners need different reading instruction than do children, learners' goals deviate from official policy mandates, and variety in the target language makes even the choice of reading materials problematic. In spite of these shortcomings, it is clear that *some* instruction in reading is better than *no* instruction in reading. This foundation in reading instruction can be applied situationally and experimentally until some wisdom is reached about best practices for the particular context and learners.

Standards-Based Reading Instruction

Several reading basals on the market reflect the current insistence on standards-based instruction. For example, *Launch into Reading, Level I* (Heinle & Heinle), an ESL reading series, specifically refers to the particular California English Language Development standard to which each lesson is connected. Lesson 13, "'Flowers' (A Poem by E. Greenfield)," addresses Reading Standard 6.3.4, "Define how tone or meaning is conveyed in poetry." Follow-up exercises ask students to use a continuum scale to rank five "ways you can learn about people's feelings and ideas" (short story, poem, magazine or newspaper article, movie or television program, and conversation), which addresses Reading Standard 2.2.7, "Interpret information from diagrams and charts" (Heinle & Heinle, 2002a).

Later in the lesson, students are asked to find the rhyming words in the poem "Flowers" (Reading 1.1.6, "Create and state a series of rhyming words") and then work with a partner to interpret a poem (Writing 6.2.4, "Write responses to literature: Organize the interpretation around several clear ideas, premises or images"). All teaching materials, the teacher's resource book, the student workbook, and the student reading book contain explicit references to standards on each page. The assessment guide (Heinle & Heinle, 2002b) contains a Language Proficiency Assessment chart, with a summary of the standards across three levels of each of the six domains (Oral Reading, Reading Comprehension, Vocabulary, Spelling, Conventions, and Writing).

Emergent Literacy

When children—or adolescents or adults, for that matter—are first learning to read, they are in the stage of *emergent literacy*, the reading and writing behaviors that precede and develop into conventional literacy. Educators now realize that most "nonreaders" actually have had much exposure to print in the culture at large and may have engaged in various informal kinds of reading. Therefore, it is the teacher's job to build on these nascent skills so that these students can "grow into reading."

Emergent literacy involves a combination of components. Emergent readers must learn to do the following tasks:

- Draw on their prior knowledge of the world to connect the printed word with its semiotic meaning. For example, most preschool children understand that a red octagonal sign at a street corner means "stop."
- Enhance their phonemic awareness by coming to understand that sounds correspond to symbols.
- Recognize a set of sight words that are frequently used in English but may not be phonetically predictable (*the* is not "ta-ha-ay").
- Acquire reading behaviors, such as handling books, borrowing and returning books to the class library, and reading for enjoyment.
- Participate in a culture of reading, sharing their pleasure in reading with others and working in the company of others to acquire meaning from books.

Most people learn new skills in an integrated way, starting from the need to learn for some purpose. May and Rizzardi (2002) use the example of a child learning to ride a bicycle. She does not spend thirty days practicing how to pedal, jumping on and off the seat twenty times, and then trying to ride; at a certain point, she just gets on the bike and goes, wobbling and falling at times, but riding. The joy of the first ride is exhilarating. In a similar way, we do not teach children to speak by having them repeat syllables until they can put together a whole word. Children speak in holophrastic utterances because they mean to communicate. Reading is a cognitive activity that must be learned in a brain-compatible way—as an organized, meaningful event.

Why? Because humans like stories.

> [W]e are story-making animals[;] . . . something deep within us impels us to cherish the product of the writer . . . . Given a modicum of reading skill, some free time, and accessibility to literary materials, people read . . . not every person, but most. People read in cramped bunks under the Arctic ice. They read 40,000 feet above the earth. They read as they have their hair cut and dried, and while they wait for the dentist. People read in bed, in the bath tub, and occasionally, sitting upright in a chair. We are literature-creating and literature consuming animals. (Carlsen, 1974, p. 24)

Most learners read and write because they see others doing it—reading directions, newspapers, or road signs for information, or notes they have written to themselves to jog their memory, or novels just to pass the time. Many English learners do not see their families reading or writing. Therefore, it takes a leap of imagination for them to see themselves as readers. It is important, then, for the classroom as a community to be a place in which reading is an everyday, enjoyable feature. This environment socializes students into a culture of literacy.

Until recently, ELD teaching for beginning English learners focussed on oral English as a necessary prerequisite to introducing written forms. However, instructional approaches that integrate language, reading, and writing skills have gained increasing favor as a means of promoting emergent biliteracy.

> By creating shared contexts, mediating students' learning through ongoing literacy activities, providing vocabulary, modeling language and literacy behaviors such as reading and writing, encouraging peer interactions, relating to students' cultural background and according high status to LEP students' first language, teachers can successfully develop language and literacy skills in multilingual classrooms. (Abramson, Seda, & Johnson, 1990, p. 72)

Using an integrated skills model (see Chapter 9), teachers can draw on students' everyday activities to help them use the tools of literacy for their own purposes. Teachers who converse with students can find natural ways to introduce written words into their stories. Finding books that correspond to children's natural interactions while playing also helps students to feel that literacy supports their interests.

One teacher might overhear two children playing with a caterpillar and as a result read Eric Carle's *The Hungry Caterpillar* to the class. A context of shared enjoyment is the key to making literacy an everyday part of life.

Language Experience Approach

The language experience approach (LEA) encourages students to describe events in their own words, which the teacher writes down and reads back so that students can eventually read the text for themselves. This process develops language by connecting students to their own experiences and activities. Because students provide their own phrases and sentences, they find the text relevant and interesting, and generally have little trouble reading it. The texts they create can be used for specific lessons on vocabulary, grammar, writing conventions, structure, and more.

The use of stories is probably the most important means by which teachers can develop oral and written language in young children. Stories come naturally to children, and in the telling and retelling they gain vocabulary enrichment, sensitivity to audience, and mastery over oral language. The same holds true for written stories as they learn to read.

> The sounds of children bathed in language—in and out of school—are not those of structured language lessons; no one is repeating sentences like "This my pencil." Instead, children create their own meanings for the drawings they design, the stories they invent, and the ideas that grow out of the many experiences they have . . . . [C]hild-oriented classrooms lack drill-like, repetitive language, but they do have a rhythm and stability that enable children to repeat—or more accurately, replay—what they are learning in the context of activities that make human sense. A word may be repeated 20 times or more, not in the senseless context of an isolated sentence, but in a range of contexts: a poem, a child-created song of drama, a caption for a drawing, a chant, a story that children beg to hear again, a game that a child plays and replays with friends, or a conversation with children or the teacher. (Genishi, 1988, p. 22)

Direct Teaching of Reading

Despite the success of approaches based on the social construction of knowledge, a generation of students is being taught how to read through a series of controlled, behaviorally based lessons. Such programs as Reading Mastery, Open Court, and Direct Instruction employ teacher-centered methods in step-by-step curricula that follow highly structured, interactive scripts (Groves, 2001). Reading Mastery requires students to be grouped in precisely measured skill levels, and Open Court expects teachers to follow a script verbatim day by day to reinforce skills (Vega, 2000). Only time will tell if the students taught in this manner learn to read for both academics and for enjoyment. Groves (2001) made the point that gifted students are not taught in such a prescriptive manner. It may be that being taught to read in such a prescriptive manner is yet another marker of social class in the United States.

Fostering Emergent Literacy In Children

- Provide an accessible, appealing literacy environment with attractive reading and writing materials.

- Include in classroom reading materials extra copies of books the teacher has read aloud, books by the same author, commercial books, student-written books, comic or cartoon books (with words), magazines, encyclopedias, and age-appropriate bilingual dictionaries.

- Encourage children to role-play or playact reading and writing activities.

- Incorporate shared book experiences using Big Books or enlarged text.

- Follow up shared reading with independent reading, small-group review of the Big Book, or work with language skills such as phonics.

- Bolster reading with chanting or singing based on reading the lyrics together.

Source: Gunning, 2009.

Teaching Students Who Are Not Literate in L1

Emergent literacy for adolescents and adults is a challenge. Many people who have never learned to read have internalized a sense of shame, stemming from a background that precluded schooling or from a deep sense of failure at having attended school with a poor outcome. Many need to experience immediate success. Collecting words from environmental print and helping students to decode it sometimes reassures the nonreaders that they can read.

A Balanced Literacy Approach

Teachers have been advised to teach using a "balanced literacy" approach, in which they employ a variety of activities to help students become better readers and writers. Across a week of instructional planning, teachers try to include the components of a balanced literacy program. Mermelstein (2006) lists and describes these components as follows:

- Shared reading (the teacher reads an enlarged text aloud as students read along; students use various strategies when they encounter difficulty)

- Read-alouds (the teacher reads a text while students listen; the teacher models thinking aloud about how to interpret the information)

- Reading workshop (students work independently, with partners, or in a small group; the teacher gives mini-lessons to teach reading strategies)

- Shared writing (the teacher composes texts with students, modeling the thought process by thinking aloud)
- Interactive writing (students and teacher write a text together; the teacher helps students build up structure and meaning)
- Writing workshop (students work independently, with partners, or in a small group; the teacher gives mini-lessons to teach writing strategies)
- Word study (which might include phonemic awareness, phonics, and/or spelling)

The Basics of Learning to Read

A variety of instructional approaches is used to teach English learners to read: teacher modeling, shared reading, reciprocal reading, guided reading, sustained silent reading, and other activities that lead the learner gradually to gain independence, confidence, and comprehension. English learners can begin to respond by pointing to words; underlining; highlighting; drawing pictures to illustrate ideas; matching words with pictures; sequencing pictures, sentences, or paragraphs; classifying words and word families; and responding to oral comprehension questions.

Within the social context of shared enjoyment between a group of readers, there are four important facets of learning to read: skill with print, prior knowledge, comprehension, and seeking meaning. When these four elements are present, it is more likely that reading will take place.

Skill with print involves understanding that the printed text contains words carrying meaning and that printed words correspond to spoken language. Reading begins when the emergent reader matches specific letters to spoken sounds and begins to look for recognizable words or parts of words in text. Skill with print comprises ten concepts:

- Language is divided into words.
- Words can be written down.
- Space separates written words.
- Letters make words and words make sentences.
- Sentences begin with capital letters.
- Sentences end with punctuation.
- A book is read from front to back.
- Reading goes left to right and top to bottom.
- Words, not pictures, are read.
- A book has a title, an author, and sometimes an illustrator. (Gunning, 2009)

In a print-rich environment, children see print wherever they turn (see Box 7.1).

Prior Knowledge That Is Useful for Reading. Word knowledge (vocabulary) is the chief hurdle faced by English learners, because reading a word successfully depends on knowing the word in the first place. Beyond vocabulary are the experience and understanding of situational context that help make sense of the world.

Box 7.1 Ideas for a Print-Rich Environment

A rich literacy environment presents ample opportunities for reading:

- Bulletin boards with words and pictures
- Aquariums and terrariums labeled with the names of their inhabitants
- Calendar with children's birthdays and other important events
- Displays of students' stories and booklets
- Student-run post office
- Library corner with book displays
- Labels on objects in several languages
- Magnetic letters, printing sets, typewriter, computers available
- Picture dictionaries, both commercial and student-made
- Listening centers with audiotaped books for read-along
- Order blanks, notepads, shopping lists at play centers

- Displays around the classroom can include different scripts and languages, as well as other alphabets and number systems. This can help to position bilingual pupils in the role of "expert" as they share their knowledge with the class.
- Labels around the room in the bilingual child's primary language can help students feel that the classroom is hospitable to diversity.
- A display of appropriate books in languages other than English might be featured, accompanied with language tapes and pictures of a country in which that language is spoken.

Source: Morgan (1992).

Source: Gunning (2009).

Once students start to read, vocabulary acquisition accelerates because general comprehension of a text allows readers to predict and infer meaning of unknown words they encounter. The teacher's job is to help students develop background knowledge through the use of other books, oral discussion, exposure to media, or use of pictures or other visual prompts combined with text in order to build schemata—that is, construct a framework of concepts that shows the relationships of old and new learning and how they are connected.

Reading Comprehension. Comprehension is the key to meaning. Readers generally form some initial hypotheses about the content or main idea of a book or a reading passage based on their expectations, title, first sentence, previous knowledge of genre, or other clues. Reading further, the reader modifies the initial prediction. Getting the gist of a reading passage is the most important concept a reader can develop, because getting the main idea makes further reading more purposeful, facilitates recall, and helps to make sense of the supporting details.

Sight Words and Phonics. Using sight words, the learner relies on visual memory to match sound with writing. Using phonics, the learner explicitly constructs the sound–symbol connection (Heilman, 2005). Each of these techniques has its place in learning basic words. Lists of sight words can be obtained from reading texts. These include

Box 7.2   Teaching Reading via the Analytic Method of Phonics

Tactics for teaching via the analytic method of phonics:

1. Planning: Make a list of easy words that include the target phonic element, for example the digraph *sh*: *cash*, *crash*, *mash*, *dish*, *fish*, and so forth. Write simple, meaningful sentences for each one, or if possible a little story that contains the words. Find pages in a common reading book that have these or other *sh-* words, including *-sh* as a final sound.
2. Teaching: Read the sentences aloud to the students in a smooth and informal fashion.

Have the students echo-read the sentences, repeating after the teacher, then repeating each underlined target word after the teacher, looking to see what sound the words have in common.

3. Guided practice: Students each make the target sound and look again at the letters that make the sound. Have students say other words with the same sound. Students choral-read the sentences and then take turns reading them aloud.

Source: May & Rizzardi (2002, p. 177).

frequently used words with unpredictable spelling, such as *the, might, could,* and so forth. Phonics can be taught using the synthetic method (bottom-up), with students first learning phonemes in isolation, then learning to blend them, and finally seeing them in the context of words. Or students can learn using the analytic method, beginning with contrasting words that contain the target phonemes and then hearing classmates generate similar words. The analytic method is illustrated in Box 7.2.

Phonemic Awareness.   Phonemic awareness has been found to be an important precursor to learning to read. Phonemic awareness, "the insight that every spoken word is made up of a sequence of phonemes" (California Department of Education, 1999b, p. 278), is considered by many to be a prerequisite for learning to read. Once children grasp the principles that words are made of phonemes represented by letters, they can benefit from phonics instruction (Tompkins & Tabloski, 2003). See Figure 7.1 for a sample diagnostic test.

Reading-Readiness Activities.   Reading-readiness activities help to develop visual discrimination, including such tasks as matching pictures and patterns, sequencing story cards in a meaningful order, and matching uppercase letters to lowercase letters. Teaching letters phonetically takes place in a sequence. First, alphabet cards introduce the name of each consonant letter and the sound it makes. Matching objects and pictures to letters helps learners to identify initial sounds. (Ending sounds can be treated in a similar way.) Then short vowels are introduced, usually in the order *a, i, o, u,* and *e*; next come the short vowels blended with consonants. Sight words (those that do not conform to phonetic rules—about 10 percent of English written words) are

FIGURE 7.1 *A Sample Individual Diagnostic Test*

Directions: Listen carefully. Which pair of words are the same?

mat	met	tall	tell
tap	tap	wing	wink
sand	sand	van	van
fail	fell	burn	but

Directions: Listen carefully. Give me another word that rhymes with

tan _____   hat _____

mail _____   pay _____

Directions: Listen carefully. Give me another word that begins like

bottle _____

dig _____

cat _____

fan _____

Source: Rubin & Opitz (2007).

memorized. Simple stories featuring short vowels help to create early success. Long vowels and vowel blends are taught next, followed by digraphs (consonants that together make a single sound, like "th").

Drawbacks of Structural Approaches.   However, reading based on phonetic awareness may not be the best approach for English learners (Flood, Lapp, Tinajero, & Hurley, 1997). Hamayan (1994) cited four reasons why structural (phonics-based and grammar-based) approaches fail to meet the needs of preliterate English learners: (1) They do not meet the learner's need to acquire an understanding of the functional aspects of literacy; (2) literacy is forced to emerge in an unnatural way and in an artificial form; (3) a focus on form without a functional context makes learning abstract, meaningless, and difficult; and (4) literacy becomes a boring chore.

Emerging Sound–Symbol Awareness.   Written English is based on the alphabetic principle, and children do need to understand that sounds correspond to letters. Teachers of English learners are encouraged to provide students with rich language experiences, including wordplay, which lead them to understand sound–symbol correspondences. During and after read-alouds, for example, teachers point out specific sound and letter patterns that occurred in the texts. Specific instruction in sound–symbol correspondence emerges best through students' own writing. Their invented or temporary spelling represents a phase on the way to conventional spelling that assists reading and writing development.

Strategies for Making Meaning.   When attempting a sentence with an unknown word, different readers use distinct strategies. One type of reader uses *semantic knowledge*. If the sentence reads, "Joey pushed open the door of the haunted . . .," that reader might guess that the next word is not *hose*, because the meaning would not make sense. Another type of reader might use *syntactic knowledge* to understand the sentence "Joey drives a small . . ." to reject the word *care* as the wrong choice for that part of the sentence. Still a third type of reader might use *orthographic shape* in decoding the sentence "Joey drove a load of trees to the paper mill," knowing that the words *pap* and *paperwork* look wrong. A single reader might use these three types of making meaning equally often or might develop a preference for one type of decoding.

Seeking meaning is natural to the mind. Some readers seek precision and are satisfied only when they can state the writer's intention with certainty. For others, a general feeling for the topic seems to satisfy. Nonetheless, the goal of the reading instructor is for students to come away from a reading passage with meaning. Because this meaning is constructed by the reader, there will always be some imperfect match between the meaning as taught and the meaning as attained by each reader. The richest of text evokes the most fundamentally meaningful, yet passionate and idiosyncratic, response. Anything less is reductionistic, to be doomed to accept the exact understandings of others rather than to glory in our own, however unique. This is the chief reason for the existence of literature.

The Three-Stage Reading Process

A common approach used in working with literature is captured by the phrase *into, through, and beyond*. Activities prior to reading prepare students to get "into" the reading. Other strategies help students read "through" the material. Finally, follow-up activities help students organize and retain their understanding "beyond" the act of reading. This three-part, sequential approach, although a popular organizing device, actually misrepresents the complexity of a classroom in which literacy is socially constructed. In reality, students are moving into, through, and beyond their own reading on an individual basis as they dip into some books, pick up and discard others, or use the table of contents and index wisely to be able to choose to read what they need. Other students surf the Internet, following links that fizzle out, downloading information to look at later, or stumbling onto topics much more exciting than their original area of interest. Therefore, the "into, through, and beyond" approach better represents reading for an entire topic rather than for a single book.

Schemata for the Reading Process

A useful overall method of teaching reading to English learners is to think of three types of schemata: cultural or content schemata, text-processing schemata, and

FIGURE 7.2   *Strategies Using "Into, Through, and Beyond"*
to Build Cultural and Content, Text-Processing,
and Linguistic and Grammatical Schemata

Schemata Type → Reading Process	Cultural and Content	Text-Processing	Linguistic and Grammatical
Into			
Through			
Beyond			

Source: Based on Jo (1999).

linguistic/grammatical schemata. These three types of schemata are applied at every stage of the reading process by using specific strategies (see Figure 7.2).

Cultural and content schemata include the categories that humans deploy to make sense of new knowledge. For example, in a recent class, prospective TESOL educators were comparing Chinese writing with alphabetic scripts. Because it was close to the Chinese New Year, a small red envelope was part of the display of Chinese writing. When non-Chinese students found that this envelope had something to do with intergenerational money transfer, their attention was immediately alerted. They asked the Chinese students, "How much money is customarily given?" "When does this occur?" "How old are you when your parents no longer give you this money?" On the other hand, interest in the writing on the envelope was low. The native English speakers had a cultural category of their own as a schema (parents giving money to children) but, conversely, had little experience with an ideographic writing system and were relatively incurious about it.

Many topics in target-language reading shut out English learners because of their lack of knowledge about the culture or the content. One teacher found teaching Jack London's story "To Build a Fire" to a middle school class frustrating because the students did not care about dogsleds or Arctic travel. Establishing a historical context is a particular challenge. Table 7.1 shows a variety of "into, through, and beyond" strategies that can be used to build students' cultural and content schemata.

Text-processing schemata are used to help students read. These can take place in all phases of the reading process (see Table 7.2) as students prepare to read, perform silent or oral reading, or evaluate what has been read. Text-processing schemata permit readers to accelerate their reading and yet retain more information.

Linguistic and grammatical schemata are built when an instructor devotes explicit attention to analysis of the structure, use, or even dialect of a text. Native speakers often find it necessary to do this in order to understand a writer's intent.

TABLE 7.1 *Strategies Used to Build Students' Cultural and Content Schemata during Phases of the Reading Process*

Phases of the Reading Process	Strategies	Suggestions for Implementation
Into	Setting goals for reading	Goals make sense in the cultural context of the classroom.
	Gaining background knowledge	Use background notes or a content or cultural briefing to understand relevant aspects of culture.
	Recognizing discipline-specific knowledge	Define particular technical terms.
	Brainstorming	Students pool their existing knowledge.
	Tactics for lexical acquisition:	
	• Previewing a glossary	If book has no glossary, students can keep a private dictionary.
Through	Understanding cultural terms and practices	Terms, beliefs, and behaviors are explained as they occur in the reading.
	Crosscultural comparison	Compare/contrast matrix or Venn diagram is used to make explicit cultural differences and similarities or to explicate content.
Beyond	Tactics for cultural understanding:	
	• Cultural perspectives	Characters are understood in their cultural contexts; rewrite ending to story from other perspectives.
	• Cultural immersions	Students put themselves in the shoes of characters of other cultures.
	• Intercultural communication	Students talk with a guest from another culture or content expert about issues raised in reading.
	Tactics for content application:	
	• Project-based learning	Read for problem solving.
	• Making posters, doing experiments	Gain additional content knowledge through hands-on experience, then read/write to report findings.

When employing these schemata with nonnative speakers of English, an occasional focus on form is helpful as they strive to understand and create longer, more intricate, and more elegant sentences. Table 7.3 specifically lists strategies that focus on form rather than content.

TABLE 7.2 *Strategies Used to Build Students' Text-Processing Schemata during Phases of the Reading Process*

Phases of the Reading Process	Strategies	Suggestions for Implementation
Into	Literary lore: • Identifying genre (e.g., fiction, reflective essay)	What structure characterizes this genre?
	• Identifying literary terms	What poetic/literary characteristics make the reading appealing?
	Previewing text: • Skimming • Scanning • Previewing • Formulating questions	What techniques can be used to process text to evaluate its usability or worth before much time is invested?
	• Semantic mapping	What can a picture or graphic reveal about the conceptual structure?
Through	Metacognition	Self-monitor and adjust.
	Tactics for text comprehension: • Identifying the main idea and supporting details	Use group discussion—the instructional conversation format, for example—to identify possible main ideas; evaluate; vote.
	Practices for critical thinking about text: • Making inferences • Problem solving	What is implied but not stated outright? What problems does the character create for others?
Beyond	Practices for review: • Taking notes • Study buddies	Make flash cards, underline, make annotations, pose questions.
	Practices for text comprehension: • Summarizing • Storytelling	Retell the text from an outline. Recall key ideas. Conduct "what if?" discussion to generate alternative possibilities.
	Practices for application: • Telegraph plot	If you had only forty words to tell the plot, what would you say?

Into Reading. "Into" activities activate students' prior knowledge by drawing from their past experiences or helping them to develop background knowledge through new experiences. Films, texts, field trips, visual aids, and graphic organizers can clarify meaning and help students anticipate the work. Brainstorming ideas about a topic is one way to activate prior knowledge and stimulate students' ideas by generating

TABLE 7.3 *Practices Used to Build Students' Linguistic and Grammatical Schemata during Phases of the Reading Process*

Phases of the Reading Process	Strategies	Definition
Into	Practices for sociolinguistic competence:	How does dialogue reflect differences between characters?
	• Observing dialect, idiosyncratic speech, social class distinctions	How does dialogue reflect the social class of the speakers or characters?
	Practices for discourse competence: • Observing point of view	Is there a narrator? Whose point of view is represented?
	Practices for metacognition: • Time management • Planning	Will the text be difficult? How much time should be allocated for mastery?
Through	Practices for vocabulary acquisition: • Guessing meaning using context	
Beyond	Practices for paragraph analysis:	What role does every part of the reading play in creating and sustaining meaning?
	• Identifying the topic sentence	Do the paragraphs have clear, coherent content?
	• Identifying logical argument	Does the order of paragraphs createan accurate flow of ideas?
	Practices for discourse competence: • Identifying story, grammar	Are the beginning, middle, and end apparent to the reader? Does the plot hold the reader's attention?

those of others. Some teachers have students make predictions about the content of a story and then put these predictions into "time capsules" that can be opened and analyzed once the text has been read. Students can discuss what happened later in the book to confirm or disprove their original predictions.

Another classroom activity that activates or develops background knowledge using all of the language processes is K-W-L (What do I *Know*? What do I *Want* to learn? What have I *Learned*?). Asking, "What do I know?" allows students to place new knowledge in the context of their own episodic memories and existing concepts, even if they have misconceptions that have to be "unlearned." Some prior knowledge may be based on experiences in the students' home cultures that are beyond the teacher's conceptualization.

It is especially important for English learners that during brainstorming and K-W-L, all ideas should be accepted. A comment made by a student may be highly relevant within that student's experience or cultural background even though it may appear inappropriate to the teacher. In the follow-up to brainstorming, the teacher can ask the student to give more detail about the comment. Once ideas are exhausted, the students and teacher together can organize the list, grouping and selecting appropriate category labels to create a beginning model from which they can work and learn.

K-W-L not only taps into what students already know but also draws from them what they would like to learn. The students list everything they know about a topic and then tell the teacher what they would like to learn. The chart is kept up throughout the duration of the unit for students to refer to from time to time. They have the opportunity to make additions and change incorrect information. When the unit is completed, they return to the chart and talk about what they have learned. By starting each topic or unit with an activity that actively engages students in reviewing their own experiences relevant to the topic, the teacher gains valuable insights.

To summarize, teachers might employ these practices before reading:

- Review goals to ensure that students have a clear purpose for reading.
- Preview the title, subheads, graphics, and other chapter aids.
- Introduce the author.
- Activate students' background knowledge of the topic.

While Reading. "Through" activities help students as they work with the text. Many teachers find reading aloud a useful strategy that gives the students an opportunity to hear a proficient reader and get a sense of the format and story line. Frey and Fisher (2007) emphasized that read-alouds may benefit English learners because students are thus exposed to fluent language role models. To build schemata for understanding what is read to them, such learners may gain comprehension from a preview-review approach. Stopping to show pictures and illustrations may also help English learners create new schemata. Teachers can "think aloud" to model how they monitor a sequence of events, identify foreshadowing and flashbacks, visualize a setting, analyze character and motive, comprehend mood and theme, and recognize irony and symbols (Anstrom, 1998).

Teachers using literature in their classrooms may find that English-language literature does not elicit the same responses from English learners as from native English speakers. By selecting materials judiciously, slowing the pace slightly, portioning work into manageable chunks, and increasing the depth of each lesson, the teacher can ensure that English learners have a fulfilling experience with literature. Myths and folktales from many cultures are now commonly available in high-quality editions with vibrant illustrations, and these can be used as a bridge to more complex works of literature. These tales often evoke a familiar response. Students can move from these folktales and myths to selected short stories by authors of many cultural backgrounds, go on to portions of a longer work, and finally progress to reading entire works.

Students can perform the actual reading in various ways. Table 7.4 offers a variety of reading methods for in-class use.

TABLE 7.4 *In-Class Reading Methods for English Learners*

Method	Description
Page and paragraph	Teacher or fluent reader reads a page; English learner reads a paragraph; group discusses what has been read.
Equal portions	Students work in pairs, and each reads aloud the same amount of text.
Choral reading	Passage is divided into sections, and various parts of the audience read various sections.
Radio reading	One student reads while others close their books and listen. After reading, the reader can question each student about what was read.
Repeated reading	Students read silently a book that has been read aloud or independently reread books of their choice.
Interactive read-aloud	Students can join in on repetitious parts or take parts of a dialogue.
Cloze reading	When reading Big Books, teacher covers certain words and students try to guess the word in context.
Nonprint media support	Students can follow along with a taped version of the book.

Source: Based on Hadaway, Vardell, & Young (2002).

To sustain students' interests in a longer work of literature, class time can be used to review the narrative to date and discuss and compare students' understanding of the assigned reading. Early language learners can use pictures from the stories they read to cue story retellings. In preparation for retelling, each student is given a set of pictures. As the story is read aloud, each student holds up a relevant picture. After the story is read, students mix up their pictures and then arrange them in order of events, telling the story as they go. A preview of the next reading can feature interesting aspects of the new passage. *Story mapping* is a way for students to use a graphic organizer to summarize the plot. Younger students can work with four boxes (Wants? Who? But? So?) to fill in their knowledge of what happens in the story (Peregoy, 2008). Older students can use the terms *characters, intent, opposition,* and *resolution*. Using this device, students can follow the story grammar, the progression of events in the plot.

In summary, teachers can help students to employ the following reading strategies:

- Paraphrase if necessary.
- Distinguish between important and unimportant information.
- Connect graphic illustrations to written text.
- Make inferences about text information.
- Compare text information to prior knowledge.

- Use visualization to enhance understanding.
- Find the central theme or gist.
- Recognize comprehension strategies and modify if necessary.

After Reading.   "Beyond" activities are designed to extend the students' appreciation of literature, usually in another medium. Poems can be written and shared with other classes or parents at a Poetry Night. Letters to authors or to pen pals encourage students to express their reactions to certain pieces of literature. Students can be movie critics and view the film representation of a text studied in class, comparing the pros and cons of the two media. Favorite parts of selections can be rewritten as a play and enacted for other classes. Students can plan a mock television show, such as a game show, in which a host asks contestants to answer questions or to act as characters or objects in the story. Students can create their own videos or films based on literature they read. Rather than adapting the work word for word, they can interpret the literary work by changing the dialogue, plot, or ending. The videos or films can be shared in a classroom film festival (Couch, 1996).

> As a follow-up to reading a work of literature, Díaz Maggioli has students bring to class a painting, a song, a sketch, or a prop that represents a character or a setting from the story, or a feeling that is evoked. Working in pairs, students challenge one another to defend their choices. (Díaz Maggioli, 1996)

After reading, teachers can help students to use the following strategies:

- Reflect on the purpose of the reading to see if purpose was satisfied.
- Determine whether prior knowledge has been updated with new insights.
- Summarize the central theme.
- Review or reread if necessary to retain information.

Students can read aloud small books that they have written.

©Rob Marmion/Shutterstock.com

Box 7.3 **Fluency and Comprehension for Older, Struggling Readers: Guided Repeated Oral Reading**

Reading programs that emphasize repeated oral reading accompanied by teacher feedback and guidance is a strategy known as Guided Repeated Oral Reading (Sousa, 2005). The feedback that the teacher provides gives readers the opportunity to modify their pronunciation so that the representation of the word in their mental lexicon continues to approach its correct pronunciation and spelling. Such practice builds accurate neural representations of vocabulary and enhances comprehension.

Focus on Acquisition Vocabulary

Vocabulary instruction is multifaceted. Students need to use a variety of strategies to gain meaning from context, including ways to guess which part of speech a word is, to look for embedded definitions in which the following text explains a word's meaning, and to find theme-related clues in the surrounding text. They can identify words with multiple meanings to avoid confusion when using them (Newman, 2006). These strategies help students to acquire words independently.

Two important goals of vocabulary acquisition are to expand the breadth and depth of existing word knowledge and to build habits of independent word acquisition. One way to assess what students already know is by asking for synonyms for new words and then involving students actively in discussing the word, associating it with familiar events and examples. By posing questions, students can quiz one another about word meanings. Word games and wordplay provide practice and motivation. Students need to build not only declarative knowledge about a word (what it means) but also conditional knowledge (when to use the word) and procedural knowledge (how to use the word—which form to use and in what context).

Preteaching Vocabulary. Part of success in reading is building schemata for comprehension. Preteaching essential vocabulary terms helps the reader get the "gist" of the reading passage during reading. It is not necessary to preteach every new word in a reading selection—minor vocabulary terms may be gained from context. Quiocho and Ulanoff (2009) offer these preteaching procedures:

- Select a few key terms. If possible, show pictures of the terms, labeling parts if necessary; have students create picture glossaries
- Give students an opportunity to work in groups to create a graphic organizer for each new word in which they separate out the parts of the word by syllables, noting what they think each part of the word means and concluding from this analysis the overall meaning.
- Ask students to volunteer connotations of the word from their personal experience.

Box 7.4   A Getting-to-Know-You Vocabulary Icebreaker

Long words can be descriptive! Students at the intermediate level of English-language development can describe themselves using "ten-dollar words."

The teacher supplies a list of thirty adjectives (including such "meaty" words as *tenacious*, *demure*, *intrepid*, and *ebullient*), and students each choose two that describe themselves. They must provide a definition of the two words and use them in sentences about themselves. Then

they use their two sentences to introduce themselves to the class. After all introductions, students complete four sentences, drawing from the total word list:

- I have a propensity toward _____
- I have an affinity for _____
- I have an antipathy to _____
- I have been known to be remiss in _____

Source: Adapted from King-Shaver & Hunter (2003).

Vocabulary Strategies.   Specific vocabulary acquisition strategies teach students to infer from context, find synonyms in apposition, make use of a subsequent list of examples of a new word, and use a dictionary. *Technical word acquisition strategies* include a glossary, sidebar, chart, or graphs. Worksheets or other kinds of practice may also help students to recognize meaning. *Word formation practice* involves compounding (room + mate = roommate), blending (motor hotel = motel), and acronyms (self-contained underwater breathing apparatus = scuba) (see Justice, 2001). Moving a new word from students' acquisition vocabulary (used in reading or listening) to their production vocabulary (used in writing or speaking) requires far more guided practice.

Mark James makes enrichment packets to teach students vocabulary using mail-order catalogs. He cuts out pictures, glues them onto index cards, and groups them into plastic bags in topic sets: fashions, sports, music, travel, baby care, and so forth. The English word for the object is on the back of the card, and a separate matching card has the English word only. Working alone or in pairs, students try to match the word and picture cards, checking their guesses with the word on the back of the card (James, 1996).

Folse (1994) uses picture cards in a small-group vocabulary matching game. All cards have the picture or word on one side only. Various card pairs are laid facedown in a random order. A student takes a turn by turning over two cards; he or she must

Box 7.5   They Have the Words on Their Backs

Michael Bailey, a twenty-six-year-old UCLA undergraduate, raised $5,000 to help pay the cost of providing middle-school students at Wilmington Middle School in Los Angeles Unified School district with free physical education shirts that

each feature a different word + definition from a bank of one hundred "high incidence" academic words and simplified definitions.

Hey! *Evident*! Throw that ball over here!

name and pronounce the picture or word. When all cards are matched, the player with the most matches wins.

Teaching Proficiency Through Reading and Storytelling (TPRS) for Vocabulary Learning.   Rather than exposing students to word lists for memorization, Teaching Proficiency Through Reading and Storytelling (TPRS) focuses on two to three target language structures (TLSs) per a ninety-minute instructional period, the complexity depending on the age and level of the learner. Gaab (2011) sets forth a set of TPRS strategies as follows:

- Write the target structure in English, then use a different color to write the meaning(s) in the students' L1.
- Use gestures, illustrations, photos, verbal explanations, props, and/or skits to demonstrate meaning in context.
- Use videos or technology to help students create their own mental images of meaning.

Collocation is growing in importance as a teaching tool because it enables students to learn vocabulary as it is used in real contexts. Using concordances, or sets of corpus, students can see "how words combine in predictable ways" in order to see recurring patterns (Hill, 2000). Although students must still devote study to individual words, seeing the word as it is actually used in a natural context permits words to be learned in appropriate phrases. Students can see verb + noun sequences ("dispute findings"); adjective + noun sequences ("unaccompanied minor"); verb + preposition sequences ("hear about"), and adverb + adjective + noun sequences ("highly irregular situation") (Conzett, 2000).

Transition Reading

Educators emphasize that students should be taught to read first in their primary language because the sound–symbol correspondence draws on words they know. Primary-language usage continues as English is acquired so that students can sustain higher-order thinking. Sometimes reading instruction in English resembles reading instruction in the L1, and sometimes it does not. Because Spanish has an excellent sound–symbol correspondence, Spanish reading instruction has traditionally relied on phonics and syllabic decoding. In contrast, Chinese is traditionally taught using kinesthetic memorization, with emphasis on drawing ideographs.

Depending on the L1, some students must learn the roman alphabet. As students who speak other roman alphabetic languages make the transition into English, they must learn to distinguish phonemes in their L1 that differ in sound but are spelled the same (*ll, b, v,* and *t,* in Spanish and English, for example), as well as learn the many exceptions to the sound–syllable correspondence between oral and written English. These various similarities and differences between English and the L1 result in some students learning English more quickly than others.

> ## PRACTICES FOR TEACHERS
> ### Reading Strategies for Students at Various Levels of Proficiency
>
> - Novice: Anticipating/predicting, skimming, gisting, scanning, extracting specific information, contextual guessing, prereading activities, simple cloze
> - Intermediate: Comprehension checks, guessing from context, clue searching, making inferences, scrambled stories, extracting specific information, skimming, scanning, paraphrasing, gisting/resume, note taking/outlining, passage completion, identifying sociolinguistic factors, understanding idioms, understanding discourse structures, understanding link words and referents
> - Advanced: Comprehension checks, guessing from context, clue searching, making inferences, cloze techniques, reverse cloze, scrambled stories, extracting specific information, skimming, scanning, paraphrasing, gisting/resume, passage completion, identifying sociolinguistic factors, filling out forms, anticipating/predicting, understanding discourse structures, understanding link words and referents

Teaching Strategies for Comprehension

Too often students do not know what to do when they cannot comprehend a text. Table 7.5 presents several learning strategies that are useful when comprehension fails.

Each of these strategies can be developed using a variety of reading selections. When introducing a new comprehension strategy, the teacher explains when the strategy is useful, models the process, and then gives the students guided practice.

Teaching Literature

More and more teachers are using literature as the core of their reading program. For an overview of the use of literature in a children's reading program, see Tunnell and Jacobs (2000). A literature-based approach to reading uses *controlled readers, text sets, core books,* and *thematic units* to provide reading experiences that are rich in meaning and interest for students. Controlled readers can be literature-based basal readers, in which vocabulary and length are tailored to the target reading level, or book sets (Story Box and Sunshine Series from the Wright Group, Literacy 2000 from Rigby) that feature Big Books and matching reader sets. Text sets are books that are related thematically (such as books on sports and hobbies, or sets of multicultural readers on the Cinderella theme) or feature the same characters in a series of adventures.

Children's literature in education, and specifically in the teaching of foreign languages, should not be used exclusively to teach communication skills or to present learners with perennial favorites of imaginative writing for youngsters.

TABLE 7.5 *Learning Strategies That Readers Can Use When Comprehension Fails*

Strategy	Description
Rereading: text-based answers	One can skim the text and find the answer. (1)
"Right there" answers	Answer is easily found in the book. (2)
"Think and search" answers	Reader needs to put together different parts of the reading to obtain solution. (2)
Rereading: reader-based answers	The reader must infer the answer: Look for answer clues from text. (1)
"Author and you" answers	Solution lies in a combination of what is in story plus reader's experience. (2)
"On my own" answers	Answer comes from one's own experience. (2)
Visual imagery	Before rereading, students discuss what pictures come to mind. Younger children can draw these pictures, and older children can use verbal description. Ask students to form mental images while rereading. (3)
Thinking aloud	Students self-monitor comprehension by asking, "Does this make sense?" as they read. What question can they ask that will help to focus what they need in order for it to make sense? (1)
Reciprocal teaching	Students predict, summarize, ask questions, and suspend judgment, using these techniques with one another. (4)

Sources: Barr & Johnson, 1997 (1); Raphael, 1986 (2); Gambrell & Bales, 1986 (3); Palinscar & Brown, 1984 (4).

Rather, its use must aim to take advantage of children's innate imaginative potential and playfulness and serve as a springboard for the students' own creativity, verbal or not. This focus is born of a deeper belief in the need for education to prepare future citizens capable both of appreciating the otherness represented (e.g., by a foreign language or culture as a source of richness and stimulus rather than as a threat) and of responding with their own creative and autonomous initiatives to the problems that arise in their lives and their community (McNicholls, 2006, p. 73).

Teachers who select literacy materials may wish to consider the following: If the text has multisyllabic words, how will these be taught—are students to decode these independently, or will these words be taught before reading? If sentences are long, are they clear, or are too many ideas presented at once? Does the content match students' prior experience, or will much time be necessary for schema building?

Students who read books that interest them are more motivated to read. A study of sixth-grade students' reading preferences found that most preferred books with scary stories, comics, and content about popular culture, sports, cars and trucks, and

Box 7.6 **Practices to Introduce a Core Book**

If an entire class is to read the same book, the following tactics may inspire them to want to read it:

- Read the title and ask students to speculate about its significance.
- Begin with questions that raise issues dealt with in the book, or create a scenario similar to one in the book and ask students how they would react.
- Read the first few pages or the first chapter aloud. Have students predict the kinds of situations that will develop or what will happen to the characters.

- Read the first few pages aloud and ask students to write about or sketch the images or pictures they see in their minds.
- Draw students into the book by asking them to share experiences that parallel those the character will experience.
- Read a provocative paragraph or scene to raise students' interest.
- Pass out a survey or questionnaire or sentence starters that you composed based on issues that surfaced during the book.

Source: Tchudi & Mitchell (1999, pp. 217–218).

animals (Worthy, Moorman, & Turner, 1999). Core books are those that are specifically featured in a statewide adoption list for all classrooms to use. These books are selected to appeal to a wide range of interests and abilities. Box 7.6 demonstrates how to introduce students to a core book so that they will want to read further.

Thematic Units. Thematic units integrate literature with science, social studies, and art/music/performing arts. The unit may be on the rain forest, the settling of the West, or other interdisciplinary topics. *Family Vacation,* a thematic unit designed by Ann García, combines five types of reading. In Lesson 1, "Visiting National Parks," the focus is on reading for facts. In Lesson 2, "Joshua Tree National Park," the students read for interest. Lesson 3, "Family Vacation at a National Park," includes reading fiction. Lesson 4, "Lake Perris, Your State Park," teaches how to read for technical information. In Lesson 5, "Local Park," students collate, compare, and evaluate information. Last, "Plan Your Own Park" (Lesson 6) leads students through an information search as they brainstorm what items an "ideal" park for their family would have and then draw a map (complete with map legend) that lays out the recreation area, picnicking facilities, restrooms, and parking lots.

Multicultural Literature. Multicultural literature helps students to see life from a variety of points of view, to compare cultures on different aspects of life, and to see their own culture represented in the curriculum. Anthologies of multicultural literature present a wealth of materials, some grouped thematically (see V. Harris, 1997; Monroe, 1999). *Multicultural Voices in Contemporary Literature* (Day, 1994) presents thirty-nine authors and illustrators from twenty different cultures. A follow-up book, *Latina and Latino Voices in Literature for Children and Teenagers* (Day, 1997), has biographies of thirty-eight authors with synopses of their work, as well as an extensive list of resources for books in English on Latino themes. Day (2003) is a follow-up extending the Latina and Latino theme.

Reader Response.   Reader response theory holds that in order to make sense of a text, readers must first make connections with it (see Rosenblatt, 1978). The teacher must create an atmosphere of trust and acceptance so that students are free to reveal their perceptions, personal feelings, thoughts, and feelings in relation to a text in a cooperative setting. Despite the emphasis on personal intellectual and emotional reactions, reader response must be guided by faithfulness to the text. The texts themselves must be of high quality, yet close enough to the readers' interest to inspire investment in the ideas.

Literature Response.   Literature response groups can develop a community of readers and help students understand the richness of literature. After reading a piece of literature (with the teacher, other adult, cross-age tutors, buddies, or individually), a group of students and the teacher meet for discussion. After each student expresses ideas about the story, the teacher opens the discussion with a thought-provoking question and guides the students to deeper understanding of, for example, figurative language, mood, and the presence of devices such as foreshadowing, flashback, and irony. These more subtle features distinguish high quality literature from hack writing, and are best mediated by teachers in appreciative, small-group discussion.

Independent Reading.   As students become better readers, they begin to read their own *self-selected books*. As they read independently, they are encouraged to use familiar techniques for comprehension—making mental images, surveying the book and making predictions, and monitoring their reading to make sure they understand. Students keep a simple reading log of the books they finish. Students who have difficulty finding books to read might benefit from a peer "book hunt" in which students interview each other and then go off to the library to find books that fulfill the partner's interests.

Several sources are available that suggest *age-level appropriate reading material*. Public libraries have detailed reference books that list thousands of children's books, including winners of the Caldecott and Newbery Medals. At one school, fourth graders prepared their own list of books and duplicated it for every child in the school. Generally speaking, children respect their teacher's recommendations and enjoy what the teacher enjoys, but if a recommended book is not interesting or understandable, the teacher's opinion begins to account for less.

Text Genres.   Some common types of information books are textbooks, which use predictable presentation styles to assist the reader. In addition to textbooks, teachers use trade books (chapter books, biographies, series books, graphic novels, and anime) that are produced for the general market; websites; picture books and photo-essays; newspapers and magazines; and authentic sources such as diaries and letters. Frey and Fisher (2007) described common features of these text genres. Textbooks, for example, often employ margin notes, graphs, photographs, and indexes to highlight information, whereas chapter books are largely text only. Graphic novels are based on pictures, with text used largely for dialogue—these are often recommended to jump-start reading for the reluctant adolescent.

Book Conferences. Book conferences with the teacher, if there is time, allow students to benefit from direct guidance. Students can use this time to share what they liked about the book, what they do not understand or what puzzled them about the book, and other personal responses. Hornsby, Sukarna, and Parry (1986) suggested this format for a reading conference: The teacher first listens to students' responses as they summarize a story or retell a particular scene and then asks students questions that encourage speculation or divergent thinking. If students confer in a group, they can ask one another questions. Occasionally, students can read their favorite passages aloud. The conference ends as students make a plan for an extension activity or for the next book they will read.

Sociocultural Affects on Literacy. When students do not like to read, schooling becomes a cycle of failure: Poor reading habits exacerbate poor academic work, leading in turn to the dislike of reading. Minority students reported to Zanger (1994) that their literacy was adversely affected in high school by their feelings of low status, negative classroom experiences due to a curriculum that alienated them from the teacher and from other students, and failure to include their home language and cultures in a respectful and meaningful way. Nieto (2008) and others have called for inclusionary, multicultural learning environments in which English learners will feel accepted and productive and will therefore work to become literate and successful in school.

How Does the Internet Affect Literacy?

Today's English learners, like other youth, engage in a connectivity that brings with it new hybrid forms of language. Multimodality, at its core, blurs the distinction between speech and writing, and reading and seeing. Although in some fundamental ways, one still decodes texts, for example, reading is no longer just a process of serial cognitive processing of linear print text; readers are now often expected to perform parallel processing of multimodal texts and images, while simultaneously texting, listening to music, and downloading images. Input and output are hybridized, overlapping and interpersonally, socially constructed.

This creates pressure on teachers to keep up with young people's restless and relentless innovations in representation. The challenge for schools is to devise ways to help young people learn, while they are immersed in the complex and ever-shifting parameters of hybrid forms of socially networked information. As Luke (2003) puts it,

> to track the fluidity and mobility of "travel" across the semioscape of links, knowledge fields, webpages, chat rooms, e-mail routes, intersubjective and intercultural relationships . . . capturing the idea and practices of flows . . . across the Internet's global terrain of signification, which operates in real time but nearly instantaneously and yet never stops (p. 402)

Box 7.7 **Online, Open-Source Reading: The Wave of the Future?**

Elementary school teachers in Florida can access a free, state-approved reading program called Free-Reading as a supplement to the state-adopted textbooks. As an open-source program, it is available for teachers to download and modify as they wish. Want to try it? Go to www.freereading.net (Toppo, 2008).

Writing Processes

Hand in hand with reading goes writing. Writing is no longer an activity that can be postponed until English learners can speak English fluently. Writing in English is not only a key to academic success, but it is also an outlet for self-expression. Hadaway and colleagues (2002) put it this way:

> The permanence of writing allows us to communicate with others across distance and across time. Yet, at the same time writing allows us to reach beyond ourselves, it also furnishes a means of looking inward. Writing is an expression outlet for self-communication, a way to chronicle our personal reactions and journeys. Finally, writing is truly the most complex of the communicative arts, incorporating reading as well as oral language. (p. 137)

Although much has been written about "the writing process," it is more accurate to use the term *writing processes*. Most writers do not simply draft, revise, edit, and publish. Rather, the process is recursive; there is much back-and-forth work—drafting to redrafting, editing to redrafting, revising to redrafting, and so forth. Many teachers teach a five-step writing process, but in a classroom with a rich learning environment, students actually work in various stages simultaneously. If teachers honor the reality of the learning process rather than trying to impose a lockstep system, the mind stays engaged throughout the struggle to "write down" and clarify thinking.

Megastrategy 7.2

Teach writing in a way that sustains interest, information acquisition, and lifelong self-expression

The Role of Writing in Academic Literacies

Students who are still in the process of acquiring English are entering colleges and universities at an unprecedented rate. The good news is that English learners are being encouraged to pursue higher education. The bad news is that few are ready to perform college-level work. Why are so many students unprepared for college writing? Students' prior academic work and social situation may hamper their ability to participate in discourse at the university level.

Just what language is needed to accomplish academic work and how students can attain mastery of that language are topics of much debate. Academic writing seems to serve a variety of functions. Some instructors use writing so that students can draw on their prior knowledge in preparation for new activities (for example, stimulating students' interests through freewriting). Some instructors expect writing to enable students to consolidate and review new information and experiences (using, for example, learning logs, journals, note taking, reaction papers, summaries, and study exercises). Others hope that by writing, students can reformulate and extend their knowledge using formal, structured reflection assignments such as lab reports, essay exams, or impromptu writing.

The field of teaching undergraduate writing and other academic skills to underprepared English learners is burgeoning in response to the "Generation 1.5" population of U.S.-educated ESL learners (Harklau, Losey, & Siegal, 1999; Roberge, 2009). ELD educators are collaborating with content-area instructors to improve the targeted writing of English learners in specific academic fields. This chapter treats writing issues as generic across age levels of English learners.

Writing as a Social Construction

Writing is no longer seen as a lone pursuit of the individual. The motivation for many students to improve their writing is not so much internal or intrinsic but rather lies embedded in the social context in which the writing takes place. As Rodby (1999) pointed out:

> motivation is not located in the individual, per se. Motivation results from a combination of factors often beyond the individual's control. It is produced by a confluence of relationships, ideologies, institutions, and activities with and in which the individual is engaged. Second, as these factors change from one context to another, either synchronously or chronologically, so does motivation. (p. 48)

Rodby (1999) described case studies of English learners who were more or less able to draw on multiple and overlapping systems of support from work, home, church, clubs, peer interactions, faculty, and social and cultural systems to revise their writing in a pre-first-year English class. These students are examples of the powerful role played by the systems in which they are immersed in influencing their literacy behavior, which in turn influenced their academic potential. This type of ethnographic study now facilitates the careful analysis of these intersecting forces as a means of designing interventions that are sensitive to context and culture.

What Do Writers Need?

Learners need time and opportunity to write as a regular means to develop their fluency. They need a real reason for writing, such as a letter exchange with a pen pal. They need a genuine audience; if students know they will be sharing their writing with their classmates, their investment increases. Students need role models, people who are using writing to fulfill life purposes. They need a safe environment for writing, with voluntary sharing, one-on-one conferences, and support for the writing at different phases of the work. They need useful feedback that blends a moderate level of error marking with a thoughtful response to the writer's composing efforts. The final need is for a sense of community, in this case others who can collaborate, validate, and support one another's efforts (Hadaway et al., 2002).

Authentic Purposes for Writing.   Sometimes writing, if it does not stem from or fulfill an authentic purpose, becomes a ghost of itself, an empty form that looks like writing but is hollow. Although some teachers assign students to write thank-you letters, journals, and stories so as to avoid having them complete worksheets, the writing on these teacher-assigned topics is often wooden and perfunctory. In contrast, Edelsky (1989) gave several examples of authentic writing: Students scolded their pen pals, offered medical advice in get-well letters, and gave Santa Claus directions so that he could deliver a motorcycle. Students who are writing just to fulfill an assignment cannot really write with a spirit that is their own. Luckily, teachers who work with students on each phase of the writing process can help them to find topics that interest them and to which they can then do justice with a dedicated effort.

Dialogue Journals.   *Dialogue journals* enjoyed a surge of popularity as a part of whole-language methodology, and many teachers employ them as a means of increasing fluency and promoting interpersonal communication. P. Jones (1991) provides a definition:

> Dialogue journals are essentially written conversations between a student and teacher, kept in a bound notebook or on a computer disk or file. Both partners write back and forth, frequently, over a period of time about whatever interests them. Their goal is to communicate in writing, to exchange ideas and information free of the concern for form and correctness so often imposed on developing writers. (p. 3)

Topics in dialogue journals are typically not assigned so that the partners are free to discuss whatever they wish. The writing is not corrected, graded, or evaluated. Most teachers keep the writing private, promising not to show the journal to a third party. Students like dialogue journals because the interaction focuses on student-generated topics; the process emphasizes meaning, rather than form; the language input that the learner receives from the teacher is comprehensible; correct grammatical forms are modeled by the teacher and thus taught indirectly; and the dialogue occurs in a private, supportive context.

Writing is often more fun if students write collaboratively. Students may enjoy writing buddy journals, a sort of diary in which a pair of students write back and forth to each other. The teacher models this by suggesting sample topics and perhaps putting a daily journal entry on the board: "Today I feel excited about the field trip. I got up extra early to find something to pack in my lunch!" (The buddy journals are less private than a teacher–student dialogue journal because every two weeks or so the students change buddies, and the new buddies have access to previous entries.)

The value of dialogue journals is that students can express themselves in written English long before they have mastered its forms and structures and are able to write narratives, describe events and problems, and even argue their points of view.

Digital Formats.   Multimedia tools are expanding the genres available to English learners. Digital storytelling allows students to incorporate pictures, video clips, and other imported and/or self-created types of media as part of the text. Creating photo-essays encourages students to document their ideas with text-enhanced photo archives. Adding voice—posting a podcast to the writing—integrates audio with visuals. Adding "tags" to the text enables others to categorize and search for texts by type. Using real simple syndication (also called rich site summary) (RSS) aggregators, readers and writers alike can subscribe to web content that is fed to their electronic in-boxes. These and other web-enhanced types of writing are explained at commoncraft.com.

Stages of Writing Development for Young English Learners

Writing behavior on the part of children who are native speakers of English reflects a series of developmental stages. The first is scribbling and drawing, as the writer attempts to emulate adult writing. At the prephonemic stage, the writer uses real letters, but the meaning stands for whole ideas. Moving on to the early phonemic stage, the writer uses letters, usually consonants, to stand for words; as the letter-naming stage follows, vowels may accompany the consonants as the writer attempts to approximate phonemic sequences. The writer then moves through a transitional phase toward conventional spelling, using "invented" or "temporary" spelling to convey meaning. If children are held to correct spelling, they write much less (Hadaway et al., 2002).

The actual spelling that children write is a fascinating indicator of their thinking and their emotions, as well as their progress in learning conventional forms. Kress (2000) looked at one child's form, *dided* ("died"), and speculated that the child was struggling with overregularization of past tense; another child, Emily, printed the uppercase *E* with four horizontal strokes instead of three, perhaps indicating that this letter carried extra signification as the first letter of her name. Emergent spelling, whether it stems from first- or second-language acquisition, is a rich source of knowledge about intellectual development.

Beginning English learners usually enter English in the transitional phase, that is, they generally catch on to the sound–symbol principle of the alphabet, even if their own language is ideographic. Beginning students can engage in interactive journal writing with their teacher or complete simple frame sentences such as "I like _____ because _____." They can copy words and sentences, or they can make their own books by copying and illustrating simple books.

Intermediate English learners can try their hands at various genres of personal and expressive writing, such as letter writing, as well as various types of academic writing such as note taking, short essays, and lists. Exercises in combining sentences help English learners to extend the length and variety of their writing. Many errors occur at the sentence level, involving adverbial and adjectival phrases and clauses, sentence fragments and run-on constructions, and collocation errors (incorrect verb + preposition combinations) (Leki, 1992).

Advanced English learners write responses to many academic assignments, such as personal or literary essays and completed worksheets, laboratory manuals, and test questions. Their writing may feature many of the issues with which native speakers struggle, such as topic focus, parallel sentence structure, and paragraph cohesion.

The Writing Workshop

The writing process approach is also called the "writing workshop." In this workshop environment students are free to talk with one another as they write. English learners can draw on other students, not just the teacher, as a resource, and can in turn use their own experiences to enrich their writing and that of their peers. The teacher's role then becomes that of facilitator and listener. The process approach involves several stages: planning or prewriting, writing, and feedback and editing.

The Writing Process: Prewriting

During *prewriting,* students are involved in using oral language to develop their need and desire to write. The prewriting phase helps students to generate, incubate, explore, test, and integrate ideas. These activities may include talking about and listening to shared experiences, reading literature, brainstorming, or creating role-playing or other fantasy activities. Mind mapping (see Chapter 5) encourages students to generate and organize their ideas graphically on chart paper or on the chalkboard. Some classes may use Inspiration, a computer program that facilitates mind mapping.

Some writers experience prolonged silent periods, whereas others report heightened emotional states or sudden bursts of productivity. Just because writing in school is tidily penciled into thirty-minute lessons does not mean that each writer can wax eloquent in a timely way. The most profound education reaches deep into the individual and, in reaching deeply, evokes emotional reaction. Teachers who respect this passion sympathize with its companion emotions. The alternative? Apathy.

The Writing Process: Drafting

The drafting stage involves quickly capturing ideas. Writers do the best they can in spelling, vocabulary, and syntax, without a concern for accuracy. This stage is followed by revision, during which students share and discuss the content and clarity of their writing, drawing on the teacher as a resource for advice and support. This step helps students to expand their thinking and communicate more expressively before editing perfects the form and grammar.

A useful aid for English learners is a *word wall* or *word bank,* which provides a visual representation of words they may need to draw on while writing. For example, a pictorial word wall for a unit on fairy tales might include matched pictures and printed words of a queen, a king, a castle, a crown, and other words that a writer might need to use. This device helps English learners to be more fluent as they draft their ideas.

In general, the use of word-processing programs has been found to motivate students to produce longer writing, with easier revision. Students using word processing were more likely to return to their writing for revision (Bitter & Pierson, 2006).

Self-Correction and Revision

Writers face similar problems as they draft. Moxley (1994) suggested using the following questions for self-evaluation as part of the revision process (questions have been shortened from the original):

1. Have I provided the details that my audience will need in order to understand the subject? What changes can I make to simplify the presentation?
2. Is my essay unified by a clear purpose or thesis? Have I provided sufficient forecasting statements so that readers will understand the organization of the essay?
3. How well developed is the content? Are all important concepts well defined?
4. Will readers find fault with my logic? Have I provided sufficient information for readers to understand my reasoning? What additional comparisons, illustrations, or analogies could I add?
5. Is the report visually appealing? Would readers better understand how I have organized my information if I used more subheadings, tables, flowcharts, or other visual aids?
6. Is my writing economical? Can I combine and edit some of the sentences to make them more vigorous?
7. Is the report grammatically and mechanically correct? (p. 109)

Digital writing workshops can help students to preserve drafts automatically. Using blogs, writers can copy and paste their original text into new posts, saving each one as a new revision. In wikis and collaborative word processors, the writer can go back to see changes from revision to revision.

Feedback through Peer Response and Writing Conferences

Students can give one another feedback through formal "sharing" meetings organized by the teacher in which students explain where they are in the writing and what help they need, read their work, and ask peers for comments; or they can be informal, student-initiated interactions. Peer response can be more valuable than teacher feedback in helping writers analyze their own drafts. Simply putting students together in groups to react to the strengths and weaknesses of a paper read aloud is unlikely to be successful with ELD students. To be useful, peer responding must be modeled and taught as part of the writing process from the beginning so that students are aware of writing for their peers as well as for the teacher.

Blogging offers writers the chance to synthesize ideas by commenting on the blog posts of others and also incorporating others' comments (via blog post) into revisions. Students are also able to hyperlink to sources of information, embed multimedia into their posts, and share their work with a larger audience while integrating their networked literacy skills into their writing (Hicks, 2009).

Group Review.   Peers are most successful as respondents when they are grouped with two other writers whose topic is similar. They can read two papers and respond to one of them. In this way, they are better prepared to become more deeply involved in the discussion of ideas and topic development, use of sources, and other substantive issues. Peer response to writing is not about editing. It should include feedback about the content, point of view, and tone of the work. The point is to focus on the communicative content of the writing and draw students together in a more respectful sharing of the messages they intend.

Writing Conferences.   Individual writing conferences with the teacher are interviews in which the teacher listens to each student talk about the work in progress, commenting and asking "following" questions (those that follow or reflect the student's comment), which lead the student toward control of the topic; "process" questions, which help the student organize and focus the writing; or "basic" questions, which ask the student to focus on the basic structure. This questioning helps the teacher understand the student's topic and focus, and models appropriate questions that students can later ask themselves as they put their thoughts on paper.

Ideally, the tone of the conference is that the writer is in charge. The writer speaks first to set the agenda and communicate the intended meaning. The teacher may then respond to specific sections ("What is the main point of this part?"), offer suggestions as alternatives, or check for understanding. The student who can restate what the instructor suggests is more likely to make substantial revisions in subsequent drafts (Goldstein & Conrad, 1990).

The Writing Process: Editing

Editing takes place after the message is complete. In this stage, which is particularly important when writing is going to be shared in a formal way, errors or mistakes in usage and spelling are corrected. Students who learn to self-edit can examine their own writing critically and improve it. The teacher's proofreading is useful only if the students can use it to improve their own writing.

If a perfected, or final, version is not necessary, students may archive their rough drafts in a portfolio without rewriting. The process has generated writing that is satisfying in its ability to capture and share ideas, which is the essence of writing for the purpose of communication. If, however, the writing is to be published or publicly shared, and students are to achieve pride of authorship, accuracy in such areas as spelling is warranted.

Error Correction

In the early stages of writing English, fluency is a much more vital goal than accuracy. With ELD students, the teacher must consider the level of their general language proficiency before making decisions about error correction. Law and Eckes (2000) suggested that with younger children and newcomers, one should encourage expression of ideas without correcting grammar. Writers should be rewarded for their courage in trying new formats and more complicated sentence syntax, and risk taking should be actively encouraged. Error correction is the process of tactfully leading students to enjoy perfecting their vocabulary, grammar, and usage.

Leki (1986) found that students are grateful for specific kinds of feedback that improve their sentence-level writing. An instructor's optimal response to any written composition errors should follow two cardinal principles: (1) Attention to the communication of meaning is paramount; and (2) the learner is better served who is guided toward self-correction.

Teachers may wish to use *restrictive correcting,* focusing on only a few types of errors at one time (Bartram & Walton, 1994, p. 80). Some instructors may set certain standards of submission before accepting a paper, such as requiring that a word-processed paper be electronically spell-checked. Table 7.6 lists frequently asked questions about correcting errors in composition and experts' responses.

Overall, instructors can assist students by prioritizing errors and developing strategies that address these, so students can monitor them effectively.

TABLE 7.6 *Questions and Answers about Error Correction in Composition*

Questions about Error Correction	Expert Answers
What is the instructor's role when responding to ESL learners' papers?	• Collaborator in response to content" • "Constructive critic in response to sentence errors" (p. 5)
Why is it important to respond to content in writing?	Most writers do attempt to address content issues that have been raised during the process of feedback from instructors.
How can the instructor effectively respond to content?	• Write specific comments that reflect a personal response. • Refer to specific text segments in the feedback. • Balance positive and negative comments.
When in the writing process should content feedback be given?	• On early drafts, mostly suggest ideas for content. • On later drafts, provide pregrading feedback.
How can the instructor respond systematically to sentence-level errors?	• Use a system, with codes. • Be selective
Should grades be given on content and sentence errors?	Some systems allow for three grades: Organization (focus and coherence), Development (logic of paragraph structure), and Language

Source: Based on Bates, Lane, & Lange (1993).

Publishing

Ways of publishing vary: A story is bound into a book for circulation in the class library, a poem is read aloud, an essay is posted on a bulletin board, a video is made of a student reading aloud, a class newspaper is circulated to the community. Desktop publishing software, usually a simple page layout program combined with a word processor, has made more readily accessible the look of professional typesetting and layout. It is easy to master the principles of laying out a newsletter page:

- Put the most important information near the top left of the page.
- Do not put two headlines side by side.
- Do not mix too many different type fonts on the same page.
- Make columns at least two inches wide.

Issues with ESL Writing

Selecting a topic can sometimes be a concern for English learners. Not all writers find a topic of a personal nature, such as a childhood experience, fruitful for generating ideas. Being familiar with a topic is no guarantee of writing ease. The fact that a topic is popular with native English speakers is no guarantee that it will enable English learners. Crosscultural dfferences abound: Japanese writers are reluctant to discuss religion, for example (see McKay, 1989), whereas students of the Islamic faith usually like nothing better (Leki, 1992).

Academic Register.   Establishing a tone suitable for school writing may be difficult for English learners, especially at the young adult level. Topics about which the student knows little (divorce, drug use) may be treated with naïveté or an excessively judgmental tone (Leki, 1992). Other tones to avoid are flippancy (disrespectful levity), sarcasm (contemptuous remarks), sentimentality (shallow feeling), self-righteousness (making a special claim to virtue), belligerence (trying to bully the reader into agreement), and apology ("poor little me") (Packer & Timpane, 1997).

Plagiarism.   The unacceptability of plagiarism may be difficult to convey. Students from other cultures may not understand the Western emphasis on originality. They may have been taught that mimicry is the highest form of respect and thus literally feel negative sanction for altering words as they are written. Students may also feel pressure to help others by letting them copy; or they may simply work together, resulting in identical copies of student work (Leki, 1992).

On a deeper level, however, plagiarism may occur because English learners feel coerced into writing in English, perhaps on account of social, academic, or economic demands on their lives; or they may feel lack of ownership over English (Pennycook, 1998). Last, students may feel that the pressure to succeed in the United States is so strong that any means justify the end. Plagiarism has been taken to new levels by the advent of the Internet and electronic databases, which allow instant access to global

Box 7.8 **Writing for Nonhumans**

Writing used to mean arranging words in a particular order to be printed with ink on the cellulose entrails of a tree. You wrote for people, and you hoped that the marks you made would leave a permanent impression upon the world. Today, writing can refer to anything from posting a one-line status update on Facebook to dashing off a 10,000-word blog entry. Your readers include not just humans but algorithms, and your goal is not immortality but a momentary piercing of the ever-shifting zeitgeist. (Madrigal, 2010, p. 173)

sources of information as well as multiple sources of term papers for sale (Bloch, 2001). The best solution to the problem of plagiarism is to invest in the writing process, give students support and accurate feedback at various stages in their writing, and offer specific guidelines and training in "textual borrowing" strategies (Barks & Watts, 2001, p. 246).

Reference Materials.   The use of dictionaries and the use of the library are two areas in which English learners may need guidance and direction. Many students rely on bilingual dictionaries, which in their brevity do not always supply accurate translations. On the other hand, if dictionaries are not frequently used in the primary language, the student may not use one in English either (Leki, 1992). Explicitly teaching dictionary skills can be of great help to students, especially those whose first language shares the same alphabet as English (see Feuerstein & Schcolnik, 1995, for an example of such instruction). International students sometimes rely on pocket translating devices, which do not always supply accurate translations.

English learners may not be familiar with the use of a library, especially if such resources are not available in their native culture. Students who know how to use a library may simply need special training to be able to make use of the library's features, such as the electronic card catalog (Leki, 1992). In other cases, students may have come to rely on the libraries within their own families, if they are among the elite, or they may never have had occasion to use a library.

Computer Technologies.   Online editing and conferencing, instant messaging, and distance learning are among contemporary uses of computer-assisted writing.

To make use of distance learning for young adult learners, Janet Raskin developed a noncredit writing course for the commercial website Englishtown.com (www. englishtown.com). Students could enroll for a variable period of time, but most stayed for about four weeks. Participants represented many countries throughout the world. The academic content consisted of one-week units on topics of general interest, such as current events, science, animals, literature, sports, business, and travel. A study guide accompanied the course, with a vocabulary preview, reading

Box 7.9   Code-Switching from Texting to Writing

More than one billion text messages are exchanged by cellphone in the United States each day. Such messages often employ short, brief sentences, abbreviations (POS = "parent over shoulder"), word puzzles (2L8 = "too late"), and emoticons such as [:x]("my lips are sealed"). Although some English teachers forbid the use of texting shorthand in classroom writing, a 2006 study by two professors at Coventry University in England found that eleven-year-olds who used texting in their schoolwork were actually better at spelling and writing. The students were adept in code-switching—from texting to standard English!

comprehension questions, directions for making maximum use of the website, instructions on how to perform the writing assignment, and guidelines for peer review. Once a week a live chat room discussion encouraged students to communicate with one another in real time. The instructor sent feedback on the paper transmitting a table of corrected text and comments (Raskin, 2001).

In summary, current approaches to literacy vary in emphasis, but the best teaching supports the following principles: (1) integration of language and content teaching, (2) use of authentic language and materials, (3) recognition of student diversity and learning styles, (4) development of cognitive strategies, (5) use and support of students' first languages and cultures, (6) importance of interaction and collaborative learning, and (7) student engagement in purposeful learning tasks (Díaz-Rico & Weed, 2010).

Exploratory Break

- Discuss the ways in which a classroom teacher can foster students' love for reading, both for pleasure and informational purposes.
- Do you consider writing a process of discovery? Explain.
- How can a teacher increase students' excitement about writing?

Chapter *8*

Learning Processes and the Imaginary

The Importance of the Imaginary

No one has fully fathomed the power of the human mind. Human history has recorded amazing feats of mental prowess: Bards, the oral historians of the ancient cultures, were capable of reciting entire epics from memory. For example, the *paha* (ceremonial singer) of the Native American tribal group Serrano was responsible for a week of oral storytelling, singing/chanting the entire history of the tribe from creation to the present during the yearly mourning ritual. Genius is manifest in many domains of human endeavor, including the literary productions of Shakespeare, Cervantes, and Solzhenitsyn; the works of mathematics savants and visionaries (Einstein, Gauss); the prodigious musical accomplishmnets of Mozart; and the artistic brilliance of Cassatt or Nevelson.

What constitutes genius in second-language acquisition (SLA)? How many languages can a human acquire in a lifetime, and to what degree? And more important for the study of SLA, what features of the human mind can be tapped to help the rest of us, the population of nongenius learners for whom SLA is "1 percent inspiration and 99 percent perspiration"?

Chapters 5, 6, and 7 offered many strategies that behavioral, cognitive, and humanistic psychologists, linguists, educational researchers, and teachers have proposed to assist the process of SLA. Yet one senses that more powerful strategies await discovery if one could tap as-yet-undiscovered powers of the human mind. In what domain would these lie? One answer lies in the domain of the *imaginary*. Imagination is the art and practice of producing ideal creations and forming clear mental images. Overall, the imaginary is an avenue toward things not yet seen. It defies definition.

Imagination is probably the oldest mental trait that is typically human; it roils through human history, surfacing in myth, dream, poetry, and the arts. The imaginary is a realm of language that can enrich us emotionally and expand our

> ### Megastrategy SET 8
> Use English to explore the imaginary

creative powers. Everyone spends time not only in the world of language but also in the imaginary; the human being "hovers between the imaginary and symbolic orders, divided into conscious and unconscious systems" (Peim, 1993, p. 62). But how can the imagination be used in SLA, which, like so many other aspects of the modern world, has long emphasized the supremacy of rationalism?

Vygotsky (1981, 1982) saw the imagination as the key to the creation of meaning. In creating imaginary situations, children learn to react not just in response to the real world immediately before them but also in accord with their internal world, the world of ideas. Imagination helps the child to separate thought from the surrounding world and rely on ideas to guide behavior. Therefore channeling this imaginative power is an important part of education and cognitive development.

Exploring the Imagination

Lozanov's Suggestopedia Revisited

Although in Lozanov's *Suggestology and Suggestopedia* (1982) he proposed learning methods that were unorthodox at the time, two strands of his work loom ever larger in importance. The first is his use of music to stimulate the brain. Recent discoveries in cognitive science have affirmed the connection between exposure to music—particularly music from the baroque era such as Bach, just as Lozanov predicted—and brain development in children. This idea is further explored later in this chapter.

> ### Megastrategy 8.1
> Explore the concept of the imaginary as a language-learning tool

The second aspect of Lozanov's work that may prove momentous in future language learning is his use of alterations in human personality to further second-language learning. He proposed that the learner assume a second identity in the second language, even taking a new L2 name, and have that persona assume the role of L2 learner. This suggestion has implications far beyond Suggestopedic technique. The assumption of an altered personality opens the door to the imaginary.

The imaginary as an underexplored realm of the human mind has potentially vast implications for the education of English learners. In the past, educators have considered the exercise of the imagination a marginal pursuit, one relegated to the visual and performing arts. Traditionally, neither of these arts has had a strong theoretical or methodological connection to SLA, perhaps because of the strong modernist rational bias in the historical and philosophical traditions of Western civilization since the Enlightenment.

As postmodern theorists, as well as psychoanalyst Carl Jung, have pointed out, the rational bias of Western education has led to certain limitations. In traditional cultures such as Bali, in which the average person spends time developing skills in, and participating in, art, music, and drama, these creative and imaginative activities help to balance "rational" pursuits, to the benefit of the whole community. How can the work of the imagination lead to increased language learning and, even more important, to increased wholeness and balance in society?

Lacan's Personality Theory and the Imaginary

Jacques Lacan, the French psychoanalyst, has had a profound influence on post-modernists through his reconceptions of personality development and his emphasis on the importance of language as a means of personal development. Lacan's work (1977) has wide-ranging potential impact for the field of linguistics (even though Lacan never contributed directly to SLA theory). A brief exploration of his work is offered here to expand a vision of possibility for educators in the creative and generative realm of the imaginary.

Lacan was a post-Freudian in the sense that he relentlessly pursued research into the function and effects of the unconscious. Lacan furthered Freud's research on the unconscious by insisting that it was a profoundly linguistic domain, with its own drives toward the production and articulation of knowledge (Grosz, 1990).

Freud viewed the ego as motivated by principles of rational compromise between the demands of physical and social reality and the impulses of the unconscious. He equates successful ego functioning with successful negotiation of reality. In contrast, Lacan argued that reality is not to be equated with successful ego functioning. The real cannot be experienced by the ego; it is a terrain without borders, boundaries, or divisions, a continuum of "raw materials" capable of representation or conceptualiza-tion only through the inferential work of the imaginary.

According to Lacan, the imaginary is the key to the child's entry into social life (Grosz, 1990), for it is the vehicle by which the child first distinguishes his or her identity from the mother and is able to interact. Through the imaginary, the child turns needs into demands, creating the earliest mechanism of self-satisfaction through the use of a symbolic system that is individual, unique, unregulated, and unrestricted. This, then, describes the freedom of the imaginary.

The stage following the use of the imagination is the use of language as a symbolic means of seeking satisfaction. Therefore, the use of the imagination precedes language. The "mother tongue" becomes a flexible and powerful tool for obtaining satisfaction not only from the first caretakers but also from the larger world. For most people, the dominant brain hemisphere seizes on language as a tool and pushes the other, more idiosyncratic symbol system—the imaginary—into subdominance.

The Imaginary and English Learning

How, then, can this affect SLA? Probably the chief factor inhibiting SLA is its marginal utility. The first language fulfills so many basic needs—for family kinship, emotional security, and job satisfaction—that there is little room for the L2 to be deeply fulfilling in the same way. Therefore, to access some motivational drive within the learner, the second language must somehow reach beyond the powers of the first language to address social and emotional functions that the first language does not. To access motivational power, the second language must reconnect with a symbolic system that is subdominant in the first language but lies dormant, connected with powerful emotions, in a sense waiting for a portal of expression. Thus, the door opens to the imaginary.

Picture a darkened theater. The curtain rises. The actors step into the spotlight wearing elaborate costumes, singing exquisite music heard nowhere else, portraying emotions exaggerated for theatrical effect. Opera, in Western culture, is often sung in a language unfamiliar to the audience. Yet tickets for major productions are sold out far in advance. Why do opera buffs submit themselves voluntarily to hours of exposure to a foreign language in an opera house when they would not do so at the office, at the beauty parlor, or in their neighborhoods?

The answer lies in the imaginary. Imagination is stimulated at the opera in a manner that is attractive, intriguing, and motivating. The challenge in SLA is to harness the power of imagination.

The Imaginary and the Development of Personality

Second-language learners must develop some capacity to imagine themselves speaking a different language. Students at different ages have differing access to the imaginary and link this to language acquisition in age-predictable ways. Cecil and Lauritzen (1994) wrote, "Young children tend to make the transition between their inner and outer worlds easily, as they intuitively alternate between the symbolism of art and language in order to make sense of their world. It should be one of the major tasks of language, therefore, to ensure that children are free to explore both sets of symbols as they mature" (p. 27).

Elementary school children who are in the personality stage characterized by Erik Erikson (1963, 1980) as "industry versus inferiority" (ages six to twelve) may see second-language learning in school as just another form of work; if they can imagine themselves as industrious workers, they can deal with the demands of learning a new skill and thus avoid a sense of inferiority.

According to Erikson, however, adolescents are in the throes of questioning their identity. The sense of self they have been developing since birth is faced with new challenges, such as choices about work, values, ideology, and commitments to people and ideas that may be new (see Marcia, 1980). Peer pressure, which at times includes social mockery from one teen to another, may inhibit students' ability to alter their image of themselves as native-language speakers and take on images of themselves as speakers of another language.

On the other hand, older, adolescent or adult learners have other personality drives, according to Erikson: the need to become intimate with the other sex, or the need to contribute to society at large. These needs may involve the imagination in new and compelling ways as one uses a second language to attract romance in accordance with one's image of the ideal lover or uses a second language vocationally or socially.

Research on the role of personality in SLA seems to have been limited to date to the study of the role of affective variables, such as inhibition, anxiety, extroversion, and so forth. No study to date has linked developmental changes in personality to the idea that SLA suffers after the learner has passed the "critical period" (see Lenneberg, 1967). In other words, researchers have not yet asked the question, "Is the difficulty in language acquisition that the learner experiences after adolescence due to personality changes?" In addition to the relative paucity of research connecting personality theory to SLA, research is also lacking on the link between the imagination and SLA.

The Imaginative Function of Language

Halliday's (1978) seven categories of language function included the *imaginative* function as that which allows the individual to create a personal world, freed from everyday boundaries, in which language is used for sheer pleasure. Despite the fact that communicative language teaching has facilitated the switch from behavioral approaches to those eliciting communicative competence and has succeeded in building curricula based on social function theory, the personal and imaginative functions of SLA remain underdeveloped.

Yet it is these functions, paradoxically, that have the most potential for intercultural communication. The result of SLA is often biculturality; the bicultural person actually has a personality structure and identity that is flexible and capable of operating in two or more very different social, intellectual, and emotional contexts. Therefore, working directly to use the personal and imaginative functions of language—that is, working with identity development and reaching into the imaginary as a semiotic system that precedes language—provides a fertile avenue of curricular development.

PRACTICES FOR TEACHERS

Honoring the Imagination of Language Learners

- Help learners embrace the notion that learning a second language involves an enjoyable leap away from everyday reality.
- Create a classroom ambience that encourages risk taking and fun.
- Give public recognition to acts of imagination, fancy, and whimsy.

Stimulating the Imagination Directly

Throughout the recent history of education, various techniques have been proposed to stimulate the imagination directly. Several of these can be adapted to the education of English learners.

Guided Imagery

De Mille's classic *Put Your Mother on the Ceiling* (1976) offers directed mental play to children that encourages them to practice creating specific visual images. The book contains a series of themed exercises that the teacher reads aloud as the students follow along in their minds; for example, Squeeze is an exercise in changing the imaginary size of objects; Being Things is an exercise in changing into things ("Be a rock. Be a mountain. Be the moon"); Camera is an exercise in turning the eyes into a camera and seeing in new ways. The excerpt below, which can be used as a listening task for English learners, provides the flavor of exercising the imagination:

> This game is called Animals. We are going to start with one little mouse, and see what we can do. Let us imagine that there is a little mouse somewhere in the room. Where would you like to put him? All right, have him sit up and wave to you./ Have him turn green./ Change his color again./ Change it again./ Have him stand on his hands./ Have him run up the wall./ Have him sit upside down on the ceiling./ Turn him right side up and put him in a corner up there./ Put another mouse in the corner up there./ Put a mouse in each of the other two corners up there./ . . . Turn them all yellow./ Have them all say "Hello" at the same time . . . . (De Mille, 1976, pp. 57–58)

Guided Fantasy Stories.   Guided fantasy stories can be used to stimulate mental creativity and personal imagery. Walker (1987) suggested a guided fantasy that begins with a teacher-directed journey that uses the framework of an imaginary trip to elicit vivid imagery. The journey begins by creating an atmosphere of relaxation and sensory awareness ("Close your eyes and just listen to the sounds around you . . . "). Note that each section of suggested wording should contain five or six such sentences. Rather than spontaneously creating such sentences, the teacher should write them out in advance. Sensory awareness is followed by wording that suggests a setting ("You hear the soft sounds of a green mountain meadow"); following this, action statements are mixed with calming statements ("A soft breeze is blowing across your face as you climb the mountain").

Further events in this sequence evoke images and actions that may include meeting a wise man, seeing far in the distance, or seeing images in cloud formations that carry a meaning or a message. As students are guided back, the wording features closing and separation statements such as, "When you are ready, you can return to the classroom." Although Walker (1987) followed such mental experiences with the exercise of writing a story, productive output is optional. For English learners, the listening experience is rich enough to provide practice in language skills.

Guided imagery as a writing prompt stimulates fluency. Magy (1991) suggested that the teacher begin with a relaxing episode and, when students are relaxed and receptive, present an image. The writing prompt "Someone I Remember" is generated by the following imagery:

> Bring to mind a picture of a feeling of a person important to you when you were growing up . . . Someone who is still living now, or someone who has died . . . someone for whom you have loving thoughts . . . your mother . . . father . . . grandmother . . . grandfather . . . aunt . . . uncle . . . or family . . . a friend . . . .
> Allow a picture of them to come into your mind . . . . Notice what they look like . . . their face . . . eyes . . . hair . . . the size of their body . . . . Notice their

clothing . . . pants . . . skirt . . . sweater . . . blouse . . . shirt . . . dress . . . maybe traditional clothing from your country . . . . How do you feel when you are with them? What smells or sounds do you associate with them? . . . cooking . . . animals . . . machines . . . perfumes . . . musical sounds . . . work sounds . . .

Share with them something about your life . . . what you are doing . . . what you are feeling . . . . Listen to them as they speak to you . . . . Listen to what they are saying . . . . Take a moment to talk with them . . . . Thank them for being with you . . . for sharing with you . . . . Look at them again . . . . Notice how you feel with them . . . .Now, slowly come back to the classroom . . . . Breathe in and breathe out slowly . . . . Open your eyes . . . . Share with a partner who you saw, what they looked like, and what you talked about. (p. 81)

Turning Imagery into Language.   Talking and then writing after this guided imagery experience helps students to share what they saw or felt with a partner or with the whole class. Students may "pass" if they do not wish to speak. Then each student writes the first draft of a composition on this theme. The role of the teacher is to read what students have written and encourage them all to stretch and expand their descriptions. They may then go through several cycles of reading the story to their peers, soliciting feedback, having the teacher correct the draft, and then writing a final version. Other topics that may stimulate the imagination and result in interesting stories are About Me, Early Memories, An Important Experience, Problems and Choices, and Plans for the Future (Magy, 1991).

Other Uses of Fantasy.   Directing an inner movie is another way of using the imagination that connects to the increased use of mental imagery to affect goal setting, boost self-esteem, and defuse anxiety. Movies of the mind (Bry, 1976) are inner pictures that bypass the limitations of the rational, analytic mind and provide an outlet for visual memory and visual imagery.

Programmed visualization (Bry, 1976, p. 51) can be used to help learners defuse anxiety, for example, in preparing for oral class reports. The teacher may lead the class members through a preliminary "movie of the mind" in which each individual visualizes the prospective audience as friendly and supportive, the information to be presented as interesting and useful, and the vocabulary involved as easy to pronounce. This stimulates the imagination to provide relaxation and emotional support.

Visualization activities are important to include in a language-learning curriculum because when in the midst of a creative process, students need to be able to consult their own personal mental images, in which are stored their experiences and emotions. In fact, the National Reading Panel (2000) found that the use of mental imagery or visualization to develop understanding of settings, plot, or characters improved students' comprehension and memory of text. Hess (1991) recommended using visualization as a lead-in to a fictional text. Students close their eyes and imagine a scene from the book, an object that plays a role in the plot, or a character they will encounter. Students can then draw the object or skim the text for its occurrence.

Creative Environments

Fashioning an environment that promotes creativity is vital to the stimulation of imaginative skills (Csikszentmihalyi, 1996). Creative thinkers have long sought out places of beauty and harmony in order to produce art. "Think tanks" are creative laboratories—for example, Xerox Park in Palo Alto and the Media Lab at The Massachusetts Institute of Technology—that attract original thinkers who wish to work in an environment that encourages creative group brainstorming.

A classroom bright with posters, unusual visual images, and colorful cultural materials sparks the emotions and invigorates the spirit. Although schools around the world vary in the degree to which they permit decoration, many exercises that stimulate the imagination depend on the introduction of a stimulating visual image. Current issues of magazines such as those in the Internet industry supply arresting visual images that can be used to promote creative language use in poetry, role play, or creative writing.

Using Images to Promote Creative Language Learning

Pictures, comics, paintings, and drawing—the use of images is a long tradition in teaching language. Kress and van Leeuwen (2006) point out that the concept of visual literacy—interpreting and learning from images—is not without controversy from those who fear that emphasizing images detracts from textual reading skills. But in the world of Google Images, Photoshop, Flickr and other visual tools, creativity can be enhanced at the same time verbal language is strengthened.

Captioning cartoons, putting speech into cartoon dialogue bubbles, making movie storyboards, guessing pictograms, discussing album covers, creating collages, and interpreting flags and insignia are but a few of the creative activities described by Goldstein (2008) that can be used to promote both first- and second-language development.

Comics.   While on the topic of visual images, one cannot neglect the use of comics and cartoons as tools to teach English. *Comics and Conversation* (Aragones, 2000) contains witty, uncaptioned cartoons that can be used to stimulate discussion. One example is a three-part comic strip in which a customer calls a waiter to his table to complain about a bug in the soup; the waiter pulls a can of insect spray from his jacket and douses the dish. This incident can be used for a quick writing exercise in which the students retell the cartoon in words or predict what happens next. Small (1993) is another source of cartoons for English-language teaching. Each cartoon is accompanied by a short vocabulary list.

Curriculum That Stimulates the Imagination

Teachers can use the imagination explicitly to facilitate SLA. This chapter presents many ways to elicit imaginative responses from elementary school children and link these to English learning. Especially in the new elementary EFL programs being instituted in Japan, Korea, and Taiwan, new methods are needed to energize English instruction.

In an EFL context, one cannot rely on the standard survival motivation used to assimilate immigrants to the United States. An ESL student needs to learn quickly the English terms for such common classroom objects as chalk and functional vocabulary such as *bathroom,* but it is probably not such a high priority for young EFL students to know this type of vocabulary in English, as they will be using the native-language term throughout their schooling. It would be more stimulating for them instead to learn words that fulfill imaginative social functions that are less frequent in the native language.

Avoiding nonsense and providing meaning are both necessary steps to stimulate the imagination. It is probably better to avoid the nonsense rhymes found in Mother Goose ("Wee Willie Winkie runs through the town, upstairs and downstairs in his nightgown"—a strange message, to be sure, and not crossculturally communicative!). Rather than relying on techniques that have been used in traditional contexts for native speakers of English, new curricular demands call for creativity and imagination.

Adolescent identity is flexible, but adolescents may find it particularly difficult to risk communicative efforts in a foreign language. It may be wise for teachers to address the identity issue openly and creatively. For example, the teacher might encourage shy Hans to take on the role of Gene the waiter, a friendly, outgoing personality. This kind of identity shift encourages students to associate the second-language use with alternative personality features that they can freely try on and discard.

Immigrants' identities may be at risk in ESL education. Immigrants may feel threatened by being asked to become "Joe" rather than "José" and may sense assimilation pressure from a teacher if asked to use an English-sounding name. Assuming a temporary identity only for the purpose of role play, and using a name that is not phonetically similar to the original, may help to sidestep this issue.

Imagination is part of a cycle in the 4-MAT learning styles system (see Chapter 5). McCarthy (1983) recommended that all instructional units begin with a personal experience that helps to connect the learner to the concepts of the unit. Throughout the unit, a return to concrete experience builds a foundation for conceptual development at a more abstract level. The cyclic use of the imagination as a vehicle for exploration, coupled with concrete experience and reflective observation, becomes a manner of teaching that appeals to multiple learning styles. This is an excellent use of the imagination for purposes of learning.

The sections that follow feature a variety of ways in which teachers can use the imaginary to develop English-language skills, including creative dramatics, poetry, and music. This is by no means an exhaustive presentation. The creative educator can invent a myriad of activities that stimulate the imagination and promote language skills.

Drama in the Classroom

Theatrical drama may be as old as human culture. The earliest dramas were connected with religious rituals, as the human stepped into a special arena of performance to call forth the divine. The theater holds a mirror to human life to show us ourselves—the "complicated, contradictory, joyful and sorrowing things that we are, the pattern of tensions between hopes and fears that constitutes human life, the inward and outward conflicts that accompany and comprise human existence" (Roberts, 1971, p. 3).

Megastrategy **8.2**

Empower the emotional imagination with drama

The opportunity to perform in a play or dramatic reading allows an ESOL student to step into the spotlight, however briefly, and experience the sense of heightened reality that is peculiar to dramatic performance. Plays are a holistic experience involving not only language but also the physical body and emotions on a conscious and unconscious level. Theater has long been accepted as part of English-language instruction, both for native speakers and in EFL courses of study. McCaslin (2000) described the connection between the imagination and drama:

Imagination is the beginning of our work. To work creatively, it is necessary, first, to push beyond the boundaries of the here and now, to project oneself into another situation or into the life of another person. Few activities have greater potential for developing the imagination than playmaking. Little children move easily into a world of make-believe, but as they grow older, this amazing human capacity is often ignored or even discouraged. The development of the imagination to the point where the student responds spontaneously may take time in some cases, but it is the first step toward satisfying participation. (p. 14)

Drama helps explore the world of emotions and nonverbal communication in the ELD classroom. Drama helps students to use reading to find meaning and then to enact that meaning in an interpersonal context. In this sense, drama and reading join forces to promote learning: "They develop the same personal resources in students, building links between print and experience, dream and reality, and self and other" (Booth, 1985, in Ernst-Slavit & Wenger, 1998, p. 31).

Drama helps students to develop problem-solving skills. The persona that students assume as they take on roles in plays or dramatic readings is the one who does the talking in English and makes the errors. This freedom to take risks allows students to relax, reduce their self-criticism, and protect their self-esteem. Taken together, drama activities have the power to transform the social structure of the classroom, bringing out dormant talent, having teachers and students cooperate on projects, and generating new kinds of face-to-face interactions.

Drama in the classroom usually takes on a variety of forms: use of classroom dramatics, whether developed by class members or performed by visitors; use of playscripts as literary text; use of role play, readers theater, puppetry, and storytelling. Each of these is examined in turn.

Many kinds of creative drama have been found to promote language development in early childhood (Mages, 2008). In particular, research has shown that creative drama stimulates oral language development, including vocabulary development, narrative development, story comprehension, story sequencing, and story recall. Story-based improvisation (reenactment of set stories) as well as enactment of child-produced stories have been shown to promote language skills. (To date, however, such research has not been extensive in dual-language settings.)

Classroom Dramatics

Classroom dramatics offer a range of performance opportunities, some as simple as role-playing from a prepared script, others as complex as staging the school version of a Broadway musical. Creative dramatics include pantomimes, improvised stories and skits, movement activities, and dramatic songs and games for which students do not need sophisticated theater skills. Dramatics provide students with a format for exploring self-perceptions and attitudes toward self and others, developing an understanding of human behavior, and participating in group work.

Drama is a language laboratory for oral communication skills, enabling students to acquire speaker–listener experiences and increase their ability to decode and encode ideas. Drama makes it possible for both teachers and students to escape from familiar patterns of language interaction and invent a new range of possibilities for their lives. As students practice dramatic improvisation and characterization, their deeper understanding of human motivation and character can give them topics for composition.

The use of drama can stimulate other language skills such as vocabulary use. Students meet new words and move these words from their passive to their active vocabulary, helping them to clarify meaning and permitting the repeated practice of unfamiliar pronunciation. This section features a variety of ways in which English learners can use drama to access the imaginary.

Types of Enactment. *Participation theater* is a technique that originated in England (Way, 1981). Plays are enacted in the classroom by a children's theater group. During the enactment, the action is stopped from time to time to invite children to suggest ideas to the actors. Children become actively engaged as they become vocally, verbally, and physically involved with the action.

Drama in education encourages students to become emotionally involved in the content they are studying by becoming the person they are studying or enacting the event: a tourist visiting the Statue of Liberty, an international student being interviewed at the U.S. consulate for a visa approval, or Paul Revere getting ready to undertake his historic ride to warn the patriots that the British soldiers are advancing on Concord. The teacher guides the study and furnishes direction and materials.

Theater in education uses professional actors to visit schools, enacting productions that provoke discussion. The touring company provides curricular materials that help teachers to introduce the play and integrate the theme of the play into curriculum units. *Forum theater* is a dramatic technique that presents to students a difficult social situation and invites the audience to step into the action as protagonists and change the outcome. Each of these types of drama has potential benefits for language development.

Two Complementary Aspects of Drama. *Informal* and *formal drama* are two complementary aspects: On the one hand, students learn to act informally and use their imagination to develop their talents in characterization and movement. On the other hand, if a formal play is staged, students become involved in reading the script; auditioning for roles; staging the play with costuming, rehearsals, and memorization; and, finally, performing it. These two processes aid each other, and each incorporates strategies that have been covered in earlier chapters, such as the use of multiple intelligence theory to develop talent, TPR to develop movement and listening skills, team building to promote cooperation, and social function theory to develop an understanding of language routines (see Figure 8.1).

Practice in sense awareness and movement precedes creative dramatics. English learners love language games such as Simon Says and Fruit Basket (each student receives a card bearing the name of a fruit; they take a chair in a circle, and when their fruit is called they must exchange places with the other fruit that is called). They may also improvise physical movements to match vocabulary words

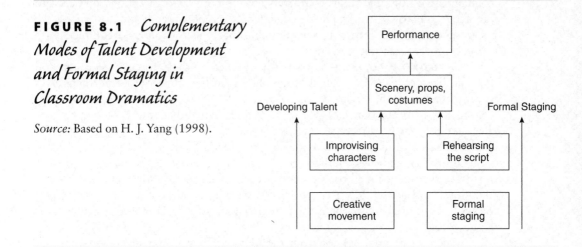

FIGURE 8.1 *Complementary Modes of Talent Development and Formal Staging in Classroom Dramatics*

Source: Based on H. J. Yang (1998).

in games such as Charades. (In a simple version of Charades, each student receives a card with an action verb to act out; they call on a peer to guess, and if that peer guesses correctly, he or she keeps the card; the person with the most cards at the end wins). These and similar routines help students to relax as they enjoy listening and learning vocabulary.

McCaslin (2000) emphasized the importance of the teacher's support for nascent playacting on the part of students:

> The sensitive teacher will not demand too much in the beginning but will accept with enthusiasm the first attempts of a beginner to use imagination to solve a problem. After the players have had the fun of seeing, hearing, feeling, touching, tasting, or smelling something that is not there, they will find that their capacity grows quickly. Through drama, the imagination is stimulated and strengthened to the student's everlasting pleasure and profit. We learn through experience. Through participation in drama and vicariously through attendance at plays, children are provided with many experiences in acceptable and exciting ways. (p. 14)

Improvisation is an important part of talent development for creative dramatization. In Object Imagination, students stare at an object provided by the teacher and make up a story about it to share with others. McCaslin (2000) suggested the following objects: a velvet jewelry box, an artificial rose, a foreign coin, an old hat, a cane, a quill pen, a headset radio, a pair of athletic shoes, a silver whistle, an old dog leash. As an additional stimulus, the teacher can provide a setting in place or time for the object: a settler's cabin one hundred years ago or the town refuse dump.

Character improvisation can take place by providing a setting, such as a bus stop, in which one by one characters come and join a group conversation. Other types of improvisation include costume improvisation, in which a vest or hat assists in imaginative thinking about character development. Improvisations that lead to interactive skits or scenes might be considered role play (see below). At times, the response to an improvisation is rich enough to become a whole play, complete with script, characters, setting, and costumes.

Character development starts with characters that are as "neurotic and unusual" as possible (McCaslin, 2000, p. 34), as well as those who lend themselves to dramatic situations, such as police officers. Students work first from character introductions ("I am the thief who . . . ") and then the characters interact. Each character belongs to the entire class, so the class as a whole can suggest that the character, say, falls in love, be kidnapped, or so forth (Wilhelm & Leverett, 1998).

Dramatizing allows children to add an emotion or personality to a text that they have read or listened to. Take any word, sentence, or short dialogue (two to four lines) and ask children to practice saying it "in character." By interpreting the words, children make them their own. This also makes language memorable (Zalta, 2006).

Students can stage scenes from the plays they read, exercising creativity by being able to rewrite the scenes in their own words or reworking the scenes in creative ways. Some rehearsal is necessary to create a successful staging, with the teacher providing assistance in blocking out the actors' movements on stage and helping the actors to convey effective emotional communication in accordance with the script.

The teacher's role in scripting is to move the script along by correcting grammar, making the lines more colorful based on the character's personality, and helping the actors to face the audience and speak loudly. Dialogue in a scene should be balanced so that all characters have approximately the same number of lines. Performances can be small, for the class only, or large, with audiences drawn from school staff, families, and other classes.

The teacher's role in rehearsal can vary. The teacher may act as a coach on the sidelines, offering suggestions to enhance staging, prompting with lines from a script, or taking actors aside for individual rehearsal. The teacher may actually take on a role in the play or assume a part briefly to get a scene back on track; such participation helps students to view the teacher as willing to experiment with characterization (Ernst-Slavit & Wenger, 1998). The teacher may act as a group facilitator, running several scenes simultaneously and moving from one to the other to provide support and direction. Seldom can a group of novices reach emotional depth and focus without the direction provided by the teacher.

Student-Made Plays. Plays can be developed and written by students using such literary sources as myths, fairy tales, and scenes from novels, stories, or popular television shows. Students can act out fables such as "King Midas and the Golden Touch." The teacher evokes the mood by asking students, "If you had only one wish, what would it be?" The teacher then intensifies the mood by showing pictures of ancient Greece while reading the story. Students choose their favorite characters and close their eyes to picture that character in a pose from the play: a princess picking flowers in the garden or Mercury watching the king from Mount Olympus. Students then develop the play from their characters.

Plays involve authentic and creative use of oral and written language skills.
©SCPhotos/Alamy

One class reads an Aesop fable every week, and each student writes a story based on that fable. The story can adhere to the original moral (such as the Hare and the Tortoise's "Slow and steady wins the race"), or it can end with a twist, showing the moral is not always true. The stories are peer-critiqued, and then the stories are turned into scripts with dialogue. Students take turns in groups turning each script into a play, and every student has a part in each script. Over a period of time, students improve their playwriting and their performance skills—and boost the cognitive level of the class considerably. (Strohmeyer, 1991–1992)

No matter what the source, the process of writing the script, rehearsing, and performing stimulates both the creative imagination and the use of English. Myths, legends, and fairy tales provide fertile story lines for drama because they are based on archetypes (the poor lad, the fairy godmother, rags to riches, the frog prince) that have evoked strong feelings and ideas through the ages. Two sources of multicultural stories that can be used for dramatization are Stern's *Tales from Many Lands: An Anthology of Multicultural Folk Literature* (1996) and Kasser and Silverman's *Stories We Brought with Us* (1994), which includes "Juan Bobo and the Pot" and "Don't Make a Bargain with a Fox." Fables open the door to creative use of scenery, music, and costume in ways that realistic stories do not.

Playscripts as Literary Text

Playscripts as reading texts can be used to teach English in various ways. Most teachers who use drama tend to use plays for which a videotaped version is available. Students can read plays in sections, perhaps after viewing a videotape of the entire performance and discussing the production and its context, language, and plot. Scripts have particular elements that must be taught explicitly, such as directions to the actors. Some plays, such as the libretto to the musical drama

West Side Story, may need an introductory passage (written by the teacher) that explains the social context of the plot and functions as a prereading warm-up (Beniston, 1996).

Reading the Play. Dialogue is a means of focusing on conversation when reading a play. One advantage of this technique is that the study of the second language is used to further understanding of discourse in general, thus avoiding the view of SLA as a compensatory or remedial activity.

Postreading exercises may be used to recap the plot and explore the characters. Each student can draw a picture of a plot event and then pair with another student to discover whose plot event comes first or last or features a given character. Students can write brief biographies of the characters that actors might use as backstory to prepare to act out their roles. As a class, they can brainstorm a list of questions they could ask each character for their opinions on the events of the plot. Students might also volunteer to be interviewed in character to answer these questions.

Viewing a Play. Seeing plays performed is a memorable experience. A field trip to a theater is a first-time experience for many English learners. If a major theater company is beyond the classroom budget, local high school or amateur productions may be a reasonable alternative. Students might enjoy studying a play before attending.

The analysis of a play to be read or viewed begins with a plot summary. What happens? Working in pairs, students tell the overall story briefly in their own words. Next, they try to recall what language they found memorable, working from their notes. What mental images does the playwright create with words? Were the words highly emotional? Was the language understandable?

Emotional impact is essential. What is the overall feeling of the scene? What emotions do the characters feel? Did the characters really interact with one another emotionally? Were the students affected by the actors? Which actors were most successful in creating a convincing character? Were the actor's lines understandable? Did any of the actors overact (make the character too much of a stereotype or make the emotions too obvious)?

Staging is an important feature to note. Did the design of the set convey a message? Was the setting realistic or tending toward the symbolic? Did the actors use the space well? Was the staging creative or boring? Were the props used well to convey the intent of each scene? Finally, encourage students to state the message of the scene in their own words. Was it hard to understand? Do they agree with it, or not?

Role Play

People are natural actors; after all, each person likely assumes a variety of roles every day. Role play is not only an excellent communicative activity in its own right, but it can also be used as a warm-up for other kinds of dramatics. Role-play activities in the ELD classroom range from rehearsal of relatively routine social interactions such as cashing a check at a bank to problem solving that involves complex conversations, whether authentic or staged. Students can practice talking by asking questions, making suggestions, demanding things, pretending to be other people, organizing themselves to solve problems, and reflecting on what happens.

Role plays can be imaginative or realistic. One simple scene takes place at a newsstand in a subway station, where a variety of customers interact with the newsstand owner. Young children can simulate a scene at a toy shop after customers have gone home, in which various toys discuss their desires. Customers in a Laundromat can pretend they have lost money in a coin slot and try to obtain a refund from the Laundromat manager. A floral delivery person can give flowers to a person at the wrong address and then try to get them back. Most problem-solving role plays are open-ended, encouraging the players to shape the conclusion (McCaslin, 2000).

Communicative Role Play.   In communicative language teaching, the social functions of language are the organizational basis for turn taking. Slots and fillers are variable forms that fulfill social functions. For example, the common pattern for a restaurant involves a sequence of communicative slots. The first slot is "The Welcome," in which the hostess or maître d' greets the customer with such phrases as "Hello, and welcome to Friday's. How many will there be?" or "Good evening! Do you have reservations?" Any of these filler phrases is acceptable. The next slot might be labeled "Being Seated at the Table," and so forth. In communicative terms, showing the role players various filler phrases helps to acknowledge that the social function can be fulfilled creatively, within a range of socially acceptable responses.

Decision Dramas.   Decision dramas combine discussion and role play. An instructional unit poses a "weighty" problem. One student in a pair takes on the role of decision maker, and the other takes the role of advice giver. Dramatizing family scenes, school situations, and other kinds of interactions helps English learners compare their reactions to certain problems with those of other students. Thus, they can clarify differing points of view, attitudes, and values. The teacher might further the discussion by asking leading questions, such as "How do you think the father felt?" Repeating the role play with characters exchanging roles also furthers understanding of other people's feelings and gives all players the opportunity to experience both sides of an issue (Radin, 2000). Personal journals can be used to explore the issues that a role play has dramatized, allowing students to reflect on their learning.

Readers Theater

Readers theater is a reading activity in which readers read stories or plays with expressive voices and use gestures to help the audience visualize the action. Through voice and bodily tension, the audience is led to imagine the scenes and characters. Because the players are reading aloud, no energy is expended on memorization, props, costumes, scenery, music, or lighting, although the performance may be enhanced with elements of stage theater.

Readers theater engages students in group work that can enhance classroom language learning. This activity motivates students' enjoyment of literature by means of creative activity and promotes reading fluency, as students are provided with opportunities to read and reread the same texts (Martínez, Roser, & Strecker, 1998). It particularly benefits weak readers, because their need for additional mediation is met as the text is rehearsed.

Texts for readers theater are chosen based on the age of the students, the length of the text, and the suitability of the language and plot to oral adaptation. Interesting characters help students to project understanding and care for their characters as they read.

Adapting Text. To adapt a text to readers theater, the teacher reproduces a selection that appeals to the students as a script, eliminating parts that are unnecessary and highlighting the characters' names on the left margin along with their lines (Young & Vardell, 1993). Dialogue sections are short, and characters use direct speech. Parts are distributed so that characters have a proportionate number of lines. A narrator introduces the play and provides background not told in dialogue.

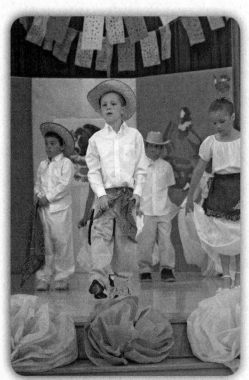

Classroom drama helps students to exercise the imagination.

Practicing and Performing. Preperformance preparation may include language development activities. The teacher reads the selection to the class, clarifying the meaning of unfamiliar vocabulary. On the second reading, students repeat each line in a choral response after the teacher. As an alternative, the teacher may read two lines and then wait for student repetition, or teachers and students may alternate lines. Students continue practicing in small groups, after which the teacher may ask for volunteers to read individual parts (Root & Dumicich, 1998). Parts may then be assigned for the reading.

During the performance, readers usually hold the script in their left hand so that the right hand is free to gesture. Pages are fastened securely to a binder, using loose rings or spiral binding so that pages turn easily and stay flat. All performers wear similar clothes to present a uniform appearance onstage (Shepard, 1994). Performers are arranged to create an interesting stage picture. Music can be used to indicate transitions between scenes. As a performer is reading, he or she directs the speech to another character if it is intended that way. Otherwise, the reader uses an offstage focus, looking up from the script as often as possible to establish eye contact with the audience.

Following the performance, students can talk about their experiences, either as performers or as listeners, or write a review for a local newspaper. Teachers can use observational checklists or rating scales as a means of evaluating students' performances, using such criteria as smooth delivery of lines, clear and distinct speech and fluent reading, creation of believable characters, listening and reacting to other characters appropriately, and mature behavior onstage. With these qualities in mind, readers theater makes a substantial contribution to students' growth in reading skills, communicative competence, and social awareness and interpersonal cooperation in the English development classroom.

PRACTICES FOR TEACHERS

Promoting Classroom Dramatics

■ Set aside a stage in the classroom illuminated by a strong lamp with a gooseneck stem; rig a portable curtain; provide a microphone stand with a heavy base on which cardboard can be taped to create stand-alone props or scenery.

■ Provide readers theater scripts with each character's parts prehighlighted.

■ Write versions of readers theater scripts with parts for a chorus that comments on the action; this involves class members who may not have a speaking part in that scene.

Puppetry

In many parts of the world, puppetry is enjoyed as a fine art, whereas in Western culture it is generally considered a child's entertainment. In recent years, with the popularity of innovative forms of theater, the use of puppets has entered the mainstream. The musical *The Lion King,* adapted from the animated movie, features giant costumes with actors dressed as puppets. Although masks and puppets go hand in hand, for the purposes of SLA, hand puppets are better than facial masks, which make it harder to produce and listen to oral language. Puppets are particularly useful for English learners if shyness, anxiety, or fear of error are inhibiting factors.

Puppet plays with cultural content can portray legends, fairy tales, or historical events, whether from the native culture or the target culture. An excellent example is the instructional unit entitled *Chinese Animal Zodiac* (C. Y. Yang, 1999), which features a puppet show starring the animals of the twelve-year Chinese zodiac cycle (rat, bull, tiger, rabbit, dragon, snake, horse, sheep, monkey, cock, dog, and boar).

Instructions for making the animal hand puppets are available on the Internet (http://familyplay.com/activities/actpuppets.html); these can then be used to act out the *Story of the Chinese Zodiac* (Chang, 1994, available from Shen's Books and Supplies in Arcadia, California).

Puppets are constructed from a variety of materials. Some hand puppets hang from strings; others are fastened to sticks, fit over the hand or fingers like a glove, or are made of everyday materials such as paper bags, bandannas, or socks. The puppeteer can manipulate the puppet in full sight of the audience or can hide behind a cloth or below the edge of a table.

Puppet scenery can be simple, with the setting established by means of dialogue. Props should match the size of the puppet in scale. Students can write their own puppet plays or adapt material from stories, poems, or fairy tales used in class. The wide range of material that can be used in puppet shows demonstrates the usefulness of puppets as language teachers. A wealth of multicultural literature is now available so that puppet shows can teach crosscultural values as well as English-language development.

Storytelling

In the world predating the printing press, storytelling was employed by many cultures not only as entertainment but also as a means of educating the young, preserving history, and transmitting cultural values and beliefs. The narrative approach to ESL and EFL education provides students with interesting and comprehensible language in a low-anxiety setting. When students hear and see stories, they are exposed to a wide variety of vocabulary and structures.

Storytelling foundations such as the New York City Storytelling Center and the Jewish Storytelling Center, together with celebrations such as the Jonesboro (Tennessee) annual storytelling festival, are promoting the return of storytelling as a human art form. Storytellers who are booked through organizations such as Art in the Schools visit schools to engage students in the firsthand immediacy of oral language events.

Delivery.   Storytelling delivery takes much practice with characterization, vocal exaggeration for effect, strong facial expressions, and dramatic use of emotion and suspense. Some storytellers add musical accompaniment or work in conjunction with a traveling minstrel. Stories can be told standing or sitting in front of the class with a dramatic flair, using props or costumes, or in a tight circle with the class drawn closely together. Visual effects, such as reduced lighting, a spotlight, or special staging, can heighten the mood. The best training for storytelling is to watch experts and learn from them and to collect stories that are interesting and entertaining for the listener.

Children absorb meaning by investing their attention and interest in the plot and characters of a story as the storyteller makes use of inflection, intonation, emphasis, and change of pitch and use of facial expressions, eye contact, gestures, and body language. Whether telling heroic tales, science fiction, biography, or history, the storyteller has a unique opportunity to build positive social attitudes and values while transporting the listener by means of the imagination to remote times, places, and cultures.

Picture-enhanced listening can more fully engage young English learners. As they listen to a story, each child holds a picture that corresponds to the characters in the story. As the children listen attentively, they each hold up the picture of the character who is featured in that part of the story. The storyteller pauses to check the children's pictures, saying the name of the character with the child. After the story is over, the children repeat the names of the pictures one by one and then work with a partner to retell the story using the character pictures. A sequential story like "The Little Red Hen" (in which the hen goes from animal to animal trying to get help with baking) works well with this exercise (Malkina, 1998).

Telling stories from their native cultures is one way that English learners can benefit, but they can certainly enjoy a well-told story from any culture of origin. Older students may enjoy preparing stories to tell younger children and thus develop poise in speaking before a group. Students may enjoy working together to prepare stories using props or other types of prompts.

Creating Stories.   Students can create stories using a flannel board with flannel characters or act out fairy tales. Many different flannel board sets, including Castle Stories (featuring six fairy tales), Dinosaurs, People (twenty-seven figures of various ages and ethnicities), Cottage Classics (interior scene for Snow White, etc.), Aesop's Fables, and others are available from Storyteller online (www.thestoryteller.com). Alternatively, a magnet board with magnetic characters (see World Discoveries) can provide a shy storyteller with props that help move the story forward.

Strip stories are fun activities in which each student in order adds a line to a story based on an intriguing picture or photo. One way to involve students in groups is the use of *story theater*. A narrator—a student who may have stronger reading skills—reads a story aloud, while others in the group perform the actions of characters or objects. This format helps students to listen and work cooperatively.

Aesop's fables may work well in this format. Students may also work cooperatively to find an alternative ending to a story, giving it a creative twist as it is retold. Students enjoy retelling stories they have heard, using props such as stuffed animals or telling the story to a favorite stuffed animal in a classroom storytelling center.

> Marna Bunce-Crim sets the stage for writing in the classroom by using storytelling to arouse students' interest. She begins by raising a question: "How many of you have a pet?" She then instructs them to think of funny or sad stories about their pets— where they got the pets, their names, and so on. As hands rise, children are invited to share their pet stories with the class. Additional "How many of you . . . " questions include, "How many of you have broken a bone or had an injury? How many of you have a funny story to tell about a brother or sister? How many of you have taken a trip or a vacation?" She also shares stories about herself and her family. By having everyone in the room share a story, she creates a feeling of intimacy and an understanding of everyone's similarities and differences. (Bunce-Crim, 1991, p. 16)

Personal Stories.   Family stories may provide anecdotes for retelling. Students may prompt stories from their relatives using openers like "Tell me about the town where you lived as a child" or "Tell me about your favorite toy when you were a child."

Personal experience stories are often best told in small groups or to a partner, because the storyteller is sharing something personal. Students may enjoy sharing these unrehearsed anecdotes with classmates, thus practicing the use of story structure: plot, characterization, elaborative details, climax, resolution, and conclusion.

Stories to Tell Our Children (Weinstein-Shr, 1992) is a collection of short quotes from immigrants to the United States. Each "story" is accompanied by a picture of its author. Readers are asked first simply to react to the story and discuss its theme briefly with a peer. After a few workbook exercises to familiarize themselves with the vocabulary, students use given discussion questions to deepen their experience with the story. They then tell a similar story to a classmate, using sentence completion as a prompt. They can meld these sentences into their own story and save these stories in a portfolio. The teacher's personal stories are also a part of the class's shared experience. Both are a part of the telling, writing, and sharing process of the class.

Steps to Storytelling. Four main steps in the process of storytelling begin with a very short story and culminate in students creating stories and books independently. These steps are listed in Table 8.1.

TPR storytelling uses mini-stories to introduce and practice vocabulary for beginning students (see Ray & Seely, 1997). A list of "guide words," core vocabulary that will move the story forward, begins each story. These are presented visually and taught through hand gestures and basic TPR techniques. The guide words act as the anchor of the storytelling. Next, a few students act out the given "mini-situation." The teacher then retells the mini-situation, using questions to boost comprehension (example: "Did she *jump* or did she *fall*?"). One or two students then retell the story, using all the guide words. The students tell each other the story in pairs and then repeat it without seeing the guide words. Finally, various students tell parts of the story to the whole group. This procedure is replicated at higher levels of language learning and extended to student-created stories.

Stories can be introduced by means of a picture cue, a mysterious object, or a photograph. As an icebreaker, intriguing sentences from a story might be cut in half and the halves distributed to all the students; each student must then find the match

TABLE 8.1 *Steps to Using the Narrative Approach*

Steps	Instructions to the Teacher
1. Telling the core story	Begin with a simple story, assisted by props or gestures. Retell several times, adding details.
2. Revising the story	Retell the story, altering the plot, characters, or point of view.
3. Creating a class story	Retell their versions to the class.
4. Creating independently	Students create their own narratives.

Source: Based on McQuillan & Tse (1998).

for his or her half. As the story is told, students listen for their sentence. After the story, the students can sequence the sentences as a story review. In a different setting, the language laboratory, half of the students can listen to one story while the other half hears a different story. After listening, students form pairs to tell the missing story to their peer, emphasizing the target form with exaggerated intonation.

One way to expand students' descriptive powers as they begin writing stories is to give pairs of students a fairy tale cut up into sentences. After each sentence of the story, students must stop to describe at greater length the character, place, or physical action. Alternatively, each pair of students can be given an index card bearing a small anecdote, with three words highlighted. Using the highlighted words only, the students must create a different story. Another option is to divide students into groups of four and make each person responsible for the time, people, action, or place. They can create story openings made up of a sentence that contains one of each element (Wong, 1996). The key that makes these exercises useful for storytelling is the final phase, in which students tell their stories in pairs to another pair (pair/share).

Something about the narrative, with its structured beginning and ending, ritual performance, and patterned sequence of events, is deeply satisfying to the emotions, powerfully stimulating to language acquisition, memorable to the mind, and conducive to crosscultural comparison and cultural enrichment. This is exactly the kind of technique sought by TESOL educators around the world.

PRACTICES FOR TEACHERS

Promoting Storytelling

- Coach students to practice storytelling often.
- Select stories with vivid emotional appeal, engaging characters, and a clearly defined theme.
- Encourage vivid and vital use of voice, face, hands, body, and props to make storytelling come alive.
- Give students training and practice in becoming attentive and responsible members of the audience.

Poetry and the Muse

The Greeks believed that poetry was a gift of the Muses, a group of goddesses who acted as the source of inspiration for poets (at that time also musicians). Although some people still believe that gifted musicians and poets have a special connection to mysterious wellsprings of talent, the love of poetry can be taught, as can the use of the imagination to produce creative writing in this genre.

Megastrategy **8.3**

Stimulate the linguistic imagination with poetry

Poetry is often excluded from behaviorist teaching because language for the classroom is deliberately simplified into structured patterns with limited, controlled vocabulary. Any literature that is used is molded into texts, which are the basis for analysis or comprehension questions. Poetry is too often an optional extra. Yet poetry can be used as the central focus of a language-teaching lesson, integrated with other forms of reading, writing, speaking, listening, and critical/creative thinking to teach English in a satisfying manner.

A Universal Language

Poetry is universal across languages. All cultures deal with its nontrivial themes such as love, nature, religion, joy, and despair. All languages employ devices of rhythm, rhyme, allusion, and figurative language to express deep emotions. From poetry we receive the language tools that make life more beautiful, meaningful, and personal. Just as important, students who write poetry can be encouraged to make the second language their own by coining words, using new words in old ways, and being freer to be more imaginative and more creative in the second language than they could be in their first.

Poetry is a gateway to personal growth. This is especially true of poetry enacted in performance. In poetic imagination, if old, we are young again; if Chinese, we can become Persian; we can become our own brother, mother, uncle; we can transmogrify into a hawk, a chrysanthemum, a syringe, or a raisin in the sun. In the poetic imagination, identity, culture, past, and future are open to change. In poetry we can share with others the journey that has brought us to the present or the bridge that connects us to the future. Poetry uses contemporary language and does not trap students in fusty archaisms. Rather, it opens doors to compacted, intense meanings that lift the language classroom, even momentarily, from the humdrum to the sublime.

Poetry is used in many ways in the SLA classroom: to reinforce English pronunciation patterns by taking advantage of the sounds and natural rhythms of a poem; to introduce students to the insights into human nature revealed through literature; and as a vehicle for discussing culture. Both reading the poems of others and creating one's own poetry stimulate the imagination and can lead to an increase in appreciation for the beauty of English as a language.

The Sound of Poetry

Language games such as tongue twisters teach sound values without being truly poetic, but they can lead to other kinds of word fun. Students working in pairs can generate lists of English words that rhyme (Humphries [1998] used *pen, red, feet, sing, cake,* and *hat* as starting words), just for the fun of using language or to teach irregular homonyms (*way* rhymes with *say,* but so does *weigh*). Making poems directly from rhymes, however, may undercut the connection between the imaginary and poetry; I believe poetry is based on communicating an insight, image, or emotion, and the rhyme should serve to enhance this original impulse. As Koch reminded us, "The effort of finding rhyme stops the free flow of . . . feelings and associations, and poetry gives way to sing-song" (1970, p. 8).

Traditional poetic structures are organized by sound. If the sound value of a particular poem is salient, poetry is worth studying for this feature alone. Using Poe's "Annabel Lee" to teach such concepts as *end rhyme, internal rhyming, stanza,* and *verse,* and having students tap or clap along with the meter, helps to convey the rhythmic basis of poetry enjoyment. Students can be assigned to memorize the poem to encourage them to master the intonation and flow of the phrases (Meloni & Masters, 1996).

Using Poetry for Speech Improvement.   Poetry can teach pronunciation if specific poems can be matched to a pronunciation pattern that the class is practicing. Solé (1998) gives practical suggestions on using poetry to teach pronunciation. Over a period of weeks, the teacher can take note of words that students are having trouble pronouncing, display these together, and ask students to make a sound poem. Reciting the poem together in pairs helps students to pronounce the words.

Poetry can teach intonation. Websites dedicated to rap musicians such as Tupak Shakur or the music of Bob Marley can teach students the rhythm of sentences. Choosing carefully poems that are appropriate for classroom use, the teacher can excerpt segments from rap music that feature rhymes made of longer, multisyllabic words. These examples assist students whose languages are monosyllabic to master the way longer words in English with multiple inflections (*inspirátion, rámificátion*) fit into sentence intonation.

Choral speaking has been used successfully with poetry to give students the opportunity for speech improvement by working on pitch, volume, rate, and tone quality of spoken English. Individual voices might alternate with the group as a whole for dramatic effect. Two groups may alternate lines or go back and forth in a call-and-response format. The choral reading may rise toward a climax, with individuals first blending into groups and then the groups into the whole.

Line-around reading gives each reader a line in turn. Sound effects (bells, drums, vocal sounds) may be added. McCaslin (2000) suggested many poems that can be used with choral speaking, including the majestic "The Creation" by James Weldon Johnson and Walt Whitman's "I Hear America Singing," which can be dramatized with pantomime. Choral reading can be used effectively to build a sense of classroom community, such as in a morning routine that brings students into oral group unison.

Poetic Listening.   Auditory input is sometimes even better than visual images because listening alone, without seeing, evokes mental images. Listening to "The Highwayman" by Alfred Noyes can bring out a sequence of images. Perhaps the students might see a young man of the 1770s clothed in breeches and lace and review a list of words such as *inn, musket,* and *galleon.* After listening to the poem, they might try to write down images that came to mind. The teacher might help the class put these images into words and write new verses to the poem. The intensity of emotion conveyed by the poem might counter the stereotype of the English as emotionally reserved!

Using Poetry Artistically.   Artistic recitation, either writing or memorizing, is an objective when working with poetry. The teacher who models this type of recitation sets the pace (see the movie *Dead Poets Society* for an example of a teacher's dramatic poetic interpretation). An interpretive reading can be recorded at home with a small handheld tape recorder and then played for the class. Dramatic lighting during the listening enhances the mood.

Types of Poems

Found poems are made from vocabulary words that students discover while reading. Collecting words and rearranging them in phrases to make a poem makes vocabulary acquisition also the work of the imaginary. Rather than having English learners simply translate a poem, Chatton (1993) suggested that they make a poem in their native language to match the English version. This could result in a dramatic dual-language choral reading.

Poems can bring together vocabulary (meaning), form (meter, intonation), and sound (pronunciation). *Haiku* poems are written in three lines (5 syllables, 7 syllables, 5 syllables) for a total of 17 syllables, capturing a single image that transmits beautifully the sense of a single season of the year (see Box 8.1 and Box 8.2). The *tanka* follows the syllabic principle of the haiku, using the pattern 5, 7, 5, 7, 7 (see Box 8.3). The *cinquain* has five lines: The first line names the topic, the second uses two or three words to describe the topic; the third line expresses action in three or four words; the fourth line expresses personal attitude in four to five words; and the last line uses a word or two to rename or reframe the topic (see Box 8.4). The *concrete* or *figural* poem has a shape that reflects its content (see Box 8.5).

Box 8.1   **Haiku: "Pretend Rain"**

Mist is not shower
Sympathy false, you're guilty
Crocodile tear-rain

Box 8.2   **Haiku: "Plum Blossoms"**

Snow-frozen white blooms
Unfurled too early, withered
Like fragile spring dreams

Box 8.3 Tanka: "Bicycle Lad"

Ped'ling, waves to me
Brown hair whipping in the wind
So far down the street . . .
I only know your hair whips
Because mine is rippling too

Box 8.4 Cinquain: "Puddle"

Puddle
After the rain
For sloshing, swashing, wading
New boots . . . I'm tempted . . .
I puddle . . .

Box 8.5 Figural Poem: Caracal Goes A-Hunting

Caracal goes   a-hunting
Nose
buried
deep
in
the
grass,
Ear-
tufts
sticking straight up above the meadow

Cultural context in poetry is important. The haiku is of Japanese origin and has been used in Japan for three hundred years. A lightly sketched picture that the reader fills in from personal memories and experiences, it often juxtaposes two unrelated subjects, which the reader connects. The poem also implies a link to a specific season. The root syllables of Japanese words, like Chinese characters, have sounds and meanings that evoke literary and historical meanings. On translation, the haiku is stripped of its cultural context and thrust unclothed into English. Yet even in translation, the subtlety lingers. Students can meet haiku from its masters. The local library may have access to a book of Japanese haiku. It is well worth the effort to preserve the flavor of the cultural origin as students write their own haiku.

Writing Poetry

Because each syllable of Chinese poetry represents a single image, poetry from China can be used to stimulate students to view English poetry in a different way. Rather than the word coming first, which often results in forced rhymes, letting the image come first tells a story or evokes a feeling by letting the poem emerge picture by picture. *The Heart of Chinese Poetry* (Whincup, 1987) offers the reader a bilingual translation of selected Chinese poems, including the original Chinese characters in an image-by-image translation. One does not have to be familiar with Chinese characters to absorb the logic of the poetry, and the visit to a dissimilar mental logic can be a refreshing stimulus to students' creativity. Students can translate the poem from the original characters, each putting the verse into English in a different way. Then they can view a short video segment such as a scene from the motion picture *Crouching Tiger, Hidden Dragon* and put the scene into a poem image by image.

Writing Poetry with Students.   The private world of dreams and desires is an inspiring source for those who wish to write poetry with English learners. Koch's *Wishes, Lies, and Dreams* (1970) offers students the chance to finish the line "I wish . . . " The world comes alive to the ear using the theme "noises." Changes in feelings over time are "poeticized" in the convention "I used to . . . but now . . . " The theme "lies" elicits the "tall tale teller" in students. "I seem to be . . . but I really am . . . " allows students to compare their public face with their private, inner world. An interesting genre that Koch drew from students was "Poems using Spanish words." The words, usually nouns or adjectives, were inserted into English stanzas for cultural effect. This bilingual format may be highly generative for English learners.

Exposure to a rich poetic environment helps students to create poems in the classroom. Koch (1970, summarized in Cecil and Lauritzen, 1994), offered a few suggestions. First, poetry should be an in-class activity. Uses of the imagination in class can become drudgery if assigned as homework. However, if students are inspired to write at home and share their work, it is cause for celebration! Students who mingle with one another to share and borrow words and ideas can write collaboratively. Idea prompts that open up the world of "pretend" encourage students to exercise their imaginations fully. If a line is unclear, asking for clarification rather than criticizing the work frees the poet from the burden of pleasing the teacher.

Scaffolding poetry, providing a temporary writing framework for a poetry pattern, is an important way to stimulate students. The scaffold can be a kind of formula for writing the poem (for example, "I dream . . . " in which each line contains a person, place, and color, as in "I dream I'm dancing with salamanders around a yellow desert campfire"). Other scaffolds can be the use of paintings that evoke mystery or provoke a rich sensory response. When students have seen and heard the models of others, written and shared a group poem, and drafted their own versions, the teacher may wish to follow a group writing process in which students solicit feedback from a trusted peer editor, confer with the teacher, and then incorporate suggestions from both sources in a final work that they can read to an appreciative audience (see Cecil & Lauritzen, 1994).

Connecting Visual and Poetic

Visual Imaginary Dramatic Arts (VIDA) (Díaz-Rico, 2001b) is a process combining art with drama and poetry to help students explore their culture, dreams, and fantasies. Two types of visual prompts are used, depending on the age of the student. For adolescents and adults, a collection of art prints is employed; each print features rich color and images that are figurative but not constricted by an easy-to-label story line. For example, Nash's "Landscape from a Dream" (1936–8) contains a beach, a hawk, transparent doors, and floating balls—all of which evoke ideas but do not constrain the imagination. The paintings are chosen with the goal of evoking archetypes and deep feelings, avoiding the display of nudity or overly disturbing images (see Appendix C for a list of paintings used in VIDA).

Students choose one from a laminated set of prints and work with a partner to create their own title for the artwork. They then find three decorator paint sample cards (obtained free from a hardware store) that match colors in the painting. The paint samples have names such as Malibu Blue or Thunder Gray. Students write the three color names on a display pad for the class to view, explaining or asking for explanations of the cultural allusions (Why "Malibu Blue"?) (Answer: Malibu is a beach community in California). They then act out one of the names in a game of Charades. This is easy and rewarding for students. Using the color names and the paintings themselves as prompts, students write a brief poem using the scaffold "Go through a portal in the painting. Meet the portal host. Bring back a message." They are encouraged to use words that evoke a rich sensory experience.

The cards from *Inner Child Cards* (Lerner & Lerner, 1992) function as the visual prompts for young children. These images feature fairies, dwarfs, and other fanciful creatures as well as the main characters of well-known fairy tales. Students can write poetry using the prompt "You are invited to a party by the figures on the card. What do you see? What do you hear? What happens then?" For both groups, acting out the poem or performing a dramatic reading adds emotion and excitement.

Students who create art during class can engage in language development activities in a variety of ways as they prepare a classroom art or photography exhibition. They can discuss with their teacher how they want their pictures matted or framed, and they can work with others to arrange floor and wall space at the exhibition. They can create an invitation to the art show and write brochures or handouts describing their work. Not all art is visual; students may wish to invite visitors to interact with the work in a performative way. Throughout the exhibition, student artists may socialize with the audience, discussing and explaining the work (Cecil & Lauritzen, 1994).

For more information on using art in education, see H. Gardner (1990).

Poetry Interpretation

Interpreting poetry with students helps to bring out both literal and figurative meanings, as well as enabling students to appreciate the sound qualities of poetic language. The beginning element of analysis is the *story line*. In a few sentences, what is the poem about: who, what, when, and where (characters, setting)? The second element is the *language* of the poem—the word choice, sound value (including assonance and alliteration), rhythm, rhyme, and use of mental images. The third element of a poem is the *emotional message*. What words are used that convey feelings? How are the images used to evoke passion, sympathy, or horror? Finally, what is the *meaning or theme* that the reader or listener constructs from the poem? Is the message straightforward or ambiguous? What do we experience that is unique to this poem, and what do we learn about the human condition?

To evaluate a student's presentation of a poem in class, teachers might use criteria that assess such aspects as choice of poem; communication of meaning, emotion, and tone; quality of delivery in terms of stance, voice, gesture, and audience consideration; and overall impact. A teacher might use the presentation as a vehicle for informal feedback to the student, using an interactive journal to open the door to continued conversation about the theme, discussing favorite lines of the poem or the student's interpretation, composing a poem in return, or writing a short reminiscence about a related personal experience.

Poem in the pocket is a technique that invites spontaneous reading. On one special day, students copy favorite stanzas of poems, and throughout the day, whether in the classroom or elsewhere in the school, another student, the teacher, or anyone else may ask the student, "What poem is in *your* pocket?" The student then responds by reciting the poem (Cecil & Lauritzen, 1994).

Events in students' lives can provide occasions for poetry expression. Students who send birthday, graduation, or holiday cards to one another can write special poems for the occasion. This opportunity gives students authentic reasons for reading and writing poetry linked to communicative events (Christison, 1982).

> Mother's Day and Father's Day were poem opportunities for
> Mr. Stillwell's Level II ESL class. The class read poems from Myra
> Livingston's *Poems for Mother* (1988) and the companion volume,
> *Poems for Father* (1989). These poems describe many kinds of mothers
> and fathers, capturing the complexity of love and the warm memories
> of shared experience as well as the mixed feelings for parents who have
> moved away. The students each chose a poetic form to adapt, writing
> their own feelings and memories in a card to illustrate and bring home.

Poetry in the Curriculum.   Theme poems can tie poetry to the curriculum. Travel is a broad theme that brings out the poet in some students. Creating an anthology of poems that focus on travel, students imagine a place they would like to visit. After collecting pictures of that locale, students brainstorm words that describe their feelings about the site and write phrases that combine in a poem about the experience. A "wish book" is the result of combining the poem and pictures. Making a transition from the imaginary to the real world, students research the climate and geographical features, compute the distance, decide the best mode of travel, and write a story about something that happens when they travel there.

Choosing poems for classroom use is based on poems having some innate, immediate appeal to the students. Poetry that goes too far beyond their developmental level may build resistance to the genre. An excellent source of poems for children is *The Random House Book of Poetry for Children* (Prelutsky, 2000); for adults, *The Norton Anthology of Modern Poetry* (Ellmann, 1988) is the classic. Children's magazines such as *Cricket* and *Highlights* can show young students that poems are written by students their own age; they may wish to submit their own poems to these sources for publication.

"Hokey" poetry seems authentic but is not really literature. Lipson's *Audacious Poetry: Reflections of Adolescence* (1992) is a collection of numerous poems, most of them written by the author, that address adolescent themes such as the dirty bedroom, work at a fast-food restaurant, and teen slang. The book attempts to evoke issues that relate to the lives of teenagers, but the poems are rhyme-driven, with shallow poetic language. Adolescents, like other human beings, need to be exposed to language drawn from the heights and depths of the human experience, rather than pandered to with language that is trite.

Form poetry (alphabet poems, list poems, etc.) can help reluctant writers use and appreciate language in a new way. Kazemek and Rigg's *Enriching Our Lives: Poetry Lessons for Adult Literacy Teachers and Tutors* (cited in Peyton, 1997) includes advice on publishing student work, suggestions on how to work on language skills while reading and writing poetry, and also some background information on familiar, popular poems. For example, the poem "Apple" by Bruce Guernsey can prompt students to brainstorm ideas about apples and what they represent, leading them to write their own "apple" poems (Peyton, 1997).

PRACTICES FOR TEACHERS
Using Poetry in the ELD Classroom

- Stimulate the poetic imagination through prompts from other media.
- Involve students actively by producing as well as consuming poetry.
- Ask a poet to visit.
- Emphasize that emotion, image, and creative word use are more important than rhyme.
- Publish students' poetry whenever possible as a keepsake.

Good poetry has great benefit for English learners, with so many styles and topics that both student and teacher are bound to find some poems that are useful and memorable. A teacher who shares personal favorites communicates his or her love of English as a language, as well as a deep commitment to understanding what it means to be a human being. Inviting poems, or translations of poems, in students' native languages also communicates the value of bilinguality and models an openness to learning about other languages and cultures. A classroom in which poetry is featured invites learning about language and about life.

Music: Listening, Playing, Singing, Creating

> *Megastrategy* **8.4**
>
> **Celebrate a sense of joy with music and other oral activities**

Music has gained increasing prominence both as a way to develop the brain and as a way to help students acquire a second language. Cognitive psychologists have connected music to the development of the brain (see Jourdain, 1998), so much so that parents of newborns now routinely rush out to buy a Mozart CD along with disposable diapers, although the effect on L1 acquisition is questionable.

Suggestopedia used music as a vital element, especially classical and early Romantic music of an emotional nature. The music accompanying Suggestopedic teaching is precise, with a clearly recognizable melody in the violin or string section and a steady bass accompaniment to the specific rhythm of sixty beats per minute (Rose, 1985). According to the tenets of accelerated learning, a set of educational methods based on Lozanov and neurolinguistic programming (NLP), a musical piece that is specifically constructed to be harmonious has a harmonious effect on the mind and body. Music has become an accepted part of English-language development, and it is valued for its ability to engage students' interest, teach language forms and functions, and transmit target-language cultural content.

Popular Music

Songs drawn from traditional sources, films, and popular music are commonly used in EFL settings, as are songs created by ESL publishers exclusively for the classroom. The old gold rush song "Clementine" is known all around the world, although it is also rather depressing ("Oh my darling . . . you are lost and gone forever / dreadful sorry, Clementine") and perhaps crossculturally obscure and grammatically incorrect ("herringboxes without topses / sandals were for Clementine").

Music in films adds a visual component as well as cultural elements. Switzerland is full of Japanese tourists chiefly because so many were taught the song "Edelweiss" in their English classes when they viewed the movie *The Sound of Music,* which the tourists associate with an Alpine setting. Technically speaking, however, American films marketed for home use cannot be shown in public contexts such as classrooms without royalties being paid to the company and artist. Purchase of a karaoke version of popular songs may be legally acceptable, as these are marketed specifically for public use.

Using popular music to teach vowel pronunciation is the goal of the program Rock Talk (Redding, 2001). Using pop and rock songs dating back to the 1960s, the program provides intensive practice on target vowels; for example, singing along

Box 8.6 **The Real *Glee***

Students attending John Burroughs High School in Burbank, California are the real-life inspiration behind the television show *Glee* (S. P. Goodwin, 2011b). The pilot episode of the show was filmed there, and members of Powerhouse, JBHS's glee club, were invited to sing with *Glee* cast members at the season 2 premiere cast party at Paramount Studios. Brendan Jennings, the glee club faculty coach, has this to say about high school choirs:

Students need something to be invested in and excited about. The important thing is that students are able to connect with each other and their school. The kids are not only learning to be great singers, but also great people. (S. P. Goodwin, 2011b, p. 11)

with the Beatles' "Eight Days a Week" encourages students to practice the phoneme common to *eight* and *days* and contrast it with that of *week*. The program comes with a tape of original recordings of the songs and a workbook that uses grammar, idiom, and essay exercises to reinforce language learning.

Music as a Cultural Tool.   Sharing cultural history with students through song is a way for many teachers to present their personal favorite songs. The Lennon–McCartney song "In My Life" provides a lesson plan that encourages personal reflection. Before playing the song, the teacher may wish to introduce the context of the song, including a brief review of the Beatles era. Playing the song through once without a specific listening assignment communicates the idea that music is, after all, entertainment that is meant for personal enjoyment. During the second playing, students are asked to jot down phrases they hear and, after listening, to compare their phrases with those of a partner. Next, students read the lyric and pick out key phrases that inspire them to think about their own lives. Using these key phrases, students write down two sentences about something in their life that has been unforgettable. This song can become part of a journal or songbook that they create throughout their course of study in which lyrics are paired with introspective or personal writing.

Music and thematic units go together. Jane Nakagawa (personal communication, 2002) created an intermediate-level English course with a discussion emphasis in which the discussion prompts were all rock and pop songs (mainly from the 1990s) that discuss global issues. She arranged the lyrics by topic, sorting them into themes such as environment, war, youth culture, race, violence, beauty and fashion, growing old, modern romance, family, materialism, AIDS, anorexia, homophobia, domestic violence, gender issues, classism, and exploitation of peoples. These songs address social problems and social justice issues, obviously for use with high school or college students.

Songs that promote justice are an integral part of Bob Peterson's teaching. Classroom discussions, freewrites, and a large spiral notebook entitled "Questions We Have" keep alive the idea that one's environment is not a given, but a process of creation, and that students themselves are active creators and shapers of that environment. Occasionally the "Questions We Have" are used as "triggers"—what Freire calls "codes" (see Chapter 2)—for classroom research projects.

Peterson (1994) offered some of the students' questions: "Who tells television what to put on? How many presidents owned slaves? If we are free, why do we have to come to school?" Peterson provided a list of songs that he has used in his classroom, among them Holly Near's "I Cried," Stevie Wonder's "Happy Birthday, Martin Luther King," Woody Guthrie's "Deportee," Phil Ochs's "There but for Fortune," and the Neville Brothers' "Sister Rosa."

Culturally Authentic Music

Commercial ESL publishers often feature music that has been reinterpreted by studio musicians, and thus copyright issues have been covered. Typical songs include a range of selections from American musical heritage, including children's songs, spirituals, traditional folk songs, and pop music. The advantage of using commercially designed sources is that songs are often accompanied by practice exercises, tips on grammatical structures, and vocabulary explanations. Another source for commercially repackaged songs is the *Kids Songs* collection (see Cassidy, 1992), which contains audiocassette and CD versions of songs that are beautifully arranged and recorded, accompanied with a book containing sheet music. The downside of commercially repackaged music is that popular songs are not sung by the original artists (see Grenough, 1998).

The loss of authenticity is cultural loss. Not using the original recording of a famous song means more than loss of a celebrity's voice. A case in point is the use of a classroom-adapted version of "This Land Is Your Land." Many such versions are upbeat, well arranged, and inviting. However, to hear the original voice of Woody Guthrie, and through that voice and that man's history to understand the Great Depression and the hope that the song conveyed in the darkest of eras, is to vote for the authentic over the ersatz. Moreover, the book *This Land Is Your Land* (Guthrie, 1998) contains several original verses to the song, which seldom appear in commercial versions, that raise some deeper questions about democracy and equity in the United States. The authentic version and voice undoubtedly convey a truer picture of American culture.

Teaching favorite songs is easier with a book of lyrics. A teacher with a guitar or piano will benefit from *Rise Up Singing*, a book containing 1,200 songs (with lyrics and source citations) drawn from the rich musical heritage of the United States. Many songs can be taught to classes even without musical accompaniment if the teacher remembers the tune. The book has a title index as well as theme and culture indexes. Broadway lyrics, old ballads, blues tunes, labor union songs—both famous and obscure—are featured, though not pop and rock songs of the last twenty years (Blood, 1992).

Jazz Chants

Teaching intonation is fun using jazz chants by Carol Graham (1988) that contain entertaining verbal interchanges set to catchy rhythms. These can give students the opportunity to work with longer texts, songs, and plays.

Students can create their own chants to promote understanding of character and plot in a poem or story. Using a three-part chart (character, action, and sound), students list what characters do or say. The teacher then introduces the pattern of a chant, and students in groups write verses using the pattern (Hetherton, 1998). This works well with *Alice's Adventures in Wonderland* or other tales with a multitude of fanciful characters.

Singing Games

Ring games, or singing games, are social events; they stem from the Middle Ages, when they were originally used for courtship. These can be used in the language classroom in much the same way as jazz chants, but they incorporate movement and gesture. They also, as a part of the rhythmic events, encourage individuals to have speaking parts. Bell (1999) described the ring game as a kind of movement-enhanced choral speaking. A simple ring game is a five-beat chant, "When's your birthday?" with the accents on *when's, birth,* and *day.* Students form a ring, lining up in chronological order of their birthdays in the year. They then begin the chant, moving left three steps on each of *when's, birth,* and *day.* Then they snap their fingers twice: This is the time when the first person in order says, "January 15" (fast—the month and day get only one beat each). Then the circle steps to the right, as all chant "When's your birthday?" This and other simple games, based on a chant with repetition and movement, break the ice and get students interacting physically as well as mentally with one another.

The best source for those interested in using music for TESOL education is Murphey's *Music & Song* (1992). Using song clips, video clips, song lyrics, discussions of the pop music industry, music with young children, even music alone, Murphey provides a complete "how to." Every activity includes a recommended language ability level and includes the approximate time to accomplish the activity. With this guide, even a tone-deaf educator has little excuse not to have the students "sing along."

PRACTICES FOR TEACHERS
Using Music in the ELD Classroom

- Select music that illuminates some facet of the target culture.
- Involve students actively by singing along, clapping, or playing rhythm instruments.
- Ask a musician, such as a colleague who plays guitar, to entertain.
- Ask students to bring in music from their native culture and see if they can provide a translation.

The Virtues of the Imaginary

Exercising the imagination directly through mental play or guided fantasy; using listening skills, visual arts, stories, or drama to stimulate language use; or practicing English through music or poetry emphasizes three facets:

- The imaginary serves the whole person; it develops new ways of thinking, new depths or understanding of emotion, and new avenues of expressing the complexity and wonder of the human experience.

- The imaginary develops language; although it is not primarily or even primordially a linguistic domain, it is a rich source of input to stimulate linguistic output, as well as providing powerful means and motivation, such as creative drama and poetry, to express language in new and creative ways.

- The imaginary is an "equal opportunity employer." It levels the playing field of language. Using imaginative functions of language, the teacher can encourage nonnative speakers to feel a sense of "pride of ownership" of English. Whatever refreshing form of language comes forth, the wise teacher rewards innovation and creativity in language use.

As a language, English is profoundly democratic. It is a language that has accepted thousands of new words from cultures all over the world. The millions of speakers of English who are not native speakers nonetheless have equal rights to use English to their benefit and enjoyment. Although to the experienced linguist the spoken language conveys precise information about social origin, class, status, and education, the imaginary knows no such boundaries of class and culture. All users of English have an equal right to use English as their own personal door to a world in which love, joy, and freedom await, along with adventure and excitement, even loss and pain. The teacher of English learners, if open to creative language use, finds delight in unusual turns of phrase. The process of language acquisition, when it takes creative turns and twists, opens language doors that the native speaker may not even know exist.

And in the imaginary, the children shall be teachers to us all. In fact, one linguist postulates that humans may owe the development of language to children:

> How, then, did [language] begin? I suggest that it began with the children, and it probably began when the earliest settlements . . . reached a sufficient density of population so that there were plenty of young children in close contact with one another, a critical mass of children, playing together all day long . . . . When it first happened, it must have come as an overwhelming surprise to the adults. I can imagine the scene, the tribe gathered together in a communal compound of some sort . . . . The children have been noisier than ever in recent weeks, especially the three- and four-year-olds. Now they begin a clamor never heard before, a tumult of sounds, words tumbling over words, the newest and wildest of all the human sounds ever made, rising in volume and intensity, exultant, and all of it totally incomprehensible to the adults . . . . In that moment, human culture was away and running. (Thomas, 1994, pp. 43–44)

In this vein, the person who acquires language with a sense of childlike wonder has an openness and curiosity that makes every day come alive with new learning. SLA, when done well, furthers the use and understanding of the first language as well. Time spent developing the imagination, in conjunction with time spent learning to communicate and learning how to learn, creates an agenda for English learning that uses powerful strategies to better the world.

Exploratory Break

- What is the most imaginative activity you have experienced in your native language? In your second language?

Chapter 9

Grammar through Integrated Language Skills and Wonderful English

English Is Democratic and Creative

Many learners of English have what Gardner and Lambert (1972) termed *instrumental motivation*: the desire to acquire a language for a specific purpose such as reading technical material or getting a job. Because in many countries a good command of English is a key to entrance into prestigious universities and attractive career prospects, students dutifully memorize vocabulary words and grammar structures. What may be missing, however, is a genuine appreciation for English as a language.

The tongue spoken by Winston Churchill, Eliza Doolittle, Louis Armstrong, and Huckleberry Finn, to mention but a few of the characters—real and fictional— whose words have held the world's attention, is replete with history, spellbinding in its poetics, and rich in nuance and connotation. Many people, however, have learned English in the form of decontextualized sentences, puzzling over structure as one would solve algebraic equations. It could be that as many English learners resent its complexity as love its gifts. How regrettable if one devoted so much time to mastering a language without acquiring a curiosity about word roots, a delight in witty puns, or appreciation of the turn of an elegant phrase.

> *Megastrategy* **SET 9**
>
> Teach language in a way that arouses a genuine interest in the history and beauty of English

English is the language of a fiercely independent people who struggled for centuries to attain personal freedoms. Freedom of speech is the first right that the American colonists demanded in exchange for approval of the Constitution. Freedom of speech is a far deeper right than a person's freedom to complain to a neighbor about high taxes. Freedom of speech includes the fundamental right of a learner to express oneself through reading, writing, speaking, and listening, and to study one's own personal and community culture as well as a larger target culture.

English as a language is not restricted by a national academy that decides what language is proper. In fact, language innovators—advertising copywriters and rap musicians, for example—continually exert pressure on English to change. The fundamental democracy of English is that all users have the right to torque the tongue to their needs and to their advantage. A learner should emerge from an English class with more diverse and creative language than on entry. The best way to do this is to integrate the study of grammar—the structure of language—with other receptive, expressive, and processing skills.

Grammar should not be the prison house of language, the subject of judgments about right versus wrong, correct versus incorrect, and acceptable versus unacceptable. Instead of being taught as a mental puzzle to be solved or as a series of rules to be memorized, grammar should be subordinated to larger, nobler purposes: the empowerment of the learner as a full-fledged member of the English community and the enhancing of the learner's freedom of expression and joy in learning English. Rules should serve not as shutters drawn against the storm of cacophony and chaos but as lenses to focus the rays of dawn at the birth of new words, postcolonial dialects, imaginative worlds of literary fancy, and calls to liberation and justice.

The sacred duty of a speaker of English is to treasure and respect the rights of others to honor English as only each individual can, by embedding in its words and phrases the depth and breadth of the struggle to be fully human. Teachers of English who remember and respect the role of English in the struggle for human rights will not use its current instrumental usefulness in the world as a tool to bind the learner to purposes that are ignoble, mean spirited, narrow, negative, or simply boring.

This chapter explores some ways in which proficiency in the structure of English can be combined creatively with other skills in the service of a deeper knowledge of the beauty, strengths, and challenges of English as a language. In this way, each learner of English can gain equal access to the rights and privileges of English as a world language.

Why Integrated Skills?

Integrated skills is an approach in which teachers and students engage in long-range units of study so that language is used for many meaningful purposes. Speaking, listening, reading, and writing are not separate subjects, taught as though they were an end in themselves. Instead, they are tools to be used in the service of something greater: exploration of the world and its complexity.

> *Megastrategy* **9.1**
> **Treat language as whole and integrate skills**

Teachers who involve the learner in thematic units, problem solving, or service learning show by these engagements that language is a tool for analysis, examination, and investigation, as well as presentation and celebration. As a part of integrated instruction, teachers provide a broad spectrum of activities that stimulate inquiry and advance language skills. Language is a preeminent tool by which students construct their own wisdom.

In an integrated skills classroom, the skills that constitute language arts are not separated. In the reading class, students might also be writing, speaking, listening, or thinking. Thematic units combine disciplines. Home and school are integrated; there is no sharp break between knowledge that stays at school and knowledge that can be brought home to enrich the home and community. As Dewey (1956) wrote, "From the standpoint of the child, the great waste in school comes from his inability to utilize the experiences he gets outside of school in any complete and free way; while, on the other hand, he is unable to apply in daily life what he is learning in school" (p. 75). An integrated curriculum—for example, growing a garden to study science, math, social studies, and language arts—mirrors the unity of real life.

Integrated Instructional Activities

Before taking a closer look at how one might integrate classroom activities by combining language skills, it is important to reexamine some assumptions about how language is learned. Table 9.1 contrasts common assumptions about language learning held by those who teach through focusing on discrete skills with those held by teachers who emphasize integrated language skills.

TABLE 9.1 *Contrasting Common Assumptions about Language Learning*

Discrete Skills	Integrated Language Skills
Mastery of oral language is a prerequisite to acquiring written language.	Oral and written language develop simultaneously.
Seeing written language interferes with acquisition of oral language.	Oral and written language can facilitate and support each other.
Skills are best taught in isolation.	Skills are reinforced by other modalities (e.g., reading by writing).
Language must be explicitly taught.	Neither oral nor written language is learned exclusively through direct instruction or specific tutoring. People learn by interacting with adults or others (e.g., older or more knowledgeable peers); by exploring the world on their own and interacting with others; and by observing others.
The teacher's role is to be language expert, language source, or language "cop."	The teacher is co-learner, explorer, and language "delightee."

Learner Output

Integrated skills furnish informative output. Output from language users gives the teacher three valuable kinds of information: a student's interests, preferred modality, and the nature of his or her interlanguage.

Students' interests are shown by their output. One student may be interested in pond fish and seek out books in English on the subject. Other students may be fascinated by graphic illustration; intricately designed web pages capture their full attention, and the words are noticed only if the visual design is appealing. Their own best work may take place using an integration of words with graphics. Some students' favorite use of language is to manage the behavior of others. The language teacher capitalizes on these interests.

Students' preferred channels of production are signaled by output. One learner may prefer conversation and learn to speak fluently before acquiring other skills; another may need to be in continual motion, perhaps willing to practice pronunciation as homework via headphones while lifting weights. With careful observation, the instructor can match activity to students' preferred information modality.

Interlanguage of the learner is revealed by output, the dynamic construction of what the learner understands about English. *Dynamic* means that the learner's system changes from day to day, even moment to moment. The learner's underlying knowledge, and hence interlanguage, is normally unstable. This instability is productive as long as the interlanguage is dynamic and growing toward improved English.

Productive Use of Errors. Errors show students' rule making is a window to the learner's interlanguage competence and learning strategies; it shows the ways in which learners are thinking about English. Teachers need to see English from the learner's point of view, paying careful attention to learners' errors to see what hypotheses they are using. Language, like other mental processes, is learned through "best guessing." In most exploratory activities, the mind uses guesswork and approximation when practicing. An atmosphere of acceptance of error helps the learner to take risks. Persistent errors, rather than random mistakes, provide insight into the learner's rule set.

Complexification, not simplification, is the key to language growth. As long as input is interesting, a learner can process a great deal of complexity and extract useful rules. Because this is not a conscious process, learners are often not aware of what they know until they try to produce output. One job of the teacher at the intermediate level of English development is to engender in the learner sophisticated communication needs that require more advanced language. This keeps language acquisition moving forward.

Content: Flexible, Thematic Curriculum

Recognizing the wholeness of knowledge, instruction is organized around broad themes that engage students in meaningful activities and focus on areas of inquiry rather than on specific skills. For example, students learn social studies by researching real-world questions that they have posed themselves. The question-driven format encourages focus on broader concepts that connect significant ideas and issues (Freeman & Freeman, 1998).

Thematic units provide a natural environment for the practice of language skills as students learn concepts in other areas of the curriculum. Through such means as filmstrips, films, videos, computer simulations, literature, nonfiction texts, and oral discussions, students are able to develop conceptual knowledge. Thematic units can incorporate history, geography, sociology, economics, values, information-seeking skills, group participation, and perhaps dramatic skills.

This move to a thematic approach to instruction has taken place primarily at the elementary level, although middle schools have also been reorganized so that content teachers can collaborate on instruction and can work together with the same groups of students. For examples of thematic integration at middle school, see Berman, Minicucci, McLaughlin, Nelson, and Woodworth (1995).

One teacher used a mind map to generate ideas for a thematic unit on spiders. The organizer is displayed in Figure 9.1. This illustrates how subjects are interwoven in thematic planning.

FIGURE 9.1 *Mind Map for Thematic Unit on Spiders*

Integrated curricula also open the door to language input from a wide range of sources. English as a language has a history of enrichment from multiple sources. Studying English as a language provides a rich, integrated look at history and linguistic change.

The History of English

Megastrategy 9.2

Arouse interest in the history of English

The rise of English is a remarkable success story. When the Romans landed in Britain nearly two thousand years ago, English did not exist. Five hundred years later, English, which would be incomprehensible to modern ears, was still spoken by very few people. Nearly a thousand years later, at the end of the sixteenth century, the time of William Shakespeare, English was the native speech of between five and seven million English subjects.

Four hundred years later, the contrast is extraordinary. Today, English is used by at least 750 million people, barely half of whom speak it as a mother tongue. Of all the world's languages, it is arguably the richest in vocabulary. The *Oxford English Dictionary* lists about half a million words, with a further 250,000 technical terms that remain uncataloged. Neighboring German has about 185,000, French fewer than 100,000.

English's teeming vocabulary is 80 percent foreign-born. Precisely because its roots are so varied—Celtic, Germanic, and Romance—it has words in common with virtually every other language in Europe. In addition, it contains extensive borrowings from Hebrew, Arabic, Hindi-Urdu, Malay, Chinese, and the languages of Java, Australia, Polynesia, and West Africa. The enormous range and varied source of this vocabulary, as much as the sheer numbers and geographical spread of its speakers, gives English unique vitality.

Supple in grammar, maddeningly inconsistent in spelling and pronunciation, English has its strengths and weaknesses. English as a world language is sustained by another elusive quality, its own peculiar genius. This genius was, and still is, essentially democratic. It has given expression to the voice of freedom from Wat Tyler to Tom Paine, to Thomas Jefferson, to Edmund Burke, to the Chartists, to Abraham Lincoln, to the suffragettes, to Winston Churchill, to Martin Luther King, Jr. It is well equipped to be a world language, to give voice to the aspirations of those who use English in developing countries as much as intercommunication among people in English-dominant nations.

The Birth of English

The story of English goes back to the earliest recorded days of Britain. Throughout its history, the island of Britain seemed to receive cultural innovation primarily through invasion and importation from overseas. The warlike Saxons invaded England when Rome withdrew its protection. They brought with them the language of Frisia, just across the English Channel to the east. With the Saxon conquest, new words came into English. For example, the Germanic prefix *wer-* meaning "turn" brought into English a host of words with the prefix *wer-* or *wr-* whose meaning involved turning. Finer clothes, in contrast to leather, could be washed and dried by wringing (turning), but this caused wrinkles. To illustrate the response of English to Germanic influence, Table 9.2 lists words that stem from the German prefix *wer-* (English *wr-*).

TABLE 9.2 *English Words Beginning with Wr-, Connoting Turning*

Word	Definition
wrap	to coil or twine about something
wreath	vines or branches twisted into a circle
wrench	to move with a violent twist
wrest	to twist something out of someone's hands
wrestle	to struggle, to twist the opponent to the ground
wriggle	to squirm, to make short writhing motions
wright	a worker who turns or forms wood on a lathe
wring	to extract water by turning cloth
wrinkle	a small furrow caused by twisting a fabric
wrist	bones that turn in the arm
writhe	to twist, as in distort
wroth	twisted up with anger
wry	to have a twisted shape or condition

By the time the Danish Vikings were able to conquer Saxon England, the land was rich with Christian monasteries containing gold, silver, jewels, and stores of food and wine. In 871 at the Battle of Ashdown, Vikings met Saxons; each took the other's measure and found that neither could prevail, so they coexisted. English became part Norse.

The ancient Saxon names for days of the week (from Old Frisen *wike*) subsequently changed. Tiew's Day, the day for the god of war, became Tuesday; Woden's Day, the day for the god of wisdom, became Wednesday; and Thor's Day, the day of the thunder god, became Thursday. Daily life mixed Saxon emotion (*weep* from Old Frisen *wépa,* to cry aloud; *laugh* from Old Frisen *hlacka*) with Vikings' food lore (*cook* from Danish *kok, ale* from Norse *öl*), Vikings' love of plunder (*weapon* has a cognate in Old Norse *vápna*), and Vikings' taste for personal comfort (*rug* from Norse *rugga; silk* from Danish *silke*).

Meanwhile, across the English Channel, Vikings who settled in Normandy viewed England as rightfully theirs. The Norman duke William the Conqueror invaded England in 1066 and subdued the whole island little by little, bringing with him continental culture. At first the Normans and the English did not mix, and the only Norman words used in English were words that a ruling class could force on a lower: *prince, duke, noble, servant, messenger,* and so forth. But before long, the English learned French, and Saxon notables sent their sons to France for education (Churchill, 1956). Gradually the two peoples intermarried, and a language developed that blended the Latin-based French with English to form Middle English.

The new language blending Anglo-Saxon and Norman French reflected a more sophisticated continental lifestyle and more abstract ways of thinking. Words from Latinate languages were used in conjunction with a noble lifestyle. Here is a description of how English changed:

> . . . a typical family lives in a Saxon *house* or *home,* or in a French *residence* or *domicile.* They eat a Saxon *breakfast* and a French *dinner* or *supper* at a Saxon *board* or a French *table,* seated on Saxon *benches* or *stools* or French *chairs.* Their Saxon *meal* or French *repast* consists of Anglo-Saxon foods like *milk, bread, broth, stew, baked meat, peas, beans, pie,* or of French foods like *cream, rolls, soup, roast, beef, pork, vegetables, fruit,* and *pastry.* They live in a Saxon *town* or *hamlet* or in a French *city* or *village.* Along the streets of the city or town you will see shops of Anglo-Saxon *bakers, builders, millers, shoemakers,* and *weavers,* alongside of French *carpenters, drapers, tailors, painters,* and *masons.* . . . [W]e see people wearing Saxon *shoes, hats, shirts, hose, gloves, coats,* and French *boots, robes, dresses, blouses, gowns, bonnets,* and *capes.* (Lambert, 1955, pp. 72–73)

The Dual Nature of English

As a result of the Norman invasion, English is a double language. For every Saxon-based word there is a conceptual double from the Latin side of the language. One may have *heart trouble,* but also a *coronary occlusion.* One may *try hard,* or *persist;* one may *request,* or *ask.* At a *party, buffet,* or *banquet,* one may *mix* or *socialize.* One may take a *snapshot* or a *photograph.* One may buy an *icebox* or a *refrigerator.* One may be *thrilled* or *delighted, joyous* or *merry, saintly* or *holy, fearful* or *intimidated,* and *desire* or *wish*. Choosing carefully among these synonyms can help to achieve just the right shade of meaning or nuance. As Lambert (1955) put it, "*sincere amity* is a little different from *hearty friendship,* and to be *welcomed heartily* is a little different from being *received cordially,* although in each case the basic meaning is the same" (p. 74).

The Latin side of the language is often used by bureaucrats who seek to use intellectual-sounding words to *hide* (*obfuscate*) simple truths: Thus, simple *slaughter* becomes *collateral damage,* and *war* becomes a *police action.* Being "let go" from a job can involve a series of euphemisms. Whether a worker hears *release of resources, involuntary separation from payroll, career-change opportunity, involuntary severance, career-transition program, reduction in force,* or *elimination of employment security,* it means the same: "You're fired!"

The English-language poet is not seduced by words derived from Romance languages. Anglo-Saxon English has the emotional power that "governmentality" lacks. Witness this stanza from the poem "Winding Down":

> Too hot! "Turn heater down." Too cold! We bicker . . .
> Lukewarm our love; stale, now flown the flicker
> That sparked that lust, so long awry.
> Where once love flowed the stream's gone dry. (Wallace, 1999)

In this poem, could *bicker* be replaced by the more modern term *argue*? The Old English word *bicker* has the emotional power that the word *argue* lacks; it connotes a battle, especially a domestic quarrel, whereas *argue* can be used in a court of law, dealing with more abstract issues. Similarly, *sparked* is more powerful than its synonym, *initiated*; *awry* is more wrong, bitter, or twisted than its counterpart from French, *astray*. In these instances, the poet has chosen words that are older, more basic, primitive, with more concrete imagery. In the process, the poet gains two more aspects of English that are poetic and pleasant: assonance and alliteration. These are discussed in the next section.

Using the Dual Nature of English for Effect.   The best writers in English have drawn conceptual elegance from the Latin side of English and emotional power and directness from Anglo-Saxon words. Shakespeare, for example, could tap from either the Anglo-Saxon, Anglo-Norman, or classical tradition. After Macbeth has murdered King Duncan, he laments what he has done:

> Will all great Neptune's ocean wash this blood
> Clean from my hand? No; this my hand will rather
> The multitudinous seas incarnadine,
> Making the green one red.

The allusion to Neptune flatters the listener who knows that Neptune is the Roman god of the sea; *multitudinous* is a long version of the word *many,* and in case the playgoers in the cheap seats miss the meaning of the graceful *incarnadine,* he translates the phrase into plainer terms: "Making the green one red."

The great writers of English have long taken advantage of the dual nature of English to draw on both sides of the language when they needed emotional power in combination with the force of intellectual abstraction. In 1775, Patrick Henry delivered a famous speech in Virginia to arouse support for the revolution that was brewing in New England. His speech reached into the hearts of his listeners by using ancient words from Anglo-Saxon English. Of the eighty-six words in this speech, try to figure out how many come from Old (pre-A.D. 1066) English:

Gentlemen may cry, "Peace, peace!"
but there is no peace.
The war is actually begun.
The next gale that sweeps down from the north
will bring to our ears
the clash of resounding arms.
Our brethren are already in the fields!
Why stand we, here, idle?
What is it that gentlemen wish?
What would they have?
Is life so dear, or peace so sweet, as to be
purchased at the price of chains and slavery?
Forbid it, Almighty God!
I know not what course others may take,
but as for me,
give me liberty—or give me death!

Whether or not Henry was conscious of this effect, only six words have Latin origin. Four of these are strung together in the powerful phrase "purchased at the price of chains and slavery"; ironically, he uses words that harken back to a time when England was conquered by the Normans to remind the listener in Latinate terms of the threat of punishment if the British are successful. The last of the six, *liberty,* that most abstract of terms, is used as the pivot point of his last, immortal phrase, linked emotionally with the final term, *death*. This is a fine example of a great speaker drawing power from both sides of the language.

Abraham Lincoln was one of the greatest writers in the history of English, writing more total words than Shakespeare. His Gettysburg Address uses both facets of English for the sake of power: ". . . we cannot *dedicate,* we cannot *consecrate,* we cannot *hallow* this ground." Only a master would follow the Latinate *dedicate, consecrate* with the ancient synonym *hallow,* with its connotation of both holiness and spookiness.

Winston Churchill's powerful language in his famous challenge to the Nazis during the Battle of Britain stems from the direct and concrete words of Anglo-Saxon English:

We shall fight on the beaches; we shall fight on the landing grounds, we shall fight in the fields and in the streets, we shall fight in the hills; we shall never surrender.

In his expression of stubborn determination, Churchill used words that could have been used in A.D. 1066 to repel the previous invader. Only the last word, *surrender,* comes from continental French.

Fortunately, despite the Norman attempt to civilize the uncouth population, throughout the centuries English has lost little of its raw, earthy spirit. One can still draw on Elizabethan English for a hearty insult if need be. In a fit of rage, one could use one or more of the following: *beef-witted, beslubbering, dog-hearted, elf-skinned, flap-mouthed, fly-bitten, fool-born, logger-headed, milk-livered, pox-marked, swag-bellied* or *toad-spotted.* What a pity these terms are mostly obsolete!

English: Innovative and Unregulated

The English used in Shakepeare's day was as open to innovation as it is today. In Shakespeare's time, people expected the playwrights to titillate them with new words, much as today's English users expect the same from advertisers. Shakespeare loved to experiment verbally. These words used by Shakespeare were all new to English in the sixteenth century: *allurements, armada, antipathy, critical, demonstrate, dire, emphasis, emulate, horrid, initiate, meditate, modest, prodigious,* and *vast.*

Disorderly Spelling.   In the centuries that followed, fiercely independent English writers considered it within their rights to spell words as they pleased. Only in the nineteenth century did people begin to attend to spelling rules, but by then it was too late; English spelling had escaped logic almost entirely. The following two sentences show the various spellings of the long "e" sound (/i/ phoneme): *Did he believe that Caesar could see the people seize the seas?* and *The silly amoeba stole the key to the machine!* Other vowels are just as disorderly; there are ten ways of spelling the long "i" sound (*bite, sight, by, dye, aisle, choir, liar, island, sign, height*) and six ways of spelling the /u/ phoneme (*boot, lute, who, sewer, through, two, Louis*).

It is not just the vowels that are unruly in English; consonants have their own lunacy. Witness the thirteen spellings of the /sh/ phoneme in English: *shoe, sugar, issue, mansion, mission, nation, suspicion, ocean, conscious, chaperon, schist, fuchsia,* and *pshaw;* the four ways of spelling the /f/ phoneme (*fat, philosophy, cough,* and *coffee*), six ways of spelling the /z/ phoneme (*zip, jazz, pads, Xerox, design,* and *scissors*); and five ways of spelling the /zh/ phoneme (*measure, vision, azure, casual, rouge*). It seems that English spelling is already too far gone to return to a simple sound–symbol correspondence. English learners have to face the fact that *come* and *dome* do not rhyme, nor *how* and *low,* nor *war* and *far.* Then there is the phonetic absurdity of *heart, beard,* and *heard.* Kant we do beter?

Semantic Oddities.   Another confusing feature of English is the fact that the same word can be used to denote exactly opposite meanings. The word *fast* can mean firmly fixed or immovable (stuck fast) or it can mean the opposite: rapid (to run fast) (origin: Old Gothic *faest,* strong, vigorous). The verb *trim* can mean to take off, to cut off irregularities (trim hedges); or it can mean to *add on,* as in decorate (trim a Christmas tree) (origin: Old English *trymman,* to make ready). The wealth of synonyms and ambiguity of meaning lend themselves to creative wordplay and riddles: Using synonyms, can you get from *good* to *bad* in five steps? (good = fine [very good]; fine = delicate [elegant]; delicate [precarious health] = ill [poor health]; ill [ill wind] = bad).

Lexical Innovation.   After 1066, England did not wait for waves of foreign language to wash ashore but went looking for it far and wide through international trade and, later, imperialism. For example, from what country are these English words taken: *cummerbund, bandanna, bungalow, calico, jungle, chintz, verandah, juggernaut, pundit, coolie, curry,* and *guru?* These terms originated from India but have long since abandoned their tropical flavor.

Nowadays, few can keep up with the lexical demands of a language in which the cyberworld coins sixteen new words in a single edition of the magazine *Wired.* The pace of technology is, if anything, accelerating; an issue of *Wired* dated July 2011 contains the following words and phrases not found in even the most recent dictionaries:

aeroroad

deck-hogging

din-quashing

footpod

gladvertising

photonic hyperhighway

sousveillance

zaptastic

The ceaseless innovation of English speakers is partially driven by technology and partly by other kinds of cultural change. In 1927, for example, two new words entered English, *airfield* and *co-pilot,* both due to airplanes. Other words entered English in 1930 that can be attributed to cultural change in general: the verbs *debut* and *hang around,* as well as the nouns *grandparent, myth, melanoma, gold digger,* and *fair shake* (Merriam-Webster, 2001b). Even further back, in the year 1789, *aristocrat* first appeared in print, as did new words from the world of politics such as *federalism, federal court, district attorney,* and *public land.* But there were plenty of miscellaneous new words that year also: *lapel, ego, immigrant, roommate, washstand,* and *tomcat;* the verbs *remodel* and *arrange;* and the adjectives *philanthropic, sickening, weathered,* and *working class* (Merriam-Webster, 2001a).

Pinker (2007) muses about the creation of new words in English:

What kind of things call out to be named? New words, one might guess, should materialize to name a concept that people need to talk about . . . But strangely enough, many concepts we long to name remain stubbornly nameless. We still don't have a name for unmarried romantic partners. (p. M9)

Not all the changes to English are welcomed by English speakers. Each time a new edition of the Merriam-Webster dictionary appears in print, critics complain about the slang words that are sanctioned. In 1961, for example, many American cultural innovations and imports from the 1950s appeared in the new edition of *Webster's*: *breezeway, split-level, fringe benefit, astronaut, beatnik, den mother,* and *zen.* However, critics ignored these newcomers and raised a ruckus about *ain't* (Pei, 1962).

Five Languages in One. Slang has been a big influence on new words in English, but it is not the only influence. In fact, one might accustom oneself to the fact that English is really five languages in one: the Anglo-Saxon tongue (Old English), words from Norman-influenced English (after 1066), English that is borrowed from other languages, slang, and scientific–technical English. Table 9.3 gives examples of these.

TABLE 9.3 *Examples from the Five Languages of English*

Anglo-Saxon (Old English)	Norman-Influenced English	English Borrowed from Other Languages	Slang	Scientific–Technical Vocabulary
hut	castle	hogan	pad space	cyberspace
like	relish		dig	:-)
seek	solicit		go for it	gopher
meet	encounter	powwow	hook up with	interface with
meeting	rendezvous	caucus	face time	synchronous interface
trade	interchange	swap		file transfer protocol
tool	machine	robot	tool	computer
get	obtain	swap	score	download
get mad	become furious	go on the warpath	go ballistic	flame
start	initiate		hit it	boot up
shoe	(podiatrist)	galoshes moccasins mukluks	Docs	boot-up (not a cognate)
mead, grog	vintner	tequila vodka alcohol	hootch	[rave drinks]
baby	infant	papoose	babe	generations of software
boss	executive	head honcho sahib	chief	Central Processing Unit
heaven	Celestial Kingdom	Valhalla happy hunting ground	bliss out	Nirvana Tao satori
gold	money	wampum	bread	credits/debits

How much time is wasted in the early stages of English-language acquisition holding students to norms of accuracy in spelling and syntax, when the same time could be spent teaching them to love the sound of words, to create elegant phrases, and to forge fresh and original sentences!

PRACTICES FOR TEACHERS

Teaching Students about the History of English

- Post favorite quotes from famous poets, politicians, or leaders—and share with students why the language is extraordinary.

- Challenge students to learn words in families that share the same Latin root (engender, generous, gentile, heterogeneous).

- Display English words from foreign languages and what they mean.

The Curiosity and Beauty of English

ESL and EFL instruction alike have invested heavily in promoting the academic success of English learners, yet students may not be exposed to the love of English. Teachers may fail to stimulate interest in learning more about English and exploring it to the limits of its immense and unique nature.

Assets of English

The English language itself has three key assets. First, gender-matching articles (like French *le* and *la*) are not required. Second, nouns and adjectives have simple endings, without a lot of morphemic declensions and inflections. Nouns can become verbs in a way that is impossible in many other languages (we can *park* our cars near the *park*, bus the children to *school*, and *school* them in English). Third, the vocabulary can be as simple or complex as the learner can tolerate. A subset of English called Special English, often used by the Voice of America, has just 1,500 words, although the *American Heritage Dictionary* contains about 200,000 of the 750,000 words amassed by the *Oxford English Dictionary* (Wallraff, 2000).

Megastrategy **9.3**

Arouse interest in English as a language

Complexities of English

Each of the assets above has an associated drawback. Although words are not declined with gendered endings, certain words are definitely associated with gender. One can be a *handsome* woman (although this seems to also indicate that the woman is not young); but to say a man is *beautiful, petite,* or *winsome* somehow undermines his masculinity. Conversely, one cannot call a woman a *hunk* or a *heavyweight* without impugning her femininity. These rules may not be obvious, but to violate them causes trouble.

The syntactic simplicity of English makes it easy to create idioms that conjoin verbs and prepositions. Who can quickly explain the differences between *sign up, sign on, sign over,* and *sign in*? Or distinguish *tune in, tune out,* and *tune up*? And the fact that nouns can become verbs (to *milk,* to *shoulder* [to *cold-shoulder*], to *partner,* to *fellowship,* to *carpool*) means that perfectly good verbs may be pushed aside by their noun counterparts, as in the replacement of the humble verb *confer* with *to conference,* the simple verb *eat* with the pseudospecific *to breakfast,* and the unadorned *write* with the fancier *to journal.*

And the ease with which new English terms are coined! Who can stay abreast of a language that can quickly combine nouns and verbs to form neologisms such as *hat hair* (mashed hairdo from wearing a hat) and *helmet hair* (squashed hairdo from wearing a bicycle or motorcycle helmet)!

English is curious, too, for the absurdity of some of its compound words. It is hard to explain how one can *drive* on a *parkway* but must *park* in a *driveway*; why there is no *egg* in an *eggplant* and no *ham* in a *hamburger*; or why *overlook* and *oversee* are opposites.

English has become even more complex with the accelerating jargon of the information age. English has even spawned subdialects consisting entirely of punctuation marks used in computer-mediated communication (emoticons, such as :-) [happy], ;-) [wink], :-o [surprised]; :-# [my-lips-are-sealed]). In addition, we now have instant messaging lingo such as BRB (be right back), TTYL (talk to you later) (Yost, 2000); INoUR (I know you are), YBS (you'll be sorry), (Mander, 2001); and number codes used conversationally (24/7, pronounced "twenty-four-seven," meaning "all day and all night"). WL C WHT HPNS 2 NGLISH as a result!

Not only are the spelling and rich synonym features of English confusing, but also English is rife with other odd peculiarities. English is not the only language to use classifiers, words that must precede particular nouns in the singular or plural. For example, in Chinese one would say "i-ben shu" (a book) but "i-ge" for many other kinds of things. But English certainly must score high among languages that feature weird classifiers (see Figure 9.2).

In some ways English has already spread confusion enough in the world by proliferating systems of measurement that people in the rest of the world are forced to reckon with, however much they might prefer the scientific simplicity of the metric: *dots per inch, picas, points, letter size/legal size, inches, feet, yard, furlong, light-years, acres, miles, pint, quart, barrel, shot, fifth, sack, carat, dram, ounce,* and *pound per square inch.* These terms are deeply implicated in both common life and technology, like it or not.

FIGURE 9.2 *Some Classifiers in English*

a pack of wolves	a piece or slice of cake
a herd of cows	a head of lettuce
a flock of birds	a scoop or dish of ice cream
a gaggle of geese	a slice of apple
a school of fish	a handful of cookies
a pod of whales	a piece or cut of meat
a cup of coffee	a stick or pat of butter
a glass of water	a spoonful or gob of peanut butter
a bunch of grapes	a coven of witches
a slice or loaf of bread	a pack of needles

Despite its deceptive simplicity of morphemes and its never-ending vocabulary innovation, English has retained its ability to host the best of the world's writers in its bosom. Naipaul, who writes in English as an Indian in exile who grew up in Trinidad, won the Nobel Prize in Literature in 2001. Nabokov, a renowned writer in English, was a native speaker of Russian. Joseph Conrad's native tongue was Polish. Yet the world is the richer for the beauty of their language and the depth of their insights.

Beauty in Nuance and Sound

In poetry the beauty of language lies in the sound value of the words, as well as in the ability of words to communicate subtle nuances of image, emotion, and meaning. Poetry permits a rarefied language that rises above the ordinary and says in a few compressed, well-chosen words what the orator cannot say in one hundred words, nor the tongue-tied lover say at all. Only in poetry could Shakespeare have a character look at the horizon and say, "But look, the morn in russet mantle clad / Walks o'er the dew of yon high eastward hill" (*Hamlet,* act 1, scene 1). He could have said, "Dawn is here," but this would have been the listener's loss.

Beauty, to the ear of the English speaker, lies in the combination of sound with meaning. Table 9.4 uses quotations from *Hamlet* to illustrate a variety of ways in which poetry can appeal to the English ear.

Of course, these devices can be combined to great effect, as in the following examples: internal rhyme combined with alliteration, as in "Till then sit still, my soul" (*Hamlet,* act 1, scene 2); assonance combined with alliteration, as in "Here's yet some liquor left" (*Hamlet,* act 5, scene 2); or meter and lexicon combined with assonance, as in "I could a tale unfold whose lightest word / Would harrow up thy soul" (*Hamlet,* act 1, scene 5). Good poetry is distinguished from the mediocre in

TABLE 9.4 *Some Sound Characteristics of Poetry**

Characteristic	Definition	Example from *Hamlet*
Assonance	Vowel sounds are repeated.	What is a man If his <u>chief</u> good and market of his time Be but to <u>sleep</u> and <u>feed</u>? A <u>beast</u>, no more . . . (act 4, scene 4)
Alliteration	Consonant sounds are repeated.	When <u>sorrows</u> come, they come not <u>single spies</u> But in battalions . . . (act 4, scene 5)
Anastrophe	Usual word order is reversed.	Madness in great ones must not <u>unwatched go.</u> (act 3, scene 1)
Internal rhyme	Rhyming words follow one another quickly.	<u>How now,</u> Ophelia! (act 3, scene 2)
End rhyme	Words rhyme at end of line.	The time is out of joint. O cursèd <u>spite</u>, That ever I was born to set it <u>right</u>. (act 1, scene 5)
Lexicon	Word choice is unusual.	Oh, Hamlet, thou has <u>cleft</u> my heart in <u>twain</u>. (act 3, scene 3)
Meter	Rhythm and flow of the line pleases the ear.	Good níght, sweet Prínce, And flíghts of ángels síng thee tó thy rést. (act 5, scene 2)

*Underlining added for purposes of illustration

that the sound serves the meaning and serves to make the poem pleasing to the ear as well as the mind. Paradoxically, the better the poetry, the more creative a relationship it breeds to the rules of sounds and syntax, which leads directly to a look at the teaching of grammar.

PRACTICES FOR TEACHERS
Helping Students Learn to Love English

- Put up a "Wacky Word Wall" or bulletin board on which students can post weird anomalies in English spelling or sounds.
- Give a prize for the week's strangest-sounding word.
- Collect and display word games or puzzles from the daily newspaper.

Teaching Grammar

The need to pay explicit attention to language structure in a classroom should be balanced by emphasis on a rich and stimulating learning environment. Second-language learners absorb and produce correctly formed sentences by listening and speaking, with the focus not on form but rather on social or academic language functions.

This is not to discourage teachers from working with students to refine sentence structures at later stages of language acquisition. The explicit teaching of grammar—that is, use of a structured text and workbook—should be part of a balanced language arts curriculum.

However, at the elementary level many teachers begin daily instruction with a misnomer called "daily oral language" (DOL). Rather than promoting fluent oral language, as would happen in an alternative activity that Cazden (1988) calls "sharing time" (students take turns telling personal anecdotes), DOL features students taking turns correcting a sentence written incorrectly on the board. Like other forms of "display knowledge" (see Chapter 11), those who already know which usage or punctuation rule is violated are quick to volunteer, whereas those who do not simply do not pay attention. Thus, DOL does not promote oral language; neither does it teach usage or grammar effectively. A systematic program of grammar is recommended as part of a comprehensive ELD program.

The topic of grammar seems to divide English teachers into three camps (Wilson, 2001). One camp, the *overt,* believes that students learn a language by mastering its grammar rules, usually by means of explicit teaching using memorization. The second camp prefers a *covert* approach, using directed inductive learning in a contextualized format (see Table 9.5). There is attention to grammar, but areas such as syntax might be taught using color-coded patterns, hands-on manipulation of sentence strips, and other ways to get students to internalize rules. The third approach to grammar, which might be called the *no-grammar* approach, expects that the mind will internalize rules by being exposed to language-rich situations. Each of these approaches might be useful in distinct situations.

Megastrategy **9.4**

Teach the structure of English explicitly but contextually

Without rules, language would be unpredictable, and speakers would have no common ground of agreement. The rules of a language govern what sounds right—for example, what is an acceptable phoneme in English. Phonemic errors cause speakers to have a foreign accent. Sometimes native speakers find this hilarious—think of Peter Sellers's character in the Pink Panther movies, Inspector Clouseau, who pronounced *bomb* as "bimb." More seriously, though, a foreign accent can serve as grounds for social and economic discrimination. Rules also govern semantics—remember how outraged Alice was in *Alice's Adventures in Wonderland* when Humpty Dumpty insisted that he could make words mean whatever he pleased? Syntax rules connect verb tense, morpheme use, and word order in a sentence.

Generally, people use the term *grammar* in two ways. One common use of the word considers what is proper and what is not. For example, the use of the subjunctive in English is often a social class marker. It takes years of schooling and exposure

TABLE 9.5 *Should Grammar Be Taught Inductively or Deductively?*

	Inductive	Deductive
Definition	Students' attention is focused on the structure being learned, and the students are required to formulate for themselves the underlying pattern—they infer grammar rules from examples (Shaffer, 1989, p. 395).	Regardless of the timing relative to the practice part of the lesson, students are given an explanation.
Advantages	• Supports cognitive research, in which the mind retains more from discovering patterns. • Focus is on end-use in meaningful situations. • Grammar is viewed as a tool or resource toward communication.	• Explicit teaching of a form results in explicit recall and production of that form on tests. • Students learn grammar metalanguage—how to talk about explicit forms.
Disadvantages	Grammar learned in a natural context does not promote learning explicit structures.	Grammatical terminology must be learned slowly—it is like its own foreign language.

Source: Adapted from Farrell (2006, pp. 47–49).

to those who use the subjunctive form correctly to say something like, "If he were related to me, I'd help him." Most commonly one would hear, "If he was related to me . . ." Aside from equating grammar to correctness, it can also mean, in general, "how sentences work."

Grammar as System

One student wrote this sentence in a draft of his master's thesis:

> ESL teachers meet more challenges from many directions than before, ESL teaching is no longer just teaching English vocabulary, grammar, or logistic knowledge only, social and psychological effects of American culture is getting more complicated, especially tragic events of terrorism on New York the impacts on ESL teaching, immigrant education are changing at rapidly speed.

Certain facets of this piece of writing defy the rules of English. First, so many disparate ideas are crammed together that they strain the bounds of sentence logic. Certainly, this excerpt demands to be more than one sentence. Second, the central clause lacks subject–verb agreement (effects . . . is getting). Third, the final phrase offends in cardinal ways; the phrase "at rapidly speed" is one that no native speaker would utter, and the morphemic error (using an adverb in a prepositional phrase) clearly betrays the writer as a nonnative speaker. The other errors, such as using a noun in place of a verb ("the impacts on" for "impacts"), article errors ("especially tragic events" instead of "especially the tragic events"), and redundancy (just . . . only) might be of less concern in the overall scheme of things; it is the basic syntax flaws that undermine the understandability of this writing.

Teachers of writing at many levels of schooling can use peer editing to help writers identify grammar errors and receive feedback. Thus, grammar is integrated into the oral conversation between editor and writer. Most teachers do not give students feedback on grammar errors in speech, preferring to recast sentences correctly as they respond to the content of students' talk. Thus, grammar is integrated into conversation. Rather than study grammar as a "stand-alone" system, it is more often studied in the context of writing correction.

Grammar and Emotion

Learning the grammar of a foreign language is not just a cognitive act; it involves feeling. Rinvolucri (1984) relates many examples of the ways in which learners react to grammar emotionally. In one story, a young French speaker really liked the *-ando* (progressive ending in Spanish) because it feels ongoing and, well, progressive. Requests can be made more emotionally acceptable using "polite" phrases: "May I go first?" No wonder incorrect use of grammar is so negatively sanctioned; people react to grammar with emotion. Rinvolucri uses this emotion in the service of teaching. He offers students sample sentences and asks them to enter them on the chalkboard under two categories: NICE and UGH! Students use their emotions to accept and reject syntactic structures.

Box 9.1 **Keeping it CRISP**

Clear, Relevant, Interesting, Short, and Productive (CRISP) is an acronym invented by Farrell (2009) as an approach to grammar instruction. Farrell follows Brown's (1994) guidelines that grammar instruction "[be] embedded in meaningful communicative contexts; contribute[s] positively to communicative goals; promote[s] accuracy with fluent communicative language; do[es] not overwhelm students with linguistics terminology; [is] lively and intrinsically motivating" (p. 349). To be CRISP is to . . .

- have a *Clear* objective so that students can follow your presentation easily;
- teach a grammar form that is *Relevant* to the forms that the students are already using;
- Make it *Interesting*;
- *Productive* means that students can use the grammar form in their lives outside the classroom.

TABLE 9.6 *Cognitive, Affective, and Drama Activities That Teach Grammar*

Activity	Description
An article's article (Definite and indefinite articles)	Students form two teams. A reader reads an article aloud but says "Bleep" instead of the articles. Students mark a score sheet with the missing article: *a, an, the,* or nothing (#). (1)
Jumping to conclusions (Comparisons with gerunds)	Students receive a survey sheet with the names of all class members. At the top of the page, they write a comparison using two gerunds (Example: *Swimming* is more fun than *riding* a bicycle). They survey the class, entering answers *Agree* or *Disagree.* (1)
Conditional chain reaction (Conditional sentences)	Students are seated in a circle. Student A makes a conditional sentence ("If Fred took a trip, he would go to Paris"). The next student uses the final clause to make a new conditional sentence ("If Fred went to Paris, he would climb the Eiffel Tower"). (1)
Shopping list (Count and noncount nouns)	Half of the students are players seated in a circle and half are reserves standing outside the circle. The first player uses a count noun ("I went to the supermarket and bought a few lemons"). The second player repeats the previous entry and must add a noncount noun (. . . some sugar). Alternate using count and noncount nouns in the sentence. A player who fails to take a turn correctly is replaced by a reserve. (1)
Brainstorming structures (Present perfect)	Give students sample prompts: Good Experiences I Have Never Had, and Bad Experiences I Have Never Had. Students brainstorm answers, and a recorder writes them on the board. (2)
Your words—My grammar (Present perfect continuous)	Write a sentence in the target structure on the board. Students must replace every word but the target with the same part of speech. (Example: Who's *been* eating my porridge?) Students write answers on board, and the class votes yes or no for correctness. (2)
I spy (Review vocabulary)	A student who is "it" says, "I spy something in the classroom. What is it?" Go around the room in order as the other students have to ask, "Is it the wastebasket?" etc. When someone guesses correctly, the next person is "it." (3)
Buffet (Prefixes and suffixes)	Students receive a list of 40 prefixes (Appetizers), 18 roots (Main Courses), and 35 suffixes (Desserts). Students try to form correct words using two or three of each (for example, "in-duct-ion"). Students check answers with a dictionary; to receive credit, the word must be accompanied by its meaning. (3) Hint: Use a book that features words of Greek and Latin origin such as Horowitz (1977).

Sources: (1) Kealey & Inness, 1997; (2) Rinvolucri, 1984; (3) Steinberg, 1983.

Grammar Games

Games for use in the service of grammar are presented in Table 9.6. Using games for this purpose serves several functions. Students have to take responsibility for learning the grammatical structures in order to play the game, and the teacher can use the game to take an informal inventory of students' mastery. The serious work of grammar mastery takes place in the context of fun, and games that last ten to fifteen minutes fully engage the learner during that time (Rinvolucri, 1984). The games in Table 9.6 are for beginning-level students, and none requires much advanced preparation.

Although some might argue that games teach grammar out of context, the social context of having fun might overrule that caveat. For the most part, grammar corrections are subordinated to the meaning that is conveyed. For example, when master's degree students are at the point of incorporating a theoretical framework into their theses, the conversation that ensues is about ideas. The last thing that comes to my mind as their adviser is to correct their grammar. The ideas that are conveyed are far more interesting and important. This same principle governs the integration of grammar into learning.

Correct Usage and Discourse Competence

Prescriptive Language and Usage Wars

Should road signs read *drive slow* or *drive slowly*? Which is grammatically correct? And what about the Apple Computer Company's former slogan "Think Different": Is that poor grammar? If *books* is the plural of *book,* what's wrong with *yous* as the plural of *you*? Are "between you and I" and "between you and me" both right, and who decides what's right and what's wrong in language, anyway? And who put *ain't* in the dictionary?

Megastrategy **9.5**

Teach respect for correct usage in English

Linguistic variation is inevitable and natural. Languages often have alternative expressions for the same thing ("steal" and "appropriate"), and a given word can carry a different meaning as a different part of speech. Languages naturally adapt to their situations of use and also reflect the social identities of their speakers. In some countries, language academies have been established to settle such matters, but English has no such regulating body. Instead, those who write dictionaries and grammars and columns in daily newspapers are often seen as authorities.

Who decides whose language is right? Some observers claim that the real issue about prescribing right and wrong language usage is one of deciding who wields power and who does not. Stigmatized forms of language are typically used by social groups other than educated middle-class professional people such as lawyers, doctors, publishers, and so on. Linguists generally argue that the language of non-middle-class social groups is no better or worse than that of educated middle-class speakers. Teachers who enjoy and honor the English that students produce balance that respect with concern that students know what is acceptable usage and are able to produce it when warranted.

In many English-as-a-foreign-language elementary classrooms, emphasis has shifted from direct instruction of grammar to a focus on communicative language teaching.
©AVAVA/Shutterstock.com

A Schema for Literature, ESL, Grammar, and Usage

A beginning teacher called me one day and asked for help; she had so many language arts books that she needed advice on how to plan the best use of students' reading and language arts time.

> I arrived at her classroom to find her sitting behind a tall stack of fourth-grade curriculum materials. She had a basal literature anthology with supplementary workbook, teacher's manual, and testing booklet; an ELD series comprising a teacher's manual, student reading books, student homework book, and testing materials; a grammar series comprising a teacher's manual and workbook; and a spelling series comprising a teacher's manual and student workbook. In addition, she had a student library with books for independent reading and many reference materials that accompanied the social studies curriculum. If she were to teach from each of these elements, her language arts period would be ten hours long! How could I help her bring order out of teacher-planning chaos? And what was the role of explicit grammar teaching in a curriculum that depended heavily on promoting reading skills?

In response to the need expressed by this fourth-grade teacher, I designed the following four-part schema to guide the teaching of reading and language arts (see Figure 9.3). Each quadrant is based on a different set of curricular materials. Assignments that combine objectives in more than one domain help to integrate these approaches. In this plan, acquisition vocabulary (learning new words) is separated from production vocabulary, which is associated with correct usage (spelling). Students are not expected to be able to spell the new words they acquire in literature, but simply to understand their meaning in context. The same might be said for concept vocabulary acquired through social studies or science. Moreover, the study of

FIGURE 9.3 *Schema to Guide the Teaching of Reading/Language Arts*

Literature:
Using the basal reader or chapter books, students learn to read for enjoyment and love of language, study character, and acquire vocabulary.

Language Arts:
Using the ESL series, content-based ESL is integrated thematically with social studies and science, and promotes critical thinking and cognitive academic language proficiency.

Grammar:
Using a grammar textbook, students learn parts of speech and correct sentence structure as a part of systematic grammar instruction.

Usage:
Students use a spelling workbook that groups words together according to similar rules. Explicit attention is paid to capitalization and punctuation in writing, as well as to handwriting.

literature is an end in itself, and students should not be required to use it to learn spelling or social studies. Thus, the selection of stories that students read is supplemented, not dictated, by thematic integration with other content domains. Last, correct usage such as punctuation, capitalization, and paragraph structure is emphasized in the context of composition, but that is by no means the sole goal of writing.

Integrating Grammar into the Curriculum

Awareness of sentence structure can be enhanced with various learning activities. Table 9.7 offers some ways to have students work creatively with sentences.

Explicit teaching of particular features of grammar and usage should, if possible, be drawn from actual (anonymous) student work. If an entire class has difficulty with a similar set of structures, it may be beneficial to use a workbook to make the instruction systematic. For example, almost all English learners have difficulty with the use of articles. Cole's (1997) *The Article Book* has exercises that go through the use of

TABLE 9.7 *Activities to Develop Awareness of Sentence Structure*

Activity	Description
Sentence expanding	Students start with a simple sentence ("The jetliner flies.") and make it into a richer sentence by adding details ("The giant, four-engine Northwest jetliner flies above the skyscrapers.").
Sentence linking	Students chain sentences together by reading a detail-rich sentence and then using a phrase from that sentence to start a new sentence. ("This evening, a storm might drop six inches of snow." New sentence: "Six inches of snow is enough to cause a big traffic jam.")
Sentence shopping	From a passage that has varied sentences, students have a "shopping list" of sentence types to find (shortest; longest; compound subject, etc.).
Sentence swapping	One student starts a story about a common subject, such as getting dressed in the morning. After writing one sentence, the student passes the paper to the next person, who writes one sentence to continue the idea.

Source: Based on Suid & Lincoln (1992).

articles and offers principles, examples, and quizzes. It is exemplary professional practice to use the right workbook for the right application.

Grammar Texts. A grammar book that presents a systematic reference for ELD writers is an indispensable feature of the curriculum. Without such an aid, a teacher cannot be expected to explain grammar points with a suitable degree of accuracy. Byrd and Benson's *Problem-Solution: A Reference for ESL Writers* (1994) is an excellent resource, covering pedagogical grammar points with clear explanations and examples. Moreover, pedagogical grammar for students at every level is a must. An excellent grammar for TESOL educators and a classic in its field is Master's *Systems of English Grammar: An Introduction for Language Teachers* (1996).

A reason to work closely with students to improve their usage skills (handwriting, correct spelling, paragraph coherence, and correct use of punctuation) is that mainstream teachers often base their expectations for students on such salient features of their written production. Therefore, ELD teachers do students a great service by emphasizing—but not overemphasizing—correct usage. As students write—whether for purposes of critical thinking, reaction to literature, or in project-based learning—some part of that writing should become a final product in which correct usage is required.

Usage Games. Games can be used to practice correct usage. Students can be given a copy of a passage in a book retyped with the punctuation removed. Students in working groups restore the missing periods, commas, and so forth. Correct usage can also be a part of various writing tasks. As students write about a trip they are planning to take around the United States, they pay particular attention to the correct use of capital letters. As they bring in a recipe from home for a class meal, they learn how to use the imperative form of the verb. Thus, correct usage and grammar can be incorporated into a host of learning activities.

A Balanced Approach to Grammar.   Teaching grammar is one part of the overall reading and language arts and content curriculum and at best is integrated with these subjects. Teachers who enjoy students' language creativity and variety while still teaching rules of language will promote English learning to high levels of academic achievement while fostering enjoyment of English. The effect that English learners have on English itself is to expand the language, as it has expanded before, to accommodate new speakers with new needs and desires. Contemporary English is undergoing the same kinds of changes that have contributed to making it the rich, flexible, and adaptable language so popular throughout the world today. The job of ELD educators is to teach that language to the world.

Exploratory Break

- To learn English grammar, do you think it is necessary to know grammatical terminology? Are you familiar with grammatical terms? If not, what is your plan as an ELD teacher to acquire terminology about grammar?

Chapter *10*

Culturally Based Language Teaching

Culture and Language Teaching

Teachers of English learners are first and foremost language teachers. But unlike those who teach English to native speakers, they are also intercultural educators. Those educators who learned English in an English-speaking culture have the advantage of an unconscious understanding of this culture, whereas those who learned English but whose primary socialization took place in a non-English-speaking environment have a different perspective. Just because one is raised in a certain culture, however, does not necessarily mean that one can explain that culture to others. Teachers of English learners benefit from education about the mutual impact of language and culture. *Intercultural educators* are experts who understand culture to the extent that they can teach about culture to others.

Studying one's own culture is a domain of learning like any other, perhaps made more challenging because people may find it difficult to see the invisible matrix in which they operate on a daily basis. Culture has many components that influence behavior at an unconscious level. Schools and teachers are cultural transmitters. Habits of teaching and learning are cultural products. Language teaching as an educational process is intimately involved with culture and its transmission.

Before beginning to explore the language–culture connection, it is important to define what is meant by culture. The following definition serves as a reminder that culture is not only about art museums and ethnic dances, but also about people's everyday lives and worldviews:

> *Megastrategy* **SET 10**
>
> **Use culture to teach language**

Culture is the explicit and implicit patterns for living, the dynamic system of commonly agreed-on symbols and meanings, knowledge, belief, art, morals, laws, customs, behaviors, traditions, and/or habits that are shared and make up the total way of life of a people, as negotiated by individuals in the process of constructing a personal identity.

To understand culture, one must look beyond the obvious to understand how values, codes, beliefs, and social relations are continually being reshaped by shifting parameters of place, identity, history, and power. Rather than individuals being excluded for differing from cultural norms, people with dissonant, flexible, complex, and hybrid racial and ethnic identities struggle to generate new meanings within accommodating contexts as they use experimentation and creativity to rework existing configurations of knowledge and power and thus extend the possibilities of being human, even in the face of an uncertain outcome.

Culture involves not only observable behaviors but also intangibles such as beliefs and values, rhythms, rules, and roles. Rather than seeing culture as an invisible, patterning force, it is more useful to see it as an active balance between the "social shortcuts" that make consensual society possible and the contributions and construction that each individual creates while fashioning a life that is satisfying.

Commenting on the language–culture connection, Strevens (1987) had this to say:

First, language is but one element of the complex, seamless fabric of the total culture of a society. Of course language is an immensely important element which informs and shapes other elements, yet is in turn shaped by them. It is not possible to say how far language influences the rest of the culture, and how far culture influences language. What is clear is that there are deep and indispensable links between the two.

Second, "language" . . . embraces much more than vocabulary, grammar, and phonology. It includes also the subtle and only partly comprehended mechanisms for interpersonal communication which are grouped under the general rubric of discourse. These mechanisms are partly linguistic, partly paralinguistic, and partly non-linguistic; they include the individual's rules for social comportment; they are subject to individual variability.

Third, difficulties of understanding in cross-cultural circumstances are other cultural as much as—or more than—linguistic in nature. (pp. 170–171)

Teachers who function as intercultural educators acquire a sense of the difficulties faced by English learners. However, many prospective teachers initially are unaware of their own cultural values and behaviors and how these might be at odds with the home cultures of students. Those who are willing to engage in self-assessment activities are often richly rewarded with a deeper understanding of their professional and personal lives. The goal of such assessment is to enable prospective teachers to sustain intercultural contact, foster culturally responsive pedagogy, and develop the skills of advocacy for, and appreciation of, English learners.

Intercultural educators use a variety of terms in cultural education (see Table 10.1).

TABLE 10.1 *Terminology Involving Culture*

Term	Meaning
Intercultural communication	Exchange taking place between two or more speakers who have been socialized into different cultures
Intercultural education	Interchange between teacher and student who have been socialized into different primary cultures
Crosscultural education	The study of how people from different cultures view and practice education (Lustig & Koester, 1999)
Multicultural education	Educational practices that ensure students equal opportunity to learn in school regardless of their gender, socioeconomic status, ethnicity, religion, physical or mental abilities, or other cultural characteristics (Boutte, 1999)
Native culture (NC)	The culture in which the primary language was acquired along with the primary socialization
Target culture (TC)	The culture in which the target language is used (the target culture for English must be specified, because English as a target language varies depending on which culture is the model, such as Australia, India, New Zealand, Canada, or South Africa, in addition to Britain or the United States; the pronunciation and lexicon vary distinctly depending on this choice.)
Bicultural	Having intimate knowledge of more than one culture
Long-term intercultural empathy	The ability to shift easily between cultural frames of reference (Bennett, 1996a, p. 15)

The Skills and Responsibilities of the Intercultural Educator

Culture influences the teaching of English to speakers of other languages in six basic ways. Each can become a component of instruction. First, the learner has learned how to learn by means of native culture patterns, values, and behaviors. Teachers who are acquainted with the norms and patterns of the native culture will better understand how students learn, especially how they learn L2. This component relates to *culturally derived learning styles and strategies.*

Second, the intercultural educator accommodates to students' culturally derived learning styles and strategies in order to deliver effective instruction. Because cultural patterns are difficult for the individual to analyze or alter, it seems unlikely that a group of learners can or will change their culturally based habits as they learn English. Teachers of English learners make whatever accommodations may be necessary to promote students' academic achievement. This component is called *culturally compatible instruction.*

Third, learning a language becomes easier when the whole personality of the learner is engaged. The learner who acquires English takes on a set of patterns, habits, and behaviors suitable to a multilingual lifestyle. Learning to add facets to one's identity rather than suffering identity conflict or loss might be called *assuming a bicultural identity.* The intercultural educator helps students to adapt to shifts in identity and values that may occur.

Fourth, the native culture and the target culture each provide rich content for instruction. However one defines culture—as literature, art, and music or as the daily life of a people—the *ideas* that language conveys give learning English meaning and purpose. Whether these ideas come from the native culture or from the traditions embodied within English, *culture can serve as academic content.*

Fifth, building on the idea of culture as content, English teaching can incorporate the comparison of cultures, both in terms of culturally based learning styles and strategies and in terms of ideas or behaviors. This component might be called *crosscultural studies.*

The sixth component is *using intercultural communication to teach English.* As an international language, English is often used by individuals who share no other common language. The use of English in intercultural communication can easily be accomplished using Internet chats, e-mail pen pals, or other forms of computer-mediated communication. In addition, many bilingual programs are set up so that English-only students can mix with non-English-speaking students during "mainstreaming" classes; all students then benefit from the opportunity to interact and to discuss this interaction as content.

This chapter outlines those general areas of culture that teachers will find most useful and then presents techniques for learning about students' cultures. Teachers can use their knowledge of students' cultures to design appropriate classroom organizational procedures and teach in a culturally responsive manner.

Culturally Derived Learning Styles and Strategies

Any learning that takes place is built on previous learning that has taken place in the context of families. Children learn verbal and nonverbal behaviors appropriate for their gender and age and observe their family members in various occupations and activities. The family teaches them about love and relationships with friends, kin, and community members. They watch as community members cooperate to learn in a variety of methods and modes. Their families give them a feeling for music and art. They learn to use language in the context of their homes and communities, to share feelings and knowledge and beliefs. Indeed, they are native speakers of the home language by the age of five and as such can express their needs and delights.

The culture that students bring from the home is the foundation for their learning. All cultures provide an adequate pattern of living for their members. Therefore, no children are "culturally deprived." Certain communities may exist without middle-class resources. Poverty, however, should not be equated with cultural deprivation. Every community's culture incorporates vast knowledge about successful living. Teachers can use this cultural knowledge to enhance students' learning in schools.

Megastrategy **10.1**

Learn about how culture affects learning

Culture is not just a collection of artifacts used by a people; neither is it just about types of food or celebrations, symbols, souvenirs, or lifestyles. And although many people use "culture" to represent "high culture" or the high-status events of elite groups, culture is not about the activities of privileged social classes. Some aspect of culture belongs to every person within a society and is embodied by everyday objects and events.

In-depth background on the culture and history of all minority groups in the United States is clearly beyond the scope of this book (see Díaz-Rico & Weed, 2010). However, all cultures share general features. These features are discussed here along with ways in which insightful teachers can use this general knowledge in their classrooms. For further reading, Buckley (2000) features a set of common parameters shared by cultures that help to organize the complex terrain of intercultural communication.

Values, Beliefs, and Practices

Values are "what people regard as good or bad, beautiful or ugly, clean or dirty . . . right or wrong, kind or cruel, just or unjust, and appropriate or inappropriate" (Lustig, 1988). Each culture uses a set of values to manage social life. Values cannot be seen, heard, or tasted, but they deeply influence social customs. Teachers concerned about the success of all their students make every effort to understand the different ways in which cultures organize individual and community behavior, ways that on the surface may not seem compatible with school practices and beliefs. To understand these differences is to help students bridge home and school differences.

Social Customs

Social customs dictate norms of daily life. These customs are paced and structured by habitual use of time and space. Conflicts may arise when teachers use *time* in different ways than families do. For example, teachers who demand abrupt endings to activities in which children are deeply engaged or pace instruction strictly by the clock may confuse and depress students whose family life is not regulated in this manner. Many teachers find themselves in the role of "time mediator," helping students meet their learning needs within the school's schedules.

Use of *space* is another aspect of cultural experience. Personal space varies; in some cultures individuals touch each other frequently, whereas in others, touch and proximity may cause feelings of tension and embarrassment. In the United States, touching often shows dominance—a higher-status individual may throw an arm around the shoulder of a lower-ranking individual, but the reverse is not acceptable.

A cultural sense of space influences the rooms and buildings in which people feel comfortable. The organization of the space in the classroom sends messages to students: how free they are to move about the classroom and how much of the classroom they "own." Space can be negotiated to provide a classroom setting in which ownership is shared.

Other symbolic systems, such as dress, personal appearance, and facial makeup, also convey meaning. In fact, these are prominent class markers in U.S. schools. The "right" clothing and accessories are considered status symbols; conversely, the "wrong" ones mark some students for ridicule. Other symbolic systems are intrinsic, such as beliefs about natural phenomena, luck, and fate. Because European-American culture views nature as something to be conquered, natural forces greater than human control cause great anxiety. People's behavior during harsh weather often demonstrates this.

Rites, Rituals, and Ceremonies

Each culture celebrates formal events such as holidays, births, marriages, and deaths with specific rites. Schools have ceremonies; in the United States, assemblies often begin with the Pledge of Allegiance. Rituals in some elementary classrooms in the United States are also relatively formal; students must line up and wait for the teacher. Greeting and welcome behaviors vary across cultures. The sensitive teacher understands how students and parents expect to be treated and incorporates some of these behaviors in conversation and instruction.

Work and Leisure Systems

Crosscultural variation is evident in work and leisure activities. In mainstream U.S. cultures, work is valued over play; that is, one's status is directly related to one's productivity, salary, or job description. Play often reinforces job status; for example, executives conduct business informally on the golf course. Young people are trained to use specific tools of play, and their time is structured to attain these skills. The expectations for work and play activities for girls and boys also vary by culture.

In work and play groups, the orientation may be to the *individual* or to the *group*. U.S. society is widely regarded as one in which the individual is paramount. In Japan, by contrast, individuals compete fiercely, but accompanying this value is a sense that one must establish oneself within a group; being singled out for attention or praise by teachers may therefore result in embarrassment (Furey, 1986).

Health and Medicine

Health and medical practices involve deep-seated beliefs because the stakes are high: life and death. Each culture has certain beliefs about sickness and health that may affect schooling, and when students come to school with health issues, teachers need to react in culturally compatible ways. Students may have health problems stemming from war trauma, culture shock, poverty, family violence, or crime, but teachers and the family may view these problems in very different ways, resulting in miscommunication. Students from some cultures may respond negatively to attention from mental health professionals or counselors.

Institutional Influences: Economic, Legal, Political, and Religious

The institutions that support and govern family and community life are embedded within cultural behavior and beliefs. In the United States, for example, religious practices are heavily embedded but formally bounded: Some citizens complain about Christmas trees in schools, but retail businesses depend on increased consumer spending at the close of the calendar year. When immigrants with strong religious beliefs encounter the largely secular institutions of the United States, cultural patterns may be challenged or cause conflict within the family.

Language-Related Behaviors and Beliefs

The role of language and nonverbal expression in communication varies widely by culture. *Kinesic* behavior, including facial expressions, body movements, postures, and gestures, enhances a verbal message. People from such cultures are highly tuned to nonverbal messages that a teacher may be sending. *Paralanguage,* the nonverbal elements of the voice, can affirm or belie a verbal message. *Proxemics,* the communication of interpersonal distance, varies widely across cultures. Last, but not least, *olfactics,* the role of smell in interpersonal communication, may constitute a factor that is powerful yet often overlooked. Even the use of silence differs dramatically across cultures. In the United States, silence is interpreted as expressing embarrassment, regret, obligation, criticism, disagreement or sorrow; in many Asian cultures, however, silence is a token of respect.

Attitudes toward language are also a part of the messages teachers send. In the example below, Hang Nguyen and her family were immersed in a new language and culture when they fled Vietnam to seek sanctuary in the United States in 1983. Hang felt that the messages her daughter received caused much conflict and unhappiness within the family:

> My daughter is bilingual, but only half bilingual because she doesn't know how to read and write. She only speaks Vietnamese. She was four years old when she came over, and she started kindergarten early. So since she was five years old she has been bombarded with the ideas "You live here. You have to speak the language. You have to learn the way to live here. Your language is not important. Your language is an embarrassment. If you learn your language you will not be able to learn English. English is the main language here." That's the message she got. It was not always obvious, but she would be told, "You need to go home and practice your English.

You need this . . . you need that . . . "and I think that was enough to poison her mind against what she stands for. (Stiel, 2002, p. 187)

Educational Systems

Educational systems in the past were designed to pass on cultural knowledge and traditions; however, in the increasingly complex and technological society of the United States, schools have shifted their emphasis. Students come to school already steeped in the learning practices of their own family and community. Many of these practices may not support the type of learning to which students are exposed in school.

For immigrant children with previous schooling, experience in U.S. classrooms may engender severe conflicts. For example, Indochinese students expect to listen, watch, and imitate. They may be reluctant to ask questions or volunteer answers. The teacher might wish to support their initial dependence while gradually introducing student-centered practices.

Teachers who seek to understand the value of education within the community can examine the following questions: What methods for teaching and learning are used in the home (e.g., modeling and imitation, stories and proverbs, direct verbal instruction)? What role does language play in learning and teaching? How are children expected to interact (observe only, ask questions, volunteer)? Understanding different perceptions of schooling is an important step toward accommodating those differences.

Culturally Compatible Instruction

Megastrategy 10.2
Align the culture of schooling and the learner's culture

Teachers can play an important role by learning about their students' communities and cultures and thus reducing the culture shock between home and school. The best way for a teacher to understand culture is to understand his or her own teaching and learning styles and then investigate to what extent each student is similar or dissimilar. Direct personal observation of social behavior or ethnographic study may be used to understand students' cultures from the perspective of the members of those cultures. This understanding can then be used to organize classroom activities in ways that promote educational achievement for all students.

The study of culture is important because groups of students may be similar in their reactions to schooling. With this cultural knowledge, classroom routines can be organized to encourage more effective learning, and information about the students' cultures can be incorporated into the content of instruction. In a multicultural classroom, there may be no single best way for students to learn. Using a variety of activities that appeal to different students in turn may be an effective strategy. The observation cycle continues as teachers watch students to see *which* approaches meet *whose* needs. The intercultural educator is sensitive and flexible.

Ethnographic Study

Ethnography seeks to provide cultural explanations for behavior and attitudes. This field of inquiry is useful in exploring the ways in which students' cultural experiences at home and in their community compare with the culture of their schools. The classroom teacher becomes not only an observer of the students' cultures but also an active participant. To understand the home and community cultures, teachers may participate in community life, interview community members, and visit homes. To understand the school culture, teachers may observe in a variety of classrooms, record and/or videotape classroom interaction, and talk with other teachers and administrators.

Self-Study

Teachers who engage in self-exploration activities that help them understand and appreciate their own origins and values may find it easier to understand the cultural behaviors of others. One can start a cultural inquiry by investigating one's personal name, asking, "Where did I get my name? Who am I named for? In which culture did the name originate?" Self-examination includes identifying one's favorite cultural customs, such as holiday traditions, home decor, and favorite foods, as well as one's stance on such issues as individual freedom, competition, and the value of work. Introspective questions help to pinpoint one's own cultural attitudes (see Box 10.1). The process is challenging and ongoing. One teacher explained how her cultural background influenced her teaching:

> I admit to being rather sheltered when I went to do my undergraduate work and then my teaching credential. Having grown up in a very European American, middle-class, suburb city, our schools were very European American. . . . [T]here were a few minorities, but we never got to know anything about them. . . . It wasn't until I was in my junior year in college that I got the opportunity to study in Costa Rica. There a whole new world opened for me. . . . [M]y year in Costa Rica taught me how different and alike we all are. Their rich cultural values, the love for family, respect for others, and their kindness were so reassuring. I finally understood the importance of learning about other cultures. (Delgado-Gaitan, 2006, p. 85)

Cultural Observations

Observations of students' cultures include looking at students' use of language within the community; etiquettes of speaking, listening, greeting, getting or giving information; values; and aspirations—in short, the categories of culture described in this chapter. When analyzing the culture of the classroom, one might look at classroom management and routines; affective factors (students' attitudes toward activities, teachers' attitudes toward students); classroom talk in general; and nonverbal behaviors and communication.

Box 10.1   Cultural Self-Study: Self-Exploration Questions

Describe yourself as a preschool child. Were you compliant, curious, adventuresome, goody-goody, physically active, nature-loving? Have you observed your parents interacting with other children? Do they encourage open-ended exploration, or would they prefer children to play quietly with approved toys? Do they encourage initiative?

What was the knowledge environment like in your home? What type of reading did your father and mother do? Was there a time when the members of the family had discussions about current events or ideas and issues? How much dissent was tolerated from parental viewpoints? Were children encouraged to question the status quo? What was it like to learn to talk and think in your family?

What kind of a grade school pupil were you? What is your best memory from elementary school? What was your favorite teacher like? Were you an avid reader? How would you characterize your cognitive style and learning style preferences?

Was the school you attended ethnically diverse? What about your secondary school experience? Did you have a diverse group of friends in high school?

What is your ethnic group? What symbols or traditions did you participate in that derived from this group? What do you like about your ethnic identity? Is there a time now when your group celebrates its traditions together? What was the neighborhood or community like in which you grew up?

What was your experience with ethnic diversity? What were your first images of race or color? Was there a time in your life when you sought out diverse contacts to expand your experience?

What contact do you have now with people of dissimilar racial and ethnic backgrounds? How would you characterize your desire to learn more? Given your learning style preferences, how would you go about this?

Source: Díaz-Rico & Weed (2010).

Interviews

Interviews are *structured* or *unstructured*. Structured interviews use a set of preselected questions to gather specific kinds of information. Unstructured interviews are more like conversations on a wide variety of topics. When learning about a new culture, the classroom teacher would be well served initially to begin with general questions and be guided in follow-up questions by the interviewee's responses. The result of the initial interview may lead to a second interview. Agar's *The Professional Stranger: An Informal Introduction to Ethnography* (1996) is a useful book about ethnographic interviewing.

Home Visits

The home visit can be a "social call" or a brief report on the student's progress that enhances rapport with students and parents and helps teachers learn what is familiar and important to their students. A short visit (twenty to thirty minutes) is best, but some hosts may expect a longer stay. Viewing the child in the context of the home provides an opportunity to observe the parent–child interaction, the resources of the home, and the child's role in the family.

Sources for Learning about Cultures

Teachers can use books, magazines, and videos to learn about other cultures, or they can draw on students, parents, and community members for insights about values, attitudes, and habits. Students generally provide teachers with their initial contact with other cultures. Through observations, shared conversations during or after school, and group participation, teachers gain understanding about various individuals and their cultures.

Educators who form relationships with parents can talk about culture and schooling. Teachers can ask students to interview their parents about common topics such as work, interests, and family history. In this way, students and parents together can supply knowledge about community life.

Community members are an equally rich source of cultural knowledge, especially about such areas as housing, popular meeting places for different age groups, and sources of food, furniture, and services. Through community representatives, respected elders, or religious leaders, teachers can become familiar with important living patterns of a community. They can also attend local ceremonies and activities to learn more about community dynamics. Websites on the Internet can introduce the curious to other cultures. The Internet can also be a source of materials for the study of students' cultures.

Culturally Responsive Teaching

The selection of a particular teaching method often reflects cultural values, whether conscious or unconscious. There may be conflict between the patterns acquired at home and those demanded by the school. However, it is not enough simply to explain children's differential school success as a cultural mismatch between home and school. Teachers who understand students' cultures invite students to learn by welcoming them, making them feel that they belong, and presenting learning as a task at which they can succeed. Teaching styles, interaction patterns, classroom organization, curriculum, and involvement with parents and the community are all factors that are within the teacher's power to adapt to achieve the goal of culturally compatible teaching.

"Culturally relevant teaching" is one approach to intercultural communication (Ladson-Billings, 1994). Prospective teachers may need to be observed closely and objectively so they can be offered feedback on practices that encourage classroom equity. Prospective teachers may also need to participate in sessions that raise self-awareness of racism in practice in the classroom (see Díaz-Rico, 1998, 2000). New forms of instruction are necessary that promote equity, and new forms of communication must be developed that allow teachers to believe in their students' capacity for high achievement and to communicate that belief to the students.

Preparing for Culturally Responsive Teaching

Gay (2002) focuses on four key areas of culturally responsive teaching that play a key role in using students' backgrounds as the basis for instruction:

- developing a knowledge base about cultural diversity (What are the cultural characteristics of various groups? What are multicultural teaching strategies?);
- designing culturally relevant curricula (What books can be used to incorporate diverse histories, stories, and images? How can we be sure these materials are free of bias?);
- demonstrating "cultural caring" by eliminating bias in the classroom and conveying a sense of equal positive attention towards all students; and
- building a learning community using intercultural communication to bring families into the school as partners, especially making available primary-language-speaking teachers and staff members.

PRACTICES FOR TEACHERS

Culturally Responsive Teaching

- Building on students' culture supports them as intellectual leaders in the classroom.
- Teaching in an integrated, coherent way helps students to feel a part of a learning community.
- Students' real-life experiences legitimate their contribution to the "official" curriculum.
- A broader conception of literacy includes literature and oratory.

Source: Ladson-Billings (1994)

Promoting Diversity as a Resource

Some critical theorists argue that ELD teaching and learning are incomplete without inclusion of a critical analysis of such issues as gender and race. Taylor (2004) described an antidiscrimination camp held in 1999–2000 for ESL students within the Toronto School District, one of the most racially and culturally diverse school districts in North America. Students representing more than seventy different language groups came together for three days of activities and discussions that explored students' personal understandings and experiences of xenophobia, ethnocentrism, linguicism, sexism, classism, and hetereosexism. Through this curriculum, students could explore their complex identities and transcultural histories, as well as gain insight into the perspectives of others.

Another source of diversity is sexual orientation. ELD teachers who establish a classroom ambiance of inclusion can foster respect for individuals no matter what their sexual orientation. Such respect can literally be lifesaving. Gay, lesbian, or bisexual adolescents who face a hostile school climate or undergo harassment, verbal abuse, or physical abuse, may become truant, drop out, or resort to suicide or substance abuse (Nichols, 1999).

> It can be an uncomfortable topic. A student...is teased because of perceived sexual orientation. Some teachers and principals don't get involved. This might seem like an issue best left out of the classroom, but there's a population of gay, lesbian, bisexual and transgender (GLBT) students who feel unsafe at school. (Martin, 2011, p. 9)

Educators have a legal responsibility to respond to students' bullying one another. GLBT teens commit suicide at three to four times the rate of other students. Martin (2011) recommends four ways educators can create safe schools for GLBT students:

- Establish a "gay–straight alliance," a student club where students can talk about issues related to sexual orientation;
- Provide anti-bullying training, emphasizing GLBT issues;
- Develop the presence of supportive staff (who are not necessarily GLBT themselves); and
- Include GLBT figures in the curriculum.

Teacher–Student Interactions

Teacher–student interaction may derive from parent–child relationships or from values transmitted by the parent toward teachers and schooling. Attitudes toward authority, teacher–student relationships, and teachers' expectations of student achievement vary widely. In the United States, respect is shown to teachers by looking at them, but in some cultures looking at the teacher is a sign of disrespect. In some parts of the world, it is acceptable to call a teacher by his or her first name, indicating that relations between teachers and students are warm, close, and informal. In other cultures, teacher–student relations are formal, without an emphasis on rapport.

> Over the past two weeks, Carol Freedman, a fourth-grade pull-out ESL teacher, noticed that Katya Stepanova, a recent Russian immigrant, had grown increasingly quiet and more withdrawn, and that she seemed very unhappy. She had stopped working with other students and kept

to herself in class. In speaking with Katya, Mrs. Freedman found that the girl was confused about life in the United States, discouraged about the progress she was making, and sad that people believed Russia was a cold and gloomy place. After that conversation, it was Carol who was dismayed and confused. How could she help Katya (Egbert, 2005)?

Classroom Organization and Curriculum

The typical classroom is that of a teacher-leader who gives assignments or demonstrations to the students, who act as audience. Teacher presentations are usually followed by some form of individual study. Learning is then assessed through recitation, quizzes, or some other performance. Any deviation from this—group work, individual projects, group problem solving, or class discussion—requires explicit cultural adaptation for students to these new ways of behaving and speaking. Teachers can help students adapt by providing clear instructions and models, and by assigning self-conscious students minor roles at first in order not to embarrass them.

Many aspects of the school curriculum are highly abstract and contain themes and activities for which some students have little point of reference. The biggest challenge for all educators is to engage students of all backgrounds equally in a stimulating, yet understandable, curriculum, with instruction organized in a way that meets their learning needs.

Assuming a Bicultural Identity

Megastrategy **10.3**

Motivate the learner to achieve cultural fluency

People communicate their identities (personality, intellectual ability, interests) to one another by means of culturally based interaction patterns. Aspects of identity are not only individual but also characteristic of subgroups in a society, and they circulate through society by means of discourse (Foucault, 1984). Cummins (1996) argued that students' success or failure is determined largely through the process of identity negotiations between teachers and students. When students learn another language and then learn by means of the second language, maintaining and supporting a strong sense of identity and self-esteem are important (Cummins, 2000b).

When people use language in any discourse context, the meaning is shaped and constrained by that context, whether it is interpersonal, institutional, or sociocultural. This in turn influences the discourse that the individual produces. Identity is shaped and determined by social configurations, distinctions, categories, and practices. Taking on new language practices inevitably requires a new set of intrapersonal configurations.

Shen (1998) found the act of academic writing in English to require cultural and ideological reformulation: "learning the rules of English composition is, to a certain extent, learning the values of Anglo-American society" (p. 124). Shen found that to obey the dictum to express her "voice" ("Just be yourself!"), she had to construct an American self, different from her Chinese self, and become *that* self: a mask that was confident, assertive, even aggressive. In the end, the identity she forged was a balance between these two aspects. In retrospect, she would have liked the instructor to help her to confront the cultural differences more directly, rather than assuming that the "real" self was the Western construct.

Technologies of the Self toward Identity Development

Teachers who use humanistic techniques, including interactive journals and self-esteem exercises, draw on what Foucault calls a "technology of the self," which he defines as a set of techniques that permit individuals to transform themselves (Foucault, 1988). But what exactly is the "self"? In fact, *self* is an elusive concept because concepts of identity differ across cultures.

The idea of the *self* in postmodern thinking has taken on certain characteristics: as multiple rather than unified identity; as a decentered site of struggle rather than a centered, essentialist core; and as a flexible, changing response to the contexts of the external and internal world rather than a fixed structure of personality (B. N. Pierce, 1995; Weedon, 1987). Modern themes of self-expression, self-fulfillment, and self-actualization have been gradually replaced in the postmodern mythos with a realization that the external world is pushing against the self with its own forms of restraint, including threats of ecological disaster, the decay of community, and the loss of universal values.

For many students, a subjective sense of self is secure within an identity based on traditional sources (family, race, neighborhood, nationality). But in the complex, technologically based contexts in which English is now used, traditional identities may not be as important as negotiated identities—specific, utilitarian aspects of personality suitable for the workplace or for instrumental relationships. Verbal language thus becomes increasingly important.

Many students from collectivist cultures see the United States as a culture that values individualism, in contrast to cultures in which self-identity is grounded at least in part by the thoughts and feelings of others in a specific referent group. In Japan, for example, self-identity is predicated on interactive reflection, with strong social pressure to subordinate one's individualism to the well-being of others. Doutrich (2000) commented on this sense of self: "Without knowing one's position and without the caring of others, the sense of self may fade . . . ." (p. 147).

Many English learners are aware that their sense of self shifts as they move back and forth from their native language to English. Doutrich (2000) described the ability to move back and forth freely between cultures, smoothly, with grace and flexibility, as "cultural fluency" (p. 142), borrowing the term from Poyatos (1984). This means one must be able to change and undergo personal transformation, as well as maintain flexibility and openness to change.

New Forms of Literacy Shape New Forms of Identity

Instant messaging (IM) not only involves reading and writing as a central part of its practice—but it also depends on the assuming of flexible identities that require a highly developed awareness of the audience and context for each exchange. (Although there are many English learners whose families lack access to the Internet, almost all young people in the United States have a cell phone used for sending and receiving texts.)

Lewis and Fabos (2005) reported the extent to which the teens they researched had to shape, perform, and elaborate their identities through electronic media in order to use IM to sound "with it":

> The identities our participants enacted in IM had to sound—and look, semiotically— like speech, but be accomplished through writing. Sam had to write her way into the textual worlds of the new group to which she wanted to belong . . . to "talk like they do . . . " [on IM]. (p. 495)

Cultural Marginality

One might ask whether the English language, as a vehicle for postmodernity, is a Trojan horse, bringing the unwanted cargo of negotiated identity into a citadel of traditional context for the self. Even if this were true, little alternative exists to global cultural change except the defiant rejection of such influences. Probably a wiser course would be to embrace biculturality as a positive outgrowth of cultural marginality (see J. M. Bennett [1993] for an exploration of the concept of "dynamic in-betweenness"), so that those who learn English can feel themselves enriched by an expanded set of personal and cultural alternatives enabling them to maintain roots in the native culture while sprouting wings in English.

Many members of oppressed groups are forced to become bicultural to work or attend school and to participate effectively in their own ethnic communities. Different behaviors are expected in the two settings. To be successful on the job usually requires proficiency in the ways of the dominant group. Because most schools reflect the dominant society, students are forced to adjust (or act "white") if they are going to be academically successful.

Many students feel caught in the pressure to assimilate or accommodate. A useful position for intercultural educators is to accept a role at the margin, and as M. Bennett (1996a) recommended, choose to associate themselves with cultural difference. In short, teachers of English learners can play an important role in helping institutions accommodate students' needs.

Culture as Content

Part of the richness and delight found in teaching English learners is the opportunity to teach and learn about culture. I confess I am a cultural traditionalist in some ways. I put ornaments on the Christmas tree every year, and I love to color Easter eggs and carve jack o'lanterns. At the same time, I can accept the gifts of cultural exchange: Christmas tree ornaments made of origami, sugar skulls celebrating El Dia de los Muertos, and multiple New Year's celebrations throughout the year. Students who are from other cultures enjoy learning the traditional symbols of American holidays and participating in seasonal pastimes, just as English-language cultures are opening up to the celebrations, customs, and beliefs of English learners. This cultural exchange generates deep feelings and emotions to enrich our mutual relations.

Why Teach Language Using Culture?

> *Megastrategy* **10.4**
>
> **Teach English using the learner's culture as well as the target culture**

Teaching English using the *learner's culture* as well as the *target culture* makes English more accessible. Teaching English to elementary students in Taiwan, for example, using the children's book *Legends of Ten Chinese Traditional Festivals* (Li, 1992) permits the students to draw on their cultural knowledge as they make sense of English. Teaching Mexican immigrant children English using a tour of Mexico as content helps them to feel pride in their heritage, and fluency is advanced much more if they know what they are talking about. Later in this section, several sample native-language cultural units for English teaching are described.

Culture of the Target Language

Teaching target language means presenting information to English learners about the cultural context of the language. If one is learning English in Australia, the target culture is that of Australian English-speaking peoples, whereas if one is in inner-city Detroit, the target culture is probably African American. In the rhetoric of English as an international language, there is no good reason for target cultures always to be those of native English speakers. Yet for purposes of illustration, I speak here of the target culture as being mainstream United States American.

Bringing rich cultural context into the classroom can motivate students to learn English.

©Big Cheese Photo LLC/Alamy

Resources for teaching American culture are vast. One might read about the Founding Fathers, country or punk rock music, African American women's liberation (hooks, 1989), schooling in Hawai'i (Jordan, Tharp, & Baird-Vogt, 1992), or Native American art. Table 10.2 offers an annotated list of reading anthologies about American culture, all at an intermediate or advanced reading level. Table 10.3

TABLE 10.2 *Resources for Readings about American Culture*

Source	Description
American Voices: Webs of Diversity (Quintero & Rummel, 1998)	Readings about aspects of American culture (multicultural education, family values, social issues) are informed by critical theory perspectives.
American Ways (Althen, 1988)	Readings offer ways to understand Americans (for foreigners who are visiting or sojourning in the United States).
The American Ways (Datesman, Crandall, & Kearny, 1997)	Readings about aspects of American culture (education, family, leisure time) are accompanied by workbook-type comprehension and vocabulary exercises.
The Yin and Yang of American Culture (Kim, 2001)	American culture—its virtues and vices—is viewed from an Eastern perspective.

TABLE 10.3 *Resources for Information about Native American Cultures*

Resource	Description
Chants and Prayers (Padilla, 1995)	Spiritual messages in the form of chants and prayers rooted in Native American oral traditions
Spirit Walker (Wood, 1993)	Poems with Native American themes, beautifully illustrated
Myths and Legends of the Indians of the Southwest (Dutton & Olin, 1995)	Brief introduction to the Hopi, Acoma, Tewa, and Zuni cultures
Great Native Americans (Copeland, 1997)	Brief illustrated biographies of forty-two outstanding Native Americans from the seventeenth to the twentieth centuries
A Rainbow at Night: The World in Word and Pictures by Navajo Children (Hucko, 1996)	Paintings by Navajo children, featuring their photographs and biographies
Native American Traditions (Versluis, 1994)	History of Native Americans in their contact with European culture, with many illustrations of cultural artifacts and historical personalities

presents a sampling of books about Native American cultures on topics ranging from art and history to rituals, stories, and prayers.

American holidays are fun to teach about, especially when they involve family activities and even more when they are about love. Valentine's Day scores high on this index. Yet as with any other cultural content, it is not enough to relate to it only at a superficial level, one of behaviors or artifacts. The most important cultural content is at a deeper level, the level of values and beliefs. Box 10.2 presents an instructional plan that teaches about some typical American holidays and shows how to have fun with Valentine's Day. Table 10.4 (p. 284) presents vocabulary associated with various holidays celebrated in the United States.

One interesting way to learn about the European roots of American culture is to use the Inner Child Cards, a fancifully illustrated deck of cards based on European folk- and fairy tales (Lerner & Lerner, 1992). (See the demonstration lesson: "Contacting the Inner Child," Box 10.6, p. 285). This promotes communicative activity and pair learning.

English Teaching Using the Native Culture

English can be taught using themes derived from native cultures. Lesson plans might feature such topics as Japanese fairy tales (see Nishimoto, 1997); Chinese fairy tales; a puppet play based on Chinese horoscope animals; a dramatization of the Chinese folktale "The Magic Sieve"; Japanese cultural artifacts such as kites, dolls, and pottery; and other topics pertaining to the native culture. These are particularly useful at the elementary school level, a time when children should learn more about their own cultures. One instructional unit compared English and Chinese proverbs and folk sayings using as a resource Chinnery and Chu's *Corresponding English and Chinese Proverbs and Phrases* (1984), a source that is useful at several levels of instruction. A similar unit can be developed using Mexican folk sayings, or *dichos* (Sellers, 1994), or Hawaiian proverbs (Provenzano, 2001).

Using the learner's culture to teach English comes with a price—teachers need to take the time to use accurate information that represents the culture in an authentic way. It is important to have a native-culture consultant available with whom to verify cultural content. In addition to presenting information about the learners' culture(s), the teacher who can act as an advocate for that culture and its customs and values shows an adaptive, integrative view about culture. This serves as a model for students to acquire this view as well.

Bias in Teaching about Culture

Teachers with good intentions but lacking a solid foundation of cultural knowledge are often guilty of cultural bias. One type of bias is trivializing the cultural content of the curriculum. The sole cultural reference may be to holidays or food, or they may have "ethnic" bulletin boards only during certain times of the year (e.g., Black History Month). Books about children of color are read only on special occasions, and units about different cultures are taught once and never mentioned again. People

Box 10.2 Instructional Plan: American Holidays and Valentine's Day

Level: ESOL speech emergence or intermediate fluency, all age levels

Objectives

1. To survey American holidays
2. To explain American Valentine's Day customs and compare with L1 customs for Valentine's Day or other similar holiday (see Box 10.3)
3. To connect culture with language: candy heart messages
4. To make Valentine cards

Task Chain 1: American holidays

- Connect vocabulary and conceptual knowledge about holidays (see Table 10.4).
- Participants practice quizzing each other on vocabulary.

Task Chain 2: American Valentine's Day/crosscultural comparison

- Participants read Box 10.3 and compare with their native cultures (pair/share, group share).

Task Chain 3: Candy heart matching (see Box 10.4)

- Play Candy Heartbreak:
  Two teams in relays (fly swatter game)
  Half of candy heart is on wall
  Instructor shows half heart; first person in line reads message, seeks matching half of heart (by message) to swat. (one point for each winning swat)

Task Chain 4: Making Valentine cards

- Participants make cards for their "Valentines."
- Use construction paper, doilies, paste, glue, adhesive tape, ribbon, scissors, stickers, candy hearts, cookie cutter shapes.
- Draw names randomly from a hat. Put a Valentine's message inside the card by selecting three adjectives that you think represent this person (see Box 10.5).
- Exchange cards.

Assessment: Vocabulary

- U.S. holiday matching quiz (based on Table 10.4)

Box 10.3 Valentine's Day Customs

Children exchange Valentine cards in elementary school. Each child brings one for each classmate. Adults buy Valentine cards for their significant others; sometimes they buy a box of chocolate for each other. A desperate lover may buy twelve red roses for his object of passion. Parents buy cards and candy for their children. The holiday used to be called "Saint Valentine's Day"; with the increasing secularization of United States culture, "Saint" has been dropped.

Box 10.4   Focus Sheet for Valentine's Day Activity

The Idiom of Candy Hearts

One of the traditions of Valentine's Day is the tiny candy heart. Below are the messages you may find on the hearts. Some messages are from the new millennium!

Traditional Messages

SWEET TALK	REAL LOVE
CALL ME	CUTIE PIE
I HOPE	ONLY YOU
I'M SURE	MY BABY

"Twenty-First-Century" Messages

E-MAIL	WHAT EVER
GOT LOVE	EZ 2 LOVE
MUCH ADO	GET REAL
COOL DUDE	UR MINE

Box 10.5   Adjectives Used on Valentine Cards

glamorous	artistic	sincere	dependable	easygoing
sensitive	friendly	competent	magnetic	perky
adventurous	attentive	imaginative	thoughtful	upbeat
even-tempered	generous	sociable	determined	elegant
expressive	gentle	stable	outgoing	personable
agreeable	sensible	courteous	tranquil	pleasant
faithful	charming	strong	passionate	energetic
ambitious	cheerful	creative	trusting	entertaining
firm	graceful	sweet	patient	polite
amusing	serious	intuitive	dynamic	wise
flexible	compassionate	deep	peace-loving	enthusiastic
articulate	hardworking	kind	unselfish	witty

Choose three adjectives that you think best describe you:

_____   _____   _____

Choose three adjectives that you would like to become:

_____   _____   _____

Interview your partner. Ask what traits he or she would like to acquire. List three adjectives that your partner would like to become:

_____   _____   _____

TABLE 10.4 *U.S. Holiday Vocabulary*

American Holiday	Vocabulary
New Year's Eve (December 31) New Year's Day (January 1)	Noisemakers, "Happy New Year!"
Valentine's Day (February 14)	Box of chocolate candy; Cupid; love notes; a dozen red roses; "Will you be my _____?,"
St. Patrick's Day (March 17)	Irish, shamrocks, green
Easter (first Sunday after first full moon after spring equinox)	Bunnies, crosses, Easter egg hunts
Fourth of July (July 4), Signing of Declaration of Independence	Firecrackers; red, white, and blue; parades; picnics; neighborhood parties
Halloween (October 31)	Candy corn, orange and black, skeletons, "Boo!," costumes
Thanksgiving (fourth Thursday in November)	Indian maize, turkey dinner, gobble gobble, cranberries
Christmas (December 25)	"Jingle Bells," Season's Greetings, Santa Claus, ornaments, red and green
Hanukkah (25th of the Hebrew month of Kislev—sometime between the end of November and the end of December)	Dreidel, menorah

from cultures outside the United States are seen only in "traditional" dress and rural settings or, if they are people of color, are always shown as poor. Native Americans may be represented as from the past. Moreover, students' cultures are often misrepresented; pictures and books about Mexico, for example, are used to teach about Mexican Americans, or books about Africa are used to teach about African Americans (Derman-Sparks and Anti-Bias Curriculum Task Force, 1988).

In her article "Educating Teachers for Cultural and Linguistic Diversity: A Model for All Teachers," Parla (1994) discussed issues related to the multicultural classroom and included information on cultural sensitivity, linguistic diversity, and teaching strategies to help teachers improve their understanding of cultural issues and translate that understanding into classroom practice.

The following checklist can help teachers assess the extent to which ethnic, linguistic, and gender biases exist in the curriculum:

■ What groups are represented in texts, discussions, and bulletin board displays? Are certain groups invisible?
■ Are minorities and women treated in a positive, diversified manner or stereotyped into traditional or rigid roles?

Box 10.6 Demonstration Lesson: "Contacting the Inner Child"

Level: High School or Adult
(intermediate fluency)

Objectives:

1. To identify key European fairy tales
2. To experience personally target-culture mythical figures and compare these with native-culture figures
3. To explore means of thinking about personal decisions and choices

TESOL Standards:

Standard 1 English language learners communicate for social, intercultural, and instructional purposes within the school setting.

Standard 2 English language learners communicate information, ideas, and concepts necessary for academic success in the area of language arts.

Warm-Up:

Brainstorm with students to see how many English-language fairy tales they can name.

Task Chain 1: European American Fairy Tales

- View *The Wizard of Oz* and identify key figures.
- Identify key figures in *Sleeping Beauty.*

Task Chain 2: Target-Culture Mythical Figures—Crosscultural Comparisons

- Cultural background: What are tarot cards? Major Arcana versus Minor Arcana.

- Each person chooses three cards from the Inner Child pack (Lerner & Lerner, 1992).
- Each pair identifies and discusses the cards, offering crosscultural comparisons if available.
- Each member of a pair orally describes two cards.

Task Chain 3: Thinking about Personal Decisions and Choices

- Using the Inner Child cards, each pair plays Turn the Corner. One partner thinks about a personal decision.
- Turn the Corner directions: Choose one card from the pack and lay it face up (card of the past). Choose another card from the pack. Lay it face up below the first card (card of the present, which "turns the corner" of your fate). Choose another card from the pack. Lay it face up beside the second card (card of the future)
- Given time, discuss personal anecdotes relating to game

Final Assessment: Thinking about Personal Decisions and Choices

1. Write a brief description of the cards that appeared in this activity. How did the images relate to your situation?
2. Self-assessment: Write in one or two sentences what you gained from this activity.

- Are the problems faced by minorities presented in a realistic fashion, with a problem-solving orientation?
- Are the materials written using inclusive language, or do they contain biased terms such as masculine forms (*mankind, mailman*)?
- Does the curriculum foster appreciation of cultural diversity?
- Are experiences and activities included besides those common to middle-class European American culture?

Crosscultural Studies

Comparing various aspects of cultures can result in rich thematic units used for teaching English. One such unit might compare communication styles in Korea and the United States; yet another might compare marketing, advertising, and product placement across several cultures. Simultaneous comparison of multiple cultures is fascinating. An instructional unit comparing Korean Chusook and American Thanksgiving, for example, should include a third celebration, El Dia de los Muertos, because many customs of Chusook are similar to the Aztec elements of picnicking at family graves. In fact, they may have originated in the same peoples, if one believes that the Aztecs migrated to the New World from the northern Asiatic peninsula. Comparing three cultures avoids the dichotomy of "my culture versus American culture."

Achieving Ethnorelativism

Megastrategy **10.5**

Teach English by comparing cultures

Bennett (1996a) called *ethnorelativism* the state of being able to accept cultural differences, adapt to them, and integrate them into our own personality. This means that one must understand culture not as artifacts, but rather as values, behaviors, and other patterns. In addition, ethnorelativism allows a discussion of cultural generalizations without stereotyping people and accepts that all cultures and races consist of varied groups of individuals, who may or may not exemplify a particular cultural predilection. Thus, one can talk about the "primary tendency" of a cultural group in relation to some trait without insisting that all people fit a particular generalization.

Many students are particularly interested in crosscultural analyses of behaviors and values. Table 10.5 presents an annotated guide to several representative books from this genre. Intercultural Press (www.interculturalpress.com) is an excellent source for books in this genre. In contrast, Table 10.6 presents books relevant to minority cultures within the United States.

Deeper Crosscultural Comparison

The only concern when comparing cultures is to ensure that the content of such comparison goes beyond the superficial aspects of culture (holidays, food, and Cinderella tales) and delves into the values that people of different cultures bring to their celebrations. This process may, however, cause some degree of discomfort.

For example, Americans who compare Halloween with the Mexican celebration El Dia de los Muertos (Day of the Dead) may find superficial similarities in costumes and sugar candy. This superficial similarity masks deeper differences, however. The sugar candy in Mexico is in the shape of skulls, and most Americans probably find it distasteful to eat a skull because of the cultural avoidance of the subject of death. The underlying dissimilarity that might prove even more distasteful to some Americans, however, is the cultural belief of the Aztecs (who may have originated the

TABLE 10.5 *Sample of Books on Crosscultural Behaviors and Values*

Resource	Description
Understanding Spanish-Speaking South Americans (Stephenson, 2002)	A study of cultural themes that underlie behaviors and beliefs in Latin America, with a focus on nine specific countries
Business Taiwan: A Practical Guide to Understanding Taiwan's Business Culture (Kenna & Lacy, 1994)	A concise guide to business practices and customs in Taiwan (including communication styles, body language and nonverbal cues, negotiating, and contracting)
Old World/New World, Bridging Cultural Differences: Britain, France, and the U.S. (Storti, 2001)	An assortment of dialogues illustrating fundamental differences in cultural behaviors and beliefs
Understanding Arabs: A Guide for Westerners (Nydell, 1997)	Insights into the complexities of nineteen distinct Arab cultures

TABLE 10.6 *Books on Minority Cultures within the United States*

Resource	Description
Multicultural Education: A Teacher's Guide to Linking Context, Process, and Content (Hernández, 2001)	Strategies for studying students' backgrounds and for adapting instruction accordingly
Educating for Diversity: An Anthology of Multicultural Voices (Grant, 1995)	Specific readings on fifteen American cultural groups, as well as other types of diversity
Multicultural Education: Issues and Perspectives (Banks & McGee Banks, 2009)	General approach to diversity, plus four-level schema on multicultural curricula (contributions, additive, transformational, and transformational + social change)
Sisters of the Yam: Black Women and Self-Discovery (hooks, 1993)	One in a series of provocative books by a black feminist writer
Crossing Cultural Borders: Education for Immigrant Families in America (Delgado-Gaitan & Trueba, 1991)	Ethnographic study of Mexican immigrants in California

celebration) that the dead are alive alongside the living. Conversely, Mexicans might look with disapproval on Americans who visit cemeteries only on a military holiday (Memorial Day) rather than for a family holiday or picnic. In this case, crosscultural comparisons that are used to deepen understanding should not be avoided when the issues become tinged with deeper emotion.

One way of comparing cultures in depth using crosscultural psychology is through a unit on mandala design across cultures. Lessons examine Crete's myth of the labyrinth and the Minotaur, Tibetan Buddhist yantra and meditation designs, the interwoven tracery of Celtic dragons and sacred trees, and the Japanese circle designs displayed on family crests. Moving back and forth from design to explanation uses visual import to support the language learning that takes place through this rich input.

Teaching Crosscultural Content

Crosscultural differences in greeting, complimenting, and showing appreciation are the bases for Nam's (2001) instructional unit on comparing customs in Korea and the United States. She uses a list of "dos" and "don'ts" as an acculturation strategy to get students talking about cultural differences. She also presents the concept of high-context culture and low-context culture (see Buckley, 2000) as a means of focusing the discussion on fundamental principles of crosscultural contrast. Key vocabulary words in this unit are such terms as *higher status, modest and humble, disrespectful,* and *make eye contact.* Nam then presents two dialogues, one in which a teacher who is a native speaker of English tries unsuccessfully to compliment a Korean student, and one in which the interaction appears to be more successful. Students complete a worksheet using a comparison circle diagram (see Chapter 5) to articulate the differences between the two dialogues; the instructor then presents a dialogue analysis that points out the cultural differences, which students discuss. This plan demonstrates the use of crosscultural comparison not only to teach English but also to compare the target and native cultures.

Using Intercultural Communication to Teach English

Classes of English learners that involve students from a variety of countries offer the opportunity to have the students communicate with one another in structured class activities. Almost any game or activity is valuable if it helps students to share their beliefs, values, and conceptions about the world.

Beyond Superficial Communication

A favorite activity on Valentine's Day in the American Culture and Language Program at California State University, San Bernardino, is the Language of Love game (MacKay, 2000). Using the game board provided, players take turns rolling dice, moving their tokens around the playing board, and drawing cards with questions that they must answer in the group (or they can pass). Sample questions are featured in Box 10.7. These questions create a deeper level of intercultural communication, involving sharing of values and personal anecdotes.

Megastrategy **10.6**

Use intercultural communication to teach English

Box 10.7 Sample Questions from "The Love Game"

Category	Sample Questions
About You	Do you think it's OK for a girl to ask a boy for a date?
Cultural Question	What kinds of things do people do on a first date in your country?
	How do people meet other people in your country?
New Expressions and Idioms	What does "to go steady" or "to go with someone" mean?
	What does "to be stood up" mean?

Source: MacKay (2000).

Using Language–Culture Resources

Teachers cannot possibly hope to provide to English learners all the language and culture resources needed to advance quickly in learning English. Classrooms are an intrinsically limited and artificial setting for language learning, yet audiovisual aids, computer access, other English learners, cultural objects, and community resources can supplement the classroom and bring real-world input. Fantini (2009) encourages the use of peer-to-peer contact:

> Students can communicate directly with other learners and other speakers anywhere in the world through blogs and e-mail, and Skype connections (especially when accompanied by a webcam) make it possible to talk in real time, face to face, with anyone anywhere in the world and at no cost! (p. 15)

Intercultural Conflict

Occasionally, interaction occurs that is not so much fun: interethnic conflict. Should this occur, techniques exist for problem solving through carefully planned intervention. First, teachers can intervene in the early stages of conflicts to defuse the problem by talking to students privately, encouraging the sharing of perceptions on volatile issues, and communicating expectations that students will be able to resolve their differences. In this way, teachers allow students to vent their feelings as a group and provide a brief period of controlled verbal expression that can serve as an outlet for frustration. A teacher must resolve to be calm and should not tolerate violence or personal attacks. The most proactive stance is to modify the classroom learning environment to include a variety of cultural content and to make provisions for varied learning approaches (Díaz-Rico, 2000).

In summary, cultural studies are a rich and rewarding part of educating English learners, whether students are learning about American culture from a distance or learning about their host culture as immigrants to an English-speaking country. Teachers of English learners play an integral role in the success of their students. In effect, the teacher is the gatekeeper for academic success, serving as an everyday implementer of social policies and values.

For prospective teachers to accept the work of achieving equity in education, they must at some point examine their own complicity in the privilege of being a native speaker of a colonial language. To sustain professional lives committed to ideals of multicultural equity and private lives enriched by intercultural participation, individuals must be able to interact with speakers of the primary language using dimensions of intercultural understanding. It is useful for prospective teachers of English learners to use tools like the ethnographic case study to obtain rich, descriptive data about the contexts, activities, and beliefs of diverse community members.

Overall, instructors who can "teach with a difference" are the best cultural ambassadors. Infusing the domains of intercultural communication and cultural study into the education of English learners has the potential of strengthening the capacity of educators to prepare diverse students to be strong, caring, contributing community members in the cultures of the future.

Exploratory Break

- If you teach a class with English learners from a variety of cultures, discuss ways that you can engage your students in intercultural communication to help them learn about one another's cultures and improve their English language proficiency in the process.

- Think of a critical incident from your own experience that might have been the result of an intercultural miscommunication on your part. How could improved cultural awareness have resolved this incident in a more positive way?

Chapter 11

Discourse in the Classrooms of English Learners

> *You must know who is the object and who is the subject of a sentence in order to know if you are the object or the subject of history. If you can't control a sentence you don't know how to put yourself in history, to trace your own origin in the country, to vocalize, to use your voice.*
>
> Nelida Piñon (in Aronowitz & Giroux, 1991, p. 114)

What Is Classroom Discourse?

Discourse analysis can be defined as the analysis of language beyond the sentence. A discourse might be characterized as "a language form associated with a particular activity, a particular kind of knowledge, a particular group of people or a particular institution" (Peim, 1993, p. 37). The study of discourse looks at language in its larger units, such as oral text (classroom talk, speeches, casual conversation) and written text (magazine articles, school assignments, signs and posters). Discourse specialists have looked at such behavior as how people take turns, how speakers use contextual cues as they interact, and how people show others they are listening. These features are heavily influenced by culture. Educators who understand how culture affects schooling can help English learners adapt to new patterns of language use.

Megastrategy SET 11

Understand cultural patterns of instruction

Linguists who analyze classroom discourse, the language that is used in teaching and learning, note that schooling in some ways sounds like everyday life yet in other ways has its own peculiar patterns of interaction. This chapter has two goals. The first is to understand the ways in which schools use language separately from the experience of everyday life, exploring in the process how this separation (which is powerful, inevitable, and potentially positive) can work to the benefit of English learners. The second is to ask how educators can affirm the voices that students bring to school.

Language Teachers at the Edge

In a surprising sense, at the beginning of the twenty-first century we have all become second-language learners. The various discourses that are circulating keep us all on edge. The "edge" in nature is the growing tip of the root where growth is possible. If possible, this is where the expert educator works, at the edge where learning takes place, a social and cultural border that functions as a horizon of opportunity.

> Central to the notion of border pedagogy are a number of important pedagogical issues regarding the role that teachers might play at the interface of modern and postmodern concerns.... [T]he concept of border pedagogy suggests that teachers exist within social, political, and cultural boundaries, which are both multiple and historical in nature.... As part of the process of developing a pedagogy of difference, teachers need to deal with the plethora of voices...that constitute any course, class, or curriculum, so as to make problematic not only the stories that give meanings to the lives of their students but also the ethical and political lineaments that inform their students' subjectivities and identities. (Aronowitz & Giroux, 1991, p. 130)

The Language and Culture of Schooling

Culture is constantly changing and accumulates based on individuals' past experiences. When someone learns a foreign language, the culture acts as a guide to the way people think, feel, and act. Culture aids in understanding not only daily life but also the ways in which people bring meaning, joy, creativity, and enrichment to this daily life. Ideally, the language used in school promotes this sense of meaning.

Megastrategy **11.1**

Understand the role of language and culture in instruction

Schooling is an enterprise in which people use language to express their culture. The language of schooling is one element in a whole set of discursive practices that shape behavior and remind the student that society is serious about participation. Nonverbal signals reinforce this message: Most school buildings are huge compared to homes; surfaces are hard, official flags wave, and shrill bells ring. Given these practices, how can the language of schooling function as a tool of improvement?

Classroom discourse is a special type of conversation. Conversation is an enterprise in which one person speaks and another listens. Intonation, pausing, and phrasing determine when one person's turn is over and the next person's turn begins. Markers signal the circulation of power. As Foucault (1979) noted, discursive practices in the modern world prepare the individual for power. Schooling can shape an average person into a "good" student using discourse. The postmodern shift has allowed teachers for the first time to use the power of language knowingly and equitably.

Good language learners are able to gain access to a variety of conversations in their communities rather than simply acquire or control a variety of linguistic forms and meanings (Norton & Toohey, 2001). The communities of practice (Lave & Wenger, 1991) in which they participate, even peripherally, provide access to the utterances of others and the cultural practices they need to become engaged in community life. This means that the community of practice in a classroom does more to create a good learner than the individual's cognition and striving.

Linguistic Features of Classroom Discourse

Linguistic features are useful ways to examine classroom discourse. Speaking is signaled by turn markers that govern who takes the floor, but listenership too may be signaled in different ways. Some speakers expect frequent nodding and some kind of listener feedback such as "hmm," "uhuh," and "yeah." In a room full of people, one might expect listening to be signaled by eye contact. The type of listener response a speaker gets can change the presentation: If someone seems uninterested or uncomprehending (whether or not they truly are), the speaker tends to slow down, repeat, or overexplain, giving the impression of "talking down."

Discourse is classified using four dimensions. One dimension is *written versus spoken*; another is *register* (formal ↔ informal); a third is *genre* (a combination of communicative purpose, audience, and format); the fourth is *monologic*, *dialogic*, or *multiparty* (how many are involved) (Celce-Murcia & Olshtain, 2000). Many kinds of analysis have been applied to the study of discourse: studies of information structure, coherence, cohesion, turn taking, and critical language analysis. This chapter focuses on the educational anthropologists' look at patterns of discourse, as well as on cognitive academic language proficiency and its incorporation into instruction.

Classroom discourse patterns involve students as active language users.
©Andresr/Shutterstock.com

What Discourse Genres Are Common in U.S. Classrooms?

Chapter 3 provided an introduction to communicative competence theory and looked at the social functions of language. To review, the seven categories of language function outlined by Halliday (1978) are *instrumental* (manipulating the environment to cause certain events to happen), *regulatory* (controlling events or the behavior of others), *representational* (communicating information), *interactional* (maintaining social communication), *personal* (expressing feelings and emotions), *heuristic* (acquiring knowledge), and *imaginative* (creating a world freed from the boundaries of everyday).

A curriculum might encourage students to perform a wide variety of verbal functions such as reporting, evaluating, questioning, and critiquing. Many other functions are not necessarily encouraged by schools but take place in schools nonetheless: interrupting, shifting the blame, threatening, accusing, arguing, demanding, and making excuses. Learners must acquire written as well as spoken competence in the effort to match forms with functions.

Academic language functions, which supplement these social functions, include explaining, informing, justifying, comparing, describing, proving, debating, and so on. Because accomplishing these functions successfully with academic content requires the use of thinking skills, there is some overlap in the terminology of academic functions and thinking skills. Chamot and O'Malley (1994) listed and described these functions.

Academic English, also called *cognitive academic language proficiency (CALP)*, is designed for abstract, decontextualized performance across a variety of content domains. Students acquire this level of proficiency in English only after a long period of successful schooling, exposure to academic language, feedback and support in its use, and explicit instruction in vocabulary, morphology, syntax, and cognitive strategies. TESOL's Statement on the Acquisition of Academic Proficiency in English reaffirms the importance of CALP: "In the past decade, research has shown that content-based instruction that focuses on the development of academic language proficiency is critical in school. LEP students are expected to learn academic content in English in order to compete academically with their native-English speaking peers" (TESOL, 2002).

Academic genres of discourse are academic functions within content areas. This chapter looks at discourse patterns to see how these are used to foster academic English.

The Recitation Pattern: A Typical Learning Encounter

Classrooms in the United States often follow a model of instruction based on what Mehan (1979) labeled "recitation." Typically, the pattern falls into three parts, called the IRE sequence. First, the teacher invites (I) an interaction by asking a question; a student responds (R), and the teacher follows with evaluation (E). Alternatively, this may be called the IRF pattern if the term *evaluation* is replaced by the term *feedback*. *Feedback* is a more accurate term because this step involves

Megastrategy **11.2**

Understand typical U.S. classroom instructional patterns

not only praise or disguised evaluation but also reformulation, repetition of the student's answer, and a summary or delivery of information.

The IRF pattern shares characteristics of other kinds of teacher talk. The teacher not only produces the most language but also takes the most turns. Questions asked in this way usually call for simple information recall, and the responses are limited to this type of thinking. The teacher tends to ask "known answer" questions in which students' responses can be easily evaluated (Pridham, 2001). The IRF pattern is easy to identify, partially because of its prevalence.

Invitation to respond:

> TEACHER: Who knows why names are capitalized? (Some students are wildly waving their hands, begging to be chosen to respond; others are averting their eyes, hoping *not* to be called on) José?

Response:

> JOSÉ: It's somebody's name.

Evaluation, or *Feedback:*

> TEACHER: That's true. Good, José.

Invitation to respond: (pattern repeats)

> TEACHER: But who can tell me what the term for that is?

Sociohistorical Features of the Recitation Pattern

The IRF pattern may have become dominant in U.S. classrooms because it matches deep-seated discourse habits of the mainstream culture. Some evidence of this exists in Heath's *Ways with Words* (1983), an ethnographic study of two communities in the rural South conducted in the 1970s. One community, which Heath called Roadville, is white and working class, while the other, Trackton, is African American. Heath described ways in which Roadville home-language practices patterned the discourse of white teachers in schools. Despite the fact that few mainstream teachers are raised in communities exactly like Roadville, the IRF is highly consonant with language patterns that Heath identified in Roadville homes.

For example, Heath detailed a typical question put to a Roadville child: "What color is that?" (1983, p. 251). This pattern, which Heath calls *display knowledge,* follows an underlying Roadville discourse value: People respond when called on by others to talk. Corollary principles are that children respond when called on by adults to talk and that, in the company of adults, children speak only when called on. One can see immediately the carryover to the recitation pattern: In class, a student waits to be called on, and when called on, the good student is ready with the answer.

The IRF is not the only discourse pattern in which the teacher dominates. In *teacher-fronted* classrooms in general (Harel, 1992), the teacher takes the central role in controlling the flow of information, and students compete for the teacher's attention and for permission to speak. In such classrooms, English learners are dependent on their ability to understand the teacher's explanations and directions. The IRF is the dominant pattern in U.S. classrooms, but traditional educational contexts around the world feature their own versions of teacher-dominated talk. Although this chapter focuses on the IRF pattern, the suggestions that follow for altering this reliance on teacher talk may hold good for other types of teacher-fronted discourse.

Instructional Features of the Recitation Pattern

The recitation pattern has shown great persistence in U.S. schools. Clearly, the IRF pattern has positive instructional features. It is often used to activate students' prior knowledge about a topic, to review material already covered, and to present new information. Teachers often use the IRF as a calming and control device, as a way of checking on the general state of group knowledge on a topic, and of evaluating the discipline and cooperation of individual students. This evaluation of the student seems to shape a teacher's academic expectations for that student. Table 11.1 shows features of the recitation pattern that work for the benefit of instruction.

Recitation Pattern: Critique

Despite its persistence, the recitation pattern is not successful for all students. Tables 11.2, 11.3, and 11.4 detail the ways in which the IRF pattern may inhibit learning for English learners. Table 11.2 looks at the invitation to bid, Table 11.3 examines the response turn, and Table 11.4 shows the feedback part of the pattern. (see Gutierrez, 1995; Gutierrez & Larson, 1994.).

Recitation Pattern: Questioning Strategies

Questions are a staple in U.S. classrooms, and it is generally through skilled questioning that teachers lead discussions and ascertain students' understanding. Questions should be framed relative to the students' proficiency levels, the sociocultural aspects of displaying knowledge, and the level of critical thinking sought in the response.

A linguistic hierarchy of question types can be matched to proficiency levels. For students in the "silent period," a question requiring a nonverbal response—a head movement, pointing, manipulating materials—will elicit an appropriate and satisfactory answer. Once students are beginning to speak, either/or questions provide the necessary terms, and the student needs merely to choose the correct word or phrase to demonstrate understanding: "Does the water expand or contract to form ice?" "Did Russians come to California from the west or the north?" Once students are more comfortable in producing language, *wh-* questions are appropriate: "What is happening to the water?" "Which countries sent explorers to California?" "What was the purpose of their exploration?"

Teachers who are sensitive to varying cultural styles are aware that in some cultures students are reluctant to display knowledge before a large group. They will take care to organize other means for students to demonstrate language and content knowledge, such as small-group discussions.

TABLE 11.1 *Instructional Benefits of the Recitation Pattern*

Discourse Feature	Benefit to Instruction
Invitation to bid	Teacher waits for silence and imposes order on student behavior.
	Teacher controls the scope of the lesson by asking selected questions.
	Teacher determines order and importance of information by posing questions.
	Teacher controls the level of language displayed in class by choice of lexicon and complexity of sentence structure.
	Teacher controls pace and rhythm of discourse.
Response	Teacher evaluates behavior of individuals by looking to see who is willing and ready to participate.
	Teacher controls potential for reward by choosing respondent.
	By acting eager to answer, students can demonstrate attention, cooperation, and responsiveness to instruction—even if they do not really know the answer the teacher expects to hear.
	Teacher controls behavior by calling on students who may not be attentive.
	Students can practice risk taking by volunteering to answer.
	Students can show knowledge from prior instruction or experience.
Evaluation	Teacher is able to evaluate students' level of oral participation.
	Teacher is able to use teacher approval as a reinforcer.
	Teacher is able to establish public recognition for those who answer correctly.
	Teacher can withhold negative evaluation by partially accepting an incomplete answer.
	Teacher can avoid direct negative evaluation by asking one student to "help" another to improve the answer.
	Teacher can elaborate on answer and expand a concept by delivering direct instruction at this point.
	Teacher can improve a poor answer by substituting more accurate terminology or restating a sentence using correct grammar.
	As teacher evaluates students' responses, he or she determines what question comes next.
	Teacher rewards some students, for example, white boys (Sadker, Sadker, & Klein, 1991), by extending the response through corrective and thoughtful dialogue.
	Teacher rewards some students, for example, compliant girls (Sadker & Sadker, 1986), for brief, exact responses that receive little extended feedback and correction.

TABLE 11.2 *Instructional Shortcomings of the Recitation Pattern for English Learners (Discourse Feature: Invitation to Bid)*

Beneficial Features in Mainstream Setting	Potential Shortcomings to Instruction for English Learners
Teacher waits for silence and imposes order on student behavior.	English learners may not appear as attentive as native English speakers because they may have difficulty comprehending instructions.
Teacher determines order and importance of information by posing questions.	English learners may need more time than native English speakers to understand questions and frame responses.
Teacher controls the scope of the lesson by asking selected questions.	Students with creative and individualistic thinking may wish to contribute related ideas outside the scope of the immediate topic.
Teacher controls the level of language displayed in class by choice of lexicon and complexity of sentence structure.	Instructional language, including vocabulary, may be too complex for English learners.
Teacher controls pace and rhythm of discourse.	Pace and rhythm of discourse may be different in students' native language, causing discomfort.

TABLE 11.3 *Instructional Shortcomings of the Recitation Pattern for English Learners (Discourse Feature: Response)*

Beneficial Features in Mainstream Setting	Potential Shortcomings to Instruction for English Learners
Teacher evaluates behavior of individuals by looking to see who is willing and ready to participate. Teacher controls potential for reward by choosing respondent.	English learners may be reluctant to bring attention to themselves because they feel insecure about their oral language, see such an action as incompatible with group cohesiveness and cultural norms, or are reluctant to display knowledge in front of others.
By acting eager to answer, students can demonstrate attention, cooperation, and responsiveness to instruction—even if they do not really know the answer the teacher expects to hear. Students can show knowledge from prior instruction or experience.	Students may lack experience in particular topics under discussion, although their background may be rich in topics that are not curriculum related.
Teacher controls behavior by calling on students who may not be attentive.	Students from cultures in which children do not make direct eye contact with adults may not appear attentive during instruction.
Students can practice risk taking by volunteering to answer.	If their culture does not reward ambiguity, English learners may be reluctant to volunteer to answer if they are not 100 percent sure their idea is correct.

TABLE 11.4 *Instructional Shortcomings of the Recitation Pattern for English Learners (Discourse Feature: Evaluation)*

Features That May Be Beneficial for Mainstream Students	Potential Shortcomings to Instruction for English Learners
Teacher is able to evaluate students' level of oral participation.	Students may need prior language development in oral participation, including turn taking, listening, and speaking.
Teacher is able to use teacher approval as a reinforcer.	Students from certain cultures may not depend on teacher for approval.
Teacher is able to establish public recognition for those who answer correctly.	Individual public recognition may be a taboo in some cultures.
Teacher can withhold negative evaluation by partially accepting an incomplete answer.	Indirect negative evaluation may be confusing for some students, leaving them with unclear concept formation.
Teacher can avoid direct negative evaluation by asking one student to "help" another to improve the answer.	

If a teacher is seeking evaluative responses requiring critical thinking by means of questioning strategies, more wait time is necessary for students to understand the question and frame a thoughtful response. Bias is avoided if all respondents are given equal feedback and support in increasing the cognitive complexity of the answer.

Whether or not they use the IRF as a default discourse pattern, teachers of English learners cannot help using teacher-fronted discourse patterns to some extent, because of the legacy of traditional teaching discourse. However, awareness of its strengths (ease of use, usefulness in controlling attention and behavior, and diagnosis of learner's responsiveness) and weaknesses (limited learner oral production, limited peer interaction, and inequity of reinforcement) may encourage teachers to limit the use of teacher-fronted discourse in teaching English.

PRACTICES FOR TEACHERS

Avoiding Overreliance on Teacher-Fronted Discourse

- Use performance-based instruction to stipulate desirable language-learning goals.
- Use task chains to plan a variety of learner activities to accomplish language-learning goals.
- Use guided practice activities that strengthen the frequency of students' oral language production.

Cooperative Learning as an Alternative Pattern

The way discourse is organized is important for language acquisition in content classes. In contrast, classrooms that feature flexible grouping patterns and cooperative learning permit students greater access to the flow of information as they talk and listen to their peers, interact with the teacher or other adult in small groups, and use their home language for clarification purposes.

In such classrooms, the style of teacher talk often changes: Teachers assist students with the learning task rather than providing error correction, they give fewer commands, and they impose less disciplinary control. The teacher orchestrates tasks so that students use language in academic ways. Students are placed in different groups for different activities. Teachers work with small groups to achieve specific instructional objectives (e.g., literature response groups, as discussed in Chapter 7, or instructional conversations, discussed below).

The Instructional Conversation (IC) as a Discourse Alternative

A collaborative team of teachers and researchers have used Vygotsky's construct of the zone of proximal development to create the IC discourse format, a semistructured group discussion. The teacher selects a theme based on the ideas presented in the literature or content in question and permits open-ended but focused exploration. Students' prior knowledge is activated by the teacher during discussion or, if lacking, is quickly supplied by the teacher as direct instruction as the conversation progresses. Throughout the discussion, the teacher draws out the participants, supporting the development of complex thinking and ensuring that statements made are supported by facts or texts (Goldenberg & Gallimore, 1991).

Small-group discussion formats and class projects mix native and nonnative speakers of English.

©Tangducminh/Dreamstime.com

IC remains at its core a conversation. Participants take turns in a connected discourse in which, ideally, the leader has no more than 20 percent of the total talk (Díaz-Rico, 1994). How can a teacher talk with eight students and leave the rest of the class unattended? An instructional aide or parent volunteer can supervise other language development centers and activities while the instructional conversation proceeds. Many teachers find that increased attention paid to the assisted thinking of students reaps great benefit, not only in teachers' increased understanding of students' thought processes, ideas, and depth but also, unexpectedly, in improved classroom discipline and students' sense of instructional co-ownership.

Learning to manage and appreciate the IC takes time. A cognitively demanding activity, it challenges the teacher to become a conversational partner. The most difficult components for most teachers are learning to keep silent and let students think and volunteer their thoughts in good time, moving the conversation forward by building on students' ideas rather than the teacher's, selecting topics that students find genuinely interesting and comprehensible, and having the patience to listen as English learners' struggle to find the words for their thoughts. However, the rewards are great; a satisfying IC is an event for which, deep down, every good teacher yearns.

PRACTICES FOR TEACHERS

Using the Instructional Conversation

- Arrange the classroom to accommodate conversation between the teacher and a small group of students according to a regular and frequent schedule.

- Have a clear academic goal that guides conversation with students.

- Ensure that student talk occurs at higher rates than teacher talk and that all students are included in the conversation according to their preferences.

- Guide conversation to include students' views, judgments, and rationales, using text evidence and other substantive support.

- Listen carefully to assess levels of students' understanding.

- Assist students' learning throughout the conversation by questioning, restating, praising, encouraging, and so forth.

Cognitive Academic Language Proficiency

During the elementary school years, and even more so throughout middle and high school, students need to acquire a completely new kind of scholastic language. In contrast to basic interpersonal communication skills (BICS), the language used for social interaction and early school adjustment, CALP constitutes academic language, which is a highly complex set of language functions required for access to, and success in, the core curriculum. BICS and CALP overlap, with more complicated social language useful for cooperative learning and teamwork. Conversational skills have been found to approach native-like levels within two years of exposure to English, but five or more years may be required for minority students to match native speakers in CALP (Collier, 1987; Cummins, 1981a; Hakuta, Butler & Witt, 2000). Students need skills in both kinds of language.

Megastrategy **11.3**

Promote the learner's use of cognitive academic language

CALP is the language needed to perform school tasks, which are often abstract and decontextualized. Students must rely primarily on language to attain meaning, especially reading and writing. Cummins (1984) called CALP *context-reduced* communication, because there are few concrete cues to assist comprehension.

The Language of Thought

Beyond words, CALP also involves systematic thought processes. It provides the human brain with necessary tools to systematically categorize, compare, analyze, and accommodate new experiences. One cannot separate words from knowledge or learning; it is not possible to say that one understands a topic but does not understand the terminology. CALP represents the cognitive toolbox needed to encode and decode this thought. CALP is key to acquiring the in-depth knowledge that characterizes the well-educated individual in a complex modern society.

Academic language features specific linguistic functions such as persuading, arguing, and hypothesizing. Accurate use of grammar and precise differentiation of word meaning are increasingly important. CALP requires a transition from the simple *use* of language to the more complex ability to *think and talk about* language—that is, metalinguistic awareness (Scarcella & Rumberger, 2000). This takes place against a background of prior knowledge, a gradual accumulation of cultural capital that helps language users understand the cultural and social uses of the language to which they are exposed. CALP is not gained entirely from either school or the home; one reinforces the other. Teachers who find ways for students' families to support CALP are able to expand those students' chances of academic success.

CALP requires complex growth in many linguistic areas simultaneously. This growth is highly dependent on the assistance of teachers, because for the most part CALP is learned in school. The complexity of CALP can be captured by examination of the five Cs: *c*ommunication, *c*onceptualization, *c*ritical thinking, *c*ontext, and *c*ulture (see Table 11.5). Many CALP skills are refinements of BICS, while others are more exclusively school-centered.

The Teacher's Role in Promoting CALP

Teachers can promote the use of CALP by ensuring that students understand and use the vocabulary of specific subjects. When comparing two numbers, a teacher might ask, "Which number is greater?" The term *greater than* is specific to mathematics,

TABLE 11.5 *Components of Cognitive Academic Language Proficiency*

Component	Explanation
Communication	Reading: increases speed; uses context cues to guess vocabulary meaning; masters a variety of genres in fiction (poetry, short story) and nonfiction (encyclopedias, magazines, Internet sources); able to "read the world" (interpret comics, print advertising, road signs)
	Listening: follows verbal instructions; interprets nuances of intonation (e.g., in cases of teacher disciplinary warnings); solicits, and profits from, help of peers
	Speaking: gives oral presentations, answers correctly in class, and reads aloud smoothly
	Writing: uses conventions such as spelling, punctuation, report formats
Conceptualization	Concepts become abstract and are expressed in longer words with more general meaning (*rain* becomes *precipitation*).
	Concepts fit into larger theories (*precipitation* cycle).
	Concepts fit into hierarchies (rain → precipitation cycle → weather systems → climate).
	Concepts are finely differentiated from similar concepts (*sleet* from *hail*, *typhoons* from *hurricanes*).
Critical thinking	Uses graphic organizers to represent the structure of thought (comparison charts, Venn diagrams, time lines, "spider" charts)
	Uses textual structures (outlines, paragraphing, titles, main idea)
	Uses symbolic representation: math operators ($<, >, +, =$); proofreading marks, grade indications (10/20 points, etc.)
	Employs many kinds of critical thinking
	Plans activities, monitors progress, evaluates results, employs self-knowledge (metacognition)
Context	Nonverbal: uses appropriate gestures (and is able to refrain from inappropriate ones); interprets nonverbal signs accurately
	Formality: behaves formally when required to do so
	Participation structures: fits in smoothly to classroom and schoolwide groups and procedures
Culture	Draws on experience in mainstream culture (background knowledge)
	Uses social class markers, such as "manners"
	Moves smoothly between home and school
	Deploys primary-language resources when required
	Maintains uninterrupted primary-culture profile ("fits in" with neighborhood social structures)
	Develops and sustains supportive peer interactions

Source: Díaz-Rico & Weed (2010)

because it eventually corresponds to the symbol ">"; *bigger* as a synonym is therefore not as useful. Rather than use the colloquial "look at," a teacher might ask students to "compare"; instead of "What do you think will happen?" they say, "Predict what will happen," and instead of "How do you explain," they ask, "What hypothesis might explain this?" These terms—*compare, predict, hypothesis*—are a part of the mental infrastructure students will need in order to succeed in middle and high school (Norton, 2007).

Teachers can use scaffolding to support students' use of CALP. Table 11.6 displays discourse moves that teachers can make to deepen a student's understanding of the concept *dense*.

Teachers may encourage English learners to repeat a term to themselves for practice. Keeping a personal glossary of terms used academically is also useful for all students. In order not to single out English learners, the teacher should not require them to repeat phrases aloud in front of other students.

TABLE 11.6 *Using Scaffolding to Help English Learners Verbalize the Concept Dense*

Scaffolding Move	Student's Talk	Teacher Talk
Open-ended question		What did you find out?
	If you put wood in the water…it…stay up.	
Restatement using correct term + probe		The wood floats? OK. What else?
	The thing…you put the thing…and it…it go down.	
Clarification		What goes down?
	The screw…the screw go down in water.	
Probe using correct term		What causes the screw to sink?
	The screw sink because it…too…it too…screw too…	
Provides choice of terms		The screw sinks because it's more dense or less dense than water?
	…More dense…	
Restates students' sentence and confirms meaning		Yes, the screw is more dense than water and so it sinks.

Some teachers confuse the terms *BICS* and *CALP* with correct versus incorrect usage of English. CALP is *not* just BICS that uses complete, grammatical sentences. Teachers further the acquisition of CALP by analyzing the conceptual and critical thinking requirements of the grade-level curriculum *and* taking the time to ensure that all students are explicitly taught such requirements. Good teachers use CALP with their students; excellent teachers ensure that students can use CALP themselves.

Without explicit attention to teaching CALP, one of three outcomes is all too common. First, educational "haves" prosper academically, whereas "have nots" do not. Those students who come to school already having acquired CALP as a benefit of a privileged home environment can draw on this prior knowledge, but English learners may lack this ability. Second, the curriculum for English learners may be watered down on the assumption that those who lack CALP cannot perform academically at a high cognitive level. Third, the acquisition of CALP is heavily implicated in the type of participatory structure established in the classroom. Students lacking CALP in English are not able to participate knowledgeably in the IRF and are often instead given a skills-based, direct instruction approach that does not encourage a constructivist learning environment.

Discourse That Affirms Students' Voices

Throughout this book, the emphasis has been on the participation of the learner in learning. Classroom discourse will always be somewhat constrained, if not stilted, if the goal of discourse is to accomplish an agenda that is solely the teacher's. It is therefore imperative that teachers situate their practice in the language needed and desired by the student. If that desire does not exist, teachers must evoke those emotions and motivations as an integral part of instruction. Instruction that is not meaningful and motivating to the learner, particularly in a second language, becomes empty.

Megastrategy 11.4

Help the learner to construct meaning

What kind of participation enhances motivation and promotes acquisition? *Co-construction of meaning* permits the learner to plan, choose, and evaluate knowledge in relation to personal needs and goals. *Communities of practice* are local. Knowledge in the community sustains and reinforces classroom learning. The school and families must work together to extend academic discourse into the home.

Every community has a distinct kind of discourse into which children are socialized. *Participatory genres* help the student to bridge the home–school divide. By working in acknowledgment of, rather than at cross-purposes with, community patterns of discourse, teachers can successfully modify teacher-fronted discourse for a particular group of learners.

In summary, teachers can use the tools of ethnography and community participation to learn what it means to have meaning, and how to help the learner gain that meaning through English-language instruction. A study of how the community uses discourse can help teachers pattern their classroom activities in ways that increase the likelihood that students' English proficiency will grow.

Exploratory Break

■ What do you think are the most useful forms of classroom participation for English learners? Discuss alternatives to the recitation pattern and ways for classroom discourse to encourage the public voice of English learners beyond cooperative groups.

Chapter *12*

Dual-Language Proficiency

Schooling in Two Languages

> Gadda ge. Dankie. Hioy'oy. Ghu long khu me-ah. Ju falem nderit. Amesegënallô. Shukran. Barak llahu fik. Merci. Mesi. Sag olun. Matur suksme. Nitsíniiyi'taki.

When I hear anyone state, "I can speak twelve languages," it always makes me wonder, "How much do people have to know in a language before they can say they can 'speak' it?" For example, if I say "thank you" in twelve languages—see above, and see Runner (2000, 2007) for more words in many languages—that does not mean I can "speak" twelve languages. How many people can say they are truly fluent in more than one language? On what level of proficiency is this based?

In many parts of the world, people undergo schooling in a language that is not their mother tongue because of government mandates, colonial legacies, or social pressure. For example, in the United States educators expect immigrants to function well in English before they graduate from high school. In Canada and elsewhere, the ability to read and write in two languages is encouraged. This chapter concerns the education of English learners in the context of bilingual programs, with an emphasis on programs that foster dual-language academic proficiency, what Cook (1999, p. 190) calls *multicompetent language use*.

Why Dual-Language Acquisition?

Most of the world's population is bilingual or multilingual. Each of the world's nations has groups of individuals living within its borders who use other languages in addition to the national language to function in their everyday lives. The term *bilingual* means able to function in two languages. Although it is the case that some bilingual speakers possess very high levels of proficiency in both written and oral modes, others display varying degrees of proficiency in comprehension and/or speaking skills along a continuum, depending on how they use their two languages.

> **Megastrategy SET 12**
>
> Develop cognitive academic language proficiency in two languages

Bilingual individuals experience cognitive and linguistic advantages when compared to monolinguals, performing better on tests of divergent thinking, pattern recognition, problem solving, and metalinguistic awareness (Cenoz & Genesee, 1998). Part of the metalinguistic advantage of the bilingual brain is enhanced operation of the executive control system, part of the prefrontal cortex that controls conscious attention, choice, and other high-level functions. As the brain switches back and forth between two or more languages (Bialystok, 2009; Kroll & Tokowitz, 2005), the brain is strengthened, eventually even developing enhanced abilities to focus, prioritize, and multi-task. Knowing a second language often opens doors into other cultures, leading to understanding of cultural differences and providing opportunities for intercultural communication. Proficiency in multiple languages is also a career enhancement in the modern world of international commerce.

A common myth is that fluency in one's primary language interferes with attaining proficiency in a second language. When a teacher supplements classroom instruction by providing reading materials in students' primary language, allows students to use their home language in the context of informal learning logs or journals, and encourages collaborative classroom work in whichever language students choose, the message that is conveyed is support for additive bilingualism, a "back-and forth process, in which one language 'teaches' the learner about the other" (Finders & Hynds, 2007, p. 136).

> **Megastrategy 12.1**
>
> Support enriched education in dual-language programs

Identifying Types of Bilingual Students

Although individuals with dual-language backgrounds are difficult to categorize, four general profiles emerge, each with different schooling backgrounds and curricular needs (see Table 12.1).

Myths about Bilingualism

"For as long as I have been working with bilingual and second-language children, I have been asked about whether a child is confused due to learning two languages and if this learning of two languages can cause a language delay," writes Deborah Jill Chitester (2007, p. 22). "The answer is generally *not*." Chitester offers a few reminders that help to counter myths about bilingualism in children:

- Children should not be labeled "bilingual" if they are English learners; they are not yet "bilingual."

TABLE 12.1 *Characteristic Profiles of Bilingual Students*

Type of Bilingualism	Characteristics
Balanced bilingual	Has achieved oracy and literacy in two languages
Monolingual/literate in native language	Is fluent and can perform well academically in one language; has had limited exposure to English, including limited cultural knowledge
Monolingual/preliterate in native language	Is fluent in, but cannot perform well orally or academically in the primary language; has had limited exposure to English, including limited cultural knowledge
Limited bilingual	Is fluent in the primary language; may be fluent in English, including cultural knowledge, but academic skills in both languages are not yet established

Source: Based on Echevarría and Graves (2011).

- Mere exposure to a second language is not significant for acquisition…just watching Dora the Explorer will not create a bilingual child.
- Just putting children of two different languages together does not necessarily lead to dual-language learning. Children need well-run, supervised bilingual "play-activity groups" in which the opportunity is available for

Box 12.1 Students with Limited or Interrupted Formal Education

One group that poses a particular challenge is the population of students with limited or interrupted formal education (SLIFE). Such students lack the requisite skills in their native or first language that are needed to transfer literacy to English.

Nearly all schools place SLIFE in an age-appropriate grade level regardless of their prior academic skills or their current level of first- or second-language proficiency. This placement requires intensive support (DeCapua & Marshall, 2011). DeCapua, Smathers, and Tang (2009) recommend the following for working with these students:

- Knowledge: understand the needs of these students; become familiar with their home countries and cultures;
- Skills: Be thoroughly trained in ELD methodology as well as basic literacy tutoring;
- Dispositions: Be flexible, creative, and patient; convey clear but high expectations for achievement; work closely with content teachers; and actively communicate with administrators, as well as parents/guardians on behalf of SLIFE.

dual-language output and interaction. These can work as early as eighteen months of age.

■ Second-language learners need a "silent period" in which to absorb foreign language sounds before they can use the language to produce speech. This should not be labeled "language delay."

Summing Up the Sociopolitical Foundations for Bilingual Programs

The four pillars of legal and legislative action underpinning the rights of language minorities to schooling are as follows (see Herrera and Murry, 2011):

■ *The Bilingual Education Act of 1968.* Title VII of the Improving America's Schools Act (formerly the Elementary and Secondary Education Act) moved away from bilingualism as a deficit and set in motion models of schooling that promoted dual-language acquisition and support for primary languages. This was later undercut by the No Child Left Behind Act of 2001, whose Title III emphasizes achievement in English rather promoting developmental bilingualism (see Ovando, Combs, and Collier, 2006).

■ *Lau v. Nichols (1974).* Ruling that bilingual students had a civil right to language support programs, this Supreme Court case prompted oversight of bilingual programs by the Office of Civil Rights (OCR).

■ *Casteñeda v. Pickard (1981).* This court case mandated that school districts had to comply with the Equal Educational Opportunity Act of 1974 and provided guidelines for OCR to use to protect the civil rights of language-minority students.

■ *Phyler v. Doe (1982).* Students cannot be denied quality schooling on the basis of undocumented immigrant status; this protects the rights of parents to insist on quality schooling.

Bilingual Education and the Teaching of English

Bilingual education, in its most basic form, incorporates three characteristics: (1) continued development of the primary language; (2) acquisition of a second language, usually English; and (3) instruction in the content areas (Ovando & Collier, 1998). A fourth characteristic is the promotion of self-esteem and pride in the primary culture. However, it is not always feasible to implement a bilingual program. When there are too few English learners to justify primary-language support, monolingual instruction takes place with an ELD component.

Program models for English learners vary widely across the United States. One could find children who speak English only and Spanish only mixed in a shared kindergarten class or a two-way-immersion first grade; a second- and third-grade combination class mixed with English-only students plus native Spanish speakers who have had previous schooling either in a Spanish-language class or in TBE; a third-grade TBE class; and other combinations of learner, language, and curriculum, including an ESL resource room. These models offer a variety of alternatives, with varying degrees of success.

This chapter specifically promotes dual immersion as the preferred model for educating English learners. In many local contexts, this approach may not be feasible. However, teachers who teach in other types of programs can compare the dual-immersion model with their own program, noting the strengths and shortcomings of each model.

Submersion (Sink or Swim)

It sounds like a nightmare. You find yourself lost in a strange building one day, surrounded by hundreds of people milling about, speaking a language you do not understand. Finally, someone smiles at you, says something, and hands you a sheet of paper covered with odd characters. He points, pats you on the back, and leaves you on your own. You recognize numbers on the paper and try to match them with the numbers on classroom doors. In a fog, you enter a room. More noise. A gentleman turns to you and says something that sounds like a question, but you have no idea what he has said. He hands you a book filled with incomprehensible writing, points to a desk, then turns away. You seem to become invisible and remain so the rest of the day, without understanding or communicating, just feeling isolated, a true nightmare.

Unfortunately, this nightmare, with slight variations, occurs time after time in the lives of beginning-level ESL students (Osgood, 2002, p. 43).

It is illegal in the United States to submerge English learners in mainstream classrooms in which no provisions are made for the language and academic needs of English learners. As a result of submersion the strongest may survive or even succeed academically (they "swim"); but the majority do not have the cognitive and academic foundation in the primary language at the time of their education in English and therefore do not attain the level of success educators might wish (they "sink"). Overall, submersion is academically disabling.

Transitional Bilingual and Structured Immersion Programs

Before examining dual-language programs, a look at two other programs will provide a contrast. Transitional bilingual education (TBE) programs support the use of the students' home languages in academic settings only during the period in which they acquire enough English proficiency to make the transition into English-only education. This subtractive view of bilingualism in effect requires English learners to discontinue the use of their native language as they increase their fluency in English (Nieto, 2008). In these programs, students receive initial instruction in most, if not all, content areas in their home language while they are being taught English.

There are numerous problems with a TBE program. It may be perceived as a remedial program and/or another form of segregated, compensatory education. It rests on the common misconception that two or three years is sufficient time to learn a second language for schooling purposes; in fact, this is not long enough for students to build cognitive academic language proficiency in either their native tongue or English. As a consequence, they may not be able to carry out cognitively demanding tasks in either English or their home language.

The following vignette illustrates the challenge in teaching reading in a transitional bilingual education classroom:

> In Ann García's fourth-grade classroom at Chaparral Hills Elementary School in Moreno Valley, California, the ethnic makeup of the 27 children consists of 22 students of Hispanic heritage, 2 European Americans, 1 African American, and 2 children of European/African American mix. Of the 22 Hispanic students, 17 are proficient in Spanish speaking and listening, and 5 are not. Of the 17 who are fluent in Spanish listening and speaking, 8 read fluently in Spanish, 6 read with a more limited capacity, and 3 do not read in Spanish. These students have attained mixed proficiency in Spanish for a number of reasons, including lack of parental support for schooling in Spanish, mixed prior exposure to Spanish reading programs, and insufficient number of qualified bilingual teachers.
>
> In this school district, as in others in California, students attend Spanish instruction only by parental request. Students who do not speak English are expected to undergo one year of structured English immersion (SEI) and then enter a mainstream classroom. Most students make the transition from education in Spanish to education in English no later than the fourth grade.
>
> Mrs. García has established six different reading groups to meet the needs of the students. The first group are Spanish readers whose skills are at the fourth-grade level in Spanish; the second group reads at the second-grade level in Spanish. The third, fourth, and fifth groups comprise those who are reading at the second, third, and fourth grades in English. The sixth "group" consists of one Spanish speaker without previous schooling whose Spanish reading is "emergent." This student requires the services of a tutor. Mrs. García continually changes the composition of the reading groups throughout the year, as some students begin to read in English and others move up to higher levels. By the end of the year, transition into English is complete, and there are no more Spanish reading groups.

Reflection reveals problems with this scenario. First, those students who are in the top reading group in Spanish may not be receiving grade-level instruction in English. They must devote extra time to English to catch up to the English-only readers, who are at the same time moving forward to the next grade level in their reading. Second, after transition, the top students in Spanish may not be the top students in reading and language arts overall, as the school's exclusive use of English favors the English-only students. Third, the fact that they cannot continue to learn in Spanish, a subject to which they have devoted three years, is a blow to students' motivation. Imagine an athlete who trained daily for three years, only to find out in the end that the sport had been canceled!

Another shortcoming of TBE is its effect on home-language use. After transition to English, conversational fluency in the home language tends to erode. Frequently, students switch to English as their primary language of communication. Research evidence suggests that this retards rather than expedites academic progress in English (Dolson, 1985), primarily because children and parents lose the benefit of a shared language for such purposes as homework help. For these and other reasons, TBE programs have not led to school success for many students (see Medina & Escamilla, 1992).

The same drawbacks that can be identified in the TBE model also hold true for students in structured English immersion programs, in which students are taught solely in English supplemented with SDAIE strategies (see Chapter 5). Although supporters of SEI programs equate increased time spent immersed in English with increased classroom learning, a key missing factor in this research is that the opportunity for dual-language proficiency is lost. Though foreign-language teaching is increasing in elementary classrooms in developed countries around the world, neither SEI nor TBE classrooms of English learners in the United States take advantage of the chance to support dual-language proficiency.

Newcomers Centers

Newcomers High School in Queens, New York, offers recent immigrant high school students a chance to transition into regular high schools after specialized preparation in English. Most of the 900 students are from China and Latin American countries, but also from countries such as Poland, Haiti, Tibet, Indonesia, India, and Bangladesh. Students spend up to half their day in English classes, grouped according to level of fluency. Beyond core academics, students enjoy classes in art, dance, music, and business. Parent turnout is good for workshops. "Our parents are new to the country," said principal Mary Burke. "We give them demonstrations and that draws them in." Students can use electronic language converters and iPods for self-paced tutorials. The library features books in 35 different languages as well as easy-to-read titles in English. After graduation, nearly 90 percent of graduates enroll in two or four-year colleges (H. S. 555, 2011).

Dual-Literacy Programs: An Introduction

Four kinds of educational programs promote the acquisition of English side by side with acquisition or maintenance of other languages. These are *developmental bilingual, second- or foreign-language immersion, two-way immersion,* and *EFL foreign-language partial immersion.*

Dual-literacy programs are also dual-oracy programs; the four language modes of speaking, listening, reading, and writing are promoted in two languages. These programs are distinguished from foreign-language programs, in which the target language is not used for content instruction.

Developmental Bilingual Programs in the United States

Also called late-exit bilingual and maintenance bilingual education (MBE), developmental bilingual programs are designed for students who enter school speaking a primary language other than English. The goal of these programs is for students to preserve and advance academic proficiency in their heritage language as they become proficient in English, leading to additive bilingualism. The major assumption in such a program is that bilingualism is a valuable asset, not only for bilingual individuals but also for society as a whole.

The goal of advancing dual-language skills has not always been the focus of bilingual education. When the federal government passed the Bilingual Education Act of 1968 (Title VII, an amendment to the 1965 Elementary and Secondary Education Act), the purpose was compensatory. Children who were unable to speak English were considered to be educationally disadvantaged, and federal aid to bilingual education was seen as a "remedial" program (Wiese & García, 1998). The focus shifted again in 1989, when MBE programs were expanded. Since that time, maintaining and developing the native language of students has become an important goal for advocates of bilingual education.

Developmental programs have been implemented mainly at the elementary level. They are rarely continued into the intermediate grades. The goals of developmental bilingual programs are maintenance and full development of the student's primary language, full proficiency in all aspects of English, grade-appropriate achievement in all domains of academic study, integration into wholly English-language classrooms, and positive identity regarding the culture of both the primary- and the majority-language group (Cloud et al., 2000).

Two studies (Ramírez, 1992; Collier, 1992) have provided considerable support for the idea that students in MBE programs have greater academic success than students who are educated in SEI or TBE programs. According to the studies, students in MBE programs, who continue to receive academic instruction in a language they can understand, are able to keep up with English-speaking students. In contrast, students in the SEI or TBE programs over time fall further behind in academic subjects. These studies lend empirical support to additive bilingual models.

One challenge for developmental bilingual programs is to achieve an adequate balance between support for the native language and ESL instruction. Children in a developmental bilingual program may be served by "pull-out" ESL instruction (L. D. Soto, 1991). If this is the case, the ESL instructor should be qualified. A far better approach is English instruction within the classroom in an integrated biliteracy model.

A particularly compelling illustration of MBE programs is the education of Native Americans. The attempt to increase the number of speakers of Native American languages is sometimes called "restorative" bilingual education. Because NCLB assessments are conducted only in English, students learning in two-way (dual) immersion programs who are spending 50 to 90 percent of their instructional time in primary-language classes are at a disadvantage on standardized (English) testing. Currently, these schools are under pressure to demonstrate adequate yearly progress (AYP) by grade 3. Thus, two-way programs are being undermined by the NCLB mandates. Cummins, Brown, and Sayers (2007) offered as an example a Navajo-language pre-K–6 bilingual program in which students had improved their oral and written English proficiency while becoming fluent and literate in Navajo. In 2002–2003, however, funding for this program ended, and the program was labeled as "underperforming" based on students' standardized test scores. The school hosting the program faced the possibility of being placed in receivership by the Bureau of Indian Affairs. This outcome underscores the fragility of restoration efforts.

Second- and Foreign-Language Immersion Programs for Majority-Language Students

Second-language immersion, also called enrichment education, provides academic and language instruction in two languages. The goal of immersion programs is additive bilingualism. Many such programs are found in Canada, where English and French both have high status for instructional purposes. In this model, middle-class, English-speaking children are instructed in French, and English is incorporated into the programs both as a subject and as a medium of instruction (W. Lambert, 1984). In the United States, a comparable schooling context is some private schools exclusive to the upper class, in which foreign languages are highly valued, even to the extent of having instruction delivered directly in those languages. In early immersion programs, the second language is introduced in kindergarten or first grade. Early partial immersion uses English about 50 percent of the time rather than delivering academic instruction solely through the second language (Cloud et al., 2000).

The enrichment immersion model is inadequate for English learners in the United States because the low status of the students' primary language puts it at risk for suppression. When the minority language is not a high-status language, few middle-class English-speaking parents will favor having their children immersed in it for instructional purposes.

Two-Way Immersion Programs for Majority-Language and Minority-Language Students

Two-way immersion (TWI) (also called two-way maintenance bilingual) groups English learners from a single language background in the same classroom with approximately equal numbers of English-speaking students. The curriculum is provided approximately at grade level in both languages. Speakers of each language develop proficiency in both their native and their second language, achieve academically through and in two languages, and come to appreciate one another's languages and cultures (Lindholm, 1994). This method enhances the status of both primary languages, promoting self-esteem and increased cultural pride and leading to increased motivation. Cummins (2000a) argued that "a major advantage of two-way bilingual programs…is that they overcome segregation in a planned program that aims to enrich the learning opportunities of both minority- and majority-language students" (p. 142).

TWI programs had been implemented in 182 schools in the United States by 1995 (Christian, Montone, Lindholm, & Carranza, 1997), and the number of schools is growing yearly. Sites are located in eighteen states ranging from Alaska to Florida, with the largest number in California and New York. Nearly all the schools (167) are Spanish–English in design, although other schools immerse students in Arabic, Cantonese, French, Japanese, Navajo, Portuguese, and Russian (with the other language in all cases being English). The grade levels served are predominantly K–6. Examples that follow focus on Spanish–English program designs.

Careful attention to a high-quality bilingual program in the context of primary-language maintenance is key to the success of TWI programs (Veeder & Tramutt, 2000). Successful dual-language programs are described in Howard and Sugarman (2007). In addition, the National Clearinghouse for English Language Acquisition has a wealth of information about two-way programs (available at www.ncela.gwu.edu).

Transfer of Literacy.   TWI is predicated on beginning literacy instruction for students in both languages. But how are skills transferred from beginning literacy instruction in Spanish to that of English? Goldenberg (1990) found that beginning literacy instruction in Spanish made extensive use of phonics-based, sound–syllable approaches that were weaker in providing opportunities to read connected text. Edelsky (1986) described attempts to introduce a reading-and-writing approach in a bilingual program in Arizona that took a phonics approach to Spanish reading. Both Goldenberg and Edelsky have advocated a balanced approach to Spanish reading instruction in which children have many occasions to interact with meaningful text.

Reading in a foreign language above the level of emergent literacy takes place through the use of both literature and subject area content, following many of the same principles as reading in the native language. Time is given in class for reading so that students working in groups can facilitate one another's comprehension. To appeal to students' varied interests, all types of content are used (magazines, newspapers, plays, novels, stories, and poems), depending also on the proficiency level of students and the level of language studied. In this way, students are assured of receiving a challenging academic program in both languages.

Criticisms of TWI.   Critics have argued that TWI delays English learning and fails to teach English to English learners. Because TWI programs teach content in the primary language, they do not emphasize communication in English, as do TBE programs. Amselle (1999) argued that "dual immersion programs are really nothing more than Spanish immersion, with Hispanic children used as teaching tools for English-speaking children." Experts concede that the greatest challenge in two-way bilingual programs is to "reduce the gap" between the language abilities of the two groups (English learners and SLLs). This gap appears as content classes in English are modified (slowed down) for English learners to "catch up," or as content delivery in the primary language is slowed for Spanish-as-a-second-language students. As Molina (2000) advised, "Without a watchful approach to the quality of two-way programs, schools will find themselves tragically exploiting the English learners they had hoped to help for the benefit of the language majority students."

Advocacy for Dual-Language Programs

Despite these criticisms, TWI is gaining in popularity in the United States. Parents of native English speakers see advantages in having their children learn academic and social skills in two languages, whereas parents of English learners see that the home language is valued. This is a win–win situation. Strong partnerships between schools and parents are needed, however, for these programs to be maintained.

Parents who are looking into a TWI program generally have three major concerns (Cloud et al., 2000). First, will the students attain as high a level of achievement in English and in the content areas as those in non-TWI programs, and will the students be able to transfer successfully to non-TWI programs after having been in the TWI program? Second, will parents be able to help their children in the language they do not know? Last, will children be able to attain a high level of proficiency in the home language? Will the identity and self-esteem of the children be fostered and the primary culture maintained and transmitted, and will students feel able to converse with native speakers in both languages?

The Role of Monolingual English Instructors in a Dual-Language Program

Educators who teach English to speakers of other languages but are not themselves speakers of another language sometimes feel threatened by bilingual programs, fearing that individuals with dual-language skills will take their jobs. However,

Dual immersion programs help children learn Spanish whose families have not maintained their heritage language.

©Ted Foxx/Alamy

many TWI models are successful in pairing a bilingual teacher with one who is not. There are many ways in which monolingual teachers can demonstrate that they value students' languages and cultural experiences. These include making literature and learning resources available in two languages; encouraging students to write in more than one language, share that writing with others, and help one another by speaking in both languages; using adults and community members who speak the primary language to assist in instruction; and advocating for literacy in two languages.

Biliteracy in a TWI Context

Complexities of Biliteracy

A TWI context is complex because the contexts of the classroom and the school together influence how children learn to use language. Students in a TWI program do not merely absorb and produce two languages; they do so while immersed in a sea of covert messages regarding social uses of two languages, effects on instruction stemming from the similarities and differences between the languages, and complications resulting from the different practices of literacy acquisition in the distinct languages (Pérez & Torres-Guzmán, 2002). This complexity is aggravated by social and educational discrimination that has historically existed in the attitudes toward and treatment of minority groups in the United States (Cummins, 1989), as well as by local social and political conditions in the community of a given school. Two additional complicating factors are the relative similarity or dissimilarity of the languages and the type of script they use. The process of language instruction within a framework of biliteracy is complex. Table 12.2 offers seven questions about dual-literacy development.

> *Megastrategy* **12.2**
>
> **Teach literacy and oracy in two languages**

A Teaching Unit in Two Languages

Let's Go to Mexico/Vamos a México is an integrated teaching unit on the culture and traditions of Mexico that Christina Panzeri-Álvarez (1998), a second-grade teacher, developed with her students. The unit comprises twenty lessons combining social studies, language arts, mathematics, art, and music. Each lesson uses Spanish and English together.

> Students first create a passport for travel to various cities in Mexico. They identify regions and states using a geographical atlas of Mexico and briefly describe the historical background of Mexico. Using travel brochures, they first choose favorite vacation destinations and then write a persuasive letter to their parents, telling why they think such a trip would be enjoyable.

TABLE 12.2 *Questions and Answers about Dual-Literacy Development*

Question	Answer
What level of oral proficiency is necessary to teach literacy?	Younger children need to develop some oral and prerequisite cognitive skills (e.g., retaining information in short-term memory). For older students, an integrated oral/literacy approach is recommended.
In what order should literacy be introduced when two languages are taught?	For speakers of a minority language, three to five years of primary-language reading instruction should take place before reading instruction in English begins. Some exposure to oral English is beneficial.
	For majority-language students in a dual-language program, some programs begin with non-English-language literacy and academics. Other programs begin with the respective primary languages in order to build on existing oral language skills.
Why should literacy be taught in one language before beginning the second?	Students' reading rates, fluency, and comprehension may be compromised if both languages are begun simultaneously. Moreover, too much time may be spent on reading at the expense of other content.
How can reading be matched to a student's language proficiency level?	Students should be familiar with the core vocabulary used in the reading; the story line should be easy to grasp.
What cultural features of texts facilitate dual literacy?	Students possess the background knowledge and life experience required to understand the text; the materials represent and honor the cultural groups present in the school and their values.
How are materials used in dual literacy judged as authentic?	The language used is natural and predictable, and the level of colloquiality versus formality is appropriate; texts are based on the literary traditions of students.
What can be done with a student who reads well in the first language and performs poorly in the second language?	Strategies can be borrowed from those designed for special needs learners: use of high-interest/low-readability materials; cued text (underlining, highlighting, margin notes); modeling and demonstration; and peer tutoring and collaborative learning.

Source: Cloud, Genesee, & Hamayan (2000).

Starting in La Ciudad de México, students explore the capital. They read "La Calle del Indio Triste" from Macías's (1996) *Leyendas Mexicanas,* draw and color a Mexican flag, and learn the "Himno Nacional Mexicano," translating it into English, noting similarities and differences in words and word order in English and Spanish, and comparing the anthem to "The Star Spangled Banner." The next lesson is a favorite: making corn tortillas, and listing and discussing the recipes that use tortillas as a basis.

Students next "travel" to the Guadalajara, "The Pearl of the West." They read about mariachi orchestras using the website www.mariachi.org. They tour the giant market (*mercado*) San Juan de Dios, also known as La Libertad (see http://vive.guadalajara.gob.mx). They role-play how to bargain at a Mexican market, use math to convert dollars to pesos, practice converting to the metric system of measurement, cook *nopales* (prickly pear cactus), and make a piñata. Moving on to Michoacán, Veracruz, and Oaxaca, they make mole, "attend" a Mexican wedding, and learn a traditional song of Veracruz, "La Bamba." At the end of the unit, students reflect on their travels and write about their favorite places.

Although this unit did not originate in a TWI setting, its emphasis on biliteracy and its theme can easily be adapted to a TWI program. Families who are familiar with various cities in Mexico are invited to show-and-tell. Students from Mexico sustain pride in their culture, and students who are not familiar with Mexico gain valuable skills in Spanish.

Box 12.1 Biliteracy through "Reading Cooperatives"

Despite ten years of primarily English-only schooling in the wake of California's Proposition 227 initiative mandating "structured" English immersion as the predominant literacy model, two teachers in Los Angeles Unified School District found that students assigned to their elementary classes had remained functionally illiterate in both English and Spanish.

Interviewing family members, the teachers realized that English-only programs had accelerated a steady extinction of Spanish from the literacy environment of the home, and that English had come to be considered an alien, foreign language. Consequently the two teachers constructed after-school "reading cooperatives" in which parents and students could engage in dialogic reading activities that combined their knowledge in Spanish as a tool to master both English and Spanish reading.

"*Leyendo juntos, crecemos*" ("Reading together, we grow") was the theme of the first evening meeting at the school. Parents, students and teachers read passages of Sandra Cisneros's *Hairs/Pelitos* in a communal reading experience followed by discussion about hair. Later a local bookstore offered parents a discount on bilingual books, and the "reading cooperatives" went on to explore chapter books. The result? Families began to enjoy reading in two languages and there was a high level of engagement with the school—and yes, test scores went up (Valls, 2009).

Box 12.2 Cultural History: Chicana Women

Martínez's *500 years of Chicana Women's History (500 Años de la Mujer Chicana)* is an invaluable reference for English learner classrooms, especially those with Spanish–English bilingual skills. Text and pictures featuring social and political issues over the long history of Mexican-American women's struggles will fascinate and enlighten English learners, provoking rich discussions and writing.

Principles of Language Transfer

Issues of language transfer are complicated not only by the complex nature of receptive and productive skills of oracy/literacy in two languages but also by the oral/literate contexts, the type of media that literacy employs with respect to simultaneous/successive exposure to languages, and, to some degree, the contrast between alphabetic and nonalphabetic languages. Expert use of strategies maximizes the probability that language acquisition will occur in sufficient depth and at a rapid pace.

Metalinguistic Awareness and Common Underlying Proficiency

Educators once believed that not speaking the dominant language of the school (in the case of ELD students, not speaking English) was a handicap that interfered with and delayed cognitive growth. This belief assumes that content and skills learned through the primary language do not transfer to English. This notion of "no interrelationship between languages" has been termed *separate underlying proficiency (SUP)* (Cummins, 1981b). The contrasting notion, *common underlying proficiency (CUP)*, is the belief that the primary and second languages have a shared foundation, an idea that Cummins (1979, 1981b) has cited much evidence to support.

Megastrategy **12.3**

Teach for transfer between the primary language and English

One common element is *metalinguistic awareness,* which refers to knowledge about the structural properties of language, including sounds, words, and grammar. It also means knowledge of language and its functions (Gombert, 1992) and awareness that there is more than one way to represent meaning, that to "realize the arbitrary nature of language in that form of language, either written or spoken language, is something different from meaning" (Yaden & Templeton, 1986, p. 9).

Metalinguistic awareness can develop either alongside primary-language acquisition or during middle childhood as the child learns to think about the linguistic system (Tunmer, Herriman, & Nesdale, 1988). A third view is that metalinguistic awareness is a result of schooling, particularly of learning to read. Up to a point, metalinguistic ability is a function of age, and students vary in this ability. To summarize best practice in promoting metalinguistic awareness, knowledge, and skills, Table 12.3 divides these into four components and prescribes practices that enhance their various components.

Teaching for Transfer: Language-Acquisition Processes

Language-acquisition processes involve mental activities that people employ to be able to communicate ideas. Two of these processes involve general cognitive mechanisms that individuals use to learn: *transfer* and *generalization*. Transfer is applying old learning to new situations, whereas generalization involves inferring or drawing conclusions in order to respond to a situation.

TABLE 12.3 *Practices That Promote Metalinguistic Awareness*

Component of Metalinguistic Awareness	Definition	Suggestions to the Teacher to Enhance Awareness
Metaphonological	Identifying the phonological components in linguistic units and intentionally manipulating them (Gombert, 1992, pp. 15, 39, 63)	■ Teach sound–symbol connection (phonics). ■ Teach word segmentation into syllables.
Metasyntactic	The ability to reason consciously about the syntactic aspects of language and to exercise intentional control over the application of grammatical rules (Gombert, 1992, p. 39)	■ Have students make good/bad judgments on the correct form of sentences (could use peer editing).
Metapragmatic	The awareness or knowledge one has about the relationships between language and the context in which the language is embedded	■ Help students to judge the adequacy of messages and their context. ■ Point out ironic, sarcastic, humorous, and polite forms of language.
Metasemantic	The ability to recognize the language system as a conventional and arbitrary code and the ability to manipulate words or phrases, without the signified correspondents being automatically affected by this (Gombert, 1992, p. 63)	■ Teach students about word denotation and connotation and nuance of meaning. ■ Expand vocabulary of synonyms and antonyms. ■ Explore word oddities. ■ Help students to find cognates between languages.

Principles of Transfer.   Educators point out that transfer can be anticipated by closely aligning contexts or by engaging in immediate and varied practice through simulations, modeling, and problem-solving situations (Perkins, 1986). Abstract transfer depends on attaining a general principle before attempting to transfer, as well as using analogies, parallel problem solving, and metacognitive reflection to build bridges from one context to the next (Fogarty, Perkins, & Barell, 1992).

Language transfer occurs when the comprehension or production of a second language is influenced by the way the first language has been acquired. Sometimes learners use rules from their first language that are not applicable to the second (*negative transfer*). As an illustration, Natheson-Mejia (1989) describes substitutions that Spanish speakers make when writing in English. These include *es* for *s* as in *estop, d* for *t* or *th* as in *broder, ch* for *sh* as in *chort, j* for *h* as in *jelper,* and *g* for *w* as in *sogen* (sewing).

Positive transfer allows people to respond appropriately and meaningfully in new language situations. The use of Spanish–English cognates—that is, words in two languages that look alike and have the same or similar meaning—is a helpful resource (Garrison, 1990; Nagy, García, Durgunoglu, & Hancin-Bhatt, 1993). The many predictable relations between Spanish and English words can assist students to expand their vocabularies with ease. For example, almost all nouns in English that end in *-ion* have a Spanish cognate: *preparation* (*preparación*); *communication* (*communicación*); *attention* (*atención*); and *action* (*acción*).

Contrastive Analysis.   Contrastive analysis compares features from L1 and L2 to predict learnability—the more the two languages differ, the more difficult the transfer. Contemporary theory recognizes the importance of the first language in a global sense and does not encourage learners to compare minute surface forms of the first and second languages as they learn.

A general cognitive strategy used by all learners is generalization. In first-language acquisition, this process is seen when young children begin to put labels on concepts. "Dada," a child may say to any male, or "ball," for any round object. *Overgeneralization* refers to situations in which the learner incorrectly generalizes a rule to cases in which it does not apply. English learners may say, for example, "I don't can do that," overgeneralizing the rule "insert *do* in negative clauses."

What kind of transfer can be expected from the first language to the second? Students can transfer sensorimotor skills (eye–hand coordination, fine-muscle control, spatial and directional skills, visual perception and memory); auditory skills (auditory perception, memory, discrimination, and sequencing); common features of writing systems (alphabets, punctuation rules); comprehension strategies (finding the main idea, inferring, predicting, use of cuing systems); study skills (taking notes, using reference sources); habits and attitudes (self-esteem, task persistence, focus) (Cloud et al., 2000); (speech–print relationships; concepts such as syllable, word, sentence, paragraph); and knowledge about the reading process.

Teachers can transform positive transfer into a learning strategy by helping students to become aware of ways in which they can draw from prior knowledge of "how language works" to make English easier. They can explicitly foster this approach by welcoming dual-language use, understanding code-switching, providing support for literacy in multiple languages, and honoring primary languages; and they can use specific strategies to help students build English proficiency on a firm foundation of primary-language proficiency.

Literary Transfer to English from Alphabetic and Nonalphabetic Languages.   The unit of linguistic representation in alphabets such as English is a symbol that represents a phoneme—even though in English, unlike, say Hawaiian and Spanish, the correspondence is not exact. Readers whose first language in nonalphabetic, however, are not used to pronouncing words for recognition and tend to rely solely on visual cues such as the shape of the word. Alco (2009/2010) recommends that beginning readers from nonalphabetic languages be given increased "bottom-up" processing, such as word recognition skills, to speed up automatic phonemic–graphemic connections.

Biliteracy and Biculturality

A bilingual/bicultural approach to teaching helps students to establish, maintain, and value the language and culture of their homes and communities as much as their skills in English (see Chapter 10).

Megastrategy **12.4**
Provide cultural support for dual-language learning

Students who are supported in both languages and are able to attain a high level of scholarship can use both languages for literacy purposes. They can develop reading and writing in the second language simultaneously with speaking and listening skills. When students are provided functional use of two or more languages, they are able to read more widely, expanding their worldview. If the teachers can draw from students' cultural backgrounds to complement learning that goes on in the classroom,

Box 12.3   **Using "Affinity Spaces" to Promote Dual-Language Development**

Immigrants can use online digital media to create elaborate literacy practices related to the development of their second language and maintenance of native language literacy, drawing upon multiple languages and media resources to learn. Using Gee's (2007) concept of "affinity spaces" W. S. E. Lam (2009) profiles two youths who used the Internet (including such sites as *Uwants, Anime Paper*, and *Gendou*) to network with others who share their interests in the Japanese comic forms of manga and anime, as well as in deeper philosophical issues. The youths, both English learners, kept up their Cantonese and Mandarin skills and their cultural knowledge of contemporary trends by frequent, creative, and complex discussion board postings.

TABLE 12.4 *A Bilingual/Bicultural Approach to Teaching*

Considerations That Guide Effective Practice	Description
Use both languages for literacy instruction.	Primary-language use permits students access to core concepts, shows respect for its value, and enhances SLA.
Develop reading and writing simultaneously with speaking and listening skills in L2.	A holistic approach does not delay literacy for the sake of oral skills.
Provide functional use of the languages.	Students can choose to use either language to communicate, depending on what the situation seems to warrant.
Use students' cultural backgrounds as a tool for learning.	Students read books in their second language about which they have had experience.
Become cultural brokers.	Teachers help students to acquire knowledge and understanding of the use of the literacy skills they are acquiring and the cultural knowledge needed to comprehend text.
Have high expectations regardless of language proficiency.	Each student works to his or her potential in an environment that communicates the faith that all will succeed.

Source: Based on Brisk & Harrington (2000).

there is more potential for involving the community in a meaningful way (see Table 12.4). Echevarria and Graves (2007, p. 88) described a case study that shows how a limited-Spanish-speaking science teacher became a role model for English learners:

> The teacher spoke Spanish with his pupils to demonstrate the value he placed on the learners' native language, and became a role model regarding the learning of a new language (Pease-Alvarez & Winsler, 1994). Though his knowledge of Spanish was quite limited, he sought help from students in using Spanish properly. He started with a Spanish translation of the key vocabulary for the topic. Students responded well to this teacher, and their English skills improved (p. 88).

The biliterate, bicultural community is a vision yet to be realized in the United States, yet models exist in other parts of the world. If English is one of the languages, it must take its place as a full, supportive partner of its sister and brother languages.

Exploratory Break

- If you were to make a visit to a dual-language immersion program in your area, what questions would you ask? Make a list. Consider the following categories:

  Curriculum

  Lesson plans/planning

  L1 support

  Second language acquisition methodology

  Assessment for placement and progress in proficiency

  Differentiated instruction

Chapter *13*

Teaching English in Context

Mr. Park was a student who had a successful business in Korea training students in grammar to pass the Test of English as a Foreign Language (TOEFL) so that they could apply to university programs in the United States. His teaching consisted of presenting sentence after sentence in English while speaking in Korean to explain the grammar structures. For him, English might have been algebra: a puzzle, a code, a complex system needing extensive explanation. However, when he applied to and was accepted into graduate school in the United States, his lack of ability to speak and understand spoken English became a challenge both for him and the instructors. In his graduate classes in the MA TESOL program, Mr. Park was silent, and after ten minutes of listening to English he would mentally drift away. Finally, I discussed with him the issue of his lack of oral/aural English. "Korean men don't have to talk," he said. I felt sorry for him, because he was somehow unable to learn to listen to or speak English.

But one of my colleagues gave me a different picture of the situation. "Quit pitying him," he said. "Mr. Park can speak English if he wants to—he just doesn't want to."

English learners have language rights, and one of those rights is not to speak English. In fact, many students of English will never need to speak English and will never learn to speak English. For them, English learning has other purposes: to attain high entrance examination scores, to read business documents, or to decode radio transmissions. In their contexts, oral/aural English may not be necessary. One kind of contextualized English is English for Special Purposes (ESP), English that is adapted specifically for science, technology, or business. Another kind of contextualized English is a dialect, a way of speaking that individuals have developed within

Megastrategy **SET 13**

Teach respect for contextual usage of English

the context of a special group of speakers. This chapter concerns these contextual uses of English.

The reading and writing that are performed in various contexts—situated literacy—are influenced by the social and institutional practices and power relations of each specific context (Barton, Hamilton, & Ivanič, 2000). This chapter addresses two issues that are normally not grouped together: *situated oracy* (listening/speaking) and *situated literacy* (reading/writing). Situated oracy, including considerations of *oral dialect,* is evinced when people talk a certain way in order to feel appropriate within a given context. Situated literacy influences the way people read and write in a given context. This chapter explores situated oracy and situated literacy in turn, as the research traditions of the two differ greatly, and then discusses what teachers can do in the classroom to communicate respect for and understanding of contextual influences on the use of the English language.

Dialects in English

Megastrategy **13.1**

Honor the dialect of the learner

Many people have had the experience of picking up the telephone and listening to the voice of a stranger. Within the first few seconds, I can usually tell if the speaker's voice is familiar. If I do not recognize the voice, I am left to rely on other cues, such as the accent and dialect of the speaker. As Wolfram (1991) noted, "It is surprising how little conversation it takes to draw conclusions about a speaker's 'background'; a sentence, a phrase, or even a word is adequate to trigger a regional, social, or ethnic classification" (p. 1).

English is spoken with regional dialects all over the world. *Dialect* refers to "any variety of language which is shared by a group of speakers" (Wolfram, 2011). Dialects are important in many languages as markers of social class, ethnicity, regional background, and other social characteristics. Although Americans like to believe they live in a casteless society, the United States seems to have inherited the British tradition of using language as a marker of social class. As Wolfram (1991) noted, "In fact, there are some who feel that language differences serve as the single most reliable indicator of social position in our society. When we live a certain way, we are expected to match that lifestyle with our talk" (p. 2).

Language varies by region, social class, and ethnic origin. In some respects, the study of dialect overlaps with other aspects of cultural study, folklore, and literature. Some people enjoy the study of dialects as a way of understanding human differences, or as a way of learning more about their own culture. This leads people to listen to others when they speak and to draw conclusions about what they hear.

As a native of Pittsburgh, Pennsylvania, I am able to identify others whose accent originates in that region. For example, they say "still mill" ("steel mill") and "dantan" ("downtown"). Certain features of the dialect were then, and still are, negatively evaluated by others. At that time, a middle-class person, hearing the sentence

"I shoulda went" instead of "I should [have] gone," automatically disapproved. In southern California, however, the use of the simple past to replace the past participle is common in the middle class and is not as negatively stigmatized. I can now listen to "You shoulda went with us" and not wince—most of the time.

Dialects and the Education of English Learners

Language educators cannot help being influenced by dialect considerations. Wolfram (1995) emphasized the importance of dialect issues for educators of English learners:

> The standard version of English provided in most ESL curricula aims unrealistically at a dialect-neutral variety of English. At the same time, the majority of ESL learners are surrounded by an array of dialects, including some well-established vernacular dialects for those who live in economically impoverished conditions.... Because many ESL learners may, in fact, speak vernacular varieties of their own languages that are comparable in status to the vernacular dialects of English, they may have already experienced language variation and bias. It thus seems appropriate to incorporate dimensions of langage variation into the ESL curriculum. (p. 1)

Issues of Dialect in EFL.   EFL and ELD contexts differ somewhat in the issues involving dialect. For those who teach English abroad, their own English dialect may be an issue. Many English-teaching programs abroad prefer to hire native speakers of English on the assumption that native speakers are more expert on the target language and culture.

A second issue is that of honoring the dialect of the learner. The English of native speakers may not be the English needed or used in the local context (Kirkpatrick, 2000). A more complex issue is that of teacher expectations. The EFL teacher may be tempted to reduce the standards of language use, believing that English used inside the artificial confines of the EFL classroom is "good enough." Finding the appropriate balance of language knowledge, pedagogical skill, dialect accommodation, and standard-language modeling is a challenge for English education in the EFL context.

A third issue in the EFL context is prejudice on the part of international speakers of English. They may discriminate against native speakers who speak a dialect.

Issues of Dialect in ELD.   In the ELD context, the issue of whether ELD teachers should model standard English is still relevant. In many urban school districts, where bilingual (Spanish–English) teachers are in demand, personnel administrators do not seem to see Spanish-accented English as a negative factor in elementary school teaching. However, the same administrators still seem to prefer to hire high school English teachers who are native speakers or who speak English without a "foreign" accent.

The second issue, that of honoring the dialect of the learner, means finding the appropriate balance between accepting and honoring the home dialect of the student and modeling and teaching standard English. In many urban schools in the United States, English learners attend classes in schools with African American students, some of whom speak African American Vernacular English (AAVE). Teachers of English learners in urban schools—or even in rural schools in which speakers of dialects interact with English learners—need to understand how to teach English in these contexts.

Prejudice is a third issue in ELD contexts. Often a speaker of a regional dialect (for example, a Puerto Rican dialect in Massachusetts) is not accorded the same respect as a speaker of standard English. Thus, dialect issues are also issues of social power and status in society.

Teachers who understand dialects understand better how to teach. In a court case in Ann Arbor, Michigan, in 1979, teachers were ordered to attend workshops on dialects because of the potential impact on the school's achievement of vernacular dialect students (Wolfram, 1991).

Students who speak nonstandard dialects are very aware that their speech creates potential difficulties in such areas as successfully acquiring standard forms for academic writing and avoiding stereotyping and discrimination if their dialect is negatively evaluated by others (see Nero, 1997). They are also aware that their very identity and deepest values are linked to their language, leading to potential conflicts in self-evaluation and acculturation. Their dialects can lead, however, to possible positive biculturality (Bosher, 1997). These factors make the role of dialect a complex variable in the language of English learners.

Before addressing the question of how a teacher deals with dialect, a look at dialect from a linguist's point of view is in order. The following section examines some common features that constitute dialects, ways in which dialects exhibit social and ethnic differences, typical attitudes toward dialects, ways in which gender influences dialect, and ways in which dialects affect speaking style. The section concludes with advice for educators.

Common Features That Constitute Dialects

Why do languages have dialects? Language differences go hand in hand with social differentiation. People may speak differently either because they are physically separated (regional dialects) or because they are socially separated (by means of economic ecology and/or social stratification). A third explanation is based on linguistic differences between the dialects themselves.

Regional Dialects.   *Regional dialects* emerge because groups of people settle in specific places, and the physical terrain keeps dialects isolated and intact. In the United States, the geographic isolation of some communities in Kentucky, Tennessee, North Carolina, Virginia, and West Virginia has given rise to so-called Appalachian English (see Wolfram, 1991). Not all geographic isolation results in regional dialects, however; the important factor is the communication links that the region maintains with other speakers. In Alaska, for example, English speakers maintain links to the larger U.S. media and have not developed significant regional variations in speech. Most linguists recognize four distinct dialects in the United States today; these can be roughly characterized as (1) New York City, (2) New England, (3) the South, and (4) everyone else.

Dialects of English around the world are equally location dependent. As individuals from these parts of the world conduct business or pleasure in their local English, it serves them well enough. It is when English is used internationally—when it is the only common language for each speaker—that differences in dialect become an issue and speakers must learn to decode one another's speech. When complex international negotiations take place, such differences are not an issue, because experts are hired to translate. Dialects become important as international English is used on a daily basis, and in these cases the issues relating to dialect have cultural implications.

It may well be, in fact, that the English spoken in Nigeria, Trinidad, Scotland, and Montana may already be mutually unintelligible. Entire lists of lexical entries differ from one English-speaking country to another: in South Africa, a *robot* is a traffic light; in England, a *lift* is an elevator, a *lorry* is a truck, and a *boot* is the trunk of a car; in Massachusetts, a *frappe* is a milkshake; and in South Asia, a *hotel* is a restaurant. English may soon find itself in the quandary of Chinese: The written language is shared, but Cantonese and Mandarin are considered distinct languages.

As an example of these cultural implications, in the colonizing of Puerto Rico, as well as in the diaspora of Puerto Ricans living in the United States, Puerto Ricans have most often interacted with people from New York and New England. Many people in the United States find New Englanders terse and think New Yorkers' speech is brusque. The way people from the southern United States speak English, in contrast, is more languid, more tropical in pace and rhythm; but southerners seldom travel to Puerto Rico. Therefore, Puerto Ricans often feel themselves remote in culture from "Americans," with little recognition of how much their values and lifestyles—even their speech habits—resemble those of U.S. southerners. Thus, regional differences in English dialects can enhance intercultural communication or, conversely, hinder the process.

Social Stratification. Dialects reflect *social stratification* due to differences in the social groups with which people affiliate. People evaluate others by means of their

Box 13.1 **Philadelphia, Can You Understand Pittsburgh?**

Despite the argument that the combined effects of national television broadcasting and a highly mobile population of the United States are creating one homogenous dialect, the cities of the United States are actually showing more diversity than ever, according to William Labov, a sociolinguist at the University of Pennsylvania. In Philadelphia, people are dropping the /L/ phoneme in the middle of a word—"New Balance" shoes are pronounced "New Ba-ance, and ""cellar" is pronounced "ce-ar" (Balzar, 1997). In Pittsburgh, "steel" is pronounced "still" (even though the "still mills" are now gone). And in Pittsburgh, the /l/ before /k/ is long gone—most people in Pittsburgh drink "/miwk/." So English learners, many of whom live in the inner city, may be learning a very local English!

language in order to establish and maintain social distinctions. If people want to be identified as part of a particular social group, they adopt the vocabulary, pronunciation, and grammatical patterns of this group (Wolfram, Adger, & Christian, 1999). This phenomenon is easy to see in the case of teenage slang. More complex is the fact that even when people's language receives negative social evaluation from mainstream English speakers, they continue to use the language of that group even if they have the choice of speaking a different way. Why is this the case?

One reason for the persistence of language dialects stigmatized by the larger society may be their association with ethnic solidarity; speaking like a mainstream person may cause the loss of one's friends or weakening of family ties. It is not uncommon for speakers to try to live in both worlds, to speak like a "hip" urbanite in the city and then to use the vernacular at home with the family.

Language can be used as a signal for social stratification consciously or unconsciously. A vernacular dialect associated with the underclass sometimes also connotes strength, toughness, and resolve. Conversely, speakers may use the pronunciation associated with an elite social class to convey erudition or knowledgability. Thus, dialect differences are socially sustained.

The Deep Syntax of Dialects   Dialects may persist because of deeper syntactic causes. The third explanation for the origin and persistence of dialects is based on linguistic analysis. Double negation within a sentence ("He don't hardly know"), which resembles the AAVE construction "The dog didn't like nobody," is found in European languages. Deletion of the copula ("You ugly") is a feature of AAVE but also of Chinese and other languages. Lack of the 's in the possessive structure (*that man hat*) is correct for specific possessive structures in English (*her hat*); lack of plural endings (*four girl*) is common in many languages; and final stop deletion (*nin' war'* for *ninth ward*) is common in other constructions in English that use midword stop deletion (*water*) or change the unvoiced to voiced consonant. Thus, dialects persist based on the ways in which languages are constructed.

Whether dialects have a regional, social, or linguistic explanation, speakers acquire a dialect of English based on that which is used by others of their region, social class, and native language. The most obvious form of dialect usage is in the sound of the language, or *accent*—how an individual pronounces words. Just because someone speaks with an accent, it does not mean that they are less competent in the language (Wolfram, 2002). In fact, as Lippi-Green asserts, "degree of accentedness, whether from LI interference, or a socially or geographically marked language variety, cannot predict the level of an individual's competency in the target language" (1997, p. 70).

How Dialects Exhibit Social and Ethnic Differences

The stakes are high when it comes to differences in social status, both in the United States and in the United Kingdom. In the United States, regional accents may be seen as quaint or charming, but listeners also use accent to judge on a range of personal qualities and capabilities, such as innate intelligence, morality, and employability (Wolfram, 1991).

Millions of U.S. residents, as well as millions of English-speaking people around the world, do not use the standard accent of the broadcast media, known in the United States as "general American" or "middle western" and in England as "received pronunciation" (Lippi-Green, 1997). Standard pronunciation has become associated with those in high-status occupations—doctors, lawyers, professionals, and executives of large companies—what Christensen (2002) calls the "cash language" (p. 176). Thus, language variation is associated with a person's economic activity. Economic discrimination based on language is enforced by means of informal, often invisible, social networks that intersect with social stratification.

Much of the social stratification that underlies linguistic discrimination is based on ethnic subcultures that manifest themselves in linguistic distinctions. Because of both racial class and prejudice, the extent of exclusion from the mainstream varies according to the number of people involved and the perceived threat these numbers create for the majority. In places like Texas, Spanish is sometimes seen as a major threat to the hegemony of English in the United States, whereas French, another language spoken just offshore in Haiti and over the border in Quebec, is not. This difference may also be due to the relative prestige of French compared to Spanish.

Linguistic influences from subcultures leak into English, and in the process the subcultures acquire some degree of acceptance. Sometimes the language sneaks in through specific customs. Japanese food has brought the language of sushi into major cities, whereas American fast-food chains have created pseudo-Spanish food items like the "chalupa." Popular cinema can also bring subculture language into the mainstream, as in Arnold Schwarzenegger's "Hasta la vista, baby."

In a major example of subculture influence on English, when European Jewish immigrants brought Yiddish to New York City, its grammar, everyday phrases, and intonational patterns became so frequently heard on the city's streets that Yiddish expressions are associated to this day with New York dialect. Table 13.1 presents a sample of expressions or lexical items of Yiddish origin (Rosten, 1982).

Many people are multidialectic, living in communities in which multiple varieties of English coexist in relative harmony and switching back and forth easily between multiple languages, each with its own repertoire of styles. To disparage the use of code-switching in the Spanish community as "Spanglish" or other such perjoratives, is, as Lippi-Green puts it, "just another subordination method with a long history" (1997, p. 233).

To overcome the negative effects of social stratification, many nonnative speakers of English seek to acquire an accent that will help them assimilate into the mainstream. On the other hand, in many cultures the dialect they speak *is* the mainstream and to acquire any other accent risks social stigma. For example, in Taiwan, Taiwanese English is the norm and to deviate much from the phonological and linguistic features of that dialect might be to risk being accused of being too American. In some cultures, being bilingual is acceptable only to a limited degree.

Attitudes Toward Dialects

People who are forbidden by law or social custom from discriminating against others on the basis of race or ethnicity may use accent as a means of social stigmatization or exclusion (Lippi-Green, 1997). Children from outside mainstream cultures or languages

TABLE 13.1 *English Expressions Derived from Yiddish*

Linguistic Term or Phrase	Example or Meaning
Alright already!	Enough!
cockamamy	ludicrous, unbelievable, cheap
chutzpa	brazen, shamelessness
dreck	utter trash; cheap, worthless
Eat your heart out!	you should feel envy
glitch	slipup
How come…	why
icky	unpleasant, nauseating
-nik	devotee (peacenik)
Now he tells us!	Finally we find out!
Phooey!	disgust
So sue me!	Just try to do something about it.
That's for sure.	agreement
What gives?	What's going on?
Who needs it?	not necessary

Source: Based on Rosten (1982).

may not find validation in school. For these students, as for others, school is not a power-neutral environment. As Foucault (1984) commented, "Any system of education is a political way of maintaining or modifying the appropriation of discourses, along with the knowledges and powers which they carry" (p. 123).

When students speak at school using the language patterns used in their homes and communities, some teachers may deem their language "deficient" and continually correct their grammar and usage. According to Wheeler and Swords (2008), such attempts often fail to teach students the speaking and writing skills they need; instead, students need to engage in critical thinking about language so they can analyze the language patterns of informal English, compare and contrast them with Standard English patterns, and learn how to use code-switching to use the appropriate language for a particular setting. Their awareness and code-switching skills can help them to become more sophisticated language users.

Teachers may unwittingly communicate a negative social evaluation to a student who is not a native English speaker by speaking louder, using shorter sentences, slowing speech, restricting vocabulary and range of topics, or signaling a patronizing attitude. The nonnative speaker's status is thus demeaned, though teachers may be unaware of the attitudes they communicate.

Americans, consciously or unconsciously, view certain "foreign" languages as more prestigious than others. French, for example, is seen as a high-status language, although the French spoken by Haitians may not be evaluated positively due to racism. On the other hand, a Slavic accent may be seen as less acceptable because of the stigma attached to this accent during the cold war. Status issues are prevalent in dialect differences among native speakers of English. Many Americans assign a positive value to British dialects (Wolfram, 1991). Pat Morrison (1994), a columnist for the *Los Angeles Times,* observed this in a radio broadcast: "Everyone knows an English accent gets you invited to lunch, but a Spanish accent gets you dirty looks."

In England some dialects are negatively evaluated by other speakers. An example of this is the conversation I had in a local bookstore with a cashier named Francesca who was fixing the cash register before my transaction could be completed.

LDR: So what happened? The drawer got stuck?

F: It was jemmed. The coin rolls got jemmed.

LDR: Oh, jammed? Where are you from? England?

F: Surrey.

LDR: I'm writing a book chapter about dialects. What accent in English is the hardest for you to understand?

F: That would be Newcastle. Up there in the north, near the border. You can't tell what they are trying to say. It's awful.

LDR: So, Surrey, is that in the south of England?

F: South, yeeeah, way down. Our speech is, you know, the right one. Oh, I shouldn't say that, should I? It's the normal one, you know.

In many parts of the world, the prestigious form of British English is considered preferable to any form of American English, an attitude perpetuated through the pronunciation requirement of the Cambridge certificate in order to teach English.

Language is central to the identification of self and group. Teachers who communicate dialect bias in the classroom do not merely damage the teacher–student relationship through prejudice or impair students' academic success through their lower academic expectations for them. Longer-term damage results from *symbolic-structural violence* (Skutnabb-Kangas, 1981), in which the student who is made to feel inferior for reasons of accent internalizes the shame associated with discrimination. Moreover, a student who is made to feel inferior internalizes a negative attitude toward learning English. As Lippi-Green (1997) stated,

> When persons who speak languages or dialects that are devalued or stigmatized consent to the standard language ideology, they become complicit in its propagation against themselves, their own interests and identities. Many are caught in a vacuum: When an individual cannot find any social acceptance for her language outside her

own speech communities, she may come to denigrate her own language, even when she continues to use it. (p. 66)

The movie *American Tongues* (http://www.pbs.org/pov/americantongues) provides an informative overview of various American dialects, American linguistic prejudice (regional, social, racial), the role of the mass media in fostering stereotypes, the way in which accents in one locale can differ by social class, and assessments and examples of AAVE. Also useful is the companion video, *Yeah You Rite,* which uses the city of New Orleans as a microcosm of dialectic variation. These tools help students hear examples of regional speech and attitudes and relate them to their own lives.

Dialects and Speaking Style

When the Australian actor Russell Crowe played a tobacco executive in the movie *The Insider*, he sounded just like a North Carolinian. How is it that actors can mimic particular regional and ethnic forms so well? Speakers may shift back and forth from vernacular dialects to more standard forms for a variety of reasons: to reaffirm ethnic solidarity, to appear well educated, or to sound "folksy." But why would a well-educated person deliberately use poor grammar?

When he was chairman of the Joint Chiefs of Staff of the Armed Forces, Colin Powell appeared before a congressional committee. Powell testified as an advocate of a pay raise for military personnel, yet he confessed to the committee that his own salary was more than adequate. "I ain't done bad," he admitted.

Why would the top military official at the Pentagon appear before the United States Congress sounding like a street punk? One would think that Powell, as the

Students speaking a nonstandard dialect of English such as speakers of AAVE, are a rich source of language input for English learners in urban schools.

©David Grossman/Alamy

child of an immigrant family from the West Indies, would feel some linguistic insecurity and be careful to use proper language before such an august body as the U.S. Senate. Quite the contrary. Powell's speech is an example of downshifting into "buddy talk" to appear manly. He was also playing a status-equalization game: He can go to the U.S. Senate and deliberately use colloquial grammar, defying negative evaluation. Thus, this style shift worked to his advantage: He could be seen as powerful, confident, and manly. With this mastery of the language game, is it any wonder that Powell's next public position was secretary of state, a job for the quintessential diplomat?

Dialect Switchings   One might think that people shift dialects solely to express or reject regional and ethnic affiliation, but the issue is complex. *Vertical dialect switching* from a more to a less stigmatized mode of speech in order to reduce negative social evaluation is frequent among all types of speakers; it is usually a function of the social setting, the person being addressed, the topic, and the purpose of the communication (Wolfram, 1991).

For speakers of English as an international language, the ability to shift styles to accommodate speakers of other dialects of English is important. The auxiliary features of language, such as social distance and touching behaviors, that accompany style shifts can enhance rapport in intercultural communication.

Instructing about Dialects   Explicit instruction in English dialects might include the use of movies showing people speaking various dialects, so that students could, by repeated exposure, learn to understand what is being said. *The Harder They Come* features Jamaican dialect; *My Left Foot*, Irish; and *Billy Elliot*, northern British English.

Pronunciation software is excellent for the specific, repetitious drills needed to work on an accent. Many such programs allow the user to record speech and then compare the recording with a norm; some even show a graphic representation of the speech tone for purposes of comparison. Students can work in the privacy of a computer laboratory.

Gender and Language Variation

Traditional studies of dialect seldom included gender differences. Several studies of social dialect in American English have shown patterns in which the women in the study tend to have a higher incidence of prestige markers than their male counterparts from the same social class and region. What accounts for this? The most substantial male–female differences have been in samples taken from the lower middle class, a class typified by its desire to move up to the middle class. In this context, because women tend to be more sensitive to prestige norms, they are more frequently seen to use language that is more characteristic of the class into which they wish to move (Labov, 1981).

Women's Speech   Women tend to use more hypercorrect forms, such as "It is I" or "He's not as fast as I." They also use more hedges, or qualifiers, when speaking, such as "I guess I'll have soup" (Lakoff, 1975). Women change pitch more to show emotion ("Oh, that's awful!"), use more expressive adjectives and intensifiers (Brend, 1975), and speak more softly and with more breathiness and higher overall pitch than men do. They may speak more indirectly overall, using more polite speech conventions (see Brown & Levinson, 1987).

English educators, both in EFL and ESL contexts, may find that male and female learners acquire different dialects of English, transferring to English the different roles and speech patterns in the native language. For example, women students may be more reticent about speaking than men, or vice versa. In such cases, a teacher might openly discuss the differences and find ways to equalize speaking opportunities; alternatively, the class might agree to divide into distinct gender groups and establish different norms. In some countries, the shifting values and social structures are permitting women to have a greater voice (Magnier, 2002), and in the long run gender differences in EFL students' learning may be less pronounced.

Gender as Powerful/Powerless Speech Gender roles, and gender-influenced dialects of English in other cultures, may affect the TESOL educator returning from abroad. In an interview in my office at the university, a native speaker of English was applying for the master's program in TESOL. I could see clearly that she had picked up some Japanese cultural habits, even though she was speaking English. She was explaining that she had forgotten to bring her transcript for the admission interview.

> "Oh, I'm so sorry," she said. "I didn't bring it."
>
> "That's OK, you can send it in later," I said. "So you have been teaching in Japan?"
>
> "Oh, sorry," she replied. "Did I tell you I taught there for four years?"
>
> "Yes, you did," I said. "Whereabouts in Japan did you teach?"
>
> "Oh, sorry," she said. "I put Osaka on the admission form, but I should have put Hiroshima *and* Osaka—they had a branch school there where I also taught."
>
> "That's OK, it's no big deal," I said. "You know, you really don't have to apologize so much."
>
> "Oh, sorry," she said.

Vernacular Dialects and Language Teaching

Because accent and intonation patterns are important in making oneself understood when speaking a foreign language, it is important for students to understand four basic ideas about dialect usage in English: (1) One's dialect, if widely used by the surrounding racial, ethnic, or cultural community, is as valid a subset of English as any other dialect; (2) it is a fact that dialects are used as a basis for discrimination, but such discrimination is based more on underlying issues of power and race relations than on the dialect alone; (3) it is common for individuals all over the world to learn more than one dialect of English and to switch, depending on the demands of the context, from one dialect to another; and (4) such features of dialect as accent can be altered, if so desired, by specific, albeit time-intensive, drill.

PRACTICES FOR TEACHERS

Teaching Dialects

- Teach students pride in their community's dialect.
- Emphasize that the ability to communicate is more important than the sound of one's accent.
- Tell students that learning to switch from formal English to informal, and from standard English to colloquial usages, is part of learning English.
- Explain that pronunciation software is useful for accent reduction.

Teaching Standard English: Whose Standard?

In a language as varied as English, there are naturally some who feel that it is important to establish a standard, or norm, against which usage is measured. Experts who publish grammar and usage books usually prescribe correct or standard language forms.

Although "standard English" is often referred to, in fact it does not exist. Generally speaking, standard American English is a composite of several subdialects spoken by the educated professional middle class. People seeking success in school and in the job market tend to adopt the language used by people in positions of power.

Informal standard English is a continuum, with some speakers speaking much as they would write formal standard English. Many speakers practice sociocultural shifts in their usage, speaking an informal vernacular with friends, coworkers, and car mechanics and then shifting to a more formal speech with superiors at work. To be *bidialectic* may mean shifting back and forth vertically, using language as a means to navigate the particular social environment.

Despite this facility, many educators feel it is their right and privilege to enforce standard English on their students. Teachers may subordinate the language of their students using a variety of messages, both overt and covert. Covert messages may range from "English is too complex for a nonnative speaker to master" to "Your language is quaint, cute, funny, or incorrect and unacceptable" to "No one will employ you if you talk that way." Teachers should not act as though it is their right to correct students in public, to reprimand them for incorrect usage, or to refuse to acknowledge them until a standard is reached ("You must answer in a complete sentence," "I can't understand you—say it again") (Lippi-Green, 1997).

Varieties of language are a result of normal social processes rather than inadequacies on the part of individual speakers. In the case of English as an international language, the youth of the world associate American English with the latest in trends and styles, and individual speakers differentiate their language with regard to these trends. Today's international English is moving at rapid speed, making it difficult to enforce standards of correctness.

The unique voice of the student is lost if educators insist on standard English exclusively in the classroom, along with the irreplaceable and priceless gift of knowledge about that individual's inner universe. Just as the worldview of the Native American is lost if the indigenous language dies away, so is the interlanguage of the student lost if no one listens. An approach that balances the need to teach standard English with the desire to find zest and delight in each individual's vernacular can make education a reservoir of English-language diversity.

Language Variety as a Goal of Instruction

The heterogeneity of the modern world presents vast register and stylistic diversity in English. These enrich language learning.

> *Megastrategy* **13.2**
>
> **Teach a variety of registers and styles**

What is a *register*? A register is a type of language used in accordance with overt or covert rules of formality and informality in a specific situation. These rules may involve conventions of intonation, vocabulary, or topic that meet the needs of the people and the tasks to be performed in that situation. A *register shift* enables a language user to adapt to these rules. Registers are usually features of situated oracy, but the term can also be applied to the use of various conventions in reading and writing that relate to the adoption of a tone of formality. For example, the tone of voice in which one reads sacred texts in church constitutes a register shift.

Some Sample Registers in Oracy

A church is a common site of what might be termed *ceremonial register*. The words of a cleric at a wedding or funeral may have the tone of solemnity, including the choice of words, "Dearly beloved, we are gathered here…" Kindergarten teachers who read fairy tales aloud use *storytelling register*, featuring a tone of wonder and suppressed excitement. Airline pilots who use the public address system of the airplane adopt a folksy, reassuring, and paternal tone—*captain register?* Automobile commercials filmed locally often use "car advertising register," a kind of frenzied tone performed by a man speaking loudly and quickly.

Some Sample Registers in Literacy

Reading and writing are as contextualized as oral activities. Reading a pornography magazine at a PTA meeting, or a gun magazine at a women's club meeting, would certainly raise eyebrows. Literacy register in the United States seems to be affected by gender, class, and occupation; teachers in the average elementary school, for example, might read *Instructor* but probably not *Business Week*. Automobile repair waiting rooms might have racing car magazines available for customers, and hospitals or clinics might offer patients a general-interest publication such as *National Geographic* in the waiting room. I once became annoyed when I saw *Investor's Weekly* in a medical specialist's office, thinking that it indicated that the doctor charged such high fees that he could invest large sums in the stock market. Literacy registers sometimes reveal more about a context than we care to know.

Register shifts seem to be age related. One difficult register for a child to master while growing up is the thank-you letter for gifts received by mail. Letter writing in general is a difficult register for most people to master, for it generally requires the writer to set an appropriate tone that mirrors the relationship between reader and writer, which ranges from business ("please make good on the product warranty") to long-distance relations ("sorry I haven't written/how are Joe and the kids?").

Gender-Typical Registers

Because certain registers are traditional, they tend to sound more acceptable if performed by the appropriate gender. For example, some people have trouble accepting a woman's voice in ceremonial register as authoritative because church ceremonies in English were traditionally performed by men. Men, on the other hand, do not seem to enjoy spending time on the telephone and therefore seldom use "gossip register," that intimate tone of chitchat some women often use with their best friends.

Teaching Oral Register Shifts

Students can be encouraged to practice a variety of oral registers in the classroom. One is *student response register*, a firm tone, spoken confidently, that reaches all other students in the room. Students can be trained to use *leadership register*, the voice of roll call, the call to line up for lunch, or the call to be quiet and listen. *Classroom presentation register* involves eye contact with an audience, confident bearing, pleasing and varied tone of voice, and an inviting sense of two-way communication with listeners. *Dramatic register* is used in a play, in the role of narrator or announcer, or in the role of storyteller. It is "larger than life," with exaggerated emotion and voice. The *storytelling register* features simplification and a sense of warmth and intimacy, no matter what the size of the crowd. Each of these registers requires situated practice with the appropriate setting, topic, and audience.

Situated Literacy and Academic Registers

What does it mean to use language for academic purposes? Chapter 11 covered in depth the academic functions of language within the cultural context of ELD, detailing those practices that promote the learner's use of academic language. Because this chapter focuses on contextualized language use, we return to the topic of cognitive academic language from the standpoint of register. Academic competence makes demands on the learner that in some ways require activities and attitudes not found in other, less literacy-dependent situations.

The Individual World of Literacy

If an educated person kept a daily reading and writing log, it might become obvious to that person that both skills are used for a wide range of purposes. In the morning, the individual might read the morning paper and perhaps make a shopping or "to do" list for the day. On the way to work, he or she might pass advertisements by the roadside. At work, literacy is situated in the workplace setting and varies greatly depending on the work tasks. For many, literacy at work has become highly computer related, depending on word processing, databases, telephone number files, e-mail, and Web-based activities; work literacy also remains highly paper related, with piles of various folders containing information, not to mention books, journals, and newsletters. At home, personal literacy might involve cookbooks, hobby materials, newsmagazines, correspondence, and bill paying. All these reading materials have their own place, time, and task orientation—situated literacy.

Megastrategy **13.3**

Teach academic registers and standard usage

Situated Literacy: Synthesis of Practices

One of the best ways for students to understand literacy and its relationship to settings, people, and tasks is for them to reflect on their own literacy practices and the everyday practices around them. Barton (2000) posed a series of questions to students: How might literacy depend on the particular roles that people take? How does gender influence participation in literacy events? How do people learn new literacies? Some students observed events in the everyday life of the community—such as rugby games, sports betting shops, or wallpaper sales—concentrating on everyday literacies rather than on those demanded by their academic tasks. In researching these practices, students developed new insights into the role of literacy in people's lives, their own in particular.

Everyday life provided an amazing range of types of situated literacy. In Barton's (2000) study, students investigated literacy in mundane events, such as having a baby, being arrested, getting a tattoo, drinking wine, playing the lottery; in working life, for example, conducting a job search at an employment bureau, consulting a staff notice board at a supermarket, and selling to customers at a home decor store; in travel, for example, viewing signs on roads, buses, and trains, as well as travel brochures; during sports activities, for example, playing darts, reading sports magazines, and attending a soccer match; and in student life, for example, reading message boards, writing graffiti, or using the laundromat.

International students at U.S. colleges may use literacy to try to figure out how the host culture works. They may find themselves studying bulletin boards around campus, inundated by notices they have no way of sorting through to separate the significant from the insignificant. They have to learn new computer literacy habits, such as using the Internet and e-mail to keep in contact with their home culture. For these students, being in an unfamiliar culture makes them reliant on the written word as a means of cultural survival and accommodation.

Gee (2000) pointed out that the New Literacy Studies described by Barton (1994), Gee (1996), and Street (1995), among others, are part of a larger movement away from the focus on the behavior of individuals that constituted behaviorist research in the early twentieth century and cognitivist research in the later part of the same century. Gee related this change of focus toward investigating the social and cultural effects on literacy to fifteen collateral movements, in addition to the New Literacy Studies. See Gee (2000) for a comprehensive list of citations comprising a reading list on the New Literacy Studies.

The individual does not exist in a vacuum but rather within a social milieu with historical, cultural, and political aspects. Literacy practices are activities within larger sets of structures that form discourses of the culture or society at large (see Mills, 1997). The literacy practices of the group shape the individual, and the individual in turn plays a part in the larger whole. The New Literacy Studies, which situate literacy in a cultural matrix, are relevant to educational literacy practices. Attention to the larger social and cultural contexts is a vital part of the work of literacy educators.

This chapter has taken two positions that argued that the concept of dialect may be seen as a facet of situated oracy. Knowing when to shift to standard English is a sociolinguistic issue, involving choice of register.

Language educators, as mentors of situated oracy and literacy, have the responsibility to create contexts in which English learners are fully supported by the activity system co-constructed by teacher and learners. This activity is purposeful, is satisfying to all members, and moves students forward in their understanding and use not only of English as their second language but also of language itself and the cultures that it conveys. This type of context brims with meaning and enjoyment. Learners deserve this high-quality environment.

Exploratory Break

- Can you identify your own dialect of English? Give examples of words and phrases that you pronounce or use that are unique to your idiolect.
- Do you think code-switching should be encouraged in the English-learner classroom? Why or why not?

Chapter *14*

Building a Community of Learners

Every neighborhood has a school. That simple building houses the American dream. In that school are classrooms, each a microcosm of society. In the best case, that class is like a close-knit family in which the members come together every day eager to share stories of their adventures, their triumphs, or their concerns. They learn together willingly, working on projects that enrich their quality of life, pushing the boundaries of their knowledge, confident that the world of learning is exciting and fulfilling.

Megastrategy **SET 14**

Make the classroom a community, and bring the community into the classroom—parents, families, neighborhoods, and culture

In many cities, suburbs, and rural areas across the United States, families speak languages other than English, and children depend on schooling to learn English. In some areas of the United States, it is the English-speaking immigrants who have settled in Native American lands, forcing indigenous people to function reluctantly in English. In EFL contexts, students grapple with the complexities of English as an academic language. Across these contexts, teachers face the challenge of building communities in the classroom in which students find positive affirmation.

McCaleb (1994) posed the issue succinctly:

How can educators create a partnership with parents and young students that will nurture literacy and facilitate participation in the schools while celebrating and valuing the home culture and family and community concerns and aspirations? (p. x)

This chapter situates the education of English learners within the life of the community and offers strategies for opening the doors of the classroom to the world. These strategies include ways in which students can use their nascent English to improve community life and ways in which themes and projects important to the community become tools for classroom teaching.

What Is a Community of Learners?

In the traditional teacher-centered classroom, the language teacher sets educational goals, maintains an effective learning environment, dispenses linguistic and cultural content, initiates and organizes learning activities, motivates students, monitors progress, and evaluates achievement. Much of the success of the learner depends on the teacher. In a learner-centered classroom, in contrast, students develop self-discipline and accountability as they accomplish learning goals, work together collaboratively, make choices about language content, and follow their own interests and talents to develop ideas and turn them into projects. This change from teacher-centered to learner-centered pedagogy is accomplished largely through group collaboration (Bassano & Christison, 1995).

From a wider perspective, a community of learners is not only a group of learners working together in a classroom, but also a classroom connected closely to a larger community; namely, the families of the learners. For English learners at the K–12 level, this environment ensures the support and active involvement of their parents or other family members and preserves the connection to their native culture that lives through their neighbors or friends. For adult English learners, the community may mean their children, their own elders, or the values and habitudes of their native culture. A "learning community" denotes a group of people who set out to gain knowledge by working together. The challenge in creating and sustaining such a community is to foster the sense of interdependency as well as productive learning.

The Classroom as a Community

In a classroom community, students feel that they are free to work with others and that they have something to contribute to the whole (Tchudi & Mitchell, 1999). Actively involving the students in decision making and collaborative interaction requires a major shift from the traditional roles of teacher and student. Both are now learners as well as teachers.

Megastrategy **14.1**

Make the classroom a learning community

Classrooms go beyond the use of cooperative learning to encourage students to be agents of change; they become sites of social transformation. What do classrooms look like when teachers listen to and learn from students?

In four contrasting scenarios that took place in Hong Kong, Lin (2001) compared classroom instruction in which students' *habitus* (Bourdieu's term for the dispositions/attitudes with which children are endowed, by virtue of their family or community socialization) was either compatible with that of the practices of schooling, incompatible with schooling, or transformed by schooling. Table 14.1 displays the four classrooms and describes briefly the contrasts in students' attitudes and teachers' behavior.

Using qualitative description, Lin showed how important it is for TESOL educators to match classroom teaching with students' social and cultural backgrounds. The teacher in classroom A benefited from the fact that students were habituated to

TABLE 14.1 *Habitus and Discourse Patterns in Four Hong Kong Classrooms*

Class	Socioeconomic Status/Habitus	Classroom Discourse Patterns	Outcome
A	Upper middle class/compatible with schooling	English is used as the language of instruction to engage students in higher-order critical thinking. Students are attentive and cooperative.	Students like English.
B	Working class/incompatible with schooling	English is used as the language of instruction, but students are cynical, bored, and resistant.	Students dislike English.
C	Working class/incompatible with schooling	English is used consistently by the teacher, but students are cynical, bored, and resistant. The teacher often has to rephrase questions into L1, and students respond in L1.	Students dislike English.
D	Working class/transformed by schooling	L1 is used as the language of instruction and explanation. The teacher gives all students individual attention in and out of class to develop their interests, skills, and confidence in learning English.	Students like English

Source: Based on Lin (2001).

the use of English in their lives, had learned to act cooperatively, and no doubt saw themselves as eventually being as successful as their parents were. English instruction was successful in this classroom because the students were already socialized at home to perform in consonance with the teacher's habits and expectations.

In contrast, classrooms B and C students disliked English because of their lack of interest, confidence, and competence. They did not expect to master English, even though they recognized its potential advantage, and this low expectation made the students feel angry and disenfranchised. These emotions were exacerbated by the teacher's insistence that they use only English, although they were uncomfortable with it as the language of instruction.

In classroom D, students brought the same habitus in English as those in classrooms B and C, but they felt more comfortable. Acceptance combined with challenge motivated students to learn English, even though they did not have the cultural capital or habitus enjoyed by the students in classroom A. The teacher spent extracurricular time getting to know each student individually. By using L1 as the language of instruction, she was able to bond with the learner, sustaining motivation when she pressured students toward high achievement. Lin (2001) called this teaching "transformative" because students made genuine progress toward a clear and attainable outcome.

To create a sense of community, then, it is helpful but not entirely necessary to be fluent in the L1 of the students. What *is* necessary is the investment in getting to know students as individuals, openness to students' creative impulses, and willingness to find ways for students to manage their own learning. However, even these ingredients are not sufficient to ensure that English teaching serves the ideals of democracy and social justice. Only the most fragile sense of community can grow within the classroom if the larger society is corrupt and uncaring.

Example Learning Communities

At San Diego State University (SDSU), the Freshman Success Program (FSP) was formed in 1991 to increase the odds that entering students would be successful in their studies. Most of the students who enrolled in the FSP were ELD or bilingual students. Other students who were not considered ELD had failed the English Placement exam and thus needed one or more remedial English classes; some of these were Generation 1.5 students (see Harklau et al., 1999; Roberge, 2009). Like many other such programs across the United States, SDSU's included a one-unit freshman seminar designed to orient students to the university and provide mentoring. What makes the FSP of interest to teachers of English learners is the composition/literacy class that was offered. This class helped students to acquire strategies for approaching different kinds of reading and writing tasks and genres, alternative discourse styles, and preparation for the exit exam that would demonstrate writing competence. This disciplinary-adjunct model not only helped the students with ELD needs but also positioned the skills of the English-for-academic-purposes faculty as valuable to the university (A. M. Johns, 2001), creating positive feelings for both student and faculty participants in the community.

Conchas (2006) studied the Medical Academy at Baldwin High School (California), a school-within-a-school that prepares students for careers in health-related occupations. A positive learning environment connected students and teachers across race, gender, and class differences. Both immigrant and U.S.-born Latinos formed a strong sense of belonging and identification with other students in the program; strong collaborative relationships led to academic success.

Critical Perspectives on Community Involvement

Critical language educators recognize that an effective curriculum is not simply a matter of "methods that work." B. Morgan (1998) brings the concerns of the community into course design through five key questions:

- Whose social values does this instruction serve?
- Whose expectations, desires, identities, and realities are reflected and promoted by the instructional activities?

- How does the classroom language complement the social concerns and priorities of the community?
- How can students learn to speak with authority in the face of a new culture in which networks of privilege may exclude them from higher education, employment, and the pursuit of happiness?
- How can dialogue with students and other members of the community help teachers to become aware of the values and habits they may be taking for granted and that may or may not meet the needs of the community?

In community centers, classrooms, or wherever ELD and EFL are taught, students do not leave their lives as newcomers, parents, employees, and family members behind. The English they learn is not "an isolated topic disconnected from social concerns" (B. Morgan, 1998, p. 19). A focus on community is a way of achieving a more locally and socially responsive way of teaching. This means building language learning on experiences and activities that are real and immediate to students.

Introducing concepts such as politics and civil rights into the ELD/EFL classroom positions English teaching in the real world. In the past, language educators believed that theories and techniques could be used independent of the local context, as though one could learn a language "culture free," in a social vacuum. However, the economic and social circumstances of students' lives underlie the mental and emotional efforts they are able to make as language learners.

Listening to the Learner

The teacher in classroom D in Lin's examples above was able to engage her students because she was a genuine part of the communicative network of the class. She spent time with them to learn about them as individuals, and in turn she communicated to them that she was a real person who worked hard on their behalf and cared about them. Brian Morgan speaks of the importance of listening to the learner as he describes his early efforts to teach EFL:

> My initial training as an ESL teacher served several important purposes. It satisfied my early assumptions about the nature of language and provided me with a body of abstract methods and techniques that might safely guide me past the various land mines of the classroom. Soon after, however, I found myself fumbling with questions from students that went beyond my limited canon and experiences. Moreover, I tended to view such moments as disrespectful challenges to my newly sanctioned authority. Usually, in these times of threatened confidence, I would call upon some greater authority: the "latest" research, famous "expert," or in more desperate occasions, the "ultimate truth" on language. These responses were not specifically intended to deceive or mislead my students. Rather, they seemed to suit my idea of what a teacher should do, say, and know in a classroom.
>
> Later, during a stint as an instructor in the People's Republic of China, chinks in my protective armor began to appear. Unfortunately, my first private impulse was to berate the "willful ignorance" of students who resisted when presented with my

"state-of-the-art" techniques to develop fluency. These methods, I assumed, were certain to work if only given a chance and a commitment. Of course, it didn't work that way, and I then embarked upon an unsettling adventure of listening to my students as much as telling them what to do. This proved more fruitful, and while I didn't always agree with them or comply with all of their requests, I started to gain a sense of their expectations and their histories, which informed their goals in learning. (1998, pp. 3–4)

The concept of listening to the learner is not new. Greene (1988) posed the question of what it might mean to listen to multiple voices in the classroom—one voice many times, one voice saying several things, or many voices with overlapping or contradictory needs. Vella (2002) emphasized that the first need of adult learners is to feel that their needs are being met with understanding and immediacy. This need to listen to the learner has generated a host of teaching techniques based on the dialogue journal. Van Deusen-Scholl (1993) described ethnographic study as a way in which prospective teachers listen intensively to English learners in a semester-long series of interviews about the progress of their English learning. Thus, heeding the needs and interests of the learner is central to the formation of a learning community.

Cultural Models within Communities.   Listening to the learner is key to translating what is said into codes for critical work (see Chapter 2). Listening is also important because each community has what Gee (1990) called *cultural models*. Only by spending time within a community can one fully understand the meanings and nuances in the terms used by members of that community. Despite the overt meanings of words, one can only plumb the cultural connotations put on these words by spending time with people for whom they carry particular significance.

Listening to the way people use language helps us understand their cultural models. One can learn any number of languages and still interpret reality using one's original cultural models. Gee (1996) made the point that all meaning is local, *customized* within specific cultures and *activated* by cultural models. Only as teachers listen carefully to students can they design instruction that meets students' needs and resist superimposing a pedagogical English that is "culture free" and thus relatively meaningless to them. Cultural models are not necessarily self-consistent and logical.

Gee described an interview with a young Latina on the topic, "Why do you think there are relatively few African American and Hispanic doctors?" In her response to this question, Marcella comes close to a cultural capital theory of society—that some people advance because their social class benefits from inherited privilege. Mixed with this tacit theory, however, is Marcella's insinuation that white people are inherently smarter than other races and thus succeed in medical school. She may have internalized a sense of racial inferiority as a result of the circulation of hegemonic ideas (in which lower classes participate in their own subjugation)—whatever the source of her belief, her cultural model is mixed, and the meaning of "success" to her is complicated by conflicting explanations for reality. (Gee, 1996)

Cultural Voices and Authentic Materials. The concept of "listening" to language learners extends from the prompts used in discussions to the writing students do in journals, essays, and stories. B. Morgan (1998) presented lesson plans that brought many topics into his adult ESL classroom: the Gulf War, community policing, the impact of immigrants on society, and the morality of bringing children into a "dangerous world." The last topic sprang from a remark that a student made about the AIDS epidemic: that reading about this global health challenge had made her wish she didn't have children. In small groups, the class discussed the prompt, "Would you advise people against having children in a dangerous future?" This caused an outpouring of personal stories and opinions.

Morgan used writings as prompts that challenged "scientific" views. He asked questions like, "Whose interests does this article serve?" This stance enabled students to examine how a seemingly neutral grammatical structure such as passive voice helps to soothe antisocial or subversive tendencies against the social order. Morgan used critical language analysis in its three levels (text, institution, and sociocultural context) to help a class co-construct awareness of the interconnecting role that language plays with power and privilege to maintain controlling social structures. This work helped the class members to confront the challenge and oppression in the life of an immigrant.

Authentic materials can bring the concerns and voices of the community into the classroom. Pfingstag (1999) passed out copies of letters to the editor from the local paper. The class discussed not only the content of the letters but also how the writers used sentence structure and vocabulary to make their points, sometimes using sarcasm ("I feel really safe in the parks now, with the policy that replaces park rangers with work release prisoners"), loaded vocabulary ("ludicrous thinking," "hoodwink voters"), rhetorical questions ("Why is it that people such as council members make decisions on matters they have no clue about?"), and dialect grammar ("This ain't your kind of town") (p. 62). Then the class wrote letters to the editor of the school newspaper to voice their opinions on controversial issues.

Not-So-Critical Perspectives on Community Involvement

Not all community involvement takes a critical stance. *A to Zany: Community Activities for Students of English* (Stafford-Yilmaz, 1998) takes a neutral approach. In contrast to Morgan's work (1998), in which students who had experienced inequities in community policing discussed their experience of discrimination, Stafford-Yilmaz's chapter on police compares police in the United States with that of the language learner's home country, discusses images of the police in the mass media, and suggests that the students invite a police officer to class. Students then write essays on whether they would want to be a police officer.

This and other activities in *A to Zany* position the class members as outsiders who interview "Americans" to ask their opinions ("Talk to an American about the speed of life in America. Ask if he or she would prefer a faster or slower life. Ask why" [Stafford-Yilmaz, 1998, p. 121]). When reading this assignment, a critical reader might ask when and where an English learner could ask such a question. Would such a conversation take place on the street or in a neighborhood? The realities of the lives of newcomers seem to be missing from this perspective on community involvement, despite the range of suggested activities.

Authentic community concerns might serve as codes for critical educators but serve as neutral language input in the hands of other educators. "Protest!" is the topic of a lesson in which students discuss controversial issues (Connell, 1999). Class members skim the content of newspaper or newsmagazine articles for answers to a teacher-prepared worksheet, write one-paragraph summaries, and share their work in pairs or small groups. The whole class then discusses the issue, comparing attitudes that people in the United States might have with attitudes of people in other countries. This approach uses authentic materials, but not those that originate in the concerns of the local community. Although this approach may engender critical thinking and discussion, it is strictly an academic exercise.

A Model for Community Involvement

Given the previous examples, one might imagine that the issue of community involvement is complex. Some people follow Bassano and Christison's (1995) approach, outlined at the beginning of the chapter, that "community" means the classroom as a community, without a systematic focus on concerns in the larger community outside. This kind of instruction positions the SLA educator as neutral to the concerns of the community. In return, critical educators have been accused of introducing content that is irrelevant to the survival skills needed by English learners.

One might think of the community-curriculum-instruction connection in four parts. Quadrant I is individually based English instruction disconnected from community concerns or social change. In quadrant II, students work in groups, but the learning does not reflect engagement with the local community. In quadrant III, the individual is engaged with the local community but not as a member of a proactive group. In quadrant IV, students are involved in both group learning and engagement with community concerns. Quadrant IV has the most potential for the learner's long-term growth and empowerment to influence society positively. This chapter uses this model to describe teaching from each quadrant.

Individual Learning.   The traditional approach to learning assumes that each learner's success is independent of another's. Quadrant I of Figure 14.1 posits individuals learning English independent of any substantive connection to a learning community.

Individual Community Engaged.   The individual can learn in a community-neutral or a community-engaged learning context. The use of authentic sources represents the movement from community-neutral instructional materials toward the input of real language as used by the community. For example, using a sample

FIGURE 14.1   *A Model of Educational Strategies for English Learners and Community Involvement*

Learner Unit	Community Involvement	
Individual	I Individual Learning Community Neutral	III Individual Learning Community Engaged
Group	II Collaborative Learning Community Neutral	IV Collaborative Learning Community Engaged

map of San Francisco as well as travel brochures, students in an English-language private school in Seoul wrote an account of an imaginary trip to the city (a quadrant I activity).

Although this activity is a creative alternative to worksheets and other language drills, this specific use of authentic materials does not in itself engage the community. Deeper aspects of engagement might shift this approach toward a more authentic interaction with the community rather than an individualized, academic exercise. First, has anyone in the students' community actually visited or lived in San Francisco? The voice of authentic experience would be an invaluable resource. Second, students might generate questions to ask a denizen of San Francisco that would help students understand daily life there. An e-mail link might be possible with students at a school in San Francisco.

Collaborative Learning.   Probably more was written on cooperative and collaborative learning in the last twenty years of the twentieth century than in all the previous history of education. Many researchers (Johnson, Johnson, & Smith, 1991; Johnson, Johnson, & Holubec, 1993; Slavin, 1983, 1991; Kagan, 1998, 1999) advocated the use of cooperative learning for elementary students. Others documented the success of cooperative learning with elementary school English learners (Cohen, Lotan, & Catanzarite, 1990; Johns, 1992; Johnson & Johnson, 1994) as well as with secondary school ELD students (Holt, Chips, & Wallace, 1992).

Cooperative learning is well established as a methodology for language as well as content instruction. How-to books abound in the use of cooperative learning in the education of English learners, an approach that came into its own simultaneously with the field's emphasis on communicative competence.

Small-group learning provides English learners with a rich discourse environment and multiple opportunities for face-to-face interaction. When students are collaborating in small groups, they have substantially more chances to practice language without worrying if their production is exactly right. This lowers their anxiety and lets them concentrate on the content of learning. They can hear and say key

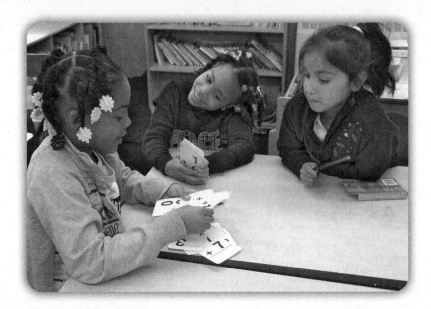

Cooperative learning helps to build a sense of community in the classroom.

©Elizabeth Crews/PhotoEdit

words and phrases and repeat them in a variety of ways until they feel comfortable with their language mastery (Faltis, 2001).

Cooperative grouping also increases the possibility that English learners will feel a part of the culture of the classroom as a whole.

> Cooperative grouping allows children to get to know each other in ways that do not happen in a whole-class setting. When left to their own devices, children tend to pick their friends from their own social or linguistic group. However, cooperative grouping gives students the opportunity to work with those they have never considered interacting with before. In such a setting, the likelihood of their becoming friends increases. (Johns & Espinoza, 1992, p. 2)

Table 14.2 summarizes the instructional use of cooperative learning with English learners. This information represents a synthesis of tips and guidelines from Bassano and Christison (1995), Cantlon (1991), and Kagan (1998, 1999).

Even in the best of circumstances, cooperative learning has its challenges. Table 14.3 (p. 358) sets these forth, offering practices for teachers to address these issues.

Many types of tasks have been designed that feature cooperative structures. These range from simply pairing students for discussion to more elaborate setups requiring extensive time for preparation and monitoring. Table 14.4 (p. 359) presents a few cooperative structures and tasks.

The jigsaw model of cooperative learning is particularly useful, in that students are individually accountable for learning their own material and for sharing their information effectively with other group members. In the jigsaw method, each member of the base team (see Table 14.4; teams are I, II, III, and IV) attends an expert group session (all the As huddle together) to study one aspect or section of the topic, and

TABLE 14.2 *Instructional Use of Cooperative Learning*

Component of Cooperative Learning	Explanation or Example
Definition	"An approach to education and a repertoire of teaching strategies based on the philosophy that students can learn effectively in small groups. Cooperative learning restructures the traditional classroom into small, carefully planned learning groups to provide opportunities for all students to work together and to learn from one another" (Coehlo, Winer, & Olsen, 1989, p. 3).
Rationales for using cooperative learning	Practice speaking and listening.
	Share information.
	Create things together.
	Learn democratic processes.
	Practice negotiating and compromising (Bassano & Christison, 1995, p. 29).
	Develop leadership, communication, decision-making, and conflict-management skills (Cantlon, 1991).
	Promote real-world team skills.
	Together Everyone Achieves More (TEAM)!
	Build positive interpersonal relations.
	Transcend differences (cliques) (Kagan, 1999).
Roles in teams	Language monitor, task monitor, timekeeper, secretary, clarifier, encourager, reporter (Bassano & Christison, 1995, p. 29).
	Materials monitor, quiet captain (Kagan, 1998).
Optimal team size	For initial start-up, dyads (teams of two) are most successful (Cantlon, 1991).
	If teams of three are necessary, have them sit side by side (Cantlon, 1991).
	Teams of four are ideal, small enough for active participation and able to be split evenly for pair work (Kagan, 1998).
Frequency of use of cooperative structures	Minimum is three times a week, but simple structures (pair/share) can be used more often (Cantlon, 1991).
Room and seating arrangements	Partners should sit side by side. If students are in fours, provide two sets of materials. No student's back should be to the teacher (Cantlon, 1991).
Role of the teacher	Teacher is the source of task, arranger of materials, accountable authority, partner in learning (Bassano & Christison, 1995).
Team composition	Heterogeneous (mixed gender, ethnicity, ability), teacher-assigned, long-term teams are preferable (Kagan, 1998).
	Random (randomly mixed ability, etc.) short-term teams break up the monotony (Kagan, 1998).
	Random teams may be a problem if all high-achieving students are in one group, or two students create mutual discipline problems (Cantlon, 1991).
	Random grouping: Use colored marbles or slips with group numbers in a jar; group students by month of birth; count off around class (Bassano & Christison, 1995).

(continued)

TABLE 14.2 *Continued*

Component of Cooperative Learning	Explanation or Example
Team management	Inform students how much time is allotted to the task; agree on a signal to stop working (clap pattern, ringing a bell, countdown) (Cantlon, 1991).
Rationale statement	Teacher explains why work is done in a team, what the benefits are, and what behavior is expected (Cantlon, 1991).
Necessary group skills	Form into groups quickly. Participate with muted voices. Establish turn-taking routines. Involve more hesitant members in group processes (Bassano & Christison, 1995).
Trust building/bonding	Build rapport by discussing favorite foods, hobbies, likes, dislikes. Do nonacademic fun activities: games, puzzles. Do academic tasks: partner reading, checking homework together (staple papers together, teacher corrects top paper) (Cantlon, 1991).
Teaching social skills	Teacher models behavior: speaking in quiet voices, taking turns, everyone participating, encouraging partner, signaling to stop (Cantlon, 1991).
Appreciation statements by peers at debriefing	"(*Name*), you helped the team by _____." "(_____), you did a great job of _____." "(_____), I appreciated it when you _____." "(_____), you are very good at _____." (Cantlon, 1991)
Clarification statements by peers	"I don't understand." "Excuse me?" "Speak more slowly, please." "Okay?" (Bassano & Christison, 1995, p. 29)
Procedural statements by peers	"It's my/your/his/her turn." "Quickly! We have four minutes." "You first, then me." (Bassano & Christison, 1995, p. 29)
Peers asking for/offering help	"Are you finished?" "I need help." "Do you need help?" (Bassano & Christison, 1995, p. 29)
Individual accountability	Students have progress conferences with instructor; groups are rated by teacher using monitoring chart; groups monitor themselves periodically using rating charts (Bassano & Christison, 1995).
Rewards (nonmaterial), avoiding message that reward involves escape from work (extra recess)	Elementary: Provide "happy grams," suggest applause, display group work, offer an audiovisual event, play a special game. Middle/high school: Use library passes, computer time, daily announcements/newsletter recognition, work displays, special privileges, team picture displays (Cantlon, 1991).
Feedback	At the close of activity, teammates write on index card: "Which question/problem gave you difficulty?" "Give examples of what you might do differently next time." "List ways in which your partners helped the team to reach its goal" (Cantlon, 1991).

TABLE 14.2 *Continued*

Component of Cooperative Learning	Explanation or Example
Anticipated difficulties	Aggression: Some students dominate and control others.
	Withdrawal: Some students are shy, embarrassed, and avoid participating.
	Apathy: Learners do not seem to care about the work of the group.
	Evasion: Students are off task.
	Egocentrism: Group members go off on their own or do not talk about their idea together.
	Complaints: Students reject one anothers' ideas and make negative comments.
	Disorderly conduct: Students damage materials, leave the group, or distress one another (Bassano & Christison, 1995).
Teacher-created difficulties	Instructions are unclear. Teacher fails to provide a rationale. Topic is boring, unfamiliar, or irrelevant. Product or process expectations are unrealistic. Strangers are expected to trust one another too quickly (Bassano & Christison, 1995).

thus has one piece of the knowledge puzzle (hence the name *jigsaw*). The ultimate learning goal is for each member of the base team to have the whole set of information, so each member must communicate what has been learned in the expert group.

In one use of the jigsaw, fifth-grade students researched "Who Discovered America?" As a warm-up, students discussed the various land and sea routes to North America. Then students went to their expert groups and each read a statement of one point of view, such as that the Vikings were the first Europeans to come to the New World, or that the first people came by way of the Bering Strait. When students returned to their base groups, they compared the information and opinions in the four readings. (Coehlo, Winer, & Olsen, 1989)

In another example of jigsaw, intermediate ESL students studied the use of persuasion in advertising by looking at three different types of ads in three expert groups and completing work sheets with questions like, "How is the ad trying to persuade you? Is it using reason, an appeal to the emotions, or an appeal to a feeling of right or wrong? Is the advertisement effective? Why or why not?" Returning to their base group, they discussed the ad they studied and completed a second work sheet summarizing the types and effectiveness of persuasion used in various ads. Students then worked cooperatively to write their own ads (Weatherly, 1999, p. 79).

TABLE 14.3 *Challenges to Cooperative Learning and Practices to Meet Them*

Challenge	Practices for Teachers
Students cannot get along.	Keep activities short and simple while students are learning how to work together.
	Group students wisely; place a socially immature student with two who are more mature.
	Teach social skills and review regularly.
Student prefers to work alone.	Provide encouragement by emphasizing importance of working in a group, giving examples from teacher's work.
	Give bonus points to class for working well together.
	Provide individual work occasionally as a "safety valve."
Student is unmotivated.	Use an interest inventory to discover students' likes and dislikes.
	Ask previous teachers what works for the student.
	Give student a role in the group in which he or she can succeed.
Student cannot keep up with others.	Let the student prepare some part of task prior to group work.
	Provide a modified worksheet for the slow student.
	Provide an alternative way for the student to perform.
Some groups finish before others.	Provide an extension or enrichment task that extends the activity.
	Two groups who finish first can compare their products.
One group works too slowly.	See if task can be modified so that all groups will finish together.
	Teacher or a member of an early-finishing group can spend some time to help a slow group.
	Let individuals take home tasks.
There is too much noise.	Monitor groups and commend those who are quiet and on task.
	Use a standard signal for noise, such as blinking room lights.
	Assign a member of each group as "noise control."

Source: Based on Ellis & Whalen (1992).

Collaborative Social Action.   Involving students in social action is a natural way to extend students' work (see quadrant IV). Project-based learning helps students to make school–community connections. *The Kid's Guide to Social Action* (Lewis, Espeland, & Pernu, 1998) is a resource for teachers who wish to help students feel socially engaged. This guide explains how students can find worthwhile endeavors: acquire "power" skills such as writing letters to newspaper editors and public officials; gather information by interviewing and surveying people; influence public opinion by making speeches; circulate petitions and proposals; raise funds; have officials make proclamations; and obtain media coverage and advertising. In this way,

TABLE 14.4 *Sample Cooperative Learning Activities*

Name of Activity	Description
Relay	Four students learn a skill; they teach it to four others; eight teach it to eight more, until everyone knows it (Bassano & Christison, 1995).
Group memory	In groups of six, give each group a line to memorize. Group members receive extra credit if everyone can say it when time is up (Bassano & Christison, 1995).
Listen, please (also called "information gap")	In this paired activity, student A has words on various cards and student B has a matching set of picture cards. Listening to the description on a card, student B must pick out the matching card (Bassano & Christison, 1995).
Sequencing task	Students put a cut-up sequence in correct order, such as a scrambled dialogue from a phone call to a friend (Bassano & Christison, 1995).
Scavenger hunt	With a stack of newspapers, group finds one of each: some good news, some bad news, weather map, letter to editor, overseas news, etc. (Bassano & Christison, 1995).
Round robin	Each person solves a problem (using one color ink) and passes the paper to the next team member, who does the next problem. Teacher corrects one sheet (Cantlon, 1991).
Jigsaw	Students receive number and letter (Ex.: I–IV, A–D). Base teams: I, II, III, IVs. Students exit base team; all As group to study one aspect, etc., then return to base team to share expertise (Cantlon, 1991).
Numbered heads together	Each student in the group has a number (1 to 4); students huddle to make sure all can respond; then a number is called and that student responds (Kagan, 1998).
Rotating review	Students visit wall charts, each with different review question; they write answers, then rotate to next chart. If they agree with what is already written, they mark it with an asterisk (Kagan, 1998).
Send-a-problem	Groups create problems and send them around the class for other teams to solve (Kagan, 1998).
Pairs compare	Pairs come up with ideas to solve a problem. When pairs are through, two pairs make a team of four and compare ideas, generating more ideas (Kagan, 1999).
4S brainstorming	While brainstorming solutions to an open-ended prompt, team members take one of four roles: Speed Sergeant enourages many responses quickly. Sultan of Silly tries to come up with funny ideas. Synergy Guru helps members build on one anothers' ideas. Sergeant Support encourages all ideas, suspending judgment (Kagan, 1999).
Group memory	Students write everything they know about a topic they plan to study, including unanswered questions that come to them. In groups of three, they read the paper to the group, and everybody adds ideas to the list. The group compiles unanswered questions and turns in a group memory sheet (Whisler & Williams, 1990).

(continued)

TABLE 14.4 *Continued*

Name of Activity	Description
Partner prediction	Teacher preidentifies places in a literature story where the students can stop to predict what happens next. They share predictions with a partner. They must then share aloud what the partner predicts.
2/4 question some more	Teacher identifies key points in a read-aloud story. Partners talk about the story so far and then discuss what questions occur to them. They share these in a team of four, then with the class (Whisler & Williams, 1990).
Panel of experts	Students read selected passages, taking notes of possible comprehension questions. In a group, students agree on four questions. One group in the room forms a panel, and others question them. Play continues until panel gets two right or one wrong; then questioning group becomes panel (Whisler & Williams, 1990).

students can feel that their energies make a difference in the world, and teachers can feel that they have a positive influence on students and their families.

Before leaving the topic of classroom community, one might look again to the theme of classroom culture (see Chapter 11). Toohey (1998) noted three instructional practices that communicate the value of individualism over collectivism. The first practice was exemplified by the maxim, "Sit at your own desk"; the second, "Use your own things"; and the third, "Use your own words and ideas." Certain ways of seating children enabled the teacher to restrict them from conversing with others. Forbidding students to lend or borrow goods restricted social relations based on sharing. Prohibiting intellectual sharing reinforced the idea that cognition is individual and not co-constructed. These practices unfortunately restrained English learners from making maximal use of peer resources in learning English, reduced their legitimate peripheral practice (Lave & Wenger, 1991), and reinforced social stratification of language "insiders" and "outsiders."

In this excellent analysis of the circulation of power within the classroom community, Toohey includes a quote from Freire (1970):

> The truth is that the oppressed are not "marginals," are not people living "outside" society. They have always been "inside"—inside the structure that made them "beings for others." The solution is not to integrate them into the structure of oppression, but to transform that structure so that they can become "beings for themselves." (p. 55)

Here we see a use of the concept of the margin. When the postmodernists see the margin as the terrain of possibility (Yúdice, 1988), they do not mean that the sole role of teachers of English learners is to induct them into the mainstream. Rather, cultural margins are a "zone of possibility"; the classroom as a community is interlaced with these possibilities of community and interpersonal growth in and among the individuals who are learning English.

Why Involve Families?

"Strong parent involvement is one factor that research has shown time and time again to have positive effects on academic achievement and school attitudes" (Ovando & Collier, 1998). The growing number of English learners in the school system clearly requires continued efforts to involve parents, families, and communities in public education. Successful program models are available to help school personnel, parents, and communities work successfully together.

Changing Definitions of Family Involvement

Every society has its view of what kind of family involvement in schools is effective and appropriate. In addition, each school has its own version. Some schools want families to be involved only in specific ways and at times determined by the staff. Other schools are run completely by parents, who control expenditures, curriculum selection, and hiring and firing of staff. This perspective on the role of the family has shifted as society has seen the rise of nontraditional and alternative family structures.

Megastrategy **14.2**

Involve families as partners in learning

As modern society becomes more complex and demanding, many social institutions are disappearing that, in the past, helped children to grow and mature. Outside of school, members of the community spent time with children, taught them values, nourished their hobbies and interests, and helped them feel that they were important. Nowadays, schools often must take on the role that neighbors, extended families, churches, and other community organizations used to play (Ada, 1995).

New beliefs are emerging about family involvement. The focus has shifted from parents to families, from a deficit view of urban families to an emphasis on the inherent strengths of families, from agendas that originate with teachers and administrators to a renewed respect for family priorities, and from the assumption that families do not want to be involved to an acknowledgment that some families are hard to reach. Because TESOL educators almost always teach in situations in which family members are non–English speaking, it is vital that teachers and administrators make a special effort to understand, and communicate with, these families.

Six types of family involvement are parenting, communicating, volunteering, learning at home, decision making, and liaison with the community (Epstein, 1995). Volunteering benefits specific classrooms as well as the school at large. Family members can help with small groups of individuals in classes or planning projects and field trips. Another helpful role is that of community liaison, whereby one person who knows many others in the community explains school programs and needs, publicizes meetings and open house activities, and musters support for extracurricular activities or parent training. (Although many educators prefer the more inclusive term *family members,* the term is used in this chapter interchangably with the term *parents.*)

Recognizing Rights of Families

Parents in the United States have numerous rights that educators must honor. These include the right of their children to a free, appropriate public education; the right to receive information concerning education decisions and actions in the home language; the right to authorize consent before changes in educational placement occur; the right to be included in discussions concerning disciplinary action toward their children; the right to appeal actions when they do not agree; and the right to participate in meetings organized for public and parent information (Young & Helvie, 1996). In other parts of the world, parents may exert power in more informal ways, using family connections that influence the behavior of school administrators, personal relationships with the teacher, or external religious or political authorities. From the teacher's point of view, family involvement should promote achievement but not disrupt instruction or privilege one student at the expense of others.

A fundamental right of all parents is school support for the home language. To deny access to native-language literacy exploits minorities (Cummins, 1989). It is important that teachers help families to understand the advantages of bilingualism in connecting students to their heritage culture, adding a cognitive dimension in broadening and deepening students' thinking, and expanding career opportunities later in life. Family support for bilingualism helps to establish expectations for high academic performance in two languages (Molina et al., 1997).

Issues in Family Involvement

Schools that have grappled with how to increase parental involvement have encountered many of the same issues (Bermúdez & Márquez, 1996; Young & Helvie, 1996). Ovando and Collier (1998, pp. 301–309) organize these issues within five areas: language, survival and family structure, educational background and values, knowledge of and beliefs about education, and power and status. From each area questions arise that serve as guides for school personnel as they build collaborations with parents. Some questions and practices for educators are presented in Table 14.5.

Myths about Families and Other Communication Barriers

Often teachers think that families of English learners are not interested in what happens in school if they are not visible at parent meetings or traditional parent–school activities. However, surveys of parents show that an overwhelming number of parents express interest in being involved in school events, activities, and decisions. They report, however, that they are often not consulted about the type of involvement, scheduling of activities, or location of events. These reports show that the myth of

TABLE 14.5 *Practices for Educators Based on Questions Regarding Parent—School Relationships*

Area of Concern	Questions	Practices for Educators
Language	How does educators' language (jargon?) affect home–school communication?	Translate jargon into plain English and then into the home language.
	Do community members support using the home language in school?	Advocate maintenance of the home language in all parent communication.
Family structure	How does the family's struggle in day-to-day survival affect the home–school partnership?	Arrange conferences at convenient times for working families.
	How do diverse family structures affect the relations between home and school?	Use the term *families* rather than *parents*. Accept the relationships that exist.
Educational background, attitudes toward schooling	Do school expectations match the parents' educational backgrounds?	Discover the parents' aspirations for their children. Do everything possible to have the school and family agree on high standards.
	What do educators assume about the attitudes of parents toward schooling?	Ensure that communication with school is always honest and positive.
Knowledge of and beliefs about education	How do parents learn about school culture, their role in U.S. schools, and the specific methods being used in their child's classroom? Would they be comfortable reinforcing these methods at home?	Family education events, family literacy classes, primary-language written and oral information, formal and informal teacher–family talks, and family tutoring training are a part of the picture.
	How do parents and teachers differ in the perception of the home–school relationship?	Not only do teachers inform parents, but interest and communication is fully two-way.
Power and status	How does the inherent inequality of the educator–layperson relationship affect the partnership?	Try to have a "family space" at the school. Parents should be informed and involved in decisions.
	Do programs for parents convey a message of cultural deficiency?	"Funds of knowledge" approach affirms and respects the knowledge of the home.
	To what degree are minority-language community members a part of the school in instructional and administrative positions?	Bilingual speakers are paid well and are considered respected assets to the school as well as to the classroom.

Source: Adapted from Ovando & Collier (1998, pp. 301–309).

so-called lack of interest that circulates in low-achieving schools may be due to poor communication between home and school.

Moreover, parents may feel intimidated by school staff and awkward about approaching school personnel. Parents are not comfortable dealing with school staff who appear to be too cold or impersonal, or who talk down to them. Some parents may feel that it is disrespectful to talk to teachers about instruction, as doing so might appear to challenge the teachers' role. Other parents may feel inadequate to deal with school authorities or may be suspicious or angry about specific incidents. These and other communication problems can be lessened if teachers of English learners are trained in effective communication strategies.

Enhancing Home–School Communication

If the teacher does not speak the same language as the family, nonverbal messages assume an increased importance. Teachers who meet family members informally as they arrive to drop off their child, at a classroom open house, or during other school events should strive to make their body language "warm" rather than cold. Teachers can show respect toward family members by, for example, rising as guests enter the room, greeting guests at the door, and accompanying them to the door when they leave.

Any notes, letters, or newsletters sent home need to be translated into the home language. If communication sent home is positive, there is more chance that it will be read. Many teachers establish a positive communication pattern by sending a consistent stream of "happy grams" describing what a student has done well. However, if a student has a problem in class, communication between home and school must be consistent and sustained. Any useful program of home–school communication is predicated on having established a rapport with parents in person.

Teachers have modified a wide range of classroom behaviors through the use of home–school notes. The most effective notes are those that focus on the improvement of academic productivity, such as the amount or quality of completed classwork or homework. In contrast, a focus on disruptiveness seldom in itself causes an improvement in academic performance.

Teacher–Family Conferences

Preparation for meetings with families enhances their chances of success. The concerned teacher makes sure that scheduled times are convenient for family members and prepares a portfolio of the student's successes. The conference might begin with a limited amount of small talk, especially if there has been a recent notable family event. Then the teacher reviews the student's performance, using the portfolio or other evidence of student work. Showing an anonymous example of a grade-level performance may make it easier for family members to put their child's performance in perspective. Listening to family members helps the teacher get a more complete view of the child. If there needs to be a plan for improvement, the teacher sets in motion definite steps, including setting a time in the near future to compare notes on the child's progress.

When parents and teachers meet in conference, they both bring with them their own school experiences—what went right and what went wrong; they are determined for schooling to be different for the child they both care about. Teachers learn to use their words with care and hope they can build a partnership with parents that works to everyone's advantage. And parents over time may realize that when it comes to their children, they still have much to learn (Gibbs, 2007, p. 20).

Three-Way Conferences.   Three-way conferences that include the student invite family members into a dialogue about their children's schooling. Students can use this opportunity to demonstrate what they know, share their accomplishments, and set new learning goals. Family members find out about their child's learning, have the opportunity to ask questions and express their ideas, and help to plan for the child's learning at home. Teachers act as guides by clarifying ideas and issues and responding to specific questions (Davies, Cameron, Politano, & Gregory, 1992). In this way, students are encouraged to follow through on their self-regulated learning.

Using an Interpreter.   The use of an interpreter for parent conferences shows respect for the home language of families. During the conference, the interpreter usually translates the client's own words as closely as possible to give a sense of the client's concepts, emotional state, and other important information. Despite the language difference, the teacher can watch nonverbal, affective responses and observe facial expressions, voice intonations, and body movements to extend communication.

Partnership with the Family.   Partnership with the family is strengthened in several ways. A positive tone communicates that the teacher likes the student and has found strengths to appreciate in that student. Keeping careful records and samples of student work shows that the grading practices are fair and that the student is making adequate progress; if not, the family should be informed early if the child falls below expectations in some area. All family contact should be documented in an activity log that includes the date, subject, and parents' reactions. In this way, school administrators can see what communication efforts have been made.

Cultural Differences in Parental Involvement.   A major difference between Russian parents and those from other cultural groups was the assertive way in which Russian parents approached classroom teachers to inquire about their children's academic progress. Although they did not speak English very fluently, Russian parents approached the teachers. The children translated for them as they inquired about homework or progress in class. This was in contrst to other parents who usually waited for their children at the gate outside (Delgado-Gaitan, 2006, p. 60).

How Families Can Assist in a Child's Learning

Schools that have a take-home library of print- and media-based materials encourage learning activities outside school. In a dual-language setting, families can work with their children in either language. Following are ways in which a volunteer, such as a family member, can help in the classroom (Enk & Hendricks, 1984):

- Dictate spelling words.
- Listen to reading practice.
- Give drills on words, phrases, and flash cards.
- Supervise games and small-group activities.
- Help with written compositions.
- Help children who were absent from class to catch up.
- Give reinforcement to children new to the class.
- Supervise individual testing.
- Set up learning centers.
- Help children publish a class newspaper.
- Supervise student committees doing research.
- Work with projectors, recorders, and listening posts.
- Repeat a lesson for a child who needs extra help.
- Teach a special enrichment skill.
- Serve as an interpreter for non-English-speaking children.
- Record primary-language stories.
- Accompany small groups to the library.

Families' Attitudes toward Dual-Language Learning.　Families may not support learning in two languages. For example, Watahomigie (1995) describes the negative reaction of parents on the Hualapai Indian reservation in Peach Springs, Arizona, when educators proposed that schools establish a Hualapai–English bilingual program. The parents had been told for over one hundred years that the native language was unimportant, and they did not believe that such instruction would benefit their children. A "high-tech" approach based on CALL, built on efforts to convince parents of its value, was eventually successful.

Family Literacy.　Family literacy projects help children achieve in school. In Fresno, California, the Hmong Literacy Project was initiated by parents to help students appreciate their cultural roots, preserve oral history, and maintain the culture through written records. Parents asked for literacy lessons in Hmong (a language that has been written for only about thirty years) and in English. The program helped families to develop not only literacy skills but also skills in math and computers, thereby allowing them to help their children academically. The Hmong parents newsletter increased communication between the school and the community, leading to greater parent participation in school activities (Kang, Kuehn, & Herrell, 1996).

In the Parents' and Schools' Learning Clubs (PASLC) program in Soweto, South Africa, parents commented that students had gaps in their knowledge about their own communities, so parents' cultural knowledge was made an explicit part of the Saturday or Sunday morning parent workshops in the form of using family praise poems, family trees, and family histories to promote literacy. Parents also suggested activities involving co-participation: experiential learning in which parents worked with children on projects, as well as activities that helped to encourage the reading habit in children, such as vocabulary games, picture interpretation, story dramatization, and use of stories, rhymes, and folktales (Mashishi, 2002).

In South London, the school system organized a Saturday School in which Somali immigrant parents could pass on to their children their cultural and religious inheritance, work with one another to share advice and information, and serve as a place for adults and young people to get to know one another. This gave the community a sense of identity and belonging (Elmi, Folarin, Moalin, & Rees, 2002).

A Model of Home–School Relationships

Faltis (2001) provides a four-level sequence for home–school relationships based on an earlier model proposed by Rasinski and Fredericks (1989). Although teachers may not be able to reach the highest level of parental involvement at a particular school site, the model presents an overall view of the possibilities. This reciprocal process is summarized in Table 14.6.

Box 14.1 offers a host of practices for involving parents in learning, ranging from providing information to learning from them about their views of education. These suggestions are drawn from Jones (1991), Díaz-Rico and Weed (2010), Fredericks and Rasinski (1990). Rather than including a separate list of suggestions from each source, I have amalgamated them in categories.

PRACTICES FOR TEACHERS

Involving Parents in Policy Decisions

- Ask representative parent committees to advise and consent on practices that involve culturally and linguistically diverse students.
- Talk with parents before and after school to encourage them to get involved in school issues.
- Make school facilities available for meetings of community groups.

TABLE 14.6 *A Two-Way Parent–School Involvement Model*

Level of Involvement	Description of Activity
I. Teacher–parent contact	The teacher learns about parents' daily experiences and initiates positive home–school contact and dialogue by chatting, making home visits, talking with community workers, and arranging for after-school homework help or tutoring to promote students' success.
II. Sharing information in the home about schooling	The teacher keeps the parents informed (in the home language if possible) about important school and community events and meetings, changes in school schedules, help available from community-based organizations, and sources of academic support, using such means as student-produced newsletters, personal notes, telephone calls, and other notices.
III. Participation at home and school	Parents, caregivers, and other concerned adults are welcomed and encouraged to come to class and to attend school meetings and social events. Parents may linger in the morning to watch reading and writing take place or to see a little poetry reading, especially if it takes place in the home language. Students may be assigned to find out about their families' knowledge of planting, banking, etc., that teachers can find a way to use and elaborate on in class.
IV. Parental empowerment in curricular decisions	After the success of the previous three levels, teachers support parents who become involved as colleagues in professional activities and decisions. Some parents form advisory committees, start community tutoring centers, and find multiple means to influence school policy and support academic learning outside the classroom. The role of the teacher is to encourage and work with parents to make these possible.

Source: Based on Faltis (2001).

Community Funds of Knowledge

Sometimes teachers believe that English learners come from homes that have limited social and intellectual resources. This inaccurate perception, based on a "disadvantage/deficiency" model, has too often led to lowered academic expectations for these students. To counteract this misconception, researchers have sent teachers as participant-observers into the homes of English learners to see what strategies and knowledge are used at home to sustain the families' well-being. Through these visits, it has become obvious that communities have "funds of knowledge" (Vélez-Ibáñez &

Box 14.1 **Practices for Educators to Involve Families in Schooling**

Providing information

- Informally chat with family members as they pick up their child after school.
- Use the telephone as an instrument of good news.
- Operate a homework hotline.
- Encourage parent-to-parent communication.
- Hold workshops for family members to learn to help children with reading skills.
- Offer materials in the home language.
- Provide bilingual handouts that describe programs available through the school.
- Make available a list of parental rights under the Bilingual Education Act.
- Send home personal handwritten notes, using a translator if necessary.
- Send home notes when students are doing well.
- Create parent–student handbooks.
- Have students write classroom newsletters.
- Welcome new families with packets delivered to the home.

Ways to showcase English learners

- Enter students in poetry, essay, or art contests or exhibits sponsored by community or professional organizations.
- Offer to train students how to read aloud at libraries or children's centers.
- Encourage dual-language proficiency as a mark of prestige in school.

Ways to bring parents to school

- Encourage family members to come to class to make crafts with students or to discuss culture, calligraphy, or family history.
- Find out if teacher–family conferences or meetings conflict with work schedules.
- Ensure that siblings are welcome at teacher–family conferences or meetings.

- Provide baby-sitting services for teacher–family conferences.
- Maintain a friendly school office.
- Establish an explicit open-door policy so that families will know they are welcome; include welcoming signs in the primary language.
- Suggest specific ways family members can help to promote achievement.
- Help students to obtain remedial help if necessary in a timely way.
- Make meetings into social events, providing food and dramatic or musical performances if time permits.
- Hold student–teacher–family breakfasts once a month.
- Schedule primary-language speakers at school events.
- Recognize family members for involvement at award ceremonies, send thank-you notes, and speak positively of parents to their child.

How families can teach teachers

- Suggest better ways to communicate.
- Provide a rich understanding of the students' role(s) in the family.
- Express the hopes they have for schooling.
- Describe students' hobbies, interests, and strengths.

Homework tips for families *(adapted from Jones, 1991)*

- Set aside a family quiet time when each person has homework or other activities to do that demand concentration.
- Establish a routine for finding out what assignments to expect.
- Make sure there is a place set aside for homework; provide paper, pencils, adequate lighting, etc.
- Check with the child to see if he or she understands the assignment. If needed, work

(continued)

Box 14.1 **Continued**

through a sample problem. Have someone to call for help if necessary.

- Check the completed assignment with the child.
- Praise the work or offer constructive improvements.

Workshops and family support groups
(adapted from Jones, 1991)

- Hold "make-it-and-take-it" workshops to construct home learning materials.
- Open a family learning center—school library or computer center—several nights

a week, with learning activities for all ages.

- Hold learning fairs—in the evening, with single-topic sessions.
- Have community members host family support groups.
- Set aside a family room at school for families to drop in and participate in informal activities, play with toys, and talk with other parents.
- Hold child and adolescent development talks.
- Conduct special workshops on reading, math, study skills, self-esteem, etc.

Greenberg, 1992) that the community has developed and drawn on over generations to create success. This knowledge can be brought into the classroom to enrich, develop, and transform the curriculum.

Megastrategy **14.3**

Affirm and build on what the community values as knowledge

Teachers need to know what children do intellectually in the everyday context of their neighborhood and families. If teachers are not familiar with the activities and responsibilities that children perform in their homes and neighborhoods, their knowledge about children's cognitive abilities will be distorted, and they will not be able to connect the curriculum with students' daily thinking. Teacher research in the community accomplishes two purposes. First, teachers who interview community members and parents become familiar with the local expertise in many areas, and they use this knowledge to teach in ways that make sense to students. Second, students feel a closer connection and increased respect for community members.

In the past, teachers may have made home visits to get to know parents or to discuss a particular student problem. In the "funds of knowledge" program (Moll, 1992), teachers visited homes to document families' knowledge in such areas as farming, animal care, construction, trade, business, and finance. By asking questions about these domains, the teacher-investigators opened up new channels of communication between home and school (González, Moll, & Amanti, 2005). Researchers found that practical activities (auto repair, music, etc.) provided rich possibilities for learning to occur (Moll & Greenberg, 1990). The ethnographic approach became a joint inquiry among the community, the teachers, and the university researchers working on the project; all met periodically to weave knowledge about family and school matters into academic content and lessons.

One teacher, aware that members of the community often built or remodeled their own homes, created a sixth-grade thematic unit on construction. Over twenty parents and community members visited the class, sharing their knowledge and skills on various aspects of construction. As the unit culminated, students wrote and gave oral reports on their design of a model community. These authentic, relevant activities elicited from students real communicative and problem-solving skills and added excitement, authenticity, and a community connection to the classroom (Moll, 1992).

Transformative School–Community Partnerships

The anthropological focus (based on culture) rather than the solely psychological approach (based on analysis of individual behavior) has widened the focus of SLA. Rather than looking at the classroom as a collection of individuals whose aptitudes, study behaviors, and motivation are responsible for achievement, educators now regard these learners as part of a larger community whose goals, aspirations, struggles, and resources form the basis on which school achievement rests. School–community partnerships are fundamental to the education of English learners.

Empowerment as a Goal

Some liberal educators look at their involvement with families and communities as "liberating" based on the belief that education has the power to create social change. Although many educators describe community involvement programs as *empowering,* Valdés (1996) questioned the use of this term. Many such programs teach parents to help their children, but they may fail to address topics such as racism, social equality, and economic exploitation. Educators have a vested interest in the financial resources of schools and families.

Megastrategy **14.4**

Form partnerships with the community to involve students in community activities and social action

According to Delgado-Gaitan (1994, p. 144) *empowerment* can be defined as a way in which a historically underrepresented group can recognize its potential and state its goals of access to resources, hence power. ELD programs are often found in neighborhood schools that do not receive the same resources as schools in affluent neighborhoods. The wealthiest school districts in the United States outspend the poorest by a factor of more than four to one (see Kozol, 1991). One might well channel the empowerment rhetoric into the election of officials who will enforce equal financial rights for neighborhood schools.

Family involvement programs may communicate the message that individual or family heroics are needed to overcome obstacles so that children can succeed. Many assumptions (individual heroics trump community building, poverty is an obstacle, students who succeed are valued the most, education should prepare students for a complex technological culture) underlie mainstream middle-class values. Other communities may hold alternative values.

Getting to Know the Community

Making friends in the community is the first step to forming and sustaining school–community partnerships. Some schools sponsor Grandparents' Day so that students can invite family members to class. Teachers may send home cards to mark the arrival of new babies or a change of residence. One teacher announces to the class at the beginning of the year that she is available to be asked to dinner on Friday nights. Knowing in advance that their invitation is welcomed, parents and students schedule her for months ahead. Teachers who take the time to shop in the neighborhood, visit community centers, or attend religious services in the community often get to see another side of students' lives.

When investigating the daily life of the community, it is particularly valuable to look at the social practices that support learning. Delgado-Gaitan (1994) spoke of the "ecocultural niche" in which families exist, involving such factors as socioeconomic level, social and political relations, religious beliefs, and relationship to the neighborhood, media, health institutions, and schools. These influence the way in which the community uses learning as a means toward power. In a modern society that uses discursive practices to circulate power (see Foucault, 1979, 1980, 1984), it is important for the existing oracy and literacy practices to be seen in their sociocultural context as a way to begin to understand the culture of the community.

School Partnerships with Community-Based Organizations

Community-based organizations (CBOs) are groups committed to helping people obtain health, education, and other basic human services that can boost students' academic achievement in a variety of ways. Their activities include tutoring students in their first language, developing leadership skills and promoting higher education goals, and providing information and support on issues such as health care, pregnancy, gang involvement, and so on. Some programs help parents to assist their children by training the parents as tutors and homework helpers (see Chapter 15).

Community Support for English Learners

A supportive community offers a home for linguistic and cultural diversity. This support takes many forms, such as fund-raising for college scholarships for English learners and providing user-friendly community services. Students can be invited to the local library to offer their stories, books, and poetry to other students, in both English and the primary language. Policies of community agencies such as the library can be influenced by teacher involvement.

Community service organizations are often run by community leaders who set the tone for the community and sometimes have strong ideas about education. Teacher-led presentations to other teachers, staff, or community members can explain ELD pedagogy. Service clubs such as Rotary and Kiwanis provide opportunities for speakers to reach the business leaders of the community with current information about multicultural and linguistic issues. These activities deliver the message that teachers are knowledgeable and interested in the community at large.

PRACTICES FOR TEACHERS
Influencing Policies of Local Libraries

- File lesson plans in the library and make specific materials accessible to students.
- Consult with those who purchase materials for school district and community libraries.
- Encourage parents to use the public library to check out books with their children.
- Justify to librarians the need for primary-language and ESOL materials.
- Ask if English learners can be involved in delivering storytelling and other programs at the library.

Communities can foster a climate of support for English learners by featuring articles in local newspapers and newsletters about their achievements in the schools and prizes they have won, by sponsoring literature and art exhibitions that feature students, and by publishing their stories written in both languages. In this way, support for ELD programs is orchestrated in the community at large.

Letters to the editor of the local paper can serve as a vehicle to persuade the public to support bilingual and ELD instruction. Teachers and other staff members can influence community public opinion in several ways.

This chapter suggests that the most successful educators are those who are connected with the communities in which they teach. In this situation, families are treated as partners and are able to affirm and support students' efforts. Parents and community alike value what is learned as useful and compatible with what the community values as knowledge. In fact, the community acts in close harmony and partnership with the school, as students take initiative and responsibility in community activities and social action (Auerbach, 2002).

PRACTICES FOR TEACHERS
Influencing Local Public Opinion

- Give presentations to community groups about ESOL programs.
- Join or begin local education–community partnership foundations.
- Be proactive in gaining newspaper coverage for school events.
- Be heard in the local newspaper editorial pages.

The Idea of Community

Not all communities are in the immediate vicinity of the classroom; today virtual communities connect English learners with others around the world. The *idea* of community, the mere imagining that such a thing exists, is sometimes enough to inspire the deepest feelings of identification (see Anderson, 1983; Norton & Toohey, 2001). Language is one of the strongest markers of group identity, and linguistic conflict is one of the bitterest sources of discord (Thornborrow, 1999). This makes the role of speech communities—and those who manage, instruct, and transform them—one of the world's strongest potential forces for cohesion or division.

Globalism affects the sense of community. "The production of electronic information radically alters notions of time, community, and history, while simultaneously blurring the distinction between reality and image" (Aronowitz & Giroux, 1991, p. 115). Global issues make peace education a priority, as members of ethnic groups who may never have spoken with one another before come together using English as a common language. Peace education can be defined as preparing students for "efforts to achieve human dignity for all people and to realize a viable global society on an ecologically healthy planet" (Reardon, 1988, in Brooks & Fox, 1998, p. vii).

Teachers of English learners face multiple challenges in connecting with community. Such education, for the most part, takes place in classrooms in which learners are socially marginalized, either because they are recent immigrants or because they live in neighborhoods in which English is not the native speech. TESOL educators who work in EFL settings may be expatriates who have much to learn from the societies in which they serve, and they may feel themselves marginalized too, by virtue of their visitor status. This means that involving the community in the education of English learners will always be challenging, but it can also be rewarding. Building a community of learners means that these challenges and rewards are shared with others, multiplying both.

Exploratory Break

- Would you rather learn a foreign language by using a cooperative-learning group experience or by yourself? Discuss specific ways that English learners can collaborate as they learn.

Chapter *15*

Project-Based Learning and Service Learning

Why Projects?

In many ways, school is inadequate preparation for real life. In school, problems are simplified, and there are usually right and wrong answers. Activities are neatly structured to fit within class periods. Knowledge is neatly divided into content domains. Teachers evaluate students' products and effort. Students know exactly what actions are required to produce good grades. Because all problems are simulations, no one lives or dies, eats or goes hungry, or is sheltered or homeless as a direct result of what goes on in class.

In contrast to the delimited world of the classroom, the real world is relatively complex and unstructured, and the stakes are enormous. The efforts of individuals and groups make a difference. Project-based learning (PBL) is an opportunity for students to take on tasks that are consequential.

Facing the Real World

Investigations based on real-world problems provide instructional tasks that are contextualized and appropriately challenging for targeted students. The English that is practiced in class is connected with the English used in real-life environments (see Fried-Booth, 1997).

Project-based learning is based on a more general learning paradigm, problem-based learning. This is a strategy that creates a culture of inquiry in the classroom, in which individuals engage in "defining problems, seeking ways of addressing these problems, collaborating with others, and being curious about the work that they do.

Megastrategy **SET 15**

Involve the learner in projects that offer long-term, meaningful learning; serve and learn in the community

Problem-based learning presents learners with real-life problems to solve" (Jordan & Porath, 2006, p. 10).

PBL is "an instructional approach that contextualizes learning by presenting learners with problems to solve or products to develop" (Moss, 1998, p. 1). PBL connects students with challenges that are motivating, putting students in charge of seeking knowledge and selecting and generating the activities they will pursue as part of completing the project (Roth-Vinson, 2001). The project approach is part of a balanced curriculum that supplements the curriculum of specific, sequential skills. Because a project is emergent and negotiated rather than fully preplanned by the teacher, it encourages students to go beyond the minimum standards of engagement (Katz & Chard, 1989).

Characteristics of PBL

Four characteristics exemplify the use of PBL in the classroom (Blumenfeld, Solo-way, Marx, Krajcik, Guzdial, & Palinscar, 1991). First, students are engaged with a *driving question* that is related to a real-world situation and applies across content areas. Second, students *conduct active research* that engages them in the study of concepts, analysis of data, and presentation of their findings. Third, *collaboration* takes place between students, teachers, and others in such a way that the learning is shared among members of the learning community. Fourth, *cognitive tools* are used that support student presentations, such as computer-based graphics, hyper-media, and telecommunication technology. Students become involved in long-term collaborative learning situations in which they identify what they need to know, assess what they already know, gather information, evaluate potential outcomes, and design and carry out activities.

Benefits of PBL

Students learn to take initiative, seek learning on their own, and take responsibility for the results of their inquiry. They experience diverse opinions and viewpoints, figure out how to negotiate with others to design a plan, and learn to agree about what to accomplish, who will be in charge of each task, and how information will be investigated and presented (Roth-Vinson, 2001). Students develop cognitive skills by posing questions, developing proposals, gathering and examining information, drawing conclusions, generating further questions, and completing artifacts. Students use technology as they learn to systematize information and develop informative presentations (Land & Greene, 2000). Even students with low proficiency in English benefit from interacting cooperatively with others while working on a high-interest topic.

In addition to promoting students' academic skills, PBL helps students to feel more integrated into the community at large. This type of learning helps both international students studying in an English-speaking country and immigrants in a new setting to feel connected in more positive ways to life outside the classroom.

Projects Are Collaborative

Although the instructional content of projects may vary depending on the setting, language proficiency level, and target language skills, it is important for projects to be collaborative. Six features of this collaborative effort are crucial (Wilhelm, 1997):

- Cooperative learning increases student collaboration.
- Individualized instructional planning and feedback are provided, even when students work in groups.
- Student self-assessment involves students in deciding their grades, combined with teacher evaluation.
- The teacher facilitates learning and provides feedback (see next sections).
- Authentic settings offer real-world significance.
- Reflection during and after the project is essential, because it is largely through reflection that people learn and develop.

Collaboration of any kind is based on interpersonal trust. Students working on projects need to become friends with one another so that they can build positive, productive working relationships, especially in classes of mixed nationality, primary languages, and cultural backgrounds. When students work together, cultural barriers fade, and students build communication skills.

Projects outside the classroom encourage language acquisition in a content-rich setting.

©Stock Connection Distribution/Alamy

The Teacher as Guide

Teachers act as coaches or tutors, providing not only cognitive help in framing issues and assessing possible solutions but also metacognitive help as they assist students to set goals, plan, monitor ongoing efforts, and evaluate progress. The role of the teacher may be to coax students along, drawing them into assuming responsibility in a given situation and then assuming the role of colleague on a problem-solving team (see Stepien & Gallagher, 1993). One of the best features of PBL is that teachers gain new opportunities to see their work as challenging. Taking on projects with students fosters the disposition to evoke creativity and problem-solving skills from students.

The way in which the students' learning is supported in the classroom has much to do with the teacher's vision of the learner. In the project-based early learning centers of the Reggio Emilia schools in Italy, teachers were interviewed about how they imagined the learner. The educators in Reggio Emilia saw the young children as "powerful, active, competent protagonists of their own growth; actors in their shared history, participants in society and culture, with the right (and obligation) to speak from their own perspective, and to act with others on the basis of their own particular experience and level of consciousness" (Edwards, 1998, p. 180). This view of the learner evolves just as the teacher's own identity evolves. In return, the role of the teacher constantly undergoes revision as students grow and mature, or occasionally regress under stress, and as the dynamics of the concerns and capacities of the students, parents, and community change.

Table 15.1 is a synopsis of C. Edwards's (1998) advice to teachers. I have taken the liberty of inventing names for each role by giving a label to the behaviors that Edwards prescribes for teachers.

Skill Integration

In the process of tackling projects large and small, students often integrate various content areas. They use a combination of receptive skills (reading and listening), processing skills (critical and creative thinking; use of graphic organizers), and productive skills (speaking and writing) as they research and discuss issues, propose and justify solutions, and design outcomes. In the process of completing projects, students learn to view knowledge as connected rather than narrowly divided by subject matter. The integration of content knowledge and language development makes PBL an ideal mode of study for TESOL education.

Design, Documentation, and Discourse

Asking students to *design* a project requires them to keep records of their plans and intentions. *Documentation* records the process of creation and design, displaying what action or thought took place and explaining the thinking that went on. *Discourse* is the analysis of communication, "a metalinguistic process in which meaning is questioned in the name of growth and understanding" (Forman & Fyfe, 1998, p. 241).

TABLE 15.1 *The Role of the Teacher in Project-Based Learning*

Teacher's Role	Associated Behaviors
Listener	Being fully attentive, and at the same time recording and documenting what is observed as a basis for decision making
Organizer and provoker of occasions: "spark"	Originating intellectual dialogue that creates excitement and curiosity; writing down what students say; reading back their comments; searching for insights to motivate further questions and group activity
Co-actor in discoveries	Playing ball with students; catching ideas and throwing them back in a way that makes the students want to continue the game
Shaper	Taking ideas that emerge from a discussion or dispute and forming hypotheses to be tested, a representation that should be attempted, or the basis for a day's activity
"Knot" finder	Helping students pinpoint sticking points, need for more information, acquisition of necessary tools or skills, or launching points for new aspects of a project
Group "rememberer"	Observing and selectively documenting work by means of assigning benchmark reflection events, reminding groups to preserve notes, jotting down ideas overheard in discussions, making a record of observations
Intervener	Knowing when to nudge and when to step back to let a group solve its own problems
Colleague	Involving other adults in the process of a project
Expector of growth	Extending the students' stamina and attention span, increasing their range of techniques and strategies, and enhancing their concentration and effort.
One who is amazed	Expecting students to do wonderfully and to experience pleasure and joy in learning
Spiraler	Engaging in cyclical teaching and learning as ideas are revisited and represented a second time

Source: Based on Edwards (1998).

Table 15.2, loosely based on Forman and Fyfe's 1998 description of the processes that underlie PBL, traces the evolution of a project from earliest discussion to culmination. This process is cyclical rather than linear, with many steps being revisited and deepened throughout the course of the project. Design leads to documentation, which engenders discourse, leading to new design, and so forth.

Children in the Reggio Emilia preschool model use project-based learning to engage with teachers in a co-constructed curriculum (Forman & Fyfe, 1998). The students in this model originate a

TABLE 15.2 *Tracing the Process of Project Development*

Stage of Development	Leads to...
Early discussion	Questions raised
Early explorations, such as drawings about questions raised	Descriptions of the problem
Descriptions from various points of view	Designs addressing the problem: plans, mind maps
Designs, symbols	More talking about the designs, becoming discourse as teachers help to deepen the dialogues, creating shared vocabulary and meanings, with symbols becoming project language
Research and exploration	Facts, displays, artifacts, notes
Collections of information	Documentation, as teacher helps to wrap rationales and explanations around exploration, becoming part of formative assessment
Partial solutions	More documentation, more design
Disequilibration: partial solutions may not work	Provocation, more searching
Collaboration: student–student, student–teacher, teacher–colleague, class–community	Co-construction of designs, plans, meaning, final products
Design of culminating activity	Performance preparation, including formative assessment
Performance	Celebration, debriefing reflection, summative assessment

Source: Based on Forman and Fyfe (1998).

question for study from their curiosity about the world; the teacher frames their inquiry in ways that allow them to delve more deeply into their questions and explore the world around them in a series of educational experiences. As students discuss what they are learning, the teacher documents their activities by displaying diagrams they have drawn, photographs of their learning activities, or quotes written down from their oral discourse. These artifacts are displayed and discussed as more language ensues and other relevant facets of the topic are explored. Switching from one modality to another gives students a variety of ways to express and explore what they are learning through the project.

Representation

A group of teachers of five-, six- and seven-year-olds at Marks Meadow Elementary School, a public school in Amherst, Massachusetts, embarked on a project called "The City in the Snow" (Forman, Langley, Oh, & Wrisley, 1998). Students prepared for the first snow of the year by recollecting how snow feels, how kids can play with it, and how the city deals with huge quantities. They drew snow scenes of skiers, snow falling on houses, and so forth. They constructed a toy village, sifted flour over the tiny buildings, and painted a large mural of a city—without snow—in anticipation. When teachers gave the children white paint to paint the snow, it became evident that some children did not fully understand that snow falls on horizontal surfaces (one child drew white snow vertically covering the walls of a house). When the students finally experienced real snow, they drew snow again, this time with more appreciation for the look of snow on the roofs and cornices of buildings. They then became fascinated with snowflakes—looking at them under a microscope, watching a video about snowflakes, and experimenting with freezing water. Last, some students tried to invent snow-making machines, revealing in their drawings their ideas about how snow is formed. Thus, the study of snow generated some emergent objectives that were not part of the original discussion.

In the project described above, teachers started the project design with the language modality used most easily by children—talking—and then moved immediately to drawing. This connection between verbal and figural representation is important for English learners, whose emergent oral language is thus supported by kinesthetic and visual activities. Viewing the drawings, the teacher learned how the students were thinking about the topic at hand, what aspects of the topic they depicted, and what their hypotheses were about how the world works. Moving to another mode of representation, in this case the simulation of the snowfall with flour, allowed the teacher to offer students another nonverbal way of looking at the situation, which was then represented again in words during collaborative discussions. In the project "City in the Snow," the cycle of design-documentation-discourse was repeated as the students broadened and deepened their experience with the topic.

The following examples illustrate the use of PBL at a variety of educational levels. They range from short thematic units of two or three weeks' duration to investigations lasting several months, with students' ages ranging from second grade to college.

Thematic Projects in the Elementary School

Elementary ESL students can benefit from working on thematic projects. Gordon (1992) described a project that involved studying different breeds of dogs. This combined relatively complicated vocabulary with comparatively simple syntax to boost students' English skills. For example, when students discussed dog breeds, the teacher employed "personality words" such as *affectionate, enthusiastic, obedient,* and *pugnacious* (p. 30). Student-generated topics sustained interest over the period of the project: Students took notes, duplicated pictures from source books into personal notebooks to use with mini-essays, and created their own books. This type of PBL helps students who are fluent in English but lacking in academic skills to sustain interest as their literacy skills in English catch up with their basic interpersonal communication skills.

Projects at Urban High Schools

The NET Team was a two-year PBL program at Denver North High School, a large urban school with 1,500 students and a predominantly Hispanic (82 percent) student body, 8 percent of whom spoke only Spanish and 25 percent of whom were English learners. Students who have difficulty learning also often have poor attendance habits, low self-esteem, minimal study skills, and low math and reading scores. The NET Team project was initiated to address these problems. Students applied to the program and, once accepted, were assigned to teacher-composed, heterogeneous groups mixed by ability, cultural background, gender, or learning style, usually with three or four members. Instruction took place in blocks of time, with two or more teachers working together in nearby classrooms (Giromini, 2001).

National History Day provided the stimulus for extensive research on the theme "Frontiers in History." Students were tasked with finding a "turning point" in history. They kept project logs, fact sheets, and annotated bibliographies; made a time line of significant dates and events; wrote a process paper explaining their research efforts; and completed a "metacognition," a five-paragraph essay that traced the project's success, failures, and lessons learned. The final project was presented to teammates, teachers, parents, and invited guests at the school's History Night. This project addressed content standards in English, history, science, and visual arts as well as workplace standards in technology, organizational skills, and communication skills.

> Southeast Asian students at a high school in Sacramento, California, created multimedia, multicultural family histories. Students connected special effects, drawings, visual text, photos, and voice-over to present their families' stories. Balderas (2001) created family history projects in which students used photos, drawings, and word-processed text to create albums that could be shared with other family members or read aloud to other classes and community groups. A list of guiding questions early in the project helped students to structure intergenerational interviews with family members.

Community-Based Projects

Anderson Valley High School, on the north coast of California near Mendocino, worked with the Anderson Valley Nursery and the North Coast Rural Challenge network to collect seeds and cuttings of native plants and restore the plants to wetlands near the high school. Students refurbished an abandoned greenhouse to propagate native plants for distribution throughout the valley. Meanwhile, at the junior high school, students spread out throughout the valley to record oral interviews with Anderson Valley elders, which they then typed and edited. Audio CDs were created to present the stories. Students collected photographs and prepared them for publication in book form (North Coast Rural Challenge Network, 2000).

Project-Based Learning in EFL

Sometimes a "vicious cycle" takes place in EFL classes in which lack of exposure to real-world English causes the learner not to use English, which in turn leads that learner to lack self-esteem and confidence in his or her English ability, which further exacerbates the lack of proficiency (Sarwar, 2000). PBL provides EFL learners a context for meaningful use of the target language outside the classroom. In Sarwar's EFL classes in Pakistan, groups of students created newsletters and books based on models they found in the library. Their products featured news, sports, business, advertisements, or whatever content they chose, with pictures to accompany the text. The final product was shared as a presentation and display.

> Mr. Hao, a ninth-grade English teacher in Beijing, designed a series of learning activities around the theme of life stories. He believes that using life stories can help students learn not only about grammar in sentences but also about the people in their families, and that these stories can anchor their experiences as society in the People's Republic of China changes rapidly. Students interviewed each other to practice before interviewing family members or neighbors to capture important events in their lives. As a culminating project, students made a class storybook. (Zhang, 2006)

Projects in Intensive English Programs

PBL can be used effectively in short, theme-focused classes for international students. Wilhelm (1999) described seven different project classes in Levels 1–4 of an intensive English program (IEP). These included Know Your City, Travel USA, The Midwest Yesterday and Today, Coffeehouse, School Visits, Creative Speaking/Drama, and Newsletter. In the Coffeehouse project, students working in groups organized a public performance in a local coffeehouse, reserving space, issuing invitations, creating the agenda, and documenting the event. In the Newsletter project class, students conducted surveys and wrote up the results in informative articles. The Travel USA project featured students acting as travel agents, "selling" the travel packages they had assembled at an open house exhibit. Communication in these classes was enhanced through the e-mail messages, activity surveys, and journal entries by which students kept the instructor informed about the progress of the projects.

Projects in Teacher Education

Candidates for a teaching credential or master's degree in TESOL can benefit greatly from working on projects themselves during their career preparation. This brings into TESOL teacher preparation programs the element of individual research design. When assigned a project, TESOL candidates learn to focus the topic, design and carry out research, and represent the results to their peers and mentors. They thus both experience the power of a creative response to authentic learning and practice the skills they will be demanding of their students who take on supervised projects of their own while learning English.

> Sam's class engaged in the collection and presentation of a teaching portfolio. He chose to write a case study about his teaching in an intensive English program (IEP) in a midsize university town. Sam's class, an oral conversation class, included immigrant students (mostly Puerto Rican) who worked in nearby manufacturing companies, spouses of Japanese international students enrolled at the university, and a Russian couple who were brought to town in a church-based resettlement program. Sam's portfolio posed the problem of these students' unequal oral participation in class and documented the attempts he had made to address the challenge. These included ways that students could contribute their personal experiences to each lesson and ways that students could make a personal commitment to increasing their participation through interactive journal communication with him. For Sam, the teaching portfolio became a useful tool in taking on the project of improving his teaching. (K. E. Johnson, 1996)

Many TESOL master's degree programs culminate in master's theses in which students perform research investigations or develop curriculum designs. For the MA in education TESOL program at California State University at San Bernardino, two students collaborated on a project in which they job-shadowed the administrator of the campus IEP and then designed their own proprietary language school. A student from Taiwan developed a theoretical model for teaching reading using film scripts and then designed a unit on Irish culture to provide students with background knowledge before viewing the movie *My Left Foot*. A student from Japan who taught at a school for international business combined theoretical insights from three domains (situated discourse, intercultural communication, and negotiation theory) to design a teaching model for intercultural negotiation.

Choosing a Project Topic

Teachers may wonder how to begin involving students in projects. In the Reggio Emilia schools described earlier, teachers observe what interests the children. Often these interests, as expressed by children's questions and speculations, evolve into a group unit. Using cycles of representation, teachers find ways to deepen the learning experience for students by combining language input (reading or listening) and output (speaking, writing, or drawing). Each class of students is unique; what works for one class may fall flat in another. Helping students to design and carry out projects is a process of trial and error.

Megastrategy **15.1**

Negotiate the project topic with the learners

One teacher used the book *Esperanza Rising* (Ryan, 2000) two years in succession as part of a fourth-grade unit on California history. In the first year, students showed interest in the young girl Esperanza's first home, a wealthy ranch in Mexico, by drawing, reporting on, and making up stories about haciendas in Mexico and comparing them to ranchero life in early California. In the second year, students showed more interest in Esperanza's second life, which followed the migrant trail in California. Those students mapped Esperanza's journeys and planned family visits to various parts of California.

Of course, the teacher's passion is a factor. One fifth-grade teacher who is a great fan of detective fiction finds new ways to share this passion year after year by turning science, social studies, or even music into a detective game. Another teacher loves adventure stories, and students who come to share a love of this genre design projects that somehow involve adventure—imagining, planning, or carrying out group adventures. Yet another teacher is a cook and organizes student projects that always seem to have some eating component. No wonder!

What PBL teachers avoid is the repetition of units year after year. Like the hoary build-a-Spanish-mission projects carried out in the fourth grades of California elementary schools, eventually the project is "used up"; that is, a given group is not likely to discover ideas or facets of the topic that are new, and the teacher is not really involved in what Halliday (1978) called "heuristic" language use. In other words, the process of learning is no longer exciting for the teacher.

Mapping the Project

In phase 1 of a project, the students and teacher devote several discussion periods to selecting and refining the topic. Good topics are those that are within the range of interest and comprehensibility for the students and closely related to their everyday experience so that they can raise relevant questions. Rich topics generate two or three weeks of exploration and cut across subject domains of the school curriculum. A mind map of the topic, delineating the questions raised and the prior knowledge of the students, helps to serve as an ongoing road map for the inquiry.

The journey of a PBL inquiry begins with questions for the class as a whole to consider. Guiding questions in this regard may be the following:

> Why are we doing this project? (What is the community issue, concern, or need this project is trying to address?) How does this project address this issue, concern, or need? If we are dealing with a problem or concern, what has created it? What kind of knowledge needs to be acquired? What can be done to prevent the problem from recurring once our project is complete? (Roth-Vinson, 2001, n.p.)

Schools may not be the best source of interesting projects. In the search for a compelling project, one must take the community's needs into consideration. A teacher who takes the time to meet community members, listen to parents, and observe firsthand the life of the community can put into perspective the concerns brought forth by students. PBL, combined with critical pedagogy, makes sensitive use of stimulus codes to generate language that originates in the social context of the community.

> Deborah, a community college ESL teacher, had a Level I class in which half the students were Japanese exchange students and the other half were Mexican immigrants. The social interaction reminded her of oil and water in the same flask; that is, the students eyed one another warily, communicated in culturally homogeneous groups, and when paired across cultures had little to say to each other.
>
> Deborah turned to Gary Soto's *Pacific Crossing* (1992), the story of a Mexican American youth who finds himself living with a Japanese family during a study-abroad program. As they read the novel together, the Japanese students explained more fully the cultural customs of Japan, and in return the Mexican students clarified the protagonist's feelings of cultural shock. The novel opened doors to discussions of martial arts, communal bathing, and other areas of interest to both groups that kept the class lively and fun. The novel as code elicited language, feeling, and cultural sharing that neither side alone would have been able to articulate, much less communicate.
>
> There was spirited debate throughout the course as members discovered their mutual love: baseball. As a group project, the class members described the baseball leagues in their home countries and shared pictures of their favorite players. Although initially the topic seemed to be of greater interest to the male students than to the females, the class went together to a local baseball game, and the women were grateful that they knew something about the game.

Topics across Disciplines

When PBL is interdisciplinary, collaboration takes place between teachers of different disciplines. Collaboration begins as teachers identify the central principles or concepts of each discipline and the target knowledge, skills, and dispositions that students will acquire. The next step is to create, discover, or define an engaging project that combines the required concepts or skills, achieving a balance between a problem that is both important and understandable for students. A division of labor among instructors distributes the work of supervision, coaching, and assessing results.

> "Zookeeper" is a collaborative project among the NET team at Denver North High School, addressing content standards and involving teachers in English, history, visual arts, and science. Students design and build a habitat for a specific animal and plant, visiting a zoo and interviewing a zoo specialist in the process. At the beginning of the project, students amass a fact sheet for each plant and animal, with the goal of fifty facts for each. (Giromini, 2001)

Envisioning Success

When the students and teacher together develop a project, with input from the community if it is a service-learning project, the most compelling image that moves the project forward is the vision of what can be accomplished. The teacher next identifies the skills that will be needed to complete the project, such as writing, computer, or interview skills, and makes plans to teach or coach these skills. The teacher also matches the identified skills or content to district, state, or national curricular frameworks or standards to justify the project as playing a substantive role in classroom learning. The next step is to select the performance indicators that will be used to determine the assessment of the project (presentation, product, etc.; "How will we know that it is good?") and to develop criteria for a successful project and/or product (Roth-Vinson, 2001).

Project Focus and Development

Megastrategy 15.2

Delimit and focus project activities

Gathering and organizing information is an ongoing process as the project takes shape. The teacher as guide helps participants locate sources relevant to the scope and focus of the project, whether books, magazines, Internet content, other print sources, or people with relevant expertise. Data that are gathered may be used to prepare a proposal or plan (for funding or other support); the plan may then include collecting further data to be analyzed as the project proceeds, data that will then be used to assess the success of the project.

Students are preparing energy- efficient light bulbs to give away to the community.
©Martin Shields/Alamy

Project Development

No matter what the goal or purpose of a project, the task of developing it has a certain structure. The elements of this structure are represented in Table 15.3. Each of these is discussed in turn in the sections that follow.

The Planning Cycle

The elements displayed in Table 15.3 seem to be in a linear, sequential order from the earliest to final stages of the project. This appearance of a linear order may, however, be illusory. Some projects contain loops in the planning cycle, in which the design changes multiple times during the project as participants' various points of view are incorporated to adjust and modify the ongoing design. The following project is an example of how plans can undergo modification during the design cycle due to such factors as the input of opinions, provision of expert data, and cost considerations:

> Fourth-grade teacher Mrs. Shim had the original idea: a four-part
> garden on the bare plot of ground beside the fourth-grade classrooms

TABLE 15.3 *Common Structure for Development of a Project*

Project Element	Description
Task representation	The information needed to perform the tasks is provided, and the task is explained to the observer.
Example of the desired product	The project is based on a model or prototype.
Guided implementation	The project is supported by such means as assistance in information acquisition and advice on project design.
Self-check (quality control)	Project designers are able to obtain feedback, using specific criteria as a guide.
Recommendation for improvement	Project designers are able to modify and correct design flaws that have been identified during the quality-checking process.
Student presentation of product	Using a combination of designers' and audience's preferred mode of representation, the student-designer makes a formal presentation of the project for purposes of assessment.
Feedback and reflection	Project designers are able to learn from feedback obtained through assessment.
Advice for mentors	Mentors are able to learn about learning by means of aggregated assessments across project results.

Source: Based on Loria, Shaltied, Pieterse, & Rosenfeld (1999).

that would show various time periods of California history by means of four gardens: Native American, Mission, Chinese American, and Victory (World War II). Another fourth-grade teacher joined the project, suggesting a Ranchero period garden and a Japanese garden. A third teacher wanted a creek bed to demonstrate the gold rush. The space allotted to the project did not change, despite these added features, and the size of each garden shrank as more components were added. Finally, each segment became one 4-feet by 8-feet area, connected by a "Walkway through Time." When research showed that the garden plants in the Mission and Ranchero periods were similar, the two periods were combined. When the project went over budget, the Japanese garden became a Zen garden with sand, a rake, and beautiful rocks—but no plants. Thus, the project changed in scope, focus, and design over an extended planning period.

Task Representation

The initial plan as imagined by the designers, the ongoing documentation, and the final product each are represented in a way that enables communication between project team members and the audience, stakeholders, or other participants in the project. The form of representation depends largely on four variables: the nature of the project, the preferred information style of the designers, the preferred information style of the audience or community participants, and the expertise and funds available. This may change during the course of the project. The following vignette illustrates how project designers struggled with the data available as a function of the nature of the project:

> As a final research project for a computer-assisted language-learning course, two students chose to document the successes and/or frustrations of a group of international students who were learning to use English pronunciation software in the campus foreign-language media laboratory. In the exploratory phase of the project, the researchers planned to make the software program available only in the presence of the researchers, who would observe and record student responses.
>
> Then one of the researchers suggested that the computer software itself could be used to store results from each usage attempt by an international student, thus allowing students to work unsupervised. The data would then be represented by computerized scores for each student. After consultation with the staff of the foreign-language media laboratory, the researchers decided that this was not feasible. Refusing to give up on the idea, the researcher called the software company to see if a research version of the software was available that could trace the process of the students as they used the software. However, no one in the company seemed to know if such a version existed.

In frustration, the researchers decided to alter the research project to focus on six students (two each at three levels of pronunciation proficiency) and to monitor them three times each in supervised, half-hour sessions with the software, as well as record the computer's performance feedback. This would result in a total of eighteen sessions, a 4.5-hour commitment for each researcher. The data would then be represented by observational entries about each student supplemented by student feedback and pre- and postsession interviews with the six students.

The preferred information style of the designer usually influences the choice of project; people who do not prefer music and know little about it are rarely comfortable with a project based on music, for example. Because teachers of English learners work in a language domain, each project should serve as the stimulus for written or oral activity; that is, explanatory paragraphs should supplement a map, and a picture should not substitute for a verbal explanation. Charts, graphs, and other graphic organizers are not incompatible with words, but rather can support and express ideas along with verbal representation.

The preferred information style of the audience, stakeholders, or other participants governs how the final results will be conveyed. Pictures that show their children working in various stages of the project may be popular with parents. If the audience comprises school district authorities, an article with pictures in a district newsletter could simultaneously inform both insiders and the public at large. If dissemination of project results takes place at a culminating event, a slide show accompanied by music might be popular. Mariachi music and folkloric dance teams reinforced the cultural content of the César Chávez Day of Service and Learning:

> The César Chávez Day of Service and Learning was exciting for all participants. On the morning of March 31, teams of students from each of a dozen elementary, middle, and high schools set up their posters in the Expert Exposition area at the San Bernardino County Museum and took turns manning their booths. Each poster described a Sustainable Products project that had taken place during a service-learning partnership between their school and a community organization. The gardens that were showcased had a variety of themes. A first-grade class with a Bird and Butterfly school garden had learned to propagate plants and then donated several butterfly-attracting bushes to a nursing home. A class of sixth graders had traced the history of favorite recipes in the Mexican diet and had raised and donated six types of plants in an information kit to local families. As the students toured from booth to booth to look at other schools' projects, they experienced firsthand the social values of César Chávez: respect for life, service to others, determination, and celebration of community.

The expertise and funds available determine the long-range durability of project results and the extent of dissemination efforts. If a school can raise money for desktop publishing, each student can receive a colorful packet of pictures on completion of a project. If a school has access to digital cameras and students can construct websites, project documentation can take the form of sites available on the Internet. Or, students can make up a song that commemorates the project and record it on audiotapes.

Example of the Desired Product

Not every project is brand-new. When a teacher implements a similar project for several years, the students in the second year have the benefit of seeing documentation or products from the first year. After students in a high school in Denver were invited to view the products from the Mexican Day of the Dead project prepared by a magnet program within the school, requests for admission to the program skyrocketed the next year. A student-run crafts market that took place in conjunction with International Day festivities was so popular that the following year parents began calling the school months in advance to be sure of the upcoming date.

Students can also benefit from viewing the efforts of others, even if those efforts are available only on a website or through other kinds of remote access.

> When high school students in Miami heard about the Memphis Blues project, in which students in Memphis, Tennessee, interviewed blues musicians to document the history and extent of the music tradition in their city, the Miami students wanted to do the same with Puerto Rican and Cuban music in Miami. Eventually they formed their own band— The Salsa Kids—and were invited to play at a national PBL conference, where they had the audience dancing in the aisles!

It is always a temptation to show students the best of past products, but it is more realistic to display a range of results as examples. Sometimes, products that turned out less successful than expected can nonetheless have a creative aspect that will inspire the next spark of creativity. In addition, it is wise to display as exemplars those that feature a range of representation styles and English skill levels.

Guided Implementation

The teacher in the role of guide plays a role long before the start of a project. The most difficult part of PBL is to involve the participants in worthy endeavors that are both comprehensible and manageable. Much background investigation must be done before a teacher can step into a complex situation and risk offering that complexity to students as a learning experience. Some research may be necessary to locate materials and make these accessible to students.

Community partners may have much to offer, such as a telephone list of contacts for reduced-price materials, a friend of a friend who knows an expert, or a shelf of books on a relevant topic. On the debit side, when the community is involved, it may be advisable to probe the goals and values of partners outside the school to ensure that students who participate are not exploited. Trust among community partners is established largely not by blind faith but by experience. Part of what the teacher learns as a guide is how to accommodate the labor, or lack thereof, of other partners.

Because a large part of students' initial motivation to become involved derives from the enthusiasm of the teacher, the most successful projects seem to be those in which the teacher is invested, whether this be in prior knowledge, skills, or disposition. The challenge of the teacher is to build within students the desire and skills to become self-directed learners and then to fade into the background as supporter, colleague, clarifier, and reminder of deadlines.

At a certain point, it is necessary to formalize a master plan for the project. Students can use a chart called "Time Line with Responsibilities" (see Figure 15.1) to organize their plans. When dividing up the work, students should start with the strengths and skills of each team member. When selecting project duties, however, good project management leaves room for team members to branch out and learn new skills (Roth-Vinson, 2001). When completed, the master plan becomes a guide for the project and should be easily accessible so that team members can check off their work when completed.

Self-Checking (Quality Control)

Metacognition plays a significant role in PBL, as it does in other parts of life. A valuable role of metacognition is to compare partial results or products against the desired criteria. At a certain point along the way, however, it may become obvious that some group members are too easily satisfied, whereas others are hard to please. Some point of satisfaction may have to be agreed on by the team as a whole, and the person(s) closest to an understanding of that point may become the agent of quality control.

A new student, a recent immigrant from Guatemala, entered Mr. Olivo's second-grade class, which consisted predominantly of English learners. As a welcome gift, she gave the teacher a homemade "God's eye," a small wooden cross wrapped with brightly colored yarn in a diamond shape. Soon two Mexican girls came shyly to the front and

FIGURE 15.1 *Project-Based Learning Time Line with Responsibilities*

Objectives of the Project	Person Responsible	Date of Proposed Completion

informed Mr. Olivo that their mothers knew how to make the "God's eye" too; the next day one of the girls brought another to class. Within a week, a "God's eye" fad swept the second-grade class. Students came up with the idea to make "God's eyes" and sell them to other students at Christmas. Mr. Olivo bought yarn and several packets of craft sticks and presented the potential sales event as a project for students. As a group, they figured out the sale price, based on a fixed number of colors and a fixed length of yarn on each "God's eye."

All went well until the actual creation of the "God's eyes." At that point, it became obvious that some children's quality level was not as good as others. Students whose efforts were rejected by the perfectionists were hurt, and some began sneakily to sabotage the work of others. Mr. Olivo called a class meeting, at which it was decided that all finished products would be stored in flat cardboard boxes until just before the sale, when a panel of three would set a variable price for each. As it turned out, by the end of October the poor craftspeople had lost interest, whereas those motivated to continue worked at lunch or at recess. At the end of the sale, no one remembered whose work was whose; and even the "God's eyes" that were not so perfect were sold anyway to those who had a nickel to spare for a present for their *abuelas*.

Recommendation for Improvement

Sometimes improvement is easy to attain by altering one's approach to a problem. However, when the project is still feasible based on a few changes yet repeated attempts at problem solving fail and an impasse is reached, it may prove helpful to seek outside expertise and advice. The frustrations along the way provide the greatest amount of learning, not only in problem solving but also in character building. Adequate prior analysis of the risks involved, finances needed, management and organization required, community's issues and values, and health and safety considerations makes projects no less challenging but more assured of success.

Project Documentation and Evaluation

Process Counts

Megastrategy 15.3

Document and assess the progress and outcome of the project

As the project proceeds, all parts of the process constitute learning. Participants take pictures, preserve planning sketches, and keep a log of activities. If one person is appointed archivist, someone may wish to check periodically to make sure there are indeed archives. Notes from participant interviews, whether in person or by telephone, make worthy archive entries. When key decisions must be made, it is advisable for a member to record the minutes of the deliberations.

Student Presentation of Product

Culminating events trigger emotional investment as students experience anticipation, excitement, and suspense. They also supply clearly visible deadlines. Students benefit from projects that include a public demonstration, because they can invite friends and family. Showcase events also create lifelong memories. Few people remember the day-to-day life of the classroom, the names of their peers in the third grade, or the pictures on the page of the ESL book they used. Few forget, however, the feeling of singing in a chorus or acting in a play. Life's events are the key to creating episodic memories.

The culminating event can be a poster presentation or bulletin board display, play, songfest, or festival. The products of ESL are words, phrases, sentences, paragraphs, pamphlets, brochures—by themselves rarely as compelling as a steam engine exhibit. Perhaps language educators should focus on more dramatic linguistic products to showcase, such as dramas.

Feedback and Reflection

In any project, the learning that takes place does not come automatically but rather results from introspection. Structured moments in which all pause and write down their feelings and thoughts capture a snapshot of ongoing activities. Here is a sample set of summative reflective questions:

> In your opinion, was the project a successful undertaking? In your evaluation, consider the following: What have you learned by participating in the project? How were project challenges met? How did the project make you feel? How may others have viewed the project? How do you think the community benefited? (Roth-Vinson, 2001, n.p.)

Planning for Assessment

Giving grades is part of the teacher's work. One of the goals of assessment is to organize learning so that it becomes visible and can be documented. Assessment should take place in multiple forms and be diverse enough to provide meaningful and relevant feedback to the participants. Multiple assessors (students, peers, teachers, and other mentors) in multiple formats ensure variety and completeness, avoiding a one-sided picture of student competence.

The teacher helps participants keep their documentation organized, reminds participants to take pictures or record activities, pauses with the group for reflection and self-monitoring, and ensures that all team members share the workload. Moreover, the teacher—sometimes with the help of a teaching assistant or paraprofessional, if one is available—keeps records of project activities for the purpose of school records, such as documenting growth of English skills or making sure that the content standards are being met.

Conducting Project Assessment

Part of the challenge of assessment is balancing high, focused expectations for achievement with the need for students to feel a sense of ownership of the project and freedom to explore its possibilities. Sometimes the process uses a form of "planning backwards," linking outcomes and standards (the end point) to student interests (the start point). A rich project environment demands resources, and teachers often steer students toward lines of inquiry in which the teacher has developed expertise and amassed supporting materials. A rich terrain of inquiry leaves room for students to make individual contributions and not feel that they are revisiting turf that is already well trod.

Quality Assessment. Various kinds of assessments have been implemented in conjunction with PBL. Because the work that students produce is in some ways unique to the project, it might at first seem difficult to find assessments that measure the quality of such disparate types of work as a book report, a budget proposal, an informational brochure, the design for a museum exhibit, a survey report, or an interview-based personality profile (C. Morrison, 2001). Creating a documentation portfolio in the course of a project may achieve the goal of archiving the work, but evaluation is still necessary. The teacher, functioning as expert audience, forms the backbone of the assessment effort.

The teacher might draw on community expertise to help assess student work. What the community appreciates in a product may after all differ from the teacher's expectation, and this disparity may provide a healthy reality check on the relevance of the instruction. Students' goals and interests are a second pillar on which evaluation rests. As a group, students may find fascinating part of a project that the teacher has undervalued, due to generational differences or peculiarities of peer culture. To answer the question "What constitutes a quality product?" one must draw on multiple points of view.

Assessing Language. For purposes of English education, however, a vital criterion is the extent to which students' language skills have improved. Many final performances or products include reports, oral presentations, or multimedia exhibits that clearly demonstrate the use of language skills. Beyond such visible evidence as success in written essays and in standardized reading scores, however, lie deeper, more intangible measures of English communication ability. Does the student show more willingness to chat with peers? Does the student engage more often in self-selected reading? Is the student more comfortable with students of different cultures and family backgrounds? Certainly, features of sociolinguistic and strategic competence, as well as measures of affect (comfort with English, self-esteem), are appropriate criteria for judging overall performance on a project.

Criteria for Project Assessment

Projects offer a wealth of learning and build real mastery of a subject because students can test themselves in real situations. Along the way, they can incorporate new understandings and constructive feedback. In addition, they permit teachers to build more complex relationships with students by providing many opportunities for meaningful discussions in contexts in which students may appreciate adult input. And the culminating events of PBL provide precious memories for all.

Designing a landmark for their city is one project that Steinberg and Stephen (1999) offer students in their book *City Works*. Through this and other such activities, students focus on community issues, learning to join adult conversations about the quality of life in their town and the role of young people within the fabric of city life. The worksheets and design activities suggested by Steinberg and Stephen can be used by teachers as templates for PBL, even though purists would hold out for students to design projects that originate wholly from the interests of the class rather than from such workbooks, inspirational as they might be. That said, *City Works,* with its emphasis on community improvement, profusion of ideas for involving local experts, and wealth of sources for community-based learning, directly ties PBL to learning within the context of the community.

The following student's reactions to the use of projects in the ESL classroom summarize well the language learning that is possible by means of PBL:

> I liked this course because there were a lot of chance to talk to classmates and American people. Especially, I liked the assignments to interview American people. I made some friends through this assignment.
>
> It gave me a chance to broaden my conversational ability, not just simple sentence, not just simple idea, but ideas that make me think more. (Wilhelm, 1999, p. 15)

Why Service Learning?

We learn as we serve. The maxim is simple, but the implications are profound. The world's greatest leaders—great in the sense of great in spirit—have urged a life of service. One example is the life of César Chávez. Chávez was a man who dedicated his life to bettering the conditions of farmworkers in California. He believed that service to others was a calling, a mission, and a way of life, not merely an obligation or an occasional act of charity. He once said, "we can choose to use our lives for others to bring about a better and more just world for our children. People who make that choice will know hardship and sacrifice—in giving of yourself you will discover a whole new life full of meaning and love" Chavez (n.d.).

Chávez was committed to the idea that service not only strengthens a community but also benefits those who serve. English learners have a strong need to feel part of the community, be that their classroom community, a community in which they are sojourners, or a community into which they have immigrated. Service learning helps students to improve their language skills, their social skills, and their understanding of the target culture. Service-learning pedagogy, with its focus on real-world experience, is a natural complement to potentially more abstract critical classroom learning. O'Grady and Chappell (2000) captured the essence of service learning as an activity in which "the academic and the experiential converge" (p. 209).

Some teachers of English learners may feel that service learning is not appropriate for their students, or that the community is not willing for English learners to be of service. These challenges can be addressed by strategies presented in this chapter.

Definitions

Service learning is a form of experiential education in which learning flows from service activities (Furco, 1996). The term has been used to describe a range of endeavors, including volunteer and community service projects, field studies, and internship programs. The National Society of Experiential Education defines service learning as any service experience that is monitored, involves intentional learning goals, and incorporates active reflection from the learner. Thus, service learning requires a balance between learning goals and service outcomes.

Jacoby and Associates (1996) supplied the following definition:

> Service learning is a form of experiential education in which students engage in activities that address human and community needs together with structured opportunities intentionally designed to promote student learning and development. Reflection and reciprocity are key concepts of service learning. (p. 5)

Across the United States, teachers are discovering that student service projects can be powerful learning tools:

> Whether children lend a hand to neighbors in need or assist their peers halfway around the world, service projects form a bridge between academic skills and real-life problem solving—and help students develop a sense of responsibility and self-worth along the way. (Bozzone, 1993, p. 65)

Community is a term that may refer to local neighborhoods or larger entities, national or global. It is important, however, that the needs identified and addressed are those defined *by the community,* which may be very different from those perceived by well-meaning outsiders. The involvement of community members in assessing needs and defining goals richly contributes to the learning outcomes of a given project.

To differentiate service learning from other types of experiential learning, Sigmon (1994) defined *community service* and *volunteerism* as types of involvement in which the focus is on service and the persons served are the chief beneficiaries. In contrast, in the case of *field education* and *internships,* the focus is largely on the learning that takes place, and the beneficiary is largely the service provider.

Service learning, as a combination of these, must be fully integrated into the curriculum of an ongoing course or program so that the learning enhances the service and the service supports the learning. Learning objectives might involve *knowledge* (to recognize the recitation discourse pattern in a classroom and to note which students respond well to it); *skills* (to practice vocabulary development activities with students using audiovisual media); or *dispositions* (to feel empathy for parents' support role in schooling, or to foster civic responsibility and citizenship).

If the service learning addresses a short- or long-term problem needing a solution, then the service might involve project-based learning. On the other hand, the service can involve such efforts as tutoring, in which the person performing the service supplies labor in an already established program. The best service-learning projects provide students with an opportunity to develop skills and knowledge in real-life situations and meet a real community need. They reinforce the connections between school and community and teach students how to work collaboratively with others to create change.

Extent of Participation

Today's students are participating in community service in record numbers. A survey of students entering college in 1994 indicated that more then 70 percent of entering freshmen reported involvement in community volunteer work in high school (Astin, Korn, & Sax, 1994). In a simultaneous survey of 9,000 undergraduates, 64 percent were involved in volunteer activities (Levine, 1994). Such volunteerism is not a color-bound phenomenon: 65 percent of white students and 62 percent of nonwhite students were involved. As Coles (1993) observed, "today's students are likely to express their lofty political and social impulses and practical desires to change the world through community service" (p. 40).

Education in America has a long tradition of service. As Smith (1994) recalled, "From the beginning, the goals of American higher education have included the preparation of citizens for active involvement in community life" (p. 55). College student community service has long been involved in such agencies as the YMCA and Greek-letter organizations. In 1961 the Peace Corps was founded by President Kennedy, followed soon after by Volunteers in Service to America (VISTA) and the National Student Volunteer Program (1969), which became the Corporation for National and Community Service (www.learnandserve.org). In 1978 the National Society for Internships and Experiential Education was established (NSIEE; as of 1994, National Society for Experiential Education, NSEE).

The White House Office of National Service was created by the National and Community Service Trust Act of 1990. During President Clinton's administration, the Corporation for National and Community Service (generally referred to as the Corporation for National Service) was created, funding the AmeriCorps national service program as well as service-learning programs in both K–12 and higher education settings through Learn and Serve America. Service learning became an integral part of education.

Components of Service Learning

A beginning component of service learning is *preparation,* laying the groundwork for understanding the problem or topics to be addressed, identifying the host community agency or site and its perception of needs, and planning the learning objectives. The sponsor or partner at the host site is involved to a greater or lesser extent in these issues.

A second component is *performing the service.* This may be simple, requiring only fixed hours for all participants at a single site; or it may be complex, involving ill-defined problems, transportation difficulties, communication challenges in relation to the host site, and multiple coordination needs.

The third component is *reflection,* in which the learner analyzes the experience, absorbs lessons from the experience, identifies areas of maximum or minimum success, and refines insights. Were the service-learning goals fulfilled? What personal or professional growth took place? What positive change took place within the organization, neighborhood, or community as a result of the service (Campus Compact, 2000)?

Benefits of Service Learning

Traditional instruction that requires students to learn within a classroom setting may not develop intellectual habits, personal understanding of the content, or the desire and capacity for lifelong learning. By encountering and addressing problems in a real-world context, students can learn under conditions that are personally relevant to their own lives and interests (Bringle & Hatcher, 1999). Service in the community educates critical thinkers. Significant and authentic work in the community gives students the opportunity to examine social structures and their effects on people (Anderson & Guest, 1994).

Service learning has been shown to have positive effects on the learner, on faculty members who incorporate service-learning experiences into the curriculum, on the educational institutions that support such experiences, and on the communities that act as hosts. Eyler, Giles, and Gray (1999) presented a summary and list of research on the effects on the learner (see Table 15.4).

In addition to listing the positive effects on students, Eyler, Giles, and Gray (1999) cited research that shows specific gains for educators: increased satisfaction with the quality of student learning, increased commitment to learning, and increased integration of service learning into courses. Communities that have been involved with service learning in return feel that service learning provides a useful service to the community and are satisfied with student participation (Eyler, Giles, & Gray, 1999).

Lopes-Murphy and Martin (2002), describing a successful community service-learning (CSL) project carried out by preservice teachers, summarized its benefits this way:

> Although our preservice teachers have gained enormously in the ways outlined and
> illustrated above, perhaps the greatest benefit of CSL is its long-range effect on the
> attitudes and practices these preservice teachers will one day bring to their own
> classrooms. Not only will the CSL students benefit from a greater understanding
> of the needs of English language learners and the confidence to teach them, but so
> will the many generations of students that these future teachers will one day
> teach. (p. 49)

TABLE 15.4 *Effects of Service Learning on Students*

Outcome by Category	Sample Positive Outcome
Personal development	Personal efficacy
	Personal identity
	Spiritual growth
	Moral development
Interpersonal development	Ability to work well with others
	Leadership
	Communication skills
Social cognition	Reduction of stereotypes
	Improved racial and cultural understanding
Sense of social responsibility	Citizenship skills
	Commitment to service
	Involvement with community service after graduation
Learning	General increase in learning and cognitive development
	Ability to apply learning to "real world"
	Improved grade point average (GPA)*
	Demonstrated complexity of understanding
	Problem analysis skills
	Critical thinking skills
Career development	General contribution
Relationship to institution of learning	Stronger faculty-student relationships
	Satisfaction with college
	Increased likelihood of graduating

*Other studies, however, show no difference in GPA between those students who were engaged in service learning and those who were not.

Source: Based on Eyler, Giles, & Gray (1999).

What Constitutes Good Service-Learning Pedagogy?

J. Howard (1993) listed several principles that distinguish good practice in service learning. Among these are the following: The instructor supplies educationally sound ways in which students can benefit from service, is prepared for a redefinition of the instructor's role, and can accept some degree of uncertainty and variation in student learning outcomes.

Students Serving Others: Some Examples

Bozzone (1993) offered a glimpse of several service projects. A group of fourth-grade students in Ashton, Maryland, raised money to build a school in a small village in Somalia about five hundred miles from the capital, Mogadishu. Students held a bake sale, asked friends and merchants for donations, and wrote to foundations and major corporations for aid. Students in Holtwood, Pennsylvania, created books to help stock the classroom libraries of Chee Dodge, a school on the Navajo Reservation at Yah Tah Hey, New Mexico. Children in a third-grade class in Lynbrook, New York, wrote an informational booklet explaining the hazards associated with discarding used batteries and ran a collection agency so that dead batteries could be disposed of properly. These vignettes illustrate how curriculum topics can be extended to become service-learning projects.

In one such program, prospective TESOL educators could choose from a number of community sites, among them an ESL classroom at a nearby elementary or secondary school, an adult basic education ESL program, a public library, and a youth center that provided after-school recreation for youth. Participants attended their site for a total of twenty hours a semester, tutoring children or adults in small groups or individually. During the experience, students maintained a journal and wrote a number of papers on specific prompts. In addition, class discussion included references to, and descriptions of, students' individual experiences at their site and the relevance of assigned readings to the service-learning project. Through a combination of readings, reflections, classroom dialogue, and the service project, the goal was to pose problems, explore power relations, and encourage student commitment to activism (O'Grady & Chappell, 2000).

Building Relationships with Service Agencies

A phase of exploration begins service learning. In schools with a long-standing commitment to service learning, a wealth of partnerships may exist with community agencies. In newer situations, extended conversations with workers at potential community sites may be necessary in order to determine the goals and needs of the host.

Reciprocity

Exposing prospective TESOL educators to diverse community settings is of great value. Merely subjecting students to readings on cultural diversity will not increase students' cultural awareness or sensitivity; they need exposure to a variety of racial and cultural groups in community-based experiences (Tellez, Hlebowitsh, Cohen, & Norwood, 1995). As Sleeter and McLaren (1995) pointed out, students and teachers are often situated, knowingly or not, in a "highly politicized field of power relations that partake of unjust race, class, and gender affiliations" (p. 6). Service-learning experiences help to create reciprocal exposure to these power relations.

White, middle-class students in particular often ignore the fact that *their* interests are being met through the curriculum and school structure, which tends to emphasize middle-class, European American values while not meeting the interests of more marginal groups. For instance, Aparicio and Jose-Kampfer (1995) described the educational downside for Latinos in public school: linguistic and cultural erasure, censure for speaking Spanish, low levels of motivation based on alienation, and inequitable placement policies. In service learning, students of diverse races, classes, and genders can mix in mutual, reciprocal projects, permitting a more open dialogue on these issues.

Identification of Community Partners

> *Megastrategy* **15.4**
>
> **Form partnerships with the community to involve students in community activities and social action**

In many instances, the manifold needs of a community partner, combined with chronic underfunding for community-based organizations, drive a community agency to seek out student help. The usefulness of each site for service learning is weighed taking into account peer support, proximity, ease of transportation, the abilities and interests of the students who will be placed at these sites, learning objectives of the curriculum, and personal and professional contacts of the instructor.

Designing A Service-Learning Project

> *Megastrategy* **15.5**
>
> **Design a service-learning project**

In a time of escalating costs of education and increased academic pressure on ESL/EFL students, it may be hard for instructors to design and supervise service-learning projects. For this reason, it is even more necessary for such projects to become an intrinsic part of the core educational effort (Jacoby & Associates, 1996). This also means that one must maintain a realistic perspective regarding what results are possible within the time allotted.

The most important steps are to determine the desired service and learning goals of the project. The community has the largest role in setting the service goals. Planning goals should be evenly distributed across community host and student participants. This distribution ensures that the outcomes are feasible given the amount of time and resources that can be realistically devoted to the project, and that both parties have a sense of ownership.

Because the school year is limited and some time is consumed at the beginning in organizing student participation and establishing working relations, it is vital to set a time line. In this way, both parties can allocate their time accordingly. Key accomplishments should be planned along the way, from initial project stages to final report, with plans for documentation. Students often feel more secure if they can plan the structure of their reflection at the beginning so that they can anticipate the types of desirable outcomes of their participation.

Determining the Learning Goal(s)

Learning goals and objectives constitute the desired outcomes for student involvement. The learning objectives may balance cognitive, affective, and participation goals. Not all the goals and objectives of a course of study or program are involved in any given project.

Proposing Performance-Based Results

Because of the experimental nature of some service-learning projects (ill-defined problems needing creative solutions), there is often no clear-cut, concrete example of an exemplary result. Despite this drawback, a statement of specific proposed outcomes is possible. The following is a statement of proposed outcomes for one of the twelve California native gardens that were proposed as a part of the California Native Gardens Partnership at CSU, San Bernardino:

> The Craftsman Garden (grade 5) at Mariposa Elementary School is a planning/planting project based on the Arts and Crafts movement of the 1920s and 1930s. The product of this project is twofold: (1) creation of a handbook for the Craftsman Garden theme, complete with connection to California curriculum standards in reading/language arts, ELD, science, and social studies; and (2) creation of an actual Craftsman Garden at Mariposa Elementary School.

> It is evident from this statement that the desired outcomes were first, a handbook, and second, an actual garden. More specific subgoals were determined during the partnership through extensive dialogue between host community members and student participants.

Monitoring and Evaluating Service Learning

Frequent feedback sessions with supervising instructors and community members are essential to the successful completion of a complex project. Problems having no

---

Box 15.1 Service Learning: Considering Virtual Volunteering

- Use foreign-language skills to translate a document.
- Design a newsletter, brochure, or logo for a service agency.

- Volunteer to proofread student papers submitted to you online.
- Communicate online with elders at a senior center.

Source: Based on Woolfolk (2007, p. 437).

Megastrategy 15.6

Perform and evaluate service

clear-cut, predetermined solution may provoke anxiety in students. It may be important to emphasize to participants that they are members of a team, that their team members may be feeling anxiety too, and that open communication is valuable. Partial goals, benchmark indicators, should be tied closely to fixed dates. All parties can check at these times to see if their expectations have been met.

The Reflective Component

According to John Dewey, reflection is an "active, persistent, and careful consideration of any belief or supported form of knowledge in light of the grounds that support it" (1933, p. 146). The overall goals of reflection are to deepen students' understanding of their experience and to enable students to "recognize themselves, name their experiences, and learn how to change existing conditions for themselves as well as for others in the community" (Keith, 1997, p. 137).

Many kinds of reflective activities can be used to support the learning in service learning. Student journals help to distribute the reflection over the course of the engagement and tie summary thoughts to specific events. Bringle and Hatcher (1999) caution that more formal reflective activities may be more satisfying than unstructured journal entries, which tend to become a mere record of activities rather than a means of tying experiences to learning objectives. They recommend various reflective exercises (see Table 15.5). In a reflective paper, each student is expected to examine his or her own learning process and attitudes toward teaching, learning, and language; integrate past and present teaching and learning experiences in the light of various learning theories; and examine his or her assumptions, values, and attitudes.

The emphasis on reflection within service learning stresses dialogue between the student and the experience, between the student and the community members, and between the student and the course concepts. As O'Grady and Chappell (2000) reminded us, students are not mere receptacles to be filled; they must engage in an active way with their own experiences and with the social consequences of their service. Therefore, service-learning programs must engage people in responsible action for the common good.

Assessing Performance-Based Results

Bringle and Hatcher (1999) invoked Bradley's three-level set of criteria for assessing the level of reflection a participant has attained (see Table 15.6). Presenting these criteria to participants in advance of their reflective writing may elicit maturity and development in their perspective about the learning experience.

Measuring the impact on participants seems to be the chief focus of reflective evaluation, but Driscoll, Holland, Gelmon, and Kerrigan (1996) also looked at the effect of such experiences on the instructor, the community, and the institution. Their conclusions show an impact on participants' self-awareness, personal development, academic achievement, independence as learners, and overall academic achievement.

TABLE 15.5 *Types of Service-Learning Reflection Assignments*

Assignment	Description
Experiential research paper	Students write a formal paper to identify a particular set of events at the service site; find an important social issue or issues underlying the circumstance; discuss multiple perspectives from which the situation could be analyzed; discover published research relevant to the issue or issues; and end with recommendations.
Ethical case study	Students raise issues that concern beliefs, values, and morals.
Class presentation	Students participate in bulletin board exhibits, panel discussions, speeches, or other creative displays. These can take electronic form such as home pages, chat room discussions, bulletin board discussions, or class listservs.
Double-entry journal	Students use the left side of a spiral-bound notebook to record events and personal thoughts, keeping the right side for formal essays that connect these experiences to class readings, lectures, or presentations. Arrows may be used as links from left to right.
Critical incident journal	Students explore thoughts and reactions to a specific occurrence that took place, tying these explicitly to learning concepts and projecting possible alternative actions that might have been taken.
Three-part journal	Students list key incidents, decisions, and interactions that took place during service learning; then they make a connection to key learning concepts, personal goals, values, attitudes, or beliefs.
Directed writing	Students match specific learning concepts to relevant features of the service-learning experience.

Source: Based on Bringle & Hatcher (1999).

Community benefits included enhanced capacity to meet the needs of individual clients, as well as economic and social benefits. These may be important results to keep in mind when designing a final evaluation of a service-learning project.

Linking the results of the service-learning experience directly to the desired goals and objectives seems the most straightforward approach to evaluating the experience (Jackson, 1993). Clearly, assessing service-learning experiences requires broadening the evaluation process and letting participants exercise a wide range of response. Promoting the active involvement of participants in evaluating their experience can be as valuable as their designing and execution of the experience itself.

The Critical Component

Service learning is an integral part of inducting prospective teacher educators into a critical perspective on the relationship between schooling, democratic principles,

TABLE 15.6 *Criteria for Evaluating Service-Learning Reflection Assignment*

Level (1 = lowest)	Description
Level 1	The reflection paper features a list or description of activities or events, with little or no apparent insight into deeper causes or reasons. The event may be described from a single perspective or aspect, without discriminating how varying perspectives did or could occur, and with some confusion of personal beliefs with facts.
Level 2	The paper evinces some broader context for events or incidents, gives cogent reasons for different perspectives, and shows an effort to distinguish fact from opinion.
Level 3	The paper shows that the writer can view occurrences from multiple perspectives, acknowledge possible conflicting goals among participants and possible contextual factors influencing behavior, and draw conclusions based on facts versus opinions.

Source: Based on Bringle & Hatcher (1999).

and existing social and power structures. In fact, critical educators have probed the whole concept of service learning to ask if, indeed, such projects truly serve the interests of the community whose needs they purport to meet. In the project described above, the originators of the project explored this issue:

> The politics of the...service learning project can be analyzed in a systematic way by focusing on the relationship among interests, conflict, and power (Morgan, 1986). In this project, the interests of the predominantly white college students were being met. They were acquiring valuable personal and professional experience in working with students from diverse backgrounds. The interests of the ESL teachers also were being met, since they acquired additional aid in the classroom. The interests of the ESL students—at least some of the students—were being met as well, since they were getting valuable one-on-one tutoring, which had the potential to increase their agility with the language.... [I]t is the parents of the Latino students whose interests are missing. Rather, it is more correct to say that we do not know whether or not their interests were met, since they were an invisible component in this project. Within the schools their children attend, within the social structure of our community, and now within this project, they have little or no power to see if their interests are served. (O'Grady & Chappell, 2000, p. 218)

O'Grady and Chappell went on to question the relationship between service learning and multicultural education, cautioning that involving students without introducing a critical perspective or deeper analysis of social, political, and economic realities can at best perpetuate a superficial understanding of such issues as the cause of inequities in school achievement; at worst, it can exacerbate existing misconceptions about minority-language groups.

Other theorists have been more deeply pessimistic about the motives and activities of those who enter communities as outsiders, undergo brief experiences and service-learning encounters, and then move on:

> [I]n the context of conflicting interests and the historical dominance of one racial and gender group over another, it is possible that "service," in and of itself, can have racist or sexist outcomes despite good intentions.... I think that, in the context of a history of dominance of one group over others, there is an incipient racism in the practice of service that cannot be avoided even if the conceptualization of it includes values and ideals we can respect and the virtues of people who practice it are above question. (Cruz, 1990, pp. 322–323)

In light of these reservations, it is clear that reflection alone cannot provide students with a transformation impetus that characterizes long-term commitment to social justice. Hand in hand with real experience in the community, educators who are exposed to critical perspectives begin to see social conditions not as individual plights, but rather as communities that are in need of systematic access to economic and social reform. When students can learn through service learning to analyze, critically reflect, and transform oppressive situations through action, they are engaged in a social reconstructionist multicultural education approach (Sleeter & Grant, 1987).

Finding Out More about Service Learning

Useful books on service learning are Eyler and Giles's *Where's the Learning in Service Learning?* (1999), J. Howard's *Praxis I: A Faculty Casebook on Community Service* (1993), and Galura, Howard, Waterhouse, and Ross's *Praxis III: Voices in Dialogue* (1995). Journal resources include the *Michigan Journal of Community Service Learning* (http://ginsberg.umich.edu/mjcsl). Lewis, Espeland, and Pernu's *The Kid's Guide to Service Projects* (1995) offers a wealth of ideas for involving students in the community. Eyring (2001) wrote about service learning as a part of second- or foreign-language education.

In *The Complete Guide to Service Learning* (C. B. Kaye, 2004), the author described a myriad of projects in which students have engaged in learning that combines classroom instruction with civic responsibility and social action. Chapters include a review of the fundamentals of service learning and a range of applications, including gardening, work with elders, literacy, and community safety.

Campus Compact (http://compact.org) lists resources for service-learning practitioners, along with extensive links to websites, news, model programs, and sample syllabi. Other general organizations are those of the National Service-Learning Clearinghouse (www.servicelearning.org) and the National Youth Leadership Council (www.nylc.org). Other links are the New England Resource Center for Higher

Education (www.nerche.org), the National Service-Learning Partnership (www .service-learningpartnership.org), and the National Service-Learning Exchange (www.nslexchange.org).

The reflective practice component of service learning is particularly vital if teachers of English learners aspire to personal, social, and intellectual growth. Pedagogical knowledge must be combined with learning experiences within a full range of social, cultural, and linguistic contexts and reciprocal teaching and learning relationships. Service that teaches forms a balanced mission for English-language educators around the world.

Exploratory Break

- What are the "pros and cons" of involving English learners in service-learning projects in the community? Do you think their level of English proficiency influences their ability to create transformational social change?

APPENDIX A

Influencing Language Policies to Benefit English Learners

Both formal and informal policies have an impact on educators. Exerting an influence on policies that affect English learners is not only a right; it is a professional obligation. Such influence can be exerted at many levels.

Policy at the Classroom Level

In the classroom, language policy means creating an educational and social climate that makes school a place where all students can succeed. When students fail to learn, schools and teachers have failed. Teachers are best able to foster dual-language proficiency by carrying out equitable, empowering instruction.

Fair educational practices require discipline and vigilant self-observation on the part of the classroom teacher. Practicing gender, socioeconomic, racial, and cultural equity requires all students to have an equal opportunity to participate. Teachers must extend mentoring to all students. Referrals to special education or to programs for the gifted should be equitable.

Teachers can incorporate multicultural inclusion into instructional plans, obtaining unbiased materials that promote positive role models from a variety of ethnic groups (see Díaz-Rico, 1993). Multicultural educational materials are readily available (see V. Harris, 1997; Nieto, 2008). Teachers can use multicultural examples to illustrate points of instruction, elicit the stories and voices of the students from various cultures, and knit together home and school for the benefit of the students. The following classroom policies promote equity and inclusion for English learners.

PRACTICES FOR TEACHERS
Promoting Policies of Equity and Multicultural Inclusion

- Feature minority languages and cultures in school shows, written communications, and displays.
- Take students' interests, languages, and backgrounds into consideration when planning instruction.

- Use materials that depict successful individuals of both genders and of various races and cultures.
- Ask an outside observer to help you guarantee that you are giving boys and girls equal access to your attention.

The social environment of the classroom can support student achievement. Equitable cooperative grouping can address status differences among students in the classroom (Cohen, Lotan, & Catanzarite, 1990). School practices in noncurricular areas such as school clubs should be nondiscriminatory. If not, a resistance culture may develop among excluded students, leading those students to reject schooling and either drop out or carry out acts of school vandalism. The social climate of the school can be one of acceptance for all students in a variety of ways.

PRACTICES FOR TEACHERS

Promoting an Equitable Social Environment

- Group culturally and linguistically diverse students heterogeneously.
- Ensure that students can win prestige positions in extracurricular activities regardless of their ethnic or cultural backgrounds.

Policy at the School Level

Exemplary teachers provide leadership, goodwill, and academic models for students, advocating funding increases for ELD and bilingual instruction, working to configure classes and class sizes to the benefit of the English learners, acting as lead or mentor teachers to help new teachers meet the needs of English learners, and developing a climate of acceptance for linguistic and cultural diversity. Teachers can collaborate and share resources to teach cooperatively, thus mutually increasing their expertise despite cultural, linguistic, or philosophical differences.

PRACTICES FOR TEACHERS

Advocating a School Climate of Acceptance for Linguistic and Cultural Diversity

- Ask for teacher assistants to help students who are making a transition to English from primary-language instruction.

- Experts in ELD or primary-language instruction should be given time to assist other teachers.

- Negotiate so that ELD and primary-language teachers are given an equal share of mentoring and supervisory assistance.

- Vote that an equitable share of budgeted resources be available for bilingual and multicultural instructional materials.

Often intercultural educators must take the lead in opposing racism. If a colleague expresses opinions that are derogatory to individuals on the basis of race, language, or culture, a teacher might respond to such comments by saying, "Why, it surprises me to hear a person like you express that kind of opinion." In this way, the person is affirmed while the derogatory sentiment is rejected.

How to Interrupt Oppressive Behavior

Essential tools in the effort to promote equity in the classroom and school environment are the skills that work toward social justice. All too frequently students join in mockery or discriminatory behaviors because they cannot stand up to peer pressure. Rather than showing no response or "going along with the crowd" in such situations, McClintock (2000) recommended that students "act toward" social justice in the following ways:

- *Educating themselves* by reading literature or case histories about how others have responded to similar situations
- *Interrupting the behavior* by indicating disapproval: "I don't think that's funny."
- Interrupting and educating others by explaining why the behavior is wrong
- Supporting others who are proactive by siding with them physically or verbally
- Replacing hurtful behaviors by initiating and organizing opposite, proactive responses

---

PRACTICES FOR TEACHERS

Opposing Racism at School

- Expect leaders in the school to set an example of respect and encouragement for diverse language abilities and cultures within the school.

- Make every effort to integrate primary-language, ESOL, and mainstream instructors socially.

- Ask school staff (e.g., office personnel) to be equally courteous to all students and visitors.
- Do not use dress codes to discriminate against some subcultures while allowing others to dress as they wish.
- Identify and abandon materials that contain images derogatory to certain races and cultures.

Schools attract community attention because of the academic excellence of their students. Certain schools garner academic laurels by means of academic competitions outside school. Activities such as academic decathlons are team efforts in which dedicated teachers can involve students from many ability levels and promote problem solving and inventive thinking. Schools can foster an academic ambience in a variety of ways.

PRACTICES FOR TEACHERS

Promoting English Learner Participation in Academic Extracurricular Activities

- Insist that teachers who sponsor academically oriented extracurricular activities receive extra pay.
- Arrange for the school to support students with funds to travel to intellectual competitions.
- Ensure that teams competing for academic awards actively solicit individuals from diverse cultural and linguistic backgrounds.
- Hold some intellectual activities, such as contests, in the primary language.

Involving Families in Policymaking

Encouraging family members to participate in school activities is vital. Chapter 14 features many ways in which families can support their children's English learning.

Policy Decisions in Local School Districts

The policies of the local school districts are shaped by the values of the community. School policies are determined by the beliefs of school board members as well as by legal precedents set by state and federal laws and court decisions. Teachers are needed to advocate programs for English learners before local boards.

PRACTICES FOR TEACHERS

Influencing School Board Policies

- Place policies before the school board in a timely manner, with clear, concise, well-researched presentations.

- Attend school board meetings to send the message that the meetings are monitored by experts on issues that affect English learners.

Professional Organizations and Service

Teachers of English learners may make presentations at districtwide conferences or school board meetings, or serve on curriculum committees. Commissions organized by state boards of education offer opportunities for teachers to be involved on advisory boards or in writing curricula or adopting textbooks. Reading articles in professional magazines can lead to submitting articles about successful classroom practices.

Participation in professional organizations such as attending district or regional conferences, serving on committees, drafting proposals, and attending committee meetings can lead to leadership positions. Professional conferences put educators in contact with language development specialists nationally and internationally. Such organizations enable new teachers to form relationships with peers outside their school site.

PRACTICES FOR TEACHERS

Enhancing Professional Expertise

- Perform ESOL-related staff training and mentoring of others, and participate in leadership training for ESOL programs.

- Attend district and regional, state, and national professional events and submit proposals for professional participation and publication.

Influencing Community Public Opinion

A supportive community offers a home for linguistic and cultural diversity. Proactive publicity and public relations can present English learners as positive contributors in the community. Letters to the editor of a local paper can serve as a means to persuade the public to support the instruction of English learners or rebut overtly racist and misinformed letters. Teachers and other staff members can influence community public opinion in several ways.

Influencing Local Public Opinion

- Give presentations to community groups about ESOL programs.
- Join or begin local education–community partnership foundations.
- Be proactive in gaining newspaper coverage for school events.
- Be heard in the local newspaper editorial pages.

Influencing Legislation and Public Opinion

State and national legislators are responsive to popular opinion as expressed by letters of support and phone calls on controversial issues. It is important for legislators to hear from professionals in the field. Bilingual education and language issues often arouse strong emotions, perhaps because language policies affect the criteria set for success in the employment vital to economic survival and success in the United States. Public policy can be shaped in a variety of ways.

Influencing Legislatures and State Policymakers

- Ask your professional organizations to send subscriptions of the organization's publications to legislative libraries.
- Join an e-mail listserv to stay informed on policy issues.
- Organize letter-writing campaigns and visit legislators personally to convey interest in issues that affect English learners.

Influencing Federal Policies

In the history of the United States, decisions about subordinate languages have sometimes been supportive and sometimes repressive. Teachers, particularly through their professional organizations, play an important role in public debate. Federal funding for innovative programs can greatly benefit English learners. Federal funds are available to design innovative programs that provide success for all students. Public opinion and lobbying efforts play a large role in determining the continuation of programs that benefit English learners. Participating in lobbying that supports these programs is a chance for teachers to use the literacy they advocate.

PRACTICES FOR TEACHERS

Influencing Federal Educational Policies

- Become informed about federal legislation that has an impact on ESOL services, and support your professional organization's lobbying efforts to influence federal legislation.

- Organize letter-writing and e-mail campaigns to convey interest in issues that affect English learners.

The National Spirit

A national spirit is created in part by individuals who voice their opinions freely. Writing letters to national magazines on a regular basis helps editors sense the opinions of the readers as national arguments are debated in the mass media. Controversial media figures also shape the national spirit. The population at large must take steps to defuse the voices of demagogues by writing letters to national networks voicing opposition to and distaste for racist viewpoints. Often, teachers of English learners who advocate on their behalf act as role models for English learners to speak for themselves and to be heard. Educators who share the culture and language of the minority communities have a natural function as community leaders.

PRACTICES FOR TEACHERS

Influencing the National Debate on Topics Such as Immigration and Support for English Learners

- Write letters of support for television and radio shows that provide a fair, balanced discussion of controversial issues.

- Write or e-mail networks to express your approval or disapproval of the content of their programming.

- Write letters to national magazines to suggest or support content about issues that affect English learners.

APPENDIX B

English Learners and Special Education

English learners, like any other cross section of today's students, may need special education services. The challenge is to identify learners with special instructional needs and then team up with resource or special education teachers to include these learners in the mainstream classroom or to arrange English-language development services in a resource room situation. Special education is a category that applies not only to those who need additional mediation but also to those who need enrichment—the gifted and talented.

Many researchers who have looked at the special education services available to English learners agree that redoubled efforts should be made to increase the academic performance of English learners in special education students; and that teachers should be actively involved during the assessment, intervention, and placement process. Efforts are ongoing to augment and improve the overall delivery of education to English learners with special education needs. But first, who are these learners? What educational and policy issues does their education raise? Educators have raised the following concerns, among others:

- How can these students' language acquisition, cultural adjustment, and emotional/motivational difficulties be distinguished from learning problems?

- What is the role of psychological counseling and other services in cases in which students are in culture shock or need help adjusting to recent immigration?

- How can a school district avoid inappropriate referrals and placements yet ensure access for English learners who are learning disabled?

- What role do cultural differences and family values play in cases in which students with classroom learning problems may require evaluation for special education services?

- What ELD instruction is most appropriate for English learners with learning disabilities or physical impairments who are placed in mainstream classrooms?

Principles That Apply to Special Education for English Learners

Several basic principles characterize fair and effective processes for determining the educational services appropriate for the English learner who may be experiencing learning difficulties.

- English learners need to become self-responsible, active students who know how to learn. They need linguistic and nonlinguistic strategies, including metalinguistic and metacognitive, that may be generalizable across learning contexts.

- Students need to understand their own learning styles and preferences, as well as discover their intrapersonal strengths and weaknesses in a variety of areas, including both linguistic and nonlinguistic (logical-mathematical, musical, and spatial) domains.

- Students need meaningful and relevant language and academic goals that promote effective communication and learning, in social as well as academic domains.

- Any education setting must provide educational content and approaches that facilitate students' ability to make smooth transitions to mainstream instruction.

- Educational decisions concerning English learners should involve ELD specialists, parents, and other professionals making collaborative, informed judgments that are based on a thorough, fair assessment of the child's language acquisition stage, culture, and individual needs and talents.

The Disproportionate Representation of Culturally and Linguistically Diverse Children in Special Education

All English learners with disabilities are entitled to a free, appropriate public education under the Individuals with Disabilities Education Act (IDEA). Currently, the assessment and placement of culturally and linguistically diverse students have become major issues in special education (Burnette, 2000). Disproportionate representation can occur in one of three ways: overidentification (i.e., students are classified into a disability category when they do not have genuine disabilities); underidentification (i.e., students' disabilities are overlooked and not addressed in their educational programs); and misidentification (i.e., students' disabilities are assigned to inappropriate disability categories) (González, Brusca-Vega, & Yawkey, 1996).

Overrepresentation in Disability Programs   In the United States, some ethnic groups continue to be overrepresented in programs for those who are mildly mentally retarded (MMR) or seriously emotionally disturbed (SED). This may be due to lack of due-process safeguards during referral and testing, improper intelligence testing in the student's second language, and inadequate training of evaluators and special educators, resulting in inappropriate placement (Coutinho & Oswald, 2007).

By the time Public Law 94–142 (the Education for All Handicapped Children Act) was passed in 1975, there were over one million children who had not been served by schools (Shapiro, 2000). Since that date, for many minority children, special education has unfortunately been the ticket not to enhanced educational opportunity but rather to overreferral, increased segregation, and educational isolation. In New York City, for example, 90 percent of special education students classified come from families who receive some form of public assistance; 44 percent come from families whose first language is not English, and 19 percent were born outside the United States (Gottlieb, Alter, Gottlieb, & Wishner, 1994).

Students from minority groups are more likely to receive stigmatizing labels such as "mentally retarded" or "emotionally disturbed" (Shapiro, 2000, p. 340). Shapiro adds,

> At a time when the trend is toward integrating special education students into general education schools and classrooms, students from minority groups are more likely to remain in separate classes or separate schools where academics are sometimes not stressed and academic failure becomes predictable. (p. 340)

Disproportionate placement in special education settings can segregate students by race, and the education that such students receive is not equivalent to that received by the general student population. Being labeled as a special education student has potentially negative effects on students' self-esteem and on teachers' perception of students (Valles, 1998). Unfortunately, expansion of disability categories to include mild learning disabilities and developmental delays has resulted in an increase in the number of bilingual students being served in remedial education classes (Connor & Boskin, 2001).

Underrepresentation in Gifted Programs   English learners are underrepresented in gifted education with the exception of Asian-American students, who are overrepresented in proportion to the general population in the United States. Such underrepresentation may be due to the inadequacy of relying solely on standardized tests for admission to such programs, the lack of training on the part of teachers to recognize diverse talents as they nominate students, the confusing nature of the nomination process for minority parents and the lack of self-nomination on the part of minority students, lack of diversity on the part of selection panels, and inadequate training of assessment personnel who act as gatekeepers for gifted programs (Ford, 1998). This may be remedied by using alternative and multiple forms of identification instruments, increasing family involvement in identification and support, and increasing awareness on the part of teachers about research on giftedness in minorities.

What Is Response to Intervention (RTI)?

The Individuals With Disabilities Education Act (IDEA) of 2004 directed school authorities to focus more on helping all children learn by addressing problems earlier, before the child is so far behind that a referral to special education services is warranted. *Response to Intervention (RTI)* is an array of procedures that can be used to determine if and how a student responds to specific changes in instructional interventions.

Students who are assessed to be below or far below basic proficiency in a given content area are given targeted intervention at higher and higher levels of intensity depending on their needs. In coordination with the regular classroom instruction, the intervention is designed to provide repeated practice until the student reaches mastery, providing short-term, rapid-paced support (M. Howard, 2009).

Proponents of RTI claim that this system assists educators to target special education only for those students who do not show a response to effective interventions and who are thus more likely (or, more likely than students who respond) to have biologically-based learning disabilities. Opponents of RTI argue that RTI may delay the individualized instruction available through special education and short-circuit or evade the provision of legal rights to students and their parents provided by IDEA.

Referring English Learners for Special Education Services

How can the classroom teacher decide if a student might have a disability requiring referral to special education? Friend and Bursuck (2002) offered insights: What needs are as yet unmet in the regular classroom? Is there a chronic pattern that negatively affects learning? Is the student's functioning significantly different from that of classmates?

The classroom teacher, together with the school ELD specialist, plays an important role in investigating the following aspects of the CLD learner's performance.

- Is there a previous history of difficulty: history of special education services, or evidence of little or no prior schooling?
- Does the student need help with basic interpersonal communication skills?
- Is there a particular academic content area in which the student needs additional mediation?
- What is the student's health record and developmental history, including vision and hearing examinations and determination of overall physical health?
- Is there a discrepancy between verbal and non-verbal learning?
- Are there perceptual disorders; if the home language is nonalphabetic, is this due to difficulty with alphabetic letters?
- Does the student experience difficulty processing language, following directions, and understanding complex language—is this increasing or decreasing as English is acquired?

- Is there limited information retention or (memory difficulty)?

- Are there problems with social–emotional functioning, such as academic frustration and low self-esteem? Limited second-language skills may influence social skills, friendships, and teacher–student relationships.

- Is there difficulty with attending and focusing such as distractibility, short attention span, impulsivity, or high motor level (e.g., finger tapping, excessive talking, fidgeting, inability to remain seated)? These may stem from cognitive overload when immersed in a second language for a long period of time or stress from culture shock, leading to withdrawal, anger, or a pervasive sense of sadness.

- Are there reading dysfunctions such as slow rate; short perceptual span; reading without expression; mispronunciation, omission, insertion, or substitutions of words and letters in oral reading; excessive physical movement when reading (squirming); reversals or repetition of words or groups of words in oral reading; lack of comprehension; inability to remember what has been read; lack of interest in reading in or out of school? Are there similar deficits in written expression? Does this happen in primary-language reading or only in English?

- Is there a discrepancy between the student's performance in the first and second languages?

If the problems above do not occur when the child receives instruction in the primary language, it is likely that the situation has resulted from second-language acquisition rather than from a learning disability. Academic proficiency in English takes several years to develop. Thus, one cannot expect a newcomer to English to demonstrate proficiency in these skills immediately. Usually a five month period of observation and educational interventions is needed to determine of a student's academic difficulties are due to English acquisition or other problems.

Testing English Learners for Special Education Services

If the School Screen Team approves the request for special education testing, parental approval is required. Certain fundamentals must be in place to ensure the validity of such testing (Gopaul-McNicol & Thomas-Presswood, 1998):

- Is the person administering testing licensed and certified, with adequate training in the administration, scoring, and interpretation of the test and ability to establish rapport and understand the verbal and nonverbal language and cultural beliefs/practices of the person being tested?

- If the test is administered in the primary language, does the tester speak the same dialect as the student, or is there a qualified translator available?

- Does the assessment have norms that represent the population group of the individual being tested?

- Does the person being tested understand what is expected from the testing situation, such as having had prior experience with test materials, such as blocks or puzzles?
- Does the person being tested have culturally appropriate test-taking behaviors, such as focus on one task at a time; ability to tolerate small interpersonal space and frequent, sustained eye contact; a reflective, methodological, analytical cognitive style; and ability to work with a male or female examiner?

Teaching Strategies for English Learners with Special Needs

Inclusion is a term often used to describe the provision of instruction within the conventional/mainstream classroom for students with special needs or talents. The mainstream classroom may include English-only (EO)/non-special education students as well as EO/special education, English learner/non-special education, and English learner/special-education, all mixed in the same classroom as a nonrestrictive setting for content instruction and language development activities. By using a variety of interactive strategies, teachers have ample opportunity to implement methods and activities that promote academic success for all students.

To address this complexity, an inclusive classroom should be equipped with additional educational resources, such as teaching assistants, lower student-to-teacher ratio, and a budget for adapted instructional materials. The chief resource in any classroom, however, is the breadth and variety of instructional strategies on which the experienced teacher can draw. The following sections suggest multiple strategies in the areas of listening skills, reading, and writing.

Adapting Listening Tasks

Suggestions about adapting listening skills accord with the three phases of the listening process: before, during, and after listening.

Before listening, directly instruct listening strategies, preview ways to pay attention, and teach students to attend to cues that denote important information. Establish a listening goal for the lesson. Arrange information in short, logical, well-organized segments, with verbal, pictorial, or written prelistening organizers to cue students to important information. Preview the content with questions that require critical thinking.

During the listening task clearly highlight what information must be remembered, summarized, or noted. Teach students to self-monitor their listening behavior during listening by using self-questioning techniques and visual imagery. After the listening task, discuss with students what was learned. Integrate other language arts and content activities as a follow-up.

Adapting Reading Tasks

Reading adaptations for included students are organized into "before," "during," and "after" reading (Smith, Polloway, Patton, & Dowdy, 2011). Prior to reading, preview reading materials to assist students with establishing purpose, activating prior knowledge, budgeting time, recognizing specific vocabulary words, and focusing attention. Explain how new content to be learned links to previous learning. Ensure that readability levels of the textbooks and trade books used in class are commensurate with the student's language level; if this is not the case, locate lower-reading-level supplements in the same topic, rewrite material to simplify the reading level, or provide chapter outlines or summaries. Provide visual aids (e.g., charts and graphs) to supplement reading tasks.

During reading, reduce extraneous classroom noise. Have students highlight key words, phrases and concepts. After reading, discuss the content, paraphrasing material if necessary to clarify the main ideas. Reteach vocabulary to ensure retention. Use brief individual conferences with students to verify comprehension.

Adapting Writing Tasks

Writing is used in two main ways in classrooms: to capture and demonstrate content knowledge (taking notes, writing answers on assignments or tests) and to express creative purposes. If the acquisition of content knowledge is the goal, students can often use a variety of alternatives to writing that avoid large amounts of written work (both in class and homework) (Smith, Polloway, Patton, & Dowdy 2011). Students may need additional time to respond in writing. A word bank on a classroom wall helps with spelling. To improve handwriting, an optional calligraphy center can help students practice elegant forms of handwriting, with correct models available of cursive styles.

If the lesson plan incorporates writing to demonstrate comprehension, the *content* rather than the *form* of writing is the critical element—it is more important to respond to errors that show factual misunderstanding than to mistakes of grammar or usage. A written outline of key content from lecture notes reduces the amount of board copying. Students can work in groups to respond when working on projects or reports, with the understanding that each member takes equal turn in writing. When students write for self-expression, they should follow a well-defined writing process, with provisions for generating ideas, drafting, and peer editing. (See Chapter 7 for a discussion of the writing process.)

Adapting Assessment

Ongoing student assessment is vital, for three reasons: to diagnose which instructional tasks and strategies are responsible for student success, to document this success, and to provide a basis for communicating progress to the student, parents, and administrators.

Direct observation can determine if the student has opportunities to speak in class, has enough academic engaged time and can complete assigned tasks, and is receiving teacher feedback for completion or noncompletion of work, correct responding, or misbehavior. Analysis of student products can help to determine which instructional activities have been successful and which may need to be modified. Throughout this process, formative assessment gives students feedback about their performance and ways they can improve.

An Individual Instructional Plan (IEP) may dictate what kinds of work will be graded and what criteria will be used to assign a letter grade to the work. Assessment activities should be detailed to the greatest extent possible when the IEP is approved so that all members of the collaborating team are aware of their roles and responsibilities Ongoing assessment monitors the extent to which the student's IEP is being fulfilled. The grading process may include teachers' descriptive comments about students' learning styles, skills, effort, and attitude. Keeping parents informed ensures that they know what they can do at home to assist their child.

Universal Instructional Design for Special Populations of English Learners

English learners with special needs include those with learning disabilities, and vision, hearing, health, and mobility impairments. Educators have begun to view the education of these learners from a unified perspective: Universal Instructional Design (UID). This goes beyond merely providing physical access for all students (e.g., wheelchair ramps and sign language translators). It ensures access to information, resources, and tools for students with a wide range of abilities, disabilities, ethnic backgrounds, language skills, and learning styles, with multiple means of representation, expression, and engagement (Burgstahler, 2002). This offers diversity of opportunities for many different students. UID recommendations are as follows:

- Use bilingual signage and Braille bilingual materials; welcome and respect aides and assistants; supply multiple reading levels of texts.
- Use assistive technologies such as screen readers and online dictionaries; make online chatrooms available for deaf and hearing-impaired students.
- Employ a full range of audiovisual enhancement, including wireless headsets and captioned video; build in redundant modes (e.g., audiotaped read-along books, typed lecture notes, and study guides).
- Insure that information is both understandable and complete; reduce unnecessary complexity; highlight essential text; give clear criteria for tests and assignments.
- Set up both heterogeneous groups (across second-language ability levels) and homogeneous groups (same language-ability level); instruct students on how to secure a conversational turn.
- Employ formative assessment for ongoing feedback.
- Offer different modes to all students so that special-needs students are not the only ones with alternatives. (Adapted from Burgstahler, 2002)

Instructional Modifications for English Learners in Special Education

Although many of the strategies recommended below are appropriate for all students, they are particularly critical for English learners who may have a learning disability:

- Use reality-based or experiential learning activities.
- Teach skills and strategies explicitly (a direct instruction model in conjunction with an experiential approach).
- Focus on content over form.
- Provide understandable input.
- Provide instruction through all learning channels—visual, auditory, and tactile.

- Monitor the student for fatigue.
- Provide "wait time" and "think time."
- Respond positively to communication attempts.
- Use questions appropriate to students' second-language acquisition stage.
- Check frequently for comprehension.
- In bilingual classrooms, use the preview-view-review technique.
- Explain behavioral expectations clearly.

Source: Adapted from Illinois State Board of Education (2002).

Special Populations of Special-Needs English Learners

Autism

> In a "sensory break area" where students with autism can take a time out if needed and calm themselves, Will plays a board game and works at casual conversation with speech pathologist Amy Gold. "Turn-taking with a game is concrete, and from this he learns about conversational turn-taking," explains Gold. (Goodwin, 2010a, p. 11)

Will is a part of a growing population of students with autism, the fastest-growing special education population in the United States. Researchers estimate that in 2009, one in one hundred children in the United States had some form of autism (Kogan, 2009). Education is considered the primary treatment for autism. Classroom interventions include behavioral training, speech and language therapy, and one-on-one work with motor disorder skills. Many of these students also require ELD services.

Visually Impaired

Modifications for the visually impaired can be thought of as a continuum, with more interventions needed for the legally blind. Instructional modifications include the following:

- Textbooks are usually translated into Braille or available in audio versions.
- Computer sound synthesis software is available such as text to speech and voice recognition.
- The instructor repeats every word put on the board, including directions to location of the words.
- Diagrams can be embossed by sticking string to cardboard.
- Field trips provide culture, exposure, and experiences to build schemata.

Hearing-Impaired

Modifications for the hearing-impaired also fall along an intervention continuum, with more interventions needed for the totally deaf. Instructional modifications include the following, adapted from Pierangelo and Giuliani (2001):

- Amplification systems are made available.
- An interpreter accompanies students in class.
- Seating is favorable to speech-reading (formerly "lip-reading").
- Audio media is captioned.
- Key points are listed on chalkboard, with note-taking assistance provided.
- Instruction is concise; the student repeats key points aloud privately to ensure comprehension.
- Teachers and peers use sign language.
- Distracting ambient noise is minimized.
- The instructor modifies speech, speaking to students face to face, with clear enunciation; gestures facilitate understanding.
- A peer buddy helps the student stay abreast of the class during oral reading.

Web Search: Organizations for Students with Special Needs

Go online to see if the following organizations offer specific suggestions for English learners with intellectual, behavioral, or sensory impairment.

- Alexander Graham Bell Association for the Deaf and Hard of Hearing.
- American Association for the Deaf-Blind (AADB).**
- American Association of Intellectual and Developmental Disabilities (AAIDD).
- American Council of the Blind.
- American Society for Deaf Children.
- Autism Society of America, Inc.*

- The Beach Center on Families and Disability.
- Attention Deficit Disorder Association.
- Children and Adults with Attention Deficit Disorders (C.H.A.D.D).*

* Website has Spanish-language translation available.
** Website makes available Americans with Disabilities Act (ADA)-compliant display modifications.

Each English learner—including those with special needs, whether for additional mediation or acceleration of instruction—is a treasure box, with his or her individual and specific talents, cultural background, and life experiences locked inside. Opening this treasure chest and releasing these talents to the world is a special challenge, providing educational adventure of the highest order.

APPENDIX C

Bibliography of Works Used for Visual Imaginary Dramatic Arts

1. "Ancient Greek I and II" by Gustav Klimt (Costantino, 1998, p. 28).
2. "Music I" by Gustav Klimt (Costantino, 1998, pp. 32–33).
3. "The Motley Life" by Wassily Kandinsky (Russell, 1969, p. 67).
4. "The Farm" by Joan Miró (Tomkins, 1966, pp. 144–145).
5. "Bikes Poster" by George Hardie (Hardie & Thorgerson, 1978, p. 77).
6. "Landscape from a Dream" by Paul Nash (Swinglehurst, 1995, pp. 40–41).
7. "The Mystery and Melancholy of a Street" by Giorgio de Chirico (Tomkins, 1966, p. 115).
8. "Mama, Papa Is Wounded!" by Yves Tanguy (Tomkins, 1966, p. 119).
9. "Dog Barking at the Moon" by Joan Miró (Tomkins, 1966, p. 145).
10. "Harlequin's Carnival" by Joan Miró (Swinglehurst, 1995, pp. 34–35).
11. "Blumenmythos" by Paul Klee (Swinglehurst, 1995, p. 8).
12. "Composition" by Edward Burra (Swinglehurst, 1995, p. 77).
13. "Bronze Ballet" by Edward Wadsworth (Swinglehurst, 1995, pp. 24–25).
14. "The Entire City" by Max Ernst (Swinglehurst, 1995, pp. 31–32).
15. Album cover, "Saucerful of Secrets" (Pink Floyd) by Hipgnosis (Hardie & Thorgerson, 1978, p. 34).
16. Album cover, "Elegy(Nice)" by Storm Thorgerson (Hardie & Thorgerson, 1978, p. 19).
17. "Apotheosis of El Tucuche" by LeRoy Clarke (Art Services International, 1995, p. 197).
18. "The Magic Wedding" by Phillipe Dodard (Art Services International, 1995, p. 138).
19. "El Mundo Mágico de JOP" by José Perdomo (Art Services International, 1995, p. 123).
20. "To Know a Veil" by Hipgnosis (Hardie & Thorgerson, 1978, p. 150).
21. "Carnival Dance" by Stafford Schliefer (Art Services International, 1995, p. 175).
22. "Gethsemane I" by Ras Akyem Ramsay (Art Services International, 1995, p. 104).
23. "Blue Night" by Christopher Cozier (Art Services International, 1995, pp. 198–199).
24. "Las Meninas" by Pablo Picasso (Wertenbaker, 1967, pp. 160–161).
25. "Unterach on the Attersee" by Gustav Klimt (Costantino, 1998, p. 97).
26. "Baby" by Gustav Klimt (Costantino, 1998, p. 105).
27. "Water Snakes (Friends) I" by Gustav Klimt (Costantino, 1998, p. 51).
28. Album cover, "Uno" by Storm Thorgerson (Hardie & Thorgerson, 1978, p. 45).

Art Services International. (1995). *Caribbean visions: Contemporary painting and sculpture* (pp. 104, 123, 138, 175, 197, 198–199). Alexandria, VA: Author.

Costantino, M. (1998). *Klimt* (pp. 28, 32–33, 51, 97, 105). New York: Knickerbocker Press.

Hardie, G., & Thorgerson, S. (1978). *The work of Hipgnosis ("Walk away René")* (pp. 19, 34, 45, 77, 150). New York: A. & W. Visual Library.

Russell, J. (1969). *The world of Matisse 1869–1954* (p. 67). New York: Time-Life Books

Swinglehurst, E. (1995). *The art of the surrealists* (pp. 8, 24–25, 31–32, 34–35, 40–41, 77). Bristol, UK: Parragon Book Service Ltd.

Tomkins, C. (1966). *The world of Marcel Duchamp 1887–* (pp. 115, 119, 144, 145). New York: Time-Life Books.

Wertenbaker, L. (1967). *The world of Picasso 1881–* (pp. 160–161). New York: Time-Life Books.

Bibliography

Abedi, J., Hofstetter, C. H., & Lord, C. (2004). Assessment accommodations for English language learners: Implications for policy-based empirical research. *Review of Educational Research, 74*(1), 1–28.

Abdoh, S. (2001). Interview on *Fresh Air,* National Public Radio, October 2.

Abramson, S., Seda, I., & Johnson, C. (1990). Literacy development in a multilingual kindergarten classroom. *Childhood Education, 67*(2), 68–72.

Ada, A. F. (1995). Fostering the home–school connection. In J. Frederickson (Ed.), *Reclaiming our voices: Bilingual education, critical pedagogy, and praxis* (pp. 163–178). Ontario: California Association for Bilingual Education.

Adams, D., & Angeles, R. (2008). Mobile devices at school: Possibilities, problems, and tough choices. *Educational Technology, 48*(1), 35–38.

Adamson, W. L. (1980). *Hegemony and revolution: A study of Antonio Gramsci's political and cultural theory.* Berkeley: University of California Press.

Agar, M. (1996). *The professional stranger: An informal introduction to ethnography.* Burlington, MA: Elsevier Science & Technology Books.

Agor, B. (Ed.). (2001). *Integrating the ESL standards into classroom practice: Grades 9–12.* Alexandria, VA: Teachers of English to Speakers of Other Languages.

Airasian, P. W. (2005). *Classroom assessment: Concepts and applications* (5th ed.). New York: McGraw-Hill.

Alcaya, C., Lybeck, K., Mougel, P., & Weaver, S. (1995). *Some strategies useful for speaking a foreign language.* Unpublished manuscript, University of Minnesota.

Alco, B. (2009/2010). An L2 reader's word recognition strategies: Transferred or developed. *The CATESOL Journal, 21*(1), 66–74.

Allen, M. J., Noel, R. C., & Rienzi, B. M. (2001). *Program Assessment Consultation Team outcomes assessment handbook.* Bakersfield: California State University.

Althen, G. (1988). *American ways.* Yarmouth, ME: Intercultural Press.

Amselle, J. (1999). Dual immersion delays English. *American Language Review, 3*(5), 8.

Anderson, B. (1983). *Imagined communities.* London: Verso.

Anderson, J. B., & Guest, K. (1994). Service learning in teacher education at Seattle University. In R. J. Kraft & M. Swadener (Eds.), *Building community: Service learning in the academic disciplines* (pp. 139–150). Denver: Colorado Campus Compact.

Anderson, N. J. (2002). Using telescopes, microscopes, and kaleidoscopes to put metacognition into perspective. *TESOL Matters, 12*(4), 1, 4.

Anstrom, K. (1998). Preparing secondary education teachers to work with English language learners: English language arts. *NCBE Resource Collection Series, no. 10.* Washington, DC: National Clearinghouse for Bilingual Education.

Aparicio, F. R., & Jose-Kampfer, C. (1995). Language, culture, and violence in the educational crisis of U.S. Latinos/as: Two courses for intervention. *Michigan Journal of Community Service Learning, 2,* 95–105.

Aragones, S. (2000). *New comics and conversation.* Studio City, CA: JAG Publications.

431

Armstrong, T. (1994). *Multiple intelligences in the classroom.* Alexandria, VA: Association for Supervision and Curriculum Development.

Aronowitz, S., & Giroux, H. A. (1991). *Postmodern education: Politics, culture, and social criticism.* Minneapolis: University of Minnesota Press.

Asher, J. (1982). *Learning another language through actions: The complete teachers' guidebook.* Los Gatos, CA: Sky Oaks.

Associated Press International (2006). Latinos moving to jobs, study finds. *Los Angeles Times,* March 7, p. A15.

Astin, A. W., Korn, W. S., & Sax, L. J. (1994). *The American freshman: National norms for fall 1994.* Los Angeles: Higher Education Research Institute, University of California.

Auerbach, E. R. (1995). The politics of the ESL classroom: Issues of power in pedagogical choices. In J. W. Tollefson (Ed.), *Power and inequality in language education* (pp. 9–33). Cambridge: Cambridge University Press.

Auerbach, E. R. (2002). *Case studies in community partnership.* Alexandria, VA: Teachers of English to Speakers of Other Languages.

August, D., & Pease-Alvarez, L. (1996). *Attributes of effective programs and classrooms serving English language learners.* Santa Cruz, CA: Center for Research on Cultural Diversity and Second Language Learning.

Baker, C. (1993). *Foundations of bilingual education and bilingualism.* Clevedon, UK: Multilingual Matters.

Balderas, V. A. (2001). Words and images that provoke informed multicultural identities. In L. Ramírez & O. M. Gallardo (Eds.), *Portraits of teachers in multicultural settings: A critical literacy approach* (pp. 71–86). Boston: Allyn & Bacon.

Balzar, J. (1997). U. S. drifting apart, in so many words. *Los Angeles Times*, June 25, A5.

Banks, J. (1991). A curriculum for empowerment, action, and change. In C. Sleeter (Ed.), *Empowerment through multicultural education* (pp. 125–142). Albany: State University of New York Press.

Banks, J. A., & McGee Banks, C. A. (Eds.). (2009). *Multicultural education: Issues and perspectives* (7th ed.). Hoboken, NJ: Wiley & Sons.

Barfield, S. C., & Uzarski, J. (2009). Integrating indigenous cultures into English language teaching. *English Teaching Forum, 1,* 2–8.

Barks, D., & Watts, P. (2001). Textual borrowing strategies for graduate-level ESL students. In D. Belcher & A. Hirvela (Eds.), *Linking literacies: Perspectives on L2 reading–writing connections* (pp. 246–267). Ann Arbor: University of Michigan Press.

Barr, R., & Johnson, B. (1997). *Teaching reading and writing in elementary classrooms* (2nd ed.). New York: Longman.

Barrett, H. (2000). Electronic portfolios—multimedia development and portfolio development: The electronic portfolio development process. Accessed on March 2, 2007, from www.electronicportfolios.org/portfolios/EPDevProcess.html#stage3.

Bartolomé, L. I. (1994). Beyond the methods fetish: Toward a humanizing pedagogy. *Harvard Educational Review, 64*(2), 173–194.

Barton, D. (1994). *Literacy : An introduction to the ecology of written language.* Oxford: Blackwell.

Barton, D. (2000). Researching literacy practices: Learning from activities with teachers and students. In D. Barton, M. Hamilton, & R. Ivanic (Eds.), *Situated literacies* (pp. 167–179). London: Routledge.

Barton, D., Hamilton, M., & Ivanič, R. (2000). Introduction. In D. Barton, M. Hamilton, & R. Ivanič (Eds.), *Situated literacies* (pp. 1–15). London: Routledge.

Bartram, M., & Walton, R. (1994). *Correction: A positive approach to language mistakes.* Hove, UK: Language Teaching Publications.

Bassano, S., & Christison, M. A. (1995). *Community spirit: A practical guide to collaborative language learning.* San Francisco: Alta Book Center.

Bates, L., Lane, J., & Lange, E. (1993). *Writing clearly: Responding to ESL compositions.* Boston: Heinle & Heinle.

Battenberg, J. D. (1997). English versus French: Language rivalry in Tunisia. *World Englishes, 16*(2), 281–290.

Becker, C. (1999). Animal psychology. In N. Shameem & M. Tickoo (Eds.), *New ways in using communicative games* (pp. 95–96). Alexandria, VA: Teachers of English to Speakers of Other Languages.

Bell, D. (1999, spring). Rise, Sally, rise: Communicating through dance. *TESOL Journal, 8*(1), 27–31.

Bembridge, T. (1992). A MAP for reading assessment. *Educational Leadership, 49*(8), 46–48.

Beniston, F. (1996). *West Side Story:* A lesson. In V. Whiteson (Ed.), *New ways of using drama and literature in language teaching* (pp. 100–103). Alexandria, VA: Teachers of English to Speakers of Other Languages.

Bennett, J. M. (1993). Cultural marginality: Identity issues in intercultural training. In R. M. Paige (Ed.), *Education for the intercultural experience* (pp. 109–135). Yarmouth, ME: Intercultural Press.

Bennett, J. M. (1999). *Aspects of marginality in second language teaching.* Presentation, annual conference, Teachers of English to Speakers of Other Languages, New York.

Bennett, M. (1996a). Beyond tolerance: Intercultural communication in a multicultural society (Part I). *TESOL Matters, 6*(2), 1, 15.

Bennett, M. (1996b). Beyond tolerance: Intercultural communication in a multicultural society (Part II). *TESOL Matters, 6*(3), 6.

Benson, V. A. (1999). Syl/la/bles and linking. In N. Shameem & M. Tickoo (Eds.), *New ways in using communicative games* (pp. 18–19). Alexandria, VA: Teachers of English to Speakers of Other Languages.

Berg, J. (2006, December 27). Immigrant children shielded from state tests, but for whose protection? *The New York Times,* A24.

Berk, L. E., & Winsler, A. (1995). *Scaffolding children's learning: Vygotsky and early childhood education.* Washington, DC: National Association for the Education of Young Children.

Berman, P., Minicucci, C., McLaughlin, B., Nelson, B., & Woodworth, K. (1995). *School reform and student diversity: Case studies of exemplary practices for LEP students.* Emeryville, CA: Institute for Policy Analysis and Research. Available online: www.ncela.gwu.edu/pubs/schoolreform/contents.htm.

Bermúdez, A., & Márquez, J. (1996). An examination of a four-way collaborative to increase parental involvement in the schools. *The Journal of Educational Issues of Language Minority Students, 16.* Available online: www.ncela.gwu.edu/pubs/nysed/languagearts/Ch08ref.pdf.

Bialystok, E. (2009). Bilingualism: The good, the bad, and the indifferent. *Bilingualism: Language and Cognition, 12*(1), 3–11.

Bigelow, B. (2010/2011). "If there is no struggle . . ." Teaching a people's history of the abolition movement. *Rethinking Schools, 25*(2), 23–29.

Bitter, G. G., & Legacy, M. E. (2005). *Using technology in the classroom.* Boston: Pearson.

Bitter, G. G., & Pierson, J. M. (2006). *Using technology in the classroom* (6th ed.). Boston: Pearson.

Bloch, J. (2001). Plagiarism and the ESL student: From printed to electronic texts. In D. Belcher & A. Hirvela (Eds.), *Linking literacies: Perspectives on L2 reading–writing connections* (pp. 209–228). Ann Arbor: University of Michigan Press.

Blood, P. (1992). *Rise up singing: The group-singing song book*. Bethlehem, PA: Sing Out Corporation.

Blumenfeld, P. C., Soloway, E., Marx, R. W., Krajcik, J. S., Guzdial, M., & Palinscar, A. (1991). Motivating project-based learning: Sustaining the doing, supporting the learning. *Educational Psychologist, 26*(3&4), 369–398.

Booth, D. (1985). Imaginary gardens with real toads: Reading and drama in education. *Theory into Practice, 24,* 193–198.

Bosher, S. (1997). Language and cultural identity: A study of Hmong students at the postsecondary level. *TESOL Quarterly, 31*(3), 593–603.

Bourdieu, P. (1977). *Reproduction in society, education, and culture* (with J. Passeron). Los Angeles: Sage.

Bourdieu, P. (1979/1984). *Distinction: A social critique of the judgement of taste*. Cambridge, MA: Harvard University Press.

Bourdieu, P. (1991). *Language and symbolic power* (Trans. G. Raymond & M. Anderson). Oxford: Polity Press in association with Blackwell.

Boutte, G. (1999). *Multicultural education: Raising consciousness*. London: International Thompson Publishing House.

Bozzone, M. A. (1993). Kids make a difference. *Instructor, 103*(4), 65–67.

Bremmer, J. (1999). *MENSA mind maze challenge*. London: Chartwell Books.

Brend, R. M. (1975). Male–female intonation patterns in American English. In B. Thorne & N. Henley (Eds.), *Language and sex: Differences and dominance* (pp. 84–87). Rowley, MA: Newbury House.

Bringle, R. G., & Hatcher, J. A. (1999, summer). Reflection in service learning: Making meaning of experience. *Educational Horizons,* 179–185.

Brinton, D., Snow, M., & Wesche, M. (1989). *Content-based second language instruction*. New York: Newbury House.

Brisk, M. E., & Harrington, M. M. (2000). *Literacy and bilingualism*. Mahwah, NJ: Erlbaum.

Brooks, E., & Fox, L. (1998). *Making peace: A reading/writing/thinking text on global community*. Cambridge: Cambridge University Press.

Brown, C. (1987). Literacy in thirty hours: Paulo Freire's process in northeast Brazil. In I. Shor (Ed.), *Freire for the classroom: A sourcebook for liberatory teaching*. Portsmouth, NH: Heinemann.

Brown, D. (1987). *Principles of language learning and teaching* (2nd ed.). Englewood Cliffs, NJ: Prentice-Hall.

Brown, D. (1994). *Principles of language learning and teaching* (3rd ed.). Englewood Cliffs, NJ: Prentice-Hall.

Brown, D. (2000). *Principles of language learning and teaching* (4th ed.). Englewood Cliffs, NJ: Prentice-Hall.

Brown, J. D. (Ed.). (1998). *New ways in classroom assessment*. Alexandria, VA: Teachers of English to Speakers of Other Languages.

Brown, P., & Levinson, S. C. (1987). *Politeness: Some universals in language usage*. New York: Cambridge University Press.

Brown, S. (2006). *Teaching listening*. New York: Cambridge University Press.

Brown, S. C., & Kysilka, M. L. (2002). *Applying multicultural and global concepts in the classroom and beyond*. Boston: Allyn & Bacon.

Brown, S. E. (2009). Making the next generation our greatest resource. *Thought and Action, 25* (Fall), 151–162.

Brutt-Griffler, J., & Samimy, K. K. (1999). Revisiting the colonial in the postcolonial: Critical praxis for the nonnative-English-speaking teachers in a TESOL program. *TESOL Quarterly, 33*(3), 413–431.

Bry, A. (1976). *Directing the movies of your mind*. New York: Harper & Row.

Buckley, L. C. (2000). A framework for understanding crosscultural issues in the English as a second language classroom. *CATESOL Journal, 12*(1), 53–72.

Bunce-Crim, M. (1991). Helping kids choose a topic. *Instructor, 101*(3), 16.

Burgstahler, S. (2002). *Universal design of instruction.* Accessed July 15, 2011 from http://www.washington.edu/doit/brochures/academics/instruction.html

Burnette, J. (2000). *Assessment of culturally and linguistically diverse students for special education eligibility.* Eric Clearinghouse on Disabilities and Gifted Education (ED #E604).

Byrd, P., & Benson, B. (1994). *Problem-solution: A reference for ESL writers.* Boston: Heinle & Heinle.

Caine, R., & Caine, G. (1994). *Making connections: Teaching and the human brain.* Menlo Park, CA: Addison-Wesley.

Caine, R., & Caine, G. (1997). *Education at the edge of possibility.* Alexandria, VA: Association for Supervision and Curriculum Development.

California Department of Education. (1986). *Handbook for teaching Pilipino-speaking students.* Sacramento: Author.

California Department of Education. (1987). *Handbook for teaching Japanese-speaking students.* Sacramento: Author.

California Department of Education. (1989a). *Handbook for teaching Cantonese-speaking students.* Sacramento: Author.

California Department of Education. (1989b). *Handbook for teaching Portuguese-speaking students.* Sacramento: Author.

California Department of Education. (1992). *Handbook for teaching Korean-American students.* Sacramento: Author.

California Department of Education. (1994). *Handbook for teaching Vietnamese-speaking students.* Sacramento: Author.

California Department of Education. (1999a). *English language development (ELD) standards.* Sacramento: Author. Available online: www.cde.ca.gov/ta/ty/el/documents.eldgrd.pdf.

California Department of Education. (1999b). *Reading/language arts framework for California public schools.* Sacramento: Author. Available online: www.cde.ca.gov/cdepress/re/pn/fd/readlangarts_frame_pdf.asp.

California Department of Education. (2010). *Resources for English learners.* Available online: www.cde.ca.gov/sp/el/er.

Cameron, A. (1988). *The most beautiful place in the world.* New York: Random House.

Campus Compact. (2000). *Introduction to service learning toolkit: Reading and resources for faculty.* Providence, RI: Author.

Canale, M. (1983). From communicative competence to communicative language pedagogy. In J. Richards & R. Schmidt (Eds.), *Language and communication* (pp. 2–27). New York: Longman.

Cantlon, T. L. (1991). *Structuring the classroom successfully for cooperative team learning.* Portland, OR: Prestige Publishers.

Carlsen, G. R. (1974). Literature IS! *The English Journal, 63*(2), 24.

Carson, J. G. (2001). A task analysis of reading and writing in academic contexts. In D. Belcher & A. Hirvela (Eds.), *Linking literacies: Perspectives on L2 reading–writing connections* (pp. 48–83). Ann Arbor: University of Michigan Press.

Cassidy, N. (1992). *Kids songs: Sleepyheads* (audiocassette and book). Palo Alto, CA: Klutz Press.

Cavanaugh, C. (2006). *Clips from the classroom: Learning with technology.* Boston: Allyn & Bacon.

Cazden, C. (1988). *Classroom discourse.* Portsmouth, NH: Heinemann.

Cecil, N. L., & Lauritzen, P. (1994). *Literacy and the arts for the integrated classroom.* White Plains, NY: Longman.

Celce-Murcia, M., & Olshtain, E. (2000). *Discourse and context in language teaching: A guide for language teachers.* Cambridge: Cambridge University Press.

Cenoz, J., & Genesee, F. (1998). Psycholinguistic perspectives on multilingualism and multilingual education. In J. Cenoz & F. Genesee (Eds.), *Beyond bilingualism: Multilingualism and multilingual education* (pp. 16–34). Clevedon, UK: Multilingual Matters.

Chamot, A. U. (1987). The learning strategies of ESL students. In A. Wenden & J. Rubin (Eds.), *Learner strategies in language learning* (pp. 71–83). Englewood Cliffs, NJ: Prentice-Hall.

Chamot, A. U., & O' Malley, J. (1987). The Cognitive Academic Language Learning Approach: A bridge to the mainstream. *TESOL Quarterly, 21*(2), 227–249.

Chamot, A. U., & O'Malley, J. M. (1994). *The CALLA handbook: Implementing the cognitive academic language learning approach.* Reading, MA: Addison-Wesley.

Chan, L. (2004). The inexorable demand for qualified ESL teachers. *Language Magazine, 3*(6), 30–31.

Chaney, A. L., & Burk, T. L. (1998). *Teaching oral communication in grades K–8.* Boston: Allyn & Bacon.

Chang, M. (1994) *Story of the Chinese zodiac.* Taipei: Yuan-Liou Publishers (available from Shen's Book and Supplies, Arcadia, CA).

Charp, S. (1996). Technological literacy for the workplace. *T. H. E. Journal, 23*(8), 6.

Chatton, B. (1993). *Using poetry across the curriculum: A whole language approach.* Phoenix, AZ: Oryx.

Chavez, C. (n.d.). Education of the heart. Accessed July 31, 2011 from http://chavez foundation.org/_cms.php?mode=view&b_code=001008000000000&b_no=2197&page=1&field=&key=&n=1

Cheng, L. (1987). English communicative competence of language minority children: Assessment and treatment of language "impaired" preschoolers. In H. Trueba (Ed.), *Success or failure? Learning and the language minority student* (pp. 49–68). Boston: Heinle & Heinle.

Chesterfield, R., & Chesterfield, K. (1985). Natural order in children's use of second language learning strategies. *Applied Linguistics, 6,* 45–59.

Children's Defense Fund. (2000). *Booming economy leaves millions of children behind: 12.1 million children still living in poverty.* Washington, DC: Author.

Chinnery, J. D., & Chu, M. Q. (1984). *Corresponding English and Chinese proverbs and phrases.* Beijing: New World Press.

Chitester, D. J. (2007). Dispelling myths of bilingualism. *Language Magazine, 7*(2), 22–24.

Chomsky, N. (1959). Review of B. F. Skinner, "Verbal Behavior." *Language, 35,* 26–58.

Christensen, L. (2002). Whose standard? Teaching standard English. In B. M. Power & R. S. Hubbard (Eds.), *Language development: A reader for teachers* (2nd ed., pp. 173–177). Upper Saddle River, NJ: Merrill Prentice Hall.

Christian, D., & Genesee, F. (Eds.). (2001). *Bilingual education.* Alexandria, VA: Teachers of English to Speakers of Other Languages.

Christian, D., Montone, C. L., Lindholm, K. L., & Carranza, I. (1997). *Profiles in two-way immersion education.* Washington, DC: Center for Applied Linguistics and Delta Systems.

Christison, M. (1982). *English through poetry.* Hayward, CA: Prentice Hall.

Churchill, W. S. (1956). *A history of the English-speaking peoples: The birth of Britain.* New York: Doud, Mead.

Cisneros, S. (1994) *Hairs/pelitos.* New York: Dragonfly Books.

Clark, A. (1997). *Being there: Putting brain, body, and world together again.* Cambridge, MA: MIT Press.

Cloud, N., Genesee, F., & Hamayan, E. (2000). *Dual language instruction.* Boston: Heinle & Heinle.

Coehlo, E., Winer, L., & Olsen, J. W-B. (1989). *All sides of the issue: Activities for cooperative jigsaw groups.* Hayward, CA: Alemany Press.

Cohen, A. (1996). *Second language learning and use strategies: Clarifying the issues. Working Paper Series #3.* Minneapolis: University of Minnesota Center for Advanced Research on Language Acquisition.

Cohen, E., Lotan, R., & Catanzarite, L. (1990). Treating status problems in the cooperative classroom. In S. Sharon (Ed.), *Cooperative learning: Theory and research.* New York: Praeger.

Cole, T. (1997) *The article book.* Upper Saddle River, NJ: Prentice Hall Regents.

Coles, R. (1993). *The call of service: A witness to idealism.* Boston: Houghton Mifflin.

Collier, V. (1987). Age and rate of acquisition of second language for academic purposes. *TESOL Quarterly, 21*(4), 617–641.

Collier, V. (1992). A synthesis of studies examining long-term minority student data on academic achievement. *Bilingual Research Journal, 16,* 187–212.

Conchas, G. Q. (2006). *The color of success: Race and high-achieving urban youth.* New York; Teachers College Press.

Connell, E. L. (1999). Protest! In R. E. Larimer & L. Schleicher (Eds.), *New ways in using authentic materials in the classroom* (pp. 52–54). Alexandria, VA: Teachers of English to Speakers of Other Languages.

Connor, M. H., & Boskin, J. (2001). Overrepresentation of bilingual and poor children in special education classes: A continuing problem. *Journal of Children and Poverty, 7*(1), 23–32.

Conzett, J. (2000). Integrating collocation into a reading and writing course. In M. Lewis (Ed.), *Teaching collocation* (pp. 70–87). Hove, UK: Language Teaching Publications.

Cook, V. (1999). Going beyond the native speaker in language teaching. *TESOL Quarterly, 33*(2), 185–209.

Copeland, P. F. (1997). *Great Native Americans.* Mineola, NY: Dover Publications.

Corson, D. (1990). *Language policy across the curriculum.* Clevedon, UK: Multilingual Matters.

Corson, D. (1999). *Language policy in schools: A resource for teachers and administrators.* Mahwah, NJ: Erlbaum.

Cosentino de Cohen, C., & Clewell, B. C. (2007). *Putting English language learners on the educational map: The No Child Left Behind Act implemented.* Washington: Urban Institute.

Couch, P. (1996). Interacting with literature via student-produced videos. In V. Whiteson (Ed.), *New ways of using drama and literature in language teaching* (pp. 106–108). Alexandria, VA: Teachers of English to Speakers of Other Languages.

Coutinho, M. J., & Oswald, D. P. (2007). *Disproportionate representation of culturally and linguistically diverse students in special education: Measuring the problem,* National Center for Culturally Responsive Educational Systems. Retrieved July 15, 2011 from http://www.niusileadscape.org/lc/Record/154?search_query=Disproportionate%20Representation

Crawford, L. (1993). *Language and literacy learning in multicultural classrooms.* Boston: Allyn & Bacon.

Cruz, N. (1990). A challenge to the notion of service. In J. C. Kendell (Ed.), *Combining service and learning: A resource book for community and public service* (vol. 1, pp. 321–323).

Raleigh, NC: National Society for Internships and Experiential Education.

Csikszentmihalyi, M. (1996). *Creativity: Flow and the discovery of invention.* New York: HarperCollins.

Cummins, J. (1979). Linguistic interdependence and the educational development of bilingual children. *Review of Education Research, 49,* 222–251.

Cummins, J. (1981a). Age on arrival and immigrant second language learning in Canada: A reassessment. *Applied Linguistics, 2*(2), 132–149.

Cummins, J. (1981b). The role of primary language development in promoting educational success for language minority students. In *Schooling and language minority students: A theoretical framework.* Sacramento: California State Department of Education.

Cummins, J. (1984). *Bilingualism and special education: Issues in assessment and pedagogy.* San Diego: College-Hill.

Cummins, J. (1989). *Empowering minority students.* Sacramento: California Association for Bilingual Education.

Cummins, J. (1996). *Negotiating identities: Education for empowerment in a diverse society.* Los Angeles: California Association for Bilingual Education.

Cummins, J. (2000a). Beyond adversarial discourse: Searching for common ground in the education of bilingual students. In P. McLaren & C. J. Ovando (Eds.), *The politics of multiculturalism and bilingual education* (pp. 126–147). Boston: McGraw-Hill.

Cummins, J. (2000b). Negotiating intercultural identities in the multilingual classroom. *CATESOL Journal, 12*(1), 163–178.

Cummins, J., Brown, K., & Sayers, D. (2007). *Literacy, technology, and diversity: Teaching for success in changing times.* Boston: Pearson.

Cunningham, C. A., & Billingsley, M. (2006). *Curriculum webs: Weaving the web into teaching and learning.* Boston: Pearson.

D'Arcangelo, M. (1998). The brains behind brain. *Educational Leadership, 56*(3), 68–71.

Datesman, M. K., Crandall, J., & Kearny, E. N. (1997). *The American ways.* Upper Saddle River, NJ: Prentice Hall Regents.

Davies, A., Cameron, C., Politano, C., & Gregory, K. (1992). *Together is better: Collaborative assessment, evaluation, and reporting.* Winnipeg, Can.: Peguis.

Day, E.M. (2002). *Identity and the young English learner.* Clevedon, Eng: Multilingual Matters.

Day, F. A. (1994). *Multicultural voices in contemporary literature: A resource for teachers.* Portsmouth, NH: Heinemann.

Day, F. A. (1997). *Latina and Latino voices in literature for children and teenagers.* Portsmouth, NH: Heinemann.

Day, F. A. (2003). *Latina and Latino voices in literature: Lives and works.* Westport, CT: Greenwood.

DeCapua, A., Marshall, H. W. (2011). *Breaking new ground: Teaching students with limited or interrupted formal education in U. S. secondary schools.* Ann Arbor: University of Michigan Press.

DeCapua, A., Smathers, W., & Tang, L. F. (2009). *Meeting the needs of students with limited or interrupted schooling.* Ann Arbor: University of Michigan Press.

Deer, J. (2001). ESP in Colombia. *English for Specific Purposes News, 9*(2), 4, 8–9.

Dehaene, S. (2009). *Reading in the brain.* New York: Viking.

Delgado-Gaitan, C. (1994). Sociocultural change through literacy: Toward the empowerment of families. In B. M. Ferdman, R-M. Weber, & A. G. Ramírez (Eds.), *Literacy across languages and cultures* (pp. 143–169). Albany: SUNY Press.

Delgado-Gaitan, C. (2006). *Building culturally responsive classrooms.* Thousand Oaks, CA: Corwin.

Delgado-Gaitan, C., & Trueba, H. (1991). *Crossing cultural borders: Education for immigrant families in America.* London: Falmer Press.

De Mille, R. (1976). *Put your mother on the ceiling: Children's imagination games.* New York: Penguin Books.

Derman-Sparks, L., & Anti-Bias Curriculum Task Force. (1988). *Anti-bias curriculum: Tools for empowering young children.* Washington, DC: National Association for the Education of Young Children.

Dewey, J. (1933). *How we think: A restatement of the relation of reflective thinking to the educative process.* Boston: D.C. Heath.

Dewey, J. (1956). *The child and the curriculum and the school and society* (comb. ed.). Chicago: University of Chicago Press.

Dewey, J. (1916/1963). *Experience and education.* New York: Collier.

Díaz-Maggioli, G. H. (1996) Never-ending stories. In V. Whiteson (Ed.), *New ways of using drama and literature in language teaching* (pp. 21–22). Alexandria, VA: Teachers of English to Speakers of Other Languages.

Díaz-Rico, L. (1993). From monocultural to multicultural teaching in an inner-city middle school. In A. Woolfolk (Ed.), *Readings and cases in educational psychology* (pp. 272–279). Boston: Allyn & Bacon.

Díaz-Rico, L. T. (1994). *Teacher education of instructional conversants for multicultural contexts.* Presentation, American Educational Research Association annual meeting, New Orleans, LA.

Díaz-Rico, L. T. (1998). Towards a just society: Recalibrating multicultural teachers. In R. Chávez Chávez & J. O'Donnell, (Eds.), *Speaking the unpleasant: The politics of (non)engagement in the multicultural terrain.* Albany: SUNY Press.

Díaz-Rico, L. T. (1999a). *Critical discourse analysis applied to second language acquisition.* Presentation, annual conference, Teachers of English to Speakers of Other Languages, New York, NY.

Díaz-Rico, L. T. (1999b). The postmodern shift: A real revolution in ESOL teaching. *TESOL Matters, 9*(1), 20.

Díaz-Rico, L. T. (2000). Intercultural communication in teacher education: The knowledge base for CLAD teacher credential programs. *CATESOL Journal, 12*(1), 145–161.

Díaz-Rico, L. T. (2001a, February). *Improving MATESOL students' academic writing.* Presentation, annual conference, Teachers of English to Speakers of Other Languages, St. Louis, MO.

Díaz-Rico, L. T. (2001b, February). *Visual imaginary dramatic arts.* Presentation, annual conference, Teachers of English to Speakers of Other Languages, St. Louis, MO.

Díaz-Rico, L. T., & Weed, K. (2010). *The crosscultural, language, and academic development handbook* (4th ed.). Boston: Allyn & Bacon.

Díaz-Rico, L. T., & Young, L. H. (1998). Promoting oral language development and cultural socialization for international university students. *Phi Beta Delta International Review, 8,* 11–26.

Díez, A., & Marchis, L. (2001). "El jardín curandero" (thematic unit). Unpublished manuscript, California State University, San Bernardino.

Di Pietro, R. J. (1987). *Strategic interaction: Learning languages through scenarios.* Cambridge: Cambridge University Press.

Doggett, G. (1986). *Eight approaches to language teaching.* Washington, DC: Center for Applied Linguistics/ERIC Clearinghouse on Languages and Linguistics.

Dolson, D. (1985). The effects of Spanish home language use on the scholastic performance of Hispanic pupils. *Journal of Multilingual and Multicultural Development, 6,* 135–156.

Doutrich, D. (2000). Cultural fluency, marginality, and the sense of self. In H. Riggenbach (Ed.), *Perspectives on fluency* (pp. 141–159). Ann Arbor: University of Michigan Press.

Driscoll, A., Holland, B., Gelmon, S., & Kerrigan, S. (1996). An assessment model for service-learning: Comprehensive case studies of impact on faculty, students, community, and institution. *Michigan Journal of Community Service Learning, 3,* 66–71.

Dudley-Marling, C., & Searle, D. (1991). *When students have time to talk.* Portsmouth, NH: Heinemann.

Dunkel, P., & Lim, P. L. (1994). *Intermediate listening comprehension: Understanding and recalling spoken English.* Boston: Heinle & Heinle.

Dunkel, P. A., Pialorsi, F., & Kozyrev, J. (1996). *Advanced listening comprehension: Developing aural and notetaking skills.* Boston: Heinle & Heinle.

Dutton, B., & Olin, C. (1995). *Myths and legends of the Indians of the Southwest.* Santa Barbara, CA: Bellerophon Books.

Echevarría, J., & Graves, A. (2011). *Sheltered content instruction: Teaching English learners with diverse abilities* (4th ed.). Boston: Pearson.

Echevarria, J., Vogt, M. E., & Short, D. (2007). *Making content comprehensible for English language learners: The SIOP model* (3rd ed.). Boston: Allyn & Bacon.

Edelman, G. (1992). *Bright air, brilliant fire: On the matter of the mind.* New York: Basic Books.

Edelsky, C. (1986). *Writing in a bilingual program: Habia una vez.* Norwood, NJ: Ablex.

Edelsky, C. (1989). Bilingual children's writing: Fact and fiction. In D. Johnson & D. H. Roen (Eds.), *Richness in writing* (pp. 165–176). New York: Longman.

Edwards, C. (1998). Partner, nurturer, and guide: The role of the teacher. In C. Edwards, L. Gandini, & G. Forman (Eds.), *The hundred languages of children: The Reggio Emilia approach—advanced reflections* (2nd ed., pp. 179–198). Norwood, NJ: Ablex.

Edwards, C., Bandini, L., & Forman, G. (1998). *The hundred language of children* (2nd ed.). Greenwich, CT: Ablex.

Edwards, K. M. (2000). *Everyone's guide to successful project planning: Tools for youth. Student guide.* Portland, OR: Northwest Regional Educational Laboratory.

Egbert, J. (2005). *Bridge to the classroom: ESL cases for teacher exploration* (Vol. 1, Elementary school). Alexandria, VA: Teachers of English to Speakers of Other Languages.

Egbert, J., & Petrie, G. M. (2005). *Bridge to the classroom: ESL cases for teacher exploration* (Vol. 1, Adult contexts). Alexandria, VA: Teaching English to Speakers of Other Languages.

Ellis, S. S., & Whalen, S. F. (1992). Keys to cooperative learning: 35 ways to keep kids responsible, challenged, and most of all, cooperative. *Instructor, 101*(6), 34–37.

Ellmann, R. (Ed.). (1988). *The Norton anthology of modern poetry.* New York: W. W. Norton.

Elmi, J., Folarin, M., Moalin, A., & Rees, S. (2002). From isolation to education: Working with Somali families in South London. In E. Auerbach (Ed.), *Community partnerships* (pp. 79–90). Alexandria, VA: Teachers of English to Speakers of Other Languages.

Enk, J., & Hendricks, M. (1984). *Shortcuts for teachers.* Carthage, IL: Fearon.

Epstein, J. L. (1995). School/family/community partnerships: Caring for the children we share. *Phi Delta Kappan, 76*(9), 701–712.

Erikson, E. (1963). *Childhood and society* (2nd ed.). New York: Norton.

Erikson, E. (1980). *Identity and the life cycle* (2nd ed.). New York: Norton.

Ernst-Slavit, G., & Wenger, K. J. (1998). Using creative drama in the elementary ESL classroom. *TESOL Journal, 7*(4), 30–33.

Ewald, F. (1992). Summary of discussions. In T. J. Armstrong (Ed. and trans.), *Michel Foucault philosopher* (p. 334). New York: Harvester Wheatsheaf.

Eyler, J., & Giles, D. E. (1999). *Where's the learning in service learning?* San Francisco: Jossey-Bass.

Eyler, J., Giles, D. E., & Gray, C. J. (1999). *Research at a glance: What we know about the effects of service-learning on students, faculty, institutions, and communities.* Knoxville, TN: Vanderbilt University.

Eyring, J. (2001). Experiential and negotiated language learning. In M. Celce-Murica (Ed.), *Teaching English as a second or foreign language* (3rd ed., pp. 333–344). Boston: Heinle & Heinle.

Fairclough, N. (1989). *Language and power.* London: Longman.

Fairclough, N. (1992). *Discourse and social change.* Cambridge: Polity Press.

Faltis, C. (2001). *Joinfostering* (3rd ed.). Upper Saddle River, NJ: Prentice-Hall.

Fantini, A. E. (2009). Identifying and using language-culture resources. *Essential Teacher, 6*(3–4), 14–15.

Farrell, T. S. C. (2006). *Succeeding with English language learners.* Thousand Oaks, CA: Corwin.

Feder, C. W. (1992). *Brain quest.* New York: Workman.

Feuerstein, T., & Schcolnik, M. (1995). *Enhancing reading comprehension in the language learning classroom.* San Francisco: Alta.

Finders, M. J., & Hynds, S. (2007). *Language arts and literacy in the middle grades: Planning, teaching, and assessing learning.* Upper Saddle River, NJ: Pearson.

Fischer, B., & Fischer, L. (1979). Styles in teaching and learning. *Educational Leadership, 36*(4), 245–251.

Flavell, J. H. (1979). Metacognition and cognitive monitoring: A new area of cognitive developmental inquiry. *American Psychologist, 34*(10), 906–911.

Flavell, J. H. (1985). *Cognitive development* (2nd ed.). Englewood Cliffs, NJ: Prentice-Hall.

Flood, J., Lapp, D., Tinajero, J., & Hurley, S. (1997). Literacy instruction for students acquiring English: Moving beyond the immersion debate. *The Reading Teacher, 50*(4), 356–358.

Flower, L. (1994). *The construction of negotiated meaning: A social cognitive theory of writing.* Carbondale: Southern Illinois University Press.

Flowerdew, J., & Miller, L. (2005). *Second language listening: Theory and practice.* Cambridge: Cambridge University Press.

Fogarty, R., Perkins, D., & Barell, J. (1992). *How to teach for transfer.* Arlington Heights, IL: Skylight.

Folse, K. (1994). Secret word. In P. Nation (Ed.), *New ways in teaching vocabulary* (pp. 67–68). Alexandria, VA: Teachers of English to Speakers of Other Languages.

Folse, K. S. (1996). *Discussion starters.* Ann Arbor: University of Michigan Press.

Ford, D. Y. (1998). The underrepresentation of minority students in gifted education: Problems and promises in recruitment and retention. *The Journal of Special Education, 32*(1), 4–14.

Forman, G., & Fyfe, B. (1998). Negotiated learning through design, documentation, and discourse. In C. Edwards, L. Gandini, & G. Forman (Eds.), *The hundred languages of children: The Reggio Emilia approach—advanced reflections* (2nd ed., pp. 239–260). Norwood, NJ: Ablex.

Forman, G., Langley, J., Oh, M., & Wrisley, L. (1998). The city in the snow: Applying the multisymbolic approach in Massachusetts. In C. Edwards, L. Gandini, & G. Forman (Eds.), *The hundred languages of children: The Reggio Emilia approach—advanced reflections* (2nd ed., pp. 359–374). Norwood, NJ: Ablex.

Foucault, M. (1973). *The birth of the clinic: An archeology of medical perception.* New York: Vintage Books.

Foucault, M. (1979). *Discipline and punish: The birth of the prison.* New York: Vintage Books.

Foucault, M. (1980). *Power/knowledge: Selected interviews and other writings 1971–1977.* New York: Pantheon Books.

Foucault, M. (1984). The order of discourse. In M. Shapiro (Ed.), *Language and politics* (pp. 108–138). New York: New York University Press.

Foucault, M. (1988). Technologies of the self. In L. H. Martin, H. Gutman, & P. H. Hutton (Eds.), *Technologies of the self.* Amherst: University of Massachusetts Press.

Fredericks, A. D., & Rasinski, T. V. (1990). Increasing parental involvement: A key to student achievement. *The Reading Teacher, 43*(6), 424–425.

Fredericks-Malone, C., & Gadbois, N. J. (2005/2006). Assessment, emotional scaffolding, and technology: Powerful allies in the K–12 world language classroom. *The NECTFL Review, 57*(2), 20–29.

Freeman, Y., & Freeman, D. (1998). *ESL/EFL teaching: Principles for practice.* Portsmouth, NH: Heinemann.

Freire, P. (1970). *Pedagogy of the oppressed* (Trans. M. B. Ramos). New York: Continuum.

Freire, P. (1973). By learning they can teach. *Convergence, 6*(1), 78–84.

Freire, P. (1987). Letter to North American teachers. In I. Shor (Ed.), *Freire for the classroom* (pp. 211–214). Portsmouth, NH: Boynton/Cook.

Freire, P. (1994). *Pedagogy of hope* (Trans. R. R. Barr). New York: Continuum.

Freire, P. (1998). *Teachers as cultural workers* (Trans. D. Macedo, D. Koike, & A. Oliveira). Boulder, CO: Westview Press.

Frey, N., & Fisher, D. (2007). *Reading for information in the elementary school: Content literacy strategies to build comprehension.* Upper Saddle River, NJ: Pearson.

Fried-Booth, D. L. (1997). *Project work* (8th ed.). Oxford: Oxford University Press.

Friend, M., & Bursuck, W. D. (2011). *Including students with special needs: A practical guide for classroom teachers.* Boston: Allyn & Bacon.

Furco, A. (1996). Service-learning: A balanced approach to experiential education. In Corporation for National Service (Eds.), *Expanding boundaries: Serving and learning.* Washington, DC: Author.

Furey, P. (1986). A framework for cross-cultural analysis of teaching methods. In P. Byrd (Ed.), *Teaching across cultures in the university ESL program* (pp. 15–29). Washington, DC: National Association of Foreign Student Advisors.

Gaab, C. (2011). Multistory construction. *Language Magazine, 10*(8), 16–22.

Galura, J., Howard, J., Waterhouse, D., & Ross, R. (1995). *Praxis III: Voices in dialogue.* Ann Arbor, MI: Office of Community Service Learning.

Gambrell, L. B., & Bales, R. J. (1986). Mental imagery and the comprehension-monitoring performance of fourth- and fifth-grade poor readers. *Reading Research Quarterly, 21,* 454–464.

Gardner, H. (1983). *Frames of mind: The theory of multiple intelligences.* New York: Basic Books.

Gardner, H. (1990). Multiple intelligences: Implications for art and creativity. In W. Moody (Ed.), *Artistic intelligence: Implications for education* (ch. 2). New York: Teachers College Press.

Gardner, H. (1993). *Multiple intelligences: The theory in practice*. New York: Basic Books.

Gardner, J. N. (1997). Keys to success. In J. N. Gardner & A. J. Jewler (Eds.), *Your college experience: Strategies for success* (pp. 1–22). Albany, NY: Wadsworth.

Gardner, J. N., & Jewell, A. J. (Eds.). (1997). *Your college experience: Strategies for success* (pp. 1–22). Albany, NY: Wadsworth.

Gardner, R., & Lambert, W. (1972). *Attitudes and motivation in second language learning*. Rowley, MA: Newbury House.

Garmston, R. (1987). How administrators support peer coaching. *Educational Leadership, 44*(5), 18–28.

Garmston, R., Linder, C., & Whitaker, J. (1993). Reflections on cognitive coaching. *Educational Leadership, 51*(2), 57–61.

Garrison, D. (1990). Inductive strategies for teaching Spanish–English cognates. *Hispania, 73*(2), 508–512.

Gay, G. (2002). Preparing for culturally responsive teaching. *Journal of Teacher Education, 55*(2), 106–116.

Gee, J. (1990). *Social linguistics and literacies: Ideology in discourses*. New York: Falmer Press.

Gee, J. (1992). *The social mind: Language, ideology, and social practice*. New York: Bergin & Garvey.

Gee, J. (1996). *Social linguistics and literacies: Ideology in discourses* (2nd ed.). London: Taylor & Francis.

Gee, J. (2000). The New Literacy Studies: From "socially situated" to the work of the social. In D. Barton, M. Hamilton, & R. Ivanic (Eds.), *Situated literacies* (pp. 180–196). London: Routledge.

Gee, J. P. (2007). *Good video games and good learning: Collected essays on video games, learning and literacy*. New York: Peter Lang.

Genishi, C. (1988). Children's language: Learning words from experience. *Young Children, 44*(1), 16–23.

Gerson, M. (2008). Don't let texting get you :-(. *The Washington Post*, April 24, A19.

Gibbs, N. (2007). Parents behaving badly. In F. Schultz (Ed.), *Annual editions 10/08: Education* (pp. 15–20). Dubuque, IA: McGraw Hill Contemporary Learning Series.

Gillett, P. (1989). *Cambodian refugees: An introduction to their history and culture*. Available from New Faces of Liberty/SFSC, P. O. Box 5646, San Francisco, CA 94101.

Giromini, E. (2001, March). *PBL and the urban experience*. Presentation, the Ninth Annual Conference on Project-Based Learning, San Francisco.

Giroux, H. (1991). Modernism, postmodernism, and feminism: Rethinking the boundaries of educational discourse. In H. Giroux (Ed.), *Postmodernism, feminism, and cultural politics: Redrawing educational boundaries* (pp. 1–59). New York: SUNY Press.

Giroux, H., & McLaren, P. (1986). Teacher education and the politics of engagement: The case for democratic schooling. *Harvard Educational Review, 56*(3), 213–238.

Glaser, S., & Brown, C. (1993). *Portfolios and beyond: Collaborative assessment in reading and writing*. Norwood, MA: Christopher-Gordon.

Glass, R. D. (2001). On Paulo Freire's philosophy of praxis and the foundations of liberation education. *Educational Researcher, 30*(2), 15–25.

Goldenberg, C. (1990). Research directions: Beginning literacy instruction for Spanish-speaking children. *Language Arts, 67*(6), 590–597.

Goldenberg, C. (1992). *Let's talk*. Videotape, University of California, Los Angeles.

Goldenberg, C., & Gallimore, R. (1991). Changing teaching takes more than a one-shot workshop. *Educational Leadership, 49*(3), 69–72.

Goldstein, B. (2008). *Working with images: A resource book for the language classroom.* Cambridge, Eng.: Cambridge University Press.

Goldstein, L. M., & Conrad, S. M. (1990). Student input and negotiation of meaning in ESL writing conferences. *TESOL Quarterly, 24,* 441–460.

Goleman, D. (1998). *Working with emotional intelligence.* New York: Bantam Books.

Gombert, J. E. (1992). *Metalinguistic development.* Chicago: University of Chicago Press.

González, N., Moll, L., & Amanti, C, (2005). *Funds of knowledge theorizing practices in households, communities, and classrooms.* Oxford: Taylor and Francis.

González, V., Brusca-Vega, R., & Yawkey, T. (1996). *Assessment and instruction of culturally and linguistically diverse students with or at-risk of learning problems: From research to practice.* Boston: Allyn & Bacon.

Goodale, M. (1987). *The language of meetings.* Hove, UK: Language Teaching Publications.

Goodwin, S. P. (2010a). Facing autism: A growing challenge for our school system. *California Educator, 15*(3), 8–14.

Goodwin, S. P. (2010b). The original *Glee* club: What makes a school's choir work. *California Educator, 15*(9), 8–11.

Gopaul-McNicol, S., & Thomas-Presswood, T. (1998). *Working with linguistically and culturally different children.* Boston: Allyn & Bacon.

Gopnik, A. (2010). Mind reading. *New York Times Review of Books,* January 3, 15.

Gordon, T. (1992). "We don't want to come to ESL": Teaching ESL to fluent, low-achieving students. *TESOL Journal, 2*(1), 30–32.

GOSERV (California Governor's Office on Service and Volunteerism). (2003). Available online: www.goserv.ca.gov.

Gottlieb, J., Alter, M., Gottlieb, B., & Wishner, J. (1994). Special education in urban America: It's not justifiable for many. *Journal of Special Education, 27*(4), 453–465.

Gottlieb, M. (1995). Nurturing student learning through portfolios. *TESOL Journal, 5*(1), 12– 14.

Gottlieb, M. (2006). *Assessing English language learners.* Thousand Oaks, CA: Corwin.

Graham, C. (1988). *Jazz chant fairy tales.* New York: Oxford University Press.

Gramsci, A. (1971). *Selections from prison notebooks.* (Ed. and trans., Q. Hoare & G. Smith.) New York: International Publishers.

Grant, C. (1995). *Educating for diversity: An anthology of multicultural voices.* Boston: Allyn & Bacon.

Grasha, A. F. (1990). Using traditional versus naturalistic approaches to assess learning styles in college teaching. *Journal on Excellence in College Teaching, 1,* 23–38.

Grasha, A. F. (1996). *Your teaching style.* Pittsburgh, PA: International Alliance of Teacher Scholars.

Greene, M. (1988). *The dialectic of freedom.* New York: Teachers College Press.

Gregorc, A. (1982). *An adult's guide to style.* Maynard, MA: Gabriel Systems.

Gregory, G. H., & Kuzmich, L. (2005). *Differentiated literacy strategies for student growth and achievement in grades 7–12.* Thousand Oaks, CA: Corwin.

Grenough, M. (1998). *Sing it! Learn English through song,* Levels 1–6, New York: McGraw-Hill.

Grosz, E. (1990). *Jacques Lacan: A feminist introduction.* London: Routledge.

Groves, M. (2000, January 26). Vast majority of state's schools lag in new index. *Los Angeles Times,* A1, A14.

Groves, M. (2001, August 20). "Direct instruction" paying off. *Los Angeles Times,* B1, B8.

Gunning, T. G. (2009). *Creating literacy instruction for all students* (7th ed.). Boston: Allyn & Bacon.

Guthrie, W. (1998). *This land is your land.* Boston: Little, Brown.

Gutierrez, K. (1994). How talk, context, and script shape contexts for learning: A cross-case comparison of journal sharing. *Linguistics and Education, 5,* 335–365.

Gutierrez, K. (1995). Unpacking academic discourse. *Discourse Processes, 19,* 21–37.

Gutierrez, K., & Larson, J. (1994). Language borders: Recitation as hegemonic discourse. *International Journal of Educational Reform, 3,* 22–36.

Hadaway, N. L., Vardell, S. M., & Young, T. A. (2002). *Literature-based instruction with English language learners, K–12.* Boston: Allyn & Bacon.

Hakuta, K., Butler, Y. G., & Witt, D. (2000). *How long does it take English learners to attain proficiency?* Santa Barbara: University of California Linguistic Minority Research Institute Policy Report 2000–1.

Haley, M. H. (2010). *Brain-compatible differentiated instruction for English language learners.* Boston: Allyn & Bacon.

Halliday, M. A. K. (1978). *Language as a social semiotic.* Baltimore: University Park Press.

Hamayan, E. (1994). Language development of low-literacy students. In F. Genesee (Ed.), *Educating second language children.* Cambridge: Cambridge University Press.

Hamers, J. F., & Blanc, M. A. H. (1989). *Bilinguality and bilingualism.* Cambridge: Cambridge University Press.

Handa, C. (2001). Digital literacy and rhetoric: A selected bibliography. *Computers and Composition, 18,* 195–202.

Hansen, J. W. (2000). Parables of technological literacy. *Journal of Engineering Technology, 17*(2), 29–31.

Harel, Y. (1992). Teacher talk in the cooperative learning classroom. In C. Kessler (Ed.), *Cooperative language learning* (pp. 153–162). Englewood Cliffs, NJ: Prentice-Hall.

Harklau, L., Losey, K. M., & Siegal, M. (Eds.). (1999). *Generation 1.5 meets college composition: Issues in the teaching of writing to U.S.-educated learners of ESL.* Mahwah, NJ: Erlbaum.

Harris, P. (2006, March). NCTE members seek to influence NCLB reauthorization. *The Council Chronicle, 15,* 1, 4.

Harris, V. (1997). *Teaching multicultural literature in grades K–8.* Norwood, MA: Christopher-Gordon.

Hart, L. (1983). *Human brain, human learning.* New York: Longman.

Haycock, K. (2001). Closing the achievement gap. *Educational Leadership, 58*(6), 6–11.

Heald-Taylor, B. G. (1987). Big books. In D. J. Watson (Ed.), *Ideas and insights: Language arts in the elementary school* (p. 85). Urbana, IL: National Council of Teachers of English.

Heath, S. (1983). *Ways with words.* Cambridge: Cambridge University Press.

Heilman, A. W. (2005). *Phonics in proper perspective* (10th ed.). Upper Saddle River, NJ: Merrill Prentice Hall.

Heinle & Heinle. (2002a). *Launch into reading, Level I: Teacher's resource book.* Boston: Author.

Heinle & Heinle. (2002b). *Launch into reading, Level I: Assessment guide.* Boston: Author.

Hernández, H. (2001). *Multicultural education: A teacher's guide to linking context, process, and content.* Upper Saddle River, NJ: Merrill/Prentice-Hall.

Herrera, S. G., & Murry, K. G. (2011). *Mastering ESL and bilingual methods.* Boston: Pearson.

Herrera, S. G., Murry, K. G., & Cabral, R. M. (2007). *Assessment accommodations for classroom teachers of culturally and linguistically diverse students.* Boston: Pearson.

Herring, S. (1996). *Computer-mediated communication: Linguistic, social, and cross-cultural perspectives*. Amsterdam: John Benjamins Publishing.

Hess, N. (1991). *Headstarts*. Essex, Eng: Longman.

Hetherton, G. (1998). Choral chant. In V. Whiteson (Ed.), *New ways of using drama and literature in language teaching* (pp. 144–145). Alexandria, VA: Teachers of English to Speakers of Other Languages.

Hetherton, G. (1999). Headline news. In N. Shameem & M. Tickoo (Eds.), *New ways in using communicative games* (pp. 67–68). Alexandria, VA: Teachers of English to Speakers of Other Languages.

Hicks, T. (2009). *The digital writing workshop*. Portsmouth, NH: Heinemann.

Hill, J. (2000). Revising priorities: From grammatical failure to collocational success. In M. Lewis (Ed.), *Teaching collocation* (pp. 47–69). Hove, UK: Language Teaching Publications.

Hinton, L., & Montijo, Y. (1994). Living California Indian languages. In L. Hinton (Ed.), *Flutes of fire: Essays on California Indian languages* (pp. 21–33). Berkeley, CA: Heyday Books.

Hodgkinson, H. L. (1998). Demographics of diversity for the 21st century. *Education Digest, 64*(1), 4–7.

Holt, D., Chips, B., & Wallace, D. (1992, summer). *Cooperative learning in the secondary school: Maximizing language acquisition, academic development, and social development*. Washington, DC: National Clearinghouse for Bilingual Education.

Hones, D. F. (1999). U.S. justice? Critical pedagogy and the case of Mumia Abu-Jamal. *TESOL Journal, 8*(4), 27–33.

hooks, b. (1989). *Talking back: Thinking feminist, thinking black*. Boston: South End Press.

hooks, b. (1993). *Sisters of the yam: Black women and self-discovery*. Boston: South End Press.

Hornsby, D., Sukarna, D., & Parry, J. (1986). *Read on: A conference approach to reading*. Portsmouth, NH: Heinemann.

Horowitz, E. (1977). *Words come in families*. New York: Hart.

Hotz, R. L. (2001, July 2). Byte by byte, a map of the brain. *Los Angeles Times*, A12.

Howard, E. H., & Sugarman, J. (2007). *Realizing the vision of two-way immersion: Fostering effective programs and classrooms*. Washington, DC: Center for Applied Linguistics.

Howard, J. (1993). *Praxis I: A faculty casebook on community service*. Ann Arbor, MI: Office of Community Service Learning.

Howard, M. (2009). *RTI from all sides*. Portsmouth, NH: Heinemann.

Hruska-Riechmann, S., & Grasha, A. F. (1982). The Grasha-Riechmann Student Learning Scales: Research findings and applications. In J. Keefe (Ed.), *Student learning styles and brain behavior*. Reston, VA: NASSP.

H. S. 555 Newcomers High School: Academy For New Americans. Accessed April 27, 2011, from http://insideschools.org/index12.php?fs=1267

Hucko, B. (1996). *A rainbow at night: The world in word and pictures by Navajo children*. San Francisco: Chronicle Books.

Huizenga, J., & Thomas-Ruzic, M. (1992). *All talk: Problem solving for new students of English*. Boston: Heinle & Heinle.

Humphries, R. (1998). Rhyme time. In V. Whiteson (Ed.), *New ways of using drama and literature in language teaching* (pp. 73–74). Alexandria, VA: Teachers of English to Speakers of Other Languages.

Hunter, J. (1997). Multiple perceptions: Social identity in a multilingual elementary classroom. *TESOL Quarterly, 31*(3), 349–369).

Hymes, D. (1972). On communicative competence. In J. Pride & J. Holmes (Eds.), *Sociolinguistics* (pp. 269–293). Harmondsworth, UK: Penguin.

Hymes, D. (1974). *Foundations of sociolinguistics*. Philadelphia: University of Pennsylvania Press.

Iberri-Shea, G. (2009). Using public speaking tasks in English language teaching. *English Teaching Forum, 47*(2), 18–23, 35–36.

Illinois State Board of Education (2002). *Serving English language learners with disabilities: A resource manual for Illinois educators.* Springfield, IL: Author. Accessed July 3, 2007 from www.isbe.net/bilingual/htmls/bilsp.htm.

Irujo, S. (Ed.). (2001). *Integrating the ESL standards into classroom practice: Grades 6–8.* Alexandria, VA: Teachers of English to Speakers of Other Languages.

Jabr, Z. (2010). *Student orientation series (SOS): English language learners.* Upper Saddle River, NJ: Pearson.

Jackson, F. M. (1993). Evaluating service learning. In Campus Compact (Ed.), *Rethinking tradition: Integrating service with academic study on college campuses* (pp. 129–135). Providence, RI: Author.

Jacobson, R. (1998). Teachers improving learning using metacognition with self-monitoring learning strategies. *Education, 118*(4), 579–589.

Jacoby, B., & Associates (1996). *Service learning in higher education: Concepts and practices.* San Francisco: Jossey-Bass.

James, M. (1996). Enrichment packets. In P. Nation (Ed.), *New ways in teaching vocabulary* (pp. 22–23). Alexandria, VA: Teachers of English to Speakers of Other Languages.

Jennings, P. A., & Greenberg, M. T. (2009). The prosocial classroom: Teacher social and emotional competence in relation to student and classroom outcomes. *Review of Educational Research, 79*(1), 491–525.

Jensen, E. (1998). *Teaching with the brain in mind.* Alexandria, VA: Association for Supervision and Curriculum Development.

Jesness, J. (2004). *Teaching English language learners K–12.* Thousand Oaks, CA: Corwin.

Jo, P. (1999). Unpublished master's thesis, California State University, San Bernardino.

Johns, A. M. (2001). An interdisciplinary, inter-institutional, learning communities program: Student involvement and student success. In I. Leki (Ed.), *Academic writing programs* (pp. 61–72). Alexandria, VA: Teachers of English to Speakers of Other Languages.

Johns, K. (1992). Mainstreaming language minority students through cooperative grouping. *The Journal of Educational Issues of Language Minority Students, 11.* Boise, ID: Boise State University Press.

Johns, K., & Espinoza, C. (1992). *Mainstreaming language minority children in reading and writing* (Fastback #340). Bloomington, IN: Phi Delta Kappa Educational Foundation.

Johnson, B. (1996). *The performance assessment handbook: Volume 1, portfolios and Socratic seminars.* Larchmont, NY: Eye on Education.

Johnson, D., Johnson, R., & Smith, K. A. (1991). *Cooperative learning: Increasing instructional productivity.* Washington, DC: George Washington University.

Johnson, D. W., & Johnson, R. (1994). Cooperative learning in second language classes. *The Language Teacher, 18,* 4–7.

Johnson, D. W., Johnson, R., & Holubec, E. (1993). *Circles of learning: Cooperation in the classroom.* (3rd ed.). Edina, MN: Interaction Book Company.

Johnson, K. E. (1996). Portfolio assessment in second language teacher education. *TESOL Journal, 6*(2), 11–14.

Jonassen, D. H. (2006). *Modeling with technology: Mindtools for conceptual change* (3rd ed.). Upper Saddle River, NJ: Pearson/Merrill/Prentice Hall.

Jones, L. (2007). *The student-centered classroom.* New York: Cambridge University Press.

Jones, P. (1991). What are dialogue journals? In J. K. Peyton & J. Staton (Eds.), *Writing our lives: Reflections on dialogue journal writing with adults learning English* (pp. 3–10). Englewood Cliffs, NJ: Prentice Hall Regents.

Jordan, C., Tharp, R., & Baird-Vogt, L. (1992). "Just open the door": Cultural compatibility and classroom rapport. In M. Saravia-Shore & Arvizu, S. (Eds.), *Cross-cultural literacy* (pp. 3–18). New York: Garland.

Jordan, E. A., & Porath, M. J. (2006). *Educational psychology: A problem-based approach.* Boston: Pearson.

Jourdain, R. (1998). *Music, the brain, and ecstasy: How music captures our imagination.* New York: Avon Books.

Jussim, L. (1986). Self-fulfilling prophecies: A theoretical and integrative review. *Psychological Review, 93,* 429–445.

Justice, P. W. (2001). *Relevant linguistics.* Stanford, CA: CSLI Publications.

Kagan, S. (1998). *Cooperative learning smart card.* Kagan Cooperative Learning Available online: kaganonline.com.

Kagan, S. (1999). *Teambuilding smart card.* Kagan Cooperative Learning. Available online: kagan online.com.

Kamhi-Stein, L. D. (2000). Looking to the future of TESOL teacher education: Web-based bulletin board discussions in a methods course. *TESOL Quarterly, 34*(3), 423–455.

Kang, H.-W., Kuehn, P., & Herrell, A. (1996). The Hmong literacy project: Parents working to preserve the past and ensure the future. *Journal of Educational Issues of Language Minority Students, 16.* Available online www.ncela.gwu.edu/pubs/nabe/brj/v18/18_34 _kang.htm.

Kaplan, R. B. (2001). The language of policy and the policy of language. *Applied Linguistics Forum, 21*(1), 1, 9–11.

Kasser, C., & Silverman, A. (1994). *Stories we brought with us.* Englewood Cliffs, NJ: Prentice-Hall.

Katz, L. G., & Chard, S. C. (1989). *Engaging children's minds: The project approach.* Norwood, NJ: Ablex.

Kaye, C. B. (2004). *The complete guide to service learning.* Minneapolis, MN: Free Spirit Press.

Kaye, H. S. (1997). Education of children with disabilities. *Disability Statistics Abstracts, 19.* San Francisco: Disability Statistics Center.

Kealey, J., & Inness, D. (1997). *Shenanigames: Grammar focused interactive ESL/EFL activities and games.* Brattleboro, VT: Pro Lingua.

Keefe, M. W. (1987). *Learning style theory and practice.* Reston, VA: National Association of Secondary School Principals.

Keirsey, D. (1998). *Please understand me II.* Del Mar, CA: Prometheus Nemesis Book Co.

Keith, N. Z. (1997). Doing service projects in urban settings. In A. S. Waterman (Ed.), *Service learning: Applications from the research* (pp. 127–149). Mahwah, NJ: Lawrence Erlbaum.

Kenna, P., & Lacy, S. (1994). *Business Taiwan: A practical guide to understanding Taiwan's business culture.* Lincolnwood, IL: Passport Books.

Kim, E. Y. (2001). *The yin and yang of American culture.* Yarmouth. ME: Intercultural Press.

Kimble, R. S. (2001). *Things to know about community resources.* Portland, ME: J. Weston Walch.

King-Shaver, B., & Hunter, A. (2003). *Differentiated instruction in the English classroom.* Portsmouth, NH: Heinemann.

Kirkpatrick, A. (2000, November 16). English as an Asian language. *Manchester Guardian Weekly Learning English Supplement, 3.*

Kirschner, M. (1993). ESP for physiotherapy. *CATESOL News, 25*(4), 5, 12.

Koch, K. (1970). *Wishes, lies, and dreams.* New York: Vintage Books.

Kogan, M. D., et al. (2009). Prevalence of parent-reported diagnosis of autism spectrum disorder among children in the US. *Pediatrics, 124*(5), 1395–1403.

Kolb, D. A. (1976). *The Learning Style Inventory technical manual.* Boston: McBer.

Kozol, J. (1991). *Savage inequalities: Children in America's schools.* New York: Crown.

Kozulin, A., & Presseisen, B. Z. (1995). Mediated learning, experience, and psychological tools: Vygotsky and Feuerstein's perspectives in a study of student learning. *Educational Psychologist, 30,* 67–75.

Kozyrev, J. R. (1998). *Talk it over! Oral communication for the real world.* Boston: Houghton Mifflin.

Krashen, S. (1981). Bilingual education and second language acquisition theory. In *Schooling and language minority students: A theoretical framework.* Los Angeles: Evaluation, Dissemination and Assessment Center, California State University.

Krashen, S. (1982). *Principles and practice in second language acquisition.* Oxford: Pergamon.

Krashen, S. (1985). *The input hypothesis: Issues and implications.* New York: Longman.

Kress, G. (2000). *Early spelling: Between convention and creativity.* London: Routledge.

Kress, G., & van Leeuwen, T. (2006). *Reading images: The grammar of visual design* (2nd ed.). New York: Taylor & Francis.

Kroll, J. F., & Tokowitz, N. (2005). Models of bilingual representation and processing: Looking back and to the future. In J. F. Kroll and A. M. B. De Groot (Eds.), *Handbook of bilingualism: Psycholinguistic approaches* (pp. 531–544). Oxford, UK: Oxford University Press.

Kubota, R. (1998). Ideologies of English in Japan. *World Englishes, 17*(3), 295–306.

Labov, W. (1981). *The study of non-standard English.* Urbana, IL: National Council of Teachers of English.

Lacan, J. (1977). *The four fundamental concepts of psycho-analysis.* London: Hogarth Press.

Ladson-Billings, G. (1994). *The dreamkeepers: Successful teachers of African American children.* San Francisco: Jossey-Bass.

Lakoff, R. (1975). *Language and women's place.* New York: Harper & Row.

Lam, W. S. E. (2000). L2 literacy and the design of the self: A case study of a teenager writing on the Internet. *TESOL Quarterly, 34*(3), 457–482.

Lam, W. S. E. (2009). Literacy and learning across transnational online spaces. *E–Learning, 6*(4), n. p.

Lambert, E. (1955). *The story of the words we use.* New York: Lothrop, Lee & Shepard.

Lambert, W. (1984). An overview of issues in immersion education. In California Department of Education, *Studies on immersion education.* Sacramento: California Department of Education.

Land, S., & Greene, B. A. (2000). Project-based learning with the World Wide Web: A qualitative study of resource integration. *Educational Technology Research and Development, 48,* 45–67.

Larking, L. (1999). Spontaneous oral development of group stories. In N. Shameem & M. Tickoo (Eds.), *New ways in using communicative games* (pp. 144–145). Alexandria, VA: Teachers of English to Speakers of Other Languages.

Larsen-Freeman, D., & Long, M. (1991). *Introduction to second language acquisition research.* London: Longman.

Lave, J. (1996). Teaching, as learning, in practice. *Mind, Culture, and Activity, 3,* 149–164.

Lave, J., & Wenger, E. (1991). *Situated learning: Legitimate peripheral participation.* New York: Cambridge University Press.

Law, B., & Eckes, M. (2000). *The more-than-just-surviving handbook* (2nd ed.). Winnipeg, Can.: Peguis.

Leki, I. (1986). The preferences of ESL students for error correction in college-level writing courses. *Foreign Language Annals, 24,* 203–218.

Leki, I. (1992). *Understanding ESL writers.* Portsmouth, NH: Boynton/Cook.

Leki, I. (1995). Coping strategies of ESL students in writing tasks across the curriculum. *TESOL Quarterly, 29*(2), 235–260.

Lenneberg, E. (1967). *Biological foundations of language.* New York: John Wiley.

Lerner, I., & Lerner, M. (1992). *Inner child cards: A journey into fairy tales, myth, & nature.* Sante Fe, NM: Bear & Co.

Leshinsky, J. G. (1995). *Authentic listening and discussion for advanced students.* Englewood Cliffs, NJ: Prentice-Hall Regents.

Levine, A. (1994, July/August). Service on campus. *Change,* pp. 4–5.

Levine, L. N. (2000). The most beautiful place in the world. In K. D. Samway (Ed.), *Integrating the ESL standards into classroom practice: Grades 3–5* (pp. 109–131). Alexandria, VA: Teachers of English to Speakers of Other Languages.

Levine, L. N., & McCloskey, M. L. (2009). *Teaching learners of English in mainstream classrooms K–8: One class, many paths.* Boston: Allyn & Bacon.

Lewis, B. (1991). *The kid's guide to social action.* Minneapolis, MN: Free Spirit Publishing.

Lewis, B. (1995). *The kid's guide to service projects.* Minneapolis, MN: Free Spirit.

Lewis, B., Espeland, P., & Pernu, C. (1998). *The kid's guide to social action.* Minneapolis: Free Spirit Publishing.

Lewis, C., & Fabos, B. (2005). Instant messaging, literacies, and social identities. *Reading Research Quarterly, 40*(4), 470–501.

Lewis, G., & Bedson, G. (1999). *Games for children.* Oxford: Oxford University Press.

Lewis, M. (1997). *New ways in teaching adults.* Alexandria, VA: Teachers of English to Speakers of Other Languages.

Li, S. (1992). *Legends of ten Chinese traditional festivals.* Beijing: Dolphin Books.

Lin, A. M. Y. (2001). Doing-English-lessons in the reproduction or transformation of social worlds? In C. N. Candlin & N. Mercer (Eds.), *English language teaching in its social context* (pp. 271– 286). New York: Routledge.

Lindholm, K. (1994). Promoting positive cross-cultural attitudes and perceived competence in culturally and linguistically diverse classrooms. In R. A. DeVillar, C. Faltis, & J. Cummins (Eds.), *Cultural diversity in schools: From rhetoric to practice* (pp. 189–206). Albany: SUNY Press.

Linn, R. L. (2000). Assessments and accountability. *Educational Researcher, 29*(2), 4–26.

Lippi-Green, R. (1997). *English with an accent.* London: Routledge.

Lipson, G. B. (1992). *Audacious poetry: Reflections of adolescence.* Torrance, CA: Good Apple.

Liu, J. (1999). Nonnative-English-speaking professionals in TESOL. *TESOL Quarterly, 33,* 85–102.

Litowitz, B. (1997). Just say no: Responsibility and resistance. In M. Cole, Y. Engeström, & O. Vasquez (Eds.), *Mind, culture, and activity* (pp. 473–484). New York: Cambridge University Press.

Livingston, M. (1988). *Poems for mother.* New York: Holiday House.

Livingston, M. (1989). *Poems for father.* New York: Holiday House.

Lo, Y-H. G. (2006). Leading the way in the new millennium: An integrated multiage EFL program in Taiwan. In M. L. McCloskey, J. Orr, & M. Dolitsky (Eds.), *Teaching English as a foreign language in primary school* (pp. 25–39). Alexandria, VA: Teachers of English to Speakers of Other Languages.

Lopes-Murphy, S. A., & Martin, D. (2002). Community service learning: Making the match between preservice teachers and ESL students. In E. Auerbach (Ed.), *Community partnerships* (pp. 41–53). Alexandria, VA: Teachers of English to Speakers of Other Languages.

Loria, Y., Shaltied, L., Pieterse, E., & Rosenfeld, S. (1999). The development of software to support teachers and their students in PBL: "The Golden Way." In B. Hasselgreen (Ed.), *Conference Proceedings for the 7th European Conference on Learning and Instruction* (EARLI). Gotenborg, Sweden: Gotenborg University.

Lozanov, G. (1982). Suggestology and Suggestopedia. In R. Blair (Ed.), *Innovative approaches to language teaching* (pp. 37–53). Rowley, MA: Newbury House.

Lugton, R. C. (1986). *American topics* (2nd ed.). Englewood Cliffs, NJ: Prentice Hall Regents.

Luke, C. (2003). Pedagogy, connectivity, multimodalilty, and interdisciplinarity. *Reading Research Quarterly, 38(3)*, 397–403.

Lustig, M. W. (1988). Value differences in intercultural communication. In L. Samovar & R. Porter (Eds.), *Intercultural communication: A reader* (5th ed.). Belmont, CA: Wadsworth.

Lustig, M. W., & Koester, J. (1999). *Intercultural competence*. New York: Longman.

Lynch, T. (2009). *Teaching second language listening*. Oxford: Oxford University Press.

Macedo, D. (1994). *Literacies of power*. Boulder, CO: Westview Press.

Macedo, D., & Freire, A. M. A. (1998). Foreword. In P. Freire, *Teachers as cultural workers* (pp. ix– xix). Boulder, CO: Westview Press.

Macías, N. G. (1996). *Leyendas Mexicanas*. Mexico, DF: Selector.

Macías, R. F. (1979). The choice of language as a human right: Public policy implications in the United States. In R. V. Padilla (Ed.), *Bilingual education and public policy* (pp. 39–57). Ypsilanti, MI: Department of Foreign Languages and Bilingual Studies, Eastern Michigan University.

MacKay, S. (2000). *The language of love*. Riverside, CA: Educational Alternatives for Students of English. Available online: www.learning-with-ease.com.

Madrigal, A. (2010). Writing for new forms. *Wired, 18*(10), 173.

Magnier, M. (2002, January 29). Battery behind the *shoji* screen. *Los Angeles Times,* A1, A5.

Mages, W. K. (2008). Does creative drama promote language development in early childhood? A review of the methods and measures employed in the empirical literature. *Review of Educational Research, 78*(1), 124–152.

Magy, R. (1991). *Stories from the heart*. Palatine, IL: Linmore.

Mahoney, D. (1999a). Shadow tableaux. In N. Shameem & M. Tickoo (Eds.), *New ways in using communicative games* (pp. 13–14). Alexandria, VA: Teachers of English to Speakers of Other Languages.

Mahoney, D. (1999b). Stress clapping. In N. Shameem & M. Tickoo (Eds.), *New ways in using communicative games* (pp. 20–21). Alexandria, VA: Teachers of English to Speakers of Other Languages.

Malkina, N. (1996). Fun with storytelling. In V. Whiteson (Ed.), *New ways of using drama and literature in language teaching* (pp. 41–42). Alexandria, VA: Teachers of English to Speakers of Other Languages.

Malkina, N. (1998). Fun with storytelling. In V. Whiteson (Ed.), *New ways of using drama and literature in language teaching* (pp. 41–42). Alexandria, VA: Teachers of English to Speakers of Other Languages.

Mander, G. (2001). *WAN2TLK? LTL BK of TXT MSGS*. New York: St. Martin's Griffin.

Mansour, W. (1999). Give me a word that . . . In N. Shameem & M. Tickoo (Eds.), *New ways in using communicative games* (pp. 103–104). Alexandria, VA: Teachers of English to Speakers of Other Languages.

March, T. (2007). The new WWW: Whatever, whenever, wherever. In F. Schultz (Ed.), *Annual editions 10/08: Education* (pp. 213–216). Dubuque, IA: McGraw Hill Contemporary Learning Series.

Marcia, J. (1980). Identity in adolescence. In J. Adelson (Ed.), *The handbook of adolescent psychology.* (pp. 159–187). New York: John Wiley.

Marlowe, B. A., & Page, M. L. (1999). Making the most of the classroom mosaic: A constructivist perspective. *Multicultural Education, 6*(4), 19–21.

Marshall, B. (1999a). Making learning happen—whose responsibility is it? (Part 1). *CATESOL News, 30*(5), 11, 12, 14, 16.

Marshall, B. (1999b). Making learning happen—whose responsibility is it? (Part 2). *CATESOL News, 31*(1), 11, 12–14, 25.

Marshall, C., & Oliva, M. (2006). *Leadership for social justice: Making revolutions in education.* Boston: Pearson.

Martin, D. (2011). The safe zone. *California Educator, 15*(6), 9–13.

Martínez, E. (2010). *500 years of Chicana Women's history (500 años de la mujer Chicana)* (5th ed.). New Brunswick, NJ: Rutgers University Press.

Martínez, M., Roser, N. L., & Strecker, S. (1998). I never thought I could be a star: A readers theater ticket to fluency. *The Reading Teacher, 52*(4), 326–334.

Mashishi, L. (2002). Using a community-based curriculum to promote literacy in Soweto. In E. Auerbach (Ed.), *Community partnerships* (pp. 107–120). Alexandria, VA: Teachers of English to Speakers of Other Languages, Inc.

Master, P. (1996). *Systems of English grammar: An introduction for language teachers.* Upper Saddle River, NJ: Prentice Hall Regents.

May, F. B., & Rizzardi, L. (2002). *Reading as communication* (6th ed.). Upper Saddle River, NJ: Merrill Prentice Hall.

Mazer, A. (Ed.). (1993). *American street: A multicultural anthology of voices.* New York: Persea Books.

McCabe, M., & Rhoades, J. (1988). *The nurturing classroom.* Willits, CA: ITA Publications.

McCaleb, S. P. (1994). *Building communities of learners.* New York: St. Martin's Press.

McCarthy, B. (1983). *The 4-MAT system: Teaching to learning styles with right-left mode techniques.* Oak Brook, IL: Excel.

McCaslin, N. (2000). *Creative drama in the classroom and beyond.* New York: Longman.

McClintock, M. (2000). How to interrupt oppressive behavior. In M. Adams, W. J. Blumenfeld, R. Casteñeda, H. W. Hackman, M. L. Peters, and X. Zúñiga (Eds.), *Readings for diversity and social justice* (pp. 483–485). New York and London: Routledge.

McKay, S., & Wong, S. (1996). Multiple discourses, multiple identities: Investment and agency in second-language learning among Chinese adolescent immigrant students. *Harvard Educational Review, 66*(3), 608–677.

McKay, S. L. (1989). Topic development and written discourse accent. In D. Johnson & D. H. Roen (Eds.), *Richness in writing* (pp. 253–262). New York: Longman.

McKenna, M. C., & Robinson, R. D. (1997). *Teaching through text: A content literacy approach to content area reading* (2nd ed.). New York: Longman.

McLaren, P. (1989). *Life in schools: An introduction to critical pedagogy in the foundations of education.* New York: Longman.

McLaren, P. (1995). Critical multiculturalism, media literacy, and the politics of representation. In J. Frederickson (Ed.), *Reclaiming our voices: Bilingual education, critical pedagogy, and praxis* (pp. 99–138). Ontario: California Association for Bilingual Education; New York: Longman.

McNamara, M. J. (1998a). Self-assessment: Keeping a language learning log. In J. D. Brown (Ed.), *New ways in classroom assessment* (pp. 38–41). Alexandria, VA: Teachers of English to Speakers of Other Languages.

McNamara, M. J. (1998b). Self-assessment: Preparing an English portfolio. In J. D. Brown (Ed.), *New ways in classroom assessment* (pp. 15–17). Alexandria, VA: Teachers of English to Speakers of Other Languages.

McNicholls, S. (2006). Using enchantment: Children's literature in an EFL teacher education context. In A. Paran (Ed.), *Literature in language teaching and learning* (pp. 71–85). Alexandria, VA: Teachers of English to Speakers of Other Languages.

McQuillan, J., & Tse, L. (1998). What's the story? Using the narrative approach in beginning language classrooms. *TESOL Journal, 7*(4), 18–23.

McWhorter, K. T. (1995). *College reading and study skills* (6th ed.). New York: HarperCollins.

Medina, M. Jr., & Escamilla, K. (1992). Evaluation of transitional and maintenance bilingual programs. *Urban Education, 27*(3), 263–290.

Mehan, H. (1979). *Learning lessons.* Cambridge, MA: Harvard University Press.

Meloni, C., & Masters, C. (1996). Experiencing the music of poetry: Poe's "Annabel Lee." In V. Whiteson (Ed.), *New ways of using drama and literature in language teaching* (pp. 76–79). Alexandria, VA: Teachers of English to Speakers of Other Languages.

Menconi, M. (1996). Country profile: Russia. *TESOL Placement Bulletin, 6*(5), 1, 3–4.

Mermelstein, L. (2006). *Reading/writing connections in the K–2 classroom.* Boston: Pearson.

Merriam-Webster. (2001a). *Word for the wise. Morning Edition,* National Public Radio, April 30.

Merriam-Webster. (2001b). *Word for the wise. Morning Edition,* National Public Radio, September 18.

Mestel, R. (2001, April 25). Childhood bullying is common, study finds. *Los Angeles Times,* A10.

Mestel, R., & Groves, M. (2001, April 3). When push comes to shove. *Los Angeles Times,* E1, E3.

Milambiling, J. (2002). Good neighbors: Mainstreaming ESL students in the rural Midwest. In E. P. Cochran, *Mainstreaming* (pp. 21–30). Alexandria, VA: Teachers of English to Speakers of Other Languages.

Mills, S. (1997). *Discourse.* London: Routledge.

Mills, S. C. (2006). *Using the Internet for active teaching and learning.* Upper Saddle River, NJ: Pearson/Merrill/Prentice Hall.

Molina, H., Hanson, R. A., & Siegel, D. F. (1997). *Empowering the second-language classroom: Putting the parts together.* San Francisco: Caddo Gap Press.

Molina, R. (2000). Building equitable two-way programs. In N. Cloud, F. Genesee, & E. Hamayan (Eds.), *Dual language instruction* (pp. 11–12). Boston: Heinle & Heinle.

Moll, L. C. (1992). Bilingual classroom studies and community analysis: Some recent trends. *Educational Researcher, 21*(2), 20–24.

Moll, L. C., & Greenberg, J. (1990). Creating zones of possibilities: Combining social contexts for instructions. In L. C. Moll (Ed.), *Vygotsky and education* (pp. 319–348). Cambridge: Cambridge University Press.

Monroe, S. (1999). Multicultural children's literature: Canon of the future. Reprinted in *Annual editions 99/00: Teaching English as a second language.* Guilford, CT: Dushkin/McGraw-Hill.

Moorman, C., & Haller, T. (2011). *A safe and orderly environment.* National Education Association. Accessed June 26, 2011 from www.nea.org/tools/a-safe-and-orderly-environment.html

Morgan, B. (1998). *The ESL classroom: Teaching, critical practice, and community development.* Toronto: University of Toronto Press.

Morgan, G. (1986). *Images of organizations.* Beverly Hills, CA: Sage.

Morgan, R. (1992). Distinctive voices—Developing oral language in multilingual classrooms. In P. Pinsent (Ed.), *Language, culture, and young children* (pp. 37–46). London: David Fulton.

Morrison, C. (2001). *Schoolwide portfolios for community acccountability: What standardized tests can't tell us.* Presentation, the Ninth Annual Conference on Project-Based Learning, San Francisco.

Morrison, G. (1997). Working in Japan. *TESOL Placement Bulletin, 7*(5), 1, 3.

Morrison, P. (1994). *Commentary: Americans speak English—But we don't understand.* Morning Edition, National Public Radio, May 23. Transcript 940016680.

Moss, D. (1998). *Project-based learning and assessment: A resource manual for teachers.* Arlington, VA: The Arlington Education and Employment Program.

Moxley, J. M. (1994). *Becoming an academic writer: A modern rhetoric.* Lexington, MA: D.C. Heath.

Murphey, T. (1992). *Music & song.* Oxford: Oxford University Press.

Murphy, J. M. (1998). *The eight disciplines.* Grand Rapids, MI: Venture Management.

Murray, D. E. (2000). Protean communication: The language of computer-mediated communication. *TESOL Quarterly, 34*(3), 397–421.

Musthafa, B. (2002). English teaching in Indonesia: Status, issues, and challenges. *ESL Magazine, 5*(1), 26–28.

Nagy, W. E., García, G. E., Durgunoglu, A., & Hancin-Bhatt, B. (1993). Spanish–English bilingual students' use of cognates in English reading. *Bilingual Research Journal, 18,* 83–97.

Nam, J-Y. (2001). *Achieving English competence in Korea through computer-assisted language learning and crosscultural understanding.* Unpublished master's project, California State University, San Bernardino.

Natheson-Mejia, S. (1989). Writing in a second language. *Language Arts, 66*(5), 516–526.

Nation, P. (1994). *New ways in teaching vocabulary.* Alexandria, VA: Teachers of English to Speakers of Other Languages.

National Center in Educational Outcomes. (2011). Accommodations for students with disabilities. Accessed April 29, 2011 from www.cehd.umn.edu/NCEO/TopicAreas/Accommodations/Accomtopic.htm

National Clearinghouse for English Language Acquisition. (2009). *The growing number of English learner students.* Accessed April 27, 2011 from www.ed.gov/about/offices/list/oela/index.html

National Reading Panel. (2000). Report of the National Reading Panel. Washington, DC: National Institute of Child Health and Human Development.

Navarrete, C., & Gustke, C. (1996). *A guide to performance assessment for linguistically diverse students.* Albuquerque, NM: EAC West, New Mexico Highlands University. Available online: www.ncela.gwu.edu/pubs/eacwest/performance.

Nelson, G. (1995). Cultural differences in learning styles. In J. Reid (Ed.), *Learning styles in the ESL/EFL classroom* (pp. 3–18). Boston: Heinle & Heinle.

Nero, S. J. (1997). English is my native language . . . or so I believe. *TESOL Quarterly, 31*(3), 585–593.

Ness, V. (1998). China: A growth market for EFL teachers. *TESOL Placement Bulletin, 8*(8), 3–5.

Newman, C. M. (2006). *Strategies for test-taking success: Reading.* Boston: Thompson Heinle.

Nichols, S. L. (1999). Gay, lesbian, and bisexual youth: Understanding diversity and promoting tolerance in schools. *The Elementary School Journal, 99*(5), 505–519.

Nicolas, S. (2005). Negotiating for the Hopi way of life. In T. L. McCarty (Ed.), *Language, literacy, and power in schooling* (pp. 29–46). Mahwah, NJ: Erlbaum.

Nieto, S. (1997). We speak in many tongues: Language diversity and multicultural education. In J. V. Tinajero & A. F. Ada (Eds.), *The power of two languages* (pp. 37–48). New York: Macmillan/McGraw-Hill.

Nieto, S. (2008). *Affirming diversity* (5th ed.). New York: Longman.

Nishimoto, K. (1997). *Japanese fairy tales* (vols. 1–4). Torrance, CA: Heian International.

North Coast Rural Challenge Network. (2000). *Voices of the valley (vols. I–III).* Boonville, CA: Author. (Contact: mmendosa@avusd.k12.ca.us)

Norton, B., & Pavlenko, A. (2004). *Gender and English language learners.* Alexandria, VA: Teachers of English to Speakers of Other Languages, Inc.

Norton, B., & Toohey, K. (2001). Changing perspectives on good language learners. *TESOL Quarterly, 35*(2), 307–322.

Norton, D. E. (2007). *Literacy for life.* Boston: Pearson.

Nunan, D. (1989). *Designing tasks for the communicative classroom.* Cambridge: Cambridge University Press.

Nunan, D. (1995). *Atlas: Teacher's extended edition, Level 2.* Boston: Heinle & Heinle.

Nunan, D. (1999). A foot in the world of ideas: Graduate study through the Internet. *Language Learning & Technology, 3*(1), 52–74.

Nydell, M. K. (1997). *Understanding Arabs: A guide for Westerners.* Yarmouth. ME: Intercultural Press.

O'Bannon, B. W., & Puckett, K. (2007). *Preparing to use technology.* Boston: Allyn & Bacon.

Ogbu, J., & Matute-Bianchi, M. (1986). Understanding sociocultural factors: Knowledge, identity, and school adjustment. In *Beyond language: Social and cultural factors in schooling language minority students* (pp. 73–142). Los Angeles: Evaluation, Dissemination and Assessment Center, California State University.

O'Grady, C. R., & Chappell, B. (2000). With, not for: The politics of service learning in multicultural communities. In P. McLaren & C. J. Ovando (Eds.), *The politics of multiculturalism and bilingual education* (pp. 208–224). Boston: McGraw-Hill.

O'Malley, J. M., & Pierce, L. V. (1996). *Authentic assessment for English language learners.* Menlo Park, CA: Addison-Wesley.

Osgood, K. W. (2002). It takes a class to teach a child: The challenge program. In E. P. Cochran, *Mainstreaming* (pp. 43–51). Alexandria, VA: Teachers of English to Speakers of Other Languages.

Ovando, C., & Collier, V. (1998). *Bilingual and ESL classrooms: Teaching in multicultural contexts.* Boston: McGraw-Hill.

Ovando, C. J., Combs, M. C., & Collier, V. P. (2006). *Bilingual & ESL classrooms: Teaching in multicultural contexts* (4th ed.). Boston: McGraw-Hill.

Owens, E. (1998). Ecuador. *TESOL Placement Bulletin, 6*(6), 1.

Oxford, R. (1990). *Language learning strategies: What every teacher should know.* Boston: Allyn & Bacon.

Packer, N. H., & Timpane, J. (1997). *Writing worth reading: The critical process* (3rd ed.). Boston: Bedford Books.

Padilla, S. (1995). *Chants and prayers.* Summerton, TN: Book Publishing Co.

Palinscar, A. S., & Brown, A. L. (1984). Reciprocal teaching of comprehension-fostering and comprehension-monitoring activities. *Cognition and Instruction, 1,* 117–175.

Panzeri-Álvarez, C. (1998). *Metacognition and language transfer for an English language development transitional program.* Unpublished master's project, California State University, San Bernardino.

Pappamihiel, N. E. (2002). English as a second language students and English language anxiety: Issues in the mainstream classroom. *Research in the Teaching of English, 36,* 327–355.

Paran, A. (Ed.). (2006). *Literature in language teaching and learning.* Alexandria, VA: Teachers of English to Speakers of Other Languages, Inc.

Parker, R. (1995). *Mixed signals: Prospects for global television news.* New York: Twentieth Century Fund.

Parla, J. (1994). Educating teachers for cultural and linguistic diversity: A model for all teachers. *New York State Association for Bilingual Education Journal, 9,*1–6. Accessed October 12, 2006, from www.ncela.gwu.edu/pubs/nysabe/vol9/model.htm.

Paul, R., Binker, A. J. A., Jensen, K., & Kreklau, H. (1990). *Critical thinking handbook: 4th–6th grades.* Rohnert Park, CA: Center for Critical Thinking and Moral Critique.

Pearson, P. D., & Gallagher, M. C. (1983). The instruction of reading comprehension. *Contemporary Educational Psychology, 8,* 317–344.

Pease-Alvarez, L., & Winsler, A. (1994). Cuando el maestro no habla Español: Children's bilingual language practices in the classroom. *TESOL Quarterly, 28*(3), 507–536.

Pei, M. (1962). "Ain't" is in, "raviolis" ain't. In J. Sledd & W. R. Ebbitt (Eds.), *Dictionaries and THAT dictionary* (pp. 82–83). Glenview, IL: Scott, Foresman.

Peim, N. (1993). *Critical theory and the English teacher.* London: Routledge.

Pennycook, A. (1994). *The cultural politics of English as an international language.* New York: Longman.

Pennycook, A. (1998). Text, ownership, memory, and plagiarism. In V. Zamel & R. Spack (Eds.), *Negotiating academic literacies: Teaching and learning across languages and cultures* (pp. 265–292). Mahwah, NJ: Erlbaum.

Peregoy, S. (2008). *Reading, writing, and learning in ESL* (5th ed.). Boston: Allyn & Bacon.

Pérez, B., & Torres-Guzmán, M. E. (2002). *Learning in two worlds* (3rd ed.). Boston: Allyn & Bacon.

Pérez de Lima, A. M. (1996). Country profile: Uruguay. *TESOL Placement Bulletin, 6*(3), 1, 3.

Perfection Learning (2000). *Who am I?* Logan, IA: Author.

Perkins, D. (1986). *Knowledge as design.* Hillsdale, NJ: Erlbaum.

Perkins, D. N. (1992). Technology meets constructivism: Do they make a marriage? In T. M. Duffy & D. H. Jonassen, (Eds.), *Constructivism and the technology of instruction: A conversation* (pp. 45–46). Hillsdale, NJ: Erlbaum.

Perrone, V. (1994). How to engage students in learning. *Educational Researcher, 51*(5), 11–13.

Peterson, B. (1994). Teaching for social justice: One teacher's journey. In B. Bigelow, L. Christensen, S. Karp, B. Miner, & B. Peterson (Eds.), *Rethinking our classrooms* (p. 38). Milwaukee, WI: Rethinking Schools Limited.

Peyton, J. K. (1997). Book review of Kazemek and Rigg's *Enriching Our Lives: Poetry Lessons for Adult Literacy Teachers and Tutors. TESOL Journal, 7*(2), 39.

Pfingstag, N. (1999). Hearing voices. In R. E. Larimer & L. Schleicher (Eds.), *New ways in using authentic materials in the classroom* (pp. 62–65). Alexandria, VA: Teachers of English to Speakers of Other Languages.

Phillipson, R. (2003). Union in need of language equality. *The Guardian Weekly, Learning English Supplement, 168*(6), 3.

Pierangelo, R., & Guiliani, G. A. (2001). *What every teacher should know about students with special needs.* Champaign, IL: Research Press.

Pierce, B. N. (1995). Social identity, investment, and language learning. *TESOL Quarterly, 29*(1), 9–31.

Pierce, L. V. (1998). Planning portfolios. In J. D. Brown (Ed.), *New ways in classroom assessment* (pp. 6–10). Alexandria, VA: Teachers of English to Speakers of Other Languages.

Pinker, S. (2007). Coming to terms. *Los Angeles Times*, September 30, M1, M9.

Pousada, A. (1999). The singularly strange story of the English language in Puerto Rico. *Milenio, 3,* 33–60. Retrieved October 6, 2006, from http://home.earthlink.net/~apousada/id1.html.

Poyatos, F. (1984). Linguistic fluency and verbal–nonverbal cultural fluency. In A. Wolfgang (Ed.), *Nonverbal behavior: Perspectives, applications, intercultural insights* (pp. 139–167). Lewiston, NY: Hogrefe.

Prabhu, N. S. (1990). There is no best method—Why? *TESOL Quarterly, 24*(2), 161–176.

Prelutsky, J. (1988). *Tyrannosaurus was a beast.* New York: Greenwillow.

Prelutsky, J. (2000). *The Random House book of poetry for children.* New York: Random House.

Pridham, F. (2001). *The language of conversation.* New York: Routledge.

Provenzano, R. (2001). *A little book of aloha.* Honolulu, HI: Mutual Publishing.

Pugliese, C. (2001, March 22). Languages go to the top of the class. *Manchester Daily Guardian,* Learning English Section, 1.

Quinn, A. (1982). *Figures of speech.* Davis, CA: Hermagoras Press.

Quintero, E. P., & Rummel, M. K. (1998). *American voices: Webs of diversity.* Upper Saddle River, NJ: Prentice-Hall.

Quiocho, A. L., & Ulanoff, S. H. (2009). *Differentiated literacy instruction for English language learners.* Boston: Pearson.

Radin, B. (2000). *Decision dramas* (3rd ed.). Studio City, CA: JAG Publications.

Raffini, J. P. (1996). *150 ways to increase intrinsic motivation in the classroom.* Boston: Allyn & Bacon.

Raimes, A. (Ed.). (1996). *Identities: Readings from contemporary culture.* Boston: Houghton Mifflin.

Ramírez, J. (1992, winter/spring). Executive summary, final report: Longitudinal study of structured English immersion strategy, early-exit, and late-exit transitional bilingual education programs for language-minority children. *Bilingual Research Journal, 16*(1&2), 1–62.

Raphael, T. E. (1986). Teaching question answer relationships, revisited. *The Reading Teacher, 39,* 516–523.

Rasinski, T., & Fredericks, A. (1989). Dimensions of parent involvement. *The Reading Teacher, 43*(2), 180–182.

Raskin, J. (2001). Using the World Wide Web as a resource for models and interaction in a writing course. In L. E. Henrichsen (Ed.), *Distance-learning programs* (pp. 61–70). Alexandria, VA: Teachers of English to Speakers of Other Languages.

Ratey, J. J. (2001). *User's guide to the brain: Perception, attention, and the four theaters of the brain.* New York: Pantheon Books.

Ray, B., & Seely, C. (1997). *Fluency through TPR storytelling.* Berkeley, CA: Command Performance Institute.

Reardon, B. (1988). *Comprehensive peace education.* New York: Teachers College Press.

Redding, J. (2001). *Music creating language experience: Rock Talk.* Presentation, CATESOL Annual State Conference, Ontario, CA.

Reese, S. (2006). When foreign languages are not seen or heard. *The Language Educator, 1*(2), 32–37.

Reid, J. (2006). New census data shows 1.3 million children have fallen into poverty since 2000. *Children's Defense Fund.* Retrieved October 12, 2006, from http://www.childrens defense.org/site/News2?page=NewsArticle &id=7887.

Reid, J. M. (1995). Preface. In J. Reid (Ed.), *Learning styles in the ESL/EFL classroom* (pp. viii–xvii). Boston: Heinle & Heinle.

Rhoads, C. (2007). What did U $@Y? Online language finds its voice. *Wall Street Journal,* August 23, A1.

Richards, J. (2008). *Moving beyond the plateau: From intermediate to advanced levels in language learning.* New York: Cambridge University Press.

Riles, G. B., & Lenarcic, C. (2000). Exploring world religions. In B. Agor (Ed.), *Integrating the ESL standards into classroom practice: Grades 9–12* (pp. 1–29). Alexandria, VA: Teachers of English to Speakers of Other Languages.

Rinvolucri, M. (1984). *Grammar games: Cognitive, affective, and drama activities for EFL students.* Cambridge: Cambridge University Press.

Roberge, M. (2009). A teacher's perspective on Generation 1.5. In M. Roberge, M. Siegal, and L. Harklau (Eds.), *Generation 1.5 in college composition: Teaching academic writing to U.S.-educated learners of ESL* (pp. 3–24). New York: Routledge.

Roberts, V. M. (1971). *The nature of theater.* New York: Harper & Row.

Rodby, J. (1999). Contingent literacy: The social construction of writing for nonnative English-speaking college freshmen. In L. Harklau, K. M. Losey, & M. Siegal (Eds.). (1999). *Generation 1.5 meets college composition: Issues in the teaching of writing to U.S.-educated learners of ESL* (pp. 45–60). Mahwah, NJ: Erlbaum.

Rodríguez, G. (2007). Flexing their word power. *Los Angeles Times,* November 26, A17.

Root, C., & Dumicich, J. (1998). Reader's theater: A primer on pronunciation. In V. Whiteson (Ed.), *New ways of using drama and literature in language teaching* (pp. 123–124). Alexandria, VA: Teachers of English to Speakers of Other Languages.

Rose, C. (1985). *Accelerated learning.* New York: Bantam Doubleday Dell.

Rosenblatt, L. (1978). *The reader, the text, the poem: The transactional theory of the literary work.* Carbondale: Southern Illinois University.

Rosenblatt, S. (2007). A lesson in adaptation. *Los Angeles Times,* February 11, B1, B3.

Rosiek, J. (2003). Emotional scaffolding. *Journal of Teacher Education, 54*(5), 399–412.

Rosten, L. C. (1982). *Hooray for Yiddish! A book about English.* New York: Simon & Schuster.

Roth-Vinson, C. (2001). *All aspects of project planning: Teaching tools for community-based learning.* Presentation, the Ninth Annual Conference on Project-Based Learning, San Francisco, CA.

Rubin, D., & Opitz, M. F. (2007). *Diagnosis and improvement in reading instruction* (5th ed.). Boston: Pearson.

Ruíz, R. (1984). Orientations in language planning. *NABE Journal, 8*(2), 15–34.

Rumbaut, R. G., & Portes, A. (Eds.). (2001). *Ethnicities: Children of immigrants in America.* Berkeley: University of California Press.

Runner, J. (2000). *"Thank you" in over 465 languages.* Available online: www.elite.net/ ~runner/jennifers/thankyou.htm.

Runner, J. (2007). *Greetings in over 800 languages.* Online at www.elite.net/~runner/ jennifers/hello.htm.

Ryan, P. M. (2000). *Esperanza rising.* New York: Scholastic Signature.

Sadker, M., & Sadker, D. (1986). Sexism in the classroom: From grade school to graduate school. *Phi Delta Kappan, 68,* 512.

Sadker, M., Sadker, D., & Klein, S. (1991). The issue of gender in elementary and secondary education. *Review of Research in Education, 17,* 269–334.

Salovey, P., & Mayer, J. D. (1990). Emotional intelligence. *Imagination, Cognition, and Personality, 9*(3), 185–211.

Samway, K. D. (Ed.). (2001). *Integrating the ESL standards into classroom practice: Grades 3–5.* Alexandria, VA: Teachers of English to Speakers of Other Languages.

San Joaquin County Office of Education. (2001). *"Way to Grow!" Service learning—The seeds to your future.* Stockton, CA: Author.

Santás, C. (1996). Finding self-access activities. In D. Gardner and L. Miller, (Eds.). *Tasks for independent language learning* (pp. 18–20). Alexandria, VA: Teachers of English to Speakers of Other Languages.

Sapon-Shevin, M. (1999). *Because we can change the world.* Boston: Allyn & Bacon.

Sarwar, Z. (2000). *Project-based learning.* Presentation, annual meeting, Teachers of English to Speakers of Other Languages, Vancouver, Canada.

Saunders, W. M., Foorman, B. R., & Carlson, C. D. (2006). Is a separate block of time for oral English language development in programs for English learners needed? *The Elementary School Journal, 107*(2), 181–198.

Scarcella, R., & Rumberger, R. W. (2000). Academic English key to long-term success in school. *University of California Linguistic Minority Research Institute Newsletter, 9*(4), 1–2.

Schifini, A., Short, D., & Tinajero, J. V. (2002). *High points: Teacher's edition.* Carmel, CA: Hampton-Brown.

Selinker, L. (1972). Interlanguage. *IRAL, 10*(3), 209–231.

Selinker, L. (1991). Along the way: Interlanguage systems in second language acquisition. In L. Malavé & G. Duquette (Eds.), *Language, culture and cognition.* Clevedon, UK: Multilingual Matters.

Sellers, J. (1994). *Folk wisdom of Mexico.* San Francisco: Chronicle Books.

Shaffer, C. (1989). A comparison of inductive and deductive approaches to teaching foreign languages. *Modern Language Journal, 73,* 395–403.

Shameem, N., & Tickoo, M. (Eds.). (1999). *New ways in using communicative games.* Alexandria, VA: Teachers of English to Speakers of Other Languages.

Shapiro, J. P. (2000). A separate and unequal education for minorities with learning disabilities. In M. Adams, W. J. Blumenfeld, R. Casteñeda, H. W. Hackman, M. L. Peters, and X. Zúñiga (Eds.), *Readings for diversity and social justice* (pp. 340–352). New York and London: Routledge.

Shen, F. (1998). The classroom and the wider culture: Identity as a key to learning English composition. In V. Zamel & R. Speck (Eds.), *Negotiating academic literacies: Teaching and learning across language and cultures* (pp. 123–133). Mahwah, NJ: Erlbaum.

Shepard, A. (1994). From script to stage: Tips for readers theatre. *The English Teacher, 48*(2), 184–190.

Shepard, S. L. (2001). Mall culture. In M. Petracca & M. Sorapure (Eds.), *Common culture: Reading and writing about American popular culture* (3rd. ed., pp. 603–607). Upper Saddle River, NJ: Prentice-Hall.

Siccone, F. (1995). *Celebrating diversity.* Boston: Allyn & Bacon.

Sick, J. (1999). So did I. In N. Shameem & M. Tickoo (Eds.), *New ways in using communicative games* (p. 117). Alexandria, VA: Teachers of English to Speakers of Other Languages.

Sigmon, R. I. (1994). *Serving to learn, learning to serve: Linking service with learning.* Report, Council for Independent Colleges.

Sillivan, S. (2000). Mastering the art of persuasion: Marketing and the media. In S. Irujo (Ed.), *Integrating the ESL standards into classroom practice: Grades 6–8* (pp. 85–111). Alexandria, VA: Teachers of English to Speakers of Other Languages.

Silverstein, S. (2007). Biding their tongues. *Los Angeles Times,* November 13, A1, A17.

Simon, R. (1982). *Gramsci's political thought.* London: Lawrence & Wishart.

Skutnabb-Kangas, T. (1981). *Bilingualism or not: The education of minorities.* (Trans. L. Malmberg & D. Crane). Clevedon, UK: Multilingual Matters.

Skutnabb-Kangas, T. (2001, March 22). Murder that is a threat to survival. *Manchester Daily Guardian,* Learning English section, 3.

Slavin, R. E. (1983). *Cooperative learning.* New York: Longman.

Slavin, R. E. (1991). A synthesis of research on cooperative learning. *Educational Leadership, 48,* 71–82.

Slavkin, M. L. (2004). *Authentic learning: How learning about the brain can shape the development of students.* Lanham, MD: ScarecrowEducation.

Sleeter, C. E., & Grant. C. A. (1987). An analysis of multicultural education in the United States. *Harvard Education Review, 57*(4), 421–444.

Sleeter, C. E., & McLaren, P. L. (1995). *Multicultural education, critical pedagogy, and the politics of difference.* Albany: SUNY Press.

Small, A. H. (1993). *English à la cartoon.* Lincolnwood, IL: NTC/Contemporary Publishing Company/Passport Books.

Smallwood, B. A. (Ed.). (2001). *Integrating the ESL standards into classroom practice: Grades pre-K–2.* Alexandria, VA: Teachers of English to Speakers of Other Languages.

Smith, M. W. (1994). Issues in integrating service-learning into the higher education curriculum. In *Effective learning, effective teaching, effective service.* Washington, DC: Youth Service America.

Smith, T. E. C., Polloway, E. A., Patton, J. R., & Dowdy, C. A. (2011). *Teaching children with special needs in inclusive settings* (6th ed.). Upper Saddle River, NJ: Prentice Hall.

Solé, D. (1998). Poetry for pronunciation, pronunciation for poetry. In V. Whiteson (Ed.), *New ways of using drama and literature in language teaching* (pp. 84–85). Alexandria, VA: Teachers of English to Speakers of Other Languages.

Sonbuchner, G. M. (1991). *How to take advantage of your learning styles.* Syracuse, NY: New Readers Press.

Soto, G. (1992). *Pacific crossing.* San Diego: Harcourt, Brace.

Soto, L. D. (1991). Understanding bilingual/bicultural children. *Young Children, 46*(2), 30–36.

Sousa, D. A. (2005). *How the brain learns to read.* Thousand Oaks, CA: Corwin.

Spears, R. A. (1992). *Common American phrases in everyday contexts.* Lincolnwood, IL: National Textbook Company.

Spener, M. (1992). *The Freirean approach to adult literacy education.* National Center for ESL Literacy Education (NCLE). Available online: www.cal.org/caela/esl_resources/digests/FREIREQA.

Stafford-Yilmaz, L. (1998). *A to zany: Community activities for students of English.* Ann Arbor: University of Michigan Press.

Steinberg, A., & Stephen, D. (1999). *City works: Exploring your community.* New York: New Press.

Steinberg, J. (1983). *Games language people play.* Markham, Can.: Dominie Press.

Stephenson, S. (2002). *Understanding Spanish-speaking South Americans.* Yarmouth, ME: Intercultural Press.

Stepien, W., & Gallagher, S. (1993). Problem-based learning: As authentic as it gets. *Educational Leadership, 50*(7), 25–28.

Stern, A. (1996). *Tales from many lands: An anthology of multicultural folk literature.* Lincolnwood, IL: National Textbook Company.

Stiel, S. (2002). An interview with Hang Nguyen. In B. M. Power & R. S. Hubbard (Eds.), *Language development: A reader for teachers* (2nd ed., pp. 185–188). Upper Saddle River, NJ: Merrill/Prentice-Hall.

Storti, C. (2001). *Old world/new world, bridging cultural differences: Britain, France, and the U.S.* Yarmouth, ME: Intercultural Press.

Street, B. (1995). *Social literacies: Critical approaches to literacy in development, ethnography, and education.* London: Longman.

Strevens, P. (1987). Cultural barriers to language learning. In L. Smith (Ed.), *Discourse across cultures: Strategies in world Englishes* (pp. 169–178). New York: Prentice-Hall.

Strohmeyer, V. (1991–1992, winter). Fables in the ESOL classroom. *TESOL Journal, 1*(2), 33.

Suid, M., & Lincoln, W. (1992). *Ten-minute whole language warm-ups.* Palo Alto, CA: Monday Morning Books.

Swerdlow, J. L. (2001). Changing America. *National Geographic, 200*(3), 42–61.

Sylwester, R. (1995). *A celebration of neurons: An educator's guide to the brain.* Alexandria, VA: Association for Supervision and Curriculum Development.

Sylwester, R. (2003). *A biological brain in a cultural classroom.* Thousand Oaks, CA: Corwin.

Sylwester, R., & Cho, J-Y. (1992/1993). What brain research says about paying attention. *Educational Leadership, 50*(4), 71–75.

Tarone, E. (1981). Some thoughts on the notion of communication strategy. *TESOL Quarterly, 15*(3), 285–295.

Tarone, E., Cohen, A. D., & Dumas, G. (1983). A closer look at some interlanguage terminology: A framework for communication strategies. In C. Færch & G. Kasper (Eds.), *Strategies in interlanguage communication* (pp. 4–14). London: Longman.

Taylor, B. P. (1983). Teaching ESL: Incorporating a communicative, student-centered component. *TESOL Quarterly, 17*(1), 69–88.

Taylor, B. P. (1987). In M. H. Long & J. C. Richards (Eds.), *Methodology in TESOL: A book of readings* (pp. 45–60). New York: Newbury House.

Taylor, L. (2004). Creaing a community of difference: Understanding gender and race in a high school ESL antiracism camp. In B. Norton & A. Pavlenko (Eds.), *Gender and English language learners.* Alexandria, VA: Teachers of English to Speakers of Other Languages.

Tchudi, S., & Mitchell, D. (1999). *Exploring and teaching the English language arts.* New York: Longman.

Teachers of English to Speakers of Other Languages (TESOL). (1997). *ESL standards for pre-K–12 students.* Alexandria, VA: Author. Available online: www.tesol.org.

Teachers of English to Speakers of Other Languages (TESOL). (2001). *Scenarios for ESL standards-based assessment.* Alexandria, VA: Author.

Teachers of English to Speakers of Other Languages (TESOL). (2002). *Statement on the acquisition of academic proficiency in English.* Alexandria, VA: Author. Available online: www.tesol.org.

Teachers of English to Speakers of Other Languages, Inc. (2006a). *PreK–12 English language proficiency standards.* Alexandria, VA: Author.

Teachers of English to Speakers of Other Languages, Inc. (2006b). *Statement of principles and preliminary recommendations for the reauthorization of the Elementary and Secondary Education Act.* Alexandria, VA: Author. Available online: www.tesol.org.

Tellez, K., Hlebowitsh, P. S., Cohen, M., & Norwood, P. (1995). Social service field experiences and teacher education. In J. M. Larkin & C. E. Sleeter (Eds.), *Developing multicultural teacher education curricula* (pp. 65–78). Albany: SUNY Press.

Tharp, R. (1989). Psychocultural variables and constants: Effects on teaching and learning in schools. *American Psychologist, 44*(2), 349–359.

Tharp, R., & Gallimore, R. (1988). *Rousing minds to life: Teaching, learning, and schooling in social context.* Cambridge: Cambridge University Press.

Tharp, R., & Gallimore, R. (1991). *The instructional conversation: Teaching and learning in social activity.* Washington, DC: National Center for Research on Cultural Diversity and Second Language Learning.

Thomas, L. (1994). Song of the canary. In V. P. Clark, P. A. Eschholz, & A. F. Rosa (Eds.), *Language: Introductory readings* (pp. 35–48). New York: St. Martin's Press.

Thompson, S., & Thurlow, M. (2002). Universally designed assessments: Better tests for everyone! *Policy Directions, No. 14.* Minneapolis, MN: National Center on Educational Outcomes.

Thornborrow, J. (1999). Language and identity. In L. Thomas & S. Wareing (Eds.), *Language, society, and power: An introduction* (pp. 135–149). London: Routledge.

Tinajero, J. V., & Schifini, A. (1997). *Into English.* Carmel, CA: Hampton-Brown.

Tollefson, J. W. (1991). *Planning language, planning inequality.* London: Longman.

Tollefson, J. W. (Ed.). (1995). *Power and inequality in language education.* Cambridge: Cambridge University Press.

Tompkins, G. E., & Tabloski, P. A. (2003). *50 literacy strategies: Step by step.* Upper Saddle River, NJ: Prentice Hall.

Toohey, K. (1998). "Breaking them up, taking them away": ESL students in grade 1. *TESOL Quarterly, 32*(1), 61–84.

Toohey, K. (2000). *Learning English at school: Identity, social relations and classroom practice.* Clevedon, Eng: Multilingual Matters.

Toppo, G. (2008). Fla. Schools approve free, online reading program. *USA Today*, January 24, 17A.

Tudor, I. (1996). *Learner-centeredness as language education.* Cambridge: Cambridge University Press.

Tunmer, W., & Nesdale, A. (1985). Phonemic segmentation skill and beginning reading. *Journal of Educational Psychology, 77*, 417–427.

Tunmer, W. E., Herriman, M. L., & Nesdale, A. R. (1988). Metalinguistic abilities and beginning reading. *Reading Research Quarterly, 23*(2), 134–158.

Tunnell, M. O., & Jacobs, J. S. (2000). *Children's literature, briefly* (2nd ed.). Upper Saddle River, NJ, and Columbus, OH: Merrill/Prentice-Hall.

Turner, T. (1990). *Brainstorms: Creative problem solving.* Glenview, IL: Scott, Foresman.

United States Census Bureau. (2001a). *The Asian and Pacific Islander population in the United States: March 1999* (update) (PPL-131). Washington, DC: Author. Available online: www.census.gov/population/www/socdemo/race/api99.html.

United States Census Bureau. (2001b). *Hispanic population in the United States (2000 March CPS).* Washington, DC: Author. Available online: www.census.gov/population/www/socdemo/hispanic/ho00.html.

United States Census Bureau. (2001c). *Census 2000 supplementary survey.* Washington, DC: Author.

Unrau, N. (2008). *Content area reading and literacy.* Upper Saddle River, NJ: Pearson Prentice Hall.

Vai, M. (1998). *The heart of the matter.* Boston: Heinle & Heinle.

Valdés, G. (1996). *Con respeto: Bridging the distance between culturally diverse families and schools: An ethnographic portrait.* New York: Teachers College Press.

Valles, E. C. (1998). The disproportionate representation of minority students in special education: Responding to the problem. *The Journal of Special Education, 32*(1), 52–54.

Valls, F. R. (2009). Cooperative bi-literacy: Parents, students, and teachers read to transform. *English Teaching, Practice and Critique, 8*(2), 114–136.

van der Woude, M. (1998). Korean students in the United States. *ESL Magazine, 1*(1), 28–30.

Van Deusen-Scholl, N. (1993). Ethnography and teacher training. In D. Freeman & S. Cornwall (Eds.), *New ways in teacher education* (pp. 187–190). Alexandria, VA: Teachers of English to Speakers of Other Languages.

Vaughn, S. (2001, July 15). Common ground for differences. *Los Angeles Times,* W1, W3.

Veeder, K., & Tramutt, J. (2000). Strengthening literacy in both languages. In N. Cloud, F. Genesee, & E. Hamayan (Eds.), *Dual language instruction* (p. 91). Boston: Heinle & Heinle.

Vega, C. M. (2000, July 12). Reaching for literacy. *San Bernardino County Sun,* A1, A4.

Vélez-Ibáñez, C., & Greenberg, J. B. (1992). Formation and transformation of funds of knowledge among U.S. Mexican households. *Anthropology and Education Quarterly, 23*(4), 313–335.

Vella, J. (2002). *Learning to listen, learning to teach: The power of dialogue in educating adults* (2nd ed.). San Francisco: Jossey-Bass.

Versluis, A. (1994). *Native American traditions.* Shaftesbury, UK: Element.

Vygotsky, L. (1981). The genesis of higher mental functions. In J. V. Wertsch (Ed.), *The concept of activity in Soviet psychology* (pp. 144–188). Armonk, NY: Sharpe.

Vygotsky, L. (1982). *Thought and language.* (A. Kozulin, trans.). Cambridge, MA: MIT Press. (Original work published 1934)

Walker, B. J. (1987). Guided fantasy series. In D. J. Watson (Ed.), *Ideas and insights: Language arts in the elementary school* (pp. 112–113). Urbana, IL: National Council of Teachers of English.

Wallace, L. (1999). "Winding down." Unpublished poem.

Wallraff, B. (2000). What global language? *Atlantic Monthly, 286*(5), 52–66.

Walt Disney Company. (1990). *Disney's children's favorites, volume 2* (audiocassette plus sing-along book). Burbank, CA: Author.

Ward, A. W., & Murray-Ward, M. (1999). *Assessment in the classroom.* Belmont, CA: Wadsworth.

Wark, M. (2001). Cyberpunk—Subculture of mainstream? In M. Petracca & M. Sorapure (Eds.), *Common culture: Reading and writing about American popular culture* (3rd ed., pp. 352–358). Upper Saddle River, NJ: Prentice-Hall.

Watahomigie, L. (1995). The power of American Indian parents and communities. *Bilingual Research Journal, 19*(1), 99–115.

Way, B. (1981). *Audience participation.* Boston: Baker's Plays.

Weatherly, S. D. (1999). I'll buy it! In R. E. Larimer & L. Schleicher (Eds.), *New ways in using authentic materials in the classroom* (pp. 73–80). Alexandria, VA: Teachers of English to Speakers of Other Languages.

Weedon, C. (1987). *Feminist practice and poststructuralist theory.* London: Blackwell.

Weinstein-Shr, G. (1992). *Stories to tell our children.* Boston: Heinle & Heinle.

Wells, C. G. (1981). *Learning through interaction: The study of language development.* Cambridge: Cambridge University Press.

Wheeler, R. S., & Swords, R. (2008). *Educational Leadership, 65*(7), 54–58.

Whincup, G. (1987). *The heart of Chinese poetry.* New York: Anchor/Doubleday.

Whisler, N., & Williams, J. (1990). *Literature and cooperative learning: Pathway to literacy.* Sacramento: Literature Co-op.

Wiese, A. M., & García, E. E. (1998). The Bilingual Education Act: Language minority students and equal educational opportunity. *Bilingual Research Journal, 22*(1). Available online: http://brj.asu.edu/v221/indext.html.

Wiggins, G. (1992). Creating tests worth taking. *Educational Leadership, 49,* 26–33.

Wilber, D. J. (2010). *iWrite.* Portsmouth, NH: Heinemann.

Wilhelm, K. H. (1997). Sometimes kicking and screaming: Language teachers-in-training react to a collaborative learning model. *Modern Language Journal, 81*(4), 527–542.

Wilhelm, K. H. (1999). Collaborative "dos" and "don'ts." *TESOL Journal, 8*(2), 14–19.

Wilhelm, K. H., & Leverett, T. (1998). Lights, camera, interaction. *TESOL Journal, 7*(4), 34–35.

Williams, B. T. (2007). Standardized students: The problems with writing for tests instead of people. In F. Schultz (Ed.), *Annual editions 10/08: Education* (pp. 71–75). Dubuque, IA: McGraw Hill Contemporary Learning Series.

Willet, J. (1995). Becoming first graders in an L2: An ethnographic study of L2 socialization. *TESOL Quarterly, 29*(3), 473–503.

Wilson, H. (2001). *Three approaches to teaching grammar.* Presentation, annual conference, California Teachers of English to Speakers of Other Languages, Ontario, CA.

Wink, J. (2000). *Critical pedagogy: Notes from the real world.* New York: Addison-Wesley.

Wolfe, P., & Poynor, L. (2001). Politics and the pendulum: An alternative understanding of the case of whole language as educational innovation. *Educational Researcher, 30*(1), 15–20.

Wolfe-Quintero, K. (1998). ESL language portfolios: How do they work? In J. D. Brown (Ed.), *New ways in classroom assessment* (pp. 11–14). Alexandria, VA: Teachers of English to Speakers of Other Languages.

Wolfram, W. (1991). *Dialects and American English.* Englewood Cliffs, NJ: Prentice-Hall.

Wolfram, W. (1995). Reexamining dialect in TESOL. *TESOL Matters, 5*(2), 1, 22.

Wolfram, W. (2002). Everyone has an accent. In B. M. Power & R. S. Hubbard (Eds.), *Language development: A reader for teachers* (2nd ed., pp. 225–230). Upper Saddle River, NJ: Merrill/Prentice-Hall.

Wolfram, W. (2011). *Exposing sociolinguistic variation: The TESOL challenge.* Plenary speech, Teachers of English to Speakers of Other Languages conference, New Orleans.

Wolfram, W., Adger, C., & Christian, D. (1999). *Dialects in schools and communities.* Mahwah, NJ: Erlbaum.

Wong, M. M. W. (1996). Time-people-action-place. In L. Schinke-Llano & R. Rauff (Eds.), *New ways in teaching young children* (pp. 104–105). Alexandria, VA: Teachers of English to Speakers of Other Languages.

Wong, M. S. (1998). *You said it! Listening/speaking strategies and activities.* New York: St. Martin's Press.

Wood, N. (1993). *Spirit walker.* New York: Delacorte Press.

Woodbury, A. (2001). *Endangered languages.* In Linguistic Society of America, "Fields of Linguistics." Available online: www.lsadc.org/web2/fldcont.html.

Woolfolk, A. (2007). *Educational psychology* (10th ed.). Boston: Allyn & Bacon.

Worthy, J., Moorman, M., & Turner, M. (1999). What Johnny likes to read is hard to find in school. *Reading Research Quarterly, 14,* 12–27.

Yaden, D., & Templeton, S. (1986). Introduction: Metalinguistic awareness—an etymology. In

D. Yaden & S. Templeton (Eds.), *Metalinguistic awareness and beginning literacy: Conceptualizing what it means to read and write* (pp. 3–10). Portsmouth, NH: Heinemann.

Yang, C. Y. (1999). *Promoting communicative competence through drama in elementary English as a foreign language.* Unpublished master's thesis, California State University, San Bernardino.

Yang, H-J. (1998). *The collaborative dramatic process in elementary English as a foreign language.* Unpublished master's thesis, California State University, San Bernardino.

Yeh, M. H. (2001). *Enhancing academic competence in English as a foreign language through multiple strategies.* Unpublished master's thesis, California State University, San Bernardino.

Yi, Y. (2009). Adolescent literacy and identity construction among 1.5 Generation students from a transnational perspective. *Journal of Asia Pacific Communication, 19*(1), 100–129.

Yost, B. (2000, June 8). E-mail lingo is reshaping language. *San Bernardino Sun,* E1, E3.

Young, M., & Helvie, S. (1996). Parent power: A positive link to school success. *Journal of Educational Issues of Language Minority Students, 16.* Available online: www.ncela.gwu.edu/pubs/jeilms/vol16.

Young, T. A., & Vardell, S. (1993). Weaving readers theatre and nonfiction into the curriculum. *Reading Teacher, 46*(5), 396–406.

Yúdice, G. (1988). Marginality and the ethics of survival. In A. Ross (Ed.), *Universal abandon? The politics of postmodernism.* Minneapolis: University of Minnesota Press.

Zalta, G. (2006). Using drama with children. *English Teaching Forum, 44*(2), 24–27.

Zanger, V. V. (1994). "Not joined in": The social context of English literacy development for Hispanic youth. In B. M. Ferdman, R-M. Weber, & A. G. Ramírez (Eds.), *Literacy across languages and cultures* (pp. 171–198). Albany: SUNY Press.

Zelman, N. (1996). *Conversational inspirations: Over 2000 conversation topics.* Brattleboro, VT: Pro Lingua Associates.

Zhang, W. (2006). Weaving the past into the present. In B. Agor (Ed.), *Integrating EFL standards into Chinese classroom settings* (pp. 105–126). Alexandria, VA: Teachers of English to Speakers of Other Languages, Inc.

Author Index

Subject Index